THE EVOLUTION AND
CLASSIFICATION OF
FLOWERING PLANTS

Charles E. Bessey (1845–1915), author of
a phylogenetic system and a set of dicta that
profoundly influenced subsequent taxonomic thought. Habitat photo courtesy of Robert B. Kaul, University of Nebraska.

The Evolution and Classification of Flowering Plants

Second Edition

Arthur Cronquist

The New York Botanical Garden
Bronx, New York 10458, USA
1988

This book is printed on acid-free paper.

The Evolution and Classification of Flowering Plants, Second Edition

Copyright © 1988 The New York Botanical Garden

Published by The New York Botanical Garden, Bronx, New York 10458, U.S.A.

Issued 14 August 1988

Library of Congress Cataloging in Publication Data

Cronquist, Arthur.
  The evolution and classification of flowering plants / Arthur
Cronquist. — 2nd ed.
    p.   cm.

    Bibliography: p.
    Includes index.

    ISBN 0-89327-332-5
    1. Angiosperms—Classification.   2. Angiosperms—Evolution.
I. Title.
QK495.A1C75   1988
582.13—dc19   88-18008
                                                                          CIP

Printed by Allen Press, Inc., Lawrence, Kansas 66044, U.S.A.

Cover: *Magnolia grandiflora.* U.S. Forest Service photo by W.D. Brush.

Contents

Introduction

This book reflects an effort to provide a short version of the general system of classification of flowering plants, together with an exposition of the theory underlying the system. The system here presented is based on that in my 1981 book, *An Integrated System of Classification of Flowering Plants*. Only a few small changes are introduced, made necessary by advances in knowledge or understanding since 1981. A more substantial revision at this time would be premature; I must leave it to my successors.

The chapters on species and speciation (not included in the first edition) are perhaps not necessary for an understanding of the system, but I take this opportunity to place my views on record. These chapters may also facilitate use of the book as a text by those so minded.

The book presents taxonomy as seen by Cronquist. I try to present a coherent story, and to expound my views on some controversial matters, but I make no pretense of equal time for opposing views. For other points of view, read other authors.

The lists of references have two functions: to lead the student into the pertinent literature, and to document the particular citations in the text. I have not hesitated to cite a secondary rather than a primary reference when it suited my purpose to do so; review papers have their uses. When similar information is available both in English and in some other language, I have usually cited the English-language reference, for the convenience of the anglophone readers who presumably make up the majority of my audience. The necessity for the serious student of the general system to get along in several languages is shown by the considerable sprinkling of references that survive this English-language bias.

Many people have helped me in one way or another during the preparation of this and antecedent manuscripts and while my thoughts were developing. A complete list would have to include nearly all of my professional associates, beginning with Ray J. Davis, from whom I took my first botany course. I cannot now recall to what extent some of my ideas are original and to what extent they spring from seeds planted in my mind by others. I must acknowledge repeated useful conversations with my colleagues Armen Takhtajan, Robert Thorne, and Rolf Dahlgren, but beyond that the list could be expanded almost indefinitely. Some names were unfortunately and unintentionally omitted from the list of nearly a hundred provided in *Integrated System.* To all, named and unnamed, my thanks. I depend on conversations with my colleagues, as well as on their published work, to help shape my thoughts. I am grateful for the continuing flow of significant reprints and prepublication manuscripts.

As with all of my books, my wife Mabel A. Cronquist has been a constant assistant and foil for my ideas. She provides the domestic milieu conducive to my work, helps me shape its presentation, and now puts it all onto the word-processor. My debt is beyond payment.

Chapter 1

Staminate inflorescences, young leaves, and
(inset) fruit of *Quercus coccinea,* the scarlet
oak. Despite the clearcut distinctions among
the several subgenera of *Quercus,* it is customary to keep them all in the same genus,
because botanists and laymen alike intuitively sense the unity of the group. An oak
is an oak is an oak. U.S. Forest Service
photos by W. D. Brush.

The Nature of Taxonomy

Taxonomy reflects man's urge to understand the pattern of diversity among organisms. Recognition of repetitive patterns in nature long antedates the origin of our own species, as should be clear to anyone who has watched a grazing or hunting animal. Conscious thought about those patterns, and efforts to organize a hierarchical scheme of classification, may be more specifically human characteristics. Such thought and efforts have roots deep in our evolutionary and social history. People in primitive, nonliterate societies the world over recognize and have names for the kinds of plants and animals that are significant to them, and at least a rudimentary classification of these basic kinds into larger groups.

Efforts to organize a more complete and formal system of classification of organisms must have begun not long after the origin of writing. In literature familiar to people in Western culture, such efforts go back at least to the classical pre-Christian Greek philosophers, who doubtless had antecedents in earlier societies. Improvement and completion of the classification of organisms have continued to occupy the attention of philosophers and (more recently) biologists until the present time, and the end is not in sight.

The discontinuous distribution of diversity in nature is evident to any thoughtful person. In an oversimplified metaphor, one might take the particular combination of characters of an individual organism to be a point on an immense chart. Points for different individuals may be entered at various positions on the chart, according to their degree of similarity and difference. When these points have been recorded for enough organisms, it will be seen that they are not randomly distributed. Instead there are clusters of all sizes and degrees of density and complexity, separated by open spaces of greater or lesser size in which there are few or no such points. A great many combinations of characters that one might imagine simply do not exist. There are no photosynthetic dogs, and probably no purple cows. Neither do we get figs from thistles.

The function of taxonomy is to provide a general-purpose system of

1

classification, which can be used by all who are concerned with the similarities and differences among organisms. Toward this end we try to group together the things that are most alike in all respects, and to separate them progressively from things they are progressively less like. In terms of the chart metaphor, we try to recognize the clusters on the chart as taxa, and to draw the lines between taxa through the empty spaces. The principal lines are drawn through the biggest gaps, and the subsidiary ones through the lesser gaps.

In contrast to the taxonomic system, there can be any number of special-purpose classifications, based mainly or wholly on some limited set of criteria. Precisely because they *are* special-purpose classifications, directed toward a limited objective, they do not and cannot serve as general-purpose systems. Each of these special-purpose systems can have its own usefulness, and does no harm if it is not proclaimed to be a taxonomic system.

In 1968 I proposed the definition that taxonomy "is a study aimed at producing a system of classification of organisms which best reflects the totality of their similarities and differences." The definition was based on the historical fact that this is what taxonomists have been trying to do at least since the time of Aristotle and Theophrastus. There is nothing new in the definition but the phraseology. Most taxonomists in the past have not even found a definition to be necessary. They knew what they were trying to do, and assumed that anyone else with any interest in the subject also knew.

In any field of endeavor, however, it is possible to confuse means with ends, or to follow a familiar procedure without thought of whether it is well adapted to one's objectives. If one is to accomplish his purpose, it is well to know what the purpose is, and to keep it constantly in mind. Even some past and present efforts to present a formal definition of taxonomy have confused means with ends, or have been proposed by people who are more concerned with some one of the many facets of taxonomy than with the need to provide a general-purpose system. In writing the present book, I have tried to keep in mind the historical and continuing function of taxonomy in providing a general frame of reference for all who are concerned with the pattern of diversity in the organic world.

Some taxonomists in recent years have misdirected too much energy into a consideration of whether or not taxonomy conforms to a definition of science based on the data and procedures of the physical sciences. Let the physicists go their way, and we shall go ours. Taxonomy is a science in that the system we devise is severely constrained by the data. It is an art to the extent that there is some room for unresolvable difference of opinion, no matter how abundant the data. I call it an artful science. The oft-repeated observation that no two taxonomists working independently will come up with precisely the same classification of any complex group reflects the nature of the biological world and inherent differences in human patterns of thought, rather than a correctable deficiency in our concepts and procedures. New data or new ways of looking at the data may be persuasive in supporting one or another previously debatable position, but it is expecting too much to suppose that all such questions are inherently resolvable to the satisfaction of all.

The view that there is an objective, hierarchically organized pattern of order in the biological world is at best an oversimplification. Above the level of the local breeding population, the pattern is a creation of the human mind, neither entirely objective nor entirely subjective. To the extent that virtually all minds addressing themselves to the subject see certain elements of the pattern in the same way, the pattern is objective. At this stage in our knowledge we may, for example, consider the modern angiosperms to be an objectively perceived taxonomic group; likewise the family Asteraceae, and indeed a great many of the usually recognized taxa at various levels in the hierarchy. On the other hand, some parts of the hierarchical taxonomic pattern are more nearly created than merely perceived; or at least different minds will perceive them differently. Each of the proposed schemes for recognizing two, three, four, five or more kingdoms of organisms has some advantages and also some serious weaknesses. I am not optimistic that the differences of opinion here can ever be resolved short of some hopefully far-distant time when some keeper of the keys decides how to program the master computer that discourages further inquiry.

The Taxonomic Hierarchy

The taxonomic system is hierarchical, like a military system. In principle, every individual belongs to a species, and every species belongs to a series of progressively larger and more broadly defined groups, up to the highest rank, the kingdom. There are some problems and exceptions, such as the occasional occurrence of hybrids between species, or the absence of enough information about many fossils to permit their secure placement in the system, but these difficulties do not seriously compromise the general principle.

Any taxonomic unit, of whatever rank, is called a *taxon* (pl.: *taxa*).

The smallest necessary taxon is the *species* (pl.: *species*). A formal definition of species is reserved for CHAPTER 2. We may now simply say that the species are the smallest groups consistently used in the taxonomic system; they are the basic kinds.

Species are grouped into progressively higher taxa. Every species belongs to a *genus* (pl.: *genera*). No individual species can belong to two genera, although taxonomists may differ as to what genus should receive a particular species. Likewise, every genus belongs to a *family,* every family belongs to an *order,* every order belongs to a *class,* and every class belongs to a *division.* The division is the botanical equivalent of the zoological phylum and is the highest (most inclusive) rank regularly used in the classification of the plant kingdom.

The six regularly used ranks in the taxonomic hierarchy of plants (species, genus, family, order, class, division) may or may not conform to the pattern we perceive in nature, but ordinarily none of these ranks can be omitted. Sometimes it is necessary to have a genus consisting of only one species, or a family consisting of only one genus, etc. The order Eucommiales contains only the family Eucommiaceae, with the single genus and species *Eucommia ulmoides* Oliver.

Additional ranks can be inserted among the standard ones, as needed. The International Code of Botanical Nomenclature provides the following set of progressively subordinate ranks: kingdom, subkingdom, division, subdivision, class, subclass, order, suborder, family, subfamily, tribe, subtribe, genus, subgenus, section, subsection, series, subseries, species, subspecies, variety, subvariety, form, and subform. The categories subvariety and subform are now rarely used, but all other ranks in the list will frequently be found in the classification of one or another group. The Code even provides that additional categories may be inserted, if an author feels the need. Monotypic groups and optional taxonomic ranks are further discussed on page 18.

Once one of the optional ranks (beyond the specified six) is introduced into the scheme of classification, it must be used throughout the next higher taxon into which it has been inserted. Thus if one recognizes a subfamily Maloideae to include certain genera of the family Rosaceae, then every genus in the Rosaceae should be included in one or another subfamily; none can properly be left without a place. Of course we cannot prevent the publication of incomplete schemes, in which for example some of the genera of a family are ignored or said to be *incertae sedis* (of uncertain position) with regard to the recognized subfamilies or tribes, but such schemes are regarded as inadequate and are not examples to be followed. It is the taxonomist's job to provide a complete scheme for any group he treats. If further information later requires some change, so be it.

Use of the optional ranks within one taxon does not commit one to the use of these same ranks in other taxa. Thus an organization of the Rosaceae into several subfamilies does not require that the Crassulaceae also be organized into subfamilies.

Finally, we should point out that taxonomy follows a *binomial system* of nomenclature. The name of any species consists of two words. The first word is the name of the genus to which the species belongs. The second word is the specific epithet, telling which species of the genus is meant. Names of genera and higher taxa can stand by themselves, but specific epithets are taxonomically meaningful only when attached to the name of the genus. *Acer* is the botanical name of a genus known in English as maple. *Acer rubrum* is the botanical name of the red maple. By itself, *rubrum* is merely the nominative neuter form of a Latin adjective meaning red. One can have not only an *Acer rubrum,* but also a *Chenopodium rubrum,* and an *Actaea rubra.*

As a bibliographic convenience it is customary to append the name (or an abbreviation of it) of the author to the name of the species. Thus in more formal discourse we would write *Acer rubrum* L., *Chenopodium rubrum* L., and *Actaea rubra* (Aiton) Willd. The abbreviation L. stands for Linnaeus, and Willd. for Willdenow. The inclusion of the name Aiton in parentheses shows that Aiton first used the epithet *rubra* for the plant, but in a different position indicating a different opinion as to its taxonomic status.

Some Principles

It is obviously a large task to prepare a system of classification that truly reflects the totality of similarities and differences among organisms. We don't know everything there is to be known about any one individual organism, let alone a species, or genus, or the more than 300,000 species that are generally considered to be plants. We know perhaps more about man than about any other kind of organism, but every student of human physiology or biochemistry is impressed by the amount we do not know. We do not know, for example, which individuals can safely smoke large numbers of cigarettes over a period of years and which ones will succumb to lung-cancer under the same conditions.

It may be argued that susceptibility to lung-cancer is not an important taxonomic character. Indeed it is not. But we know that it is not, only because it does not correlate strongly with other characters found to be important in human taxonomy because they are correlated among themselves.

Several important principles can be illustrated by this one example: (1) Taxa are properly established on the basis of multiple correlations of characters. (2) The taxonomic importance of a character is established by how well it correlates with other characters; i.e., the taxonomic value of a character is determined a posteriori rather than a priori. (3) An important feature of taxonomy is its predictive value. If studies had shown that susceptiblity to tobacco-induced lung-cancer were confined to one race, then (1) this character would be correlated with a whole set of other characters; (2) it would thereby become a significant taxonomic character; and (3) we would accurately predict that a person known on the basis of other characters to belong to a nonsusceptible race could smoke without fear of developing lung-cancer as a result. In actuality susceptibility to lung-cancer is not obviously correlated with race and has no taxonomic significance.

Because our information is always incomplete, we can never be sure that any taxonomic scheme truly reflects the totality of similarities and differences among the organisms considered. From a limited amount of data we extrapolate a general scheme of classification. Some taxonomists have been notably better than others at perceiving patterns and producing taxonomic systems from scanty information, but all systems are subject to correction or even complete reconstruction as the data may require. Much of taxonomic theory is concerned with how best to extrapolate from the necessarily limited data to the complete classification.

The distinction between morphological and chemical characters is conceptually useful, but not as fundamental as it may at first seem. All morphological characters have a chemical foundation, as does life itself.

What we call chemical characters are simply characters not known to have a significant morphological expression. They may be just as important to the plant as the overtly morphological characters, or even more so, but we must suppress the temptation to extrapolate broadly from a limited data-base. Chemical characters are just as subject to variation as morphological ones, and must be evaluated with the same degree of caution.

As we shall point out in CHAPTER 5, the sequence of nucleotides in DNA and RNA provides a potentially very useful source of information on phyletic branching. At the same time, such information is of much less value in characterizing or delimiting taxa. Genes are important to the organism, and to us, not for their own sake but for what they do. They are important because of their influence on the phenotype. In order to understand the phenotypes, we begin by trying to distinguish genetic from environmental influences. In pursuit of understanding genetic differences we are led eventually to the gene. We cannot expect to have a high batting average, however, in predicting phenetic effects from genic structure. A chemical difference in the genes that seems small to us might have a disproportionately large phenotypic effect, and vice versa. We can no more predict the phenotype directly from the genes than we could have predicted the double helix from a study of nuclear physics.

Although all kinds of information ought theoretically to be equally important in taxonomy, morphology has traditionally been the mainstay of the system, and it remains so today. This is so partly because morphological information is more readily available than chemical or physiological information, and partly because of the way our minds work. No matter how wide a range of characters is considered in arriving at a classification, we must ultimately come up with groups (at least in the eukaryotes) that can be recognized morphologically in order for the system to be generally useful.

Our eyes are our primary means of learning about the world. Vision provides an instantaneous wealth of data for our minds to organize. We see size, form, color, and pattern. Most important of all is pattern. Our evolutionary heritage conditions us to its recognition, classification, and incorporation into our memory-bank. Those of our potential ancestors who could not at a glance distinguish a sabre-toothed tiger from a deer, did not live to become our ancestors.

In contrast to its facility in manipulating pattern-data, the human mind is not very good at remembering point-data and making simultaneous comparisons among many individual items. Here we are far surpassed by computers, which on the other hand are very inept with pattern-data that have not been broken into bytes. The taxonomic use of computers to manipulate point-data is discussed on pages 49–51, under the heading NUMERICAL TAXONOMY.

The Natural System

The concept that there is, or ought to be, a natural system that best reflects the essential nature of different sorts of organisms is an ancient one, going back at least as far as Aristotle. In *De Partibus* he wrote, "the method then that we must adopt is to attempt to recognize the natural groups—each of which combines a multitude of differentiae, and is not defined by a single one as in dichotomy."

Little progress toward a natural system, above the level of the genus, was made for more than 2000 years after Aristotle. In the middle of the 18th century Linnaeus (1753), the revered "father" of taxonomy, arranged the genera of angiosperms according to his Sexual System, which depended largely on the number of stamens and carpels in the flower. Linnaeus admitted that his system was artificial, and that it would eventually be superseded by a natural system, but he felt that information and understanding were yet inadequate for the production of such a system. He (1751) did provide a separate "fragment of a natural system" in which he listed certain groups of genera that he thought belonged together. We now agree with many, but not all, of the suggestions he made.

Linnaeus' successors immediately set to work to devise a natural system. Michel Adanson, Bernard and Antoine Laurent de Jussieu, Robert Brown, and especially Augustin Pyramus de Candolle made signal contributions, and by the middle of the 19th century most of the families of angiosperms that we now recognize had been perceived as natural groups. The meaning of "natural" was nebulous, but the groups were recognized all the same.

The concept of organic evolution, first made scientifically respectable in 1859 by Charles Darwin in his monumental *Origin of Species,* provided the missing rationale: that the natural system reflects evolutionary relationships. Darwin was well aware of the significance of the evolutionary concept to taxonomy. In Chapter 14 he wrote:

> ". . . the Natural System is founded on descent with modification. . . . the characters which naturalists consider as showing true affinity between any two or more species, are those which have been inherited from a common parent, all true classification being genealogical. . . . community of descent is the hidden bond which naturalists have unconsciously been seeking."

Taxonomists quickly adopted the concept of organic evolution and made it their own. A natural system must reflect evolutionary relationships, and if it could be shown that any particular taxonomic group was not monophyletic, but came instead from diverse ancestors, then that group had to be abandoned as polyphyletic and therefore unnatural. For example, as soon as taxonomists came to believe that the Sympetalae were not a monophyletic group, but rather a group of diverse origins which had independently achieved the sympetalous condition, then the group Sympetalae had to be abandoned and its members reassigned according to their probable evolutionary relationships.

The reasons why an evolutionary classification is preferred to one that cuts across evolutionary relationships are simple. Only if our taxa represent truly evolutionary groups will new information, from characters as yet unstudied, fall into the pattern that has been established on a relatively limited amount of information. If the system is to have predictive value, if it is to reflect the totality of similarities and differences in addition to the formal critical taxonomic characters, it must have an evolutionary foundation. Artificial classifications, using a few arbitrarily selected characters, are easy to devise, but they do not have the predictive value of a natural classification; new information will not tend to fall into line.

A perceptive reader may note that here we are using the term predictive value in a slightly different sense than on an earlier page. A proper taxonomic system has predictive value not only for previously studied characters on unstudied individuals, but also for characters that have been studied only in related taxa, or which indeed are wholly unstudied or unknown. The predictions will not always be correct, but they have a much better than random chance of being so. The more closely related the taxa, the more likely they are to be similar in characters as yet unstudied.

A closely related, complementary reason why a sound taxonomic system must be evolutionary is that the gaps in the distribution of diversity reflect evolutionary history. In a taxonomic system an attempt is made to draw the lines between groups through the gaps in the pattern of diversity. The detection of these gaps, the unraveling of evolutionary history, and the establishment of a taxonomic system are closely interrelated processes.

As we shall see, the gaps in the pattern of diversity are often relative rather than absolute. Sometimes it is useful to think of a distributional curve with humps and hollows of various sizes. The hollows may not all go down to the base-line, but it is still useful to draw the lines in the hollows instead of through the humps. The fewer the units lying near or astraddle the boundary, the easier the system is to comprehend and use, and the greater the likelihood that the system is truly natural. In setting up our system we try to define our groups so as to have few or no intermediates.

The evolutionary relationships among certain groups of organisms are attested by the fossil record. Our concepts of the phylogeny and taxonomy of the vertebrates, for example, have been profoundly influenced by the evidence from fossils. In many instances the fossils not only provide connecting links between distinct modern groups, but they also furnish a series of steps between the ancestral and modern forms. The series of fossils connecting the modern horse with the Eocene *Hyracotherium* (*Eohippus*), a three-toed mammal the size of a small dog, is a familiar example. In this as in other cases the fossils do not provide such a simple, straight-line series as some people have supposed, but they clearly illustrate the general course of evolution in the group.

The fossil record is much less helpful to students of angiosperm taxonomy than to students of vertebrate taxonomy. The several reasons why this is so are best explored after some further consideration of taxonomic principles and the relationship between taxonomy and evolution. At this point we can say that the fossil record as now understood makes few absolute demands on the taxonomic system, but does limit the number of schemes that can be seriously considered. It would, for example, fly in the face of the fossil evidence to consider that the palms lie at the evolutionary base of the monocots, or that the Caryophyllidae take their origin in the lower Cretaceous. For the foreseeable future, the classification of angiosperms must be based primarily on modern plants, but present and future makers of general systems ignore the fossil record at their peril.

The felicitous marriage between phylogeny and taxonomy has been showing some signs of strain for the past several decades, and some reconsideration of the relationship is in order. The rigor with which the monophyletic requirement is interpreted makes more difference than was at first apparent. All taxonomists agree that evolution is responsible for the pattern of diversity that we observe in nature, but there is now substantial disagreement about just how closely taxonomy can or should reflect phylogeny. We shall return to this question after the necessary consideration of some other matters.

Typological Concepts

Much has been written about the dangers and faults of typological thinking in taxonomy. Although serving as a useful corrective to unnecessary rigidity, such commentary often overlooks the fact that a certain amount of typology is necessary not only in taxonomy but in other kinds of thought as well.

The endless array of natural and artificial objects must somehow be organized in our minds into a set of named categories, in order that we may think about them and communicate our thoughts to others. Consciously or unconsciously we seek repetitive patterns so that we may not be lost in the jungle of diversity. The small child who points to something and asks his mother, "What?," is trying to establish categories and names, and the one who calls a stranger "daddy" is at least making progress. He has recognized the category that other people call man, and has only to establish the right name for it.

We all have type concepts for chair, bed, table, window, house, road, mountain, river, lake, and countless other objects, as well as for plant, animal, tree, snake, parasite, and human. We have a mental picture, in greater or lesser detail, of what something ought to be like to fit into each of these categories. The fact that a chaise longue is somewhat intermediate between a bed and a chair does not interfere with the utility of the type concepts for chair and bed. A person unfamiliar with a chaise longue will simply consider it an unusual chair, or an unusual bed, or something between a chair and a bed, and the person who sees a great many chaises longues will develop a type concept and learn the name for this category as well.

Plant taxonomists necessarily have type concepts for taxonomic groups, such as moss, fern, gymnosperm, monocot, dicot, Magnoliales, Asteraceae, *Helianthus,* maple, sugar-maple, etc. We cannot think effectively without them. The fact that it is possible to develop a type concept for a group does not prove that it is a natural, acceptable taxonomic group, but on the other hand any proposed group that does not permit the establishment of a type concept is of doubtful value.

It should of course be understood that the taxonomic types we refer to here are biological rather than nomenclatural. The nomenclatural type may or may not be biologically typical; all that is necessary is that it fall within the confines of the group.

The Value of Characters

Ideally, the comparative studies on which taxonomic conclusions are based should include all characteristics of all species of a group, and of many individuals throughout the geographic range of each species. Morphological comparisons should include not only the obvious floral and vegetative structure, but also the various kinds of micromorphology, as observed with both the light microscope and the electron microscope. Equally, attention should be given to all phases of physiology in its broadest sense, from habitat requirements and genetic compatibilities to serology and chemical analysis.

Practically, this ideal is not yet attainable or even in sight. Acquisition of the requisite information in chemistry, physiology, and micromorphology is a time-consuming procedure which we have as yet hardly more than begun. It is clear on the basis of experience as well as from a priori theory that information from these sources is going to be increasingly useful in the continuing development of our taxonomic and evolutionary scheme, but at present it cannot be applied with any consistency because the gaps in our information bulk so much larger than the actual data.

We have by now become accustomed to the idea that obvious morphological characters of any sort do not have a fixed, inherent taxonomic significance. A character that distinguishes families in one order may distinguish genera in another family, or species in another genus, or it may vary on a single individual of another species. For example, the Boraginaceae may generally be distinguished from the Verbenaceae by having alternate leaves, in contrast to the opposite leaves of the Verbenaceae. (There are, to be sure, some other differences between the two families.) Within the family Scrophulariaceae the arrangement of leaves is usually a good generic character, some genera having the leaves opposite, others alternate. Within the genus *Cornus,* the species *Cornus alternifolia* (Fig. 1.1) has alternate leaves, whereas most of the other species have opposite leaves. In the common sunflower, *Helianthus annuus,* the leaves near the base of the stem are opposite, but the others are alternate. In each case the taxonomic importance of the character is determined after the groups have been perceived.

It is always tempting to assume that the more recondite characters are inherently more stable and thus more important than the ones that are easily observed, but the assumption is unwarranted and gives rise to unfortunate and unnecessary error. There is no more correlation between

Fig. 1.1. *Cornus amomum* (LEFT) and *Cornus alternifolia* (RIGHT). These two species, although closely related, differ in a character (leaf arrangement) that usually marks groups of generic and higher rank.

the taxonomic value of a particular bit of information and the difficulty of obtaining it than between the efficacy of a medicine and its taste. It is the experience of taxonomists that the more recondite characters are subject to the same problems as the more obvious ones.

How, then, may taxonomic groups be recognized, and taxonomic systems set up, if particular characters do not have inherent importance? The answer is that sound taxonomy proceeds by the use of multiple correlations. Some progress has been made in recent decades in the use of computers to help recognize or at least to demonstrate these correlations, but in the past they have been made almost entirely by inspection. The groups are perceived on the basis of all the available information, and the critical characters are selected thereafter. Thus it can be stated, as a general principle, that *individual characters do not have a fixed, a priori importance; a character is only as important as it proves to be in each individual instance in marking a group that has been recognized on the basis of all the available information.* The value of characters is established a posteriori.

The principle of a posteriori evaluation of characters has been known to good taxonomists for more than two centuries. In his *Philosophia Botanica* Linnaeus (1751) gave some examples of variation in the value of characters, and then coined the aphorism, "Scias characterem non constituere genus, sed genus characterem." (It isn't the character that makes the genus, but the genus that makes the character.) The principle holds true at all taxonomic levels.

Each generation of taxonomists must learn the a posteriori principle anew. It is a lesson that comes hard. Consistency in the evaluation of characters is psychologically more appealing. Unfortunately, such consistency often does not give us groups that conform to the actual pattern of diversity in nature. It does not *consistently* group the things that are most alike in all respects, and separate them progressively from things that are progressively less like.

On the other hand, we have found from experience that certain characters and kinds of characters are *more likely* to be important than others. Floral characters are more likely to be important than vegetative characters, and the arrangement of parts, either floral or vegetative, is likely to be more important than their size or shape. But in all cases the likelihood is only a likelihood rather than a certainty. The proof of the pudding remains in the eating. The position of the ovary in the flower commonly marks families or even orders (e.g., Apiales, Campanulales, Cornales, and Dipsacales, all with inferior ovary), but in the Rosaceae it marks only subfamilies (e.g., the Maloideae with inferior ovary, the other subfamilies with superior ovary), and in the genus *Saxifraga* some species have the ovary wholly superior, others have it partly inferior, and a few have it more or less completely inferior.

There is just enough consistency in the value of particular characters from one group to another to mislead the unwary. Because the structure of the pod is so commonly useful in marking genera of legumes, an American botanist (P. A. Rydberg) of a past generation dismembered the large and highly natural genus *Astragalus,* recognizing 21 genera in the New World alone. Unfortunately, the resulting segregate genera were ill-defined, and as it now appears, not even in all cases natural. As one of my professors said, you could take a plant in one hand, and Rydberg's treatment in the other, and not know what genus to put the plant into. The structure of the pod does provide many specific characters in *Astragalus,* but it does not provide an adequate basis for fragmentation of the genus.

There is a story, hopefully true, that Rydberg climaxed a discussion with another botanist by shaking his finger in her face and saying, "The trouble with you, Miss Eastwood, is that you are not consistent!" The adamant answer was, "Mr. Rydberg, you can hang consistency!" Passions aside, we may say that consistency in anything is fine, so long as it does not get one into unnecessary trouble. In taxonomy, consistency must always be secondary to the primary objective of recognizing natural groups on the basis of all the available information.

Although we may now disagree with Rydberg on some taxonomic principles, he was a talented and productive botanist, working at a time when many "new" species were still being discovered in the American West. His *Flora of the Rocky Mountains and Adjacent Plains* was a standard reference work for several decades.

In the exploratory stage of plant taxonomy, when the flora of a large region is only becoming known, taxonomists must of necessity assign values to characters on the basis of their past experience. An imperfect classification, which must be changed as more information becomes available, is better than no classification at all. It is no reflection on the ability of our predecessors that their classifications must frequently be changed to accommodate new data. We may hope that our successors will be equally tolerant as they adjust present classifications to take account of the coming flood of micromorphological and chemical data.

OWNBEY'S PRINCIPLE

One of the interesting things that has turned up in evaluating the significance of taxonomic characters is that *the presence of a structure or substance is more likely to be important than its absence.*[1] We can now give a genetic explanation of why this should be so, and at the same time strengthen our conviction that it really is so. Studies in genetics and developmental morphology have amply demonstrated that individual phenotypic characters are commonly governed by a complex system of genes, rather than by a single gene unaffected by others. The appearance of a particular characteristic in the phenotype requires a whole genetic system, and if two individuals or allied taxa share the same structure then they probably also share the same genetic system governing its development. If any one of the essential genes in the system is lost, then the structure fails to develop, and a plant that lacks a particular structure may differ by only a single gene from one that has it. It has been demonstrated that peloric (regular-flowered) forms of the common snapdragon (Fig. 1.2) differ from the ordinary bilabiate form in only a single pair of genes, but this does not mean that the complex, irregular corolla of the snapdragon arose from a regular-flowered ancestry by a single mutation; a complex system of genes is certainly required instead.

Even an individual chemical component in the cell often represents the end product of a biosynthetic chain that can be broken at any link. Anthocyanin is a familiar example. The production of purple-flowered sweet peas by crossing two different white-flowered strains has often been studied in beginning genetics under the heading of factor interaction. Each of the white-flowered strains in this cross lacks one of the essential links in the biosynthetic chain leading to the formation of anthocyanin. The F_1 hybrid, although it is heterozygous for genes governing two of these factors, has all the links intact and produces purple flowers.

The betalains are a unique group of pigments that in the angiosperms are known only in the order Caryophyllales. The restriction of betalains to this group of families is one of several characters that lead us to believe that the group really does hang together. The presence of betalains in the Cactaceae is one of a number of characters that leads modern taxonomists to the conviction that this family, whose affinities were once obscure, is properly associated with the Caryophyllales. On the other hand, the apparent absence of betalains from the family Caryophyllaceae is not necessarily of any great moment. It does suggest the possibility that this family may not belong with the others in the order to which it gives its

[1] This concept is elucidated by Marion Ownbey in Ownbey and Aase, 1955.

Fig. 1.2. Peloric (Fig. 1.2a, 1.2b) and normal (Fig. 1.2c) flower-types of the common snapdragon, *Antirrhinum majus.* Courtesy of the George W. Park Seed Co., Greenwood, S.C. Peloric snapdragons differ from the ordinary type in only a single pair of genes.

name, but the suggestion is not borne out by further study. The similarities in several other features combine to support the traditional concept of the group. It is in fact still uncertain whether the absence of betalains from the Caryophyllaceae is a primitive feature within the order or reflects a reversion from a betalain-ancestry within the group. In the former case, the character should have more importance to the intraordinal classification than in the latter, but in either case the information now available strongly supports the traditional association of the Caryophyllaceae with the other families of the order.

It is well known that apetalous genera, species, or individuals occur in various groups of plants that usually have petals. It is now generally believed that the apetalous condition in angiosperms usually reflects the loss of petals rather than an original absence, and that this loss has occurred repeatedly in various groups only distantly related to each other.

It is of course also clear that the absence of a character may reflect the complete absence of the genetic system that would be required to produce it. There is no reason to believe that the prokaryotic organization of the protoplast of bacteria and blue-green algae could be transformed into the eukaryotic organization typical of other plants by merely supplying one or two genes missing from an otherwise complete system, nor is there any reason to think that the gymnosperms could be induced to form an angiospermous ovary merely by supplying a missing gene or so.

Thus we are led on both theoretical and practical grounds to the conclusion that the absence of a character is a less reliable guide to taxonomic affinities than its presence.

The Size and Delimitation of Taxa

Any useful system of classification must concern itself with both the objects being classified and the characters used to differentiate the groups. The scheme must permit the units to be assigned to the proper groups, and the groups should be characterized, however imperfectly, by something more than a mere list of the units to be included. The taxonomic system is no exception.

It is obviously desirable that each taxon be sharply delimited and well characterized. The existence of intermediate forms, which could as well be assigned to one group as the other, is disturbing to our sense of order. It is even more disturbing to find a unit which on the basis of the critical distinguishing character belongs to one group, but which appears, on the rest of the evidence, to be more closely related to another group. Obviously the system should, insofar as possible, be devised to avoid such flaws.

From the standpoint of understanding and remembering the scheme of classification, it would be useful if all units of a given rank contained the same number of subordinate units, if differences among units of the same rank were always of the same nature, significance, or importance, and if all characters had a fixed value in the scheme of classification. Thus it would appeal to the orderly sense of our minds if all taxonomic orders contained 10 families, all families 10 genera, and all genera 10 species, or even if all orders contained 10 families, all families 20 genera, and all genera 40 species. Likewise it would be appealing if the arrangement of leaves on the stem (alternate, opposite, or whorled) always marked genera within a family, but never species within a genus nor families within an order.

In practice, any such consistency in the taxonomic scheme is impossible. The objectives of uniform size of groups and uniform weight of characters often clash and cannot both be achieved at the same time. It is also, unfortunately, impractical to insist that there never be any intermediates between recognized taxa, however much the existence of these interme- diates may disturb our sense of propriety. All of these objectives, however, are properly kept in mind by the taxonomist.

If a small group is so different from others that it cannot be included elsewhere without undue difficulty, it is kept as a separate unit. Thus we have some genera with only one species, some families with only one genus, and some orders with only one family. The genus *Casuarina* as traditionally defined contains perhaps 50 species, but it is the only genus of the family Casuarinaceae, which in turn is the only family of the order Casuarinales. Among the gymnosperms, the well known maidenhair-tree, *Ginkgo biloba,* is the only living species of its genus, family, and order.

On the other hand, if a large and mentally unwieldy group can be divided by using a few characters of less evident importance, or by ignoring the existence of a few transitional units, it may be useful to undertake the division. Thus the genera in such large and closely knit families as the Apiaceae, Asteraceae, and Brassicaceae are notoriously difficult to define. In order to have any genera at all, we must use relatively trivial differ- entiating characters, and even then be prepared to face the existence of transitional species. In the Asteraceae we would otherwise confront the prospect of including the whole subfamily Asteroideae (Tubuliflorae), with probably more than 15,000 species, in a single genus. At the beginning of the 20th century one disgusted botanist did include all species he had to consider in the family Brassicaceae within the single comprehensive genus *Crucifera,* but his treatment has been generally ignored. In such a large group, an imperfect organization is better than no organization at all.

The larger the group, the greater the mental pressure to divide it, even if minor characters must be used and some intermediates must be arbi- trarily placed. Conversely, the smaller the group, the greater the differences must be between it and its relatives, if the group is to be maintained. The family Bataceae, consisting only of the genus *Batis* with two species, has usually been maintained in a distinct order of uncertain affinities, the Batales. More recently it has been suggested, largely on the basis of the pollen and the secondary metabolites, that another small family, the Gy- rostemonaceae, should also be included in the Batales. The differences between the two families seem too formidable to permit their merger into one family, however, and the position of the two-family order in the general system is still debatable.

We are thus led back to the principle of seeking the best compromise among the often conflicting objectives of the taxonomic system. As a general-purpose system, the taxonomic system cannot properly serve any one purpose so faithfully as to exclude some other legitimate purpose altogether. There can be as many special systems as there are special purposes, but only the taxonomic system tries to balance all these needs against one another in a single scheme. It should be no surprise that taxonomists often differ about how best to meet the multitude of conflicting objectives.

The fact that recognizable groups are not always sharply limited should not be surprising. The evolutionary concept provides the basic rationale for the taxonomic system. All terrestrial eukaryotes, no matter how distinctive, are connected through a common ancestry tracing back to the unicellular flagellates and eventually to the precursors of the anaerobic autotrophic bacteria. If the fossil record were complete, then all significant gaps between groups would disappear. At any particular time-level there are gaps, but these gaps developed only through the extinction of intermediate forms after evolutionary divergence. It is only to be expected that extinction of the connecting forms will progress irregularly, and that at any given time there are perceptible groups which are still connected by an evolutionary remnant of transitional forms. Asa Gray once observed that the several segregates of the genus *Gilia* just fail as genera, "by want of a little extinction." Most students of the Polemoniaceae now regard these segregates as distinct genera, in spite of the connecting species.

McVaugh's Principle

In 1945 Rogers McVaugh put forward an important operating principle for the delimitation of satellite genera, which is worthy of quotation in full:

> "Any segregate genus should be sharply delimited; that is, any species which is intermediate in one or more respects toward a more inclusive genus should be relegated to the latter. The retention of the anomalous species in the more inclusive genus will change its limits, if at all, but very slightly, and only in this way can the segregate genus be precisely defined."

The idea doubtless long antedates McVaugh, but I have not seen it so clearly stated elsewhere. A more generalized statement of the thought is that it is frequently useful to define one group narrowly and a related larger group more broadly, so that the smaller group is well characterized, even though the larger one remains diffuse. I have repeatedly used McVaugh's principle in defining groups here recognized, as for example in the definitions of the Laurales with respect to the Magnoliales, and the Malvales with respect to the Theales and Violales.

The Level or Rank of Taxa

As we have noted, the formal taxonomic hierarchy provides for species, genera, families, orders, classes, and divisions, in ascending sequence, within the plant kingdom. Every species belongs to a genus, every genus to a family, every family to an order, and so on.

The number of levels of relationship that we wish to recognize in any particular group may or may not coincide with the number provided in the required set. If there are too many required categories for the number of levels to be recognized, the categories are telescoped together by having monotypic groups. Thus the order Plumbaginales contains only the family Plumbaginaceae, the family Paeoniaceae contains only the genus *Paeonia,* and the genus *Linnaea* contains only the species *Linnaea borealis.*

If there are not enough categories for the number of levels of relationship that we wish to recognize, additional categories may be inserted, as we have noted on page 4. Thus the species of the large genus *Carex* are organized into four subgenera and numerous sections, and the genera of the Asteraceae are organized into about 13 tribes. The Asteraceae provide an especially interesting case, because botanists consider them to be the only family of an order Asterales. Thus we seem to have at once too many and too few standard categories to treat this family adequately. This brings us to the question of the level at which groups should be recognized.

Aside from infraspecific taxa, the only taxonomic category with an inherent rank is the species. The nature of species and infraspecific taxa is discussed in CHAPTER 2.

It is perfectly clear that natural, recognizable groups of species, and groups of such groups, exist. The ranks at which these groups should be received are not inherent in the nature of the group, but depend on subjective individual judgment. The criteria on which that judgment should be based are recondite. They come down to personal evaluation of the importance of the differences and the size and coherence of the group, in the context of the system as a whole. Since we have already pointed out that individual characters cannot reasonably have a fixed, inherent taxonomic value, any evaluation of the importance of the characters marking a group is likely to be difficult and subject to unresolvable differences of opinion.

In spite of these inherent difficulties, a very considerable agreement has grown up regarding the groups to be recognized as genera and families of angiosperms. In part, at least, this agreement involves typological thinking. If the circumstances permit, we try to define genera in such a way that one can recognize a genus from its aspect, without recourse to technical characters not readily visible to the naked eye. Thus a person who is familiar with one species of *Typha* can readily recognize other species of *Typha* when he first sees them; familiarity with a few species of *Acer, Aster,* and *Solidago* will permit one to recognize other species of these genera; etc.

In the case of the maples, the typological concept that "a genus ought to look like a genus" has clearly influenced the traditional definition of the group. There are enough well correlated differences in the flowers and inflorescences of various species of *Acer* to permit the recognition of several genera with characters just as strong as those of genera in other families, but the trees all "look so much like maples," because of the opposite, usually palmately lobed leaves and characteristic double samaras, that it is customary to define the genus broadly.

The trouble with such typological concepts is that they often do not provide a clear answer. Although it is possible to learn to recognize an *Aster*, or a *Carex*, or a *Polygonum*, or a *Quercus*, or a *Solidago* by its general appearance, it is equally possible to learn the sections or subgenera of these and many other genera in the same way. There is nothing but custom and individual opinion to determine whether the segregates from these genera should be held as distinct genera or considered as sections or subgenera of more broadly defined genera. Custom, in such matters, is merely the sum of a series of individual opinions, plus inertia.

To at least some degree, the same sort of typological concepts that influence our thinking on genera also operate at higher taxonomic levels. It is customary to maintain the Verbenaceae as a family distinct from the Lamiaceae in spite of the fact that there is no clear break between the two families. The reason is that the differences are so pronounced that it is much easier to maintain two different but fairly clear concepts than a single rather amorphous one. Exactly the same situation exists regarding the Apocynaceae and Asclepiadaceae.

On the other hand, many of the families and orders of angiosperms, especially among the dicotyledons, are difficult to recognize by their aspect, without recourse to technical characters that may not be readily visible to the naked eye. This situation is in contrast to that among the vertebrates, in which the families and orders, although sometimes recondite, are in general much more readily recognizable. Some of the reasons for this difference are explored in later pages.

It should by now be clear that there is good reason to allow custom to enter into the decision on the rank at which a group is received. Since the rank is not inherent in supraspecific groups, it is only by giving some weight to custom that any stability in the taxonomic scheme can ever be achieved. A good operating principle is to maintain the existing classification whenever it can be defended on natural grounds, and to avoid changing the rank of groups if no significant change in the concept of their relationship to each other and to other groups is involved.

On the other hand, if a traditional arrangement runs counter to evolutionary relationships, then it should give way to a more natural arrangement when such can be devised, no matter how heavy the weight of tradition. Until some two decades ago, it had been customary for nearly two centuries to hold *Franseria* and *Ambrosia* as distinct, but the work of Willard Payne (1964) made it necessary to combine these two genera. He demonstrated that *Ambrosia* consists of several groups of *Franseria* that had independently undergone further coalescence of the involucral bracts, thus attaining the morphological characters of *Ambrosia*. The closest relationships of the various groups of *Ambrosia* (as traditionally defined) are not with each other but with diverse species of *Franseria*. Lloyd Shinners had independently reached the conclusion a few years earlier that the two genera should be combined, but he did not develop the essential argument that the distinction runs counter to natural relationships. As a sidelight we may note that from the standpoint of formal nomenclature (as contrasted to phylogeny), *Ambrosia* is the older name, and therefore the enlarged genus consisting of traditional *Franseria* and traditional *Ambrosia* must be called *Ambrosia*.

In some cases custom is divided and is likely to remain so. Distinguished precedent can be found for treating the legumes as three closely related families, or as three well marked subfamilies of a single broadly defined family. No one questions the relationships; it is only the rank of the groups that is in dispute. Here is the legitimate, but narrow ground for difference between taxonomic splitters, who would recognize as many taxa at each level as the evidence permits, and the lumpers, who would recognize as few as possible. The splitter prefers to recognize the agreed units at a higher taxonomic level, the lumper at a lower one. There are no objective criteria to determine who is right. Those who compare the system here presented with the conceptually similar scheme of Takhtajan will note that he often splits where I lump, although in this case we both recognize the three groups of legumes as distinct families that collectively constitute an order. In the traditional Englerian scheme the legumes are recognized as a family of the order Rosales, with three subfamilies.

The problem of lumping and splitting also exists at the specific level, as shown by Hooker's advice (Hooker & Thomson, 1855, p. 35) that botanists should seek "to determine *how few*, not *how many*" species make up the flora of a region. However there is now, as we shall see, a good measure of agreement on the criteria for recognizing species, and the differences between lumpers and splitters mainly come down to how liberally we should interpret the requirements in borderline cases. There is no ultimate authority in such matters, as indeed there is not in any scientific endeavor.

Competitive Exclusion, Ecologic Niches, and Taxonomic Groups

The principle of competitive exclusion has profoundly influenced taxonomic and evolutionary thought among zoologists for the past several decades. The principle is usually stated at the specific level, as for example, "in equilibrium communities no two species occupy the same niche" (Hutchinson, 1965, p. 27). Another formulation is given by Hardin (1960) as "complete competition cannot coexist." Recent concepts about vertebrate taxonomy are permeated by the application of this same thought to higher taxa.

Students of mammalian taxonomy, and of vertebrate taxonomy in general, are accustomed to seeing a fairly good correlation between the major taxonomic groups and broad ecologic niches (adaptive zones). As long ago as 1953 (p. 349), George Gaylord Simpson (Fig. 1.5) elevated this correlation to a principle: "The event that leads, forthwith or later, to the development of a higher category is the occupation of a new adaptive zone." This is a natural corollary of competitive exclusion. For a large part of the animal kingdom, at least, it appears to be basically sound if one is not too rigidly doctrinaire in applying it. As we shall see, its application to the plant kingdom is much more limited. The angiosperms as a unit fit the principle, but the classes, subclasses, orders, and families of angiosperms very often do not—at least not in any obvious way.

The whole structure of a higher animal is intimately correlated with the way it makes its living—where it lives, what kind of food it eats, how it captures that food, and how it keeps from being used as food by something else. Most birds (class Aves) are adapted to flight, whereas most other vertebrates are not. Among the mammals, the whales and porpoises (order Cetacea) are adapted to life in the ocean, never coming out on land; two families of carnivores (Phocidae and Otariidae, including the walruses and various sorts of seals) are adapted to a marine habitat, but return to land to breed; most other mammals are primarily terrestrial. Only one order of mammals, the bats (Chiroptera) has developed true flight. The rodents (order Rodentia) and the rabbits (order Lagomorpha) are gnawing animals, whereas most other mammals are not. The dogs (family Canidae) and the cats (family Felidae), although they are both carnivores (order Carnivora), have different habits of catching, attacking, and eating their prey, and these differences are reflected in the appearance of the two families.

Taxonomists of vertebrates are accustomed to seeing a high degree of morphologic integration in the animals they study. Everything must fit together and work effectively with everything else. A given feature of structure A implies something about structure B, which in turn implies something about structure C, and so on. It is perhaps an exaggeration to say that if you give a vertebrate taxonomist a few miscellaneous bones from an animal, he can without fail reconstruct the whole animal, but it is not a very great exaggeration. This integration in fact applies not only to the morphology, but to the physiology and life-style as well. The human jaws and digestive system clearly show that we are adapted to being basically omnivorous, rather than basically carnivorous or basically herbivorous. The structure of our hands shows that they are used for manipulation rather than for walking, and such structure and use imply something about our brain.

The overwhelming problem for animals in general is food. Having given up (in the course of evolution) the ability to make their own food, they depend directly or indirectly on the food-makers, the plants. Motility, a nervous system, a tightly integrated morphology, indeed all of the characters that we think of as distinctly animal, relate eventually to nutrition. These characters, in turn, permit animals to do many things that plants cannot do well, if at all; e.g., to fight, to exercise territoriality, to choose their mates, to move, as individuals, from one habitat or area to another, and to use active rather than passive means to escape from being used as food by something else. With all these abilities, animal populations are still faced by an absolute limit of food supply. Directly or indirectly the food supply limits the size (or at least the potential size) of the population. Once a group has adopted a particular sort of food and way to obtain it, the evolutionary pressure is toward perfecting the adaptation to its particular mode of life. All ecologic niches are filled by one or another group which is so well adapted to its niche that other, less well adapted groups cannot easily invade.

Only on a newly formed, isolated oceanic island is there any unfilled niche not soon invaded by well adapted populations from nearby. When a few kinds of animals are introduced to such islands, there is a rapid adaptive radiation into many of the unfilled niches. Freed from the necessity to compete with better adapted animals occupying the same niche, individuals that are relatively poorly adapted can still survive and reproduce, giving rise to a new evolutionary line which may become better adapted to that niche and eventually block new phylads from entering it. The Hawaiian honey-creepers provide a famous example of the ecologic and morphologic diversity that can burst forth from an undistinguished ancestry under such circumstances.

The same relaxation of competition leads to rapid and extensive evolutionary change in plants of oceanic islands, as witness the famed Hawaiian silverswords (*Argyroxiphium,* Fig. 1.3), which are related to the tarweeds (Madiinae) of California. The contrast between the evolutionary behavior of plants on oceanic islands and those on continental land masses is not so striking as that for animals, however, because even on the mainland a given taxonomic group of plants often includes highly diverse ecologic types.

Because of the general correlation of structure, appearance, ecologic niche, and taxonomic affinity, many of the families, orders, and classes of vertebrates are well known to the general public and have well established common names. Such common names as fish, shark, reptile, snake, lizard, bird, hawk, owl, penguin, squirrel, kangaroo, and monkey may serve as examples. These are genuine common names, reflecting a folk classification that does not depend on formal scientific taxonomy. Many other taxonomic groups, though not necessarily recognized in purely folk-classification, are so easily grasped that they have become familiar to a large part of the general public. It is not here suggested that folk-classification of vertebrates conforms in all respects to the formal taxonomy, but only that a great many of the higher taxa are recognized on sight not only by the taxonomist but also by the general public.

How different is the situation among angiosperms! Each of the obvious ecologic niches for land plants is occupied by species representing diverse families and orders, whether these niches are conceived of in terms of habitat, growth habit, method of pollination, method of seed dispersal, or various combinations of these and other features. Even such specialties

Fig. 1.3. *Argyroxiphium sandwicense,* a species of Hawaiian silversword. From *Island Life,* copyright by Sherwin Carlquist, 1965. Courtesy of Sherwin Carlquist.

as parasitism, entomophagy, mycotrophy, the succulent habit, the megaphytic habit, and the mangrove habit have evolved repeatedly in different families and orders. Competitive exclusion does not stare the observer in the face. Its operation is more limited, more muted, less effective than among vertebrates, and one must look to find examples.

A single family of angiosperms may occupy widely diverse ecologic niches. The large and highly natural family Asteraceae includes trees, shrubs, vines, succulents, megaphytes, and ordinary herbs, the herbs being annual, biennial, or perennial, the perennials sometimes monocarpic (i.e., flowering only once and then dying). The leaves of the woody species are evergreen in some and deciduous in others; in some species they are reduced to scales, and photosynthesis takes place mainly in the stem. The plants occur from tropical to arctic and antarctic regions, from the tidal zone to above timberline in the mountains, in open or forested places, in very dry to very wet or fully aquatic habitats. Some species are adapted to alkaline or very salty soils, some to seleniferous soils, some to serpentine soils, some to cliff-crevices, some to shifting sand-dunes, and some to disturbed sites around human habitations. Most of them carry on photosynthesis in a perfectly ordinary way, but some have crassulacean acid metabolism, and some others use the C_4 pathway. Various species are insect-pollinated, bird-pollinated, self-pollinated, or apomictic. The achenes are distributed by wind, or by animals (in any of several ways), or have no very obvious means of dispersal. Yet the family is so well defined that if it is taken in its customary broad sense there is not a single genus about which there is any doubt as to its inclusion or exclusion from the family.

The thoroughgoing structural differences that mark the higher taxa of vertebrates have no real parallel among the higher taxa of angiosperms. Differences in growth habit, which might perhaps be roughly compared to the evident differences among the higher taxa of vertebrates, occur repeatedly *within* the higher taxa of angiosperms, especially among the dicotyledons, and they are at best useful chiefly in combination with more technical characters of flowers and fruits. The ancient folk-classification of land plants into trees, shrubs, and herbs cuts squarely across the natural taxonomic arrangement.

Once the angiospermous condition has been achieved, the obviously adaptive changes that can take place mostly occur so easily and frequently that they tend to mark species and genera rather than larger groups. Or, as in the case of some evolutionary changes in the structure of xylem, the same selective forces operate so consistently throughout the group that the sharing of advanced features provides but little indication of relationship. The vast majority of angiosperms make and use essentially the same kinds of foods, using the same raw materials which are obtained in the same way, and they rely on the same source of energy for photosynthesis. As we have seen, the families and orders, by and large, are not restricted to well defined or even approximately mutually exclusive ecologic niches.

Plants do compete with each other for space, light, water, and minerals, but the number of devices available to them in this competition is relatively limited, and most of the changes are genetically not difficult, at least among the dicotyledons. Variation from one habitat to another is often gradual, so that a phylad may move from one to another without ever being deprived of an appropriate habitat. Evolutionary changes that result in better general adaptation, such as those affecting the structure of the conducting tissues, are available to and have been adopted by many different groups. The concept of adaptive peaks, separated by adaptive valleys, is more significant for plants at the specific and generic levels than above them.

Even at the specific level, natural selection often favors greater ecological amplitude for plants than for animals. The plant cannot move from place to place. It must grow where the seed lodges, or not at all. An ability to survive and reproduce in a less than optimal environment is therefore favored. Each of the several different species of trees intermingled in a forest may have slightly different optimal requirements, yet some individuals of each species may actually be growing in sites to which one of the other species is a little better suited.

The plant must of course be adapted to its environment if it is to survive and leave offspring, but the plant system is more loosely integrated and more tolerant of casual variation than that of animals. *Verbesina alternifolia,* an eastern American species of the Asteraceae, usually has the stem evidently winged by the decurrent leaf-bases, but the occasional individuals with wingless stems are under no obvious selective disadvantage. Anyone who has been responsible for laboratory instruction in a beginning taxonomy course will recall how often students happen upon flowers that are unusual in some way and do not fit the formal description for their species or genus. There may well be some selection against such morphologically deviant individuals, or the characters would be even less stable than they are, but the selection is not so rigorous as is customary in animals. More of the deviant plants survive and reproduce, even though in the long run they or their descendants may lose out in the competition with more ordinary individuals of the species.

The separate character-complexes for various organs of plants are only rather loosely articulated. The growth-habit is certainly important to the plant, but each of several growth-habits is compatible with each of several types of flower and fruit, the one exerting relatively little influence on the other. The independence of the various character-complexes is only relative rather than absolute, however. Samaras and nuts are certainly better adapted to trees than to low herbs.

Even within such a seemingly well integrated structure as the flower there are two separate sets of adaptations, one relating to pollination, the other to seed-dispersal. Again, each of several different methods of pollination is compatible with each of several different methods of seed-dispersal. The adaptations for seed-dispersal do not reach their full development until the fruit is mature, but the gynoecium is the precursor to the fruit, and the structure of the gynoecium is an integral part of the set of characters relating to seed-dispersal.

The number of genuine common names of angiosperms that conform at all closely to the major taxonomic groups is very limited. Grass, palm, orchid, lily, and cactus might be suggested as possibilities, but even for some of these the conformity is not very good. Some members of the family Euphorbiaceae occupy in Africa the niche commonly occupied by cacti in America, and these euphorbiads look so much like cacti that only a botanist would make the distinction. On the other hand, only a botanist would recognize some tropical American epiphytic cacti (such as the Christmas-cactus) as being cacti at all. Most of the Cyperaceae and at least some of the Juncaceae would be considered as grasses by many people without botanical training. The name lily is often applied to a great many plants that do not belong to the Liliaceae, and some of these are not at all closely related to the "true" lilies. The name orchid does conform fairly closely to the Orchidaceae, but this conformity is due in large part to the interest of horticulturists and the influence of botanists. The vast majority of Americans would not recognize the vast majority of orchids as being orchids, and the situation is no different in the tropics where the orchids are much more abundant than they are in temperate regions. Only the palms are left as a widely recognized folk-taxon that compares closely to a scientific one. A few cycads would pass as palms to many people, but here the confusion is probably no greater than in many folk-groups of vertebrates. We may note in passing that the palms and some of the other taxa mentioned in this paragraph are monocots. As we shall see, the monocots labor under special handicaps that make habital changes more difficult for them than for the dicots.

The difficulty in recognizing higher taxa of angiosperms afflicts even trained taxonomists. There are some tendencies and some intangibles of aspect that can be learned, but most taxonomists will not even try to identify unfamiliar material that does not have flowers or fruits. Even when flowers, fruits, and vegetative parts are available it may take some time to determine the family of a plant belonging to one of the less familiar groups.

The orders of angiosperms are even more difficult than the families. Except for the problem of whether certain groups, such as the legumes, should be lumped into one large family or split into several smaller ones, there is pretty general agreement as to which genera go into which families. A few genera are booted about from one family to another, and some others are doubtfully attached to particular families for lack of a better place to put them, but the proportion of these is small indeed. The arrangement of families into orders, on the other hand, still arouses active and major disagreement among competent botanists. In all systems, the orders of angiosperms are apt to be nebulous and ill-defined, and their formal characterization studded with exceptions. In many manuals the keys for identification bypass the orders and go directly to the families. Some botanists go so far as to say that the orders can be defined only by the lists of families to be included. Others are more hopeful and believe that natural orders with a reasonable degree of coherence can be characterized, even though the individual characters are subject to exception. I belong to the latter group.

At the level of genera and species many taxa of both plants and animals are readily recognized and have acquired genuine common names. Alder, beech, birch, dandelion, elm, goldenrod, hickory, manzanita, maple, oak, rose, and violet are a few of the many folk-names that conform fairly well to botanical genera, and such names as sugar-maple, silver-maple, black maple, red maple, striped maple, paper-birch, cherry-birch, yellow birch, and red oak, white oak, black oak, post-oak, and bur-oak show that species as well as genera are often recognized. The present generation of city-bred Americans may be unacquainted with most or all of these plants, but our pioneer forebears knew and had names for these and many other genera, sections, and species. The English colonists, familiar with oaks at home, had no difficulty in recognizing the American species of *Quercus* to be oaks, although the species were different. Nor did it take them long to learn and recognize the wholly new (to them) and unfamiliar genus *Carya*, for which they adopted an already existing Amerindian name. (*Carya*, *Hicoria*, and hickory are all variants of the same Amerindian word.)

Gardeners, even casual ones, have become acquainted with many genera and species of plants, and the botanical generic or sectional names have often been taken over into common speech. Azalea, ageratum, calendula, chrysanthemum, cosmos, cyclamen, dahlia, petunia, phlox, rhododendron, and verbena are familiar examples.

Here again it is not suggested that common names and folk-classification at generic and infrageneric levels conform closely to formal taxonomy (for they do not), but only that many botanical genera, sections, and species, in contrast to the higher taxa such as families and orders, are readily recognizable by their general appearance. Many of the characters that enable people to recognize genera and lesser taxa by their appearance are doubtless adaptive. On the other hand, few systematists would deny that related genera and species sometimes differ chiefly in technical characters that are obscure to the layman and have no very obvious ecologic or adaptive significance. Some of these characters are presumably governed by genes that are useful for some other, less obvious effect, but alternative explanations relating to molecular drive (to be discussed later) and the supply of mutations should not be ruled out.

The Phylogenetic Concept in Taxonomy[2]

THE MONOPHYLETIC REQUIREMENT

We have, thus far, developed the principles that taxonomy attempts to provide a general-purpose system based on multiple correlations, that the value of a character is determined a posteriori, that the presence of a character is more likely to be important than its absence, and that a proper taxonomic system must reflect evolutionary relationships. We have also discussed evolutionary channelling in relation to ecologic adaptation and competitive exclusion, and touched on the point that there is some room for difference of opinion as to how best to portray the almost infinite diversity of nature in a necessarily finite and formal taxonomic system. The relationship between taxonomy and evolution now requires some further consideration.

It has become practically axiomatic that a taxonomic group must be monophyletic, and that a polyphyletic group is per se unnatural and must be abandoned. Too rigid an adherence to the rule, however, would wreak havoc on our system, without providing anything useful to replace it. Over and over again it appears, when enough evidence has been assembled, that the nearest common ancestor of a group would have to be excluded from the group on phenetic grounds and referred to an ancestral one. Or groups that are distinct for the most part have a common evolutionary base that can only be divided arbitrarily.

Anyone who has tried to perceive truly monophyletic kingdoms of organisms will recognize the problem. In the traditional two-kingdom system (plants and animals) either the plants or the animals must be polyphyletic at the unicellular flagellate level, depending partly on whether one accepts the classical or the endosymbiotic hypothesis of the origin of photosynthetic eukaryotes. Taking a different approach, we find that the break between prokaryotes and eukaryotes is presently sharp enough, but

---

[2] I here use the terms phylogenetic and monophyletic in the classical taxonomic sense, not in the drastically altered sense promoted by cladists.

the recognition of the prokaryotes as a separate kingdom merely shifts the problem to how to organize the eukaryotes into kingdoms or subkingdoms. It is possible to carve out a limited number of major groups of mainly multicellular organisms (with some permissible variation according to the predilections of the carver), but at the level of unicellular flagellates the groups are confluent. The unicellular flagellates grade into multicellular organisms among several (or many) lines, some of the lines closely parallel, others widely divergent. All of the presently fashionable schemes for the classification of eukaryotes must tolerate a lack of strict monophylesis at the unicellular flagellate level, whether the designers and users of such schemes realize it or not. Bremer and Wanntorp (1981) emphasize the lack of monophylesis in familiar schemes, but are not much happier about Leedale's (1974) 18-kingdom attempt at monophyly.

To take another example, the angiosperms probably do not have a single common ancestor short of the gymnosperms. The possible ancestry of the angiosperms and the evolution of the characters that mark the group are discussed in subsequent chapters. We anticipate the results in the following paragraphs, in order to make the point about lack of strict monophylesis. The characteristic xylem vessels of angiosperms have evidently originated several times among primitive members of the group. Stages in the development of the closed carpel, usually regarded as an essential feature of angiosperms, can be observed among living members of the archaic order Magnoliales. Within the Magnoliales one can also see all stages in the evolution of the angiosperm stamen from the presumably ancestral microsporophyll with embedded sporangia. Furthermore, it seems clear, on the comparative morphology of living species, that the development of the closed carpel and the typical angiospermous stamen took place in several related evolutionary lines within the Magnoliales. Differentiation of the perianth into calyx and corolla has likewise taken place independently in various families, as has also the origin of petals from staminodes.

One line of speculation (no more than that, but perhaps the most plausible speculation at the present time) is that the angiosperms were started on their way by a mutation in a regulatory gene in something like *Caytonia,* causing the microsporophylls and megasporophylls to function reproductively while otherwise still in an embryonic state. One can scarcely suppose that such a mutation changed a gymnosperm immediately into an angiosperm, whatever its evolutionary consequences. Under this hypothesis the most recent common ancestor of the angiosperms would have been a gymnosperm.

These are not isolated examples. As we have noted, it often appears when enough evidence has been assembled, that the common ancestor of a group would have to be excluded from that group on phenetic grounds and referred to an ancestral one. In the Asteraceae it seems likely that the common ancestor to all species of *Baccharis,* if we had it, would be an *Archibaccharis,* the common ancestor to all species of *Archibaccharis* would be a *Conyza,* and the common ancestor of all species of *Conyza* would be an *Erigeron.* The most archaic existing species of *Erigeron,* in turn, would on morphological grounds be just as well referred to *Aster,* and in fact it was first described as *Aster peregrinus* Pursh. (In this case it happens that the basal item goes with the derived group, but if a few of the right species were to die out, then this nearly ancestral species would be more at home in *Aster.*) Carrying things back another step, it seems likely that the nearest common ancestor to all the genera in the tribe Astereae, if we had it, would be better placed in the Heliantheae. If I am wrong about these examples, there are plenty of others to take their place.

The foregoing examples of difficulty with the monophyletic requirement are based mainly on comparisons of modern organisms and are thus subject to the challenge that the phylogeny may have been incorrectly interpreted. The fossil record of plants, or our understanding of it, is in general not good enough to provide unequivocal examples. We must work with the evidence we have.

The same lack of strict monophylesis has also been considered to permeate vertebrate taxonomy, where the fossil record is heavily relied on for phylogenetic interpretations. Simpson concluded in 1945 that

> "it is not probable on the basis of present knowledge that all the animals here included in the Mammalia arose from the Reptilia as a single species, genus, or even family, but it is not suggested on this account that some of them should be returned to the Reptilia or that another class be created for them. They certainly arose from a unified group of reptiles of much smaller scope than a class, perhaps a family or perhaps a superfamily, and for practical purposes this is an adequate fulfillment of the requirement of monophyly."

There is now such a ferment in vertebrate taxonomy associated with cladistic theory (discussed on subsequent pages), that a botanist can scarcely predict whether Simpson's views on the importance of close parallelism in animal evolution will ultimately prevail. Whatever their durability with regard to animals, they still seem very applicable to plants. In general, it appears that whenever we do get reasonable evidence on the history of characters that mark major taxonomic groups, at least of plants, these turn out to have developed through parallel evolution in various closely related but separate lines which collectively make up the ancestral stock of the group.

In the same vein, Ernst Mayr (1974, p. 111) points out that "The 'Adam' of the new phyletic line almost invariably belongs to the ancestral taxon." Mayr has long been known as a strong exponent of the monophyletic requirement in taxonomy, but clearly he recognizes that there are limits to its proper application.

Should we then divorce taxonomy from phylogeny, returning to the nebulous pre-Darwinian concepts of a natural system? Not at all. The marriage is highly useful and clearly worth saving. It is the evolutionary concept that has given meaning to the whole idea of a natural system, just as Darwin said it would. Furthermore, it is the fact of evolution and evolutionary relationships that permits taxonomy to have predictive value. Because of their common ancestry, the members of a natural group tend to share many recondite characters beyond the obvious ones that permit us to recognize the group.

If the monophyletic requirement is interpreted loosely rather than strictly, most of the conflict between phylogeny and taxonomy disappears. Monophylesis and polyphylesis are not such utterly distinct things as the terms would suggest. There is a continuous gradation from the strictest monophylesis to the most utter polyphylesis in proposed taxonomic groups. (Species that originate by a single act of chromosome doubling following hybridization may be taken to represent the strictest monophylesis.) In order to be natural and acceptable, a taxonomic group must fall somewhere toward the monophyletic end of this scale. Simpson has proposed (in the paper previously quoted) the useful rule of thumb that if a taxonomic group of particular rank is derived wholly from another group of lesser rank, that is a sufficient degree of monophylesis for taxonomic purposes.

It thus appears that a workable taxonomic system cannot provide a perfect reflection of evolution, no matter how abundant the evidence on which it is based. Indeed, the more abundant the evidence, and the better our understanding of phylogeny, the clearer it becomes that the correlation between phylogeny and taxonomy must be general rather than exact. However, the phylogenetic concept still proves the underlying rationale for the natural system. Taxonomy can provide only a somewhat muddy reflection of evolution, but a reflection all the same.

PARALLELISM

Once we admit the necessity for a broad interpretation of the monophyletic requirement, we are committed to the position that similarities due to evolutionary parallelism, as well as those due strictly to inheritance from a common ancestor, provide some indication of relationship and should be considered in the formulation of the taxonomic system. As long ago as 1912 Wernham pointed out that "critical tendencies are no less important than critical characters." He went on to say that

> "the general relation between the significant features of the ancestry and those of the descendants is, that in the former the characters in question are not constant throughout the group, nor may they be completely evolved. In other words, we are dealing with *tendencies* to characters, and not with the critical characters themselves, in the case of the ancestry. In the progeny, on the other hand, the characters are constant and completely evolved; and the line which unites ancestor and descendants represents the transition between the tendencies and their realization."

In order to understand why similarities due to parallelism give any indication at all of phyletic relationships, we must consider something about the mechanisms of evolution. We are here concerned with these processes only insofar as they bear on the establishment of a general system of classification of angiosperms. There is already an abundant literature on the mechanisms of evolution per se.

One way to think about the evolutionary process is to divide it into four components: an autonomous component, a reproductive component, a selective component, and a chance component. At this point we wish to focus on the autonomous and selective components.

One thinks immediately of gene mutations as constituting the bulk of the autonomous component in evolution. Within the broad category of gene mutations we should consider not only the classical, purportedly random changes, but also the internally directed changes—gene conversion and duplicative transposition—that are collectively called molecular drive. Polyploidy, aneuploidy, transpositions, and inversions are also important, especially because they contribute to the establishment of barriers to interbreeding. Discussion of these latter changes, involving whole chromosomes or substantial parts of chromosomes, is reserved for the chapter on species.

It is commonly said that gene mutation is at random. This is true in some senses. We can neither control nor predict the time and place of individual mutations. Furthermore, there is no credible evidence that mutations are specifically directed toward suiting the organism to its environment. Neither do known mutagens foster mutations toward resistance to the mutagen.

Mutation is not at random, however, in the sense that one mutation is as likely as any other. On the contrary, some of the possible mutations in any given gene are more frequent than others, and the mutation rate in opposite directions at the same locus (from a_1 to a_2 and back from a_2 to a_1) is likely to be different. Furthermore, the rate and direction of mutations in a given gene are governed not only by the intrinsic nature of the gene but also by the other genes it is associated with—the remainder of the genotype of the organism. Some genes have very pronounced effects on mutation in some other genes. As long ago as 1941 Dobzhansky summarized this situation by saying that mutability, like other characters, is under partial genetic control.

Looking at things from the opposite end, the chances of producing and fixing a particular mutant gene depend largely on what you start with. Any mutant gene that can be fitted into the functioning economy of the organism is likely to differ from its immediate predecessor in only a single nucleotide sequence. The greater the number of such differences between two functioning genes, the less—astronomically less—the likelihood that the changes occurred simultaneously as a single mutation.

Thus we are led inescapably to the position that insofar as mutation is a controlling force in evolution, the greater the genetic similarity between two groups the greater is the likelihood that they will produce similar mutations, have similar evolutionary potentialities, and undergo parallel evolutionary change. Furthermore, groups that have undergone parallel evolutionary change may well have been rather similar to begin with.

Evolutionary progress is like scientific progress in that when the time is ripe the same advance may be achieved by different individuals (or taxa) of similar background.

It is clear that the nature of the supply of mutations imposes limits on the evolutionary possibilities of any group, providing more raw material for selection to act on in some directions than in others. The influence of differential mutation rates is often so strong that a group appears to be predisposed to evolve in a certain direction. Wernham's comments on critical tendencies, referred to above, are largely a reflection of these genetic facts, as is also Vavilov's law of homologous series in variation (Vavilov, 1922).

On phenotypic as well as genotypic and mutative bases, different groups have different evolutionary potentialities, and not all evolutionary pathways are open to any one group. At the grosser levels this is of course immediately obvious. An oak doesn't have much chance of evolving into a carnivore, nor is a cat likely to develop photosynthesis. We have noted that once evolution has progressed beyond the unicellular flagellate stage, the evolutionary barrier between the plant and animal modes of life is essentially insuperable. We have seen that evolutionary channelling is on the whole more effective in higher animals than in higher plants, but no group has a clean slate, with all possibilities equally open.

Aside from the necessity of having the proper mutations, a group undergoing evolutionary change must at all times remain well enough adapted to the environment so that its individuals can compete, survive, and leave offspring. The greater the difference between the old structure or way of life and the new one being adopted, the greater the difficulty of maintaining adaptation during the change.

Thus, insofar as natural selection is a controlling force in evolution, the greater the phenetic similarity between two groups the greater is their potentiality to undergo parallel evolutionary change. Since the heritable features of the phenotype depend on the genotype, the foregoing sentence is equally true if the word genetic is substituted for phenetic.

We therefore come to the general principle that *evolutionary parallelism tends to indicate relationship,* and that it should be given due weight, along with other factors, in arriving at taxonomic conclusions. If the similarities resulting from parallelism are numerous and pervasive, and especially if they do not all relate to a single ecological change, then the ancestors were probably very similar to begin with. This is true regardless of whether one believes that all evolutionary trends must be explained in terms of survival value, or whether one believes that some trends chiefly reflect the kind and frequency of mutations rather than natural selection.

There is every gradation in evolutionary history from close parallelism among basically similar groups to convergence between essentially different groups. We do not classify bats with birds simply because both groups have learned to fly. Neither do we group *Cuscuta* with *Cassytha* simply because both are twining parasites. In each of these cases there are other important differences between the two groups that reflect their very different evolutionary history.

Our point here is that the taxonomic significance of parallelism and convergence must be evaluated in the light of all the information about the characteristics and evolutionary history of the group. It is destructive to the system to dissolve a taxonomic group merely because some of its important characters turn out to reflect close parallelism instead of absolute monophylesis. The more we learn about phylogeny the more examples of close parallelism we find, and the fewer examples of apparently strict monophylesis in phenetically recognizable groups remain. We must use phylogeny as an aid in developing a conceptually useful natural classification, not as a scrambler to obscure the patterns.

We shall see that the evolutionary history of angiosperms is so beset with parallelism as to indicate a basic genetic homogeneity of the whole group. The taxonomic and phyletic significance of similarities in individual characters must therefore be interpreted with the greatest of caution. To take the simplest hypothetical case, taxa A and B share the putatively advanced character alpha, to the exclusion of taxon C, but taxa B and C share another putatively advanced character beta, to the exclusion of A. Which similarity reflects consanguinity, and which reflects parallelism? Or do both similarities reflect parallelism? This problem is not an imaginary devil, conjured up to frighten the innocent. It is a daily fact of life and a trial to any taxonomist concerned (as we all should be) with evolutionary relationships. Talk to anyone who has studied any angiosperm family of considerable size, and he/she will tell you, in effect, "my group is shot through with parallelism."

Cladism

We must address ourselves to a theory of taxonomy that was proposed by Willi Hennig (1950, 1966) and subsequently adopted in major part by a school of true believers who have come to be called cladists. The term refers to an emphasis on evolutionary branching (Greek *klados,* branch) at the expense of other taxonomic concerns such as amount of divergence. Clade versus grade is an old question in taxonomy, which traditionally has been thought to require some sort of compromise in which both are considered. The following discussion is abbreviated from my 1987 critique.

Hennig's views attracted little attention, and still less support, until a revised version of his book was published in English in 1966, 16 years after the German original. Soon thereafter his essential concepts were adopted and then promoted with messianic zeal by a group of taxonomic theorists, most of them zoologists. Recently an increasing number of botanists have taken an interest in cladism, although often with some reservation. Cladistic theory has generated an extensive, often polemical literature. The theory is still developing and changing in ways that could not have been foreseen by Hennig, and what may be said about the concepts and procedures of one cladist do not necessarily apply to another.

The essential distinctive feature about Hennig's approach is that he considered a group to be monophyletic (and thus taxonomically acceptable) only if it includes *all* the descendants from the most recent common ancestor. The traditional (and still widely accepted) view is that a group can still be considered monophyletic (and thus taxonomically acceptable) even after some of its more divergent branches have been trimmed off. This seemingly simple difference has profound consequences to the taxonomic system. In Hennigian classification, organisms are ranked entirely on the basis of recency of common descent, that is, on the basis of the most recent dichotomy in the inferred phylogeny. The *amount* of divergence scarcely enters into the picture.

The first corollary of the Hennigian definition of monophyletic is that no existing taxon can be ancestral to any other existing taxon. The descendent must be included in the same taxon as its ancestor. Hennig expounded this thought at some length. We shall return to this matter a few pages further on.

Several terms introduced or sponsored by cladists are useful and are becoming widely accepted. Notable among these are polarity, apomorphy, synapomorphy, plesiomorphy, symplesiomorphy, and sister group. **Polarity** refers to the direction of evolutionary change in a particular structure or character. Given two or more states for a particular character, which state came first and is ancestral to the other(s)? The term is devoid of any value-judgments as to which state is more elaborated or reduced or selectively useful than the other(s). Once polarity is established, the prechange condition is said to be **plesiomorphic**, and the post-change condition is said to be **apomorphic**. Like polarity, these terms simply indicate the direction of change, without value judgments. If there has been progressive evolutionary change from character state A to B to C, then B is apomorphic with regard to A, but plesiomorphic with regard to C. The nouns apomorphy and plesiomorphy may of course be used in appropriate grammatical context for apomorphic and plesiomorphic states. A **synapomorphy** is simply an apomorphy shared by two or more species through a common inheritance. Sometimes synapomorphies are called shared derived characters, but this latter term is less explicit, because it does not clearly exclude apomorphies that are shared via parallelism instead of via common inheritance. A **symplesiomorphy** is a plesiomorphy shared by two or more taxa, presumably through common inheritance. **Sister groups** are taxa or clades that share a common ancestor not shared by any other taxon or clade. The nearest cladistic relative of any taxon is its sister group. The concept of sister groups does not provide for the possibility that one existing taxon may be derived directly from another existing taxon. Such a concept of relationship is excluded from cladistic theory.

For our purposes, it may be useful to separate cladistic theory into two parts: The method of arriving at a scheme of relationships (cladogram), and the establishment of a taxonomy reflecting the cladogram. I am sympathetic to much of the first part, but I see fatal error in the second.

Distinction among homology, homoplasy, and analogy is important for all taxonomists, but absolutely crucial for cladists. The basic concepts are simple enough. **Homologous structures**, whether similar or not, have a direct evolutionary relationship, either as a synapomorphy, or as a plesiomorphy and its apomorphic derivative, or as different apomorphies from the same plesiomorphy. **Homoplastic structures** are similar or identical apomorphies that arose independently in parallel fashion from the same plesiomorphy. **Analogous structures** are presently more or less similar, because of evolutionary convergence from different plesiomorphies. Although easy in theory, these concepts grade into each other in actual practice. There is a considerable literature on how to distinguish true homologies from mere homoplasies, and both of these from analogies (see Roth, 1984).

For taxonomists who see close parallelism as a normal process in the evolution of new taxa, the distinction between homology and homoplasy is interesting and often useful, but not necessarily vital. According to this school of thought (to which I belong), many of the seeming homologies among presently similar or identical structures would dissolve into homoplasies if their evolutionary history were known in precise detail. Only a rather loose correlation between taxonomy and evolutionary history is required, and homoplasies can be accepted as part of the pattern. For cladists it is quite another matter. Only strict homologies can be used in the construction of a cladogram, and homoplasies must be rigorously excluded from consideration.

One of the problems with traditional phylogenetic trees is that the arborist seldom explains in detail why the relationships must be as presented. Some generalities of evolutionary trends may be given, but usually without exegesis. The basis for discrimination between similarity by common descent and similarity by parallelism or convergence is likely to be unexplained, as is the basis for recognition of evolutionary reversals. Many of Bessey's (1915) classic dicta on evolutionary trends reflect the strobilar hypothesis of floral evolution, but the explanation for them is scanty. Most of us now agree with nearly all of his choices, but the reasons for our agreement are diffuse and seldom presented. Even though we accept most of his views on evolutionary trends (polarity), we no longer take his phylogenetic tree ("Bessey's cactus") seriously, partly because we assess the significance of parallelism differently than he did. With most of us, as with Bessey, a good deal of intuition goes into the construction of a phylogenetic tree, and my intuition may differ from yours. Those who boggle at the term intuition in this context may prefer to speak of heuristic interpretation.

One of the fundamental and laudable aims of cladists is to increase the amount of objectivity and repeatability in the discovery and representation of evolutionary history, and correspondingly decrease the amount of subjectivity and intuition. To this end they have established a set of formal procedures.

POLARITY

Once the characters or character-states to be considered have been recognized, the first step is to determine polarity. Which end of an evolutionary sequence is which? Is the woody habit ancestral to the herbaceous, or vice versa?

Most cladists try to determine polarity of character-states within a group primarily by comparison with a related group, called for this purpose an **outgroup**. If only one of a pair of character-states under consideration is found in the outgroup, then that state is considered to be plesiomorphic (primitive) in the ingroup. Obviously a great deal depends on the choice of the outgroup, and this is a subjective matter. Much discussion has been devoted to how to choose an outgroup. In theory the outgroup should preferably be the sister group of the group under study.

In practice the recognition of sister groups and choice of outgroups often present difficulties. There may be some doubt as to which of several related taxa is the true sister group of the group under consideration. The sister group, once identified, may not be sufficiently distinctive to provide answers. It may show some or many of the same pairs of character-states as the group under study. Then it may become necessary to choose a more distantly related outgroup. Some cladists use two or several outgroups.

Comparison with outgroups to establish polarity is not conceptually new with cladists, but the terminology and the formalization of the method are new. More traditional taxonomists should have no difficulty in grasping the method, which we have been using informally all along. Though helpful under proper constraints, the method is also fraught with the possibility of error. We should use it to help clarify our thinking, but not let it become our master.

The use of outgroups to establish polarity depends on the assumption that resemblance is more likely to reflect homology than homoplasy or convergence. If all advanced characters were uniquely received, then the outgroup method would work perfectly. Given a character with two known states in a particular phylad, the advanced (apomorphic) state would have been derived only once, and any sister group would show only the primitive (plesiomorphic) condition. Conversely, the greater the frequency of parallelism or convergence, the less dependable is outgroup comparison to establish polarity. Instead of being uniformly primitive with regard to the character under consideration, the outgroup may be uniformly advanced; it may have acquired the advanced state independently, and members with the ancestral state may all have become extinct.

Possibly the greater appeal of cladism to zoologists than to botanists until now is partly a reflection of the difference in the amount of parallelism in plants and animals. The relative lack of morphological integration in plants, and the poor correlation of evolutionary advances with adaptive zones and ecologic niches, combine to permit rampant parallelism, in contrast to the more rigid evolutionary channelling in animals.

Beginning with Hennig himself, most cladists have recognized some auxiliary criteria beyond outgroup comparison in the determination of polarity. Indeed the outgroup method is only vaguely implied by Hennig rather than clearly stated, and it is his disciples who have formalized it and elevated it to a position of primacy.

One of these auxiliary criteria, with which no one will quarrel in principle, is the fossil record. A character that appears substantially earlier in the fossil record than any alternative state should be regarded as primitive. Thus, on the basis of the fossil record, monosulcate pollen is more primitive than any sort of triaperturate pollen, and within the angiosperms tricolpate pollen is more primitive than triporate or multiporate pollen. Present-day cladistic theorists tend to downplay the fossil criterion, however, by questioning both the adequacy of the fossil record and the taxonomic assignment of the fossils. The relative importance attached to the fossil record is not central to cladistic theory. One may emphasize it or deemphasize it, and still be a cladist.

Comparative ontogeny can also be used to help determine polarity. The relationship between ontogeny and phylogeny is discussed on page 57.

Still other auxiliary methods are sometimes used in the assessment of polarity. We need not explore them here, because they do not significantly affect the general theory. We must of course approve of any procedure that increases the accuracy of the evaluation.

My own thought is that we should keep in mind Neil Stevens' description of the scientific method (delivered in a presidential address to the Botanical Society of America at Chicago in 1947) as "doing your damnedest with the problem at hand." We should use whatever evidence we can get to establish polarity, and that evidence is not restricted to the methods enumerated above. We should for example keep in mind that every organ or character should have a logically plausible evolutionary history. New structures ordinarily arise by modification of pre-existing structures, rather than appearing full-blown without a logical antecedent. This principle is expressed in an aphorism, the origin of which I have been unable to trace, that "organs do not arise functionless." We should avoid leaving anything hanging from an evolutionary skyhook if there is a reasonable alternative, and should prefer an interpretation of polarity that helps to tie groups together in a logically plausible scheme.

We should be wary of an interpretation of polarity that appears to be counter-selective. Counter-selective changes may in fact sometimes happen, or a change that appears to be counter-selective may reflect a change in selective pressures relating to a changed ecological niche, but seemingly counter-selective polarity should be a cause for careful reconsideration.

CONSTRUCTION OF A CLADOGRAM

After polarity of characters has been established, the next step in cladistic procedure is the preparation of a cladogram showing phylogenetic relationships among the taxa. Basic cladistic theory is primarily concerned with existing species, rather than with fossil or with higher taxa either living or fossil. With some adjustments it is possible to apply the same principles to fossils and to supraspecific taxa, but at this point it is useful to focus on modern species.

Under ideal conditions the cladogram will show strictly dichotomous branching. The progressive evolution of new apomorphies can be shown on the internodes of the cladogram. If only a few characters and species are to be considered, all this can be done mentally and manually. We try all the theoretically possible cladograms that reflect the presumed polarity of characters, and select the one that is the most **parsimonious**, i.e., the one that has the fewest parallelisms and reversals and thus the fewest branches. Parsimony in this sense reflects the use of Occam's Razor: Explanations should not be unnecessarily complicated.

In all but the simplest cases, the number of theoretically possible cladograms is likely to be so large that it is necessary to use a computer to find the most parsimonious one. There are likely to be some parallelisms and even reversals of characters in any group of significant size, and the unaided mind simply cannot consider all the theoretical possibilities. Even with the aid of a computer, some trichotomies or polytomies may remain, and the cladogram is said to be not fully resolved.

There is often room for some subjective manipulation in the construction of a cladogram. There are diverse sorts of computer programs, all aimed at parsimony, but likely to take different routes to approach it. If you do not like the initial results, use a different program, or add some new characters for the computer to work on, and see what emerges. Such actions are not necessarily culpable or wrong, but they compromise the objectivity claimed by cladists for their methods. Cladistic procedure is not uniquely immune to the necessity for subjective decisions.

In theory, we can never be sure that the most parsimonious cladogram for a complex set of evolutionary changes has been discovered, and that continued operation of the computer might not turn up a still more parsimonious one. For greatest confidence in the results, we should run several different programs until the results converge to approach identity.

Unfortunately, the search for the most parsimonious cladogram may lead to several or many equally parsimonious ones. This is especially a problem in botanical cladistic studies, in which the number of equally parsimonious trees may run into hundreds, with an even larger number that are only one or two steps longer than the most parsimonious one(s). Then the cladist must choose the one intuitively preferred, or accept only those features that are common to all of these most parsimonious cladograms, leaving the other decisions unresolved.

We can all agree that in any field of study the simplest explanation that provides for all the evidence has a better chance of being right than a randomly chosen more complicated explanation. It does not necessarily follow that the most parsimonious cladogram is correct or even has the best chance of being correct. There is so much evolutionary parallelism among the angiosperms that we should not balk at accepting something more than the absolute minimum number of steps if the additional parallelisms (or avoided reversals) make sense in other respects. We should therefore prefer the most parsimonious cladogram that takes into account all the available evidence as to the probable evolutionary history of the group. As the late Edgar Anderson put it orally to me (and doubtless to others), we should try to find out what has been going on in the evolution of a group, and shape our taxonomic and phylogenetic concepts accordingly.

The possible accuracy of any cladogram must be evaluated cautiously. If we could come up with an absolutely parsimonious cladogram for any considerable group of organisms, with each apomorphy occurring only once, we should feel very good about it, and have some confidence in its accuracy. In practice, such absolute parsimony is an unattainable goal. Evolution does not work that way. In any sizeable group, the number of steps required to produce the observed pattern is always greater (and usually substantially greater) than the number of polarized characters. Our confidence in the correctness of the resulting cladograms must decrease with the increase in number of steps required for a given number of characters. As more and more parallelisms and/or reversals must be admitted, the chance that the resulting most parsimonious cladogram is correct must also diminish. If there is a lot of parallelism and/or reversal going on, why should we suppose that there has not been more of it than the most parsimonious cladogram would show? It seems to me that as the number of excess steps over characters increases, the probability must also increase that the most parsimonious cladogram is not correct. If the number of polarized characters is w, and the number of steps in the most parsimonious cladogram is x, then the actual number of phylogenetic steps is x plus y, y being the number of undetected steps. As x increases in relation to w, y also increases in relation to x. The most parsimonious cladogram may still have the best chance among all the alternatives of being correct, but the probability of its being actually correct decreases as x increases in relation to w. Of course, not even the most ardent cladists maintain that the most parsimonious cladogram is necessarily correct, but the likelihood of error might reasonably have some bearing on our willingness to base our taxonomy on the cladogram alone.

We may note at this point that a cladistic approach cannot start with a *tabula rasa.* The whole concept of outgroup comparison for assessment of polarity assumes that conceptually useful groups have already been recognized. The cladistic analysis may lead to significant, even drastic changes in groupings and concepts of phylogeny, but the resulting groups and concepts inevitably bear some recognizable resemblance to those assumed at the beginning. Complete objectivity in taxonomy or any other complex subject is an unattainable will-o-the-wisp. There is a large subjective component even in the choice of which characters to use, and which to ignore as insignificant.

The procedures advocated by cladists for producing a scheme of evolutionary relationships (a cladogram) have the virtue of being repeatable and subject to rational challenge. By specifying a procedure, they foster logical thought and analysis. They require the taxonomist to explain the reasons for decisions on polarity and the basis for claiming to have produced the most parsimonious cladogram. Another taxonomist may debate the original definition of the ingroup, the choice of outgroups, and the adequacy of the computer operation (algorithm, in computerese). This is all to the good.

An important weakness of cladistic analysis as now practiced is that it does not use all the evidence that might be relevant, especially in discerning polarity. It converts the procedure into an elegant minuet rather than an unbridled search for truth and understanding. Cladograms as now produced commonly incorporate the false assumption that phylogenetic changes have occurred in a selective vacuum, with changes in opposite directions being equally acceptable, and parallelism no more likely than reversal. Granted that conditions of selection may change, and that reversals do sometimes occur, we should be reluctant to incorporate counter-selective changes into a cladogram merely to obtain a slight increase in parsimony. It would of course be possible to set up computer programs that favor parallelisms over reversals, but that would compromise the objective of parsimony.

In my view, the preparation of a formal cladogram can be a useful tool in an effort to understand phylogeny. Polarity of characters should be established on the basis of all the available information, instead of being limited to outgroup comparison. Selection of the most likely cladogram should be based not only on parsimony, but also on the plausibility of the implied evolutionary scenario. Sometimes the most plausible cladogram will be one or a few steps longer than the most parsimonious one(s). We shall return to this matter in the discussion of the evolution of xylem structure (CHAPTER 5).

From Cladogram to Taxonomy

The fundamental problem in cladistic theory, as I see it, is getting from the cladogram to the taxonomy. The fatal flaw arises from the insistence of Hennig and his followers that the term monophyletic can properly be applied only to a group that includes *all* the descendants of the clade that represents the most recent common ancestor, coupled with the assertion that only monophyletic groups are acceptable taxa. The logical and necessary corollary is that no existing taxon at whatever rank can be ancestral to any excluded taxon. The descendant must necessarily be included in the same taxon as its ancestor. A group that includes some but not all of the descendants of the nearest common ancestor is said to be paraphyletic (a pejorative term, to cladists) rather than monophyletic, and is not considered to be an acceptable taxon. As we shall see, this interpretation is destructive to the taxonomic system.

Species

Carrying cladistic theory to its logical conclusion, no existing species can be ancestral to any other existing species. Instead we can have only evolutionary dichotomies. In the process of producing two descendant species, the ancestral species must cease to exist. This is of course palpably untrue. To the extent that we know anything at all about speciation, we know that many new species arise as geographically peripheral isolates of other species (see CHAPTER 3). The ancestor and descendant continue to coexist for an indefinite time, until one or the other eventually dies out or evolves into something else. There are other modes of speciation, some producing true dichotomies, but these need not concern us here.

The problem of the putative disappearance of an ancestral species when it gives rise to a daughter species does not bulk large in the cladistic literature. I have posed the question verbally to a number of my cladistic friends, and received three different answers, all unsatisfactory.

The first such answer is that in budding off a new species through a small segment of its population, the ancestral species has lost some of its essence and has therefore become a different species. Any such loss from the ancestral population is no greater, however, than the sort of loss that is occurring constantly as particular local populations are wiped out while others are being established. Species populations are always in a state of flux, but no one regards such small changes as meriting formal taxonomic and nomenclatural recognition. *Homo sapiens* would still be *Homo sapiens* if the population on some island were wiped out overnight by a volcanic eruption, or if a few individuals were rocketed off to another planet where under different conditions of selection their descendants might evolve into *Homo* something else.

The second answer is to admit that the ancestral species does continue to exist, but to say that its continued existence cannot (or at least need not) be shown on the cladogram. We must show the dichotomy and say sotto voce that one of the ultimate clades is really the same as its prebranch ancestor. It is like saying, "Yes, we know that John Smith is alive and well, but his continued survival is inconvenient for us, so let's pretend he is dead and proceed to divide up his estate." The kindest way to treat such nonsense is to dismiss it as sophistry.

The third answer, exemplified by Donoghue and Cantino (1988), draws a distinction between Hennig's methodological principles (which they support) and his understanding of speciation. He (and they) admit that a species need not actually die in the process of giving birth to another, but for methodological purposes he (and they) find it useful to delimit species temporally at the branch points. Donoghue and Cantino also emphasize the difficulty of being absolutely sure that any existing species is truly ancestral to another. This third answer seems to be a combination of the first two, and is equally unacceptable to me.

Some of my cladistic friends now admit in conversation that a species may continue to exist after producing one or more descendant species, but their cladograms do not show it. The continued presentation of cladograms showing (when fully resolved) only simple dichotomies even at the level of species is at best misleading. It encourages cladists to continue to think in terms of the immediate disappearance of the ancestral species, even when they know better, and it permits them to avoid facing the internal contradiction that species, but not higher taxa, may continue to exist after producing descendants.

Reticulation

Botanical cladists face an additional problem not often presented to our zoological brethren. Cladistic theory, at least in its pristine form, does not provide for reticulate evolution. Many botanical species have originated by hybridization, either at the diploid level or more often through allopolyploidy. Obviously these cannot be handled in an ordinary cladogram, which would be seriously distorted if no special provision were made. The problem is not fatal if it is diagnosed in time. Species of hybrid origin must be recognized, by the same means available to traditional taxonomists, and removed from the initial set. After the primary cladogram has been made for the remaining taxa, the hybrids may be inserted, forming anastomoses.

Higher-level Taxa

Much of cladistic theory is written as if one must always start with a cladogram at the level of species, and then proceed to a hierarchical classification. Actually proceeding in this way would limit the method to those groups in which the specific taxonomy of virtually all members is well understood. We might have a chance with the vertebrates, in which the species are fairly well known, but in more speciose groups, such as angiosperms and insects, we would be lost.

In practice, many cladists apply the method to larger groups by taking genera, families, orders, or classes as the basic units to be shown on the cladogram. Such an extrapolation of the method is not fatal or even inherently improper, but it does introduce some complications that should be recognized and addressed.

Even more than with species-level cladograms, these higher-level cladograms depend on a proper assignment of polarity. Any working taxonomist of angiosperms knows that virtually all of the characters, even the most critical characters, of most large genera and higher taxa are studded with exceptions. These taxa are not analytic, but are described as polythetic or congregational. That is, they have been produced by the mental accretion of one species (or higher group) to another and another and another. Of course we try to come up with taxa whose characters are as consistent as possible, but real consistency is an abstract and unreachable goal. Anyone who has ever tried to make a workable natural key to the families and orders of angiosperms, or the genera of Asteraceae or Apiaceae or Brassicaceae, will know what I mean.

In trying to design one of these higher-level cladograms, one must decide which of two or more character-states within a given group shall be assigned as standard for the group. It would be misleading to take the most common character-state as standard. Phylogenetic relationships are *up and down* the evolutionary lines, not across them, as Bessey (1915) pointed out long ago. Thus in order to do the job right it is necessary to take the most plesiomorphic condition as standard, even if only a very few members have that feature.

Cladograms of higher-level taxa are always oversimplifications of evolutionary history. A single internode on the clade may cover the acquisition of two or several or many individual apomorphies. It is customary to show these by numbered cross-bars, with each number explained in the subscript. It should not be supposed, however, that all of the apomorphies on a given internode were achieved at one time in a great leap forward. On the contrary, the assumption must generally be that they were achieved separately and individually in a series of speciation-events. Given the pervasive parallelism in the angiosperms, probably some of them were achieved more than once even within the course of a single internode on the cladogram. Thus the nice clean lines of these higher-level cladograms are simplified representations of a much more complicated actual phylogeny. That is not in itself bad, so long as the makers and users of such diagrams recognize the simplification and take account of it in their thinking.

The problems of cladistic theory at the higher taxonomic levels are immense and cannot be swept under the rug. The refusal to admit paraphyletic taxa means that related taxa can be characterized (and defended as proper taxonomic groups) only by differences in their advanced characters. They must have different synapomorphies. If all the consistent differences between two phenetic groups lie in the presence of advanced characters in one group and their absence in the other, then the two groups cannot be separated taxonomically.

Rigorous application of these principles would destroy our taxonomic system, without producing anything useful to replace it. The cladistic association of crocodilians and birds in one major taxon (Wiley, 1981), as opposed to lizards and turtles and snakes in another, is a paradigm case. Some cladistic loyalists defend this classification as a better representation of the actual similarities and differences among organisms than the more traditional classification into reptiles and birds. I can only say that they do not live in the same conceptual world that I do. They must of course march to the drummer they hear, but must we follow them? I hear a different drummer.

Unfortunately the case of the reptiles and birds is not an isolated example. By cladistic theory, group after group would have to be broken up or dissolved and replaced by taxa that may reflect the sequence of phyletic branching but have little to do with overall similarities that can be grasped by biologists in general. The embryophytes and certain green algae (which ones might still be debated) would have to be included in a major taxon from which other green algae are excluded. Those of us who believe that the monocots originated from primitive dicots could not draw a taxonomic distinction to match. The monocots might still be monophyletic (in the Hennigian sense) in such a scheme, but the dicots would be paraphyletic and unacceptable as a taxon. The list could go on and on, and little would be left of groups that can be recognized by inspection.

Let us take another example here. The greatest gap in the biological world is that between prokaryotes and eukaryotes. Our understanding of the world is much enhanced by a formal recognition of the distinction. Yet such recognition is forbidden by cladistic theory, because the essential differences reside entirely in the advanced characters that have been acquired by eukaryotes but not prokaryotes. In cladistic terminology, the prokaryotes are a paraphyletic group. Cladistic theory requires that we seek to identify which group of prokaryotes is the closest to the ancestry of the eukaryotes, and then somehow associate these with the eukaryotes in a taxon from which other prokaryotes are excluded. Either that, or we must dissolve the prokaryotes into so many narrowly defined kingdoms that none of them can be ancestral to the eukaryotes. Some cladists are in fact proceeding with just such endeavors. If one accepts the endosymbiotic hypothesis of the origin of certain organelles, the problem is still further complicated.

There is something fundamentally wrong with any theory of taxonomy that does not permit the recognition of the prokaryotes as a major taxonomic group and their separation from the eukaryotes at a high taxonomic level. Fundamentally wrong, that is, if we are seeking to have a general-purpose system, which best reflects the totality of similarities and differences among organisms and which can be used by all who are concerned with such differences. Probable evolutionary history has a large role to play in the construction of such a general-purpose system, but the sequence of phyletic branching is not the whole of evolutionary history. The *amount* of divergence and the size of the gaps between groups must also be taken into account. Consideration of phylogeny is an important means in the construction of a taxonomy, and the reflection of phylogeny has even become one of the ends of the system, but it is not the sole end. The system must reflect the pattern of similarities and differences, and be useful to people who do not belong to the ingroup. Otherwise taxonomy would be turned into an arcane sport, interesting only to members of the club. A new general-purpose system would then have to be invented. Cladists may contrive to steal the name and aura of taxonomy, but they cannot terminate the need for a general-purpose system. Cladistic taxonomy is a prime example of letting a narrowly limited set of means become the end.

There are some other, perhaps less fundamental problems with the application of cladistic theory to the classification of higher taxa. One is that rigorous exclusion of paraphyletic taxa must often lead to an unusual degree of either lumping or splitting. We may take our examples here from a recent book by Rolf Dahlgren et al. (1985) on the classification of monocotyledons. These authors are heavily influenced by cladistic theory, but they do not uniformly exclude paraphyletic groups. They apologetically retain the Lemnaceae and Araceae with the accustomed definitions, in spite of their explicit agreement with the general view that the Lemnaceae take their origin in the Araceae through something like *Pistia*. In order to avoid paraphyletic groups here, either the Lemnaceae would have to be included in the Araceae, or the Araceae would have to be divided into segregate families so narrowly defined that none of them could be considered ancestral to the Lemnaceae. It might then become necessary to include *Pistia* in the Lemnaceae or to make a separate family for it, depending on the precise details of the cladogram to be developed.

In contrast to their treatment of the Lemnaceae, Dahlgren et al. submerge the Orchidales in the Liliales, on the ground that the Liliales would otherwise be a paraphyletic group. Dahlgren wrote to me that he would have no objection to the continued recognition of the orchids as an order, but this permissiveness is not reflected in the published treatment. On cladistic principles, inclusion of the orchids in the Liliales could be avoided if the Liliales were divided into a sufficient number of narrowly defined segregate orders so that no one of these segregates could be considered directly ancestral to the orchids. Perhaps these imperatives of cladistic theory have something do to with the extraordinarily large number of small, narrowly defined families that these authors recognize in the Liliidae (Liliiflorae of their treatment), but even more splitting would be required to justify the retention of the Orchidales as an order.

A recent paper by Dahlgren and Bremer (1985) illustrates the current status of efforts to clarify relationships among the angiosperms by cladistic methods. These authors treat 35 families of Magnoliiflorae, Nymphaeiflorae, and Ranunculiflorae (collectively equalling Magnoliidae sensu Cronquist) plus 3 families of monocotyledons, 3 families of the Caryophyllales, and a sprinkling of 8 other families that I would refer to the Dilleniidae, Caryophyllidae, and Hamamelidae. Discouraged about the possibility of successful outgroup-comparison, the authors consider that "Within the dicotyledons . . . the possible synapomorphies are few and vaguely formulated and homoplasy due to parallelism and reversal is abundant." I have no quarrel with these conclusions. Using 61 characters for these 49 families, subjectively polarized according to their own view, they produced "more than 100 equally parsimonious solutions" with 225 steps in the cladogram. Some alternative assumptions about polarity, following Burger's (1981) views on early angiosperm evolution, also led to more than 100 equally parsimonious cladograms, in this case with 226 steps. By adding only two steps to their 225-step cladogram, they opened up numerous other possibilities. The one cladogram that they chose to present, following their own concepts of polarity, associates the 3 monocot families most closely with the 4 families from their set that I would include in the order Nymphaeales. Whether this association is maintained in the other cladograms of the series is not made clear. The one cladogram following Burger's polarity that they chose to present associates the 3 families of monocots with two of the nymphaealean families, but widely separates them from the other two. I am perfectly comfortable with the phyletic association of monocots and Nymphaeales, even though I retain the Nymphaeales in the dicots. In my opinion monocots diverged from the dicots during the Lower Cretaceous, evolving from ancestors that were much like (and ancestral to) the modern Nymphaeales.

One of the few definite conclusions that Dahlgren et al. draw from their study is that the Magnoliiflorae form a "paraphyletic assemblage of orders and families toward the base of the tree." This conclusion should surprise no one; indeed the authors find it "hardly surprising." They go on to say that the three larger orders (Magnoliales, Annonales, and Laurales, in their definitions) of Magnoliiflorae "are also probably cases of nonmonophyletic, mainly plesiomorphic assemblages." Again, no surprise, given cladistic terminology and definitions. The authors do not address themselves to the drastic taxonomic consequences implicit in their conclusions under cladistic theory.

My comments about the Dahlgren and Bremer paper do not imply that cladistic techniques can never be used to help clarify major relationships among angiosperms. I do say that any such possible help does not appear to be in the immediate offing, and that here as elsewhere the rigid exclusion of paraphyletic groups would be destructive to the system. Of course it all depends on what you are trying to do.

Sister Groups

Another corollary of the Hennigian definition of monophyletic is that sister groups must have equal taxonomic rank, regardless of whether or not they are comparable in number and diversity of subordinate taxa. One of a pair of sister groups might have undergone repeated evolutionary branching and extensive diversification to produce a thousand or more species, whereas the other might have only one, which does not differ very much from the most similar member of the first group. No matter; coming from the same branch-point, they must have equal taxonomic rank.

Traditional taxonomy allows subjective ranking of sister groups, depending more on the amount of difference than on the antiquity of the dichotomy. No one objects to the recognition of *Ginkgo* (represented by only one modern species) at a high taxonomic rank. Here both the morphologic distinctiveness of the *Ginkgo* phylad and its long and diversified fossil history contribute to the consensus, although the precise rank may still be debated. In contrast, taxonomists who regard the Nymphaeales as the sister group of the monocotyledons do not generally consider that these two groups must have equal taxonomic rank.

One difficulty in cladistic theory that for a time seemed important is the number of taxonomic ranks required. Although Hennig did not explicitly say so, it is implicit in his discussion of sister groups that formal taxonomy should show every dichotomy in the cladogram. In a fully resolved cladogram, each supraspecific taxon would then consist of two and only two subordinate taxa, and so on down to the end of the line. Consistent adherence to this procedure would tremendously inflate the number of necessary ranks, and leave the rank of any group forever at the mercy of the possible discovery of additional dichotomies in its ancestry. Although some of the early cladists accepted this idea in principle, its impracticality soon became evident to all.

Now it is generally accepted among cladists that a given taxon of a particular rank may embrace two or more nodes of the cladogram, and

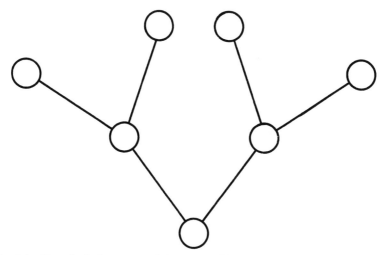

Fig. 1.4. Hypothetical two-stage cladogram, as discussed in the text.

thus have more than two subordinate taxa at the next lower rank. Just how many nodes may be covered in each case is a subjective matter. Here again the vaunted objectivity of cladism has given way to the same sort of subjectivity that afflicts more traditional taxonomy.

FOSSILS

There is an inherent problem in trying to apply cladistic principles and methodology to fossil groups. If all the species that ever lived were known as fossils, there would be a species at every branch-point on the cladogram. Consider the simple two-stage cladogram shown in Figure 1.4, with a species at each node. The basal species cannot be assigned to either of the primary branches. If it were arbitrarily assigned to one of them, then that branch would be a paraphyletic group, taxonomically unacceptable to a cladist. Neither can the basal species be treated as a taxon coordinate with each of the two branches, because then the taxon for said basal species would be paraphyletic. The same problem would exist at each node, and classification would be impossible.

Of course, not all past species are known as fossils; most of them in fact are not. It is the absence of fossil species (or higher taxa) at most of the branch-points that permits at least some approach to a cladistic classification of fossils.

The gaps in the fossil record may not result entirely from the vagaries of chance preservation. There is something in the concept of punctuated equilibria, as advocated by Gould and Eldredge (1977) and others. I do not suppose that major taxa arose full-blown from single macromutations, but a change from one Bauplan to another might have required only a relatively few mutations in regulatory genes. The species participating in such a series of changes might well have been unstable and short-lived, and they might have consisted only of small local populations. Such transitional species would be much less likely to be preserved in the fossil record than common and widespread subsequent species that fully exploited the possibilities of the new Bauplan. Thus the cladist and the classical taxonomist alike can make use of the evident gaps in the fossil record as they go about constructing a taxonomy.

Still, it must be supposed that some modern taxa, whether cladistically or otherwise defined, took their origin in extinct groups that *are* represented in the fossil record. This is a source of comfort to classical taxonomists, but a plague to cladists. Avoidance of paraphylesis in recognized taxa becomes more and more difficult as progressively more fossil groups are included in the general scheme.

Inclusion of fossils in the same general scheme as modern organisms also inflates the number of categories and ranks in a system biased toward the recognition of sister groups at equal rank. Even if a complex, multirank scheme were completed, it would forever be subject to upset as more fossils are discovered or closely analyzed. Every new introduction into the scheme would be likely to set in motion a game of musical chairs affecting all the later members of the group, so that new ranks would constantly have to be invented to provide for everything.

Cladists are well aware of these problems, but they are not agreed as to how to meet them. There are essentially four basic possibilities: 1. Fossils may be cast into outer darkness and not classified at all. 2. Fossils and recent organisms may be separately classified. 3. Fossils and recent organisms may be classified in a single scheme and all treated the same way. 4. Fossils and recent organisms may be classified together but treated differently. Option 4 may be subdivided according to the way fossils are treated as compared with modern organisms.

Each of these approaches has a degree of logic and its own set of problems. Wiley (1981) discusses the options and associated problems at some length. He eventually settles for including fossil and modern organisms in the same scheme, but treating them differently, so that the fossils scarcely bear on the classification of modern organisms. Wiley's approach seems the most practical for general application, but it compromises the fundamental cladistic principle of not accepting paraphyletic groups. If paraphyletic fossil groups are acceptable, why not paraphyletic modern groups? The convolutions necessary to provide for fossils in cladistic classification may remind some readers of a bit of doggerel that begins, "Poor old lady, she swallowed a fly."

PROGNOSIS

The useful parts of cladistic theory will eventually be incorporated into classical taxonomy, and the disruptive parts rejected. Already the terms sister group, apomorphy, and plesiomorphy are becoming familiar in taxonomic discourse. The explicit, character by character consideration of probable polarity is all to the good, but hardly revolutionary. Parsimony will become an important but not absolutely controlling factor in the computer-assisted production of acceptable cladograms. Construction of a formal taxonomy will continue to have a large subjective component, and paraphyletic groups will continue to be taxonomically acceptable. Cladograms will limit the number of taxonomic schemes that can be seriously considered, but any complex cladogram is likely to be compatible with more than one such scheme. There is already some movement in the direction here predicted, as evidenced by Duncan's (1980) acceptance of paraphyletic taxa in an otherwise cladistic approach.

Numerical Taxonomy

Numerical taxonomy, or phenetics, represents another recent approach to taxonomy, dating from the late 1950's. It is similar to cladistics in some ways, but opposite in one fundamental respect. It resembles cladistics in that it provides a formal system of procedure aimed at repeatability, that the data on which the conclusions are based must be presented, and that a computer is used to produce a dendrogram. It differs essentially from cladistic taxonomy in that the emphasis is put on the actual characters of the organisms, rather than on the putative phylogeny. The dendrogram produced by a pheneticist looks much like a cladogram, but it is instead a phenogram, intended to show present similarities and differences.

Numerical taxonomists take Michel Adanson (1727–1806) as their patron saint. Adanson (1763) was far ahead of his time in urging the use of many characters, without a priori weighting, to establish natural families of plants. However valid in principle, his scheme failed in execution, and its reception was not improved by his rejection of Linnaean nomenclature and his use of eccentric phonetic spelling. He was only a minor historical figure in botany until he was rehabilitated by the phenetic school.

In numerical taxonomy, an effort is made to consider and record as many characters as possible, without any initial weighting. That is, no character is assigned any greater importance at the beginning of the study than is any other character. The characters must of course all be translated into simple yes or no qualities, to permit the data to be fed into a computer. Then the computer is instructed to produce a dendrogram reflecting all the data. After the groups have been established, the characters that most consistently mark them can be determined, and these become the important taxonomic characters. As is proper in taxonomy, weighting is a posteriori rather than a priori. The method can be used to organize individual species into similarity-groups, or it can be used to organize species or higher taxa in the same way. The computer does not assign ranks to the groups in the phenogram; this must be done arbitrarily by the taxonomist.

The greatest practical problem with numerical taxonomy is the inordinate amount of time required to gather and record the data and turn them into a form that can be entered into a computer. The human mind is very good at recognizing and remembering morphological patterns, but these patterns must be broken down into simple yes or no point-data for the computer. Anybody can ordinarily distinguish a cat from a dog at a glance, but how do we translate the visible pattern into a set of point-data for the computer? It can be done, but not easily or quickly. Furthermore, since the numerical approach eschews a priori weighting, numerous characters that might otherwise be quickly passed over must be laboriously analyzed and recorded. Any taxonomist worth his salt is likely to perceive the answers by inspection long before the data are ready for the computer. On the other hand, such perception does not tell anyone else why the conclusions must be what they are.

Once the data have been computerized, we must instruct the computer how to proceed. Much effort has been devoted to the construction of proper programs (algorithms, in computerese), and the reasons for preferring one to another have been explored at length. Different programs are likely to give different results in taxonomically difficult groups. Part of the difference lies in how aggressively the computer is instructed to form clusters. Some programs even incorporate an adjustable factor to govern the aggressiveness of the clustering procedures. With this factor set at one extreme, the computer will peel off one unit at a time, in contrast to all the rest. At the other extreme, it will make every effort to produce groups of equal size at each dichotomy. Normally the factor is set somewhere between the two extremes, but its position is arbitrary. In spite of the complex mathematical arguments, the choice of algorithms and placement of the variable factor are likely to be governed mainly by how well we like the results.

All of this procedure in numerical taxonomy is an attempt to formalize what taxonomists have long been doing informally. Instead of trying to revolutionize taxonomic theory, numerical taxonomy tries to duplicate as closely as possible the results that would otherwise be obtained by inspection and taxonomic intuition. Taxonomy characteristically proceeds by the recognition of multiple correlations. In numerical taxonomy these correlations are done by a computer, and the data are made available for anyone to examine. The computer can be jiggered in various ways to approach the human mental operation. It can even be programmed for whatever degree of a priori weighting might be desired. It is all done openly, so that each step is subject to rational challenge.

Aside from how to instruct the computer, the main theoretical problem with numerical taxonomy is that it is not readily amenable to the consideration of phylogeny. It considers only the results, not the evolutionary pathways to them. As we have noted, some concern for possible phylogeny is useful in enhancing the prospect that a taxonomic scheme really reflects the totality of similarities and differences rather than just the characters we have studied. Not surprisingly, numerical taxonomists tend to downplay the importance of phylogeny in taxonomy. If the cladists are done in by Scylla, the numerical taxonomists are almost equally at risk from Charybdis.

Although the human mind is adept in handling pattern-data, it is not very good at remembering and cross-comparing large sets of point-data. Here it is far outdone by the computer. Bacteria, for which point-data are numerous and pattern-data few, are therefore particularly suitable for the numerical approach. The senior author of the currently standard text-book of numerical taxonomy (Sneath & Sokal, 1973) is a bacteriologist.

However valuable the numerical method may be in some groups or in some circumstances, it does not relieve the taxonomist of the necessity to use good sense, particularly in selection of the sample. Herbaria in well collected regions tend to become heavily weighted toward the unusual, with an increasing representation of hybrids, hybrid-segregates, and odd-balls of various sorts. If these unusual specimens are treated just like anything else, they will distort the results. Too careful a selection of the sample can be just as bad. Some years ago a young botanist, here nameless, tried to show by a numerical approach that his own earlier neoclassical revision of a saxifragaceous genus was sound. Using greenhouse-grown plants that he considered to be typical of each of his taxa, he induced a computer to come up with the same classification he had previously proposed. If you let me choose my own sample, I can demonstrate as many species of *Homo* as you wish.

Wagner Groundplan-Divergence Method

Despite the serious problems in both cladistic and numerical taxonomy, the urge to formalize taxonomic methods and make the results more surely repeatable is still legitimate. I have no quarrel with those who go about it in a reasonable manner.

The Wagner groundplan-divergence method is such an effort to for-malize the production of a proper cladogram that reflects the kind and amount of divergence as well as the position of the branch-points. Taking its origin in W. H. Wagner's doctoral thesis (1952) (Fig. 1.5), it antedates the burgeoning of both numerical and cladistic taxonomy. A more recent exposition is provided in his paper of 1980. Wagner's recommended procedure is essentially as follows:

1. Delimit and characterize the species by normal taxonomic meth-ods.
2. Remove species of hybrid origin from the set. These may be inserted later, after the basic Wagner-tree (a kind of cladogram) has been produced.
3. Determine polarity of characters, from whatever evidence is available, including but not limited to the outgroup-comparison method.
4. Hypothecate a common ancestor primitive in all characters con-sidered. This putative ancestor represents the groundplan.
5. Set up a chart (familiarly called Wagner's bull's-eye) with con-centric semicircles about a common base-point that represents the hypothetical common ancestor to all species in the group.

Fig. 1.5. Some biologists who have made important contributions to our concepts of the relationship of phylogeny to taxonomy. ABOVE, George Gaylord Simpson (1902–1984). Photo courtesy Department of Library Services, American Museum of Natural History. BELOW LEFT, Robert F. Thorne (1920–). Photo courtesy of Robert F. Thorne. BELOW RIGHT, Warren H. (Herb) Wagner (1920–). Photo courtesy of Warren H. Wagner.

Occasionally this may be an actual existing species. The first semicircle (nearest the base-point) represents divergence from the groundplan in one character; the second represents divergence in two characters; etc.

6. Following a relatively simple set of logical rules explained by Wagner, and starting with the species that diverge the least from the groundplan, manually construct the most parsimonious cladogram. Branch-points on the cladogram may be represented by existing species or extinct hypothetical species. Species that have diverged in the fewest characters from the groundplan appear on the semicircle(s) nearest the base-point. Species that have diverged in more characters appear on progressively more remote semicircles. All species are eventually connected by lines to the base-point (representing the groundplan) on an assumption of maximum parsimony in the evolution of individual apomorphies. Thus both the cladistic relationships and the degree of evolutionary advancement are shown on the chart.

All this can be done manually if relatively few species are to be considered, and if parallelisms and reversals are not numerous. With more species, and with more parallelisms and reversals, the phylogenetic accuracy of the results begins to be problematical, just as in Hennigian cladistic procedures. The operator may eventually be overwhelmed by the number of essentially arbitrary choices to be made. Still, the method may be helpful in clarifying the thinking of the taxonomist, as well as in presenting conclusions. It does not require any false or counter-intuitive assumptions. It will not reliably detect all parallelisms and reversals, but neither will any other method. It may help to identify lineages within the group, which the taxonomist may wish to recognize at some intermediate formal level.

Although usually presented as a means of considering species within a genus, the Wagner groundplan-divergence method is theoretically applicable to genera within a family, and to higher taxa. In practice its utility at the higher levels is progressively limited, because of the pervasive parallelism and mosaic evolution in angiosperms. It may be impossible to assign a genus, family, or order to any one semicircle on the bull's eye, and the choices tend to become arbitrary.

Further Comments on Polarity, Relationships, and the Taxonomic System

Formal procedures for assessing polarity of characters and relationships among taxa have some advantages as noted, but they also have some inherent weaknesses. They lend themselves to the easy assumption that all one needs to do is follow a specific set of rules, and the answers will emerge. Like so many other easy assumptions, this one is false. In taxonomy there can be no substitute for trying to consider all the relevant evidence in order to come up with a scheme which provides for that evidence. We should be wary of attaching overwhelming significance to any one piece or sort of evidence if it does not fit the rest of our information. When something doesn't fit, it is well to reconsider the situation to see if a new and better synthesis can be achieved. This is in accord with the classical Hegelian procedure of thesis, antithesis, and synthesis. It is not unusual to find, however, that the best synthesis we can make still leaves some things which do not fit. We must make our decisions and construct our system on the weight of the evidence, always admitting that new evidence may require a change in the interpretation.

A loose correlation of primitive characters in angiosperms with other primitive characters, and advanced characters with other advanced characters, has been empirically perceived by many botanists for more than half a century. In a series of papers from 1949 to 1982 Sporne has vigorously exploited this perception to establish putative polarity for a series of characters, eventually 30 in all. Polarity for a few characters was first assigned on the basis of the fossil record, and then other characters were added by statistical correlation. The adequacy of the fossil record (as interpreted when Sporne began his work) to establish any polarity at all might be challenged, but in fact most of Sporne's suggestions support or are at least compatible with modern theory on angiosperm evolution. Thus he considers that the primitive angiosperms were woody plants with alternate leaves and regular, hypogynous flowers with numerous distinct petals or tepals, numerous stamens, binucleate pollen, numerous carpels, anatropous, bitegmic, crassinucellar ovules and endospermous seeds. So far, so good. On the other hand, he also considers toothed, stipulate leaves and unisexual flowers to be primitive. Reasons for disagreement with these latter conclusions are presented seriatim in CHAPTER 5.

A seemingly self-evident but often overlooked fact is that in seeking relationships of a terminal group we should start not with the more highly evolved members but with the more archaic ones. Bessey (1915) expressed this same principle by saying that relationships are up and down phyletic lines, rather than across them. Thorne (1963) (Fig. 1.5) has more recently emphasized the same thought. If probable polarity of characters can be reasonably postulated, then we should focus our attention on the more archaic members of the group, which have retained the greatest number of primitive characters. Sometimes this approach will disclose what Thorne (1963) has called nonmissing links. The Aristolochiaceae seem isolated and without obvious relatives if one focuses on the large genera *Aristolochia* and *Asarum*. Consideration of the archaic genus *Saruma*, on the other hand, shows that the ancestry of the Aristolochiaceae should lie in or near the Magnoliales. Even without such linking genera, it may be possible to extrapolate backwards to find a plausible ancestor for a group. The Apiales form a distinctive order, but if they were deprived of the single advanced character of epigyny they would be quite at home in the Sapindales.

One of the most difficult aspects of the classification of angiosperms is the instability of the characters that mark families, orders, and higher taxa. We follow good taxonomic theory in assembling groups on the basis of all the available information, and then assigning weight to the characters a posteriori, according to how well they mark groups. So what do we find? It seems that everything has an exception, or more likely several exceptions. On the basis of clustering of the taxa we may feel confident that we have recognized proper affinity-groups, but sharp phenetic limits are more the exception than the rule. With some allowance for lumping and splitting, there is wide agreement among taxonomists as to which genera of angiosperms go into what families, but mutually exclusive phenetic definitions of the families are in many cases apparently impossible. We may be able to prepare synoptical keys that show the critical characters of most members of the families and orders, but an effort to prepare a workable key to the families on a worldwide basis, with each family appearing only once, is an exercise in pure frustration.

The families and higher taxa of angiosperms are therefore largely *polythetic* or *congregational* rather than analytic. We put a genus into the family that it is most like in all respects, particularly if there is some other genus already in the family to which it appears to be closely allied. But in doing so we may bring in a character otherwise foreign to the family. Splitters may pursue a sharper definition of families and orders by recognizing a series of small satellites around a major group, but this creates its own problems in comprehension and memory, and some failure of the critical characters must be admitted if we are to retain any major groups at all.

Any taxonomic system should be compatible with a logically plausible phylogeny that is not beset with internal contradictions. The evolutionary history cannot specify the precise taxonomy, but it limits the number of schemes that can be seriously considered. For example, the known fossil record would militate strongly against any effort to put the palms at the base of the angiosperms, or even at the base of the monocotyledons.

If one accepts the strobilar hypothesis of floral morphology and evolution (see CHAPTER 5), as most of us now do, then we need no formal analysis to conclude that sympetaly is an apomorphic character, as is also the absence of a perianth. The strobilar hypothesis is itself an intuitive effort to find a way to make sense of the diversity in floral structure. Its general acceptance rests not on any specific proof but on the fact that many botanists have found it the best basis for a logically plausible evolutionary scheme that accounts for all the data. The general abandonment of the Englerian framework for the classification of the families of angiosperms into higher taxa comes from the recognition that its basic premise (simple flowers are primitive) does not permit the construction of a logically plausible evolutionary scheme. What may have been tenable on the evidence in 1888 is not tenable on the evidence of 1988. We do not know how much of what we now believe will be tenable in 2088. Assessment of polarity of characters is further discussed in CHAPTER 5.

Regulatory Genes and Their Consequences

In a strict sense, plants and other organisms inherit DNA, not characters. Processes of growth and differentiation may be profoundly influenced by small differences in the regulatory genes. These govern the time and vigor of activity of the ordinary (i.e., structural) genes, which code for proteins. Evolutionary change is most easily accomplished through gradual but progressive changes in ontogeny, controlled principally by the regulatory genes. Eventually an organ may be transformed into something quite different from its evolutionary antecedent, with or without some remaining ontogenetic evidence of the nature of the change. Floral ontogeny may or may not suggest that a free-central or basal placenta in various angiosperms is essentially carpellary in evolutionary origin. The plant is under no compulsion to maintain the organographic distinctions that we find mentally useful.

One of the possible effects of mutations in regulatory genes is change in the relative timing of various ontogenetic processes. Some one or several aspects of ontogeny may be accelerated or decelerated, hastened or postponed, in comparison to other aspects. Maturity in some features may be postponed out of existence, so that the organism remains permanently juvenile in these characters. All such evolutionary changes may be covered under the term **heterochrony**. Many evolutionary theorists divide heterochrony into **neoteny**, in which otherwise juvenile individuals attain sexual maturity, and **paedomorphosis**, in which the juvenile condition is prolonged or retained in only some one or a few features. The distinction is often difficult to draw in individual instances, and I prefer to use the more general term.

Control of ontogeny by regulatory genes is at the heart of the aphorism that *organs do not arise functionless.* New structures ordinarily arise by evolutionary modification of pre-existing structures, rather than starting as useless bumps that acquire a function thereafter. Ordinarily some function must be retained throughout the evolutionary process, although the function, just as the structure, may be gradually modified. Thus, petals may be modified stamens, or modified sepals, but they do not originate (phyletically) as useless bumps. Sepals are modified leaves, and stamens are modified microsporophylls, which are modified leaves. Leaves are modified stems, stems are modified parts of a thallus, and a thallus is a modified cell-colony. Guard-cells are modified epidermal cells, and epidermis is modified parenchyma.

The persistence of vestigial organs or tissues in various groups of plants and animals also reflects evolution by changes in regulatory genes. At some stage in the ontogeny of a particular structure its further development is simply turned off. One might think of the result as an extreme effect of heterochrony.

It is widely and I think correctly believed that the later in ontogeny a particular apomorphy is introduced, the less likely it is to affect other characters. Selection therefore favors late rather than early ontogenetic introduction of evolutionary changes in morphology, no matter how valuable they may be. The late ontogenetic introduction of changes of course contributes to the persistence of vestigial structures.

It is also widely believed, on empirical rather than theoretical grounds, that once established, a particular change is likely to appear progressively earlier in the evolutionary descendants of the group. For example, Bailey (1944) considered that certain changes in the anatomy of xylem in angiosperms have "worked their way backward in ontogeny from the secondary xylem through the primary xylem."

It is not so widely known that fundamental ontogenetic change can sometimes be introduced with little or no effect on the mature morphology. One of the most striking examples is provided by the flower of *Stylidium*. According to Sattler (1973) only the stigma in *Stylidium* arises from the gynoecial primordium. Another primordium produces the inferior ovary and the stylar column with its adnate androecium. In *Stylidium* it is easy enough to see that reliance on ontogeny alone would lead to ludicrous error in the interpretation of floral morphology and evolutionary history. There must be other potential errors that are not so obvious.

A corollary of late rather than early ontogenetic introduction of evolutionary change is that the early ontogenetic stages, being least likely to be affected, may provide some evidence as to the ancestral condition. The correlation of ontogeny with phylogeny was discovered empirically long before regulatory genes, or genes of any kind, were recognized. As long ago as 1866 Haeckel proposed a so-called biogenetic law, that "*ontogeny is a recapitulation of phylogeny.*" A literal application of this concept is absurd, as Gould (1977a) has hammered home in characteristic style. Yet there is enough truth in it to make it worth remembering. It is no accident that seeds of dodder (*Cuscuta*) germinate in the ground, and that the basal parts of the plant deteriorate only after the twining stems have developed haustoria attaching them to the host.

It is virtually axiomatic that the greater the effect of a mutation, the more likely it is to be counterselective, since it is likely to disrupt a functioning adaptive syndrome. Yet we should not ignore the possibility that on rare occasions a mutation with major effects might be accepted into a genome and become standard. The "systemic mutations" postulated by Goldschmidt (1940) to result in occasional "hopeful monsters" do not seem quite so absurd now that the action of regulatory genes is coming to be understood. Gould (1977b) has deliberately put Goldschmidt's idea into modern dress in connection with the concept (Gould & Eldredge, 1977) of punctuated equilibria in the evolution of supraspecific groups. In my view, the more monstrous the less hopeful, but it does seem possible to introduce a major change in the structure of an individual organ in a single jump by an appropriate mutation or transposition of a regulatory gene.

The possibility for such abrupt major changes seems somewhat better in plants than in animals, because of the relative laxity of morphological integration and evolutionary channeling in plants. Hilu (1983) has catalogued a number of fairly large abrupt changes in angiosperms that are governed by single-gene mutations. Some of these are simple loss-mutations, disrupting a biosynthetic chain or an ontogenetic pathway and forcing the plant back to an earlier evolutionary level. Others affect taxonomically usually important characters such as the number of carpels and stamens. Even such an apostle of evolutionary gradualism as Stebbins concedes (1974, p. 286) that sympetaly in some common families "may have arisen simply by chance fixation of genes favoring an intercalary basal meristem in the corolla."

If many taxonomic characters in angiosperms are selectively insignificant, as they appear to be, then the possibility of abrupt evolutionary change is further enhanced. No adaptive syndrome need be disturbed. Connation and adnation of parts might often reflect relatively small ontogenetic changes under simple genetic control, as might some details of placentation and ovular structure. Unitegmic ovules might (at least in theory) be derived from bitegmic ones through a single regulatory change of no importance to the plant. The changes we consider to be taxonomically important must not happen very often, or they would not *be* taxonomically important, yet many of them have in fact originated independently a number of times, producing the parallelism that bedevils taxonomists trying to decipher phylogeny. Some of this parallelism appears to be selectively neutral, as suggested above, but some of it also is clearly adaptive. Competitive exclusion simply does not act as effectively in plants as in animals.

Selected References

Abbott, L. A., F. A. Bisby & D. J. Rogers. 1985. Taxonomic analysis in biology. Computers, models, and databases. Columbia Univ. Press. New York.

Adanson, M. 1763. Familles des Plantes.

Bailey, I. W. 1944. The development of vessels in angiosperms and its significance in morphological research. Amer. J. Bot. **31:** 421–428.

Baranova, M. A. 1972. Systematic anatomy of the leaf epidermis in the Magnoliaceae and some related families. Taxon **21:** 447–469.

Berlin, B., D. E. Breedlove & P. H. Raven. 1973. General principles of classification and nomenclature of folk biology. Amer. Anthropol. **75:** 214–242.

Berlin, B., D. E. Breedlove & P. H. Raven. 1974. Principles of Tzeltal plant classification. Academic Press. New York & London.

Bessey, C. E. 1915. The phylogenetic taxonomy of flowering plants. Ann. Missouri Bot. Gard. **2:** 109–164.

Bremer, K. & H.-E. Wanntorp. 1981. The cladistic approach to plant classification. Pages 87–94 *in* V. A. Funk & D. R. Brooks (eds.), Advances in cladistics. The New York Botanical Garden. New York.

Burger, W. C. 1981. Heresy revived: The monocot theory of angiosperm origin. Evol. Theory **5:** 189–225.

Carlquist, S. 1965. Island life. Natural History Press. Garden City, New York.

Crisci, J. V. & T. F. Stuessy. 1980. Determining primitive character states for phylogenetic reconstruction. Syst. Bot. **5:** 112–135.

Cronquist, A. 1963. The taxonomic significance of evolutionary parallelism. Sida **1:** 109–116.

Cronquist, A. 1968. The evolution and classification of flowering plants. Houghton Mifflin. Boston.

Cronquist, A. 1969. On the relationship between taxonomy and evolution. Taxon **18:** 177–193.

Cronquist, A. 1975. Some thoughts on angiosperm phylogeny and taxonomy. Ann. Missouri Bot. Gard. **62:** 517–520.

Cronquist, A. 1981. An integrated system of classification of flowering plants. Columbia Univ. Press. New York.

Cronquist, A. 1987. A botanical critique of cladism. Bot. Rev. **53:** 1–52.

Dahlgren, R. & K. Bremer. 1985. Major clades of angiosperms. Cladistics **1:** 349–368.

Dahlgren, R., H. T. Clifford & P. F. Yeo. 1985. The families of monocotyledons. Springer-Verlag. Berlin.

Darwin, C. 1859. On the origin of species by natural selection.

Dobzhansky, T. 1941. Genetics and the origin of species. 2nd ed. Columbia Univ. Press. New York.

Donoghue, M. J. & P. D. Cantino. 1988. Paraphyly, ancestors, and the goals of taxonomy: A botanical defense of cladism. Bot. Rev. **54:** 107–128.

Duncan, T. 1980. Cladistics for the practicing taxonomist—An eclectic view. Syst. Bot. **5:** 136–148.

Eldredge, N. & S. J. Gould. 1972. Punctuated equilibria: An alternative to phyletic gradualism. Pages 82–115 *in* T. J. M. Schopf (ed.), Models in paleobiology. Freeman, Cooper. San Francisco.

Goldschmidt, R. 1940. The material basis of evolution. Yale Univ. Press. New Haven.

Gould, S. J. 1977a. Ontogeny and phylogeny. Belknap Press of Harvard Univ. Press. Cambridge, Massachusetts.

Gould, S. J. 1977b. The return of hopeful monsters. Nat. Hist. **86(6):** 22–30.

Gould, S. J. & N. Eldredge. 1977. Punctuated equilibria: The tempo and mode of evolution reconsidered. Paleobiology **3:** 115–151.

Grant, V. 1982. Punctuated equilibria: A critique. Biol. Zentralbl. **101:** 175–184.

Haeckel, E. 1866. Generelle Morphologie der Organismen: Allgemeine Grundzüge der organischen Formen-Wissenschaft, mechanisch begründet durch die von Charles Darwin reformirte Descendenz-Theorie. 2 vols.

Hardin, G. 1960. The competitive exclusion principle. Science **131:** 1292–1297.

Hennig, W. 1950. Grundzüge einer Theorie der phylogenetischen Systematik. Deutscher Zentralverlag. Berlin.

Hennig, W. 1966. Phylogenetic systematics. Trans. by D. D. Davis & R. Zangeri. Univ. Illinois Press. Urbana.

Hilu, K. W. 1983. The role of single-gene mutations in the evolution of flowering plants. Evol. Biol. **16:** 97–128.

Hooker, J. D. & T. Thomson. 1855. Fl. Indica.

Hull, D. L. 1984. Cladistic theory: Hypotheses that blur and grow. Pages 5–23 *in* T. Duncan & T. F. Stuessey (eds.), Cladistics: Perspectives on the reconstruction of evolutionary history. Columbia Univ. Press. New York.

Humphries, C. J. & V. A. Funk. 1984. Cladistic methodology. Syst. Assoc. Special Vol. **25:** 323–362.

Hutchinson, G. E. 1965. The ecological theater and the evolutionary play. Yale Univ. Press. New Haven.

Leedale, G. F. 1974. How many are the kingdoms of organisms? Taxon **23:** 261–270.

Linnaeus, C. 1751. Philosophia botanica.

Linnaeus, C. 1753. Species plantarum.

Mayr, E. 1969. Principles of systematic zoology. McGraw-Hill. New York.

Mayr, E. 1974. Cladistic analysis or cladistic classification? Z. Zool. Syst Evolut.-forsch. **12:** 94–128.

Mayr, E. 1981. Biological classification: Toward a synthesis of opposing methodologies. Science **214:** 510–516.

Mayr, E. 1982. The growth of biological thought. Belknap Press of Harvard Univ. Press. Cambridge, Massachusetts.

McNeill, J. 1982. Phylogenetic reconstruction and phenetic taxonomy. Zool. J. Linn. Soc. **74:** 337–344.

McVaugh, R. 1945. The genus *Triodanis* Rafinesque, and its relationships to *Specularia* and *Campanula*. Wrightia **1:** 13–52.

Ownbey, M. & H. C. Aase. 1959. Cytotaxonomic studies in *Allium*. I. The *Allium canadense* alliance. Res. Stud. State Coll. Washington Suppl. 1.

Payne, W. 1964. A re-evaluation of the genus *Ambrosia* (Compositae). J. Arnold Arbor. **45:** 401–430.

Roth, V. L. 1984. On homology. Biol. J. Linn. Soc. **22:** 13–29.

Sattler, R. 1973. Organogenesis of flowers. A photographic text-atlas. Univ. Toronto Press. Toronto.

Simpson, G. G. 1944. Tempo and mode in evolution. Columbia Univ. Press. New York.

Simpson, G. G. 1945. The principles of classification and a classification of mammals. Amer. Mus. Nat. Hist. Bull. 86.

Simpson, G. G. 1953. The major features of evolution. Columbia Univ. Press. New York.

Sneath, P. H. A. & R. R. Sokal. 1973. Numerical taxonomy. Freeman. San Francisco.

Sporne, K. R. 1949. A new approach to the problem of the primitive flower. New Phytol. **48:** 259–276.

Sporne, K. R. 1980. A re-investigation of character correlations among dicotyledons. New Phytol. **85:** 419–449.

Sporne, K. R. 1982. The advancement index vindicated. New Phytol. **91:** 137–145.

Stebbins, G. L. 1974. Flowering plants. Evolution above the species level. Harvard Univ. Press. Cambridge, Massachusetts.

Thorne, R. F. 1963. Some problems and guiding principles of angiosperm phylogeny. Amer. Naturalist **97:** 287–305.

Vavilov, N. I. 1922. Law of homologous series in variation. J. Genetics **12:** 47–89.

Wagner, W. H. 1952. The fern genus *Diellia*: Structure, affinities, and taxonomy. Univ. Calif. Publ. Bot. **26:** 1–212.

Wagner, W. H. 1980. Origin and philosophy of the groundplan-divergence method of cladistics. Syst. Bot. **5:** 173–193.

Wernham, H. F. 1912. Floral evolution: With particular reference to the sympetalous dicotyledons. New Phytol. **11:** 373–397.

Wiley, E. O. 1981. Phylogenetics. Wiley. New York.

Young, D. A. 1981. Are angiosperms primitively vesselless? Syst. Bot. **6:** 313–330.

Chapter 2

Claytonia virginica, a species showing extraordinary variability in chromosome-
number. Photo courtesy of Walter Lewis.

Species and Infraspecific Taxa

The Folk Concept of Species

The species is an ancient folk concept, which biologists have adopted and shaped to their own use. It is the common experience of naturalists, in whatever part of the world, that the individual plants and animals they see can be mentally grouped into a number of taxa, in each of which the individuals are basically alike. In societies that are still close to nature, each of these taxa with any importance to the society has a name.

The idea that species consist of reproductively compatible individuals has a firm foundation in folk knowledge. Any farm boy knows that horses beget horses, donkeys beget donkeys, and that if you breed a jackass to a mare you get a mule, which begets nothing. The reproductive processes in plants are not so obvious to the unlearned, but it is clear enough to all concerned that wheat grains produce wheat plants, clover seeds produce clover plants, and mustard seeds produce mustard plants. Reproductive continuity is an essential part of the folk concept of species.

The other part of the folk concept of species, to go along with reproductive continuity, is that you can tell them apart by looking at them. Together these two criteria result in the recognition of conceptually useful groups. Each species encompasses a certain range of variability, but within any local area the distinctions between species are usually clear. Folk taxonomy of course does not address itself to things that are not perceived as being of any importance or intrinsic interest, but for the things that do attract attention it serves its purposes well enough. It operates in blissful ignorance of the possibility that there may be reproductive barriers between things that are otherwise essentially alike.

A Bit of History

It is no secret among biologists that there are frequently practical problems in applying the folk concept of species to the often bewildering diversity among individuals in nature. In trying to meet such problems, biologists have sought a more precise formulation of the concept. One can read in the works of various 18th- and 19th-century biologists definitions that sound very modern, emphasizing either reproductive isolation or discontinuity of variation, or both, as the essential specific criteria. These were produced at a time when heredity was only vaguely understood, but they are nonetheless very respectable efforts at definition.

One might suppose that the burst of knowledge about genetics in the first two or three decades of the 20th century would lead to an improved understanding of the nature of species. In the long run it did, but initially it fostered as much confusion as clarity. The mutation theory of de Vries, published in 1901 and 1903, envisioned the frequent saltatory origin of species by genetic change in a single individual, or by concurrent repetition of the same change in a series of similar individuals. Biologists such as Lotsy (1914) proposed definitions that would in effect treat each recognizable genotype as a separate species. In 1918 C. Hart Merriam recognized 78 species of grizzly and big brown bears in North America. These are all currently considered to belong to a single species, *Ursus arctos,* which is widespread throughout northern Eurasia as well as in western North America. A school of thought fostered in the United States by N. L. Britton and in the Soviet Union by V. L. Komarov considered that anything worthy of a name should be called a species, thus raising to specific rank many taxa considered by others to be of only infraspecific importance.

I have read learned efforts to defend the naming of individual apomicts as distinct species, on the basis of absolute genetic barriers among them. This approach led to the proposal of thousands of specific names in such genera as *Taraxacum* and *Hieracium,* producing utter taxonomic confusion. Such treatments are simply not useful in understanding and communicating the pattern of diversity in nature, and not many of us take them seriously any more.

During this period of confusion there remained a considerable body of both plant and animal taxonomists who retained the traditional concepts of species, but their voices were often lost in the storm.

By 1930 it was becoming clear that any really useful concept of species would have to be grounded in the traditional folk concept. In that year Du Rietz presented an admirable review of the fundamental units of biological taxonomy, and produced a definition of species that still has some relevance today. In his view, species are "the smallest natural populations permanently separated from each other by a distinct discontinuity in the series of biotypes." The existence of barriers to interbreeding between species is implicit in this definition, and explicit in his accompanying discussion. Du Rietz did not really address himself, however, to the problem of reproductive barriers not accompanied by other detectable differences. His definition, often cited in the decades immediately after its publication, is seldom repeated in print today.

In the late 1930's definitions were being produced that explicitly relied on reproductive isolation as the essential specific criterion. I well remember being exposed in graduate school to the then relatively new definition by Dobzhansky (1937) of a species as "that stage of evolutionary progress at which the once actually or potentially interbreeding array of forms becomes segregated into two or more separate arrays which are physiologically incapable of interbreeding."

It was at once obvious to me and others that Dobzhansky's formulation was too severe to be botanically useful. It would, for example, sweep great numbers of different species and even genera of orchids into a single species. The barriers to hybridization among orchids rest to a considerable extent (not entirely!) on adaptations to specific pollinators. If you will transfer the pollen yourself you can produce hybrids between very different kinds.

By 1951 Dobzhansky had relaxed his definition to read that species are "groups of populations the gene exchange between which is limited or prevented in nature by one, or a combination of several, reproductive isolating mechanisms. In short, a species is the most inclusive Mendelian population." That brought his formulation into essential harmony with the one proposed in 1940 by Mayr and rephrased in 1942 to read that species are "groups of actually or potentially interbreeding natural populations which are reproductively isolated from other such groups." Here the emphasis is placed on what actually happens in nature, rather than on what can be induced experimentally.

Inadequacy of the Reproductive Criterion for Species

Proponents of the specific criterion of reproductive isolation use the term biological species for the taxa so delimited. I am not sure who first introduced the term. Mayr used it in 1942 in such a way as to suggest that it was relatively new. By the mid-1950's there was a well established school of thought, especially among zoologists, that the real species in nature are these "biological species."

Appropriation of the term biological species for reproductively defined species implies that species defined on any other criteria cannot be biologically meaningful groups. Many adherents of the reproductive species concept have moved from Dobzhansky's original position—that the reproductive criterion is useful precisely because species as so defined are essentially similar to traditional taxonomic species delimited on less clear criteria—to the position that reproductively defined species are conceptually superior to species defined on other criteria. The term taxonomic species has sometimes been used in a pejorative way, in contrast to the putatively really meaningful biological species. This attitude amounts to nothing less than attempted theft. The traditional naturalist's concept of species has a long-established prior claim to the term, and has been an integral part of taxonomic usage and thought for more than 200 years. If the concept can be sharpened up and made more useful by emphasis on the criterion of reproductive isolation, well and good. But if so-called biological species turn out to be significantly different in many instances from taxonomic species, as indeed they do, then a new term might better be coined for the new concept, one that does not invite confusion with taxonomic species. I shall refer to reproductive and phenetic species-concepts, both equally biological.

There are some serious practical problems with the reproductive species-concept, as we shall see, but for the past several decades the majority of zoologists (or at least the vertebrate zoologists and many of the entomologists) have managed to live with them. They accept the difficulties as the price for a clear and generally applicable rule. One of these difficulties is the necessity to admit the existence of sibling species, which are reproductively isolated but difficult or impossible to define phenetically.

Botanists have in general been less receptive than zoologists to the reproductive species-concept. One's expectations from a classification may be a factor in the difference. Most taxonomists start as field-naturalists, with a basically phenetic species-concept, but experiences differ according to the group being studied.

Anyone of reasonable intelligence who applies himself can learn to recognize most of the kinds of vascular plants in a local flora. Several or many individuals of a kind are likely to grow together, and the plant stays put while it is being examined. Any attentive eye can grasp the pattern, and learn to recognize another member of the same group at the same or a different site. There are real discontinuities between species, and individuals can regularly be identified. It may even be possible to recognize the occasional hybrids between some otherwise discrete species. Things are not always quite that simple, but the budding botanist develops the feeling that the kinds of plants are really different, and that one can consistently recognize them by looking at them.

The budding zoologist encounters a somewhat different situation. Some kinds of animals go in flocks or herds, but more commonly one sees only an individual or two, often only from a distance. A bird is likely to fly away while one is focusing field-glasses on it. The opportunity to examine several individuals at leisure in the field is distinctly the exception rather than the rule. Sharp boundaries between species can still frequently be seen, but positive identification is often prevented by the circumstances. One must settle for saying, maybe that was a downy woodpecker and maybe it was a hairy woodpecker, or maybe that was a Cooper's hawk or maybe it was a sharp-shin; I didn't get a good enough look at it. The number of amateur ornithologists who keep life-lists of species shows that field-identification is indeed possible under proper circumstances, but the same people must constantly puzzle over the identity of something not seen quite clearly enough for certainty. A degree of frustration in making positive identifications becomes the norm. The budding entomologist soon learns that field-identification of any but the commonest kinds of insects is a parlous task; one needs a microscope.

Thus zoologists may not develop the same degree of feeling as botanists do that species can consistently be recognized in the field. It may therefore not be such a jolt to think that some species can not in fact be identified simply by looking at them with the naked eye or a hand-lens. The substitution of a reproductive species-concept for an initially phenetic concept may then seem like normal and proper refinement of theory. The field-botanist, on the other hand, finds the phenetic species-concept basically satisfactory, and is likely to resist a concept that interferes with identification.

The reproduction definition of the species has a certain psychological appeal. On first consideration it seems to provide a simple and theoretically sound solution to an otherwise intractable problem. Simple answers are always attractive. Scientists and philosophers alike use Occam's Razor ("Explanations should not be unnecessarily complicated") to cut through tangles of unduly complex theory. We should note, however, that Occam's Razor does not gut *all* complicated explanations, but only those that are *unnecessarily* complicated.

Like so many other simple answers to complex questions, the reproductive concept of species often produces less than satisfactory results, or the initial simplicity dissolves into dubious complexity in practice. Phenetically very similar organisms may in fact be intersterile. A sterility-barrier may be fairly readily detectable microscopically, as in the case of different levels of ploidy, or it may reside in such inscrutable details that it can be discovered only by experimental efforts at hybridization. Actual interbreeding in nature between genetically compatible individuals or groups may be heavily influenced by variable and unstable environmental factors. The taxonomic status of geographical isolates must be assessed intuitively; even the experimental success or failure of interbreeding between such isolates may be inconclusive, because experimental conditions are not natural conditions. Experimental demonstration that A will not breed effectively with B does not preclude the possibility that both are compatible with C. There may even be a complex and unpredictable pattern of interfertility and intersterility among groups A . . . Z. Natural hybrids between two putatively different groups may show varying degrees of reduction of fertility or competitive ability. Breeding groups simply cannot be recognized or defined without some recourse to phenetic features. The number of required experimental efforts at hybridization would be astronomical, and even if performed would not be definitive because the natural conditions of breeding and competition cannot be duplicated experimentally. Assessments of whether or not organisms belong to the same gene pool are in practice based primarily on phenetic similarities and differences. If individuals are phenetically alike, they are considered to be conspecific until a reproductive barrier is demonstrated. So much for the simple answer.

Actual interbreeding and gene-flow among phenetically similar, genetically compatible local populations is often much more restricted than the reproductive definition of species might lead one to suppose. It depends on the population-structure, the method of pollination, and the method of seed-dispersal. Geographic continuity, wind-pollination, and effective means of long-distance dispersal of seeds obviously favor such interbreeding, whereas geographical fragmentation, self-pollination or insect-pollination, and short-distance dispersal-mechanisms have the opposite effect. A species that appears on the map to have a continuous distribution may (and in fact usually does) actually consist of numerous local populations that are separated by distances greater than the ordinary distance to which seeds and/or pollen are effectively distributed. Even if the population is essentially continuous over the major part of the range of the species, it is likely to be broken up into small local populations toward the periphery of its range. The Mendelian populations so dear to the hearts of evolutionary theorists simply cannot embrace any very large number of individuals. Plants growing a thousand kilometers apart have virtually no chance to interbreed effectively, no matter how continuous the population. For any individual, the chance of producing a hybrid with an individual of another species growing nearby may well be greater than the chance of breeding with a conspecific individual a long distance away.

Although most botanists have always been skeptical of efforts to define species on reproductive criteria alone, a number of them did try to use the concept during the 1940's and 1950's, a few even into the 1960's and beyond. Perhaps the most persistent and influential of these was Verne Grant (Fig. 3.1), whose beautifully written books have nurtured generations of graduate students. By 1981 he had retreated to the position that "biological" (i.e., reproductively defined) species are not necessarily the same as taxonomic species, which he considers (as do other taxonomists) to be "the basic unit of formal classification."

As we have noted in CHAPTER 1, the morphologic-physiologic system of plants tends to be more tolerant of casual variation than that of animals. It is not so necessary for everything to fit exactly with everything else for the plant to survive. One result of this laxity is that many plants tolerate interspecific hybridization better than do animals. Obviously there must be some selection against extensive hybridization under most conditions, or the species involved would merge and lose their identity. Yet there is often enough tolerance of alien genes to permit the hybrids not only to survive but also to reproduce. Regardless of genetic theory, plant taxonomists have long been accustomed to the thought that the boundaries between species are often blurred by hybridization.

A Renewed Practical Species Concept

In spite of the many problems, the species is a useful and indeed necessary mental concept. Genetically and phenetically coherent sets of individuals with a recognizable geographic range and an understandable

Fig. 2.1. Some botanists who have made important contributions to our understanding of the nature of species. TOP LEFT, (George) Ledyard Stebbins (1906–). Photo courtesy of Leslie Gottlieb. TOP RIGHT, Wendell Holmes (Red) Camp (1904–1963). Photo from The New York Botanical Garden Library. BOTTOM LEFT, (Francis) Marion Ownbey (1910–1974). Photo by Terry Jacobsen, courtesy of The Marion Ownbey Herbarium, Washington State University. BOTTOM RIGHT, Edgar Anderson (1897–1969). Photo courtesy of The Missouri Botanical Garden Library.

role in nature do exist, and these sets have discernible, if sometimes hazy, limits.

As early as 1943, Camp (Fig. 2.1) and Gilly pointed out the diversity of sorts of populations that are embraced in the taxonomic species. They recognized 12 sorts, as follows:

1. Homogameon: A species which is genetically and morphologically homogeneous, all members being interfertile.

2. Phenon: A species which is phenotypically homogeneous and whose individuals are sexually reproductive, but which is composed of intersterile segments.

3. Parageneon: A species with relatively little morphological or genetical variation throughout its range but which contains some aberrant genotypes; all of its individuals are interfertile.

4. Dysploidion: A species composed of morphologically similar members of a dysploid series, the individuals of which are sexually reproductive.

5. Euploidion: A species whose individuals are sexually reproductive and which is composed of segments with a common origin arranged in a euploid series; the segments are morphologically separable although similar in appearance, but because of differential responses to various environments, appear to intergrade.

6. Alloploidion: A species derived by allopolyploidy; its individuals, although usually highly variable, are interfertile.

7. Micton: A species often of wide distribution, the result of hybridization between individuals of two or more species; all individuals are interfertile with themselves and with the ancestral genotypes.

8. Rheogameon: A species composed of segments of reasonably marked morphological divergence whose distributions are such that gene interchange may take place in sequence between them; individuals of contiguous segments are interfertile.

9. Cleistogameon: A species which, in part, reproduces by cleistogamy.

10. Heterogameon: A species made up of races which, if selfed, produces morphologically stable populations, but when crossed may produce several types of viable and fertile offspring. The most notable examples of this type are several species of *Oenothera*. The plants have large chromosome rings and balanced lethals, and are referred to in the literature as permanent translocation heterozygotes.

11. Apogameon: A species containing both apomictic and nonapomictic individuals.

12. Agameon: A species consisting of only apomictic individuals.

Camp and Gilly provided the belated theoretical foundation for a practical species-concept that long antedates any real understanding of genetics. The names that they proposed for the several different sorts of species have not been widely adopted, but it is generally agreed that all the listed types do exist and must in practice be treated as species. There are also various combinations and intermediates among their 12 sorts, so that it may be difficult to assign a particular species unequivocally to any one of them.

Still other sorts of population structure might be recognized among species. For example, self-pollination in chasmogamous flowers provides an imperfect approach to the obligate self-pollination of cleistogamy. The segments of a rheogameon are by implication geographical. There may also be ecological differentiation within a geographic area, or some combination of geographical and ecological differentiation. Polyploid pillar complexes and polyploid-apomictic complexes, discussed a little farther on, must also be added to the list.

Subsequent to the evident failure of the strictly reproductive species-concept, most plant taxonomists have adhered to a more traditional and practical concept in which phenetic (especially morphologic) divergence is of critical importance. In 1978 I tried to formalize the concept under which most of us actually work, as follows: *Species are the smallest groups that are consistently and persistently distinct, and distinguishable by ordinary means.* This very generalized definition sets the limits within which taxonomists may reasonably disagree. We may differ as to how consistent is consistent, how persistent is persistent, and how ordinary are ordinary means, but any group that does not meet each of these tests at least to some reasonable degree is not to be considered a species.

It may be worthwhile to take the definition apart and see why each piece is necessary. First, species are the *smallest* groups that meet the remaining criteria. If the group can be subdivided into smaller groups that meet these tests, then it is these smaller groups that should be treated as species.

Second, species must be *consistently* distinct. This means that all, or a very large proportion, of the individuals under consideration must clearly belong to one group or another, and not somewhere in between. You cannot arbitrarily slice off one end of a unimodal curve of variation and call it a species, nor can you split such a unimodal curve in the middle or toward one side. Either there must be an absolute discontinuity of variation, or at least there must be a bimodal curve. Taxonomists may reasonably differ as to how close the low point between the peaks of the curve must come to the base line, and different genera may call for different standards, but the test must be met at least to some degree if the group is to be called a species.

Third, species must be *persistently* distinct. There must be reasonable assurance that all or the vast majority of the offspring of the members of a given species for the foreseeable future will also belong to the same species. The so-called cinnamon bear in the United States is consistently distinguishable from the black bear, but it is not persistently distinct. Cinnamon bears and black bears regard themselves as the same sort of animal, and they breed together without hindrance. Thus the offspring of a cinnamon bear may be black, or vice versa. The two types, although *consistently* distinct, are not *persistently* so, and therefore they belong to the same species. We must remember that in delimiting species we are using the morphology to help us recognize natural populations, not just cataloging morphological diversity.

It can be seen that hybridization between groups will reduce the degree to which they meet the test of persistence, and often also the test of consistency. The more freely two groups hybridize, the more doubtful their separate specific status becomes. The precise frequency of hybridization that will invalidate a potential specific distinction varies from genus to genus, and also according to the opinion of the individual taxonomist. The place where the line is drawn is arbitrary, but the test is a real one.

Finally, species must be distinguishable by *ordinary means.* The phraseology here is deliberately loose. Means that are ordinary in one group may not be ordinary in another. An electron microscope and a fully equipped laboratory may be ordinary means for a bacterial taxonomist. The bacterial species that can be distinguished by such means may play very different roles in nature, and our understanding of the world is much enhanced by the seemingly fine distinctions. A compound microscope with an oil-immersion lens is an ordinary means for a mycological taxonomist. Mycologists find the distinctions they can draw at this level of observation to be biologically meaningful, and mostly they see no need to go further and use an electron microscope in defining species. Taxonomists considering vascular plants of ordinary size are reluctant to give specific status to things that cannot be distinguished with a hand-lens, or at most with a dissecting microscope giving up to 20 or 40 diameters magnification. Even if such a microscope is needed to identify a dried herbarium specimen with certainty, the plants as they grow in nature can probably be recognized with the naked eye after one has become familiar with the group. Vascular plant taxonomists find the distinctions they can draw at this level of observation to be biologically meaningful, and mostly they see no need to go further in search of specific characters.

To the extent that taxonomists differ as to what constitutes ordinary means, they will differ in certain instances as to the circumscription of species. Presumably everyone has an ultimate sticking point, at which he/she will cry "Hold! Enough!"; but that sticking point will vary from individual to individual. I can readily imagine that taxonomists might reasonably differ as to the level of magnification they are willing to use in examining megaspores of *Isoetes* to determine specific differences.

It will rightly be pointed out that the definition of species I am propounding is so generalized that it leaves a great deal of room for individual interpretation and difference of opinion. My answer is that such is the nature of the world. The definition merely sets the limits within which reasonable taxonomists may disagree.

Any attempt at a more precise definition will merely limit its application. Additional criteria that may help to clarify the taxonomy of one group will be useless or destructive in another. Any effort to specify the precise amount of intergradation that can be admitted between species is likewise foredoomed. The species in *Rudbeckia* are all sharply limited, if you define one or two of them broadly. These clear limits encourage us to take a broad view of *Rudbeckia fulgida,* which otherwise might conceivably be divided into several ill-defined segregates. An insistence on the same degree of distinctness in *Senecio* would only cause confusion. It is necessary to give specific recognition to a great many North American taxa of *Senecio* that are only about as distinct as varieties in some other genera. The species one would arrive at in *Senecio,* if he/she insisted on really sharp interspecific distinctions, would be so large, amorphous, and internally diversified as to be conceptually useless. Polyploid-apomictic complexes, such as in *Crepis,* are sometimes only arbitrarily divisible into species. The definition I propose can be adapted to serve in all these cases, by varying the severity of one or another of the criteria.

The "biological" species concept emphasizes the criterion of reproductive isolation, at the expense of phenetic discontinuity, when these two criteria are in conflict. The definition here presented focuses attention on the criterion of phenetic discontinuity, but actually it requires that both criteria be met. Phenetic discontinuity between groups cannot persist in the absence of a barrier to interbreeding. Reproductive isolation is a necessary corollary of persistent phenetic discontinuity.

Despite the lack of precision in formal definitions of the concept of species, most plant taxonomists do in fact agree on specific limits of most of the taxa they study. The extensive published examination of areas of disagreement tends to obscure the wide agreement that does exist. We don't write very much about the things we agree on.

We have noted that there must be some sort of barrier to effective interbreeding for two groups to maintain themselves as distinct species. The nature of the barrier is immaterial, so long as it works. (Some readers may be acquainted with the thought that it does not matter whether a cat is black or white, so long as it catches mice.) Simple distance may be a sufficient barrier. The distance must be great enough to be formidable for the passage of both pollen and seeds. A population confined to eastern Asia has virtually no chance for reproductive continuity with a population confined to eastern North America. There is a familiar pattern of closely related, vicariant species in these two areas. Probably in most cases there is some other barrier, or set of barriers, in addition to distance, but for purely taxonomic purposes it is not necessary to determine whether these other barriers exist or not. The two populations are reproductively isolated, and may be expected to remain so for the foreseeable future.

Effective transfer of pollen from one species to another may be impeded in various ways. The nectar or other reward for pollinators produced by plants of different populations may be available only to mutually exclusive groups of insects, which accordingly do not move from one species to another. The taxonomic sense of bees has also frequently been noted as an isolating mechanism. On a given trip from the hive, a bee may simply prefer to visit flowers of only one species. Sometimes the pollinators are less choosy, and pollen is transferred indiscriminately from one species to another. Such species can maintain their populational integrity only by means of post-pollination barriers. Often the stigma and style in a given species permit more rapid growth of pollen from the same species than from a different, though related one. Thus even if the transfer of pollen is more or less random, *successful* pollination is likely to be intraspecific.

There is a wide range of isolating mechanisms that act at later stages in development. The hybrid embryo may be incompatible with the endosperm of the developing seed. Or the gene-products from the two sets of chromosomes may not interact effectively, so that the seedling is weak and not competitive. Or the hybrid may be vigorous but meiotically unstable, so that seed-set is reduced. Or the hybrid may be vigorous and fertile, but not have a niche in which it can compete with other species.

Very often two or more individually imperfect isolation mechanisms combine to produce a strong barrier. On simple arithmetic, 3 independent isolating mechanisms, each 80% effective, would collectively be more than 99% effective.

In the foregoing discussion emphasis has been placed on morphologic characters as specific criteria. This does not mean that other characters should not be used in arriving at a system of classification. The number, size, and shape of chromosomes, the secondary metabolites, pollinators, anatomical and micromorphological characters, geography, habitat, sterility barriers, and other features may all be taken into account in reaching a classification which puts together the things that are most alike, and separates them from the things they are less like. Unexpected diversity in one or more of these features may prompt a reconsideration of the morphological evidence. It is only necessary, at the end, that the species be distinguishable by ordinary means.

There is inevitably some room for difference of opinion in many instances as to how to weigh the data that bear on the possible recognition of two closely allied species or a single more variable one. Sometimes additional data can decisively swing the scales, but sometimes not. Some situations are inherently marginal and capable of more than one taxonomic interpretation. Taxonomy is not physics.

Species as Ecologic Units

Every species has its own geographic distribution and ecological limits. The most ubiquitous terrestrial species of all, at least among organisms of macroscopic size, is our own (*Homo sapiens*). One of the most widespread species of plants is the bracken fern, *Pteridium aquilinum,* sensu lato. Each of these species has a very complex morphologic-ecologic population-structure. Although highly diversified, each of the two is absolutely sharply limited. There is every gradation from such widespread, complex species to very local species consisting of only a few individuals forming a single local population. Such very local species often occur on an unusual substrate, such as serpentine rock. On the other hand, there did not seem to be anything very unusual about the habitat of *Franklinia alatamaha,* which was found only twice in the wild (near the Georgia-South Carolina border), and which now exists only in cultivation.

We normally expect a species to show some sort of ecogeographic coherence. It may be ecologically diversified within a given region, but the variation should be continuous. The geographic range may be fragmented, especially toward the margins, but the peripheral isolates should be ecologically comparable to the main mass of the population. We do not expect a species to grow on the alpine summit of a mountain, and on the dry plains around its base, unless it is also on the intervening slopes.

If a species were defined to include only a local population on Pikes Peak in Colorado, and another on the Mississippi delta, we would immediately suspect something wrong. Any proposed specific circumscription that does not make ecogeographic sense should be reconsidered, with a view to coming up with a more reasonable one. Unexpected things may sometimes happen, but we should make sure that we have adequately considered the evidence.

Students of zoological taxonomy characteristically find that each species plays a unique role in the economy of nature. The theory is expressed in the *principle of competitive exclusion,* discussed in CHAPTER 1. One may wonder about the unique role of each of the hundreds of recognized species of *Drosophila* in the Hawaiian Islands, but still the idea stands up well enough in general so that it must be taken seriously.

Competitive exclusion does not stare at the botanical taxonomist with anywhere near the intensity that it does at his zoological counterpart, and relatively little attention has been devoted to it in the botanical literature. It is not unusual to find two or more congeners with broadly overlapping habitats and geographic ranges, so that the species often grow together and seem to be exploiting the habitat in the same way. The fact that the several species do not have identical limits of geographic range or habitat tolerance suggests that there may be some undetected ecological differences where they grow together, but botanical taxonomists have not often found this approach to be helpful. Instead of distinct ecological niches and competitive exclusion, we are accustomed to seeing a pattern of multiple overlaps, both geographically and ecologically.

Yet there is something in competitive exclusion, even for plants. We see many examples of a principle often attributed to the ichthyologist David Starr Jordan, that the nearest relative of a species will be found not in the same region, but in a similar habitat in a different region, separated by some sort of barrier to migration. Some of these examples reflect disruption of a once more continuous range, as in the classic eastern United States-eastern Asia disjunctions. Others doubtless result from speciation by geographically peripheral isolates, as propounded by Mayr (1954 et seq.), or from some sort of geographic speciation. How much ecological change may have occurred in such speciation-events is generally problematical. Jordan's principle holds true often enough for plants to be worth keeping in mind, even though it is far from being universally applicable. It is of course perfectly compatible with the principle of competitive exclusion.

Zoologists are accustomed to seeing situations in which two geographically overlapping species are ecologically differentiated in the area of overlap, even though they may have a wider amplitude elsewhere. These are not so common, or at least not so obvious, in plants. A possible example is provided by *Phlox condensata* and *P. tumulosa,* two morphologically rather similar but ecologically differentiated species in the western American cordillera. *Phlox condensata* characteristically occurs at higher elevations than *P. tumulosa,* which has a relatively limited range in Nevada and adjacent Utah. In the Charleston Mts. of southern Nevada, not far outside the geographic range of *P. tumulosa, P. condensata* descends to 1800 m, which would be a perfectly appropriate elevation for the missing *P. tumulosa*. The example is not clear-cut, however, inasmuch as *P. condensata* is largely restricted to high elevations in other places outside the range of *P. tumulosa*.

On an earlier page we noted that species should be biologically meaningful. We normally expect related species to play different roles in the economy of nature. Either they exploit the environment in different ways, or they play comparable roles in different geographical areas. This ideal is often not realized in fact. Different criteria must then be weighed against each other in an effort to arrive at a mentally useful classification.

If two groups are so obviously and sharply different that they can easily and consistently be distinguished, then we do not worry very much about whether they play different roles in nature. They may occur together and seem to be exploiting the habitat in just the same way, but no matter. We need not seek hidden ecological differences to justify the taxonomic separation. Often we see modally different but widely overlapping habitat-requirements, as in many of the species of oaks in eastern United States. The populations maintain themselves as different, because of effective (not necessarily perfect) barriers to interbreeding.

The Reality of Species

Until Darwin's time, biologists in general believed that species exist in nature and are merely recognized by taxonomists. After 1859 the situation did not seem so simple. It was only to be expected that at any given time there would be some groups at the threshold of specific differentiation, and biologists might reasonably differ about the taxonomic status of such groups. The developing understanding of genetics during the first two decades of the 20th century seriously undercut the idea that species are real entities. Many biologists came to believe that they are purely arbitrary concepts. The necessity for such concepts was usually accepted, but their arbitrary nature was emphasized. During the past several decades the pendulum has swung the other way.

The thesis and antithesis here are subject to rational synthesis. Individuals exist. Each individual has a particular phenotype. Successful interbreeding in nature is restricted to groups of individuals that are similar in most respects. There are gaps of all sizes in the distribution of diversity in nature. Many combinations of characters that might be imagined simply do not exist. (Again, the example of the photosynthetic dog.) In producing a taxonomic scheme, we try to recognize the clusters and draw lines through the gaps between them. The smallest clusters that are separated by reasonably evident gaps from other such clusters are the species. Usually, although not always, the continuity within a cluster is reinforced by interbreeding. Interbreeding between different clusters, on the other hand, is restricted or impossible. The story of the man who had hybridized a parrot with a cobra ("He doesn't know what kind of animal it is, but when it talks, he listens!") may be a good joke, but it is a biological impossibility.

The distribution of diversity in nature, strongly influenced by breeding patterns, is such that the number of potentially satisfying mental organizations is not infinite or even large, but always very small. Very often there is only one mentally satisfying organization at the species-level for a particular genus or portion of a genus. To that extent, species exist in nature and are merely recognized by taxonomists. On the other hand, sometimes there are two or more organizations of a small group that might be seriously entertained. One such organization might appeal to one taxonomist, and a different one might appeal to another. To that extent, the species is merely a creation of the mind, but the choices are always limited.

From Easy to Difficult Cases

Many groups have a relatively simple taxonomic pattern and present no continuing problem in specific classification. No one questions the distinctness of the four species of *Luina* (a western American genus of Asteraceae), although some taxonomists would see three genera here instead of one. Neither does anyone now propose to divide any of these species. The specific criterion of morphological continuity within species, and discontinuity between species, supports an inference of similar continuity and discontinuity in breeding behavior. Furthermore, the four species are ecogeographically differentiated inter se. One need not be taxonomically astute to come up with a satisfactory scheme of species here.

Many other groups that are ambiguous on first consideration are clarified by further study. The lingering question of whether the Chinese *Liriodendron* is specifically distinct from the American one now seems to be resolved. They are different, and anyone who knows what to look for should have no trouble in telling them apart. (An easy character is that the tepals of *L. chinense* lack the orange splash near the base that marks *L. tulipifera*. There are also some more recondite anatomical and chemical differences.) The two have no opportunity to interbreed in nature, but their close relationship is supported by the fact that they can be hybridized experimentally.

The greatest problems come when the criteria of reproductive behavior and phenetic differentiation are to some degree dissociated. Groups that must be regarded as distinct species on the basis of phenetic differentiation and phylogenetic relationship may hybridize so extensively as to be confluent. Conversely, autoploidy or other cytological changes may introduce a barrier to interbreeding not accompanied by other recognizable differences. Alloploidy can introduce both of these seemingly opposite complications at once. Groups that are clearly distinct on the diploid level may be morphologically confluent through a series of alloploids that breed more or less freely among themselves but are genetically isolated from the basic diploids. Polyploid-apomictic complexes present the most difficult problems of all. We shall discuss these and some other problems. Our necessary attention to the difficulties should not obscure the continuing value of the species as a conceptual unit. We have some fleas, but no *Treponema*.

HYBRIDIZATION

It is well known among taxonomists that some groups are prone to hybridization, and others not. The whole family Apiaceae produces remarkably few interspecific hybrids. Although I have seen many species of this family, and frequently two members of the same genus growing together, I have never seen anything in the field that I took to be a hybrid. Hybrids in the large genus *Carex* (Cyperaceae) are rare, and when produced they are likely to be sterile, even though the parent species may look much alike. Hybrids among the multitudinous species of *Astragalus* are equally uncommon.

Many genera of the Asteraceae, on the other hand, are notorious for hybridization. *Aster, Helianthus, Senecio,* and *Solidago,* for example, are familiar large North American genera in which hybridization is rampant. There are still humps and hollows in the curve of distribution of phenotypes, but the hollows frequently do not go down to the base line. One cannot escape the problem simply by expanding the specific concept, because the expansion must proceed beyond the point of absurdity. A great many North American species of *Senecio* are only about as distinct as one would normally expect of varieties, but it would not help to put 50 taxa of the most diverse aspect and ecology into a single amorphous and still ill-defined species.

Some genera in other families show similar problems. Hybridization is the key to understanding what is going on in *Mertensia* (Boraginaceae). In the Beartooth Mts., along the Montana-Wyoming border, I have seen a local hybrid swarm of *M. ciliata* and *M. alpina,* two species of markedly different aspect that belong to two different sections. The population formed a semicircle about a large natural rock-pile on a local summit, with no indication of human disturbance. At one end of the semicircle the plants were clearly *M. ciliata,* and at the other end clearly *M. alpina.* Between the two ends there was a gradual transition from one species to the other. This is not an isolated instance, although it was indeed striking in the field. Obviously these two species do not everywhere breed together so successfully as at that one place, or the populations would merge into one. Some sort of barrier to successful interbreeding is essential to the maintenance of specific distinction, but in many groups the barriers are low enough to permit occasional or frequent transgression. Our zoological friends would be appalled.

Extensive hybridization (and associated back-crossing) are especially likely in disturbed habitats. Here two species that are ordinarily segregated ecologically may come into contact in a new habitat not already preempted by species adapted to it through selection. As long as the site remains unstable, the hybrids continue to be formed, even if they are less fertile and/or less competitive than the parent species. Some of the hybrids or hybrid segregates may even be better adapted to the site than either original parent. Edgar Anderson (1948; Fig. 2.1) coined the flamboyant term **hybridization of the habitat** for such disturbances that foster hybridization.

Sometimes the hybridization between related species is so pervasive that genes leak from one to the other, diluting the taxonomic distinctions. This process was named **introgressive hybridization**, or **introgression**, by Anderson in 1949. The concept antedates the term, but for some years prior to Anderson's studies the influence of zoological thinking had led many botanists to discount the significance of hybridization. One might say that he made it respectable again to think of hybridization as an important natural process rather than as an occasional anomaly. Enlarging on Anderson's concept, Harlan and de Wet (1963) have coined the term **compilospecies** for widespread, variable species that pick up characters of diverse other species through hybridization in areas of contact.

Many putative examples of introgression have been reported during the past several decades. I have myself postulated (together with T. M. Barkley) that the variation in leaf form of *Senecio aureus* in the Gaspé region of Quebec reflects the absorption of a local population of *S. pseudaureus* that had reached the area by migration (from the western cordillera) along the retreating ice-front several thousand years ago. The trouble with such explanations is that like other phylogenetic speculations they are merely plausible reconstructions of a vanished history that may be subject to some other interpretation. Some of the supposed examples have not withstood careful reconsideration. From a theoretical standpoint, however, introgression can reasonably be supposed to be a fact of botanical life. Numerous horticultural creations have amply demonstrated the feasibility of transferring desired genes from one species to another by hybridization and selection.

SELF-POLLINATION

Natural populations of most species of plants are to a large degree cross-pollinated. Unisexuality, heterostyly, proterogyny and proterandry, and varying degrees of self-sterility are common means of promoting cross-pollination. Following standard genetic and evolutionary theory, we must suppose that cross-pollination confers a long-term evolutionary advantage, by providing a continuing supply of new and different genotypes on which selection may act. In the short run, however, self-pollination may often be more advantageous. Once an effective genotype has been established, there is no need to disrupt it by outcrossing.

Aside from dioecious groups, neither cross-pollination nor self-pollination is 100% obligate. Outcrossing groups, in particular, can tolerate a degree of selfing without significantly reducing the amount of genetic recombination.

Many ordinarily self-pollinated species have particular means of providing for occasional outcrossing. The stemless blue violets of eastern United States have inconspicuous cleistogamous flowers at the base that set abundant seed. The more showy, chasmogamous flowers in this group set only a little seed, but enough to provide for continuing genetic recombination. Likewise, the species of the *Dichanthelium* group of *Panicum* produce conspicuous, open-pollinated inflorescences that set very little seed, and many cleistogamous inflorescences, largely concealed in the leaf-sheaths, that set seed freely. Some of the small-flowered species of *Gilia* in western United States produce only a little nectar and are ignored by bees in most years. They are self-compatible and set seed without the need for cross-pollination. In dry years, when the supply of flowers of all kinds is relatively limited, the bees perforce exploit this poor source of nectar, and some cross-pollination results (Grant & Grant, 1965, and personal communication from V. Grant).

Selfing may be restricted through a competitive advantage of foreign over self pollen. In at least some cases, the advantage reflects differential rates of growth of pollen-tubes. Such cryptic incompatibility favors any foreign pollen that may reach the stigma, without compromising seed-set in the absence of foreign pollen. This phenomenon has been demonstrated in species of several families and is presumably widespread (Bowman, 1987).

From a taxonomic standpoint, self-pollination is important for its effects on population-structure. A large set of minutely differing self-perpetuating lines may come to exist. Members of different lines may grow side by side and appear to be specifically distinct. Only when a large number of such lines are studied do the distinctions that are at first perceived disappear. Even the seeming stability of the individual lines is likely to be ephemeral. Occasional cross-pollination is followed by Mendelian segregation and the establishment of new lines that likewise appear to be stable on first inspection. In self-pollinated groups it behooves the taxonomist to be especially careful to study a widely representative sample before attempting any taxonomic organization. One might suspect that the inordinate number of species of *Euphrasia* recognized by some European botanists could be reduced to a tolerable number by a reconsideration in the light of their breeding behavior.

Sometimes an outbreeding species may have an inbreeding twin, the latter usually with smaller and/or less showy flowers. Species of *Oenothera* and *Camissonia,* in the Onagraceae, provide some well studied examples. The taxa that make up such a pair have fundamentally different population-structures, and it is conceptually useful to think of them separately. Yet the actual measurements may be confluent even when the populations are readily distinguishable in the field. Emphasizing the population-structure, Peter Raven (e.g., 1969) has treated the members of a number of such pairs in *Camissonia* and other genera of Onagraceae as different species. Some other taxonomists, emphasizing the overall similarity and morphologic confluence, have treated these same pairs at the varietal level. In the particular examples at hand, I follow Raven in according specific recognition to the different taxa, but the alternative interpretation could also be defended. Even if one finds it useful to treat these particular pairs at the specific level, there are other pairs in which the morphologic difference between the breeding groups is less obvious, or the breeding pattern itself is less stable. In nature there is no inherent dividing line between clear differentiation of such pair-members, partial differentiation, and scarcely discernible differentiation.

Many outbreeding species throw occasional inbreeding mutants. These may be so similar to the bulk of the population as to escape detection, or they may catch an observant eye. A very local inbreeding derivative of the normally outbreeding annual species *Stephanomeria exigua* in Oregon has been named *S. malheurensis* by Leslie Gottlieb (1978). The population faces an uncertain future, since it varies in number from year to year and apparently never consists of as many as a thousand individuals. Only the most careful observation permits the recognition of this taxon. It is of inherent theoretical interest because of its bearing on the origin of self-pollinated taxa in general. Thus there may be some justification for giving it a name, but at the present time it is only a species in process of being born, or more likely stillborn. Doubtless many more such inbreeding mutants could be discovered by intensive study, but the utility of providing names for all of them would be doubtful indeed.

Aneuploidy

Variation in chromosome number within a species or larger taxonomic group may be mentally organized into two types: Polyploid (or euploid) series, in which the successively larger numbers reflect the addition of whole genomes; and aneuploid (or dysploid) series, which show no such pattern. An aneuploid series may have adjacent numbers, such as 6, 7, and 8, or there may be gaps of various sizes. Sometimes, as in *Claytonia virginica* (discussed farther on) there is aneuploid variation around the numbers of a euploid series.

Aneuploid increase in chromosome number can take place by duplication of whole chromosomes. In many species some individuals have one or more extra chromosomes beyond the basic diploid or euploid set. These supernumerary chromosomes may or may not have an evident phenotypic effect. Certainly they provide the possibility of future evolutionary divergence in which they acquire vital metabolic roles and become incorporated into stabilized genomes. There may be supernumerary chromosomes in even more species than the printed record suggests, because of a tendency to sweep discordant new counts under the rug.

Aneuploid increase can also take place by accidental bisection of the chromosome through the centromere. Thus a metacentric chromosome can be converted into two telocentric ones. These would of course not be subject to further such increase unless and until they had been converted to metacentric structure by happenstance transfer of material from other chromosomes to the end with the centromere. Chromosome fragments without a centromere would tend to be lost during cell division.

In the Juncaceae and Cyperaceae, families in which many species have a diffuse centromere, aneuploid increase may take place by simple fragmentation of chromosomes, without any other change. The large numbers of small chromosomes in many members of these families may simply reflect such fragmentation. The difficulty in counting so many tiny chromosomes may contribute to an impression of even more variability than actually exists.

Aneuploid decrease in chromosome number may take place by cytogenetic accidents in which all or the major part of the genetic material of a chromosome is transferred to and incorporated into one or more other chromosomes. Such aneuploid reduction, associated with taxonomic divergence, has been shown in many genera. The western American genus *Chaenactis* provides a particularly interesting and well documented example. Kyhos (1965) presents convincing evidence that the relatively mesic species *C. glabriuscula*, with $n = 6$, has given rise separately to two desert species with $n = 5$, *C. fremontii* and *C. stevioides*. No one questions that the three taxa are specifically distinct, and it is clear that an existing species has given rise to two other existing species. Cladists may be allowed to cry in their beer.

Haplopappus gracilis provides an especially interesting case of infraspecific descending aneuploidy. Most members of this species have only two pairs of chromosomes, the lowest number known in vascular plants. A few local populations, which fall well within the range of morphological and ecotypical variation of *H. gracilis,* have four pairs of chromosomes. Ray Jackson (1962) has described these latter plants as *H. ravenii*. The four chromosomes of a genome of *H. ravenii* are collectively only a little longer than the two of typical *H. gracilis*. It appears that the now abundant form with $n = 2$ originated by unequal translocations that resulted in two essentially end-to-end mergers, with only one centromere being retained for each of the two resultant long chromosomes. First generation hybrids of the two cytotypes are as vigorous and floriferous as the parents. The problem comes at meiosis, when less than 10% of good pollen is produced. According to the concepts expounded in this book, all these plants should be considered to belong to a single species. The only basis for recognizing *H. ravenii* as distinct is an a priori assumption that the sterility barrier introduced by the cytological difference is taxonomically controlling.

There is also at least one local population of *H. gracilis* in which some individuals have $n = 3$, two of the chromosomes being relatively short, and the third one much longer. Experimental hybrids between the $n = 2$ and $n = 3$ forms are fertile. Meiosis tends to produce some reduced cells with two long chromosomes, and others with one long and two short chromosomes. Different plants of the same local population have $2n = 4$, $2n = 5$, and $2n = 6$ chromosomes. Here, by anybody's standards, the difference in chromosome numbers is taxonomically insignificant. Hybrids of the $n = 3$ and $n = 4$ strains have not been attempted.

Phacelia ranunculacea provides another taxonomically interesting case of aneuploidy. As reported by Chuang and Constance (1977), this self-pollinated annual species consists of two geographically separated cytotypes. Ozarkian plants have $n = 6$, and Appalachian ones have $n = 14$. Aside from the chromosome numbers, these authors have been unable to detect even micromorphological differences between the two cytotypes. We do not know whether the two cytotypes are interfertile, because the structure and small size of the flowers have frustrated efforts at outcrossing. The authors unequivocally keep the two cytotypes in the same species, and I agree. I would see no harm, however, in treating them as different varieties. The two groups are geographically separated, implying the possibility of an ecological difference, and they do meet the tests of consistency and persistence, failing only the test of ordinary means.

It is easy enough to find examples in which aneuploidy fails as a specific character, just as it is easy to find examples of the failure of classical morphological characters. In any individual case, however, the initial assumption must be that aneuploidy suggests taxonomic divergence. The signal should no more be ignored than the sound of a gunshot in hostile territory.

POLYPLOIDY

The Nature and Origins of Polyploidy

Polyploids are individuals with 3 or more complete sets of chromosomes per cell, instead of the ordinary (diploid) number of 2 sets. Usually the number is a multiple of 2, e.g., tetraploids (4 sets), hexaploids (6 sets), octoploids (8 sets), or even higher numbers. Using the conventional symbol x to represent one complete set of chromosomes, we may speak of 4x, 6x, 8x, etc. Odd numbers of sets, as in triploids (3x) and pentaploids (5x) also exist, but these can be maintained from one generation to another only by specialized reproductive methods.

Recognition of polyploidy dates from a paper in 1917 by Winge (p. 533). He noted numbers of $2n = 18$ and $2n = 36$ in different species of *Chenopodium,* and numbers of $2n = 18$, $2n = 36$, $2n = 54$, $2n = 72$, and $2n = 90$ in different species of *Chrysanthemum*. Polyploidy was soon recognized as an important factor in speciation, and the following 3 decades saw the establishment of a complex structure of theory and terminology.

Polyploids may originate in nature by two means, somatic doubling and the production of unreduced gametes. We are not here concerned with the experimental induction of polyploidy by the use of colchicine, which interferes with spindle activity during cell division.

In somatic doubling, mitotic division of a vegetative cell is misdirected so that the daughter chromosomes that ought to be assembled into two nuclei are all brought together into a single nucleus, which thus becomes tetraploid instead of diploid. It is in fact not unusual for individual tetraploid cells so produced to be scattered amongst the much greater number of ordinary diploid cells in the plant. If the cell-lineage from such a newly produced tetraploid cell gives rise eventually to a flower or an inflorescence, then the eventual sperms and eggs will be diploid rather than haploid. If the flower is self-pollinated, or if pollen is transferred from one flower to another on the same tetraploid branch, then any seeds that are produced will have tetraploid embryos. If the pollen is transferred to another plant, or to another ordinary flower on the same plant, then the prospect is to produce a triploid.

Many species of plants produce a small percentage of unreduced pollen and unreduced embryo-sacs, more in some species than in others. The resultant sperms and eggs have as many chromosomes as the somatic cells of the parent. If the plant is diploid, then so are these unusual sperms and eggs. If the diploid sperm is transferred to an ordinary egg (or vice versa), then again we have a triploid. In the relatively rare event that a diploid sperm (from an unreduced pollen-grain) unites with a diploid egg (from an unreduced embryo-sac), then we have a newly produced tetraploid.

Origin of polyploidy by somatic doubling of chromosomes appears to be rare. One of the few documented examples is provided by the famous Kew primrose, *Primula kewensis* (Newton & Pellew, 1929). This is a spontaneous horticultural hybrid between *P. floribunda* and *P. verticillata*. Like its parents, it is a diploid, $2n = 18$, but it is ordinarily sterile. On at least three occasions (1905, 1923, 1926) it set tetraploid seeds. The cytological mechanism for the first two occurrences is not known. The third time, the tetraploid seeds were produced on tetraploid branches of an otherwise diploid plant. These tetraploid branches must reflect somatic doubling.

It seems clear that most natural polyploidy results from the production of unreduced gametes (Harlan & de Wet, 1975). Documented examples are numerous. Some of these spontaneous polyploids occur within an otherwise normal diploid population, producing polyploids that look much like the diploids. Others occur in interspecific hybrids, which because of meiotic disturbances are particularly prone to the production of unreduced gametes.

Once a tetraploid population has been established, by whatever means, the way is open to higher levels of ploidy via unreduced gametes. Two unreduced tetraploid gametes can produce an octoploid. A single unreduced tetraploid gamete can fuse with a diploid gamete (produced by normal reduction in a tetraploid plant) to form a hexaploid. Furthermore, a hexaploid can be formed by hybridization between a tetraploid and an octoploid, without the direct intervention of meiotic irregularity.

Polyploids in which all the chromosomes are derived from a single species are called autopolyploids, or **autoploids**. Those in which the several sets come from two or more distinct species are called allopolyploids, or more briefly, **alloploids**. There are both theoretical and practical problems with this apparently simple distinction. The theoretical problem comes from possible difference of opinion about specific limits. The same plant may be considered an autoploid or an alloploid according to taxonomic opinion as to the proper classification of its diploid antecedents. The practical problem comes in determining the origin of the different sets. This problem is often exacerbated by a degree of reassortment of chromosomes among the sets in subsequent generations of the polyploid. The continuity of the spectrum from autoploidy to alloploidy does not vitiate the usefulness of the concepts, however, any more than the continuity of the visible spectrum of light vitiates the utility of the concepts of red and blue.

Most newly produced polyploids, especially autoploids, have larger cells than their diploid progenitors. The large cell-size may or may not be reflected in large size and greater vigor of the whole plant (Fig. 2.2). In selected instances, natural polyploids can be distinguished from diploids simply by counting the number of stomates visible in representative samples of leaf-epidermis in a microscopic field. The polyploids, having larger cells, have fewer stomates per unit area.

A great many natural polyploids, on the other hand, have cells about the same size as those of diploids, and can be recognized only by counting the chromosomes. It is supposed, perhaps correctly, that natural selection eventually brings the cell-size of the polyploids back down to that of the diploids.

Polyploidy may induce subtle physiological differences that affect the optimum conditions for growth and competition. Thus the polyploids may eventually come to occupy somewhat different habitats than their diploid ancestors, or they may develop a different geographic range. On the other hand, plants of different ploidy-levels may grow intermingled, without any evident ecological differentiation, or there may be a seemingly helter-skelter pattern of local geographic replacement with only the weakest suggestion of ecological correlation, as in *Chaenactis douglasii* (Mooring, 1980).

The obvious major problem faced by any new polyploid is that of meiosis. Autoploids have too many chromosomes for normal pairing. Any individual chromosome of an autotetraploid has 3 homologues, and thus 3 possible pair-mates at first metaphase in meiosis, instead of only one. At higher ploidy-levels the number of possible pair-mates is correspondingly larger. The result is likely to be an irregular clustering of chromosomes at first metaphase, instead of normal pairing. In addition to some normal pairs, there may be some sets of 3 or 4 (more in higher polyploids) and some unpaired orphans. Anaphase segregation may then lead to irregular and unbalanced genomes in the microspores and megaspores and eventual gametes. Plants are more tolerant of such chromosomal anomalies than animals, but there are limits to tolerance. A functional gamete must ordinarily contain at least one full complement of chromosomes with no omissions; too many unbalanced duplications also interfere with function. Thus the autoploids suffer some reduction in fertility, and some of the seeds that are produced are inviable or give rise to weaklings that cannot survive the competition in nature.

The production of some clusters (instead of pairs) of chromosomes at meiosis is considered a marker of autoploidy, but the reverse is not nec-

Fig. 2.2. Diploid (LEFT) and autotetraploid (RIGHT) snapdragons, the tetraploidy induced by colchicine. Photo courtesy of the W. Atlee Burpee Company.

essarily true. Obviously selection will favor the establishment or restoration of normal pairing. In polyploid wheat there is a Mendelian factor that promotes normal pairing at meiosis, thus complicating the problems of breeders trying to identify genomes of different origin.

Allotetraploids face a somewhat different version of the same basic problem. In theory every chromosome has one and only one potential pair-mate at meiosis, but in life things are not so simple. If the parent species are very closely related, there may be some cross-matching, so that a chromosome derived from one parent species may pair with a nearly homologous chromosome from the other parent species. Such cross-matching (sometimes accompanied by clumping) may result in reduction of fertility, but any viable offspring that are produced will have more chromosomes derived from one parental species than from the other. Continuation of this mismatching for generation after generation may lead to the formation of a tetraploid swarm with all possible combinations of the chromosomes of the two original parents. The two extremes in such a series are scarcely if at all to be distinguished from ordinary autoploids, although as a result of former crossing over they may carry some bits and pieces of the genome of the other species.

Such an instability of allopolyploids is very common. *Primula kewensis,* often thought of as the type example of an allotetraploid, is in fact unstable in this way and does not maintain its identity over a series of generations. On the other hand, if the original parents have just the right degree of relationship, the allotetraploid may be stable and have a chance to make its way in the world if it can find a niche where it can compete successfully. If the parents are too distantly related, the hybrid (and any alloploids that may subsequently be produced) is likely to be weak and noncompetitive; if they are too closely related, the alloploids are unstable. Stable allotetraploids are sometimes called amphidiploids, in reference to the establishment of what is functionally a new diploid by addition of the genomes of the two parents.

It was at one time thought that nearly all apparent autoploids in nature had been reconstituted as such by the breakdown of alloploids. Stebbins, in particular, promoted this view and was influential in its acceptance by others. His interpretation has now been largely abandoned. There are too many examples that are more easily or even necessarily interpreted as straightforward autoploidy, and if direct formation of autoploids can happen in these cases, it can happen in others as well. Occam's Razor favors the simpler interpretation when a more complex one is not required.

Autoploidy

Autoploidy, even without other complications, introduces an immediate barrier to hybridization with the ancestral diploid. The triploids ordinarily produced by such hybridization face meiotic problems and are largely sterile. Yet the barrier is not necessarily insurmountable. The tendency toward the production of unreduced gametes that was responsible for the origin of the tetraploids continues unabated in the remaining diploids. The continuing dribble of unreduced pollen from the diploids is potentially functional on the tetraploids, permitting a limited one-way flow of genetic material through hybridization. This appears to be true, for example, in some members of the *Artemisia tridentata* complex. Imperfect though it may be, however, the ploidy-barrier is as effective as barriers of other sorts among many generally (and necessarily) accepted species.

Proponents of the reproductive definition of species must necessarily treat plants of different ploidy-levels as belonging to different species. Species so defined are impractical, because it becomes necessary to count the chromosomes for certain identification. Even within what appears to be a homogeneous local population, some individuals may be diploid and others tetraploid. I know of no significant support among present-day taxonomists for using ploidy-level as a sole and sufficient criterion for specific distinction, although some have embraced the concept in the past.

The next line of defense, for those who would emphasize the taxonomic significance of polyploidy, is to say that differences in ploidy-level are so consistently accompanied by tangible morphological differences that a difference in ploidy-level carries a presumption of specific distinction. Under this approach, if we look carefully enough we may expect in nearly all cases to find morphologic differences to go with the cytological one. In North America, Askell Löve has been the most vigorous proponent of this point of view, but there have been others as well. The theoretical problem of distinguishing between autoploidy and alloploidy, and between original and reconstituted autoploids is thus bypassed, since in either case there is a presumption of specific difference.

It is easy enough in many instances to find some morphological difference between an individual or local population known to be diploid and another known to be tetraploid. The problem is to determine whether or not the correlation holds in other individuals or local populations of the same group that have not yet been studied cytologically. Often it does not.

Nearly half a century ago, when the often larger size of tetraploids was a promising new tool for taxonomic analysis, a beautiful study of *Polygonatum biflorum* appeared to show that it actually consists of two species, *P. biflorum* sensu stricto, diploid and relatively small, and *P. commutatum,* tetraploid and more robust. The numerous plants of intermediate size were considered to be sterile triploids, as indeed some of them were. Unfortunately, the correlation disappeared under further study. There may be an average difference in size according to the level of ploidy, but it is overwhelmed by inter- and intra-populational variation. Some of the diploids are as large as any of the tetraploids, as was discovered by Marion Ownbey in further (but I believe still unpublished) study over a period of years. The specific distinction therefore cannot be maintained unless ploidy-level is taken as the sole and sufficient criterion. In this instance it may be noted that the variation in size and general vigor in the group had caught the attention of taxonomists long before a cytological difference was suspected. It is easy to forgive the initial error of the diligent student (Ruth Peck Ownbey) and her enthusiastic, influential mentor (Edgar Anderson).

So what is a taxonomist to make of autoploidy in any particular case? It is a warning flag to show that all is not so simple as it may seem on the surface. One should look carefully to see if plants on different levels of ploidy can in fact be distinguished by other means. If so, then some sort of taxonomic segregation may be in order. It depends on the amount of difference, the consistency of the difference, and the degree to which the potential segregates approximate the kind of taxa one is accustomed to finding in homoploid groups.

In theory there should be all degrees and grades from a condition in which the diploids and tetraploids are otherwise indistinguishable, to one in which anybody can tell them apart with no difficulty. Furthermore, we should expect all degrees of ecogeographic segregation (from none to perfect), which may or may not be correlated with the amount of morphological difference. That is in fact exactly what we find.

Accordingly, related populations that differ in ploidy-level may be given no taxonomic recognition, or they may be distinguished infraspecifically, or they may be treated as closely related but distinct species. The spectrum of possibilities is continuous, but the number of taxonomic ranks is finite and limited. The decisions must often be arbitrary, and taxonomists may reasonably differ about some of them.

In practice there may be some bias toward accepting such ploidy-pairs as species even when the morphological differentiation is incomplete. Thus many taxonomists now accept *Lotus tenuis* (diploid) as distinct from *L. corniculatus* (tetraploid), and *Nasturtium microphyllum* (tetraploid) from *N. officinale* (diploid), even though the morphological differences are a bit tenuous. On the other hand, not many find it necessary to recognize the diploid and tetraploid phases of *Epilobium angustifolium* (discussed farther on) at the specific level.

Alloploidy

Any newly produced alloploid is potentially a new species, but only potentially so. Probably most of them soon disappear, either through meiotic irregularity or through failure in competition. A few of them do succeed, and there have been some notable examples even during my own lifetime.

One of the most interesting and thoroughly documented cases of very recent alloploid speciation is the origin of *Tragopogon miscellus* from *T. dubius* and *T. pratensis,* and *T. mirus* from *T. dubius* and *T. porrifolius.* Marion Ownbey (Fig. 2.1) was the close observer, if not quite the midwife, of both births.

There are three common and widespread species of *Tragopogon* in the United States, *T. dubius, T. porrifolius,* and *T. pratensis.* All are introduced from Eurasia. All are diploids with $2n = 12$ chromosomes. They are well known to hybridize occasionally. The hybrids, never abundant, are largely sterile; at most only about 2% of the flowers set seed. Segregating F_2 hybrids have been grown experimentally, but are rarely seen in nature. Any possible leakage of genes from one species to another by back-crossing is not obvious.

In the summer of 1949 Marion Ownbey found a small colony of off-spring of the *T. dubius-porrifolius* cross in Pullman, Washington, and another in nearby Palouse, Washington. Furthermore, he found two small colonies of offspring of the *T. dubius-pratensis* cross in Moscow, Idaho, a few miles from Pullman. Members of these four colonies differed from ordinary F_1 hybrids in their greater vigor and much greater fertility. On a colony basis, observed fertility ranged from 52% to 66%, but some individuals in a colony were more fertile than others. Cytological examination showed the plants to be allotetraploid, $2n = 24$. Ownbey (1950) described both sets of allotetraploids as new species (*T. miscellus* and *T. mirus*).

As Ownbey's colleague at Pullman at the time, I thought it a bit premature to designate these plants as new species. We had no assurance then that either set would stabilize genetically and survive the rigors of competition to become a well established population. As it happens, both did so over the course of the next several decades. *Tragopogon miscellus* in particular has expanded to consist of millions of plants, now fully fertile, spread over parts of at least four states, Washington, Idaho, Montana, and Wyoming.

There has been ample physical opportunity for these same amphiploids to be produced elsewhere in the United States and also in Europe, but nothing has come to botanical attention, and Ownbey did not find anything morphologically comparable to them in the European descriptive literature. The odds against the virtually simultaneous formation of two such amphiploids in the same group in one small area must be astronomical, but it happened.

Tragopogon miscellus provides a relatively simple case of the origin of an allotetraploid species through hybridization of diploids, followed by doubling of the number of chromosomes. There are also more complex cases, such as that of the natural tetraploid Eurasian species *Galeopsis tetrahit*. This has been experimentally synthesized in complex fashion from its diploid ancestors, *G. pubescens* and *G. speciosa* (Müntzing, 1932). The experimentally produced first generation hybrid between the two diploids did not closely resemble *G. tetrahit*. A chance triploid among plants of the second hybrid generation presumably resulted from the fusion of a reduced and an unreduced gamete of the F_1 hybrid. Back-crossing of this triploid to *G. pubescens* yielded a single seed on the triploid, which gave rise to a tetraploid plant. The tetraploid is presumed to have resulted from the fusion of a normal haploid sperm of *G. pubescens* with an unreduced egg of the triploid. A subsequent generation of the tetraploid was produced by selfing. The resulting tetraploid set, although not entirely stable cytologically, closely resembled *G. tetrahit* morphologically and was in fact fully interfertile with it. Although the origin of *G. tetrahit* is complex, the taxonomic situation is fairly simple. Just as with *Tragopogon miscellus,* the tetraploid is fertile with itself, and does not hybridize effectively with its diploid ancestors.

Species that are distinct at the diploid level may be more or less confluent at the tetraploid level. In some such cases, the allotetraploid is cytologically unstable, producing offspring with varying assortments of the chromosomes of the parental species. A few generations of such reassortment may produce a complete range of combinations, from an essentially reconstituted autotetraploid of one parent, at one extreme, to an essentially reconstituted autotetraploid of the other parent at the other. All of these recombinant forms may (or may not) be fully interfertile, but they are not necessarily equally competitive. Thus there may (or may not) come to be some clustering of tetraploid types about the ancestral diploids. Even the seemingly reconstituted autotetraploid may be carrying portions of chromosomes of the other species, because of crossing over during some previous generation.

Autoploidy, no less than alloploidy, may foster hybridization between taxa that do not hybridize effectively at the diploid level. Meiosis in the hybrid at the diploid level may be irregular, because the chromosomes of the two species are not fully homologous. At the tetraploid level, on the other hand, each chromosome in a hybrid has a homologue to pair with, so that meiosis can proceed normally. As with the originally allotetraploid populations, the frequency of recombinant types in nature may come to depend on their effectiveness in competition, and on the existence of habitats to which they are better adapted than either of the diploids. Sometimes, as in some members of the *Artemisia tridentata* group, it is a close call whether two morphologically and ecologically differentiated taxa should be considered as distinct species because of the genetic isolation of the diploids, or as infraspecific groups because of the free hybridization among the tetraploids.

The examples and discussion of polyploids up to this point have emphasized cases at the tetraploid level and in which the parents had the same number of chromosomes. More complex cases abound. Diploids with very different basic numbers may also give rise to polyploids. *Aster ascendens,* with $n = 13$, probably arose from hybrids of *A. occidentalis* ($n = 8$) and *A. falcatus* ($n = 5$) or a close ally (Allen, 1985). Polyploids may be hexaploids, or octoploids, or have even higher numbers. Triploids, pentaploids, and other odd-numbered polyploids may also occur. Most of these latter are sterile or unstable, unless they can reproduce apomictically. The *Rosa canina* group in Europe, however, manages to maintain stable pentaploidy in a sexual setting, the sperms being haploid and the eggs tetraploid (Gustafsson, 1944).

The classic study of the *Sanicula crassicaulis* group by C. Ritchie Bell (1954) provides a fine example of some of the complexities in polyploid groups. The plants that Bell treated as *S. crassicaulis* var. *crassicaulis* comprise tetraploids, hexaploids, and octoploids. It seems probable that the tetraploid is an allotetraploid, derived eventually through hybridization between the diploid species *S. laciniata* and *S. hoffmannii* (or near antecedents of these species). The tetraploid shows considerable morphological diversity, with a degree of geography and local ecologic correlation, but the variation is continuous. On the other hand, the tetraploid is sharply set off from the diploid presumed parents. The hexaploids and octoploids can be securely distinguished from the tetraploids only by cytological examination, although some of them vary in the direction of *S. laciniata*. Plants at different levels of ploidy frequently grow intermingled, and the cytotypes may be morphologically distinguishable at a given site. At another site they may differ in other ways, or the morphological differences may even be reversed. On the basis of morphologic-geographic correlations and other evidence Bell considered that "different populations of the higher polyploids of *S. crassicaulis* have probably had independent and somewhat different origins."

Another octoploid in the same complex, which Bell treated as *Sanicula crassicaulis* var. *tripartita,* is morphologically more distinctive and has a limited geographic range to the north of that of other members of the group. Bell concluded that this octoploid resulted from past hybridization between hexaploid *S. crassicaulis* var. *crassicaulis* and still another diploid, *S. bipinnatifida*. A case might be made for treating var. *tripartita* as a distinct species. In a letter to me, Bell stated that "I believe these plants are always distinct and that they could very easily be considered as distinct species . . . but I decided that no violence was done to their integrity by giving them varietal status and that this status would best point out the affinity between these octoploids and the rest of the *S. crassicaulis* complex (of which they are definitely a part)."

If Bell had studied a more limited sample of the *S. crassicaulis* complex he could easily have come to the mistaken conclusion that the tetraploids, hexaploids, and octoploids were distinct species with clear and consistent morphological markers.

Pillar Complexes

Some sets of polyploids link not just two diploids, but several. The differences among the diploids may be comparable to those among ordinary species, but the specific differences are bridged by the polyploids. The polyploids may be less abundant than the diploids, or equally abundant, or more abundant. The apt metaphor **pillar complex** is applied to groups in which the distinct diploids may be compared to separate pillars covered by a continuous roof of polyploids.

The taxonomic treatment of pillar complexes is a vexed question, with ample room for legitimate difference of opinion. If the complex has only a few pillars, and these phenetically not too far apart, it may be useful to adopt an expanded specific concept and include all members of the group in a single species. An infraspecific organization based on the individual diploids (pillars) may then be undertaken, with the roof being sawed up to associate the diverse polyploids with the diploids they most resemble. *Rudbeckia fulgida,* with three basic diploids, may be an example.

Often a pillar complex embraces so much diversity that taxonomists do not find it useful to put everything into one species. The *Phacelia magellanica* complex is such a group. It consists of about two dozen ultimate taxa in North America, and a smaller but uncertain number in South America. Most taxonomists recognize more than one species here, but they differ as to how many. In a consideration of the taxa occurring in the United States (mainly California), Heckard (1960) recognized 13 species and 20 ultimate taxa. One of these species was represented only by diploids, five by both diploids and tetraploids, five only by tetraploids, one by both tetraploids and hexaploids, and one only by hexaploids. The polyploids include both autoploids and alloploids, and the taxa collectively form a morphological continuum. A comparison of any one "species" in the group with its nearest ally would reasonably lead to the inclusion of both in the same species, but one or both of these subunits intergrade in turn with one or more taxa in the group, so that the whole group is inextricably linked.

In such complexes no one treatment is wholly satisfactory. The decisions are largely subjective, and many of them are open to reasonable challenge. One tries to carve out "species" and infraspecific taxa that as nearly as possible approximate the morphological, ecological, and geographical nature of taxa in ordinary diploid groups, in such a way as to leave as few doubtful or intermediate forms as is reasonably possible. In my own treatment of this group for *Intermountain Flora* (1984) I recognize two infraspecific taxa that Heckard does not, but I combine some other taxa that he separates. This does not necessarily mean that either of us is right or wrong, but only that my subjective judgment differs from his in some details. The hierarchical system essential to taxonomy does not permit the classification to show the many fine gradations of differentiation among natural populations. We must choose from among a limited set of formal categories.

Combined Polyploidy and Aneuploidy

The greatest diversity of chromosome numbers within a species is provided by a combination of polyploidy and aneuploidy. The higher the level of ploidy, the less important the addition or subtraction of a few chromosomes becomes to the plant. We shall consider here only the examples of *Draba verna* and *Claytonia virginica*. These are selected precisely because they *are* extreme cases that may provide some guidance for the consideration of less extreme ones.

Draba (*Erophila*) *verna* is an annual, mainly self-pollinated species that is fairly widespread in Europe and the Near East. Known chromosome numbers in natural populations range from $2n = 14$ to $2n = 64$, with three gaps in the series. Plants with $2n = 94$ have also arisen in cultivation.

Based on studies of plants of northeastern Europe, Winge (1940) proposed to recognize four species, founded on chromosome number and fertility. He considered plants with $2n = 14$ to form one species, plants with $2n = 24$ to form another species, plants with $2n = 30-40$ to form a third species, and those with $2n = 52-64$ to form a fourth. Experimental study showed the four groups to be mutually intersterile or nearly so, but within each group plants even of different chromosome numbers were interfertile. The possible numbers for plants outside of Winge's study area have scarcely been explored, although $2n = 16$ has been reported for some plants introduced into the United States. Individual self-pollinated lines are often distinguishable by morphological minutiae, but no consistent morphological features have been alleged to characterize the four cytological groups. The current generation of European taxonomists has wearied of *Draba verna,* and it is now customary to treat the species broadly to include the whole array of cytotypes described by Winge.

Claytonia virginica is a cormose perennial, outcrossing species that is widespread in eastern and central United States. Reported chromosome numbers range from $2n = 12$ to more than 100. The series is continuous from 12 to 37, including odd as well as even numbers, and fragmented above that. Plants of slightly or widely different chromosome number often grow intermingled without any evident morphological distinction, and it is presumed that these different cytotypes hybridize freely. There is often some small aneuploid variation between underground and aerial parts of the same plant, or between different branches of a shoot.

Walter Lewis (Fig. 2.3) has studied these plants over a period of years. In 1977 he and John Semple proposed to organize the chromosome numbers into 3 series, based eventually on x = 6, x = 7, and x = 8, with most plants being diploid, triploid (but fertile!) or tetraploid, often with superimposed aneuploidy. Some cytotypes are considered to reach a ploidy-level of as much as 24x. It is unclear whether some cytotypes reflect aneuploid variation from an ordinary polyploid number, or result from the addition of different numbers. Thus $2n = 30$ might be an aneuploid variant of $2n = 32$ or $2n = 28$, or it might reflect the addition of $2n = 14$ to $2n = 16$. Possibly some are one and some are another.

Nobody currently pretends to see more than one species in this cytological tangle. There is, however, a weak tendency toward morphologic-geographic segregation of the 6 and 7 cytotypes on the one hand and the 8 cytotypes on the other, with the former being more southern and having narrower leaves than the latter. Some botanists, including myself, try to recognize two varieties on this basis, but the distinction is parlous.

Some other species of *Claytonia,* such as *C. caroliniana* and *C. lanceolata,* show similar but less dramatic variation in chromosome number.

APOMIXIS

Apomixis is here defined in the traditional sense as the setting of seed without fertilization. The various cytological-embryological means by which this is accomplished have been catalogued and elucidated by Steb-

Fig. 2.3. Some botanists who have made important contributions to our understanding of the nature of species. TOP (LEFT TO RIGHT): Jens C. Clausen (1891–1969); William M. Hiesey (1903–); David D. Keck (1903–). Photo courtesy of Carnegie Institute of Washington. BOTTOM LEFT, Harvey M. Hall (1874–1932). Photo courtesy of Carnegie Institute of Washington. BOTTOM RIGHT, Walter Lewis (1930–). Photo courtesy of Walter Lewis.

bins (1941) and later by Gustafsson (1946, 1947). All routes of apomixis share the feature that normally the seedlings are genetically identical to the parent. From a taxonomic standpoint the different routes are equivalent.

Apomixis sometimes occurs at the diploid level in otherwise ordinary populations. Here the taxonomic problems are essentially the same as in self-pollination. Much more often apomixis is associated with polyploidy and interspecific hybridization. In some groups there appears to be a direct sequence, in that hybridization leads to alloploidy, which leads to apomixis.

More often than not, apomixis is to some degree facultative rather than wholly obligate. There may be enough sexual reproduction to keep the pot bubbling, and enough apomixis to permit any fortuitously formed, highly competitive genotype to maintain itself without change. Interspecific hybrids and hybrid segregates can thus reproduce with a minimum of meiotic hazards, while still retaining the capacity to throw an occasional potentially stable new genotype.

The most difficult groups of all to treat taxonomically are the polyploid-apomictic complexes. These have all the problems of polyploid pillar complexes, with the additional complication that individual genotypes, however produced, may perpetuate themselves indefinitely by setting seed apomictically.

The population-structure in polyploid-apomictic groups is a subtle and addictive trap for the naive or unwary taxonomist. In a local area it may be possible to distinguish several constant and readily recognizable apomicts, persuading even perceptive field-botanists to describe them as distinct species. Unfortunately, in other areas there may be different sets of apomicts, filling in the gaps that were at first perceived. Seemingly distinctive individual apomicts may be discovered and named, only to be tied back into the larger group when other apomicts are discovered. The slightly more sophisticated taxonomist, bemused by the actual or potential constancy of apomictic lines, may come to rely on minutiae to distinguish purported species. In such genera as *Hieracium, Taraxacum,* and *Crataegus,* thousands of scarcely differing species may at length be described, leading to a state of chaos in which even the specialist cannot consistently put the same name on the same thing. Such dedicated specialists (here nameless) have even identified specimens taken from different branches of the same plant as different species.

In their treatment of North American *Crepis* in 1938 Babcock and Stebbins proposed a method to approach such groups: Identify the sexual diploids, base the specific concepts on these, and assign the polyploid apomicts (and sexual polyploids, if any) to one or another species according to which diploid they most resemble. Only those apomicts (or sets of similar apomicts) that appear to be essentially different from any of the sexual diploids are treated as separate species ("agamospecies").

Their application of this method to *Crepis* was eminently successful, and their taxonomic treatment is still viable half a century later. They organized the morphologically continuous polyploid-apomictic complex that embraces most of American *Crepis* into 9 species. Seven of these included both sexual diploid and polyploid (mostly apomictic) forms. Only two wholly apomictic species were recognized.

Here, as elsewhere, things are not so simple as they may at first seem. These authors considered *Crepis modocensis* to consist of two morphologically distinguishable and geographically isolated sexual diploids, linked by a swarm of apomictic polyploids. Stebbins now assures me that the two diploids, treated as the foundation of different subspecies, are so similar that they might be expected to hybridize freely, given the physical opportunity. That is not made clear, however, in the original publication. We may recall that the treatment of geographic isolates is one of the unresolved problems in the reproductive ("biological") concept of species. One must say "actually or *potentially* interbreeding," and assessment of the potentiality is generally subjective.

It seems only prudent to try to identify the sexual diploids in studying any polyploid-apomictic complex, but every group presents its own difficulties in taxonomic interpretation. In considering eastern American *Antennaria* Stebbins (Fig. 2.1) now finds it better to treat the sexual diploids as narrowly defined species, distinct from their polyploid (both sexual and apomictic) derivatives. I myself find the earlier approach (à la *Crepis*) still useful in this group, but the matter might reasonably be debated.

In sum, it may be said that in polyploid-apomictic groups, as in sexual pillar complexes, one tries to carve out "species" that are as nearly as possible comparable to ordinary sexual species in morphologic, ecologic and geographic features. In so doing, one tries to take due account of the nature of the sexual diploids, and also to draw the lines through whatever hollows there may be in the curve of distribution of phenotypes, rather than through the humps.

What's Going on Here?

The late Edgar Anderson used to say that a taxonomist should be trying to figure out, "What's going on here?". It is good advice. In any taxonomic study we are extrapolating from a limited set of data to conclusions about populations that are generally too large to be studied in individual detail. In the exploratory stage for any region, taxonomists have enough to do simply to name and catalog the things that are obviously different. As exploration goes on, and names and specimens accumulate, it becomes necessary to reconsider the classification. Such reconsideration is best done in the light of an understanding of the population behavior and conditions of selection for the group. Is there self-pollination? Apomixis? Polyploidy? Aneuploidy? Ecogeographic differentiation? Is hybridization rare, fairly common, or rampant, and what kinds of barriers limit it? Is there progressive evolutionary adaptation to exploit a particular habitat or way of life? Just what is going on here? We ignore such questions only at the risk of producing unperceptive classifications that fail to help us understand the nature of the world.

Infraspecific Taxa

A Bit of History

In pre-Darwinian times, when species were generally regarded as divinely created, variety was a convenient catchall rank for plants deviating from the norm of a species. The species was considered to be the basic population, and the varieties were appended to it. Taxonomists mostly thought and wrote of a species *and* its varieties. Distinctive individual oddballs, horticulturally derived or maintained types, and minor local populations differing from the standard for the species could all be covered in this one category.

Gradually taxonomists came to realize that some species might consist of two or several more or less equal subunits. It might be difficult to decide which of these was the species proper, and which were the varieties to be attached to it. Nomenclatural considerations sometimes led to the designation of a minor segment as the species proper, and a major segment as the variety, to the annoyance of the taxonomist.

Although taxonomists were quick to seize upon the evolutionary concept as providing the rationale for the patterns they observed, most of them were not so quick to realize that the nature of infraspecific taxa would have to be reconsidered. The concept that the species consists of its varieties, none more basic than the others, did not make its way into the International Code of Botanical Nomenclature until the Stockholm Congress in 1950. Vestiges of the pre-Darwinian concept of varieties as appendages of the species persist in the work of some taxonomists even today. In polytypic species it is likely to be assumed that the simple binomial refers only to the nomenclaturally typical phase, unless the broader concept is clearly indicated. A widely used manual for identification of vascular plants in northeastern United States, published as recently as 1950, still largely adhered to the archaic concept of varieties as appendages of the species.

With the increasing emphasis in the late 19th century and into the 20th century on species and infraspecific taxa as self-perpetuating natural populations, taxonomists began to purge the horticultural varieties and unstable natural variants from the formal system of classification. Horticulturists were loath to give up their own use of varieties, and thus there was for some decades a confusion between horticultural and taxonomic varieties. The confusion is only now being resolved by the substitution of the term **cultivar** for what had been called horticultural varieties.

The category **subspecies** has a somewhat shorter and less checkered history than variety. It was introduced in 1805 by Persoon, for taxa almost but not quite worthy of specific rank. Subspecies in that sense was not a substitute for variety, but a different, higher rank within the species. A subspecies might or might not have attached or included varieties.

For nearly a century after its introduction, the subspecies was a seldom used rank. The first serious attempt at an international code of botanical nomenclature, taken at a meeting convened in Paris by Alphonse de Candolle in 1867, permitted the use of subspecies only as an intercalary rank between species and varieties. This interpretation of subspecies remained in the International Code through the Vienna (1905), Brussels (1910), Cambridge (1930), and Amsterdam (1935) versions. It disappeared from the Stockholm (1950) version of the Code through an exercise of editorial license that was not formally challenged thereafter. Since 1950 the International Code has been neutral about subspecies and varieties, permitting either to be used without the other, and also permitting varieties to be used within subspecies.

An important paper in 1898 by the influential botanist Richard von Wettstein promoted the use of subspecies for taxa that replace each other geographically and intergrade in the contact zone. Many of these subspecies had been taken as distinct species when first encountered. Here we see the use of subspecies as the principal infraspecific category, with varieties being brushed aside as inconsequential.

The American Code of Botanical Nomenclature, dating from 1904, recognized only one infraspecific category, the subspecies, and relegated variety to horticultural usage. Also in America, a school of thought descending from Harvey M. Hall used the subspecific category largely in order to emphasize the real taxonomic significance of the groups so designated, in contrast to the often insignificant varieties of past taxonomists. This approach also freed its practitioners from the necessity to adopt inconvenient names for the recognized subspecies, since the literature was not then burdened with a plethora of priorable subspecific epithets. It also provided an opportunity for the taxonomist to impress his personal stamp on the classification of a group through a series of nomenclatural innovations, often for taxa that had in fact been previously recognized as varieties. The widespread use of the subspecific category by zoological taxonomists doubtless also had some influence on botanists, although this has seldom been noted in print. Similar considerations, aside from the American Code, led to the increasing use of subspecies by European authors.

Many plant taxonomists, the world around, have continued to use variety as the principal or only infraspecific category, in spite of the change in practice by their fellows. Nowadays one taxonomist's subspecies is likely to be another's variety. The recent trend, especially among those who consider themselves in the vanguard of taxonomic progress, is to use subspecies as the only infraspecific category—altogether in harmony with Hall and with the otherwise defunct American Code.

There would be no great harm in the substitution of terms and ranks were it not that a few species are so complex that more than one infraspecific rank is needed for adequate classification. In my own experience most such species need a rank to be inserted between the ordinary infraspecific taxa and the species. This is precisely what was envisioned by the several versions of the International Code prior to 1950, with the variety as the ordinary infraspecific category, and the subspecies to be intercalated between variety and species in particular cases as needed. Thus I find it necessary to swim against the stream, and continue to use variety as the ordinary infraspecific category.

There are other possible alternatives to provide an infraspecific hierarchy. One would be to invent a new rank, between the subspecies and the species, to be used occasionally as needed. There is nothing contrary to the Code in this, inasmuch as the creation of new ranks is clearly permitted. Even so, I find it unappealing. Another alternative would be to use subspecies as the ordinary infraspecific rank, and add varieties when two ranks are required. The problem here is that such varieties would mostly be comparable to the subspecies in other groups, and the hierarchical subspecies would not really be comparable to ordinary subspecies.

The question of subspecies versus varieties is perhaps a tempest in a teapot, but the Code as we have it has consequences for both the choice of epithets and their rank. The correct epithet at subspecific rank is not always the same as at the varietal rank. Furthermore, since the two ranks are nomenclaturally independent, a formal transfer is required to change from one to the other.

ECOTYPES

No species with any considerable geographic range or ecological amplitude is likely to be genetically or phenetically uniform throughout. Careful studies of both plants and animals have consistently shown that any gene-locus with more than one allele is likely to have different frequencies of these alleles in different local population. If a species is mentally divided into different geographic or ecologic segments on any basis, even a purely arbitrary one, the segments may be expected to differ in the frequencies of individual alleles.

Many, probably most, such differences result from different conditions of selection in different places. Any local breeding population will reflect the influence of selection in its particular area, regardless of what may happen elsewhere in the range of the species. The adaptation cannot be expected to be perfect, because conditions of selection are themselves in a continuous state of flux. Furthermore, what Ernst Mayr (1942) has called the founder principle may limit the local gene-pool on which selection may act.

In 1922 Göte Turesson (p. 533) proposed the term **ecotype** to cover any segment of a species arising through selection as a genotypical response to a particular habitat. It was soon demonstrated that a species might have numerous ecotypes, that the boundaries among these are often vague, and that there may or may not be morphological markers for the physiological differences. The ecotypes within a species might be variously characterized and defined, according to one's outlook, and there can even be ecotypes within ecotypes. From a taxonomic standpoint, it is impractical to try to characterize, define, and name all the ecotypes within most species, especially inasmuch as many of them can be identified only through exacting experimental studies. On the other hand, it now seems obvious that recognized infraspecific taxa should be self-perpetuating populations, and that these might be expected to correlate in most if not all cases with ecotypic differentiation. The concept of ecotypes is useful to taxonomists, but ecotype is not a formal taxonomic category.

The most convincing way to demonstrate ecotypic differentiation is by transplantation. Plants of the same species but from different habitats may be grown in a uniform garden, or they may be reciprocally transplanted, each into the habitat of the other. A clump may be divided, and its parts planted in different habitats. Turesson used principally the uniform garden approach.

Just as Turesson's work was coming to fruition, Harvey M. Hall (Fig. 2.3) independently began a more ambitious program in California in 1922, using both the reciprocal transplant and the uniform garden methods. This followed on some of his own earlier work in Colorado with Frederic E. Clements, the most influential ecologist of the time. Hall's junior associates in California were David D. Keck and William M. Hiesey. Hall died prematurely in 1932, just as the Danish botanist Jens Clausen was being recruited to join the team. Under Clausen's leadership the work was completed. The first major publication of the Clausen, Keck, and Hiesey results, in 1940, is a landmark in taxonomic history. Subsequent publications by these same authors focused on evolution through alloploidy (1945), and again on ecotypical differentiation in *Achillea* (1948). Finally, in 1958, Clausen and Hiesey published a broad theoretical study on the genetic structure of ecologic races. These works profoundly influenced taxonomic thought, and the trio Clausen, Keck, and Hiesey (Fig. 2.3) is as well known among taxonomists as the double-play combination Tinker to Evers to Chance is among baseball buffs.

Transplant studies may also demonstrate that particular morphologic features are plastic rather than genetically fixed. *Viola sagittata* has notably long petioles when grown in the shade, and much shorter ones in sunny sites, but the difference is a direct response of the individual to the habitat (Yost, 1987). Even some astute field-botanists have been misled to suppose a specific difference here, and the plants of open sites have passed in recent ecological literature as a distinct species under the name *V. fimbriatula*.

VARIETIES

Many species are more or less divisible into populations sufficiently distinct to warrant some taxonomic notice, but not well enough set off to be called species. These infraspecific groups fail to some degree to meet one or another of the three criteria (consistency, persistence, and ordinary means) that mark species. Most of the infraspecific taxa that we find useful to recognize meet the tests of persistence and ordinary means, but are confluent with other segments of the species. The hollow between the humps of the curve of distribution of phenetic features does not come close enough to the base line warrant recognition of the humps at the specific level. There must be some sort of barrier to free interbreeding between infraspecific taxa, or they would lose their identity, but the barrier need not be genetic. It may be the means of pollination, or ecotypic selection, or simple distance, or some combination of factors.

Ordinary infraspecific taxa are here considered to be varieties, although as we have noted many taxonomists now treat them as subspecies. Different varieties of a species usually show some ecologic and/or geographic segregation. Sometimes they occur in similar habitats but in different geographic regions, which may be confluent or disjunct. Or the varieties may occur in different habitats in the same region.

Often the varieties combine a degree of geographic and ecologic separation, both imperfect. The two varieties of *Viguiera multiflora* have different but widely overlapping geographic ranges in western United States. Variety *multiflora* grows in more mesic habitats than the dryland var. *nevadensis,* and has a somewhat more northern and eastern distribution. In Utah, where both are common, var. *multiflora* is usually at higher elevations (and thus in more mesic habitats) than var. *nevadensis.*

Sometimes the ecogeographic pattern is more complex. *Oenothera caespitosa* provides a case in point (Wagner et al., 1985). It consists of some 5 varieties, apparently all interfertile. Aside from var. *marginata,* they are fairly well segregated geographically as well as morphologically. Variety *marginata* largely blankets the range of the other varieties, except that var. *caespitosa* also extends well out onto the northern Great Plains, where it is the only variety. Variety *marginata* intergrades with all the other varieties, which also intergrade with each other where their ranges meet. Because of obscure but apparently significant small differences in habitat-preference, var. *marginata* only seldom actually grows with the other varieties, in spite of the map sympatry. There is enough intergradation among the several varieties to frustrate any attempt at specific recognition. Equally, the varieties have enough populational and phenetic integrity to warrant some taxonomic distinction.

Not infrequently the differentiation of a species into geographic varieties is imperfect in that extreme individuals from one region may resemble typical individuals from the other. Such is the case, for example, with the two varieties of *Erigeron speciosus* in western United States, which differ in leaf-shape and amount of pubescence. The bulk of the northwestern segment of the species, in Washington, Oregon, northern Idaho, and western Montana, clearly belongs to var. *speciosus.* Equally, the bulk of the southeastern segment of the species, in the Rocky Mountain region as far north as central Idaho and southwestern Montana, clearly belongs to var. *macranthus.* There is some variation in the critical taxonomic characters within each of these two regional groups, however, so that extreme individuals of one variety might well be identified as belonging to the other, in the absence of geographic data. Identification based purely on morphology would produce substantially similar geographic distributions for both varieties.

Cryptantha cinerea, mainly in central and southwestern United States, provides a somewhat different example. Variety *abortiva,* mainly in Nevada and southern California, is fairly well characterized, but the remainder of the species is only very imperfectly differentiated into variety *jamesii,* of the high plains east of the Rocky Mountains, and var. *cinerea,* of the intervening area. Whatever justification there may be for recognizing these latter two varieties rests in morphological tendencies and averages associated with geographic distribution, rather than in stable differences.

We are properly suspicious of the significance of proposed varieties that show neither geographic nor ecologic segregation. There is no inherent reason, however, why we might not sometimes have varieties occupying the same habitat in the same geographic area, but held apart by an imperfect barrier to interbreeding. I believe that such situations do exist, but not surprisingly they are all subject to debate.

The circumboreal species *Epilobium hornemannii* appears to be a paradigm case. Leaving aside some Beringian plants of limited habitats, the species as here defined consists of two widespread varieties of essentially similar habitat and geographic distribution, the var. *hornemannii* and the var. *lactiflorum*. The two look much alike, but typically differ in size and color of the petals (short, white petals in var. *lactiflorum,* longer, anthocyanic petals in var. *hornemannii*). The two characters are only imperfectly correlated, however, and the measurements are confluent. All students of the group agree that these two very similar taxa hybridize frequently, which is not surprising in view of the rampant hybridization in the whole section *Epilobium*. Some authors have treated the two infraspecifically, but others have treated them as different species in spite of their basic similarity and considerable intergradation. One current student of the genus defends the latter position on the basis that infraspecific taxa must show some ecogeographic differentiation, and that therefore the choice is between recognizing the two as distinct species and uniting them entirely. I see no reason to place such strictures on the qualities of infraspecific taxa. Just as species are of various sorts, so are subspecies and varieties. Procrustes is properly confined to classical mythology.

Epilobium angustifolium, mentioned on an earlier page, provides a marginal case of differentiation of a species into varieties (Mosquin, 1967). Numerous counts show that diploid and tetraploid segments of the species have widely overlapping geographic ranges, with a tendency toward some ecologic differentiation in the area of overlap. The range of morphologic variation in the circumboreal diploid is completely encompassed within that of the more variable, often larger-leaved and more hairy tetraploid, which is mainly North American and tends to be more southern than the diploid. The situation is complicated by the fact that a hexaploid from Japan appears to be morphologically identical with the diploid. Names are available for the diploid and tetraploid cytotypes, at both the varietal and the subspecific level, but the taxonomic utility of the separation is debatable.

Senecio pauperculus provides a marginal case of geographic differentiation into varieties without the complication of polyploidy. The flowerheads of cordilleran plants of this species average larger than those of plants of eastern North America. The cordilleran plants have accordingly been segregated by some authors as var. *thomsoniensis,* in contrast to the more eastern var. *pauperculus.* On the other hand, so much of the cordilleran population has heads in the size range of var. *pauperculus* that taxonomic recognition is of doubtful utility, and the monographer (Barkley) declines to draw a distinction.

Cases such as those of *Epilobium angustifolium* and *Senecio pauperculus* fade insensibly into ordinary infraspecific variation that does not warrant taxonomic notice. *Erigeron provancheri* was based on extremely depauperate plants from a difficult habitat along the estuary of the St. Lawrence River in Quebec. It appears distinctive in the field, but plants cultivated in the Botanical Gardens at Montreal became much like ordinary small plants of the widespread and variable species *E. philadelphicus*. There has evidently been some ecotypic selection, but the morphologic expression is magnified by the direct effect of the environment.

Machaeranthera canescens is a widespread and highly variable species in western United States. In southeastern Washington there appears to be a strong ecotypic differentiation between relatively small plants on the Palouse Prairie, and much larger and coarser plants at a lower altitude near the Snake River, as for example near Wawawai. If the species occurred only in this small area, the two ecotypes might well be recognized as varieties. In the context of the species as a whole, however, the differences are insignificant.

SUBSPECIES

A very small minority of species, probably less than 1%, is sufficiently complex to warrant a hierarchical infraspecific organization, with subspecies interposed between the variety and the species. *Achillea millefolium, Cannabis sativa, Descurainia pinnata,* and *Erigeron peregrinus* may serve as examples. Often the subspecies are geographic. We shall discuss the first two examples.

Achillea millefolium is a highly complex circumboreal species, containing both tetraploids and hexaploids, that has so far resisted efforts to organize a satisfactory taxonomy on a regional basis. No one has yet presented a comprehensive treatment of the species throughout its geographic range. It is clear enough that most of the individuals in western United States belong to a tetraploid phase that has been called *A. millefolium* subsp. *lanulosa*. The subspecies has a wide ecological amplitude, and might conceivably be divided into a number of varieties. One such is a dwarf, alpine and subalpine ecotype with dark-margined phyllaries, called var. *alpicola,* which taxonomists have found easy enough to recognize. The situation presents a dilemma to taxonomists who recognize only one infraspecific category. In 1940 Keck treated *A. lanulosa* as a species, with subspecies *alpicola* in addition to the more widespread and variable nomenclaturally typical subspecies. In so doing, he also had to recognize the northwest coastal hexaploid *A. borealis* at the specific level, in spite of the fact that *A. borealis* and *A. lanulosa* are only weakly characterized morphologically and can be securely distinguished only by the number of chromosomes. Subsequent studies (Tyrl, 1975) have emphasized the morphologic and geographic continuity of the tetraploids and hexaploids in western North America, making their distinction as separate species scarcely tenable. The geographic and taxonomic limits of subspecies *lanulosa* are not yet clear. Possibly it should include most of the native population in eastern as well as western United States. Another native American tetraploid, mainly northeastern subarctic, has dark-margined phyllaries like var. *alpicola,* but it has flat leaves as in typical hexaploid European *A. millefolium,* instead of airily three-dimensional leaves as in subspecies *lanulosa* (including its var. *alpicola*). The name *A. millefolium* var. *nigrescens* has been used for this subarctic phase. The taxonomy of *Achillea millefolium* sensu lato remains to be clarified, but it seems evident that an infraspecific hierarchy will be necessary.

   Cannabis sativa presents a different sort of example (Small & Cronquist, 1976). The species has long been cultivated in Eurasia, for fiber towards the north, and for psychoactive cannabinols toward the south. Numerous counts indicate that the plants are all diploids with $2n = 20$. They are wind-pollinated, and the pollen is airborne for long distances. There do not appear to be any sterility-barriers within the group, and all investigated characters are confluent. Wherever the species is cultivated, it also escapes and grows wild. Wherever it grows wild, it is also cultivated, or is known or might reasonably be supposed to have been cultivated in the past. No original native wild population can now be securely recognized.

   The species consists of two geographic subspecies that reflect the efforts of selection in cultivation over several thousand years. The northern subspecies *sativa* has soft, easily rotting, not much branched stems from which the fibers can readily be extracted at the proper stage of decay of the surrounding tissues. Its cannabinols (specific secondary metabolites) include only a small proportion of the psychoactive delta-9-tetrahydrocannabinol. The southern subspecies *indica* has hard, often more branching stems, and its cannabinols include a considerable proportion of delta-9-tetrahydrocannabinol; the plants require a relatively long growing season to mature.

   Cultivated forms of both subspecies have persistent, easily harvested fruits with a high percentage of germination when planted. Wild-adapted plants, on the other hand, have quickly deciduous fruits with variable dormancy. The deciduous condition is marked morphologically by a collar or constriction shortly above the base of the fruit. Wild-adapted plants also tend to be smaller, and to have smaller fruits, than their cultivated equivalents. It appears that over the course of a century or so the wild-adapted syndrome can be reconstituted by natural selection after cultivation is abandoned. Thus each of the two subspecies may be divided into a variety adapted for cultivation, and a variety adapted for growing wild: *Cannabis sativa* subspecies *sativa,* with varieties *sativa* (cultivated) and *spontanea* (wild); and subspecies *indica,* with varieties *indica* (cultivated) and *kafiristanica* (wild).

FORMAE

   A third infraspecific category, the forma, still has some limited currency. It is a lesser rank than subspecies or variety. Developing practice over the past century has limited the use of **formae** to distinctive phenotypes of no persistent populational significance. A pubescent, purple-flowered species may have an occasional glabrous deviant, which is likely to be named f. *glabra* or f. *tonsa,* and an occasional white-flowered deviant, which is likely to be named f. *alba* or f. *albiflora.* The rare individuals that are both glabrous *and* white-flowered might be referred to either form, or a purist might name still another form to accommodate them. Actual practice here is not fully reconciled with the International Code of Botanical Nomenclature, which would require an automatic tautonymous forma to cover all the diverse individuals not included in other named formae. Any possible continuing utility of the category forma is limited to the provision of names to be used by enthusiastic amateurs who insist that a plant that looks different needs a name. Nearly all taxonomists now feel that two infraspecific categories are quite enough to meet normal taxonomic needs.

Probably most named formae are Mendelian variants. There is no doubt that some Mendelian variants are so striking that people are likely to assume that they must be taxonomically significant. *Betula uber,* with small round leaves, appears to be merely a Mendelian variant of *B. lenta.* Known from only a few individuals in a single stream-drainage in western Virginia, *B. uber* has been considered a rare and endangered species. It grows intermingled with *B. lenta,* and many of its seeds develop into apparently normal plants of *B. lenta. Betula uber* might defensibly be treated as a forma of *B. lenta* by those who still feel the need of a name. No new combination is here proposed.

We should note here that taxonomists often use the term form (without the terminal *a*) in a nontechnical sense, equivalent to phase, which has no nomenclatural status.

CONCLUSION

None of the foregoing examples of infraspecific variation is beyond the possibility of challenge or reinterpretation. Many other examples could be provided if necessary. It is clear enough that the kind of variation here described does exist.

Infraspecific taxa, like species and higher taxa are recognized, defined, and named as an aid to understanding the pattern of diversity in nature. For our own purposes we find it necessary to try to organize the infinite diversity of nature into a formal pattern with a limited number of ranks and taxa, but nature is not constrained by our needs.

We do not generally find it useful to name infraspecific taxa that cannot be characterized morphologically, but there is no inherent reason not to do so in particular species if it helps our understanding. The two subspecies of *Cannabis sativa,* discussed above, are characterized mainly by secondary metabolites and stem anatomy, rather than by external morphology. Anyone who does not find this distinction useful can simply and quite properly call the plant *Cannabis sativa.* In this as in all other species that have infraspecific taxa, anyone who wants to stop at the specific level can do so, and still have a name for the plant.

Epilogue

Nothing can be more certain than that the foregoing discussion of species and infraspecific taxa does not exhaust the possibilities. Taxa may intergrade in part of their contact zone, and remain distinct in other areas of contact. A series of infraspecific taxa may form a geographic ring, with the terminal members behaving as distinct species where they come into contact; this is apparently not so common in plants as in animals, or at least it has not been so often recognized. Different morphological, cytological, and ecogeographic patterns may be superimposed, so that a taxonomic organization on one basis cuts across the others. The permanent translocation heterozygotes found especially in some members of the Onagraceae present their own set of problems. No formal set of rules can adequately foresee all cases. Ultimately the taxonomist must produce a treatment that appeals to the mind as the best conceptual organization of the diversity that exists in nature.

Selected References

Allen, G. A. 1985. The hybrid of origin of *Aster ascendens* (Asteraceae). Amer. J. Bot. **72:** 268–277.

Anderson, E. 1948. Hybridization of the habitat. Evolution **2:** 1–9.

Anderson, E. 1949. Introgressive hybridization. Wiley. New York.

Babcock, E. B. & G. L. Stebbins. 1938. The American species of *Crepis*. Carnegie Inst. Washington Publ. **504.**

Bell, C. R. 1954. The *Sanicula crassicaulis* complex (Umbelliferae): A study of variation and polyploidy. Univ. Calif. Publ. Bot. **27:** 133–230.

Bowman, R. N. 1987. Cryptic self-incompatibility and the breeding system of *Clarkia unguiculata* (Onagraceae). Amer. J. Bot. **74:** 471–476.

Camp, W. H. & C. L. Gilly. 1943. The structure and origin of species. Brittonia **4:** 324–385.

Chuang, T. I. & L. Constance. 1977. Cytogeography of *Phacelia ranunculacea* (Hydrophyllaceae). Rhodora **79:** 115–122.

Clausen, J. & W. M. Hiesey. 1958. Experimental studies on the nature of species. **IV.** Genetic structure of ecological races. Carnegie Inst. Washington Publ. **615.**

Clausen, J., D. D. Keck & W. M. Hiesey. 1940–1948. Experimental studies on the nature of species. **I.** Effect of varied environments on western North American Plants. Carnegie Inst. Washington Publ. **520**, 1940. **II.** Plant evolution through amphiploidy and autoploidy, with examples from the Madiinae. Carnegie Inst. Washington Publ. **564**, 1945. **III.** Environmental responses of climatic races of *Achillea*. Carnegie Inst. Washington Publ. **581**, 1948.

Cronquist, A. 1978. Once again, what is a species? Biosystematics in agriculture. Beltsville Symposia in Agr. Res. **2:** 3–20.

Cronquist, A., A. H. Holmgren, N. H. Holmgren, J. L. Reveal & P. K. Holmgren. 1984. Intermountain flora volume four, the Asteridae (except Asteraceae). The New York Botanical Garden. New York.

Dobzhansky, T. 1937. Genetics and the origin of species. Columbia Univ. Press. New York.

Dobzhansky, T. 1951. Genetics and the origin of species. 3rd ed. Columbia Univ. Press. New York.

Du Rietz, G. E. 1930. The fundamental units of biological taxonomy. Svensk. Bot. Tidskr. **24:** 333–428.

Gottlieb, L. D. 1978. *Stephanomeria malheurensis* (Compositae), a new species from Oregon. Madroño **25:** 44–46.

Grant, V. 1981. Plant speciation. 2nd ed. Columbia Univ. Press. New York.

Grant, V. & K. A. Grant. 1965. Flower pollination in the phlox family. Columbia Univ. Press. New York.

Gustafsson, A. 1944. The constitution of the *Rosa canina* complex. Hereditas **30:** 405–428.

Gustafsson, A. 1946, 1947. Apomixis in higher plants. Lunds Univ. Arskr. N. F. Avd. 2. **42(3),** 1946; **43(2),** 1947; **43(12),** 1947.

Harlan, J. R. & J. M. J. de Wet. 1963. The compilospecies concept. Evolution **17:** 497–501.

Harlan, J. R. & J. M. J. de Wet. 1975. On Ö Winge and a prayer: The origins of polyploidy. Bot. Rev. **41:** 361–390.

Heckard, L. R. 1960. Taxonomic studies in the *Phacelia magellanica* polyploid complex with special reference to the California members. Univ. Calif. Publ. Bot. **32:** 1–126.

Heiser, C. B. 1973. Introgression re-examined. Bot. Rev. **39:** 347–366.

Jackson, R. C. 1962. Interspecific hybridization in *Haplogappus* and its bearing on chromosomal evolution in the Blepharodon section. Amer. J. Bot. **49:** 119–132.

Jackson, R. C. 1965. A cytogenetic study of a three-paired race of *Haplopappus gracilis.* Amer. J. Bot. **52:** 946–953.

Kyhos, D. W. 1965. The independent aneuploid origin of two species of *Chaenactis* (Compositae) from a common ancestor. Evolution **19:** 26–43.

Lewis, W. H. & J. C. Semple. 1977. Geography of *Claytonia virginica* cytotypes. Amer. J. Bot. **64:** 1078–1082.

Lotsy, J. P. 1914. Prof. E. Lehmann über Art, reine Linie und isogene Einheit. Biol. Centralbl. **34:** 614–618.

Mayr, E. 1940. Speciation phenomena in birds. Amer. Naturalist **74:** 249–278.

Mayr, E. 1942. Systematics and the origin of species from the viewpoint of a zoologist. Columbia Univ. Press. New York.

Mayr, E. 1954. Change of genetic environment and evolution. Pages 157–180 *in* J. Huxley, A. C. Hardy & E. B. Ford (eds.), Evolution as a process. Allen & Unwin. London.

Merriam, C. H. 1918. Review of the grizzly and big brown bears of North America (genus *Ursus*) with description of a new genus *Vetularctos*. N. Amer. Fauna 41.

Mooring, J. 1980. A cytogeographic study of *Chaenactis douglasii* (Compositae, Helenieae). Amer. J. Bot. **67**: 1304–1319.

Mosquin, T. 1967. Evidence for autoploidy in *Epilobium angustifolium* (Onagraceae). Evolution **21**: 713–719.

Müntzing, A. 1932. Cytogenetic investigations on the synthetic *Galeopsis tetrahit.* Hereditas **16**: 105–154.

Newton, W. C. F. & C. Pellew. 1929. *Primula kewensis* and its derivatives. J. Genetics **20**: 405–467.

Nomenclature Commission of the Botanical Club of the American Association for the Advancement of Science. 1904. Code of botanical nomenclature. Bull. Torrey Bot. Club **31**: 249–264.

Ownbey, M. 1950. Natural hybridization and amphiploidy in the genus *Tragopogon.* Amer. J. Bot. **37**: 487–499.

Ownbey, R. P. 1944. The liliaceous genus *Polygonatum* in North America. Ann. Missouri Bot. Gard. **31**: 375–413.

Persoon, C. H. 1805–1807. Synopsis plantarum. . . .

Raven, P. H. 1969. A revision of the genus *Camissonia* (Onagraceae). Contr. U.S. Natl. Herb. **37**: 159–396.

Small, E. & A. Cronquist. 1976. A practical and natural taxonomy for *Cannabis.* Taxon **25**: 405–435.

Stebbins, G. L. 1941. Apomixis in angiosperms. Bot. Rev. **7**: 507–542.

Turesson, G. 1922. The genotypical response of the plant species to the habitat. Hereditas **3**: 211–350.

Tyrl, R. J. 1975. Origin and distribution of polyploid *Achillea* (Compositae) in western North America. Brittonia **27**: 187–196.

Vries, H. de. 1901, 1903. Die Mutationstheorie. Versuche und Beobachtungen über die Entstehung von Arten im Pflanzenreich. Veit. Leipzig. 2 vols.

Wagner, W. L., R. E. Stockhouse & W. M. Klein. 1985. The systematics and evolution of the *Oenothera caespitosa* species complex (Onagraceae). Missouri Bot. Gard. Monogr. Syst. Bot. **12**: 1–103.

Wettstein, R. von. 1898. Grundzüge der geographisch-morphologischen Methode der Pflanzensystematik. G. Fischer. Jena.

Winge, Ö. 1917. The chromosomes, their numbers and general importance. Compt. Rend. Trav. Lab. Carlsb. **13**: 131–275.

Winge, Ö. 1940. Taxonomic and evolutionary studies in *Erophila* based on cytogenetic investigations. Compt. Rend. Trav. Lab. Carlsb. (sér. Physiol.) **23**: 41–74.

Yost, S. E. 1987. The effect of shade on petiole length in the *Viola fimbriatula-sagittata* complex. Brittonia **39**: 180–187.

Zavada, M. S. 1984. The relation between pollen exine sculpturing and self-incompatability mechanisms. Pl. Syst. Evol. **147**: 63–78.

Chapter 3

Primula kewensis, the sterile hybrid from
which the fertile allotetraploid can arise.
New York Botanical Garden photo.

Speciation

Zoological Theory

Since so much of evolutionary theory is dominated by zoologists, it is well to begin our discussion of speciation with a brief review of current zoological thought. Ernst Mayr (Fig. 3.1) has been particularly important in both the development and the general acceptance of these concepts. Among his many publications, we here cite only those of 1942, 1954, 1963, and 1982.

In Mayr's view, nearly all speciation is based on rapid change in small populations forming peripheral geographic isolates of more widespread species. Mayr notes that the founder principle[1] has a significant influence, but the most important thing is rapid fundamental change under the driving force of selection in a small population. Mayr postulates a genetic revolution and the subsequent reconstruction of the genotype. That is how the metaphorical adaptive peaks (inhabited by species) and adaptive valleys (largely uninhabited) come to exist. Geographical isolation of the emerging new species during its genetic revolution is considered to be essential so that it can escape the stabilizing influence of hybridizing with the parent population. Mayr discounts other modes of speciation, and in particular he does *not* consider geographical subspecies to be way-stations on the road to speciation. In 1963 (p. 513) he bluntly stated that "when a new species originates, it is almost invariably from a peripheral isolate." Other theorists have pointed out that the Sewall Wright effect[2] might also influence the process of speciation as postulated by Mayr. He does not deny this, but he makes little of it.

The concept of adaptive peaks and adaptive valleys, originally proposed

---

[1] In 1942 Mayr proposed the term *founder principle* for the establishment of a new local population of a species by one or a few original founders, which perforce carry only a small fraction of the total genetic variation of the species.

[2] Sewall Wright pointed out in 1931 that in a small population the accidents of survival and death may result in the fixation or loss of individual genes regardless of selection.

by Simpson (1944) for higher taxa such as families and orders, has been enthusiastically applied to species as well by Mayr and others. Among botanical theorists, Stebbins (1950 et seq.) in particular has promoted the idea, and it is now firmly fixed in both the botanical and zoological literature. In recounting this bit of history I do not challenge Simpson's idea and its subsequent application to species as well as higher taxa. Indeed I find the concept very useful.

There has been some continuing and now growing uneasiness among zoologists about the universality of Mayr's classic concept of speciation (vide White, 1978). Both the necessity for a genetic revolution and the inability of a subspecies to evolve into a species are questioned. Mayr's concepts remain dominant, however, and it is to these that we must address ourselves in considering speciation among flowering plants.

Kinds of Speciation

Different authors have proposed various classifications of the modes of speciation. This is not so much a matter of right and wrong as one of mental convenience. All such classifications are imperfect. In anybody's scheme, there are examples that do not fit nicely into any one category. Still, we need some sort of organization to facilitate consideration and understanding.

For our purposes, I find it useful to treat speciation under the headings of *quantum speciation* (Grant's term), *local ecologic speciation, geographical speciation, phyletic speciation,* and *speciation by hybridization.* Quantum speciation as here used includes not only speciation in peripherally isolated populations as described by Mayr, but also speciation by catastrophic selection as described by Lewis, and various sorts of abrupt (often cytologically based) divergence by small populations within the geographic range of a species.

QUANTUM SPECIATION

Mayrean Speciation

It seems likely that much of the speciation in flowering plants results from rapid change in geographically peripheral isolates, as postulated by Mayr for animals. This has been described so often in zoological literature, and repeated so often by botanists, that it seems unnecessary to expound at length on it here.

In spite of the attractiveness of the theory, guaranteed examples are not numerous. The theory anticipates that the newly formed species will typically expand their ranges, rather than remaining as peripheral isolates. Therefore the original geographical relationship cannot be expected to continue indefinitely.

Some plausible examples of Mayrean species do exist among North

American plants. *Solidago cutleri,* in the mountains from Maine to northern New York, and *S. spithamea,* of the Blue Ridge in North Carolina and Tennessee, may both be presumed to be derived from the more northern, widespread *S. multiradiata. Solidago multiradiata* does not now reach the range of either of these peripheral isolates, but it may be presumed to have done so at times during the Pleistocene. *Senecio antennariifolius,* a shale barren endemic in Virginia, West Virginia, and Maryland, is very closely allied to the widespread western dryland species *S. canus.* It is not implausible to suppose that *S. canus* may have ranged much farther to the east during the postglacial hypsithermal period several thousand years ago, and that the descendants of these immigrants were able to survive only in the relatively xeric conditions of the shale-barrens.

Island archipelagos provide some of the best opportunities for maintenance of something resembling the original geographic relationships of Mayrean species. Putative examples have been much discussed in the zoological literature, less so in the botanical. *Scalesia,* a genus of Asteraceae endemic to the Galápagos Islands, may provide a botanical example. Although there is now some range-overlap, each of the 9 species appears to have a major island that is its unique home-base (if the two halves of Isabela Island, now connected by a narrow isthmus, are counted separately).

Speciation by Catastrophic Selection

Based on his studies of *Clarkia,* Harlan Lewis (Fig. 3.1) in 1962 put forward the idea of catastrophic selection as a method of speciation. *Clarkia* is a western American genus of annual plants which characteristically grow in marginally dry sites that are not dependably habitable over any long series of years. The local populations are scattered and individually subject to being wiped out in bad years. In spite of these conditions of selection, the genus has not evolved variable dormancy of seeds, and none of the species is a successful desert-annual. Genetic barriers to hybridization are typically strong, depending in large part on cryptic but detectable structural rearrangements of the chromosomes. There are a number of species-pairs in which one member is more drouth-resistant than the other. Bees frequently go from one species to another, without making a distinction.

Lewis reasonably supposes that in a bad year a local population may be reduced to only a few of the most drouth-resistant individuals. If these plants are also cytologically unusual, and especially if they carry some factor that favors the formation of new cytotypes, they have the potentiality to evolve into a new species. Freed from local competition with the parental type, and protected from immediate hybridization with it, the new group may in only a few years be able to accomplish a cytological repatterning, a genetic minirevolution, and emerge as a distinct species. The expectable drop in fertility during reorganization is immaterial, so long as the population survives until a new stability is attained.

Fig. 3.1. Some biologists who have made important contributions to our understanding of speciation. TOP LEFT, Arthur R. Kruckeberg (1920–). Photo courtesy of Arthur R. Kruckeberg. TOP RIGHT, Verne E. Grant (1917–). Photo courtesy of Verne E. Grant. BOTTOM LEFT, Ernst Mayr (1904–). Photo courtesy of Ernst Mayr. BOTTOM RIGHT, (Frank) Harlan Lewis (1919–). Photo by Herman Kabe, courtesy of the Department of Biology, University of California at Los Angeles.

Subsequent restoration of contact between the new species and its parent can be expected to lead to a degree of niche-partitioning. At any given site the numerically smaller group will be at a reproductive disadvantage because of the wastage of seeds as sterile hybrids. Such a disadvantage might be overcome if the initially smaller group were favored by selection. Then the tables could be turned, and the initially larger but less well adapted group would lose out through a combination of selection and eventually seed-wastage.

Some of the genetically isolated species of *Clarkia* recognized by Lewis are morphologically only minimally different. One might suspect that intensive study would disclose still other genetically distinct breeding-groups that are not morphologically recognizable. I never promised you a rose-garden.

In terms of the genetic processes, catastrophic speciation is not fundamentally different from speciation in geographically peripheral isolates, as postulated by Mayr. Both would come under quantum speciation as defined by Grant. Lewis' idea has been favorably received, and the term catastrophic selection has entered the language of taxonomists and evolutionary theorists. It is certainly not the principal mode of speciation, but its application in particular cases is widely admitted. One of my friends in another country has even referred to the use of antibiotic drugs as causing a sort of catastrophic selection in pathogenic bacteria.

Speciation by catastrophic selection would seem to have its greatest potentiality in groups of annuals in which the seeds all germinate as soon as external conditions are favorable. Both variable dormancy and the perennial habit would subject the survivors of catastrophe to continuing competition and genetic influence by the parental population. Desert-adapted perennials will hunker down during a drouth, blast any flowers that had begun to form, and turn all their resources to individual survival.

Other Variants of Quantum Speciation

It is not clear that the genetic change in quantum speciation need be so substantial as to constitute a revolution. Not many cases have been so thoroughly investigated as to constitute reliable examples of genetic revolution, or the avoidance of it, in speciation of either plants or animals. Instead we have the intuitive perceptions of taxonomists who have considered large numbers of species to a lesser depth. Not much has been written about genetic revolutions by botanists not steeped in zoological theory. I believe I am with the otherwise silent majority, however, in questioning the revolutionary imperative. All that is really needed is the introduction of a barrier to interbreeding (aside from pure geography), accompanied by a morphological marker.

Most taxonomists have been properly skeptical of the adaptive importance of all taxonomic differences. The characters marking species or higher taxa may be selectively significant, or they may not, in different instances. Davis and Gilmartin (1985) consider that the differentiation of morphologically recognizable plant species is frequently rapid and random in direction. I concur.

Cytological change may drive or set the stage for speciation even in the absence of geographic isolation. Alloploidy, discussed in the previous chapter, provides the most striking examples of cytologically based sympatric speciation. Here we have virtually instant speciation. Newly produced autoploids, on the other hand, are not generally regarded as distinct species, but they have the potentiality of becoming so after further evolutionary change.

Cytological differences other than polyploidy may also lead to speciation. It is my impression (again intuitive) that a great many common and widespread species are constantly spewing out cytological variants that are to some degree intersterile with the principal population. Most of these soon disappear, either through direct competition, or through wastage of reproduction potential by unsuccessful back-crossing. The few that survive over several generations are potentially new species.

If these breeding minigroups do not have morphological markers, they are likely to remain undetected unless they are happenstancely caught up in some experimental study of breeding behavior. The existence of intersterile breeding groups in some species is well known. By zoological standards they would be considered to be sibling species when discovered. As we have pointed out, the botanical community has mostly given up such efforts at taxonomic separation, after some initial flirtation with the idea.

If these newly arisen breeding groups do have morphological markers, then they *may* merit recognition as new species. I say *may* rather than *do,* because one needs to consider the amount of difference, and the potential permanence of the group. We have discussed in the previous chapter the necessity that differences between species be detectable by ordinary means. Furthermore, many of these new groups do not survive the test of competition, and it seems pointless to burden the literature with names for ephemeral populations.

I point out two examples of potential new species, both probably ephemeral, from my own field experience. *Salix arctica* is a dwarf arctic-alpine willow with a circumboreal distribution. It normally has pubescent capsules. In 1955, in the Beartooth Mts. of Montana, Mrs. Cronquist and I found a considerable population of this species, plus a few similar plants with glabrous capsules and a slight, intangible difference in aspect. Presence or absence of hair on the capsules is ordinarily a good specific character in *Salix,* although like other characters, it is not infallible. At this site there were also some intermediate plants, (more, in fact, than those with glabrous fruits) with slightly hairy capsules and distinctly reduced fertility. In the field it appeared that the glabrous-fruited phase was being overwhelmed by hybridization with the more abundant typical phase. The reproductive problems of these plants with glabrous fruits are exacerbated by the fact that *Salix* is dioecious; self-pollination is not available as a means of preserving an unusual type. Because of the partial sterility of the intermediates, it does not seem likely that the difference here is governed by a single pair of ordinary Mendelian factors. The glabrous-fruited population (if one may call it that) consisted of so few individuals, with such doubtful prospects for long-term survival, that it did not seem to merit a name. I have not been back to look for it since. There is no obvious reason why the same individuals might not still be there, inasmuch as the plants are long-lived perennials that tend to become colonial. The question is whether this small set can and will escape from the genetic influence of *S. arctica* and establish itself as an independent population. I doubt it, but it could happen.

Three species of tall *Mertensia* grow in the LaSal Mts. in Utah. In 1962 Noel Holmgren and I found a small local population (a few individuals) that we took to represent a fourth species, marked by its relatively slender creeping rhizome and distinctly petiolate middle cauline leaves with a broadly rounded or subtruncate base. The other three species have a soft, thick taproot and/or branching caudex, and are somewhat taller and have more tapering, subsessile middle cauline leaves. The unusual plants were growing near some plants of *Mertensia franciscana,* one of the tall species. There were also some intermediate plants, which we took to be hybrids. Hybridization, sometimes even between species of different sections, is a major cause of taxonomic difficulty in *Mertensia,* so the presence of such hybrids did not seem surprising. What is surprising is that I have found no other evidence of the existence of this putative fourth species. The LaSal Mts. are accessible and have attracted the attention of botanists for many years. Possibly these unusual individuals belong to a rare and local species awaiting rediscovery. More likely they represent a potential new species that has not yet (and probably will not) become permanently established. Our collection did not help its chances.

Self-pollinating mutants of outcrossing species have an immediate opportunity to establish a new line that may become a new species. As noted in the previous chapter, *Stephanomeria malheurensis* appears to be such a new species caught aborning. It is still very much like its ancestor, *S. exigua,* with which it grows.

Some more easily recognizable autogamous species differ from their outcrossing probable ancestors mainly in a syndrome of characters associated with self-pollination. Some examples in *Camissonia* and *Oenothera* were noted in CHAPTER 2. The time and number of steps required for the change are debatable, but the evolutionary sequence seems plain enough. There is no reason to suppose that either geographical isolation or local ecologic features are involved.

Local Ecologic Speciation

Local genetic diversification in association with the habitat ranges from minimal to profound. Different species react differently to the same physical opportunity for evolutionary change. The scattered shale-barrens in the Ridge and Valley Province of the southern Appalachian Mts. provide some examples. The dominant trees on these sites, such as *Quercus prinus* and *Pinus rigida,* are smaller and scrubbier than in more favorable places, but not otherwise obviously different. It is not immediately evident whether the difference in size and vigor is genetic, or a direct response to the habitat, or some combination of the two. In any case it does not appear to be taxonomically significant.

The widespread eastern American species *Solidago arguta* is represented on the shale-barrens by a morphologically more or less recognizable ecotype that has been called var. *harrisii,* but in my view this is unjustified. Too many specimens would be misidentified in the absence of geographic and ecologic information.

Different shale-barrens harbor three closely related erect species of *Clematis* section *Viorna* (*C. albicoma, C. coactilis,* and *C. viticaulis*) in a complex geographic pattern. *Clematis albicoma* and *C. viticaulis* hybridize in the two places where they are known to occur together, and they might conceivably be treated as varieties of a single species. *Clematis coactilis* apparently remains distinct. The only obvious relatives of these three species are *C. addisonii, C. fremontii,* and *C. ochroleuca. Clematis addisonii* is another local species with a restricted habitat in the same general area (dry limestone hills in western Virginia), *C. fremontii* is Ozarkian, and *C. ochroleuca* occurs from New York to Georgia, but mostly farther east than the shale-barrens, on the Piedmont. *Clematis ochroleuca* might be the ancestor of the other eastern species, or they may all be derived from some extinct ancestor that had a wider range. Whether the speciation in these restricted habitats was helped along by geographic isolation at the time is not clear. In any case, we now have some distinct species, and a marginally distinct pair.

Taenidia integerrima, in the family Apiaceae, is fairly widespread in open woods in eastern United States. Its only near relative is *T. montana,* a shale-barren species. The range of *T. montana* is wholly enclosed within that of *T. integerrima,* and the two come into frequent local contact. *Taenidia montana* looks very much like *T. integerrima,* but it smells different, and the fruit is compressed in a different direction. Because the direction of compression of the fruit is usually a good generic (or even tribal) character in the Apiaceae, these two species were for many years considered to form two monotypic genera, referred to different tribes. It now seems perfectly clear (Cronquist, 1982), however, that each species is the closest relative of the other, and that together they form a taxonomically rather isolated genus. The two species are cytologically so much alike that no gross cytological barrier to interbreeding can be postulated, but careful study has not disclosed any hybrids between them. The lack of hybridization is perfectly in character for the family, in which interspecific hybridization is in general rare. The obvious interpretation here is that *T. montana* has evolved from *T. integerrima* through ecotypic differentiation for a specialized habitat. No one was there to see it happen, but the onus of proof is on anyone who might propose a different history. There is no need to postulate geographic isolation at some time in the past as a necessary factor in the process.

The shale-barrens also harbor a number of other endemic species and varieties, of diverse origins. *Trifolium reflexum* and *Phlox buckleyi* are taxonomically isolated, and their history is doubtful. *Senecio antennariifolius* and *Eriogonum allenii* are allied to western American species, the range of which is now far distant from the shale barrens. *Paronychia montana* is evidently allied to the widespread eastern American species *P. fastigiata,* of which it is sometimes treated as a variety. *Oenothera argillicola* is considered to be a relict of the first *Oenothera* to invade eastern United States, at some time prior to the Pleistocene. It or its immediate ancestor appears to have been involved in the subsequent evolution of the complex heterozygote *Oe. parviflora,* which is now widespread in eastern United States. Clearly the shale-barren habitat has fostered ecotypic differentiation and speciation.

The granite outcrops on the southern Piedmont (in Georgia and extending into Alabama and South and North Carolina) provide some even more striking examples of ecotypic evolutionary change. Most of these outcrops are flat, and they are known as flatrocks, but the largest one, Stone Mountain, is a massive boulder 200 m high. The flatrocks (plus Stone Mountain) harbor a number of endemic and near-endemic taxa, but I here confine myself to a consideration of four.

Coreopsis grandiflora var. *saxicola* occurs mainly on the flatrocks and Stone Mountain. It is so well marked by the fimbriate-lacerate wings of its achenes that for some years it was thought to be a distinct species, but it intergrades completely with var. *grandiflora.* The widespread var. *grandiflora* blankets the range of var. *saxicola,* and sometimes occurs with it on the flatrocks. The story is complicated by the fact that var. *saxicola* also occurs in some rocky sites in Arkansas, far from the Georgia flatrocks. It seems clear enough that var. *saxicola* is an ecotypical variant of *C. grandiflora* that has not yet reached the specific level.

Sedum pusillum is a well defined dwarf annual species endemic to the granite flatrocks (and Stone Mountain). It is loosely allied to *Sedum ternatum* and *S. nevii,* which mostly occur somewhat farther north in the Southern Appalachian region. No existing species can be assumed to be necessarily its direct ancestor. With or without the help of geographic isolation, it presumably evolved in response to the severe habitat in which it grows.

Diamorphia cymosa, another flatrock endemic, looks superficially much like *Sedum pusillum,* but it is so distinctive in technical morphological features that it is considered to form a monotypic genus. It does not resemble *S. pusillum* cytologically. There is every reason to suppose that it arose from some species of *Sedum,* but on present evidence we can only speculate about which one. A Mayrean genetic revolution seems to be required to explain this species.

Amphianthus is a monotypic genus of the Scrophulariaceae, with only the species *A. pusillus.* It is confined to the shallow, ephemeral pools on the flatrocks (and Stone Mountain). It appears to belong to the tribe Gratioleae, but it has no obvious close relatives. Genetic revolution indeed.

Serpentine outcrops provide another specialized habitat that encourages ecotypic differentiation and speciation. Like the shale-barrens and the

Georgia flatrocks, they harbor populations showing all degrees of taxonomic distinction from their forebears. The antecedents of many serpentine endemics are plain, but those of others are obscure. Arthur Kruckeberg (1986; Fig. 3.1) has pointed out that the cruciferous genus *Streptanthus* shows all stages of speciation on serpentine in California and southwestern Oregon, from interfertile and morphologically similar ecotypes adapted to serpentine and nonserpentine substrates, to species so distinctive as to have no obvious near allies.

It may also be instructive to consider *Erigeron bloomeri* var. *nudatus,* confined to the serpentine outcrops of southwestern Oregon and adjacent California. For more than half a century after its discovery this was regarded as a well defined local species, differing most notably from the more widespread, evidently hairy *Erigeron bloomeri* in being essentially glabrous. In 1947 I reduced *E. nudatus* to varietal status under *E. bloomeri,* because the distinction between them is not always clear. Later I learned that some plants of small serpentine outcrops in central Oregon, well removed from the range of var. *nudatus,* are morphologically intermediate between the two varieties. The suggestion is that the physiological features of ecotypic adaptation here are directly reflected in the morphology.

Various other specialized habitats encourage ecotypic differentiation and eventual speciation, without the need for geographic isolation. Shifting talus slopes, sand-dunes, estuaries, salt-flats, vernal pools, gypsum, seleniferous rock, and the clay derived from volcanic tuff are examples. One cannot say that geographic isolation would not facilitate speciation even in specialized habitats, but it does not appear to be essential.

GEOGRAPHIC SPECIATION

The ecogeographic patterns of related species are exceedingly diverse. Speciation by rapid change in small, geographically peripheral populations, as envisaged by Mayr, might be expected to encompass ecological change in many instances, leading to a complex pattern of overlap as the new species expands its area. The range of a species may wax and wane with changes in climate and competition. Thus the present range of a species cannot be a sure guide to its mode and place of origin.

Even so, we see some patterns of geographical replacement that seem very comparable to the patterns of geographic variation seen within species. Some of these geographically adjacent taxa are only marginally distinct, so that one taxonomist might treat them as different species, and another as varieties of the same species. *Helianthus californicus, H. nuttallii,* and *H. giganteus* are geographically replacing species, but they are not sharply separated. One would be tempted to treat them infraspecifically, were it not for the consequent questions about the taxonomy of the rest of the genus. *Phacelia crenulata* and *P. ambigua* replace each other geographically in western United States, the latter species being more southwestern and adapted to a warmer climate. They are so closely allied that some botanists have treated them as varieties instead of species. *Phacelia in-*

tegrifolia, with a range to the east of *P. ambigua* and to the south of *P. crenulata,* is only a little more distinct, but nobody proposes to unite it with the other two. In the Great Basin floristic province, *Cryptantha flava* and *C. confertiflora* are closely related, geographically replacing taxa. These have usually been treated as different species, but I would not be surprised if the varietal rank eventually proved to be more appropriate. *Penstemon* section *Glabri* presents another sort of geographical replacement pattern in western United States. Here we have some 30 narrowly defined but usually fairly sharply distinct species, with generally only one in a given area.

It is hard to be sure in any particular case, but I see no reason why some of the geographic species here cited might not have arisen as geographic varieties. One would not want to have to presuppose different modes of origin according to whether a pair of closely related taxa is treated at the varietal or the specific level.

In theory, geographic speciation might also come about by the extinction of the central member(s) of a series of geographic varieties, leaving distinct end-pieces. I do not know of any botanical examples not subject to some other interpretation.

Speciation via fixation of geographic variation is not a new idea, but has been held by many biologists in the past, beginning with Darwin himself. The idea went into eclipse after Mayr's contrary proposal in 1954 and his subsequent vigorous promotion of the view that rapid change in peripheral isolates is the dominant mode of speciation. By 1982 Mayr had retreated only slightly, noting that

> "The term 'peripherally isolated' becomes somewhat ambiguous in species with low population density and very much reduced dispersal facility. In such cases a species may consist of numerous more or less isolated colonies and a new colony may be founded in a previously vacant portion of the species range. Yet even such a founder population would go through the same steps of inbreeding and homozygosity as if it were isolated beyond the periphery of the species range."

In spite of Mayr's influence, however, geographic speciation is intuitively perceived by so many practicing taxonomists that the idea has refused to die. Grant (1977, 1981), among others, now accepts it as a simple fact of life.

PHYLETIC SPECIATION

Species may also arise by gradual mass transformation of one into another over a long period of time. At any one time the population consists of only a single species, but the differences accumulate over many generations, so that the later members of the lineage differ from their far-distant antecedents as much as contemporary related species differ from each other. Grant (1977) gives the example of two late Cenozoic elephants, *Elephas planifrons* and *E. meridionalis,* as such **successional species.**

An unequivocal demonstration of phyletic speciation, resulting in successional species, can come only from the fossil record. Because angiosperms are not so well integrated morphologically as vertebrates (see CHAPTER 1), angiosperm fossils are rarely adequate to permit identification of species in the modern populational sense. What passes as one species among the fossils may actually embrace several things that would be considered different species if we had them today. Paleontological species of angiosperms are simply not dependably comparable to neontological ones.

We can, however, get circumstantial evidence for phyletic speciation in association with the disruption of a broad geographic range into two parts, eventually producing what are called **vicarious species**. Vicarious species need not remain vicarious forever. Climatic and continental changes may permit them to expand their ranges and come into contact again. The following paragraphs about Appalachian-Ozarkian vicariants form an expanded version of my comments in Takhtajan (1986).

The northern part of the Appalachian Floristic Province (and of the North American Prairies Province as well) was repeatedly glaciated during the Pleistocene epoch. The Missouri and Ohio rivers mark the approximate southern limit of the glaciation. Farther east, the terminal moraine runs the length of Long Island, off the coast of New York. To the south, the Coastal Plain has been repeatedly inundated, in whole or in considerable part, not only during the Pleistocene interglacials, but also at intervals during the Tertiary period. The Mississippi embayment, an extension of the Coastal Plain, reaches north to southern Illinois.

The combination of glaciation on the north and flooding on the south has repeatedly pinched off the Ozarkian area (mainly southern Missouri and northern or northwestern Arkansas) from the main body of the Appalachian Province. On the west, the forests of the Ozarkian area are limited by increasing aridity, as the Appalachian Province gives way to the North American Prairies Province.

Thus there has tended to be a Southern Appalachian center, and a smaller, drier, less diversified Ozarkian center in which plants of the Appalachian Province have survived the vicissitudes of climate, and within which new taxa have evolved during the course of geologic time. During the interglacial periods some of these species have extended their ranges into the areas freed from ice-cover. Others have not been able to expand their ranges, either because of specific habitat-requirements, or because of depletion of genotypes during times of stress (these being perhaps merely different aspects of the same problem), or for other reasons as yet undetermined. Vicariant populations migrating northward from these two refugia may or may not differ significantly, and if they do differ, they may or may not retain their differences when their ranges come into contact and they have a chance to hybridize.

Often it is possible to recognize a species-pair, one member in or originating from each center, even though their ranges may now overlap. Among such species-pairs are the following, with the Appalachian species listed first in each case: *Hamamelis virginiana* and *H. verna*; *Castanea pumila* and *C. ozarkensis*; *Carya glabra* and *C. texana*; *Hypericum punc-*

tatum and *H. pseudomaculatum*; *Ribes rotundifolium* and *R. missouriense*; *Asclepias perennis* and *A. texana*; *Aster sagittifolius* and *A. drummondii*; *Echinacea laevigata* and *E. purpurea*; *Helenium brevifolium* and *H. campestre*; *Helianthus angustifolius* and *H. salicifolius*; *Helianthus atrorubens* and *H. silphioides*; *Marshallia ramosa* and *M. caespitosa*; *Parthenium auriculatum* and *P. hispidum*; *Prenanthes roanensis* and *P. aspera*; *Prenanthes serpentaria* and *P. barbata*.

The differentiation between some of the Appalachian and Ozarkian taxa has reached (or maintained) only an intraspecific level. Among such examples are *Arenaria patula* var. *patula* and var. *robusta*; *Hydrangea arborescens* var. *arborescens* and var. *discolor*; *Heuchera parvifolia* var. *parvifolia* and var. *arkansana*; *Asclepias incarnata* var. *pulchra* and var. *incarnata*; *Helianthus occidentalis* var. *dowellianus* and var. *occidentalis*; and *Solidago ulmifolia* var. *ulmifolia* and var. *palmeri*.

Not surprisingly, some of these now or formerly vicarious Appalachian and Ozarkian taxa have evolved just to the vague boundary between varietal and specific differentiation. *Helianthus atrorubens* and *H. silphioides* intergrade to some extent where their ranges now meet. I somewhat uneasily follow the monographer (Heiser, 1969) in treating them at the specific level. In a genus of more sharply defined species these two would be better treated as varieties.

The Appalachian-Ozark vicariance is complicated by the fact that the same constriction and expansion of ranges has occurred several times as a result of repeated glacial and interglacial episodes. We do not know which of the episodes resulted in which taxonomic divergence. Possibly some of the effects were cumulative, so that varieties after one glaciation became species after the next.

The celebrated eastern American-eastern Asiatic disjunction between related taxa also provides examples of vicarious species that can be presumed to be derived by gradual divergence from a common ancestor. *Liriodendron tulipifera* and *L. chinense,* discussed in the previous chapter, epitomize the historical relationship. I see no reason to suppose that either of these modern species had to pass through a bottleneck of population size and undergo a genetic revolution to produce the specific distinction.

SPECIATION BY HYBRIDIZATION

In the previous chapter we considered speciation by alloploidy following interspecific hybridization. New species can also arise at the diploid level through hybridization. It does not seem likely that this is a frequent method, but there are a few apparently well documented cases.

Straw (1955, 1956) reports on the probable relationships among four diploid species of southern California, *Penstemon centranthifolius, P. grinnellii, P. spectabilis,* and *P. clevelandii,* all with $2n = 16$. These occur in different habitats, although with some overlap, and they also have different major pollinators. *Penstemon centranthifolius* is pollinated by hummingbirds, *P. grinnellii* by carpenter bees (*Xylocopa*), *P. spectabilis* by wasps (*Pseudomasaris*), and *P. clevelandii* by small solitary bees (Anthophoridae) and to some extent by hummingbirds. *Penstemon spectabilis* is very much like the natural hybrid between *P. centranthifolius* and *P. grinnellii,* and *P. clevelandii* is very much like the natural hybrid between *P. centranthifolius* and *P. spectabilis.* The difference in pollinators appears to be an important factor in the continued existence of the four discrete, self-perpetuating populations. It is supposed that the two populations thought to be of hybrid origin would have had but little chance of establishing a continuing identity had not each been adopted by a pollinator that makes little or no use of the parent species. Absent such a lucky break, the hybrids might have failed to be pollinated, or if pollinated their posterity might have been lost through back-crossing to the more abundant parents.

Lewis and Epling (1959) report on the probable relationships among three diploid species of *Delphinium* in southern California. These are all pollinated by bumblebees (*Bombus*), which visit them and other species of *Delphinium* indiscriminately, insofar as proximity permits. *Delphinium hesperium* occurs in relatively mesic oak woodland, *D. recurvatum* in alkaline drylands dominated by *Atriplex,* and *D. gypsophilum* in grasslands that are intermediate between the other two habitats in water-stress. *Delphinium hesperium* and *D. recurvatum* do not now occur together, although they may have done so at some time in the past. Their ranges now approach within five miles of each other in part of their area. The range of *D. gypsophilum* overlaps that of both the others. Experimental hybridization of *D. hesperium* and *D. recurvatum* yielded variable F_1 plants of rather low fertility. Some of the experimental back-crosses of these hybrids to *D. recurvatum* were fairly fertile and very similar to wild *D. gypsophilum. Delphinium hesperium* and *D. recurvatum* are cytologically rather unlike, although both have the same number of chromosomes ($2n = 16$). It appears that the reconstitution of a cytotype fairly similar to that of *D. recurvatum* was an integral part of the process of establishing the hybrid population that became *D. gypsophilum.* Once stabilized, *D. gypsophilum* was apparently able to outcompete both parents in the intermediate area.

A small complicating factor in the *Delphinium* story is that the natural population of *D. gypsophilum* includes both diploids and tetraploids. It may be supposed that tetraploid *D. gypsophilum* arose directly from diploid *D. gypsophilum.* How good it is to be freed from the dogma that natural autoploidy is only an illusion produced by breakdown of an alloploid. Occam's Razor is still sharp.

Sexual, Diploid, Outbreeding Species as the Main Actors in Evolution

The complexity of species populations may divert our attention from the differences in the roles of diverse sorts of species in long-term evolution. Clearly it is the sexual, diploid, outbreeding species that carry the load of long-term evolutionary advance. As Wagner (1970) among others has pointed out, "A kind of evolutionary noise is produced through the repeated origin of populations with deleteriously modified life cycles in which the advantages of diploidy, sexuality, outbreeding, and species purity are counteracted or cancelled." Inbreeding and apomixis may be temporarily successful, but they are evolutionary blind alleys, from which escape is difficult. Polyploidy, particularly at the higher levels, is also likely to lead to a dead end. Hybrids seldom lead to significant evolutionary change, although a few of them, even allotetraploids, may be effectively diploidized and enter the main stream of evolution.

Selected References

Cronquist, A. 1982. Reduction of *Pseudotaenidia* to *Taenidia* (Apiaceae). Brittonia **34**: 365–367.

Davis, J. I. & A. J. Gilmartin. 1985. Morphological variation and speciation. Syst. Bot. **10**: 417–425.

Grant, V. 1977. Organismic evolution. Freeman. San Francisco.

Grant, V. 1981. Plant speciation. 2nd ed. Columbia Univ. Press. New York.

Heiser, C. B., et al. 1969. The North American sunflowers (*Helianthus*). Mem. Torrey Bot. Club **22(3)**: 1–218.

Keener, C. S. 1967. A biosystematic study of *Clematis* subsection Integrifoliae (Ranunculaceae). J. Elisha Mitchell Sci. Soc. **83**: 1–41.

Keener, C. S. 1983. Distribution and biohistory of the endemic flora of the Mid-Appalachian shale barrens. Bot. Rev. **49**: 117–149.

Kruckeberg, A. R. 1986. An essay: The stimulus of unusual geologies for plant speciation. Syst. Bot. **11**: 455–463.

Lewis, H. 1962. Catastrophic selection as a factor in speciation. Evolution **16**: 257–271.

Lewis, H. & C. Epling. 1959. *Delphinium gypsophilum,* a diploid species of hybrid origin. Evolution **13**: 511–525.

Mayr, E. 1942. Systematics and the origin of species from the viewpoint of a zoologist. Columbia Univ. Press. New York.

Mayr, E. 1954. Change of genetic environment and evolution. Pages 157–180 *in* J. Huxley, A. C. Hardy & E. B. Ford (eds.), Evolution as a process. Allen & Unwin. London.

Mayr, E. 1963. Animal species and evolution. Harvard Univ. Press. Cambridge.

Mayr, E. 1982. The growth of biological thought. Belknap Press of Harvard Univ. Press. Cambridge, Massachusetts.

Murdy, W. H. 1968. Plant speciation associated with granite outcrop communities of the southeastern Piedmont. Rhodora **70**: 394–407.

Simpson, G. G. 1944. Tempo and mode in evolution. Columbia Univ. Press. New York.

Stebbins, G. L. 1950. Variation and evolution in plants. Columbia Univ. Press. New York.

Straw, R. M. 1955. Hybridization, homogamy, and sympatric speciation. Evolution **9**: 441–444.

Straw, R. M. 1956. Floral isolation in *Penstemon.* Amer. Naturalist **90**: 47–53.

Takhtajan, A. L. 1986. Floristic regions of the world. Univ. Calif. Press. Berkeley, Los Angeles.

Vickerey, R. K. 1978. Case studies in the evolution of species complexes in *Mimulus.* Evol. Biol. **11:** 405–507.

Wagner, W. H. 1970. Biosystematics and evolutionary noise. Taxon **19:** 146–151.

White, M. J. D. 1978. Modes of speciation. Freeman. San Francisco.

Wright, S. 1931. Evolution in Mendelian populations. Genetics **16:** 97–159.

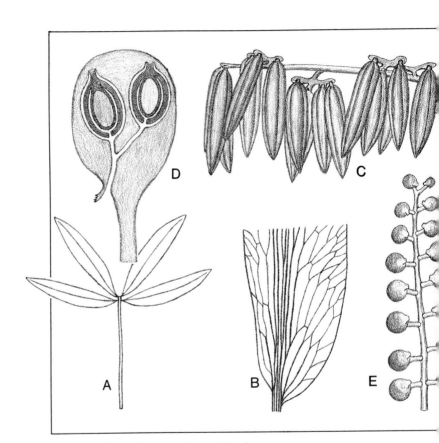

Chapter 4

Caytonia. A, leaf, ×⅔. B, base of leaflet,
×4. C, microsporophyll, ×16. D, cupule,
showing two ovules, ×12. E, megasporophyll, ×2. All figures after T. M. Harris.

The Origin of the Angiosperms

The origin of the angiosperms was an "abominable mystery" to Charles Darwin, and it remains scarcely less so to modern students of evolution. It is clear that they are vascular plants, related to other vascular plants, that they belong to the pteropsid rather than the lycopsid or sphenopsid phylad within the vascular plants, and that their immediate ancestors must have been, by definition, gymnosperms. Beyond that, much is debatable. We begin our consideration here by a review of the distinctive features of angiosperms.

Characteristics of the Group

The most distinctive features of angiosperms, as opposed to gymnosperms, are the enclosure of the ovules in an ovary, the further reduction of both male and female gametophytes, and the unique "double fertilization" that leads to the development of an entirely new food-storage tissue in the seed, the endosperm. The term endosperm is sometimes also applied to the food-storage tissue of gymnosperm seeds, which consists of the body of the female gametophyte. This is, however, wholly different from the true endosperm of angiospermous seeds. The latter arises from an endosperm nucleus produced by the fusion of a sperm nucleus with typically two nuclei (or the product of fusion of two nuclei) of the female gametophyte.

Although these several differences clearly represent evolutionary modifications (apomorphies) from the situation in gymnosperms, their survival value is debatable The enclosure of the ovules in an ovary is often thought to provide additional protection, but this is hard to verify by observation. Although the ovules of both conifers and cycads are briefly exposed to the air at the time of pollination, they are during their subsequent development as effectively covered and protected by the cone-scales as angiosperm ovules are by the ovary. The value of protecting the ovules and developing seeds from injury or predation is not in dispute, but differences in the efficacy of various ways of doing so are not so clear.

Seeds of angiosperms typically mature much faster than those of cycads or *Ginkgo*. The interval between pollination and maturity of the seed in angiosperms is commonly only a few months, sometimes only a few weeks, in contrast to a year or two in these gymnosperms. Roughly half the time between pollination and seed-maturity is typically occupied by the development of the pollen-tube and the parallel development of the receptive female gametophyte in these gymnosperms. Cycads produce massive female cones, with large ovules, before fertilization. In *Ginkgo* the whole seed, except the embryo itself, is formed before fertilization, which occurs after the seeds have fallen from the tree. The absence of embryos from the seeds of fossil pteridosperms suggests a similar ontogenetic pattern. The whole subclass Cycadicae (including the pteridosperms and some other fossil groups as well as the cycads proper) seems to be locked into a slow, perilous, and wasteful reproductive process, which may have characterized all of the early gymnosperms.

If the angiosperms are derived from cycadican gymnosperms, as postulated here, then it seems reasonable to suppose that the small ovules and accelerated development of the seeds in angiosperms have some survival-value in reducing wastage and exposure to environmental hazards.

It has been suggested that the origin of the endosperm nucleus in angiosperms by triple fusion provides a stimulus to rapid development of the seed. The thought is interesting, and possibly true, but perhaps too facile. *Post hoc* is not always *propter hoc*. The Caryophyllales and a number of other angiosperms get along well enough with diploid perisperm as the food-storage tissue of the seed; a triple fusion nucleus is formed in normal angiospermous fashion, but it does not lead to the production of endosperm. In the Onagraceae the endosperm nucleus is formed by fusion of a sperm with only one nucleus of the 4-nucleate embryo-sac, and the resulting endosperm is diploid. A slightly different slant on the relationship of double fertilization to ovular development is provided by Willemstein (1987), who suggests that formation of the endosperm nucleus triggers the commitment of food resources to the fertilized ovule. It is not immediately evident, however, why the formation of the zygote itself could not serve as the trigger, without the complication of double fertilization.

It is easy enough to see an advantage in the angiosperm reproductive cycle as compared to that of cycads and their ancestors, but the comparison with conifers is more complex. *Pinus* takes two years, like the cycads, and fertilization occurs about a year after pollination. *Araucaria* and *Agathis* show a similar pattern. Pinaceous genera other than *Pinus,* however, proceed more expeditiously. Fertilization takes place only a few weeks after pollination, and the seeds mature in a single growing season. Since the development of the female gametophyte and growth of the cone are triggered by pollination, these genera do not commit substantially more energy in advance of the prospect of seed-set than do the angiosperms. Acceleration of maturation of the seeds in certain conifers is not entirely a recent innovation. The Jurassic conifer *Athrotaxites,* among others, apparently matured seed during the course of a single year.

There is presumably a reason why all gymnosperms are woody, whereas angiosperms have been able to exploit both the herbaceous and the woody habit. If all the gymnosperms took as long to set seeds as do the cycads, *Ginkgo,* and some conifers, then the answer might be simple: Only a woody plant has time to complete the process. Because some conifers (and at least some of the Gneticae) do proceed more rapidly, that answer is at best insufficient. Possibly the pycnoxylic wood of conifers does not provide a good base for the evolution of an herbaceous habit. The manoxylic wood of cycadicans might provide a better base, but the seeds take too long to mature. (The terms pycnoxylic and manoxylic are explained on a later page in this chapter.)

Two other characteristic but taxonomically less dependable features of the angiosperms may be more important than the morphology of the ovules and ovary in explaining the success of the group. One is the exploitation of insects and other animals as agents of pollination. The second, and perhaps more significant, is the evolution of a more complex and efficient conducting system, both xylem and phloem. The xylem vessel, in particular, appears to be of critical importance.

Most gymnosperms are wind-pollinated. In order for wind-pollination to be effective and economical, there must be many individuals of a kind, preferably growing close together. (Anyone who has ever tried to grow just a few hills of corn, well separated from any large corn-field, will recognize the problem.) Even so, great quantities of pollen are wasted. A huge amount of metabolically precious protein must be produced, only to be thrown to the winds, never finding its mark.

Pollination by insects and other animals requires a much smaller amount of pollen and does not require such large populations for efficiency, but the difference is not all pure gain. The plant must produce something, such as nectar, which will attract the pollinators, and it must also use some energy in producing petals or other structures that help guide the pollinator to the source of the supply. A greater waste is in a sense traded for a lesser one.

In taking up insect-pollination, angiosperms have exploited a previously neglected evolutionary opportunity, yet without wholly giving up the old (anemophilous) way. Unlike some other evolutionary opportunities that are exploited by one or another group of organisms, this one does not have insurmountable barriers to exit. A considerable number of angiosperms have reverted to wind-pollination, even though they doubtless had insect-pollinated ancestors. Thus in a sense the angiosperms have an extra string to their pollinating bow, permitting them to occupy diverse ecological niches.

The pollen of most angiosperms is distinctively different from that of nearly all gymnosperms. Angiospermous pollen typically has a tectate-columellate exine structure. The tectum (roof) is supported by a series of columns arising from the foot-layer of the exine. In many of the more advanced angiosperms the tectum is perforated, and in a few it is even lost, so that the collumellae are free-standing on the foot-layer, but this latter condition is clearly secondary (apomorphic).

A relatively small number of angiosperms do not have tectate-colu-mellate pollen. A few have a virtually solid and structureless exine. These include some archaic families, such as the Degeneriaceae and Eupoma-tiaceae, but also some more advanced ones, such as the Bataceae and Gyrostemonaceae. Some of the Magnoliidae and Hamamelidae have a loosely granular rather than columellar infratectal structure. The Anno-naceae, a fairly archaic family, include all transitions from virtually struc-tureless exine to tectate-granular and tectate-columellate exine (Le Tho-mas, 1980, 1981). This may indeed be the sequence of evolution from the solid to the tectate-columellate type, as Walker (1976, 1984) supposes, but if so the road has been traveled more than once by different groups of primitive angiosperms, and some groups have even made the return trip. Furthermore, the oldest known angiosperm pollen, from Hauterivian deposits in Israel, is tectate-columellate (Brenner, 1987).

Modern and fossil gymnospermous pollen presents a wide range of exine-structure, from solid to granular or elaborately alveolar. Often it is bilayered, and the outer layer is then frequently but not always saccate. The tectate-columellate exine-structure of angiosperms is virtually lacking in gymnosperms. A few tectate-columellate Triassic pollen-grains (Cornet, 1977) are generally supposed to have been produced by gymnosperms of unknown nature. Given the age of these grains and the lack of definitively angiospermous megafossils in pre-Cretaceous strata, the supposition seems plausible. The pollen (*Classopollis*) of some Jurassic conifers might also be described as tectate-columellate (Chaloner, 1976). Here as elsewhere we are confronted with evolutionary parallelism in characters that do not appear to be subject to competitive exclusion.

The xylem vessel confers probably the most important competitive advantage that most angiosperms have over most gymnosperms, provid-ing faster and easier transport of water. It does not appear, however, that the earliest angiosperms had vessels; these were a later invention in the group. The probable evolutionary history of vessels in angiosperms is discussed in CHAPTER 5.

The vast majority of gymnosperms are wholly dependent on tracheids for the movement of water from the roots, up through the stems, and into the leaves. Tracheids are less efficient conductors than vessels; given an adequate supply they simply cannot deliver the same rate of flow.

A few gymnosperms (the Gneticae) and even a few vascular cryptogams have more or less well developed vessels, but, for reasons unknown, they have not been able to exploit the evolutionary opportunity thus seemingly opened to them. Perhaps the Gnetican vessel evolved too late, after the angiosperms had already pre-empted the field.

Having a less ample and assured water supply than angiosperms, gym-nosperms must perforce have more rigorous means of transpiration-con-trol to meet the same degree of evaporative stress, or they must be better able to survive desiccation. It is no accident that gymnosperms tend to be sclerophyllous, and to have a more xeromorphic aspect than most angiosperms.

The necessary control of transpiration entails restriction of photosynthesis as well. Anything that permits the exchange of gases necessary for photosynthesis will necessarily permit the evaporation of water also. Thus the advantage of vessels over tracheids in conduction of water leads to an advantage of most angiosperms over most gymnosperms in the rate of photosynthesis. Individual kinds of gymnosperms may have other adaptations that permit them to survive in competition with angiosperms, but it is only in special circumstances that gymnosperms in general have a competitive advantage.

The most extensive of the special habitats in which gymnosperms (as represented by the conifers) do seem to have a competitive advantage over angiosperms is in the boreal forest region of North America and Eurasia. Here the evergreen habit of the conifers, made possible by their sclerophyllous leaf structure and resistance to desiccation, permits them to carry on photosynthesis on any day when the conditions are right. In the same region angiospermous trees are bare most of the time and must produce great quantities of new leaves each year, only to drop them at the end of the short summer. In this northern region the sun, being at a lower angle in the sky, does not cause as much evaporative stress as it does in lower latitudes. Thus there is a more favorable p/e (precipitation/evaporation) ratio, so that the lack of vessels is not such a great handicap.

The boreal forest does have some angiospermous trees, notably species of *Betula* and *Populus,* just as the deciduous forest to the south has some conifers, but the dominance of the conifers reflects a set of environmental conditions more favorable to them than to angiospermous trees in general. It is noteworthy that the angiospermous trees which do grow in the boreal forest have relatively soft wood. At temperatures below -40, ordinary frost-resistance mechanisms fail, and only species with soft wood can survive the formation of ice crystals between the cells.

The phloem of angiosperms characteristically has sieve elements and companion cells. The sieve element and its associated companion cell(s) arise from the same individual meristematic cell. The sieve elements are characteristically set end to end, forming sieve tubes with more or less transverse sieve plates. In contrast, the sieve elements and associated parenchyma cells of gymnosperms are usually less regularly arranged, and in any case there is no direct ontogenetic relationship between a sieve element and an associated parenchyma cell or row of parenchyma cells. Furthermore, the sieve elements of gymnosperms mostly have lateral sieve areas and are not clearly aligned to form sieve tubes.

One may surmise that the sieve tube-companion cell structure of the phloem of angiosperms is more efficient than the less highly organized structure of the phloem of gymnosperms, but it is only a surmise. If there is any experimental evidence for a greater efficiency of the angiosperm phloem, I am not aware of it. Neither is it easy to see how the more complex structure might actually contribute to efficiency. Possibly terminal sieve plates are better than lateral sieve areas.

There is no obvious reason why gymnosperms should not have developed a complex phloem of angiospermous type. We know only that they did not (except, of course, in the group that became the angiosperms). Nor is there any obvious reason why the several features that collectively separate the angiosperms from the gymnosperms should all have evolved concomitantly. The concomitance is not perfect: There are some archaic angiosperms that lack vessels, and others in which the carpels are merely folded and unsealed at anthesis. Development of the pollen tube is obviously correlated with enclosure of the ovules, and double fertilization doubtless results at least in part from the extreme reduction of the female gametophyte, but otherwise there seems to be no inherent reason why these several advances should have occurred in concert. They are not parts of a necessarily interlocking system; each could operate without the others.

Recently it has been suggested (Regal, 1977; Burger, 1981; Doyle & Donoghue, 1986) that the potentiality of angiosperms for rapid speciation is an important factor in their diversity and dominance, permitting fine tuning to a myriad of slightly different ecological opportunities. The argument, especially as elaborated by Doyle and Donoghue, is that carpel closure is the critical factor. It allows experimentation with new means of dispersal (independent of seed structure), and thus more frequent establishment of geographically isolated local populations in which rapid speciation might occur. Furthermore, closure of the carpel entails germination of pollen on a stigma, providing a new source of potential isolating mechanisms fostering speciation. Pollination by insects (or other animals) instead of by wind further promotes speciation involving coadaptation of plant and pollinator. It may all be so. The idea needs to be batted around a bit to see what turns up.

Thus it is not clear how much each of the several characteristic features of angiosperms contributes to establishing their competitive superiority over gymnosperms. The advantage of angiosperms under most conditions, for whatever reasons, is of course documented by the fact that they have ousted the gymnosperms from dominance over most of the land surface of the earth.

On the basis of present information it seems that the origin of the angiosperms as we know them was fortuitous. One may speculate that the genetic revolution (à le Mayr) which permitted the development of angiospermous reproductive structures also shattered the stability of other characters such as the structure of the xylem and phloem. For the present, at least, that is mere speculation. Another time things might have happened differently.

The angiosperms evidently fit Simpson's dictum, previously quoted, about the relationship of taxonomic groups to adaptive zones. The changes in structure of xylem and phloem, combined with the changes in the reproductive apparatus and pollination mechanism, certainly do put the angiosperm into a very broad but distinctive new adaptive zone. As a result, they have become the dominant vegetation of the earth. We shall see that the application of Simpson's dictum to the families and orders of angiosperms is much more dubious.

The Fossil Record

PROBLEMS IN ASSEMBLING THE BITS AND PIECES

The low degree of morphological integration among angiosperms, discussed in CHAPTER 1, severely limits the usefulness of fossils in tracing the evolutionary history and dating the origin of taxonomic groups. The difficulty is compounded by the frequency of parallel evolution, leading to the formation of very similar individual structures in groups that are otherwise not very similar and presumably not closely related. Angiosperm fossils characteristically occur as dispersed pollen, leaves, fruits, seeds, pieces of wood, and occasionally a more or less intact flower or inflorescence. Rarely is one part connected to another. Without such connections, we can have no assurance that postulated reconstructions are correct. I well remember the published reconstruction (which I will not dignify with a bibliographic reference) of a *Magnolia*-like flower based on a single fossil thought to resemble the petal of a *Magnolia*. To my skeptical mind this fossil might as easily have been compared to a sow's ear.

Some of the oldest recognizably angiospermous pollen, from Barremian deposits in the Lower Cretaceous, has been called *Clavatipollenites. Clavatipollenites* is very much like the pollen of the modern genus *Ascarina,* in the Chloranthaceae. Even so, we cannot confidently date *Ascarina* or the Chloranthaceae from the Barremian. Even if *Clavatipollenites* is in the direct ancestry of *Ascarina,* as it may be, it is perfectly possible that some of the now characteristic features of the Chloranthaceae did not evolve until long after the characteristic structure of the pollen—the more so because *Clavatipollenites* corresponds to the putatively primitive pollen-type in the Chloranthaceae.

Virtually all assignments of age to particular taxonomic groups contain the implicit assumption that presently correlated characters were also correlated in the past. We may be reasonably confident that Pleistocene maple leaves were borne on maple trees that produced ordinary maple fruits, but such confidence must diminish with increasing age of the fossil. The older the fossil, the greater the possibility that the extrapolation from one structure to another is incorrect. Even if the fossil group is in the line of ancestry from which the modern group evolved, the fossil group may not then have attained the critical taxonomic features of the modern group. Worse, the fossil may actually represent an extinct, unrelated group that was convergent toward the modern group in some particular features. *Caveat emptor.*

The most abundant fossils of angiosperms consist of leaves and pollen grains. Even when the leaves and pollen are preserved in the same deposits, it is difficult at best to be confident in associating the two kinds of structures. Our sample of fossil leaves is undoubtedly biased toward woody plants, from which leaves suitable for fossilization may be abscised intact. Leaves of herbs may wither and fall off, but such withered leaves are fragile and not very suitable for fossilization. The fossil pollen record is also biased. Pollen distributed by wind is produced in much greater quantity than other sorts of pollen, and is likely to be better represented in the fossil record. Thus more can reasonably be read into a lack of wind-distributed pollen in a particular deposit than into a similar lack of leaves associated with herbaceous stems. We shall see that it is possible to distinguish pollen adapted to distribution by wind from other pollen, and be right most of the time.

Wood fossilizes well, but is perhaps less informative than leaves and pollen. Difficult as it is to identify fossil leaves and pollen as representing particular families or genera, the satisfactory identification of wood is apt to be even more parlous. The unusual types may be recognized readily enough, but too many families and genera present too much the same range of variation to permit confident identification of much of the more ordinary wood. Furthermore, the techniques for studying fossil wood are more complicated and time-consuming than the techniques for studying leaves and pollen. For these reasons, fossil angiosperm wood has attracted relatively little critical attention. Vesselless wood thought to be that of a dicotyledon has been reported from the Aptian in Japan, but the distinction of such wood from that of gymnosperms is problematical. Vesseliferous wood can be dated with some certainty from the Albian, and more doubtfully to the Aptian, but it would be rash to identify the fossils to family or even to order.

The Earliest Angiosperms

It now seems fairly well established that the known fossil record of the angiosperms does not antedate the Early Cretaceous. A few pollen grains from the Triassic and Jurassic might pass for primitive (monosulcate) angiosperm pollen, but they are not associated with angiospermous leaves. A few Triassic and Jurassic fossil leaves (e.g., *Furcula, Sanmiguelia*) could pass for unusual angiosperms, but they are not associated with putatively angiospermous pollen. Some undoubted fossil palm trunks (*Palmoxylon*) from Utah turn out to be of Tertiary rather than Jurassic age as had at first been supposed.

Beginning in the late Hauterivian stage of the Lower Cretaceous, we find a more or less continuous record of evidently angiospermous pollen, and from the Barremian stage onward we find angiospermous leaves as well as pollen. Furthermore, the Lower Cretaceous fossil record shows a progressive diversification of both pollen and leaves. The fossils do not tell us when and from what the angiosperms originated, but they do indicate that the evolutionary expansion of the group did not antedate the Cretaceous.

Until only a few decades ago, the early angiosperm fossil record, based largely on leaves, was generally interpreted to mean that the angiosperms were already well diversified at the time of their first appearance in the Lower Cretaceous. Thus a long, unknown fossil history was postulated. Alternatively, an explosive initial radiation was thought to have given rise to a wide array of families in a relatively short time. By 1960 paleobotanists were becoming uneasy about the casual identification of fossil leaves with modern genera, which seemed to seat many and diverse families in the Early Cretaceous. Studies of fossil pollen by various paleobotanists during the 1960's showed much less diversity in early angiosperm fossil pollen than would have been expected on the basis of the leaves.

The dam broke with the publication of James Doyle's paper in 1969 on the fossil pollen in the Potomac Group (mainly Lower Cretaceous) deposits along the east coast of the United States. Instead of sudden appearance in great diversity, the angiosperm pollen record here showed gradual diversification from the bottom to the top of the deposits. The oldest (Aptian) deposits showed only monosulcate, presumably primitive pollen. Progressively younger deposits showed the progressive appearance of tricolpate, tricolporate, and eventually triporate pollen, all very much in harmony with the sequence that had been proposed in 1948 by Armen Takhtajan largely on the basis of modern pollen. Clearly a reconciliation of megafossil and microfossil interpretation was in order.

Several years of joint study of the Potomac fossils by Doyle and Leo Hickey (both Fig. 4.1) produced the reconciliation, presented in detail in 1976. Hickey had already begun his study of angiosperm leaf fossils, with particular emphasis on patterns of venation. His 1973 paper on the architecture of dicotyledonous leaves laid the foundation for a much sounder classification and identification of fossil leaves. Virtually all identifications of Early Cretaceous leaves with modern genera disappeared as a result. Instead it was shown that in the leaves, just as in the pollen, there was a gradual diversification throughout the Lower Cretaceous and on into the Upper Cretaceous. This diversification of pollen and leaves (further discussed in CHAPTER 5) was accompanied by a progressive increase in the abundance of angiosperms, at the expense of gymnosperms.

Thus the picture was changed from one of great initial taxonomic diversity to one of progressive increase in both diversity and abundance, after an initial appearance of a rare and relatively homogeneous group.

In presenting any historical account of the growth of scientific understanding, it is necessary to emphasize the contributions of a limited number of workers. These contributors rarely work in mental isolation, however. Many people contribute both to the data-base and to an atmosphere that fosters the growth of ideas. I well remember hearing from both Leo Hickey and Jack Wolfe about 1970 that many of the early Lower Cretaceous leaf fossils bear a remarkable resemblance to leaves of modern Winteraceae (about which more anon). Had my circle of acquaintances been broader, I might well have heard the same thing from other paleobotanists in other countries. The intellectual ferment was palpable.

Fig. 4.1. Some botanists who have made major contributions to our understanding of the possible ancestry and early evolutionary history of the angiosperms. TOP LEFT, Leo Hickey (1940–). Photo courtesy of Leo Hickey. TOP RIGHT, Irving W. Bailey (1884–1967). Photo from Harvard University Archives. BOTTOM LEFT, Peter Endress (1942–). Photo courtesy of Peter Endress. BOTTOM RIGHT, James A. Doyle (1944–). Photo courtesy of Rudolf Schmid.

Possible Ancestors

What sort of gymnosperms may have been ancestral to the angiosperms is still an open question. The fossil record, which as we have pointed out has had a somewhat limited usefulness in clarifying relationships among the various groups of angiosperms, is up to the present even less helpful in determining their ancestry. Morphologically, the angiosperms are so sharply limited and so well set off from all gymnosperms that a series of hypothetical connecting forms must be postulated to tie them to anything at all. Here the "missing link" is indeed still missing—or at least has not been recognized. It is of course possible that Krassilov (1973) is right in saying that "If the origin of the angiosperms is still a mystery, the explanation should be found not in the gaps of the record but in the deficiencies of current evolutionary concepts." My trouble is that I have not been able to think of a better approach. The connections proposed by Krassilov have been adequately dealt with by Doyle (1978).

When a disease has many remedies, probably none of them is very good. Likewise, when a taxonomic group has many different suggested ancestors, the case is probably not very good for any of them. So it is with the angiosperms. Most of the orders of living and fossil gymnosperms have at one or another time been suggested as possible ancestors. If the gymnosperms (division Pinophyta) are organized into three subdivisions—the Pinicae, Gneticae, and Cycadicae, as in the system of Cronquist, Takhtajan, and Zimmermann (1966)—the Pinicae may quickly be eliminated from serious consideration, the Gneticae may be excluded after more careful study, and only the Cycadicae (including the seed ferns) remain as possible ancestors to the angiosperms. For this discussion the Glossopteridales and Caytoniales are associated with the Cycadicae, and the Ginkgoales with the Pinicae along with the Cordaitales and Pinales. I am aware of Meyen's controversial reorganization of the major classification of gymnosperms (1984), but it impinges on our consideration mainly in that he associates the Glossopteridales (Arberiales) and Caytoniales with the Ginkgoales rather than with the several orders of the seed fern to cycad phylad. If the Glossopteridales and Caytoniales are excluded from the Cycadicae, then it is not so easy to say that the ancestry of the angiosperms must be sought in that subdivision.

Pinicae

Nothing in the Pinicae offers any reasonable prospect of being ancestral to the angiosperms.

The seed-bearing apparatus of the Pinicae and that of the angiosperms follow distinctly different lines of evolutionary specialization. Ontogenetically, carpels are the serial homologues of leaves. The seed-bearing organs of the Pinicae are variously modified but never distinctly leaf-like. Possibly they are modified telomes or telome-systems that have never been vegetative leaves; or possibly they are much reduced and modified leaves. In the Cordaitales and Ginkgoales the ovules are obviously terminal on slender stalks; in the Cordaitales these ovuliferous stalks are aggregated into apparently simple cones (strobili), which are themselves loosely grouped into clusters. In the Pinales the female cones are compound, and the ovules are borne on "ovuliferous scales" that are axillary to the primary bracts of the cone. The ovular apparatus of the Taxales is even more specialized. The possibility of deriving the angiosperm flower from such a structure seems remote, the more so when we recall that the primitive angiosperm flower is thought to be bisexual, whereas the cones of the Pinicae are uniformly unisexual.

Neither is there anything in the leaves to suggest a relationship to the angiosperms. Nothing in the whole subdivision Pinicae has net-veined leaves, whereas net venation is standard among the angiosperms and occurs also in some of the Cycadicae. Even the monocotyledons, which are customarily said to have parallel-veined leaves, have abundant cross-connections between the main veins. Aside from the matter of anastomoses, pinnate venation appears to be basic to the early angiosperms, but is wholly unrepresented in the Pinicae. Many of the Cycadicae, in contrast, have pinnate venation, with or without anastomoses.

Wood of the Pinicae also compares poorly with that of angiosperms. Students of gymnosperms find it useful to classify gymnosperm wood (both fossil and modern) as pycnoxylic or manoxylic. **Pycnoxylic wood** has small tracheids with circular bordered pits, and narrow rays. **Manoxylic wood** has relatively large tracheids with either circular bordered or more often scalariform-bordered pits, and multiseriate, very high rays; the proportion of parenchyma is relatively high, and secondary growth is often rather limited. These distinctions are not absolute, but they work well enough to encourage continued use of the two categories.

Pycnoxylic structure first appears in the secondary wood of Middle Devonian progymnosperms, which retain the presumably primitive scalariform pitting of tracheids in the primary xylem. Pycnoxylic structure is carried on through the Cordaitales, Pinales, Taxales, and Ginkgoales, which make up the subdivision Pinicae as here considered. Except for the Cordaitales, members of these orders generally have circular bordered pits even in the primary xylem, lacking scalariform pitting altogether. Pycnoxylic structure in the secondary wood is also characteristic of the Gneticae and Glossopteridales and some of the early pteridosperms, with some reservation (as noted in a subsequent paragraph) about some of the Gneticae.

Manoxylic structure is regarded as derived and is found in the Lyginopteridales, Bennettitales, and Cycadales, which make up the core of the Cycadicae. Angiosperms regarded as archaic resemble the manoxylic group in having large tracheids, scalariform pitting, and multiseriate rays. Based on a somewhat shaky interpretation of the fossil record, it appears that in the manoxylic groups of gymnosperms, scalariform pitting has replaced the ancestral circular bordered pitting in the secondary xylem. This change might be regarded as a retention of juvenile structure (as in the primary xylem) in the later-formed (secondary) tissues. It is opposite to the change in more advanced pycnoxylic groups, in which even the primary xylem has circular bordered pits. These changes in wood structure might reflect heterochrony, as discussed later in this chapter.

GNETICAE

The Gneticae resemble the angiosperms in several respects and were at one time taken seriously as their possible ancestors. The Gneticae are dicotyledonous (not an unusual feature in gymnosperms), and they differ from all other gymnosperms in having vessels in the secondary wood. The female gametophyte of the Gneticae is more reduced than that of other gymnosperms. In *Gnetum* (Fig. 4.2) there is no suggestion of an archegonium, and fertilization takes place while the female gametophyte is still partly in the free-nuclear condition. The ovules of the Gneticae differ from those of most gymnosperms and resemble those of most angiosperms in evidently having two integuments instead of only one. *Gnetum* has net-veined leaves and is very angiospermous in general appearance; indeed *Gnetum gnemon* could easily pass for *Coffaea arabica* when in sterile condition, and I am told that the two have been confused in some college greenhouses. The unisexual, scaly-bracted strobili of *Gnetum* and other Gneticae might be compared, without too much stretch of the imagination, to the catkins of some amentiferous angiosperms, such as the Salicaceae and Betulaceae. It is therefore not surprising that some credence was once given to the idea that the Gneticae, and particularly *Gnetum* itself, might be closely allied to the angiosperms.

Unfortunately, first appearances are not borne out by further study. Changes in our concepts of evolutionary relationships among the angiosperms have thrown a different light on the similarity of the Gnetican strobilus to the catkins of the "Amentiferae." As we shall see, the Amentiferae are now considered to be a heterogeneous group with reduced flowers. The primitive angiosperm is thought to have had bisexual flowers, with a well developed perianth, numerous stamens, and several or numerous separate carpels, each flower representing a complete bisexual strobilus. Such flowers would be most difficult to derive from the unisexual, scaly-bracteate, compound strobilus of the Gneticae. The similarity between the Gnetican strobilus and the aments of some angiosperms is now seen as superficial and due only to a degree of convergence. Any phyletic connection between the two groups would have to antedate the development of such similarity in this respect as does exist.

The possible significance of dicotyledonous embryos in an assessment of the relationships of the Gneticae to the angiosperms is presently dubious. The angiosperms may well be derived from polycotyledonous rather than dicotyledonous ancestors. *Degeneria,* one of the most archaic existing angiosperms, has three or four cotyledons in most of the embryos.

Fig. 4.2. *Gnetum gnemon.* Photo courtesy of the Field Museum of Natural History.

Dicotyledony is widespread in the gymnosperms, and polycotyledony occurs mainly in conifers (and not all of these). In other respects the conifers seem a most unlikely choice as the source of the angiosperms.

The reduction and loss of the archegonium in the female gametophyte has evidently occurred within the confines of the Gneticae. *Ephedra* has normal archegonia. In *Welwitschia* a specialized cell that is probably homologous with the archegonial initial functions directly as an egg. In *Gnetum,* as we have noted, fertilization takes place while the gametophyte is still in a partly free-nuclear condition. Given the difference in gross reproductive apparatus between the Gneticae and the angiosperms, it appears that any connection between the two groups must involve pre-Gnetican ancestors with more primitive strobili. Therefore the reduction and loss of the archegonium in the Gneticae must have occurred subsequent to the split. The similarity in this respect, then, is due to parallelism, and merely reflects the general tendency toward reduction of the gametophyte among the vascular plants as a whole. This analysis of the evolution of the female gametophyte in the Gneticae would of course have to be modified if we were to accept Meyen's wide separation of *Ephedra* from *Gnetum* and *Welwitschia,* but I do not think that the case for a close relationship of *Gnetum* to the angiosperms would be substantially improved.

The significance of the double integument in the Gneticae must be evaluated in the light of the fact that the ovule in this group, as in other gymnosperms, is orthotropous. There is good reason to suppose that the ovules of angiosperms, in contrast, are primitively anatropous. Anatropous ovular structure is discussed on a subsequent page of this chapter in connection with the Caytoniales. Students of the Gneticae think that the outer integument in the group is derived from a pair of appendages beneath the ovule and has nothing to do with the outer integument of angiosperms.

The vessels of the Gneticae, once thought to provide strong evidence of relationship to the angiosperms, now present difficulties rather than support for the concept. As Irving Bailey (1944; Fig. 4.1) pointed out, the perforations of the vessel members in angiosperms apparently evolved by the dissolution of the pit-membranes of scalariform-bordered pits. A connection to gymnosperms with manoxylic wood is therefore suggested. In the Gneticae, in contrast, the wood is pycnoxylic (in terms of the size and pitting of the tracheids), and vessels appear to have evolved through modification of circular bordered pits of a typically coniferous type. The present structures may be similar, but they got there by different routes; the similarity reflects evolutionary convergence. The angiospermous vessel therefore cannot (in Bailey's view) be derived from the Gnetican vessel; any possible connection between the Gneticae and the angiosperms must antedate the origin of vessels in both groups.

Bailey's emphasis on the phyletic importance of the difference between the vessels of the Gneticae and those of the angiosperms has been challenged by Muhammad and Sattler (1982). Investigating the wood of the two species of *Gnetum,* they found some vessels with scalariform-bordered perforation plates, and a complete range from circular bordered pits typical of conifers to angiosperm-like scalariform pits. Thus it would be possible to interpret the wood structure of *Gnetum* as presenting the foundation for a change to an angiospermous type. The multiseriate rather than uniseriate wood-rays of the Gneticae would also lend some support to this thought. There are still problems, however, because it appears that vessels originated *within* the angiosperms, rather than being inherited from some hypothetical common ancestor with the Gneticae. The basically pycnoxylic wood of the Gneticae may not be the absolute barrier to an angiospermous relationship that Bailey took it to be, but it is a negative rather than a positive factor. It is something to be overcome, rather than evidence of affinity.

The potentiality to develop vessels exists in vascular cryptogams as well as in the seed plants. Xylem elements that fit the morphological criteria for vessels occur in such phyletically diverse genera as *Pteridium, Selaginella,* and *Equisetum,* as well as in the Gneticae and the angiosperms. Only the latter groups have capitalized on the water-conducting potentiality of a vessel system, but evidently not much can be made of this similarity in terms of phylogenetic relationship.

The fossil record of the Gneticae is scanty and equivocal. Neither leaves nor pollen nor any other fossils can clearly be referred to *Gnetum,* although the possibility must be admitted that some of the leaves which pass as angiosperms are actually gnetoid. Striate, ellipsoid-fusiform pollen-grains resembling those of *Ephedra* (but not *Gnetum*) occur as far back as the late Triassic, and are abundant in some Lower Cretaceous deposits in West Gondwanaland (Africa plus South America). These do nothing to tie *Ephedra* or other Gneticae to the angiosperms or anything else. No support for a close relationship between the Gneticae and the angiosperms exists in the known fossil record as presently interpreted.

We have left, then, mainly the habit and the net-veined leaves of *Gnetum* to support a relationship to the angiosperms. That is simply not enough. All considered, there is enough similarity between *Gnetum* and the angiosperms to invite a careful comparison, but the weight of the evidence disclosed by the comparison is heavily against the origin of the angiosperms from the Gneticae. It is possible that the Gneticae and the angiosperms are sister groups, as postulated by Crane (1985) and by Doyle and Donoghue (1986), but it appears that any connection between them would have to be found in the Cycadicae.

CYCADICAE

Having discounted the Pinicae and Gneticae as prospective ancestors to the angiosperms, we turn to a consideration of the Cycadicae. The Cycadicae are here considered to consist mainly of 5 orders, the Cycadales, Glossopteridales, Bennettitales, Lyginopteridales (Pteridospermales), and Caytoniales. A few other possibly Cycadican fossils, such as the Jurassic and early Cretaceous Czekanowskiales and Dirhopalostachyaceae, are insufficiently known to warrant detailed consideration here, but there is nothing among them that seems more promising than the several orders here discussed. Collectively the Cycadicae may provide most or all of the features necessary for a prospective ancestor of the angiosperms, but there are problems with any one of the orders.

Cycadales

Among the five orders listed, only the Cycadales are represented by living species. The rest are known only from fossils of Cretaceous or earlier age. Fossil Cycadales are known from as far back as the Permian period, long enough ago so that age alone poses no barrier to the possibility of deriving the angiosperms from them.

The gross structure of the leaves and stems of cycads does not suggest that of primitive angiosperms. Cycads have large, pinnately compound leaves. The fossil record of angiosperms, in contrast, indicates that simple leaves are basic to the group, and compound leaves evolved later. Modern cycads have unbranched stems. Some fossil cycads have a more or less branched stem, but there are no axillary buds and branching is adventitious. Thus the correspondence between cycads and angiosperms in gross stem structure is not very good. The cycads do have manoxylic wood, which is a point in their favor as potential ancestors.

The structure and arrangement of the reproductive parts of cycads pose serious difficulties to an ancestral position for the group. The cycads are dioecious, with well developed male and female cones on different individuals. The primitive angiosperm flower, in contrast, is thought to be bisexual. Granted that the megasporophylls of *Cycas* are somewhat foliar in aspect, the sporophylls of cycads in general seem too specialized to provide a good starting point for stamens and carpels. Furthermore, the cycads have nothing that could easily be homologized with the second integument of angiosperms. On the basis of vascular anatomy and for other reasons some students of cycads consider that the seemingly single integument actually represents two fused integuments, but that is no help in getting to angiospermous structure.

Any cycad-like ancestor of angiosperms would need to have bisporangiate strobili and branching stems. These characters would make the plant not a cycad but more nearly a pteridosperm. The cycads themselves are generally conceded to have evolved from pteridosperms. Thus any evolutionary connection between the cycads and the angiosperms probably lies in a common ancestry in the pteridosperms.

Glossopteridales

The Glossopteridales figure in speculation on the ancestry of the angiosperms mainly because of a paucity of other good candidates. They have net-veined leaves, but the venation does not really resemble that of most angiosperms. Their fructifications were borne on or associated with the upper surface of the leaves (fine for a pre-angiosperm), but were so complex and specialized in their own way that they do not provide a good starting point for angiospermous structure. The wood was pycnoxylic. A change to manoxylic structure must be envisaged if the angiosperms are to be derived from this group. The Glossopteridales were abundant and diversified in the Permian, but they waned in the Triassic, and the fossil record only doubtfully carries them into the early Jurassic. Somehow we must get across something like 60 million years to get to the first known fossil angiosperms. The gap may not be fatal to a connection, but it is not encouraging.

The principal proponents of a glossopterid origin of the angiosperms have been Melville (1969) and Retallack and Dilcher (1981). Melville based his argument primarily on the similarity of the net venation of the leaves of glossopterids to that of a few carefully selected modern angiosperms. Aside from being anastomosing, glossopterid venation compares poorly to that of most angiosperms, however, and in particular it does not resemble that of early angiosperm fossils. As Meyen (1973) gleefully noted, glossopterid leaf venation is also very similar to the venation in the wings of certain butterflies. Meyen's well taken point is that there is a limited number of ways to meet particular structural challenges, and the same way may be discovered by more than one group. Venation like that of the glossopterids may possibly have been an evolutionary precursor to that of angiosperms, but not necessarily so, and we see no such connections in the fossil record.

The full angiospermous syndrome of leaf venation includes several orders of veins anastomosing to form a hierarchical reticulum, usually with veinlets ending freely in the areoles. To this we should add that the early angiosperm leaves in the fossil record have a rather poorly organized pinnate venation, with primary lateral veins of irregular size arising at irregular distances and diverging at irregular angles from the midvein. Net venation in the glossopterids and other net-veined gymnosperms (except *Gnetum*), in contrast, shows a midvein and only one order of reticulate venation. The lateral veins arising directly from the midrib are no different from the others in the reticulum, and there are no veins ending freely in the areoles. There is no more reason to tie angiospermous venation to that of the glossopterids than to that of any other net-veined gymnosperms.

Retallack and Dilcher base their much more cautious argument for the possibility of a glossopterid connection mainly on the fructifications. Admitting that glossopterid fructifications are not really like those of angiosperms, they propose a complex and mainly hypothetical series that might be thought to provide a basis for a transition. To me their argument seems more hopeful than plausible, and it minimizes the problems presented by wood structure, leaf venation, and 60 million years. It is not an impossible scenario, merely an unlikely one.

Bennettitales

The Bennettitales are another group of Cycadicae that have figured in speculation on the ancestry of the angiosperms. Taking their origin late in the Triassic, the Bennettitales were abundant throughout the Jurassic and well into the Cretaceous. Thus they were physically available at the right time for the connection. They had bisporangiate strobili with the pollen-bearing organs below the ovulate ones, as a good pre-angiosperm should. Some of them had branching, monopodial stems with manoxylic (even scalariform-pitted) wood and simple, more or less net-veined (though scarcely angiosperm-like) leaves. Furthermore, they had dicotyledonous embryos, as do the cycads and some other gymnosperms, but as we have been this may or may not be a feature of primitive angiosperms.

Some other characters of the Bennettitales present serious problems to an angiospermous affinity. The structure of the cones, in particular, militates against an ancestor-descendant relationship. The microsporophylls were pinnatifid or pinnately compound and bore numerous synangia. It is possible to conceive of the evolution of angiospermous stamens from such organs, but a major transformation would be necessary. The structure of the ovulate portion of the strobilus is even less promising in terms of a possible ancestry to the angiosperms. The numerous ovules were borne on a dome-shaped central organ (metaphorically comparable to a receptacle) and were interspersed with slender scales. Each ovule was orthotropous and long-stalked. There was nothing that could realistically be compared to a carpel.

If we mentally deprive the Bennettitales of these specialized features, we are again back in the seed ferns (Lyginopteridales). Like the cycads, the Bennettitales are generally considered to be derived from the seed ferns.

Lyginopteridales

In recent years it has become customary to suggest the seed ferns as ancestral to the angiosperms, *faute de mieux*. It is a long way, both morphologically and chronologically, from any known seed fern to an angiosperm, but each of the differences could logically be bridged in the course of evolution. A long chain of unknown ancestors must be postulated, but there is nothing inherently unlikely about any of the requisite evolutionary changes.

The pteridosperms had large, usually pinnately compound leaves, and some of the species were net-veined—though not in angiospermous fashion. The stems were either simple or branched, but there were no well defined axillary buds. Most or all of the species had a definite cambium, although (as in cycads) the proportion of secondary tissues was not high. Although some of the earlier members of the group, in particular, were more or less pycnoxylic, most of them were manoxylic, as those terms were described on an earlier page. The megasporophylls and microsporophylls of pteridosperms were probably often borne on the same plant. They were not aggregated into definite strobili, but the fact that the Bennettitales do have strobili shows that the potentiality existed in the pteridosperms. We have noted that the primitive angiosperms probably did not have vessels, and that the tendency to develop vessels exists in diverse groups of vascular plants. The absence of vessels from the pteridosperms is therefore not at all incompatible with their being ancestral to the angiosperms.

The ovules of pteridosperms were borne on the margins of the megasporophylls, or on one or the other surface. The primitive position of the ovules on the angiosperm carpel has in the past usually been considered to be marginal, but more recently it has been suggested that the ovules were on the upper surface instead. The question is considered in the following chapter. Apparently either position is compatible with an origin of angiosperms from seed ferns, although the marginal position provides a larger set of possible ancestors.

The seeds of pteridosperms were much more primitive than those of any known angiosperms. They evidently had a large female gametophyte, like most other gymnosperms, but not one pteridospermous seed has yet been found to contain an embryo. Possibly the embryo developed well after the apparent ripening of the seed, as in their descendants, the modern cycads, and also in *Ginkgo*. The ovule apparently had only a single integument.

The origin of the second integument in angiosperm ovules is not yet fully understood. The single integument of gymnospermous seeds in general is believed to have arisen by fusion of a set of leaf-segments or telomes beneath the megasporangium, at a time in evolutionary history when the leaf was scarcely more than a modified set of branching stems, i.e., when the evolutionary differentiation of the typical megaphyll from the branching stem systems of the rhyniophytes had not yet been completed. The pteridosperms commonly had one or several ovules collectively subtended by a cupule that is believed to be of syntelomic origin like the integument. It is not difficult to suppose that a cupule containing only a single ovule could become further modified to form a second integument. That is only a supposition, but no other reasonable supposition comes to mind. The possible origin of the second integument from a cupule is further discussed under the Caytoniales.

The origin of sepals from leaves, and of petals from both sepals and stamens, is amply documented within the angiosperms, so that these characteristic structures pose no barrier to associating the angiosperms with any group of gymnosperms we wish to consider. The characteristic double fertilization of angiosperms, with the attendant development of a triploid endosperm, evidently relates to the extreme reduction of the female gametophyte; it provides no indication at all of the relationships of the group. Reduction of the gametophyte is a general trend throughout the vascular plants as a whole; this trend has merely been carried farther in the angiosperms than in other groups.

Thus it appears that all of the characters in which angiosperms differ from the seed ferns could have evolved from a pteridospermous ancestry. The combination of branching stems with manoxylic wood, large, sometimes net-veined leaves, and leaf-like megasporophylls presented by some pteridosperms provides a better base from which to evolve an angiosperm than the combination of characters in any of the other groups so far discussed.

Still, a great deal of change must be envisaged to get from a pteridosperm to an angiosperm, and the time problem is horrendous. Classic pteridosperms scarcely survive the Lower Permian. Instead of the 60 million year gap that we emphasized in discounting the glossopterids as possible ancestors, we face a gap of more than a 100 million years. One would like to find a more recent putative ancestor, possibly something that was itself derived from the pteridosperms. That brings us to the Caytoniales.

Caytoniales

The Caytoniales are represented by several small families (perhaps only one genus to each, when the different organs are associated), and extend from the Triassic through the Cretaceous. They are generally considered to have been derived from the pteridosperms, and they have often been treated as advanced members of that group. They have pinnately or palmately compound leaves. The leaflets have a midvein and variously open or net venation. The net venation is of the sort found in some other Cycadicae, and does not closely resemble that of angiosperms. Based on rather scanty evidence, the wood was probably manoxylic.

The fructifications of the Caytoniales are the most interesting parts, from the standpoint of a possible relationship to the angiosperms. Both the megasporophylls and the microsporophylls were pinnately compound, but we do not know how they were arranged, or even if both sorts were produced on the same plant. The megasporophylls in *Caytonia* consist of a slender central axis with the cupules pinnately arranged along the margins. In *Umkomasia* the megasporophyll is a pinnately branched axis, with the cupules more or less pinnately arranged along the branches. In both genera the cupules are recurved, so that the terminal opening lies alongside the base of the stalk. In *Caytonia* each cupule contains numerous small, orthotropous ovules, but in *Umkomasia* the cupule has only a single distally exserted ovule. *Ktalenia*, of Aptian (Lower Cretaceous) age, resembles *Caytonia* in critical features of leaves and cupules. It requires no great imagination to visualize the Caytonialean cupule as the evolutionary precursor of an anatropous ovule, with the cupular wall transformed into an outer integument.

In some of the earlier literature the cupules of *Caytonia* were compared to the ovary of angiosperms. The comparison is obviously faulty, inasmuch as the angiosperm carpel appears to be equivalent to a complete megasporophyll, whereas the Caytonialean cupule is only a small part (equivalent to a leaflet) of a megasporophyll bearing a number of cupules.

It was not until Ledyard Stebbins (1974) revived Gaussen's (1946) previously neglected comparison of the cupule with an anatropous ovule that the Caytoniales regained a proper place in speculation on the origin of the angiosperms. Stebbins even sees the zigzag micropyle of miscellaneous angiosperms (including some archaic ones) as an evolutionary vestige of a slightly excentric position of the single surviving ovule in the cupule.

Even with the comparison of a Caytonialean cupule to an anatropous ovule, we are not home free in drawing a connection to the angiosperms. The Caytonialean megasporophyll was slender, rather than broad and flat as in putatively primitive angiosperm carpels. To see a connection, we must visualize the expansion of the rachis of the megasporophyll to foliar form, or we must await the discovery of an as yet unknown relative of *Caytonia* with more leaf-like megasporophylls.

The microsporophylls of the Caytoniales have no advantage over those of various other Cycadicae in terms of providing an evolutionary base for the angiosperm stamen. Neither do they have any special disadvantages of their own. A major reduction and condensation must be envisaged to get from any fossil Cycadican microsporophyll to an angiosperm stamen. Yet some of the modern cycads have moved significantly in that direction.

The net venation of the leaves of some Caytoniales is no better and no worse than that of glossopterids and some pteridosperms as a possible precursor of net venation in the angiosperms.

Monosulcate, nonsaccate pollen might be a plus in the evaluation of a group of gymnosperms as possibly ancestral to the angiosperms, but it is not a *sine qua non*. Within the Caytoniales as here treated, *Caytonia* has saccate pollen, but the Upper Triassic genus *Peltaspermum* has nonsaccate pollen. Saccate pollen is regarded as an advanced condition in gymnosperms, facilitating (but not required for) wind-pollination. A change to other methods of pollination would obviously favor reduction and loss of the air-sacs. Thus saccate pollen in the ancestry of the angiosperms cannot be ruled out a priori. Indeed the recent discovery that pollen of *Lactoris* has small sacci (Zavada & Taylor, 1986) emphasizes the possibility that the ancestors of the angiosperms may have had saccate pollen.

The major advantages that the Caytoniales have over the Lyginopteridales as possible ancestors to the angiosperms are that the Caytoniales existed at the right time, and that the recurved cupule provides a very plausible base for the anatropous, bitegmic angiosperm ovule.

Heterochrony the Answer?

The apparent exclusion of one after another group of gymnosperms as plausible ancestors to the angiosperms raises the possibility of fundamental error in our approach to the question. Takhtajan (1976) has suggested that the problem could be minimized by supposing that neoteny played an important role in the origin of the group. I prefer to use the more general term heterochrony, to avoid the fine distinctions among the terms neoteny, paedomorphosis, and progenesis, all of which refer to changes in the timing of development of different tissues and organs. Takhtajan uses the term neoteny in a broad rather than a narrow sense; in his usage it is equivalent to heterochrony as used here.

The net result of heterochrony is apt to be that some structures either develop precociously or remain permanently juvenile, while others mature in normal fashion. It is supposed that heterochrony may be governed by changes in regulatory genes, which control the timing and intensity of function of the structural genes. The once scorned "hopeful monsters" of Goldschmidt (1940) now seem more plausible, at least in theory, through the possible effects of regulatory genes. Heterochrony, under one or another name, has been suggested by numerous authors as an avenue of escape from specialization in animals, providing the possibility for the origin of major new taxa based on alteration of generalized juvenile rather than specialized mature structures.

Heterochrony may indeed provide the answer we are seeking. The simple leaves of early angiosperms may be merely juvenilized cycadican leaves that have not yet assumed their mature, compound structure. Nemejc (1956) considered that the angiosperm leaf is neotenic, as have several later authors. Manoxylic secondary wood in many cycadicans may have originated from the ancestral pycnoxylic wood through heterochrony. Even some of the modern cycads show progressive juvenilization in some features, including the presence of scalariform rather than pitted tracheids in the secondary xylem (Chrysler, 1937). Carlquist (1962), among others, has postulated that by means of heterochrony (paedomorphosis, in his terminology) primitive characters might migrate into the secondary xylem from their "refugium" in the primary xylem.

The strobilar hypothesis of the angiosperm flower is highly compatible with a heterochronous origin. The flower may be compared to a juvenile vegetative shoot, with a short axis (as in a vegetative terminal bud), and with the floral leaves retained in a permanently juvenile condition. As Agnes Arber (1937) pointed out a half a century ago, "the flower might indeed be described as corresponding to a vegetative shoot which remains in a condition of permanent infantilism." The complex microsporophylls and megasporophylls of many Cycadicans might well be transformed by heterochrony into laminar stamens and folded but open carpels, such as we see in some modern archaic angiosperms.

The pervasive evolutionary reduction of the gametophyte in vascular plants in general is an expression of heterochrony. The gametes are produced at a progressively earlier stage in the development of the vegetative body, the further development of which is curtailed.

We have noted that one of the most important functional differences between angiosperms and gymnosperms is that the angiosperms generally pass through the stages from pollination to maturity of the seed much faster than most gymnosperms. The speed minimizes the exposure of the seeds to environmental hazards, and it opens the way to an herbaceous growth-form. The herbaceous habit itself, in angiosperms, may be regarded as heterochronous, in that the flowers and fruits are produced on plants that are vegetatively immature as compared with their ancestors.

If heterochrony is the key to understanding here, then the absence of transitional forms in the fossil record is less daunting. The early members of the group might be only marginally suited to survive and reproduce, but with a simplified basic structure they would have the potentiality for further rapid evolutionary change and diversification. The evolution of an adaptive syndrome of features, pushed by selection, might be expected to lead to the early extinction of the less well adapted ancestors. All this is pure speculation, but it is harmonious with what we know or believe about competition, selection, population genetics, and the mechanisms of gene action.

Heterochrony or no, it still appears that the Cycadicae offer better possibilities for the ancestry of the angiosperms than either the Pinicae or the Gneticae. In the Cycadicae we find in various members the features of leaves, wood, microsporophylls, pollen, and megasporophylls that might provide a suitable foundation for the origin of the angiosperms.

Imperfectly known though they are (and perhaps partly *because* they are imperfectly known), the Caytoniales appear to provide the best bet among the Cycadicae.They were there at the right time, and they suggest a possible origin for the anatropous, bitegmic ovule. This tentative conclusion is not really at odds with frequent speculation in the recent past that the ancestry of the angiosperms lies in the seed ferns. The Caytoniales are generally regarded as descendants of the seed ferns and are sometimes even included in that group.

Where did it Happen?

Where remains as much a mystery as *from what*. The angiosperms are basically a tropical group. The fossil record clearly shows that they did not penetrate into cooler regions until well after the initial diversification in the tropics. Phylogenetic analysis based on modern species leads to the same conclusion. We can dismiss speculation from the 19th century that they originated in northern regions and spread southward. Beyond that, the field is open.

The best evidence, if we could get it, would be from the fossils. Being unable to establish a direct connection with the gymnosperms, we are also unable to specify the locality on the basis of the fossils. We can say that the venation of many of the earliest angiosperm leaves in the Potomac deposits (eastern USA) is remarkably like that of the modern Winteraceae, a family now essentially confined to the continents derived from Gondwanaland. That may suggest something about the evolutionary history of angiosperm leaves, but it does not help us settle on a place of origin.

The fossil pollen record is scarcely more enlightening. Monocolpate angiosperm pollen first appears in the uppermost Hauterivian of Israel and the United Kingdom, and soon thereafter in widely separated Barremian deposits—England, eastern North America, and equatorial Africa. Tricolpate grains appear a little later, in the Aptian, in Brasil, Israel, and equatorial Africa, and then in Europe and North America in the Albian. One can scarcely visualize the simultaneous origin of the angiosperms in both Laurasia and Gondwanaland, but evidently the early members of the group got around fast enough to produce what seems like a simultaneous appearance in the fossil record. A million years is time enough for a lot of migration (especially with fewer barriers between continents), but it might not show up clearly in our efforts to date Barremian fossils.

Lacking clear evidence from the fossils, we may consider the modern distribution of the more archaic families of angiosperms. In so doing, we should keep in mind the inherent bias toward Gondwanaland in the distribution of tropical climates. Africa, South America, Australia, and all the South Pacific islands east of Wallace's Line belong to Gondwanaland. The Cretaceous tropical flora of North America (a portion of ancient Laurasia) has essentially disappeared. Indigenous tropical plants in modern North America are descendants of Tertiary and Quaternary immigrants from South America. Thus only southeast Asia and the associated islands (west of Wallace's Line) represent a possible Laurasian center of origin or survival of ancient angiosperms. Even here, we should note that the bulk of India is a portion of Gondwanaland that has drifted north into contact with Asia, pushing up the Himalaya Mts. along the juncture.

I think it is useful here to restrict our consideration to those families that are woody and have uniaperturate or uniaperate-derived pollen. My comparison thus differs from that of Schuster (1972), who also included a number of families with triaperturate pollen. His rough balance of archaic Laurasian and Gondwanaland families in the southwest Pacific region depends on that inclusion. Without these triaperturate families the balance swings heavily toward Gondwanaland. Schuster is of course right that the present southwest Pacific region should be considered as two regions in terms of angiosperm history. Australia and the islands to the east of Wallace's Line were far removed from southeastern Asia in the early Cretaceous, and only much later drifted into their present position. The possibility that there might have been some microcontinental fragments in between is only a minor complicating factor that does not seriously compromise the basic separation.

The families Winteraceae, Degeneriaceae, Himantandraceae, Eupomatiaceae, Austrobaileyaceae, Annonaceae, Magnoliaceae, Lactoridaceae, Myristicaceae, Canellaceae, Amborellaceae, Trimeniaceae, Monimiaceae, Gomortegaceae, Calycanthaceae, Idiospermaceae, Lauraceae, Hernandiaceae, Chloranthaceae, and the less consistently woody Piperaceae and Aristolochiaceae qualify for consideration. Seven of these 21 families are confined to the Australian plate. These are the Degeneriaceae, Himantandraceae, Eupomatiaceae, Austrobaileyaceae, Amborellaceae, Trimeniaceae, and Idiospermaceae. Two other families, the Winteraceae and Monimiaceae, have their headquarters in the same area, although they also occur in other parts of Gondwanaland. The Lactoridaceae and

Gomortegaceae are South American. The Canellaceae occur in Africa, Madagascar, and tropical America. The Myristicaceae and Annonaceae are widespread in tropical regions, but more probably of Gondwanic rather than Laurasian ancestry. The Lauraceae, Hernandiaceae, Chloranthaceae, Piperaceae, and Aristolochiaceae are widespread, not easily assignable to either Gondwanaland or Laurasia. Only the Magnoliaceae and Calycanthaceae are primarily Laurasian. The Calycanthaceae are closely allied to the Australian Idiospermaceae. Neither is clearly more advanced than the other, so they cancel each other out in this assessment.

Angiosperms with primitively unsealed carpels (Degeneriaceae, some Winteraceae, and, in a peculiar way, the Eupomatiaceae) all belong to the Gondwanaland group. The Winteraceae and Amborellaceae, with primitively vesselless wood, are both in the Gondwanaland group. The only other dicot families with primitively vesselless wood are the Tetracentraceae and Trochondraceae (one species each), which have triaperturate pollen and occur in eastern Asia. These two families are widely regarded as providing a link between the archaic subclass Magnoliidae and the somewhat more advanced subclass Hamamelidae. They figure in the origin of the Hamamelidae, but not in the origin of the angiosperms.

Some authors, such as A. C. Smith (1971), would divide the heterogeneous families Winteraceae and Monimiaceae into sets of smaller and more homogeneous families. Such segregation would contribute to the numerical imbalance of archaic families in favor of Gondwanaland.

Thus, to the extent that modern distribution is meaningful, it suggests that the angiosperms may have originated in Gondwanaland, and more particularly on the Australian plate. The first clear formulation of that concept may have been by Irving Bailey (1949), who advised those interested in the origin of the angiosperms, "Look West, young man, towards the remnants of Gondwanaland!" Against an Australian origin of the angiosperms is the fact that angiosperm pollen in Australia appears significantly later than in West Gondwanaland.

Speculation about a "cradle of the angiosperms" that is based on an assumption of stable continents fixed in their present positions is not meaningful and will be not discussed here.

We should not let our eagerness to find an answer lead us to go beyond our evidence. Given the apparent speed with which early angiosperms moved between Gondwanaland and Laurasia, modern endemism is a weak reed to support any conclusion about the origin of the group. For the present we much endorse the view of Doyle (1978) that "it would be premature to localize the origin of angiosperms on one side of Tethys rather than the other. . . ."

My gut-reaction? Gondwanaland.

Selected References

Arber, A. 1937. The interpretation of the flower: A study of some aspects of morphological thought. Biol. Rev. **12**: 157–184.

Bailey, I. W. 1944. The development of vessels in angiosperms and its significance in morphological research. Amer. J. Bot. **31:** 421–428.

Bailey, I. W. 1949. Origin of the angiosperms: Need for a broadened outlook. J. Arnold Arbor. **30:** 64–70.

Brenner, G. J. 1987. Paleotropical evolution of the Magnoliidae in the Lower Cretaceous of northern Gondwana. Amer. J. Bot. **74:** 677–678.

Burger, W. C. 1981. Why are there so many kinds of flowering plants? BioScience **31:** 572, 577–581.

Carlquist, S. 1962. A theory of paedomorphosis in dicotyledonous woods. Phytomorphology **12:** 30–45.

Chaloner, W. G. 1976. The evolution of adaptive features in fossil exines. Pages 1–13 *in* I. K. Ferguson & J. Muller (eds.), The evolutionary significance of the exine. Academic Press. London.

Chrysler, M. A. 1937. Persistent juveniles among the cycads. Bot. Gaz. **98:** 696–710.

Cornet, B. 1977. Angiosperm-like pollen with tectate-columellate wall structure from the Upper Triassic (and Jurassic) of the Newark supergroup, U.S.A. Amer. Assoc. Strat. Palyn. 10th Annual Meeting, Tulsa. Abstr. 8–9.

Crane, P. R. 1985. Phylogenetic analysis of seed plants and the origin of angiosperms. Ann. Missouri Bot. Gard. **72:** 716–793.

Crepet, W. L. 1984. Advanced (constant) insect pollination mechanisms: Pattern of evolution and implications vis-à-vis angiosperm diversity. Ann. Missouri Bot. Gard. **71:** 607–730.

Cronquist, A., A. Takhtajan & W. Zimmermann. 1966. On the higher taxa of Embryobionta. Taxon **15:** 129–134.

Doyle, J. A. 1969. Cretaceous angiosperm pollen of the Atlantic coastal plain and its evolutionary significance. J. Arnold Arbor. **50:** 1–35.

Doyle, J. A. 1978. Origin of angiosperms. Ann. Rev. Ecol. Syst. **9:** 365–392.

Doyle, J. A. & M. J. Donoghue. 1986. Seed plant phylogeny and the origin of the angiosperms: An experimental cladistic approach. Bot. Rev. **52:** 321–431.

Doyle, J. A. & L. J. Hickey. 1976. Pollen and leaves from the mid-Cretaceous Potomac Group and their bearing on early angiosperm evolution. Pages 139–206 *in* C. B. Beck (ed.), Origin and early evolution of angiosperms. Columbia Univ. Press. New York.

Eckert, G. 1965. Entwicklungsgeschichtliche und blütenanatomische Untersuchungen zum Problem der Obdiplostemonie. Bot. Jahrb. Syst. **85:** 523–604.

Gaussen, H. 1946. Les Gymnospermes, actuelles et fossiles. Trav. Lab. Forest. Toulouse. Tome II, vol. 1, fasc. 3, chap. 5. Les autres Cycadophytes. L'origine cycadophytique des Angiospermes.

Goldschmidt, R. 1940. The material basis of evolution. Yale Univ. Press. New Haven.

Gould, S. J. 1977. Ontogeny and phylogeny. Belknap Press of Harvard Univ. Press. Cambridge, Massachusetts.

Harris, T. M. 1951. The relationships of the Caytoniales. Phytomorphology **1:** 29–39.

Hickey, L. J. 1973. Classification of the architecture of dicotyledonous leaves. Amer. J. Bot. **60:** 17–33.

Krassilov, V. A. 1973. Mesozoic plants and the problem of angiosperm ancestry. Lethaia **6:** 163–178.

Krassilov, V. A. 1977. The origin of angiosperms. Bot. Rev. **43:** 143–176.

Krassilov, V. A. 1984. New paleobotanical data on origin and early evolution of angiospermy. Ann. Missouri Bot. Gard. **71:** 577–592.

Le Thomas, A. 1980–1981. Ultrastructural characters of the pollen grains of African Annonaceae and their significance for the phylogeny of primitive angiosperms. Pollen & Spores **22:** 267–342, 1980; **23:** 5–36, 1981.

Melville, R. 1969. Leaf venation patterns and the origin of the angiosperms. Nature **224:** 121–125.

Meyen, S. V. 1973. Plant morphology in its nomothetical aspects. Bot. Rev. **39:** 205–260.

Meyen, S. V. 1984. Basic features of gymnosperm systematics and phylogeny as evidenced by the fossil record. Bot. Rev. **50:** 1–111.

Muhammad, A. F. & R. Sattler. 1982. Vessel structure of *Gnetum* and the origin of angiosperms. Amer. J. Bot. **69:** 1004–1021.

Nemejc, F. 1956. On the problem of the origin and phylogenetic development of the angiosperms. Acta Mus. Nat. Pragae **12B:** 59–143.

Regal, P. J. 1977. Ecology and evolution of flowering plant dominance. Science **196:** 622–629.

Retallack, G. & D. L. Dilcher. 1981. Arguments for a glossopterid ancestry of angiosperms. Paleobiology **7:** 54–67.

Schuster, R. M. 1972. Continental movements, "Wallace's Line" and Indomalayan dispersal of land plants: Some eclectic concepts. Bot. Rev. **38:** 3–86.

Smith, A. C. 1971 (1972). An appraisal of the orders and families of primitive extant angiosperms. J. Indian Bot. Soc. Golden Jubilee Vol. **50A:** 215–226.

Stebbins, G. L. 1974. Flowering plants. Evolution above the species level. Belknap Press of Harvard Univ. Press. Cambridge, Massachusetts.

Takhtajan, A. L. 1948. Morfologicheskaya evoliutsiya pokrytosemennykh. Izdatel'stvo Mosk. Obshchestva Ispytalel. Prirody. Moskva.

Takhtajan, A. L. 1976. Neoteny and the origin of flowering plants. Pages 207–219 *in* C. B. Beck (ed.), Origin and early evolution of angiosperms. Columbia Univ. Press. New York.

Taylor, T. N. & S. Archangelsky. 1985. The Cretaceous pteridosperms *Ruflorinia* and *Ktalenia* and implications on cupule and carpel evolution. Amer. J. Bot. **72:** 1842–1853.

Thomas, H. H. 1925. The Caytoniales, a new group of angiospermous plants from the Jurassic rocks of Yorkshire. Philos. Trans. Ser. B, **213:** 299–363.

Tiffney, B. H. 1984. Seed size, dispersal syndromes, and the rise of the angiosperms: Evidence and hypothesis. Ann. Missouri Bot. Gard. **71:** 551–576.

Walker, J. W. 1974a. Evolution of exine structure in the pollen of primitive angiosperms. Amer. J. Bot. **61:** 891–902.

Walker, J. W. 1974b. Aperture evolution in the pollen of primitive angiosperms. Amer J. Bot. **61:** 1112–1137.

Walker, J. W. 1976. Evolutionary significance of the exine in the pollen of primitive angiosperms. Pages 251–308 *in* I. K. Ferguson & J. Muller (eds.), The evolutionary significance of the exine. Academic Press. London.

Walker, J. W. & A. G. Walker. 1984. Ultrastructure of Lower Cretaceous angiosperm pollen and the origin and early evolution of flowering plants. Ann. Missouri Bot. Gard. **71:** 464–521.

Westoby, M. & B. Rice. 1982. Evolution of the seed plants and inclusive fitness of plant tissues. Evolution **36:** 713–724.

Willemstein, S. C. 1987. An evolutionary basis for pollination ecology. Doctoral thesis, Rijksuniversiteit of Leiden.

Zavada, M. S. & W. L. Crepet. 1986. Pollen grain wall structure of *Caytonanthus arberi* (Caytoniales). Pl. Syst. Evol. **152:** 259–264.

Zavada, M. S. & T. N. Taylor. 1986. Pollen morphology of Lactoridaceae. Pl. Syst. Evol. **154:** 31–39.

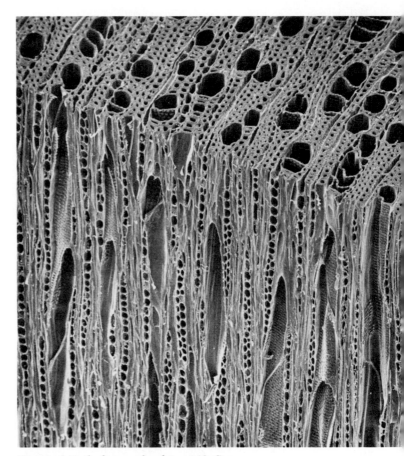

Chapter 5

Wood of *Nothofagus solandri,* ×140. Scanning electron micrograph courtesy of B. A. Meylan and B. G. Butterfield. From "The Structure of New Zealand Woods." 1978.

The Evolution of Characters

The Determination of Primitive Characters and Evolutionary Trends

The idea that organisms show a series of progressive differences from a basic type long antedates any general belief in organic evolution as such. Naturalists of the 17th and 18th centuries were preoccupied with the establishment of a *Scala Naturae* in which every group would have its place according to its relative complexity or advancement. As long ago as 1813, A. P. de Candolle (p. 135) referred to primitive and advanced characters ("Pour connaître le veritable nombre absolu des organs d'une plant, il faut, par la théorie des soudures, ou celle des avortemens, le ramener au nombre qui paraît le type primitif de sa classe . . ."), and he proposed a taxonomic "serie lineare et par conséquent artificielle."

Present-day biologists, steeped in evolutionary tradition, find it hard to see how their predecessors could entertain such thoughts without also grasping the concept of organic evolution. ("We think our fathers fools, so wise we grow; our wiser sons no doubt will think us so.") There were, of course, some stirrings of evolutionary thought long before Darwin, but if de Candolle and others like him had any inklings of evolution, they carefully avoided saying so. They wrote, and seemingly thought, in terms of logically successive modifications from a basic type, sometimes as if they were trying to retrace the steps in the mind of the Creator.

All efforts at a natural system assume that there is a way, if we can discover it, to arrange things into a scheme that is more logical than other possible schemes. We have noted that the establishment of natural groups requires the perception of multiple correlations. The methods of establishing a "natural" sequence among groups of the same rank in such a scheme are purely subjective and intuitive. Differing schemes, once pro-

159

posed, are subjectively judged by how well everything fits into place, and by the number and importance of internal contradictions in the scheme.

As we have noted in an earlier chapter, such concepts of natural relationships are readily transformed into evolutionary concepts. The necessity for every taxon to have a logically possible antecedent is thereby re-emphasized, and a new light is cast on the significance of fossils. However, the consideration of fossils does not change the fact that the propriety of a scheme is judged by how well it provides for the available evidence.

The well known system of Adolf Engler (Fig. 5.1), although pre-evolutionary in origin, was considered by its author to reflect evolutionary relationships among the families and orders of angiosperms. That view, although defensible at the time, is no longer tenable. The system and its concepts do not now meet the test of providing for all the evidence. In the 12th (1964) edition of the Engler Syllabus, Engler's successors in effect admitted that a major reorganization is necessary, and indeed they undertook such a reorganization of the monocotyledons.

The greatest weakness of the Englerian system is that it does not distinguish adequately between primitive simplicity and simplicity through reduction. Inasmuch as most students of the subject now agree that floral reduction has been a pervasive (though not exclusive) trend within the angiosperms, the flaw is fatal.

By 1926 (14a: 136–137) Engler had realized that the flowers of the Amentiferae are simplified rather than primitively simple, and he argued that their extreme reduction indicated the great antiquity of the group. Such an argument misses the whole point of a phylogenetic system. An essential requirement of any phylogenetic system is that one start with the groups which are least modified from the ancestral prototype, rather than with those which have undergone the most change.[1] All groups are of equal age, if one takes in all the ancestors as well as the members of the group. It is only if one bases concepts of age on the members that would actually be referred to a particular group that groups differ in age and a phylogenetic system becomes possible.

The search for a general arrangement and set of principles that will permit everything to fall into place has led taxonomists to revive, modify, and expand the concepts first clearly expounded by de Candolle (Fig. 5.1) in 1813. The treatment by George Bentham (Fig. 5.1) and J. D. Hooker in the *Genera Plantarum* was a lineal descendant of that of de Candolle. Although it was published over a period of years from 1862 to 1883, it was pre-Darwinian in concept, and its authors never claimed anything else. It was, however, an important historical link in the progression from de Candolle's natural system to the avowedly phylogenetic system of C. E. Bessey.

In 1915 Bessey published his epochal paper, "The phylogenetic taxonomy of flowering plants," in which he set forth the principles on which a phylogenetic system should be founded, a list of putatively primitive

---

[1] I here use the term phylogenetic in the traditional taxonomic sense, not in the restricted sense of cladistic theorists.

Fig. 5.1. Some botanists who have made distinguished contributions to the system of classification of angiosperms. TOP LEFT, Augustin Pyramus de Candolle (1778–1841). TOP RIGHT, Adolf Engler (1844–1930). BOTTOM LEFT, George Bentham (1800–1884). BOTTOM RIGHT, Armen L. Takhtajan (1910–).

characters, and an outline of a system incorporating these ideas. Although the system itself is now generally conceded to be faulty in execution, most of his principles (stated as dicta) are widely accepted. (The most notable exception is that alternate leaves are now usually considered to be more primitive than opposite, in contrast to Bessey's view.) We are all—or nearly all—Besseyans.

It is conceivable that some completely new set of concepts will at some future time displace the modified Besseyan concepts now in vogue. The ultimate failure of the very useful and highly regarded Englerian system to be compatible with the accumulating information should inspire some caution about the durability of present ideas. Yet the prognosis is for evolution rather than revolution. Even the replacement of Englerian concepts by Besseyan ones was not such a change as it might seem. Large blocks, and groups of blocks, of the Engler system remain in all present systems, merely rearranged with respect to each other. I choose not to cite some clearly unsuccessful efforts at a revolutionary new interpretation of floral morphology during the past few decades.

One of the principles that Bessey enunciated and which modern taxonomists stress is that within any one phylad the evolution of different organs may proceed at different rates. At any one time any particular group will probably present a mosaic of relatively advanced and relatively primitive characters. One result of this fact is that no one family of angiosperms has all the primitive characters which are known among modern angiosperms; each of the archaic families is more advanced in some respects than in others.

On the other hand, highly primitive and highly advanced characters are seldom mixed helter-skelter. Within very broad limits, primitive characters do tend to be associated, and advanced characters likewise. A plant that is at the bottom of the ladder in one respect is not likely to be on the top rung in others. The Ranalian complex was postulated as primitive on grounds of floral morphology long before the primitive nature of the xylem in so many of its members was even suspected. The statistical correlations among primitive characters established by Sporne were discussed in CHAPTER 1.

In the present taxonomic climate, we cannot omit some consideration of outgroup-comparison, a favorite tool of cladists in establishing polarity of characters. In a sense, outgroup comparison is merely a formalization of what taxonomists have been doing since Darwin (vide Jeffrey, 1983). To determine polarity as between character states A and B, in a given taxon, we look at the situation in related taxa. We cannot simply say, however, that if the outgroup shows only character state A, then character state B must be derived (apomorphic). Perhaps the outgroup had both character states in the past, but the species with state B have all become extinct. Given the pervasive parallelism in so many characters of angiosperms, we cannot dismiss or even minimize such a possibility. We must instead try to fit concepts of polarity into a logically plausible evolutionary scheme that is compatible with the evidence.

We have a special problem in applying the method of outgroup-comparison to angiosperms as a whole. To what should we compare them? One would get very different results by using the modern representatives of the Cycadicae, Pinicae, or Gneticae as the outgroup. If we use them all, they cancel each other out. There simply is no modern group that can be accepted as a conceptually useful sister-group to the angiosperms. If the views put forward in this book are correct, then the cycads may provide the best comparison, but the two groups do not connect phyletically short of the Paleozoic seed-ferns. The fossil record of angiosperms flatly contradicts the idea that compound leaves are primitive in the group, yet that is the conclusion we would reach by using the cycads as the outgroup.

Neither can we afford to be closely constrained by considerations of parsimony. Here again, parallelism is the undoing of the criterion. Given the amount of parallelism among the angiosperms, small differences in parsimony between alternative phylogenetic schemes are scarcely significant. We must seek a phylogenetic scheme that makes sense, parsimonious or not. If one of two otherwise equally plausible schemes is much more parsimonious than the other, then of course the more parsimonious scheme is preferred. William of Occam was perfectly correct in saying that explanations should not be unnecessarily complicated.

Often our efforts to establish polarity must depend on the mental reconstruction of a logically plausible ancestor for the group. Better to have something logically plausible than something implausible, of course. Yet we should always be cautious about the probable accuracy of such reconstructions. As Ledyard Stebbins has pointed out in conversation, it is highly unlikely that we could properly reconstruct classical Latin from a study of the modern Romance languages. For one thing, it would probably never occur to us that Latin had no articles. Likewise, it may well be that some of the characters of the original angiosperms have completely disappeared. Still, a flawed scheme may be better than none, so long as we recognize the possibility of error. We should realize that the game is crooked, but also that it is the only game in town.

To recapitulate, all ideas of what is primitive and what is advanced depend ultimately on how well these ideas fit into a coherent scheme in which every character has a logically possible evolutionary history, and every group has a logically possible ancestor. The best evidence on polarity, when we can get it, comes from the fossils. The fossil record as now understood puts significant constraints on interpretations of polarity in the angiosperms, but many of the tentative conclusions must be based on less direct, less reliable evidence.

Characters of the Primitive Angiosperms

If the evolution of the angiosperms from their gymnospermous (perhaps Caytonialean) ancestors followed the now familiar pattern of parallel developments in a set of closely related lines, there may never have been an original angiosperm that was ancestral to all other angiosperms. Each of the several features that collectively mark the angiosperms as a natural group may well have evolved separately in different lines, and separately in each line from the other critical characters, with only a loose overall correlation among the different advances.

Indeed this is exactly what seems to have happened with regard to the xylem, phloem, and gross structure of the flower. Diverse surviving members of the archaic subclass Magnoliidae retain one or more primitive (presumably ancestral) features, but are more advanced in other respects. The Winteraceae and some other small families do not have vessels, but do have sieve-tubes. The Winteraceae have uniporate rather than the presumably primitive monosulcate pollen, and stages in closure of the carpel can be seen in living species. *Austrobaileya* has vessels, monosulcate pollen, and closed carpels, but it has a very primitive, gymnosperm-like phloem, with elongate, overlapping sieve-elements that do not form typical sieve-tubes. *Degeneria* has laminar stamens, monosulcate pollen, and unsealed carpels that have the ovules on the adaxial surface, but it has vessels and sieve-tubes. Other examples could be given.

Double fertilization, the extreme reduction of the female gametophyte, and germination of the pollen grain at some distance from the ovule are characteristic angiosperm features that are regularly present in archaic as well as advanced living members of the group. These features are not known in living gymnosperms,[2] and they may be regarded as definitive angiosperm characters. There is no good reason to believe, however, that they evolved in any different way from the anatomical and gross floral characters. Germination of the pollen grain remote from the ovule is obviously concomitant with the closure of the carpel, and the later stages of this process can still be seen among living angiosperms. Unexpected things are not necessarily always impossible, but it is not to be expected that the fossil record can ever provide evidence on the origin of double fertilization. Stages in the reduction of the female gametophyte might conceivably be preserved, however, in some as yet undiscovered fossils connecting angiosperms to the ancestral gymnosperms.

If we accept the heterochronic origin of the angiosperm flower from a gymnosperm strobilus, as cautiously suggested in the previous chapter, then it is conceivable that the whole series of events leading to the evolution of angiosperms might have resulted from a single Goldschmidtian mutation in a gene regulating strobilar growth. It stretches credulity beyond the breaking point, however, to suppose that such a mutation would immediately establish also the characteristic male and female gametophytes and double fertilization of angiosperms. A strictly monophyletic origin of the angiosperms can be envisaged only if we take the postulated heterochronic condensation of the strobilus as the critical defining feature. The syndrome of floral and vegetative features characterizing the angiosperms as we know them took shape only through parallel evolution in a set of related taxa.

Only a few of the characters of the primitive angiosperms can be es-

---

[2] In a few gymnosperms the pollen can germinate successfully on the cone-scale adjacent to the ovule, but it still does not have far to go to get to the micropyle.

tablished on the basis of the fossil record. We can be reasonably sure that they were tropical woody plants with simple, entire leaves that had a poorly organized pinnate net venation. The pollen-grains were ellipsoid (the shape of an American football) and monosulcate. The size of the early fossil grains and their surface ornamentation suggest insect-pollination rather than wind-pollination. If we accept the suggestion provided by the cupules of *Caytonia*, the ovules were anatropous and bitegmic. All of these ideas about the characters of primitive angiosperms, except for the poor organization of the leaf-venation, were conceived by a number of phylogenists prior to any proper interpretation of the fossil record. They were expounded, for example, by Takhtajan in 1959 and by myself in the first (1968) edition of this book. The fossils now give us some confidence that the conclusions reached by extrapolation from modern taxa are indeed correct.

Concepts of polarity in other characters of angiosperms are necessarily based on a comparison of extant taxa. Such comparison must of course be done with due attention to the condition in various gymnosperms, and to the establishment of an internally consistent phylogenetic scheme that provides for all the data.

In spite of the fact that such a plant probably never existed, it is useful to think of a hypothetical primitive angiosperm which had all the primitive features now shown in diverse living angiosperms, but which did not have any characters not shown in living angiosperms. The evolutionary trends may then be considered character by character, and we may eventually arrive at a better understanding of the relationships among the families and orders of the group.

This hypothetical primitive angiosperm was an evergreen woody plant (not necessarily a tree) of moist, tropical places with an equable climate. It had alternate, simple, entire, exstipulate leaves with pinnate net venation of a poorly organized sort. The stomates were paracytic, or of mixed and unstable types. The nodes were unilacunar with two leaf-traces, or perhaps trilacunar with three traces. It had an active cambium, with elongate, vertically overlapping initials, but the wood had no vessels and no pronounced annual rings. The tracheids were very long and slender, with long, tapering ends and numerous scalariform-bordered pits—altogether fern-like. The wood parenchyma was diffuse, and both uniseriate and multiseriate rays were present. The phloem had elongate, vertically overlapping sieve-elements with lateral sieve-areas, but no terminal sieve-plate; thus there were no true sieve-tubes.

The flowers were borne singly at the ends of leafy branches, and were relatively large, with numerous, spirally arranged, somewhat leaf-like tepals. One might say, with equal propriety, that the perianth was not differentiated into calyx and corolla, or that the perianth consisted wholly of sepals, with no petals. The stamens were numerous, spirally arranged, relatively large, and laminar, with no differentiation into filament and anther. The microsporangia were embedded in the broad, flat, sessile blade of the stamen. The tepals, stamens and carpels may all have had three leaf-traces and three primary veins each, from trilacunar nodes, or some of them may have had the more primitive double trace from a unilacunar node, like the leaves.

The pollen-grains were ellipsoid, with a single long sulcus. The exine had a raised-reticulate surface ornamentation; internally it may have been either solid or more probably tectate-granular. The grains were binucleate at the time of transfer. The division of the generative cell to form two sperms occurred after the germination of the grain. Pollination may have been effected by beetles that chewed and ate parts of the flower.[3] There were no nectaries and no nectar.

The flower had several or many separate carpels, each probably stipitate at the base, the stipe being equivalent to the petiole of the leaf. Each carpel was folded along the midrib so that the margins were brought together and the morphologically upper (adaxial) surface was concealed. The margins of the carpel were merely loosely appressed to each other rather than anatomically joined, and the ovules were probably borne on the inner surface of the unsealed carpel. The margins of the carpel bore a tangle of glandular hairs so that the carpel, although anatomically unsealed, was effectively closed. These hairs formed, in effect, an elongate stigma, on which the pollen-grains germinated. The fruit opened at maturity, releasing the seeds.

The ovules were anatropous, each with two integuments and a massive nucellus. There were several or rather many potentially sporogenous cells in the young ovule, although only one of these went on to produce an embryo-sac. The embryo-sac was of the familiar, monosporic, eight-nucleate type. Double fertilization occurred, leading to the formation of a copious, triploid endosperm and a small embryo that was still immature at the time of ripening and discharge of the seed. The endosperm was probably of the nuclear type, i.e., it had a free-nuclear stage in early ontogeny. The embryo had two or possibly several cotyledons, and germination was epigaeal, i.e., the cotyledons were brought above the ground during germination.

A plant with the foregoing features would not fit into any modern family, but it would fit well enough into the order Magnoliales. We cannot now visualize in any detail what a pre-Magnolialean angiosperm might have been like.

HABITAT AND GROWTH HABIT

It seems clearly established that the tropics are the original home of the angiosperms. Both the fossil record and the less direct lines of evidence lead to the same conclusion.

All the pre-Albian and early Albian fossil angiosperm pollen and leaves come from regions that were tropical at the time. Axelrod (1959) considered that the fossil record shows a gradual expansion of angiosperms from

---

[3] The beetle-pollination syndrome in angiosperms is certainly ancient, but it may not be absolutely basal. See pages 217–218.

tropical regions into progressively cooler ones. Hickey and Doyle (1977) agree in principle with Axelrod's interpretation, with some refinements in detail that do not concern us at this point.

By far the largest number of species of angiosperms occur in the tropics. A large proportion of these species are highly frost-sensitive. The frost-line, south of which (in the Northern Hemisphere) freezing temperatures never occur at ordinary altitudes, is a very real barrier to the northward spread of tropical plants. To most species, the barrier is insurmountable. At sea level the frost-line lies a little north of the Tropic of Cancer, and it crosses Florida near the southern tip of the state. A similar frost-line lies near the Tropic of Capricorn in the Southern Hemisphere. Between these two frost-lines the angiosperms are represented by great hordes of species, and every botanical expedition into the less frequented areas still brings back its quota of "new" species. As one crosses the frost-line and moves toward the pole, the number of species of angiosperms per unit area progressively decreases, and probably not more than a thousand species occur north of the Arctic Circle. A similar thinning out occurs in the Southern Hemisphere.

Resistance to cold is clearly an adaptation in the angiosperms, not an ancestral feature. This adaptation takes two principal forms, both of which are commonly shown by the same species. The first and most important is a physiological resistance to the harmful effect of freezing temperatures. The second is some means of reducing transpiration when the soil is frozen. Another adaptation found in many species is the development of strengthening tissues that reduces the likelihood of mechanical damage when the leaf is physiologically wilted.

Direct resistance to the effect of low temperature is a continuously variable character among the angiosperms as a whole, ranging from complete frost-sensitivity to an ability to survive temperatures well below 40 degrees below zero (on either the Fahrenheit or the Celsius scale) in arctic and antarctic species. Several factors contribute, in varying combinations, to this type of resistance. Among them are: (1) increase in osmotic potential and thus direct resistance to freezing; (2) increased resistance to coagulation of the protein when desiccated; (3) increased permeability of the plasma membrane to water, permitting ice to form in intercellular spaces instead of within the cell; and (4) decreased structural viscosity of the protoplasm, making it less susceptible to mechanical injury by ice crystals.

Freezing of the soil during the winter makes the soil water much less available to plant roots and thus causes a physiological drought. Winter-killing of plants is often due to desiccation resulting from this drought, rather than to the direct effect of low temperature. Anything that reduces transpiration therefore promotes resistance to frost-injury.

The deciduous habit, the herbaceous habit, and the sclerophyllous habit are all adaptations to a climate in which vegetative activity cannot be carried on uninterruptedly throughout the year. Leaves give up their water to the air much faster than the stem, which has a smaller surface/volume ratio and is likely to be more fully waterproofed. If green leaves are to be retained throughout the winter (or dry season), they must be able to go into a dormant state and withstand a high degree of desiccation. Such leaves commonly have a high proportion of strengthening tissue and are known as sclerophylls. Without this strengthening tissue they would doubtless be much more subject to fragmentation during the dry season.

In moist, tropical regions with an equable climate, growth is often continuous. New leaves are always forming, and old ones are always falling. The terminal bud never goes into a prolonged state of dormancy, and it has no specialized bud-scales. Some species have periodic flushes of growth, followed by relative quiescence, even when moisture is plentiful, but even these species generally remain green throughout the year.

Different seasonal water-relations call forth different evolutionary responses in growth-habit. In moist, temperate regions (with a definite winter), or in tropical regions with alternating wet and dry seasons, the deciduous habit allows trees to make the best use of the effective growing season. If the dry season is too severe, or if the wet season is not wet enough, the deciduous habit does not furnish an adequate buffer against desiccation, and perennial herbs (often grasses) are favored instead. In desert country, where the dry season may be both severe and prolonged, annual herbs are favored. These can survive the dry season, or several years of drought, in the form least vulnerable to death by desiccation— as seeds. The sclerophyllous habit in angiosperms is favored chiefly in regions with a Mediterranean climate—one characterized by moist, mild winters, and hot, dry summers. Warm deserts also frequently have many small-leaved sclerophylls. Succulents are favored by moderate to fairly severe water-stress in warm regions. I do not mean to suggest a mutually exclusive partitioning of the land-surface for different growth habits according to water-relations and temperature. Succulents, small-leaved sclerophylls, and annual herbs get along well together in warm deserts, and other habitats likewise support plants of different habit. My point is that once we get away from the species-rich moist tropics, dominated by evergreen angiosperm trees, environmental conditions call forth the evolution of different growth-habits (according to the climate), often with fewer species per unit-area. In the dicotyledons, these diverse growth-habits can all be interpreted in terms of changes from ancestral tropical evergreens.

In addition to the seasonal climates noted above as favoring the deciduous habit, Hickey (personal communication) has recently suggested a third possibility. He considers that the deciduous habit may well have originated in the late Cretaceous and early Tertiary at high latitudes in response to seasonal darkness, even in tropical conditions without a winter or a dry season. It may be so, but that does not exclude other possibilities. The deciduous habit has doubtless originated several or even many times.

Trees in temperate regions typically produce all their leaves in a burst of growth in the spring. The leaves are preformed in the winter-bud, and they quickly expand to full size at the beginning of the growing season. Following this rapid growth, the apical meristem goes dormant and forms a winter-bud that is covered and protected by characteristic modified bud-scales. The leaves that have been formed in the spring remain on the tree all summer and are shed at the approach of winter.

The common tulip tree (*Liriodendron tulipifera,* Magnoliaceae, Fig. 5.2) occurs in temperate regions and shows winter-dormancy, but it betrays its tropical ancestry by its pattern of growth. The well developed stipules cover and protect the growing bud, and there are no other bud-scales. New leaves are produced throughout the growing season, and the first-formed leaves of the year are already dropping in June. Growth merely stops in the fall, and is resumed in the spring. The pair of stipules that covers the bud all winter becomes somewhat sclerified, but they are otherwise unmodified. The first two or three leaves that open in the spring do not attain full size, but they are otherwise normal.

The Salicaceae show a closer approach to the typical behavior of deciduous trees. They have ordinary winter-buds with one or more bud-scales and with preformed embryonic leaves, but after these leaves have expanded in the spring the bud continues to grow, producing new leaves during much or all of the growing season. The leaves are usually all retained until the general leaf-fall in the autumn.

It seems obvious that *Liriodendron* and the Salicaceae represent successive way-stations between the typical tropical growth-pattern and the typical temperate one. This is not to suggest that the two groups are closely related; indeed they are not. Here as elsewhere, similar changes have occurred repeatedly in diverse groups.

An interesting factor that tends to confirm both the woody habit and the tropical habitat of the ancestral angiosperms comes in the probable relationships of the herbaceous and temperate-zone groups to woody and tropical ones. Over and over, it appears that herbs are derived from trees, that temperate groups are derived from tropical ones, and, in combination, that herbaceous groups of temperate regions are derived from woody tropical groups. Thus the largely temperate and herbaceous Apiaceae (Umbelliferae) come from the mainly tropical and woody Araliaceae, and there is indeed no very sharp line between the two families. Within the Fabales, the relatively archaic family Caesalpiniaceae is largely tropical and woody, and the most advanced family, the Fabaceae, is mostly temperate and herbaceous. Likewise the Brassicaceae (Cruciferae), mostly herbaceous and of temperate regions, relate to the more archaic family Capparaceae, a largely tropical and subtropical group with many woody members. Botanists whose experience is concentrated in the North Temperate Zone may think of the Boraginaceae as a temperate, herbaceous group with a gynobasic style, but the more archaic members of the family, such as *Cordia,* are tropical woody plants with a terminal style.

It should be emphasized that the evolution of herbs from trees and the adaptation of tropical groups to colder climates has occurred not just once, but many times. In general, it may be said that the herbaceous groups of angiosperms relate not directly to each other, but separately to the woody "core" of the division. Among important recent authors, Hutchinson (e.g., 1973) was the only one to disagree on this matter. He believed in an early and fundamental dichotomy between herbaceous and

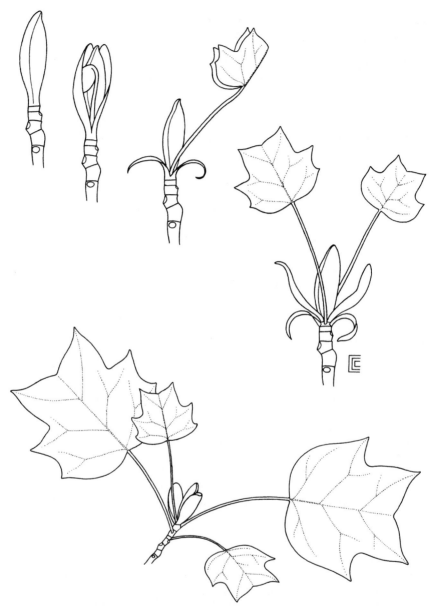

Fig. 5.2. *Liriodendron tulipifera*, the tulip tree. Successive stages in the development of a winter bud at the beginning of the growing season.

woody angiosperms. The effects of this belief on his system of classification contributed substantially to the fact that his system was never widely adopted.

These separate herbaceous groups are of all ranks, from species to class. The genus *Cornus* (Fig. 5.3), with about 50 species, is mostly woody, but it has two essentially herbaceous species, *C. canadensis* and *C. suecica,* which clearly have a woody ancestry within the broadly defined genus. Here the evolution of herbaceous species has occurred within the temperate zone, rather than concomitantly with a migration from the tropics. The large family Rubiaceae is chiefly tropical and woody, but two small tribes, the Rubieae and Spermacoceae, are chiefly herbaceous and have many temperate as well as tropical species. The Primulaceae are chiefly herbaceous and occur mainly in temperate and warm-temperate regions, but the other two families (Myrsinaceae and Theophrastaceae) generally referred to the Primulales are both tropical and woody. The order Campanulales is largely herbaceous and occurs both in tropical and temperate regions. The ancestry of this well marked order is to be sought in the complex of sympetalous orders that has often been called the Tubiflorae, which has woody, herbaceous, tropical and temperate members, the woody forms being mostly tropical. The whole class Liliopsida (monocotyledons) is largely herbaceous, although there are some woody members of a special type, such as the palms. The origin of the monocots is to be sought in the archaic subclass Magnoliidae of the dicotyledons. The more archaic members of the Magnoliidae are woody.

Aside from the Nymphaeales, about which more anon, herbaceous dicots seem to have been few and rare before the latest Cretaceous. The fossil dicot leaves found in Cretaceous deposits mostly appear to have been abscised intact from the stems—a feature of woody rather than herbaceous plants. Because much of the Cretaceous fossil pollen is not clearly assignable to a family, we cannot be sure how much of it may have been produced by herbs, but pollen that can be identified with herbaceous groups of dicots does not become common until about the beginning of the Miocene epoch. Thus the fossil record is compatible with and gives some support to the idea that in dicots the woody habit is primitive and the herbaceous habit derived. The status of the monocots as a very early herbaceous offshoot of woody dicotyledons is discussed in a subsequent section.

Because herbaceous angiosperms are evidently derived from woody ones, it is easy to fall into the error that all woody plants are primitively woody, and therefore more archaic than any herbaceous relatives they may have. We have become accustomed to the idea that evolutionary trends are essentially irreversible, and that a character once lost is never regained, at least not in the same form. These comfortable thoughts have a factual basis, but they are not strictly and universally correct.

Evolutionary trends have all degrees of stability, from those which are so vague and subject to reversal that they can scarcely be recognized as trends, to those which fasten an inescapable grip on the destiny of the

Fig. 5.3. *Cornus florida,* the flowering dogwood (LEFT), an arborescent species, and *Cornus canadensis,* the dwarf cornel (RIGHT), an herbaceous species. Photo of *C. canadensis* courtesy of Charles C. Johnson. Inset photo *C. florida* by W. H. Shaffer, U.S. Forest Service.

group. Reduction of the gametophyte appears to be a universal trend in vascular plants, although a new twist is given to this trend in those angiosperms that have more than eight nuclei in an embryo-sac. Many stable and persistent trends are known in the animal kingdom. These are often associated with progressive specialization and adaptation to an ecological

niche or zone, and the trend is obviously driven by natural selection. As we have seen, the correlation of major taxa of angiosperms with ecologic niches is often obscure, and irreversible trends of specialization are correspondingly less frequent and conspicuous. It is interesting to note that one of the most tantalizing and thoroughly documented evolutionary reversals in the animal kingdom relates to a character whose adaptive significance is obscure—the progressive coiling and uncoiling of the shells of certain ammonites during the Paleozoic era.

Returning to the question of woody versus herbaceous angiosperms, I think it is clear enough that the herbaceous habit has its advantages for certain habitats. Thus the change from woody to herbaceous could well be driven by natural selection. However, we have noted that the evolutionary barriers between different niches for angiosperms are relatively low and easily crossed. So long as they retain the genetic potentiality for secondary growth, herbs have the evolutionary opportunity to reverse their field and become woody plants. The possibility of such a reversal depends on how much of the genetic mechanism has been lost. Some herbs have no cambium at all, some have cambium within the vascular bundles but not between them, and others have a complete cambial cylinder that connects the vascular bundles as well as passing through them.

Many herbaceous Asteraceae fall into this last group, with a complete cambial cylinder, and furthermore the cambium is very active and produces a considerable amount of secondary tissue. Arthur Eames once remarked to me that *Solidago* is a perfectly good woody plant, so far as the cambium and secondary xylem are concerned. It is an herb only because the stem dies down to the ground every year. There is a lovely story about an American wood anatomist of some decades ago who claimed to be able to recognize any arborescent genus in the world by its wood. Another botanist, with deliberate dissimulation, cut down a vigorous specimen of the common sunflower (*Helianthus annuus*) late in the season and sent a piece of xylem for identification. He was delighted to learn that his plant was an African leguminous tree.

It should not be surprising if some herbs that have retained most of the necessary genetic information should revert to the woody habit. Indeed this appears to have happened several times in the Asteraceae, to mention only one family. The more obvious examples, however, have only gone back so far as to become shrubs (e.g., *Chrysothamnus, Olearia, Baccharis,* spp. of *Artemisia*). Each of these cited groups ties back into the rest of the family through related herbaceous rather than woody taxa. There are also some apparently primitively woody members of the archaic tribe Heliantheae in this family.

Only a few sizable dicotyledonous trees can pretty clearly be assigned an herbaceous ancestry. Stebbins (1974) has pointed to *Phytolacca dioica* (Phytolaccaceae) and several species of *Pisonia* (Nyctaginaceae) as examples. Woody members of these families have anomalous secondary growth, producing alternating concentric rings of xylem and phloem from successive cambia that originate de novo in the pericycle. It is the nature of the secondary growth which gives us some confidence that the woody habit reflects a reversion. Perhaps we would not usually recognize the reversion in a tree with normal secondary growth. Among the monocots, the palms very probably have an herbaceous ancestry, but their anatomy is wholly different from that of typical trees.

It has been suggested that the herbaceous habit originates from the woody one by heterochrony, i.e., the plant flowers while still vegetatively juvenile, and the later stages of vegetative ontogeny are curtailed or postponed out of existence. It is certainly true that it is the secondary xylem which makes woody stems woody, and that in the very youngest stages, before the cambium has begun to function, a woody stem often has essentially the same anatomy as an herbaceous one, with epidermis, cortex, and a ring of vascular bundles separated by medullary rays which connect the cortex to the pith. Conceptually, then, a tree evolves into an herb by blooming and dying (or dying back to the ground) while still vegetatively juvenile.

Heterochrony is not the whole story, however. The evolutionary progression in modern families is commonly from trees to arborescent shrubs to smaller shrubs to perennial herbs. Thus there is a progressive decrease in the size of the mature plant. To some extent this change in size reflects a decrease in the age at which the growth curve flattens out, and thus it might still be interpreted as a sort of heterochrony, but such an extension of the meaning of the term tends to rob it of its conceptual utility.

Heterochrony can also be invoked to explain the change from herbaceous perennial to annual duration. Most perennials do not flower until they are several years old. Some flower the first year, however, and year after year thereafter. Such plants are potentially annual, for if they were killed at the end of the first year the life cycle would continue unbroken and they would be functioning as annuals. The cultivated tomato is such a plant. Perennial in its native habitat, it is cultivated in temperate regions as an annual, succumbing to frost at the approach of winter. The common perennial plantain (*Plantago major*) also blooms the first year and thus can function as an annual.

It has traditionally been supposed that the primitive angiosperms were trees. Certainly one can see all transitions among modern angiosperms from large trees to medium-sized or small trees to arborescent shrubs to smaller shrubs to perennial herbs and then annual herbs. Under the simple and logical assumption of a basic unidirectionality in the major evolutionary changes in habit, the trees would be considered to be primitive, and the other types progressively more advanced. The occasional reversal from herbaceous to woody habit could then be dismissed as evolutionary noise.

Now things appear to be more complex. Stebbins (1965, 1974) has suggested that the earliest angiosperms, or their immediate gymnospermous predecessors, were shrubs rather than trees, that they grew in semiarid or seasonally dry tropical habitats, and that their leaves were strongly reduced in size and venation in association with the habitat. Up to the present, these proto-angiospermous xerophytes are purely hypothetical. We have no evidence of them in the fossil record. Doyle and Hickey (1976) and Hickey and Doyle (1977) tentatively accept Stebbins' proposal, and add that the immediate successors to these plants were riparian shrubs in which the leaves were again expanded under conditions of a more ample and assured water supply. Of this latter group we have abundant fossil evidence.

There is a certain logic to this two-part hypothesis. Climates suitable for xerophytic shrubs evidently existed in the Jurassic and early Cretaceous in the parts of Gondwanaland represented by the modern continents of Africa and South America. Such xerophytes might be able to compete with then-existing long-lived gymnosperms in unstable habitats requiring rapid maturation for survival. Depositional evidence indicates that the early angiosperm fossils of the Potomac deposits in the present eastern United States grew in unstable habitats, specifically stream-margins. The area was at that time tropical or subtropical, bordering on the Tethys Sea and not far distant from Gondwanaland. In these riparian habitats, shrubs would certainly have a better chance to mature and reproduce than trees. The peculiar venation of these early leaf fossils (further discussed in a subsequent section) can easily be interpreted as reflecting expansion of a previously small and xeromorphic leaf. The early appearance in the record of probable monocots and the aquatic herbs that foreshadow the modern Nymphaeales (discussed later) is easier to fit into the picture if their immediate ancestors were riparian shrubs rather than forest trees. The idea is further strengthened if the monocots were, as I believe, aquatic in origin. For whatever it may be worth, we may note that the growth habit of archaic modern angiosperms such as the Magnoliales is just as compatible with a shrubby as with an arborescent ancestry for the angiosperms; both shrubs and trees are well represented in the group.

This set of speculations about the historical development of the growth habit of early angiosperms is of course just that. Aside from the virtual certainty of a woody ancestry for the group, we have no clear proof for the scheme. What we do have is a logically coherent and phyletically plausible hypothesis that provides for the available evidence, some of which is otherwise difficult to explain. It is certainly more satisfying than anything we might come up with by relying on outgroup comparison.

ARRANGEMENT AND STRUCTURE OF THE LEAVES

Arrangement

The fossil record as now known does not indicate the ancestral arrangement of the leaves in angiosperms. Lower Cretaceous fossils showing the attachment of leaves to stems are not numerous. What few we have include both alternate- and opposite-leaved types, going back about equally far into the Aptian. No conclusion can be drawn on this evidence.

The concept that angiosperm leaves are primitively alternate (spirally arranged) rather than opposite or whorled rests essentially on the fact that alternate leaves appear to be basic for most vascular plants, with the notable exception of the Equisetophyta. Derivation of monopodial branching from the ancestral dichotomous branching of the rhyniophytes, by unequal growth and overtopping, leads naturally to an alternate arrangement of the appendages of the stem.

Among the angiosperms as a whole, alternate leaves are much more common than opposite ones, and the opposite-leaved forms are scattered at various places on the evolutionary tree rather than being concentrated in the Magnoliidae or any other one group. The main trunk of the family tree of angiosperms consists of alternate-leaved rather than opposite-leaved groups. Whorled leaves are still less common and need not be considered as potentially primitive within the angiosperms.

The origin of opposite leaves from alternate ones is not an immutable trend. Like some other trends, it is subject to reversal for no obvious reason. Within the large family Asteraceae, it is perfectly clear that opposite leaves are primitive and alternate leaves are advanced. Many species, such as the common sunflower (*Helianthus annuus*) represent a transitional stage, with the lower leaves opposite and the upper ones alternate. Members of the tribe Heliantheae show a progressive heterochronic advancement of the time of transition from early opposite-leaved growth to later alternate-leaved growth.

Although most of Bessey's dicta on evolutionary trends in angiosperms are still regarded as sound, he erred (or so we now believe) in considering opposite leaves to be primitive. His conclusion reflects an overemphasis of the principle of recapitulation applied to the fact that the cotyledons of dicots are opposite. The recapitulation principle ("Ontogeny is a recapitulation of phylogeny") often provides useful hints as to the course of evolution, but it is so beset with exceptions and special cases that it should never be regarded as definitive. The opposite position of the cotyledons in dicots may reflect nothing more than the suppression of the first internode in a very condensed embryo.

The adaptive significance of changes in the arrangement of leaves is obscure.

Form and Venation of the Blade

The simple, entire, pinnately net-veined leaf has been postulated as primitive within the angiosperms by many botanists. If there has been any recent dissent, it has not been loud. As long ago as 1915 Bessey considered the simple, net-veined leaf to be primitive in the group.

Simple, entire, pinnately net-veined leaves are by far the most common type in the woody members of the archaic subclass Magnoliidae. A plant may be primitive in some respects and more advanced in others, but on a statistical basis primitive characters do tend to hang together, and a plant that is primitive in several respects has a good chance of being primitive also in the next feature to be considered. It has therefore seemed reasonable to suppose, in the absence of any significant evidence to the contrary, that the common leaf-type in the woody members of the Magnoliidae (under whatever name) is the primitive type for angiosperms as a whole.

Now the fossil record gives strong support to the conclusions based on neontological evidence. All of the pre-Albian angiosperm fossil leaves are simple, and most of them are entire and pinnately net-veined. The step-by-step origin of pinnately lobed and then pinnately compound leaves in the putative forerunners of the Rosidae can be traced in the Albian segment of the Potomac deposits. Palmate venation and palmate lobing also appear in the Albian, notably in some platanoid fossils that may be forerunners of the modern Hamamelidae (Hickey & Doyle, 1977).

The dichotomous, free, Ginkgo-like venation of the leaves of *Circaeaster* and *Kingdonia* is more easily explained as a modification that simulates an ancient pattern than as a primitive survival. The family Circaeasteraceae, consisting of these two monotypic herbaceous genera, is referred to the Ranunculales, but is considered to be advanced in its orthotropous, unitegmic, tenuinucellate ovules and reduced, apetalous flowers. A formal out-group comparison supporting this evolutionary interpretation of leaf-venation in the family could doubtless be produced, but it would only document the obvious.

What was not postulated by comparison of modern species is the nature of the pinnate venation in most of the earliest angiosperm leaves. The primary lateral veins are of unequal size, they arise from the midvein at irregular distances, and they diverge at various angles. Branching and

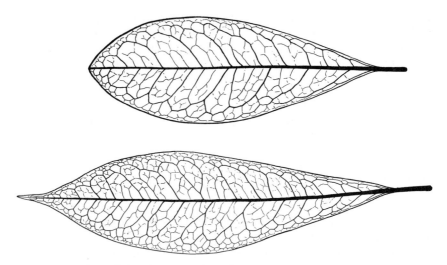

Fig. 5.4.   Leaves of *Zygogynum pancheri* (ABOVE), and *Drimys piperita* (BELOW), showing irregularly pinnate venation characteristic of the Winteraceae and many Lower Cretaceous angiosperms. Drawings by Bobbi Angell.

anastomosing from these primary lateral veins are also irregular, producing areolae of irregular size and shape. The best comparison with modern leaves is to those of some members of the Winteraceae (Fig. 5.4). In the Potomac deposits a regular progression can be traced from such leaves to leaves with a more complex and regularly organized venation. I do not suggest that the plants producing these leaves with irregular venation should be assigned to the Winteraceae, but only that the modern Winteraceae have retained this particular primitive feature from the distant past. Each of the families of the Magnoliales has its own combination of primitive and more advanced features.

The fossil record with regard to leaf venation is compelling. The question is, what does the record mean in terms of the ancestry of the angiosperms? As we have noted, Hickey and Doyle suggest that the poorly organized venation reflects expansion of a previously small and xeromorphic leaf, under more favorable moisture-conditions. Their explanation is plausible, and I don't know of any other.

The documented origin of compound leaves from simple ones during the late Lower Cretaceous does not justify automatic assumptions about the polarity of simple and compound leaves in particular groups of modern angiosperms. Each group must be studied on its own before a conclusion can properly be reached. Some go one way, and some the other.

Some compound-leaved species or genera have obviously originated from simple-leaved ancestors within their own family during the Tertiary, quite independently of anything that may have happened in Albian pre-Rosids. It can hardly be otherwise with the compound-leaved species of *Bidens, Coreopsis,* and *Cosmos,* in the Asteraceae. This basically simple-leaved family makes its first appearance in the fossil record (as dispersed pollen) near the end of the Oligocene. *Pedicularis,* in the Scrophulariaceae, likewise appears to have originated from simple-leaved ancestors in its own family, as does *Polemonium,* in the Polemoniaceae. Other examples could be cited.

The compound leaves characteristic of the Fabales and Sapindales may well trace back to the Albian pre-Rosids, but in both of these orders there are some modern members with secondarily simple leaves. In the legumes the compound leaf has repeatedly been reduced to a unifoliolate leaf, and the joint at the base of the remaining leaflet may then be suppressed, so that the leaf is truly simple. All stages, for example, exist in the single genus *Crotalaria,* but it is not to be supposed that other simple-leaved legumes take their origin in *Crotalaria.* They relate to individual other genera instead. The simple, palmately lobed leaves of *Acer* (Sapindales) must surely have a compound-leaved ancestry. Likewise the simple leaves of *Cotinus,* in the mainly compound-leaved family Anacardiaceae. Within the species *Rhus aromatica* (Anacardiaceae) we can trace the origin of simple leaves in var. *simplicifolia* from the trifoliolate leaves of var. *trilobata.*

The repeated origin of compound leaves from simple ones, and simple leaves from compound ones, should dissuade phylogenists from assigning overwhelming importance to this one character. Like other characters, it works when it works, and doesn't work when it doesn't work. Its importance in any particular group depends on its correlation with other characters. Thus, the compound leaves of the Juglandales should certainly be taken into account in any assessment of probable relationships, but they do not preclude the association of this order with the otherwise mainly simple-leaved subclass Hamamelidae. There is some difference of opinion about whether the Urticales should be included in the Hamamelidae, but no one proposes the exclusion of *Cannabis,* with palmately compound leaves, from this otherwise mainly simple-leaved order.

Efforts have been made to interpret simple and compound leaves in terms of adaptive significance. There is something in this, but perhaps not very much. I can see that pioneer trees in disturbed habitats might reap some advantage from having large leaves that quickly fill in the available space in the sun. From the standpoint of architectural engineering, such leaves might better be compound, so that wind-resistance is minimized. *Cecropia,* a tropical pioneer tree, comes to mind. In *Cecropia* the leaves are technically simple, but so deeply lobed that functionally they are palmately compound. Doubtless there are other niches in which either simple or compound leaves are favored, but there are many habitats in which the two do equally well.

The widespread climax oak-hickory forest in eastern United States illustrates the latter point. Oak-leaves are simple, and hickory-leaves compound. Trees of the two genera commonly grow intermingled, are similar in gross aspect, and appear to be making their living in the same way. Individual species of both genera have different environmental optima and limits, but these cut across the differences in leaf-form. Many other communities also include simple-leaved and compound-leaved species, without any evident sorting into ecological niches on this basis.

Stomates

The evolutionary history of the stomatal apparatus in angiosperms is still not entirely clear. In the simplest stomatotype, called anomocytic, the guard-cells are bounded by ordinary epidermal cells, without specialized subsidiary cells. It is logical to assume a priori that the anomocytic type is primitive, but the assumption is not necessarily correct. Both anomocytic and paracytic stomates (with a subsidiary cell flanking each guard-cell) are evidently of ancient lineage. Stomates of *Asteroxylon*, from the late Lower Devonian Rhynie beds, are anomocytic, but Banks (1976) has discovered paracytic stomates still earlier in the Lower Devonian.

The situation within the angiosperms is complex. Past assumptions that the anomocytic type is primitive are difficult to reconcile with the distribution of stomatotypes in modern taxa. As Margarita Baranova (1972) has shown, the bulk of the species of Magnoliales and Laurales have paracytic stomates, with a subsidiary cell flanking each guard-cell. Exceptions, such as *Takhtajania* (Winteraceae) and *Liriodendron* (Magnoliaceae), both with anomocytic stomates, are easily explainable as individual apomorphies. The members of these two orders (Magnoliales and Laurales) that do not have paracytic stomates do not form a natural assemblage, but are related only through the paracytic core of the group. These two orders (or the Magnoliales alone) are now widely regarded as the most archaic existing angiosperms.

Thus on the basis of comparison of modern species it appears that the paracytic stomatotype is primitive in the dicotyledons, and the other types derived. I don't know of any anomalies or internal contradictions resulting from a general application of this concept throughout the modern dicots. So far so good.

The monocots are equally susceptible to the same interpretation. Stebbins and Khush (1961) proposed that in the monocots the progression has been from 4 subsidiary cells (tetracytic) to 2 (paracytic) to none (anomocytic). Taking a different view of the probable evolutionary history of the monocotyledons, I see the pattern of stomatal evolution differently. Most of the members of the archaic subclass Alismatidae with emersed leaves have paracytic stomates, although some few are tetracytic. The Commelinidae are also basically paracytic, with a few tetracytic members. Tetracytic stomates are heavily concentrated in the Arecidae and Zingiberidae, although some members of both of these groups are paracytic. Anomocytic stomates are largely concentrated in the advanced subclass Liliidae, although some stomates in this group are paracytic and others tetracytic. Without calling on a computer for verification, I suggest that the most parsimonious interpretation here is that the paracytic stomatotype is primitive (plesiomorphic) for the class, and that tetracytic and anomocytic stomatotypes have repeatedly been derived from it.

The fly in this neontological ointment comes from a recent paleontological study by Upchurch (1984). He finds that early (Aptian?) leaves of the Potomac Group fossils are all unstable as to stomatotype, with paracytic, hemiparacytic, anomocytic, laterocytic, and weakly encyclocytic stomates characteristically intermingled on the same leaf. Only later in the Potomac deposits do more stable stomatotypes emerge. He therefore suggests that "the uniformly paracytic stomatal pattern characteristic of Magnoliales, generally considered primitive for flowering plants, may actually be derived from the variable condition found in Zone I leaves." One can hardly argue against the suggestion.

Upchurch's study raises the possibility that some nonparacytic stomates in modern angiosperms may be more or less stabilized segregates from the unstable early pattern, rather than more recent deviates from the paracytic type. *Platanus,* with mainly (but not exclusively) laterocytic stomates, might be a good candidate for such an interpretation. In contrast to many Lower Cretaceous leaves that have in the past been incorrectly associated with modern genera, the Albian platanoids are now thought by careful paleobotanists to be forerunners of modern *Platanus.* These Albian platanoids have intermingled paracytic and laterocytic and weakly encyclocytic stomates. *Trochodendron, Tetracentron,* and several other laterocytic Hamamelidae should presumably have the same interpretation as *Platanus.*

Based on the foregoing and other information, Margarita Baranova (personal communication and in press) considers that both the paracytic and the anomocytic stomatotypes are ancient in the angiosperms, even though in many modern species it appears that the anomocytic type has arisen from the paracytic.

The concept that paracytic stomates are primitive and other types derived still seems proper for the more advanced groups of angiosperms. It should come as no surprise that whereas the Rubiales are mostly paracytic, their more advanced relatives the Dipsacales, Calycerales, and Asterales are generally anomocytic. The possibility of reversals should always be entertained, but I don't know of any shining example.

Upchurch's study includes a number of detailed stomatal and other epidermal features beyond classical stomatotypes as such. He concludes that the "stratigraphic trend in cuticle types supports the concept that the subclass Magnoliidae includes the most primitive living angiosperms."

The adaptive significance of these changes in the stomatal apparatus is still speculative. One would assume a priori that increasing anatomical differentiation might have some functional importance, but direct evidence is notably lacking. It is even harder to see selective significance in the decreasing differentiation represented by the origin of anomocytic stomates from paracytic ones.

Stipules

The nature and evolutionary origin of stipules are debatable. They have no evident forerunner in the gymnosperms. The few very early fossil angiosperm leaves that are attached to an axis show no trace of stipules.

The oldest fossil stipules I know of are those of *Liriophyllum populoides,* from Upper Albian of Colorado. These have been discussed by several authors, most recently by Dilcher and Crane (1984). They appear as distinctive, well defined wings fully 1 cm wide at the base of the petiole. *Liriophyllum* may or may not be closely related to the modern Magnoliaceae, but it probably does belong to the Magnoliales.

Within the subclass Magnoliidae, only the Magnoliaceae, Lactoridaceae, and some of the Nymphaeales clearly have stipules, and those of the Nymphaeales are of an unusual type. Stipules are common enough, however, in the Hamamelidae and in the basal families of the Rosidae and Dilleniidae. In the Caryophyllidae many Polygonaceae have well developed stipules, but most other members of the subclass lack them. In the Asteridae stipules are found mainly in the Rubiales and some related families of the Gentianales. It has been estimated that 40% of all woody species of dicots have stipules, but only 20% of herbs do.

I suggest that stipules arose in some of the early Magnoliidae as petiolar flanges that helped to protect the terminal bud. The stipules of the modern genus *Liriodendron* (Magnoliaceae), although largely free from the petiole, still serve this function. These thoughts are not entirely original with me, but I am not sure who first voiced them.

Descending from these early stipulate species is a long line of stipulate angiosperms. In most of these the stipules are more or less reduced or vestigial, and the protective function has been taken over by bud-scales. Sometimes the stipules have taken on other functions. In *Robinia* and some other legumes they have been transformed into spines. In some species of *Acacia* these stipular spines are much enlarged and harbor ants that vigorously resent disturbance. It is not hard to see potential survival-value here. In species of *Lathyrus* the persistent stipules are enlarged and obviously photosynthetic, functioning in effect as an additional pair of leaflets on the compound leaf.

In the Rubiaceae the stipules have become interpetiolar on the stem, instead of being appendages of the leaf-base. These interpetiolar stipules have coarse, glandular or mucilaginous trichomes (colleters) on the inner surface, and the stipular apparatus clearly serves to protect the terminal bud. In *Galium,* of the same family, the stipules are transformed into ordinary leaves, and the leaves are whorled. In *Galium bifolium* each node has two ordinary, opposite leaves, and between them two smaller leaves. The smaller leaves are presumably modified interpetiolar stipules, although they lack colleters. In a number of species of *Galium* each node bears a whorl of 4 similar leaves, and in still others there are more than 4 (up to as many as 12) leaves in a whorl. Once the whorled pattern is established, the number of leaves in a whorl is governed by the ontogenetic pattern in the terminal bud; a change in symmetry changes the number of leaves.

It appears that well developed stipules sometimes arise abruptly in diverse groups that are otherwise exstipulate or have only vestigial stipules. Most of the Sapotaceae are nearly or quite exstipulate, but *Ecclinusa* has well developed stipules. *Ecclinusa* does not appear to be archaic within the family, and thus it seems unlikely that its stipules have been inherited unchanged from a distant past. Instead we have what seems to be an atavistic reversal, possibly resulting from mutations that restore suppressed links in the ancestral biosynthetic chain for the production of stipules. A similar explanation seems to be called for to explain the well developed but slender and seemingly functionless stipules of many individuals of *Viburnum ellipticum,* in a family (Caprifoliaceae) that is generally regarded as basically exstipulate. If my views on relationships are correct, the Caprifoliaceae arose from the stipulate family Rubiaceae. Other examples of apparently renascent stipules could be chosen from other families.

Apparent stipules may also arise de novo from the petiole or leaf-blade in otherwise exstipulate groups. Here again the Caprifoliaceae are instructive. *Lonicera hispidula* appears to have connate interpetiolar stipules. Other species of *Lonicera* are exstipulate, but a number of them are connate-perfoliate. In *L. hispidula* the uppermost pair of leaves on a twig are connate-perfoliate. It requires no great stretch of the imagination to suppose that in this species these seemingly stipulate leaves are actually connate-perfoliate, with a petiolar constriction shortly above the perfoliate base.

The Asteraceae are generally considered to be exstipulate, but here too there is a scattering of species with stipule-like structures that appear to be of recent origin. *Artemisia vulgaris* has laciniately about twice-cleft leaves. At the base of the leaf, more or less removed from the main part of the blade, there is a pair of small, irregularly cleft lateral lobes. In a normally stipulate group these would doubtless be called stipules, but here they are interpreted as additional lobes of the blade. *Aster undulatus* is a heart-leaved aster, closely allied to several other heart-leaved asters. The middle and upper leaves of this species (but not its relatives) vary from sessile and cordate-clasping to evidently petiolate, with the petiole enlarged and auriculate-clasping at the base. If we could not so easily see the connection to a merely cordate-clasping base, and if the family were not regarded as essentially exstipulate, these petiolar flanges would doubtless be interpreted as stipules.

On the evidence adduced above, it appears that many stipulate modern angiosperms have a stipulate ancestry tracing back to the Cretaceous, quite possibly the Lower Cretaceous. The fact that stipule-like structures have evidently arisen de novo in diverse genera of modern angiosperms suggests the need for caution, however, in assuming that all stipules as we now see them have a unified common ancestry. Given the evolutionary plasticity of the group, the laxity of selective constraints, and the muted action of competitive exclusion, there is no inherent reason why history might not have repeated itself in several phylads. I am impatient with arguments about whether apparent stipules in one or another family are true stipules or only pseudostipules.

Exstipulate angiosperms clearly have diverse origins. Exstipulate members of the Magnoliidae probably do not have a stipulate ancestry. Most of the exstipulate members of the more advanced subclasses of dicotyledons probably do have a stipulate ancestry, but the loss has occurred independently in various groups. The monocots appear to be primitively exstipulate, as befits their very early divergence from the dicots. The stipules of *Potamogeton* are evidently derived from the leaf-sheath, and have nothing to do with the stipules of dicotyledons.

On the basis of correlations of primitive and advanced characters, Sporne (1956 and elsewhere) considers that stipules are primitive in the angiosperms. I suggest that in this case the method has led him astray. The burgeoning of stipules in some early dicotyledons, followed by their decline in more advanced groups, has produced a spurious correlation of stipules with other primitive characters. Statistics are fine, but like any other data they must be interpreted in the light of all the available evidence.

Vascular Structure

Nodal Anatomy

The nodal anatomy of angiosperms and its taxonomic significance have been much discussed, but uncertainties remain. Branch stems characteristically have two traces from a single gap in the stele, not only in the angiosperms but also in ferns and many gymnosperms. In these other groups the leaves generally also have two traces departing from a single stelar gap.

Two-trace, unilacunar nodes are uncommon in the angiosperms, but they do exist in several families, notably in some woody members of the Magnoliidae (Austrobaileyaceae, Chloranthaceae, Calycanthaceae, Gomortegaceae, Lactoridaceae, Lauraceae, Trimeniaceae). It seems reasonable to suppose that here the two-trace, unilacunar node may be a primitive survival. It is more difficult, however, to see a primitive survival in similar two-trace, unilacunar nodes found in some (not all!) members of such advanced families as the Solanaceae, Verbenaceae, and Lamiaceae.

If the two-trace, unilacunar node is regarded as primitive, then it seems reasonable to visualize a phylogenetic progression to the one-trace, unilacunar node, and thence to other types, such as the three-trace unilacunar, three-trace trilacunar, and multilacunar. Unfortunately, this interpretation presents some problems. Some one-trace unilacunar nodes are clearly at the end of a reduction-series from three-trace trilacunar through three-trace unilacunar to one-trace unilacunar. It therefore becomes necessary to visualize the derivation of the single-trace, unilacunar node via two different routes. Indeed most of the unilacunar groups outside the Magnoliidae would seem to have a trilacunar ancestry.

In contrast to the views of Bailey (1956) and his associates, Benzing (1967) considers that the two-trace, unilacunar node is probably not primitive in the angiosperms, and he suggests that "the primitive node in the Angiospermae, and possibly in all seed plants, is one-trace, unilacunar or trilacunar." Single-trace nodes are not common in the angiosperms, nor

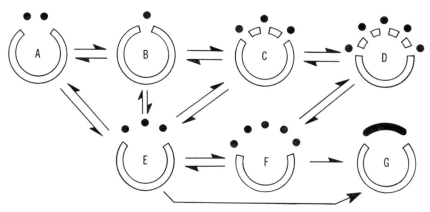

Fig. 5.5. Possible phylogeny of nodal anatomy. **A,** two-trace, unilacunar. **B,** one-trace, unilacunar. **C,** trilacunar. **D,** multilacunar. **E,** three-trace, unilacunar. **F,** multitrace, unilacunar. **G,** compound single-trace, unilacunar. Adapted from James E. Canright, The comparative morphology and relationships of the Magnoliaceae. IV. Wood and nodal anatomy. J. Arnold Arbor. **36:** 119–140. 1955.

is there any concentration of them in the Magnoliidae. I cannot say that Benzing is wrong, but adoption of his point of view would not leave us with a more tractable set of problems than exist with Bailey's approach.

On the basis of comparison of modern taxa, it appears that the various nodal types are freely interconvertible in the course of evolution (Fig. 5.5). No assumption of unidirectionality, from whatever starting point, is compatible with a general system based on multiple correlations of characters.

The adaptive significance of most of the changes in nodal anatomy of angiosperms is obscure. The multilacunar node, as seen for example in the Apiales, may reflect merely the large size of the leaf. Reduction of the leaf-blade in some of the Apiaceae has not affected the petiole, which remains broad and sheathing, with many traces from the base.

Xylem

Concepts of primitive and advanced xylem structure are based on the xylem itself and do not depend on preconceived notions of the relationships among the families of angiosperms. Here, as in floral evolution, there seems to be only one general way of organizing the bewildering diversity into a coherent evolutionary pattern. It is reassuring to find a general, though loose, correlation between primitive xylem and primitive floral structure.

The primitive angiosperm tracheid is slender and elongate, with long, tapering, overlapping ends and numerous scalariform bordered pits, very much like a typical fern tracheid. Phyletically, each of these transversely elongate pits becomes divided into a horizontal row of shorter, rectangular pits. These rectangular pits then become more rounded, and eventually they become spirally or irregularly arranged.

Tracheids function both as strengthening and conducting elements. Specialization towards strength, at the expense of conduction, leads to the xylem fiber. Specialization towards conduction, at the expense of strength, leads to the xylem vessel.

Fibers are usually more slender than tracheids, with a thicker wall and a smaller (often nearly evanescent) lumen. The pits are usually fewer and smaller than in tracheids, and are often imperfectly developed. They are always of the circular rather than the scalariform or rectangular type. Fibers in which these changes have been carried to the greatest extreme are called **libriform fibers**; cells intermediate between typical fibers and typical tracheids are called **fiber-tracheids**. Wood with highly specialized fibers is likely to be highly specialized in other ways as well.

The primitive angiosperm vessel-segment is much like the primitive tracheid, differing only in the absence of the closing membrane from some of the numerous scalariform pits of the long, slanting end-walls. Phyletic specialization (Fig. 5.6) leads to shorter, broader vessel-elements with somewhat thinner walls and less sloping, more nearly transverse end-walls with fewer and larger perforations. Ultimately there is a single large perforation extending fully across the wholly transverse end of the vessel-segment, so that the vessel might be compared to a series of barrels stacked end on end, with the end-walls knocked out. Concomitantly with these changes, the pits on the lateral walls undergo the same set of evolutionary modifications as they do in tracheids, so that eventually the lateral pits are round and scattered. Vessel-segments with a single large pore at each end are said to be simply perforate; those with two or more perforations at each end are said to be multiperforate, or (if the perforations form a ladder-like configuration) scalariform. There are also some other possible variations in vessel-structure that would appropriately be considered in a more detailed treatment.

Scalariform vessels are known in more than a hundred families of angiosperms, some of them, such as the Ericaceae and Caprifoliaceae, rather advanced on other grounds. In most of these families, simply perforate vessels are intermingled with scalariform ones. Families with only scalariform vessels are much less numerous, and most of them (e.g., Austrobaileyaceae, Chloranthaceae, Degeneriaceae, Eupomatiaceae, Idiospermaceae) belong to the Magnoliidae. With few exceptions, all vessels in herbs of all families of dicots are simply perforate. This is another line of evidence which strengthens the belief that within the angiosperms herbs are derived from woody ancestors.

Only a few angiosperms (Amborellaceae, Tetracentraceae, Trochodendraceae, and Winteraceae) are primitively vesselless, and all of them are woody plants belonging to the Ranalian complex. (The Tetracentraceae and Trochodendraceae are here referred to the subclass Hamamelidae, but they are archaic within their subclass and evidently allied to the Magnoliidae.) A few herbaceous aquatic angiosperms both within and without the Ranalian complex lack vessels (e.g., Hydrostachyaceae, Lem-

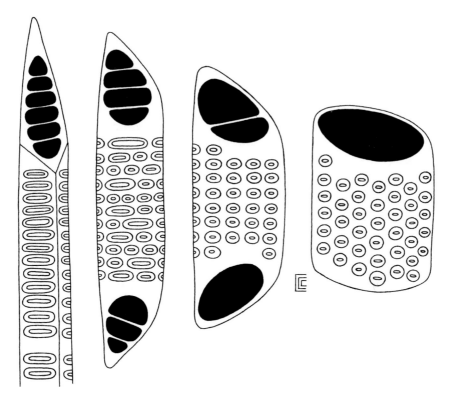

Fig. 5.6. Evolution of types of vessels. LEFT, scalariform. RIGHT, simply perforate, with circular bordered pits.

naceae, Podostemaceae, and most of the Nymphaeales), but this absence probably reflects a secondary loss, related to the aquatic habitat.

It may be significant that all the herbaceous angiosperms which lack vessels also lack a functional cambium. In the dicotyledons vessels are at first (phyletically) restricted to the secondary xylem, after which they appear progressively earlier in the ontogeny of the primary xylem. In a plant having vessels only in the secondary xylem, suppression of cambial activity would also eliminate vessels. The relationship of the aquatic habitat to the absence of vessels is further discussed in CHAPTER 7, dealing with the monocotyledons.

David Young (1981) has recently proposed that the presence of vessels is basic to the angiosperms, and that all vesselless members of the group have a vesseliferous ancestry. He maintains that a more parsimonious cladogram of relationships among archaic dicotyledons can be produced on this assumption than on the traditional assumption that vessels arose within the angiosperms. His study has been criticized on technical procedural grounds by cladistic colleagues, and it is notably deficient in leaving the monocotyledons entirely out of consideration. Sherwin

Carlquist (1983, 1987) has forcefully refuted Young's interpretation, on the basis of comparative anatomy of the xylem (not just the vessels) among archaic angiosperms.

The fatal flaw in Young's argument in his implicit assumption that gain and loss of vessels are equally likely. On the contrary, presence of vessels has an obvious survival value in terrestrial angiosperms, and loss of vessels would be counter-selective. Gain or loss of vessels therefore cannot be considered equally likely. His conclusion here exemplifies the peril of neglecting to consider, in the words of the late Edgar Anderson, "what is going on here?" None of us was there to see it all happen, and we should of course remain permanently open to the consideration of new evidence or new ways of looking at old evidence, but we should not mindlessly put ourselves in thrall to a mechanical method that excludes such an important factor as survival value.

Primitive xylem has well scattered vertical files of wood parenchyma cells, and has both uniseriate and multiseriate rays. Evolutionary advance leads to a clustering of the vertical files and their restriction to certain parts of the xylem, e.g., to the last-formed wood of the season, or to the sheaths surrounding the vessels. Concomitantly with these changes, one or another of the two types of rays may be suppressed. The secondary wood of many herbs lacks rays entirely.

The several different evolutionary advances in xylem structure tend to proceed more or less in unison, but this is only a tendency rather than a definite rule. Even more than with some other characters, evolutionary modification of the xylem has independently followed the same course in many different lines, so that sharing of one or several advanced features provides but little indication of relationship. Wood anatomy is useful in phyletic studies mainly in negating relationships that might otherwise be suggested. A group with primitive xylem is not likely to be derived from a group with highly specialized xylem. Neither are taxa with very different advanced features likely to be closely related.

Carlquist (1975) has attempted a comprehensive interpretation of xylem structure in relation to ecological adaptation. I am receptive in principle, but uneasy about some of the proposed explanations. The subject certainly merits more careful attention than it has received from most phylogenists. Even if some changes prove to be necessary, it is a beginning.

Phloem

Phloem undergoes a series of evolutionary changes comparable to those of the xylem. As with xylem, families that are considered to be specialized on other grounds tend to have specialized phloem. Specialized phloem and specialized xylem also tend to go together.

The primitive sieve-element in angiosperms is long and slender, with groups of minute pores forming scattered sieve-areas along the longitudinal walls and the very oblique end-walls. The sieve-elements are progressively modified to be shorter, with more definite end-walls that come to be perpendicular to the axis. The sieve-areas are progressively more restricted to the end-walls and more sharply defined, with larger pores, and the sieve-areas on the lateral walls become obscure or vestigial. The several sieve-areas on the end-wall eventually coalesce (phyletically) into a single sieve-area. Highly advanced phloem has sieve-tubes composed of short sieve-tube-elements stacked end to end, with each end-wall consisting of a single transverse sieve-plate with large openings. The similarity of the changes in the evolutionary origin of sieve-tubes and vessels is obvious.

Companion-cells are (so far as known) universally distributed among the angiosperms. They show no obvious evolutionary trends, except that the sieve-elements of more advanced phloem are likely to have two or more companion-cells, as viewed in cross-section, instead of only one. The report some years ago that *Austrobaileya* does not have companion-cells now appears to be erroneous.

Primitive angiosperm phloem has a considerable amount of parenchyma intermingled with the sieve-tubes and companion-cells, but has few or no hard cells. More advanced phloem has little or no parenchyma, but often has bands of fibers. "The story of evolutionary modification seems to be one of increase in complexity from a simple type, consisting wholly or largely of 'soft cells' to one that has also sclerenchyma cells of one or more types variously arranged, and to a secondarily simple type, consisting largely or wholly of sieve tubes and companion cells" (Eames, 1961).

Some angiosperms have phloem internal to the primary xylem as well as external to it, so that the vascular bundles are bicollateral. The presence of internal phloem is a useful taxonomic character, but, like other characters, it must be evaluated with some caution. It is fairly consistently present in certain families and even orders (e.g., the Myrtales), and absent from other groups. The families with internal phloem are all fairly well or highly advanced, as contrasted with the Magnoliidae, but they do not form a single taxonomic group. Internal phloem has evidently originated several times.

The adaptive significance, if any, of internal phloem is obscure. It confers no obvious advantage, and the species which have it differ so much in other respects and occur in such a wide variety of habitats that it is hard to think of it as merely an incidental side-effect of the genes controlling some other important character.

The progressive complexity of angiosperm phloem, as compared to that of gymnosperms, and especially the evolution of sieve-tubes from gymnospermous sieve-elements, are presumably correlated with increasing efficiency in conduction. Unfortunately I do not know of any experimental data bearing on the assumption.

Cambium and Vascular Bundles

The length of cambial cells is correlated with the length of the xylem and phloem cells formed from them. The progressive evolutionary decrease in the length of vessel-segments and sieve-tube-elements is accompanied by (and ontogenetically due to) a decrease in the length of the fusiform cambial initials.

Aside from the change in length of the fusiform initials, the evolutionary history of cambium in angiosperms in mainly one of reduction in activity and area. The change from woody to herbaceous habit is governed by a number of other factors in addition to cambial activity, but there is a further reduction series among the herbs. Some herbs have a complete cylinder of active cambium and form a complete cylinder of secondary xylem and phloem, but in many others the secondary vascular tissues are formed only within the bundles, and the cambium between the bundles forms only parenchyma-cells or is completely inactive. Most monocots and a considerable number of herbaceous dicots have no functional vascular cambium at all.

A few monocots, notably some of the Agavaceae and Aloaceae, have a specialized, atypical cambium that produces complete vascular bundles and other tissues. This cambium appears to be a newly originated tissue, derived by a continuation of activity in the primary thickening meristem. It is analogous to typical cambium, rather than homologous with it. This is an example of the fact that a structure once completely lost is not likely to be regained in exactly the same form, even under strong selective pressure.

The primary vascular structure of primitive herbs is essentially like that of woody plants. In cross-section, the stem shows a single ring of vascular bundles, separated by relatively narrow medullary rays. Evolutionary modification leads to an increase in the proportion of soft tissues in the primary body, accompanied by a more definite separation of the vascular bundles (i.e., an increase in the width of the medullary rays). This change in proportions may well relate to the changed functional and structural requirements of an herbaceous stem as compared to those of a tree.

Stems with scattered vascular bundles, as seen in monocots and a few dicots (e.g., Nymphaeaceae) are clearly advanced, in comparison to stems with the bundles in a single ring. The adaptive significance of the change to scattered bundles is obscure.

INFLORESCENCES

The diversity of inflorescences is seemingly endless. Certain patterns or tendencies can be observed, but no scheme of classification of inflorescences is even roughly satisfactory. Another facet of the problem is that the evolutionary history of inflorescences is not at all clear. If it were clear, a satisfactory classification would be more easily devised, or if a satisfactory classification had been devised, the evolutionary history might more easily be discerned.

The most familiar and at the present time the most useful classification of inflorescences recognizes two major types, the cymose (determinate)

(Fig. 5.7) and racemose (indeterminate) (Fig. 5.8). The analysis of probable evolutionary history here presented is made in terms of this classification.

Although an inflorescence as a whole may have either determinate or indeterminate (or mixed) sequence of flowering, the flower is always terminal to its own shoot. Growth of the shoot terminates in the formation of a flower. Given a possible ancestry of the angiosperms in megaphyllous derivatives of seed-ferns, it seems reasonable to suppose that primitively each flower was relatively large and terminal to its own leafy branch. The flowers were not aggregated into distinct inflorescences. The same organization could be expressed by saying that the plants had many uniflorous inflorescences well removed from each other, each terminal to its own shoot. Large, solitary, terminal flowers are commonly seen in the Magnoliaceae and some other families of Magnoliidae. The known fossil record does not clearly show the course of evolution in inflorescences, but it does show that the large, solitary, terminal flower, as seen in *Archaeanthus linnenbergeri,* existed as long ago as the Albian-Cenomanian boundary (Dilcher & Crane, 1984). Small flowers of chloranthoid type are also known from the Upper Albian (Friis et al., 1986).

Termination of apical growth, attendant on the development of a flower, may well have encouraged lateral branching not far beneath the flower. Apical dominance is well known in vegetative shoots: Remove or inactivate the terminal bud, and one or more suppressed lateral buds will begin to grow. In any case, three-flowered and two-flowered cymules (dichasia and monochasia, respectively) are very common components of inflorescences.

If one can assume dichasia and/or monochasia as basic organizational units, it becomes possible to develop a series of other types by logical modification of these. Whether such a logical series conforms in all respects to the course of evolution is uncertain, but at least it provides a reasonable conceptual framework for the organization of the data. The strobilar hypothesis of floral evolution was no more than such a set of logically progressive modifications from a conceptually basic type when it was first informally advanced by de Candolle in pre-Darwinian times.

If a primitive dichasium is considered to be relatively loose, with the two side-branches originating at different levels on the shoot axis, then an open compound cyme can readily be evolved by repeated branching of the successive orders of branches. Such a compound cyme, with a more or less pyramidal or ovoid shape, can be converted into a classical (strictly racemose) panicle by a progressive shift in the growth-pattern, so that the lower branches develop before the upper ones. The classical panicle is in fact not a very common type of inflorescence. Most so-called panicles actually show a mixture of determinate and indeterminate growth, often with the terminal flower of each branch developing before the lateral flowers. Compound inflorescences with mixed determinate and indeterminate growth have appropriately been called mixed panicles.

Proliferation of a more compact dichasium, with opposite or subopposite lateral branches, leads to compound dichasial cymes such as are

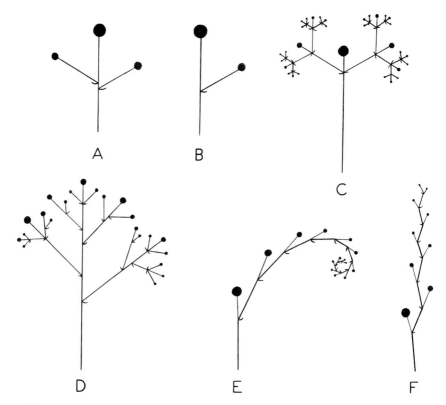

Fig. 5.7.   Some types of cymose inflorescences. **A**, dichasium. **B**, monochasium. **C**, dichasially branched cyme. **D**, compound cyme. **E**, helicoid cyme. **F**, scorpioid cyme.

seen in many members of the Caryophyllaceae and Rubiaceae, among other families. This type of inflorescence is seen especially in plants that have opposite leaves, but opposite-leaved plants may also have other types of inflorescences.

Condensation of the internodes of a compound cyme, without reduction of the ultimate pedicels, leads readily to an inflorescence having the form of an umbel, but with a more or less distinctly determinate sequence of flowering. Such inflorescences are well exemplified by *Allium* and many other members of the Liliaceae. Careful anatomical study confirms the basically cymose nature of these determinate umbels. There is no doubt here that the relationship of the two types of inflorescence is truly evolutionary rather than merely conceptual.

Reduction of the pedicels as well as the branches of an originally cymose inflorescence leads to heads of the sort seen in the Dipsacaceae and certain Rubiaceae (e.g., *Cephalanthus*), among other groups. These heads typically retain a more or less distinctly determinate sequence of flowering, but some of them (e.g., *Cephalaria*) are mixed, with the outermost (low-

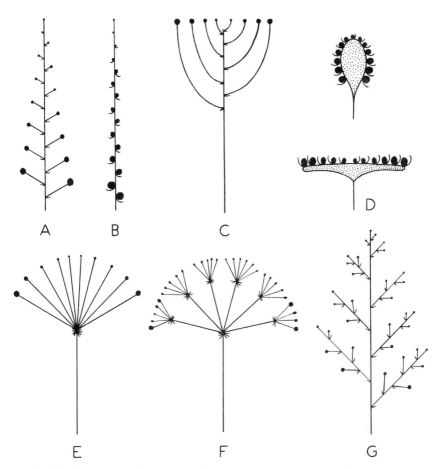

Fig. 5.8. Some types of racemose inflorescences. **A,** raceme. **B,** spike. **C,** corymb. **D,** head. **E,** umbel. **F,** compound umbel. **G,** panicle.

ermost) row of flowers blooming immediately after the terminal flower. Here too there is no doubt that we have a truly evolutionary progression. The next step is shown by the Asteraceae, in which centripetally flowering heads are arranged in a still cymose secondary inflorescence. No evolutionary relationship among these families is here implied.

In the ancestry of the Asteraceae, it appears that condensation of the inflorescence into a head preceded the change from cymose to racemose sequence of flowering. In some other groups the reverse seems to be true. The heads in *Trifolium,* for example, seem to be merely condensed racemes.

A special type of modified cyme that superficially resembles a raceme or spike is the sympodial cyme, in which the apparent main axis consists of a succession of short axillary branches. Each flower is terminal to its true axis, but the side-branch originating just beneath the flower produces its own terminal flower with another side-branch just beneath it, so that theoretically the inflorescence can elongate indefinitely by producing a branch just below each flower.

Sympodial cymes are of two sorts, helicoid and scorpioid. In a helicoid cyme the branches are all on the same side of the developing axis, so that the inflorescence is curved or circinately rolled. Often the inflorecence is conspicuously circinate when young and progressively straightens out or unrolls as flowering proceeds. In a scorpioid cyme the branches are alternately on opposite sides of the developing sympodial axis, so that the axis has a zig-zag appearance. Helicoid cymes are commoner than scorpioid ones and are especially frequent in the Boraginaceae and Hydrophyllaceae.

In the less modified forms of sympodial inflorescences, each of the successive lateral branches that make up the apparent axis is subtended by a bract, so that the axillary nature of these branches is not hard to see. Superficially, it appears that the main bract is on the opposite side of the stem from the flower, instead of directly beneath the flower.

In more highly modified sympodial inflorescences these bracts are suppressed, and only the coiled or zig-zag form of the apparent axis remains to distinguish the inflorescence from a true raceme or spike. Bractless zigzag racemes, as seen for example in *Smilacina stellata,* are really modified scorpioid cymes.

Indeterminate inflorescences may be classified as racemes, panicles, corymbs, umbels, spikes, or heads. All of these types have in common the fact that the lowest or outermost flowers bloom first, and flowering progresses toward the top or center. A typical raceme has an elongate central axis from which the individual pedicels arise. Each pedicel is axillary to a bract. Flowering progresses evenly from the bottom upwards, and theoretically the axis may continue to elongate and produce new flowers indefinitely. It is as if an ordinary vegetative axis had been modified in just two respects: The leaves are reduced to bracts, and every axillary bud develops into a short lateral branch with a single terminal flower.

Such a simple and nicely symmetrical inflorescence as a raceme ought logically to be a primitive type, but apparently it is not. True racemes are not notably abundant in the more archaic families. They are common instead in such more advanced families as the Brassicaceae, Fabaceae, and Scrophulariaceae. In a number of taxa racemes pretty clearly have a cymose ancestry. In species of *Campanula* and *Saxifraga,* for example, racemes appear to be derived from mixed panicles by suppression of the secondary branches, and we have already noted that zig-zag racemes are likely to be sympodial cymes.

On a conceptual, if not always an evolutionary basis, the other types of indeterminate inflorescences may all be considered as modified racemes. Thus a panicle is a branched raceme, a corymb is a raceme with elongate lower pedicels and relatively short axis, an umbel is a raceme with the internodes suppressed, a spike is a raceme with the pedicels suppressed, and a head is a raceme with both the internodes and the pedicels very short or suppressed.

Each of the forms of racemose inflorescence has its cymose counterpart. Within the racemose type, it appears that racemes may be derived from panicles, and vice versa, that spikes, corymbs, and umbels may be derived from racemes, and that heads may be derived from racemes or spikes or umbels, but some of these types can also be derived from their cymose counterparts. The rose family is particularly noteworthy in having a wide variety of both racemose and cymose inflorescences, with many doubtful or transitional types.

The adaptive significance of the evolutionary changes in the inflorescence is obscure. If it makes any difference to the plant whether the inflorescence is racemose or cymose, or whether it is monopodial or sympodial, the fact is not obvious. Certainly there is no evident correlation between the different types and ecological niches. Something might be made of the difference between relatively large, well separated flowers that individually attract pollinators, and smaller flowers that are grouped into showy inflorescences, but this distinction cuts across all the others and brings together groups that are dissimilar in other respects and not closely related. The culmination of the emphasis on the inflorescence as the attractive unit is seen in such disparate groups as the Asteraceae and the genus *Euphorbia*. The advantage, if any, of such pseudanthia over ordinary buttercup flowers is not clear.

FLOWER STRUCTURE

General Considerations

The primitive angiosperm flower may be visualized as having numerous, spirally arranged, rather large and firm tepals, numerous, spirally arranged, laminar stamens, and numerous, spirally arranged, unsealed carpels. All of these characteristics can be found individually among modern members of the Magnoliales, but not combined in the same species or even in the same family.

Some members of the Magnoliaceae, such as *Magnolia stellata* and *Aromadendron* spp., have the tepals, stamens, and carpels all spirally arranged, with large, more or less petaloid tepals that are not differentiated into sepals and petals. *Degeneria* has laminar stamens and unsealed carpels. If these putatively primitive features of *Magnolia stellata* and *Degeneria* could be combined into one flower, this flower would closely approach, in external morphology, the theoretical archetype for the angiosperms. We should note at once, however, that the Winteraceae have more primitive (vesselless) xylem than either the Magnoliaceae or the Degeneriaceae.

Many of the tendencies in floral evolution can be grouped under the general heading of aggregation and reduction. The receptacle is shortened, so that parts of all kinds are brought close together, in a series of cycles rather than an elongate spiral. The number of parts of a given kind is reduced from many to few, and parts of a given kind become connate with each other, and parts of different kinds may become adnate to each other. Parts of any given kind may even be lost completely. We have already noted that a repetition of this same set of aggregative and reductive processes leads to the formation of pseudanthia such as those of the Asteraceae and Euphorbiaceae, but here we are concerned only with evolutionary changes within the individual flower.

Another set of tendencies is toward elaboration and differentiation of parts. These two seemingly opposed tendencies may both be expressed in the same structure. Sympetaly reflects the evolutionary union of ancestrally distinct petals, but many sympetalous flowers are also irregular, with some of the corolla-lobes different from others.

There is in fact only the very loosest correlation among the various advances in floral structure. The different advances do not in general depend on each other, and it may be expected that any particular kind of flower chosen at random will show some relatively primitive and other relatively advanced features. Sympetalous flowers may also be polysepalous (Sapotaceae), and polypetalous flowers may be synsepalous (*Silene*). The calyx may be synsepalous but regular in flowers with polypetalous but irregular corolla (many legumes). Dioecism occurs sporadically from the Magnoliales to the Asterales, and also in the monocots. Sympetalous plants may have separate carpels (*Kalanchoe*), and polypetalous plants may have united carpels (many families).

The lack of close correlation among the various advances in floral structure extends to advances in vegetative structure as well. There is, however, a very loose and general correlation among the various advances. The Ranalian complex (roughly equivalent to Magnoliidae) well illustrates both the fact that the correlation exists and the fact that it is only very loose. The group was established as the most archaic among the angiosperms largely on the basis of traditional floral morphology, but it is also in this group that the most primitive xylem and phloem in angiosperms has been discovered, and many members have primitive (uniaperturate) pollen as well. On the other hand, every individual member of the Ranalian complex shows a combination of primitive and more advanced features, and some members, such as the Canellaceae, even have a compound pistil with parietal placentation.

The "morphological integration" that often permits students of vertebrates to reconstruct an entire animal with considerable accuracy from one or a few bones simply does not exist among the angiosperms. Another facet of this same situation is that higher plants, being nonmotile and lacking a nervous system, do not have their structure so precisely prescribed by the environmental requirements as do the animals. This brings us back to the fact, mentioned in the first chapter, that the higher taxa of angiosperms are in general not well correlated with ecologic niches, and are correspondingly difficult to recognize at a glance.

Unisexuality

We have noted that the primitive flower is perfect, having both stamens and pistils. Unisexual flowers are derived from perfect ones. An intermediate type has more or less well developed parts of both sexes, but with only one sex functional. The Sapindaceae very often have seemingly perfect but functionally unisexual flowers. Many maples, in the related family Aceraceae, have staminate flowers with an evident but abortive ovary, and functionally pistillate flowers with more or less well developed stamens. A special case of unisexuality is shown in a number of genera of the Asteraceae in which the disk-flowers are functionally staminate. In the Asteraceae the style elongates at anthesis, pushing the pollen from the anther-tube, and it retains this function even when the ovary has been phyletically lost.

Monoecious and dioecious groups are derived from perfect-flowered ancestors through a variety of intermediate states that often involve the presence of both perfect and unisexual flowers on the same individual. A number of families, such as the Asteraceae and Cyperaceae, run the gamut from perfect flowers to monoecism and dioecism, with diverse transitional states. Dioecious species of *Carex* clearly have a monoecious ancestry within the genus. Dioecism in the Simaroubaceae, on the other hand, has evidently been attained through polygamo-dioecism, in which some individuals of a species bear staminate and perfect flowers, and others bear pistillate and perfect flowers.

Any effort to read the evolution of sexuality in flowers in the opposite direction faces a serious problem in evolutionary mechanics. New structures typically arise by evolutionary modification of old ones. Even though the function may change in the course of evolution, some function is retained throughout the process. It is difficult to visualize the origin of new structures as useless bumps, which then undergo progressive evolutionary elaboration until they at last achieve a function.

The adaptive significance of the change from perfect to unisexual flowers and eventually unisexual individuals is difficult to assess accurately. Obviously it is a means of restricting and eventually preventing self-pollination. The advantages of cross-pollination must be balanced, however, against the possible reduction in seed-set through failure of pollination.

Unisexuality is merely one of several means by which angiosperms meet the evolutionary need to maintain a high level of outcrossing, and it may be assumed to share the same advantages as, for example, self-sterility. Thus one could see some utility in monoecism or even polygamo-dioecism, which might provide an adequate mix of outcrossing and high seed-set. It is not easy, however, to see how survival value could spark the further change to dioecism. In addition to the decreased likelihood of pollination, the species is burdened with the necessity of producing all its seeds on only half of its individuals. Whatever may be the reasons why dioecism is favored in higher animals, it is difficult to see how they could operate in angiosperms, in which no active cooperation between different individuals is required or even possible. The fact that something is hard to see or understand does not prove that it is only mythical, but a bit of skepticism is in order. The long-doubted Homeric legend of Troy turned out to have a solid basis in fact, but the once widespread belief in unicorns did not.

It is interesting to note that species of some dioecious genera, such as *Antennaria* (Asteraceae), have taken to apomixis, with chiefly or wholly female populations. One is tempted to speculate that apomixis in *Antennaria* is an evolutionary response to the disadvantages of dioecism, but the widespread occurrence of apomixis in other groups with perfect flowers makes such speculation hazardous. At least, one must admit that the wholly apomictic species of *Antennaria* have surrendered any possible advantage to be obtained from their dioecism.

Neither monoecious nor dioecious angiosperms, nor the two groups collectively have any habitat-requirements or other features in common to suggest that they are particularly suited to any ecologic niche in contrast to species with perfect flowers.

The Perianth

It is clear enough that the tepals of the more archaic angiosperm families are modified leaves, and like ordinary leaves they often have three vascular traces. In this group it is often difficult to distinguish between the tepals or sepals and the reduced leaves (bracts) subtending the flower. The bracts pass into the tepals as one proceeds up the pedicel.

It appears that in the vast majority of families sepals are homologous with the tepals of a primitively undifferentiated perianth. In some cases the ancestral undifferentiated perianth has become differentiated into two cycles, the calyx and the corolla. In other cases the ancestral undifferentiated perianth has been reduced to a single cycle, the calyx, whereas the corolla, if present, has a different ancestry.

It now seems well established that the apparent sepals in the Portulacaceae and Basellaceae are, in an evolutionary sense, modified bracteoles, and that the apparent petals are modified sepals. Usually there are just two sepals in these families, just as there are two bracteoles subtending the flower in many other families. *Lewisia rediviva* (Portulacaceae), however, has several sepals, commonly five to nine. The plant has no ancestral memory that its sepals are merely bracteoles, and it is under no compulsion to retain the original number.

Aside from the special case of the Portulacaceae and Basellaceae, petals are of two different origins. Some are modified tepals, representing the inner members of an ancestrally undifferentiated perianth. Others are essentially staminodes. Convincing examples of both of these two modes of origin can readily be found.

The single genus *Magnolia* provides all transitional stages from an undifferentiated perianth with an indefinite number of tepals, to a well differentiated perianth with a definite number of sepals and petals, each in a single cycle.

Petals in the Nymphaeaceae, Ranunculaceae, and many other families appear to be staminodial. *Nymphaea* has often been cited as a genus showing a complete transition between stamens, staminodes, and petals in a single flower. The basic homology here seems clear. In the Ranunculaceae the petals commonly have the additional peculiarity of serving as nectaries. In the German botanical literature these nectariferous petals have often been called "Honigblätter" (honey-leaves), but by traditional standards they are petals all the same. In some other genera of the same family, such as *Coptis* and *Helleborus,* the staminodial nectaries do not look like petals, but here again the homology seems clear.

The extra petals of "double" flowers of many different kinds are staminodial, and it may well be that in such families all petals are eventually of staminodial origin. *Mentzelia* (Loasaceae) provides an especially instructive example. Most species of *Mentzelia* have numerous stamens. Some species have five petals and no staminodes. Others have five petals and five more or less petaloid staminodes that may have a vestigial anther at the tip. *Mentzelia decapetala* has ten petals, all essentially alike, although close examination shows that the inner five are a bit narrower than the outer five.

It was once hoped that the number of vascular traces might distinguish sepals from petals, or at least distinguish staminodial petals from others, but this character has proven faulty. It was noted that sepals commonly have three traces, like ordinary leaves, whereas petals commonly have one trace, like stamens. This feature was thought to provide a critical distinction between sepals and petals. Unfortunately, the hypothesis was based on false premises. Stamens in some families, such as the Degeneriaceae, have three traces. In *Umbellularia californica* (Lauraceae) the perianth is imperfectly differentiated into sepals and petals (Kasapligil, 1951). The sepals have three traces, but the petals have one fully developed median trace and a pair of imperfectly and irregularly developed lateral traces. The next step would be the complete loss of the lateral traces. Thus the presence of three traces in a petal does not preclude the possibility that it is of staminodial origin, nor does the presence of only a single trace prove that it must be staminodial. Certainly the presence of three traces in a perianth-member does not show conclusively that it cannot be a petal.

It therefore becomes necessary to revert to a pragmatic definition of sepal and petals, based primarily on position, but taking other factors into account as seems necessary to the case. There is a general tendency in angiosperms for the perianth to be divided into two functionally and morphologically differentiated series. The outer series is called the calyx, and the inner series the corolla.

In flowers that have both a calyx and a corolla, the sepals are customarily green and more or less foliaceous in texture, serving primarily to protect the developing flower-bud; the petals, on the other hand, are brightly colored (or white) and serve to attract pollinators. This distinction does not always hold true, however. Sometimes, as in many of the lilies, the sepals are showy and essentially like the petals. In some groups, such as in *Aquilegia,* the sepals are petaloid in texture and function but different in structure from the petals. The sepals may even be larger and more showy than the petals, as in *Delphinium* and *Aconitum*. These last three genera all belong to the Ranunculaceae, in which the petals function as nectaries.

In some groups the sepals have other specialized functions, as in *Valeriana*. *Valeriana* has epigynous flowers with the sepals at first inconspicuous and circinately inrolled. At maturity the sepals are plumose and fully extended, serving to facilitate the distribution of the fruit by wind.

When the perianth consists of only a single cycle it is customary to call that cycle a calyx and its members sepals (although it is not incorrect to call them tepals). This is true even when the members of this single cycle are very petaloid, as in *Clematis* and *Anemone*. Only when there is clear evidence that the true calyx has been lost, as in some members of the Apiaceae and Asteraceae, are the members of this single-perianth cycle called petals (or collectively the corolla). This terminology is in part arbitrary, but it is not out of harmony with the probable evolutionary history. In most cases in which the perianth consists of a single cycle called sepals, it is to be presumed that these are descended from the tepals of an undifferentiated perianth.

When the flowers have no corolla, the calyx is often corolloid. The family Nyctaginaceae is strictly apetalous, but most of the species have a corolloid calyx. In some species of *Mirabilis,* including the common four-o'clock (*Mirabilis jalapa*), this corolloid calyx is subtended by a calyx-like involucre of five basally united bracts. One would be tempted to interpret such flowers as having an ordinary calyx and corolla, were it not that some other species of *Mirabilis* have two or more flowers within the calyx-like involucre. In both structure and function, the flowers of *Mirabilis jalapa* are comparable to ordinary flowers that have a differentiated calyx and corolla, but they have achieved this condition by a different route. Because of the existence of a series of transitional forms, it is useful in this case to define the parts on the basis of homologies rather than on appearance and function.

Froelichia, in the Amaranthaceae, provides another example in which evident homologies govern the morphological interpretation of the flower. *Froelichia* has what appears to be a small but otherwise fairly ordinary sympetalous flower, with epipetalous stamens attached at the sinuses between the five corolla-lobes. Comparison with other members of the Amaranthaceae shows, however, that these flowers are better interpreted as having a filament-tube with alternating sterile and anther-bearing lobes. Transitional stages are shown by various genera. It would not be helpful to make radically different interpretations of homologous floral parts within the same family.

In floral parts of all kinds the general evolutionary progression is from a large and indefinite number of parts to a small and definite number. Stages in the change from spirally arranged perianth-members of indefinite number to cyclically arranged ones of definite (and usually smaller) number can be seen in various members of the Magnoliidae. *Magnolia* presents a good series from one type to the other among its various species. Here, as elsewhere, the same evolutionary tendency is independently expressed in many lines, so that the common possession of an advanced (apomorphic) character is no guarantee of relationship.

Reduction in number of tepals from numerous and indefinite to few and definite in number commonly results in the formation of a single cycle (compressed spiral) of sepals and a single cycle of petals. The two cycles are not continuous; instead they are offset so that the petals and sepals spread on alternate radii. The petals are said to be alternate with the sepals.

Two sets of sepals, or two sets of petals, offset from each other in the manner of a set of sepals and a set of petals, are much less frequently seen. *Liriodendron* (Magnoliaceae) and many of the Annonaceae have three cycles of three tepals each. The outer set is usually interpreted as sepals, and the two inner sets as petals. Some of the Sapotaceae, such as *Manilkara* and *Mimusops,* have two cycles of sepals, and some species of *Mentzelia* have two cycles of petals.

Except for members of the Magnoliidae, the possession of more than one cycle of sepals, or more than one cycle of petals, is always secondary rather than primitive. In the Sapotaceae the bicyclic calyx apparently results from an increase in the number of sepals, correlated with a change in their arrangement. The number of petals is also increased in these genera, but the corolla is sympetalous and the increased number of petals is therefore maintained in a single cycle. In some other members of the Sapotaceae, such as *Calocarpum* (a segregate from *Pouteria*), the number of sepals only is increased, but the basically spiral arrangement is maintained, and there is no distinction into two sets. We have already noted that the petals of the second cycle in *Mentzelia* are essentially staminodes; the more archaic species of *Mentzelia* have only five petals in a single cycle.

It should be noted that cycles of perianth-parts are, in origin, compressed spirals. Often this can be seen on close inspection, as in the common quincuncial arrangement of sepals, which represents a very tight spiral on a 2/5 phyllotaxy. The two outermost sepals are wholly exposed, the two innermost ones are wholly included, and one sepal has one margin exposed and the other included.

The tendency for the perianth to consist of an outer, protective part (the calyx) and an inner, attractive part (the corolla) is obviously functional. The frequent secondary reduction or loss of petals, often accompanied by abandonment of insect-pollination, is more difficult to explain. Perhaps it results in some cases from pleiotropic effects of otherwise useful genes, and in others from happenstance counterselective fixation in small populations. We have noted in CHAPTER 1 that a change in a single gene can break a biosynthetic chain and prevent the development of a complex, multigenically controlled structure.

The change from numerous, spirally arranged perianth-parts to fewer, cyclic ones reflects the general trend toward condensation that permeates floral evolution. Conceivably this particular manifestation of the trend might reflect simple economy, but it is a bit difficult to see enough advantage in it to provide much selective force. Perhaps an abundant supply of the right mutations, with or without a small selective advantage, would provide the requisite impetus.

As Stebbins (1967) has emphasized, the number of floral parts of a kind may also undergo evolutionary increase. Most such increases affect parts that have not yet been reduced to definite cycles, so that the number is commonly given in botanical descriptions merely as "numerous." Such phyletic increases in parts that are already numerous easily escape attention. Increases in numbers of parts that have already been reduced to one or two cycles are much less common, but they undoubtedly occur. Some probable examples have already been mentioned here, and others are documented by Stebbins.

Fibonacci Numbers

The most common number of sepals or petals in the dicots is five, in the monocots three. Sets of four also occur, less commonly, in both groups. Other numbers, except for the large and indefinite numbers in some of the more archaic families, are relatively rare. It is probably significant that the numbers three and five both belong to the Fibonacci series.

Leonardo Fibonacci (Leonardo of Pisa, born about 1170, died after 1240) was the most distinguished mathematician of the European Middle ages. We are concerned here only with his numerical series, the Fibonacci series, in which, starting with 1, each succeeding number is the sum of the two previous numbers. The series therefore proceeds 1, 1, 2, 3, 5, 8, 13, 21, 34, 55, ...

It is well known that Fibonacci numbers figure in phyllotaxy, typical phyllotaxies being 1/3, 2/5, 3/8, 5/13, etc. These arrangements are not so different as might at first appear. If they are put in terms of the arc of a circle that they represent, the higher phyllotaxies progressively approach a figure of 137.5+ degrees. Two-fifths of a circle is 144 degrees; three-eights of a circle is 135 degrees; five-thirteenths of a circle is 138.6− degrees; eight-twenty-firsts of a circle is 137.14+ degrees, etc. The same figures may also be expressed as angles of divergence between successive leaves in the phyllotactic spiral. The ultimate angle toward which the higher phyllotaxies converge is called the Fibonacci angle.

Efforts to explain why phyllotaxy follows such a pattern usually center about the geometry of close packing. I am not fully satisfied with any of them, but I have nothing better to offer. This is a problem in morphogenesis, rather than in taxonomy or phylogeny per se, and it will not be further pursued here.

Inasmuch as the various sorts of floral appendages are in the last analysis all homologous with leaves (at least they are serial homologues), it seems reasonable to consider their arrangement as a facet of phyllotaxy. It is easy enough to see that the quincuncial arrangement of sepals and petals in many flowers reflects the presence of two complete spirals of parts of each kind in a 2/5 phyllotaxy. When the two spirals of sepals are compressed into what amounts to a single cycle, the sepals are nicely spaced at angles of 72 degrees around the circle. If one sepal were added in the same sequence, it would fall directly in front of the first sepal, and subsequent numbers in the same progression would likewise fall in front of other sepals. Such additional sepals might be expected to be superfluous. Given a 2/5 phyllotaxy, 5 is the only number of sepals that can be symmetrically arranged to give a uniform coverage without superfluity. The same sort of argument applies equally to the number of petals. The number 3, so common in monocots, reflects a 1/3 phyllotaxy. Symmetrical arrangements of 8 and 13 are also theoretically possible, and indeed they are occasionally seen in species of *Ranunculus* and other genera.

Except for some primitive kinds of flowers with indefinite numbers of parts, the sepals and petals do not form a continuous spiral. Instead the petals are in their own compressed spiral separate from that of the sepals, and the two series are offset so that each petal is midway between two sepals. Occasionally there may be the same sort of separate cycles in parts of the same kind. Thus flowers with 4 petals, as in the large families Brassicaceae and Onagraceae, probably have two cycles of petals each, arranged in a 1/2 phyllotaxy, the second cycle being offset at 90 degrees from the first. In a few kinds of plants, such as some species of *Pouteria,* some flowers have 5 quincuncial sepals, whereas other flowers on the same plant have 4 sepals arranged in 2 pairs like those of the Brassicaceae. The change in number and position of the sepals is basically a reflection of the change in phyllotaxy.

Fibonacci numbers also appear frequently in inflorescences, as in the number of rays in an umbel, and in the numbers of involucral bracts, ray-flowers, or total flowers in the heads of the Asteraceae. Here, as in numbers of perianth-parts, these numbers apparently reflect the phyllotaxy. Numbers above 5 are often unstable, however, and actual counts in a series of individuals may show a considerable range of variation, with the Fibonacci number being merely the high point on a more or less normal curve of distribution.

Sometimes there is even a bimodal curve, with the two high points being adjacent Fibonacci numbers, such as 8 and 13, or 13 and 21. Here we have the seeming anomaly of a bimodal curve that lacks taxonomic significance. *Senecio canus* shows a bimodal curve in the number of principal involucral bracts, with high points of 13 and 21. I was at first tempted to try to distinguish two species on this basis, but with further study it became evident that the more vigorous individuals, or the larger heads in a given inflorescence, tended to center about 21, whereas the less vigorous individuals, or the smaller heads in an inflorescence, tended to center on 13.

Bimodal curves of Fibonacci numbers sometimes do reflect specific differences, however. *Bidens frondosa* has five to ten (typically eight) outer involucral bracts, whereas the closely related *B. vulgata* has ten to 16 (typically 13). *Tragopogon dubius* characteristically has 13 involucral bracts on the primary head in well developed plants, the number sometimes varying down to eight in later heads or on depauperate plants. The closely related *T. pratensis* generally has eight involucral bracts, regardless of vigor.

Union of Parts; Hypogyny, Perigyny, and Epigyny

Under the strobilar hypothesis of floral evolution, floral leaves of a given kind are ancestrally separate and similar to each other. Separate sepals may at a later stage in evolution be joined (connate) to form a synsepalous calyx. Separate petals may be joined to form a sympetalous corolla. Separate stamens may be joined by their filaments to form a filament-tube. Separate carpels may be joined to form a compound ovary. Evolutionary change may also lead to differences among parts of a given kind, whether these are separate or connate.

Parts of different kinds may also come to be joined (adnate) through evolutionary change. Stamens may appear to arise from the petals, or from the corolla-tube, instead of directly from the receptacle. The sepals and petals may be collectively joined at the base. Still other possibilities exist.

One expression of the tendency for floral parts of different kinds to become attached to each other is the frequent fusion of the basal parts of the calyx, corolla, and androecium. The compound structure thus formed is called a hypanthium, or floral tube. The hypanthium often resembles the calyx in texture, so that the petals and stamens appear to be inserted on the calyx-tube. In some plants, such as many legumes, the proper calyx-tube extends well beyond the hypanthium, with no obvious change in texture. In others, such as *Prunus* and many members of the Rosaceae and Saxifragaceae, the hypanthium is coextensive with the apparent calyx-tube; the stamens, petals, and apparent calyx-lobes all diverge from the rim of the hypanthium. The different floral organs making up the hypanthium may also be adnate to different levels, so that the stamens appear to be attached to the calyx-tube lower down than the petals.

It is customary and convenient to define the hypanthium in terms of external descriptive morphology rather than on evolutionary homologies. In the Monimiaceae and a few other families the hypanthium is probably an expanded receptacle with an interval separating the carpels from the other floral appendages. Vascular anatomy suggests that the lower part of the hypanthium in *Rosa* is actually the hollowed-out edge of the receptacle, and that only the upper part consists of the fused bases of the sepals, petals, and stamens. In external appearance, however, the hypanthium of *Rosa* is a single discrete structure, well differentiated from the other parts of the flower, and bearing the sepals, petals, and stamens at its summit.

Flowers that have a hypanthium and a superior ovary are said to be perigynous. Perigynous flowers become epigynous (phyletically) by adnation of the hypanthium to the ovary. Sometimes, as in many of the Saxifragaceae, only the lower part of the ovary is adnate to the hypanthium, and the ovary is only partly inferior, the flower partly epigynous.

Or, as in many Onagraceae, the hypanthium may extend well beyond the wholly inferior ovary.

Epigyny may also originate in other ways. In the Rubiaceae and Campanulaceae it appears that the bases of the calyx, corolla, and androecium are all fused to the ovary wall, without any history of a separate hypanthium. The Rubiaceae, with inferior ovary, are generally admitted to be closely related to but more advanced than the Loganiaceae, with superior ovary. Two genera with hypogynous flowers, *Pagamea* and *Gaertnera,* form a sort of connecting link between the two families. On formal morphological characters they should be referred to the Loganiaceae, but they find their nearest relatives in the Rubiaceae instead. If epigyny in the Rubiaceae has a perigynous ancestry, there is no indication of it in the species alive today. Although most of the Campanulaceae have the ovary wholly inferior, some few members are essentially hypogynous, and others have the ovary partly inferior in varying degrees. Here again there is no history of a separate hypanthium.

Less commonly, the ovary may become inferior by submergence in the receptacle. This appears to be true in the Santalaceae. A complicated version of receptacular epigyny has been proposed to explain the floral structure in the Cactaceae (Boke, 1964).

The fact the perigyny and epigyny can be derived from hypogyny by different routes necessitates some caution in the construction of phylogenetic trees or parsimonious cladograms. What appears on first consideration to be one apomorphy may actually be two or three different ones.

Sequence of Maturation of Floral Organs

Inasmuch as a flower is essentially a condensed short shoot with specialized leaves, one might a priori expect the floral appendages to mature in serial sequence from the outside (or bottom) to the inside (or top). A little investigation shows that the situation is often much more complex. The first question is how maturity is to be judged. The stamens are mature when they shed their pollen, but the carpels are not truly mature until the fruit is ripe. In *Ranunculus* and some other genera the calyx is commonly deciduous at about the time of anthesis. In many others it persists but does not enlarge materially. In still others, such as *Hyoscyamus* and *Physalis,* it is both persistent and accrescent, investing the mature fruit; the carpels and sepals thus mature simultaneously, long after the petals and stamens have fallen.

If one judges maturity by the time of anthesis, there are still problems. The calyx obviously must open before the corolla can expand, but the stamens and carpels do not necessarily follow in sequence. The androecium and gynoecium may mature at essentially the same time, or either one may mature before the other. Both protandry and protogyny are well known in many widely differing families. The flowers may even be self-pollinated in bud, long before the perianth has opened. These numerous

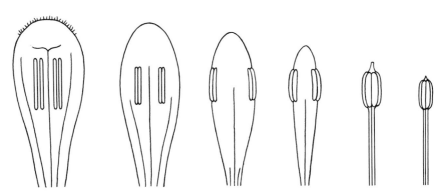

Fig. 5.9. Idealized series from the laminar stamen of *Degeneria* (LEFT) to the typical angiosperm stamen with filament and anther. Transitional forms such as those shown here exist among several families of the Magnoliales.

deviations from a simple serial sequence doubtless represent "advances" (apomorphies) from the ancestral type, but they occur in so many different groups as to provide little or no significant information for the general system at the level of families and orders.

When the floral parts of a given kind form only a single cycle, it is usually difficult or impossible to see any sequence of maturation among them, and even the sequence of initiation may be difficult to determine or subject to apparently random variation. When they are more numerous and form a spiral or several cycles, they often mature (or at least are initiated) in serial sequence. Here again one might expect the sequence to be from the outside inwards, and here again the facts do not wholly conform to the expectation.

The stamens in polystemonous androecia may be initiated in either centripetal or centrifugal sequence, according to the taxonomic group. Polystemonous members of the Magnoliidae and Rosidae are usually centripetal, whereas those in the Caryophyllidae and Dilleniidae are usually centrifugal. Unfortunately, the taxonomic distinction on this basis is less reliable than was once supposed. Thus the Punicaceae (Myrtales, Rosidae) are reported to be centrifugal, in contrast to the centripetal Myrtaceae in the same order (Mayr, 1969). Polystemonous members of the Begoniaceae (Violales, Dilleniidae) are reported to be centripetal (Merxmüller & Leins, 1971), instead of centrifugal as might be expected in the Dilleniidae. The Loasaceae show both sequences in the same family. The Loasoideae are reported to be centrifugal, and the Mentzelioideae centripetal (Leins & Winhard, 1973). In the Winteraceae the sequence of initiation of stamens may be unstable even in a single flower, according to Endress (1986).

We must now suppose that the sequence of initiation of stamens is reversible, although it does not seem that reversals happen very often. Like other taxonomic characters, this one sometimes fails. The failures compromise its usefulness but do not vitiate it. The existence of both sequences within a single taxonomic group is ample reason to pause and reconsider, but it does not by itself require dissolution of the group. We may note in passing that one order which has been considered to embrace both types (the Rhoeadales) is now generally divided on other grounds into two orders. One of these, the Papaverales, turns out to have centripetal stamens, whereas the other, the Capparales, has centrifugal stamens. The possibility that the centrifugal sequence is correlated with a secondary increase in number of stamens is discussed on page 210. I have no idea of the possible selective significance of the sequence of initiation of the stamens.

Although the developmental sequence does appear to have some taxonomic value in groups with spirally arranged stamens, it is perhaps more variable in groups with cyclic stamens. In both *Oxalis* and *Geranium* it is reported by Eames (1961) that the sequence of development may be in either direction.

Stamens

We are so accustomed to seeing typical stamens, with slender filament and sharply differentiated anther, that it comes as something of a shock to see the laminar stamen of *Degeneria*. Here there is neither anther nor filament, but a broad, somewhat petal-like, sessile lamina, with two pairs of elongate pollen-sacs embedded on the abaxial side, well removed from the tip. This stamen furthermore has three vascular traces from the base.

There is now little doubt that the laminar stamen with embedded pollen-sacs, as seen in *Degeneria* (Fig. 5.9) and some other Magnolialean genera, is a primitive type. All transitional stages between laminar, three-trace stamens and typical single-trace stamens with filament and anther can be seen within various members of the Magnoliidae—indeed even within the family Magnoliaceae. The prominently exserted connective seen in so many members of the Annonaceae is merely a vestige of the ancestral lamina.

It is not certain whether the primitive position of the embedded pollen-sacs is on the adaxial or the abaxial side of the laminar stamen. Both positions can be seen: abaxial in *Degeneria* and *Galbulimima,* adaxial in *Austrobaileya* and *Magnolia*. I am not convinced that the difference in position has any great phylogenetic importance. A simple ontogenetic change, possibly of little or no selective significance, could govern the position. We cannot expect the plant to have an ancestral memory telling it which side of the ancestral microsporophyll bore the sporangia. Plants do not directly inherit characters: they inherit genes. Neither are the plants bound by our morphological concepts. Changes that seem radical to us may be insignificant to the plants.

Once the stamen has been reduced to the familiar anther-filament form, the orientation of the pollen-sacs is easily modified. Introrse and extrorse orientation can sometimes been seen in different genera of the same family, as in the Lauraceae. The position may even change ontogenetically;

certain palms are reported to have the stamens introrse in bud but extrorse at anthesis. Introrse orientation is much more common in "typical" stamens than extrorse, and probably more extrorse stamens are only secondarily rather than primitively so. Most of the more archaic members of the Hamamelidae have latrorse anthers, an otherwise uncommon type.

Reduction of the androecium from many stamens to few has occurred a number of times, and probably in more than one way. The ordinary way is for the indefinite spiral to be organized into several cycles, after which whole cycles may be dropped out at once. Thus the progression might go from numerous and spiraled, to four cycles, to three cycles, to two cycles, to a single cycle. These several cycles are offset from each other in the same way that the cycle of petals is offset from the cycle of sepals. Thus the outermost set of stamens is normally alternate with the petals (and opposite the sepals), the next set is opposite the petals, and so on.

Either the inner or the outer cycle of stamens may be the first to be lost. In several families (e.g., Caryophyllaceae, Geraniaceae) which commonly have two sets of stamens, the outer set is opposite the petals, suggesting that a third set, outside the other two, has been lost. This condition is called obdiplostemony. Eames (1961) pointed out that the sequence of development of the cycles does not necessarily conform to their position in the flower. Eckert (1966) considered that obdiplostemony frequently reflects changes in the details of floral ontogeny, rather than reflecting the loss of an outer set of stamens. At the present time the phylogenetic significance of obdiplostemony is at best debatable.

Two cycles of stamens may also be condensed into one with or without loss of some members. Eames (1961) notes that "In the papilionate Leguminosae, the ten stamens may arise as two whorls but, in maturity, form one; differential growth brings the two whorls together. . . ." Many species of *Acer* with a 5-merous perianth have 8 stamens in what appears to be a single cycle, as do many members of the related family Sapindaceae. There is some anatomical evidence to support the view that here we have a melding of two cycles, with a loss of some members.

When the stamens are reduced to a single cycle, these are usually alternate with the petals, suggesting that they belong to either the first or the third ancestral set (counting from the outside). Sometimes, on the other hand, the single cycle of stamens is opposite the petals, as in the Primulaceae, suggesting that only the second cycle (or the fourth) has been retained.

The genus *Mitella*, in the Saxifragaceae, provides an especially instructive example of the reduction of two sets of stamens to one. Some species, such as *M. nuda*, have stamens in two sets, one set opposite the sepals, the other set opposite the petals. Other species, such as *M. pentandra*, have a single set of 5 stamens, these opposite the petals. Still other species, such as *M. breweri*, have a single set of 5 stamens, opposite the sepals. The two different groups of five-stamened species reflect the loss of different sets of stamens. The segregation of the five-stamened species as a distinct genus, which has been proposed by some taxonomists, is therefore indefensible. The two groups of five-stamened species relate not directly to each other, but separately to the ten-stamened ancestral type.

Another way that numerous, spirally arranged stamens can be reduced to a single cycle is for the stamens to be grouped into fascicles, and the number of stamens in each fascicle then progressively reduced by fusion or abortion. Each such fascicle is usually alternate with a petal, opposite a sepal.

An early stage in this sort of reduction is shown by *Paeonia,* in which the tendency toward fasciculation can be demonstrated only by careful ontogenetic anatomical studies (Hiepko, 1964). In the Dilleniaceae, the single genus *Hibbertia* shows all conditions from numerous, free stamens to five fascicles of stamens, to five separate stamens, and thence to only a single stamen. In the Clusiaceae, *Hypericum* has a similar series from numerous, separate stamens to five fascicles of three stamens each. These several groups all have centrifugal stamens, but a similar apparent reduction series associated with grouping into fascicles exists in the Myrtaceae, which have centripetal stamens.

We should note at this point that in a great many plants with numerous stamens the androecium is supplied by a limited number of trunk-bundles from which the individual stamen-traces arise. On this basis Stebbins (1974) has mounted a comprehensive challenge to the now traditional interpretation of stamens as individual microsporophylls that are archetypically numerous and arranged in spiral sequence. He maintains that the serial homologues of tepals and carpels in the flower are not the individual stamens (when these are numerous) but stamen-clusters associated with the trunk-bundles. He explicitly revives the telomic interpretation of the androecium that was put forward many years ago (1937) by Wilson at a time when the telome-theory of Zimmermann (1930) was still a bright and shiny new idea of undetermined limits. In my opinion the telome-theory is indeed useful in understanding the Paleozoic evolution of many vascular cryptogams and early gymnosperms, but it has no place in the morphology of the angiosperms.

Stebbins' interpretation is difficult to harmonize with the abundant evidence from comparative morphology of the Magnoliales that stamens are indeed sporophylls and not telomes. Even though the androecium of *Degeneria* is supplied by a limited number of trunk-bundles, I balk at the concept of the series of changes that would be necessary to produce the present morphology and arrangement of these stamens from ancestral clusters of telomic stamens. It is an unnecessary complication, vulnerable to Occam's Razor. Instead I would read the series the other way: Evolutionary reduction in the number of stamens frequently begins in the vascular supply, with numerous individual traces being combined into a limited number of trunk-bundles. Then the spirally arranged stamens of many Magnoliidae and the separate stamen-traces in some of them, need no special explanation; these groups have simply retained the ancestral condition. We may now call on the mid-Cretaceous fossil *Archaeanthus* (Dilcher & Crane, 1984) to document the antiquity of the arrangement of numerous stamens in spiral sequence.

Without invoking the telome-theory, some botanists have thought that polystemony associated with centrifugal initiation of stamens reflects a secondary increase from a previously unicyclic or bicyclic androecium. Here again the limited number of trunk-bundles is seen as phylogenetically significant. No challenge is raised to the thought that stamens in the angiosperms as a whole are primitively numerous and spirally arranged; only centrifugal stamens are thought to be secondarily numerous.

There are two principal problems with this interpretation. One is the wide distribution of trunk-bundles in centripetal as well as centrifugal taxa. The other is the probable interconvertability of centripetal and centrifugal sequences. Stebbins notes the presence of trunk-bundles in *Degeneria, Cercidiphyllum, Kadsura,* and at least some members of the Annonaceae, Ranunculaceae, Papaveraceae, Rosaceae, and Myrtaceae, all considered to be centripetal. Trunk-bundles can hardly be interpreted to indicate secondary polystemony in centrifugal androecia, but not in centripetal ones. Likewise the presence of both centripetal and centrifugal stamens in the Myrtales (as noted on an earlier page) is difficult to reconcile with an interpretation that only centrifugal androecia reflect a secondary increase.

Data on stamens in the Alismatales also undercut the theoretical evolutionary significance of the sequence of initiation. In both the Alismataceae and the Limnocharitaceae the genera with numerous stamens have trunk-bundles from which the individual stamen-traces arise. In the Alismataceae the stamens appear to be spirally arranged, but they are actually in several centripetally originating cycles, with successively fewer members in the upper cycles. In the closely related family Limnocharitaceae the stamens (when numerous) are centrifugal (Kaul, 1967a, 1967b, 1968).

All this is not to deny the possibility that some groups of polystemonous angiosperms may have oligostemonous ancestors. Perhaps some do, but we need better evidence than trunk-bundles and centrifugality.

The very large number of stamens in some families, such as the Aizoaceae, Cactaceae, and Malvaceae, doubtless reflects an increase from a more moderate (but still polymerous) number. In the Malvaceae the very numerous anthers are bisporangiate and monothecal and doubtless represent separated half-anthers.

My present thought is that stamens of indefinite number may increase or decrease, but that once the process of organization into cycles and/or fascicles has begun, significant reversals are rare. I do not understand the origin of centrifugality, but I do not believe that it results from a secondary increase in the number of stamens.

Once the stamens have been reduced to a single cycle, the number of stamens in the cycle may be further reduced, so that there are fewer stamens than petals. This has happened, for example, in the Scrophulariaceae and Lamiaceae, both of which typically have five corolla-lobes and only two or four functional stamens. In both of these families it is perfectly clear that one or more stamens have been modified or lost, and the missing stamens are often represented by vestigial parts. In some of the Scrophulariaceae, such as *Penstemon,* the fifth stamen has a well developed, more or less modified filament but no anther.

Increase in number of stamens, once they have been confined to a single cycle, is much less common. In some of the Sapotaceae the number of stamens has probably increased concomitantly with an increase in the number of sepals and petals, but the number is still not large. In *Adoxa* each stamen has evidently been divided longitudinally; the stamens are borne in pairs at the sinuses of the corolla, and each stamen has only a single pollen-sac. The recently discovered genus *Sinadoxa* shows an intermediate stage, with bifurcate filaments, each fork terminated by a single pollen-sac.

Pollen

Pollen-grains have a dual wall. The inner layer, or intine, is cellulosic, relatively simple in structure, and much alike from one taxonomic group to the next. It does not fossilize well, and it is destroyed by the acetolysis used in the preparation of modern pollen for study. It has been largely ignored by systematic palynologists. The exine, in contrast, consists of carotenoid polymers called sporopollenin. It is structurally complex, and the structure often differs in consistent ways from one taxon to the next. It is highly resistant to biological and chemical degradation, and it fossilizes in exquisite detail. Electron microscopy (both SEM and TEM) has vastly expanded the range of features of the exine that can be observed. Palynology, with emphasis on the exine, has accordingly played an increasing role in taxonomic and evolutionary studies of angiosperms during the past several decades.

A mixture of miscellaneous, mainly lipid material derived from the tapetum is commonly deposited on the surface of the pollen-grains in angiosperms. This material is called pollenkitt. It makes the pollen sticky, facilitating group transfer during pollination. In anemophilous angiosperms the pollenkitt is mainly deposited on or transferred to the cavities in the exine, so that the surface remains dry and the grains can be individually dispersed (Hesse, 1981).

Pollenkitt has not been found in gymnosperms (including *Gnetum*) so far examined. Thus it appears to be an apomorphic feature of angiosperms.

The most plausible evolutionary interpretation is that pollenkitt originated in association with entomophily early in the history of angiosperms. Evolutionary return to anemophily in various taxa was accompanied by sequestration of the pollenkitt beneath the surface of the pollen-grain, and sometimes also by a reduction in the amount. This interpretation lends some support to the view, posited on other grounds, that entomophily is basic to the angiosperms.

Differences in the shape of the pollen-grains and more especially in the structure and ornamentation of the wall provide many valuable taxonomic characters. The most useful of these characters, from a broad-scale point of view, is the number of germ-furrows (colpi). These furrows are elongate strips in which the wall is relatively thin and elastic. Usually each furrow contains a particularly thin (or rupturable) spot, the germinal pore, through which the pollen-tube may emerge. Sometimes these germinal pores are dissociated from the furrows, or the pollen-tube may emerge from a germinal furrow that shows no specialized germ-pore.

Most angiosperm pollen-grains fall into only two general types, uniaperturate and triaperturate, from which some less common types have been derived. Uniaperturate pollen-grains have a single germinal furrow or pore, usually across the end opposite to the contact-zone of the members of the tetrad. Triaperturate grains primitively have three germinal furrows radiating like the lines of a trilete mark, but at the opposite end from where a trilete mark would be if there were one. (A trilete mark is the three-parted ridge or scar that marks the contact-lines of a tetrahedral tetrad of spores.) Typically the three germ-furrows of a triaperturate grain are fairly short and well separated; sometimes they stand at the angles of the grain.

Uniaperturate grains are characteristic of the monocots, some members of the Magnoliidae, and all Cycadicae, including the pteridosperms. Triaperturate grains occur in the bulk of the dicots and are almost unknown elsewhere. Each of these two main types appears to have given rise to multiaperturate and inaperturate types, which are found in both monocots and dicots. The multiaperturate type may arise by cross-partitioning of one germinal furrow into several, or by saltatory increase. Change from one aperture to three is apparently a rare event, which has happened successfully only a few times in the history of the angiosperms, but further increase is apparently easier and has happened repeatedly. Inaperturate grains are a derived type with a very thin exine but no special place for germination. The more appropriate term holo-aperturate has sometimes been applied to them, but has not come into consistent usage.

In more precise descriptions of triaperturate grains it is customary to distinguish between strictly tricolpate grains (in which the furrows lack pores or especial thin spots), tricolporoidate grains (in which there is a suggestion of a germ-pore in each furrow), tricolporate grains (in which each furrow has a specialized germ-pore), and triporate grains (which have germ-pores but not furrows). More loosely, the term tricolpate has in the past often been used to cover all the types with three furrows, whether or not these are provided with pores, but this usage is now passé.

A similar distinction is made among uniaperturate pollen-grains, with the term monosulcate often being substituted for monocolpate sensu stricto. Uniaperturate grains with a very large round opening are often described as ulcerate, especially if the margins are irregular. The terminology is still developing and changing.

I share in the consensus among palynologists that evolutionary progression in apertures has been from colpate to colporoidate to colporate to porate. Within this series there are many grades, refinements, and special conditions, not here discussed. As we have noted, the holo-aperturate type is also considered to be derived, resulting from a pervasive reduction of the thickness of the exine.

It is generally agreed that the uniaperturate type of pollen-grain is primitive among the angiosperms and that the triaperturate type is derived from it. Real intermediates between the two types are few and difficult to interpret, however, and there has been some controversy about how one type is derived from the other. It does not appear that there is a simple stepwise progression from one to two to three. The relatively few biaperturate pollen-grains appear to be separately related either to uniaperturate or to triaperturate forms, but they do not suggest an evolutionary connection between the two fundamentally different types.

Perhaps the most likely hypothesis for the origin of triaperturate grains is that of Tom Wilson (1964), which was inspired by his observations in the Canellaceae (Magnoliales). In all members of the Canellaceae that have been studied, most or all of the pollen is of an undistinguished, monosulcate type. Some species, however, have a small percentage of other sorts of grains intermingled with the more common ones. Some of these unusual grains have the single furrow bent at the middle, so as to be broadly V-shaped. Others differ from the V-type in having a short side-spur at the point of the V, so that the furrow is Y-shaped (trichotomosulcate). It is but a short step from such a Y-shaped furrow to three separate furrows. Exactly this sort of serial change appears to have happened in the palms, which show all transitions from monosulcate, through trichotomosulcate, to virtually tricolpate, and in *Sclerosperma mannii* triporate. Such a direct series has not been shown, however, in the dicots, to which triaperturate grains are otherwise restricted.

It may be significant that some Albian (late Lower Cretaceous) pollen-grains, called *Asteropollis,* have a star-shaped sulcus with four to six arms radiating from a center. It should not be difficult to convert such a grain into one with several separate, radiating furrows, as seen in some other Albian pollen that has been called *Stephanocolpites fredericksburgensis.* (I here pass by the strictly nomenclatural problem associated with this name.) James and Audrey Walker (1984) find a close similarity between these two sorts of Albian pollen-grains and those of the modern genera *Hedyosmum* and *Chloranthus,* respectively, in the Chloranthaceae. *Ascarina,* also in the Chloranthaceae, has monosulcate pollen that compares well with some other Lower Cretaceous (even Barremian) pollen, called *Clavatipollenites.* If four to six apertures can be derived from one in this way, three should be no harder. Yet the actual transitional types are scarce. We may note in passing that I am not so optimistic as the Walkers about the possibility that other features of the plants that produced these Lower Cretaceous grains are equally comparable to features of the modern Chloranthaceae. Neither do I suppose that most of the early Lower Cretaceous leaf-fossils should be referred to the Winteraceae simply because of similarities in venation of the leaves.

The adaptive significance of the changes in number and distribution of the germ-furrows and germ-pores is obscure. With a little stretching of the imagination one might suppose that grains with germ-pores are more efficient than those with only germ-furrows, but the competitive advantage, if any, must be vanishingly small. A case might be made that triaperturate grains could have a small advantage in timing of germination, because of the better prospect that one aperture will be juxtaposed to the stigmatic surface. (A comparison might be made to the red throats of nestling birds; the bright color is of no importance to the species, but likely to be vital to the individual.) But why then do most species get along with just three apertures, whereas others progress to a multi-aperturate structure? Why have so many parallel lines within the Caryophyllales progressed from triaperturate to multiporate? Why do the vast majority of monocots get along with just one aperture? Why have the Zingiberales progressed to a holo-aperturate structure? I pose the questions, but I do not offer any answers.

Aside from apertural features, the polarity of evolutionary change in the structure of the exine of angiosperms is only partly resolved. There is a continuous morphological series from solid to cavitate to tectate-granular to tectate-columellate. The three latter types may collectively be called interstitiate, meaning that there is a nonsolid interstitium between the solid foot-layer and the upper layer or tectum. The tectum itself may be imperforate (solid and continuous) or perforate (with scattered holes into the interstitium). In a few angiosperms, said to be atectate, the tectum is lost but the columellae remain.

The tectate-columellate structure is by far the commonest type in the angiosperms, to which it is almost entirely limited. A few presumably gymnospermous tectate-columellate and tectate-granular pollen-grains are known from pre-Cretaceous deposits, extending even as far back as the Triassic (Zavada, 1984). These are not associated with angiospermous leaves or other angiospermous organs, and some are associated with gymnospermous fructifications.

It is possible that the evolutionary sequence of exine-structure in the angiosperms is exactly the same as the morphological sequence just described. Such archaic families as the Magnoliaceae and Annonaceae show all transitions from solid through tectate-granular to tectate-columellate. The Degeneriaceae, Himantandraceae, and Eupomatiaceae (all Magnoliales) have a solid exine. So far so good.

There are some problems, however, with the concept that the solid exine is primitive. A few more advanced families, notably the Bataceae and Gyrostemonaceae, also have a solid exine. Here it must be supposed that the solid condition has been derived from a tectate-columellate one. That is not immediately fatal to the hypothesis. Reversals occur in other characters, and they might also occur in the structure of the exine. Still, it is well to take another look at the evidence. Among both modern and fossil gymnosperms, the most common exine-structure is spongy or alveolar, essentially the type that the Walkers designate as cavitate, rather than solid. *Caytonia,* the glossopterids, the modern cycads, and many of the seed-ferns (though not the Bennettitales) agree in having a cavitate exine. Doyle (1978) concludes that "From a paleobotanical perspective,

relatively homogeneous and granular exines appear secondarily specialized from alveolar or spongy types rather than vice versa." As we have
noted in CHAPTER 4, the oldest known angiosperm pollen, from Hauterivian deposits in Israel, is tectate-columellate. Would we recognize
otherwise similar pollen of the same or greater age, but with a solid or
cavitate exine as being angiospermous? Perhaps not. So let us be cautious
about the evolutionary status of the solid exine in angiosperms, while
tentatively accepting the remainder of the sequence, from tectate-granular
to tectate-columellate and eventually atectate. The possibility that the
exine in the earliest angiosperms or their immediate ancestors was saccate
has been discussed on page 150.

In most angiosperms the pollen-grain has two nuclei when it is shed
from the anther. One of these, the generative nucleus, later divides to
produce two sperm nuclei. In a considerable number of taxa the generative
nucleus divides before the pollen is shed, so that the grains are trinucleate.
This early division of the generative nucleus apparently represents one
more step in the progressive compression of the gametophyte that characterizes vascular plants in general. In considering binucleate and trinucleate pollen-types, the student should remember that both types produce
mature male gametophytes with three nuclei; the difference lies in when
the generative nucleus divides.

Some whole orders, such as the Caryophyllales, have trinucleate pollen
in nearly all members. Other orders and individual families include both
binucleate and trinucleate types. No taxonomic grouping can properly be
based on this character alone, any more than on any other single character.
It does appear, however, that the change is not easily reversed. There are
no binucleate groups of significant size that clearly have a trinucleate
ancestry.

The number of nuclei in the pollen-grain is strongly (though not perfectly) correlated with a syndrome of physiological features. In general,
binucleate pollen has a high storage-longevity, and can easily be germinated in vitro. Genetic incompatibility operates through substances in the
ovary or style that act only after the pollen-grain has germinated. Trinucleate pollen, on the other hand, usually has a low storage-longevity,
and it is not easily germinated in vitro. Genetic incompatibility usually
operates at the stigma, preventing the pollen from germinating. Brewbaker
(1967) has suggested that

> "The syndrome of differences between II and III pollen can
> best be explained by assuming that the second mitotic division
> deprives the pollen grain of reserves essential for germination,
> for prolonged storage, and for the growth (albeit limited) into
> styles prior to inhibition by incompatibility alleles. These re-
> serves are perhaps made available to pollen only by genetically
> compatible stigmas, perhaps only following the action of pol-
> len-released enzymes. . . ."

The physiological consequences (or associates) of the trinucleate condition in pollen are so far-reaching that they must be assumed to be part

of an intricate mechanism associated with adaptation and survival. For the most part, however, the details of the operation of the mechanism still escape us. One might speculate that inhibition at the stigma would reserve the style for compatible pollen-tubes, but it is not clear that this would really make any difference to the plant.

Trinucleate pollen obviously should have a strong survival-value in plants that produce flowers beneath the surface of water, where binucleate pollen might well germinate without reaching a stigma. Effective underwater pollination by trinucleate pollen occurs in some or all genera of at least 19 families of diverse affinities, but there are also several genera that get along with binucleate pollen under similar conditions. In some groups the evolution of trinucleate pollen evidently preceded the evolution of submersed flowers; the pollen was preadapted to submersion, rather than selected by it.

Before the physiological consequences of the trinucleate condition had been discovered, the change from binucleate to trinucleate appeared to be unrelated to adaptation and survival. Here we have an example of the hidden significance of a seemingly trivial morphological character. The proportion of other seemingly trivial characters that will turn out to have a real importance remains to be discovered.

Pollination

Flowers of modern angiosperms are pollinated by such diverse agents as wind, water, insects of various orders, birds, bats, and even nonflying mammals such as placental and marsupial mice. They may also be self-pollinated. When the Amentiferae were generally regarded as primitive angiosperms, wind-pollination was regarded as primitive, but with the ascendancy of the Besseyan school of thought, wind-pollination has come to be considered a secondary condition, usually associated with floral reduction.

There are some obvious, though imperfect, correlations of the size and structure of pollen-grains with the method of pollination in modern angiosperms. Wind-distributed pollen tends to be relatively small (usually less than 25 microns in largest diameter), thin-walled, smooth or nearly so, and nonadhesive, in contrast to insect-distributed pollen, which tends to be larger, thicker-walled, variously sculptured, and sticky. These correlations are obviously functional, and need not reflect common ancestry. Wind-distributed pollen is necessarily produced in relatively large amounts. Pollen-deposition in bogs and other places favoring preservation is heavily biased toward anemophilous types. Pollen distributed by birds, bats, and nonflying mammals is essentially similar to insect-distributed types and need not be separately discussed here.

In spite of these correlations, it is not always possible to determine the mode of pollination from the size and appearance of the grain. There is a considerable overlap in size between wind-distributed and insect-distributed pollen. Furthermore, some insect-distributed pollen is smooth,

and some wind-distributed pollen is sculptured. Some species are pollinated partly by wind and partly by insects (vide *Solidago speciosa,* page
220).

It should come as no surprise to find that the fossil record is somewhat
ambiguous as to the evolutionary history of pollination in the angiosperms. Hauterivian pollen from Israel is in a size range (up to 25 microns)
compatible with either entomophily or anemophily, but on the basis of
surface ornamentation and infratectal structure Brenner (unpublished)
considers that it is probably entomophilous. Barremian and Aptian pollen
includes nothing (so far as I know) that is unmistakably adapted to distribution by wind. Some of it is of a size that clearly indicates entomophily,
but much of it could have been either one.

The common and widespread Barremian-Aptian fossil *Clavatipollenites
hughesii* provides a case in point. It is about 25 microns across, and
reticulately sculptured. It is also virtually identical to the pollen of the
modern genus *Ascarina,* in the Chloranthaceae. *Ascarina* has reduced
flowers and is mainly or wholly wind-pollinated. Walker and Walker
(1984) consider that *C. hughesii* was in fact distributed by wind, whereas
some other Barremian-Aptian pollen was distributed by insects. Of course
we have no assurance that *C. hughesii* was produced by plants otherwise
similar to *Ascarina.* Maybe, maybe not. Even if there is a direct ancestor-
descendant relationship, some of the other features of *Ascarina* may have
been acquired long after the stabilization of the pollen.

Taking insect-pollination as basic for the angiosperms, the Walkers
further postulate, largely on the basis of fine details of exine-structure,
that none of the Barremian-Aptian pollen is primitive in all respects.
Therefore they suppose that the initial diversification of the angiosperms
antedates the Barremian. Thus they see no problem in the existence of
both entomophilous and anemphilous types in such ancient angiosperm
pollen.

If the primitive method of pollination is judged on the basis of modern
angiosperms, the evidence is heavily in favor of entomophily. The stro-
biloid flower widely regarded as primitive is obviously better adapted to
entomophily than to anemophily. The archaic order Magnoliales, generally regarded as basal, is essentially entomophilous.

It is now widely believed that many or most of the primitive angiosperms were pollinated mainly by beetles that chewed and ate bits of the
perianth and androecium. Several of the existing magnoliid families (Calycanthaceae, Degeneriaceae, Eupomatiaceae, Himantandraceae, Magnoliaceae, Nymphaeaceae, and many Annonaceae) are still chiefly or wholly
pollinated in this way. These taxa mostly have little or no nectar and no
obvious nectaries, but some of them have more or less specialized, nonse-
cretory "food-bodies" consisting of surficial pads or apical knobs of succulent tissue on the tepals, stamens, and staminodia. These food-bodies
may superficially resemble nectaries.

Recent studies, especially by Leonard Thien and his associates (1980,
1983, 1985), have shown that beetles do not have the field all to themselves
as probable pollinators of the early angiosperms. The single archaic family

Winteraceae includes species pollinated by thrips (Thysanoptera, pollinators of spp. of *Belliolum*), archaic moths (Lepidoptera, pollinators of spp. of *Zygogynum*), and flies (Diptera, pollinators of spp. of *Tasmannia*), as well as beetle-pollinated (spp. of *Drimys*), wind-pollinated (spp. of *Belliolum*), and self-pollinated (*Pseudowintera*) types. Thien considers that the Diptera, in particular, probably have a long-standing role as pollinators of angiosperms, being associated especially with species that have relatively small flowers and produce some nectar. So let us hedge a bit and say that beetles were among the most important, but probably not the exclusive insect pollinators of early angiosperms.

The nectaries of diverse angiosperm families have little in common beyond the production of nectar. Species of some magnoliid genera (e.g., *Tasmannia, Magnolia, Liriodendron,* and *Nymphaea*) do secrete some nectar, but mostly not in localized areas. It apparently diffuses out from the surfaces of the tepals, stamens, and even the carpels, or sometimes more specifically from the stigmas and connectives. In many of the Ranunculaceae some of the stamens are modified into nectariferous staminodia. These are apparently homologous with the petals of *Ranunculus,* which have a basal-adaxial nectary. In some of the "apetalous" families, such as the Proteaceae and Salicaceae (*Salix*), the nectaries probably represent a reduced and modified corolla. In many other families the nectaries are actually reduced stamens. In the Malvales the nectaries consist of tufts of hair at the inner base of the sepals. Parts of the carpels and receptacle may also function as nectaries. The septal nectaries that are so widespread in the monocots probably take their origin in nectariferous lateral surfaces of separate carpels, or in intercarpellary portions of the receptacle.

The inference to be drawn is that nectaries evolved several times independently after the angiosperms were already highly diversified. This brings us back to the thought that the primitive pollinators of the angiosperms were chewing insects such as beetles, rather than nectar-sippers such as bees, flies, and butterflies. Even the moth (*Sabatinca*) that pollinates spp. of *Zygogynum* is a pollen-eating chewer rather than a nectar-sipper. Pollination by birds and bats is also doubtless more recent than beetle-pollination, because here again the principal attractant is nectar. Birds may have been physically available as pollinators early in angiosperm history, but bats apparently did not even exist until the angiosperms were already well diversified.

The Coleoptera (beetles) are well known as fossils as far back as the Permian period. Since the angiosperms are presumably post-Permian, the Coleoptera were physically available as possible pollinators from the beginning. The Diptera and Hymenoptera date from the Triassic, but only in forms such as midges and crane-flies (Diptera) and saw-flies (Hymenoptera), which are not and presumably never were important pollinators. The bees and most of the higher Diptera, which are now important pollinators, first appear in the fossil record in early Tertiary time, but they may actually have arisen during the Cretaceous period; the paucity of Cretaceous fossil insects of all sorts makes any conclusion hazardous. However, most or all of the early Tertiary bees belong to extinct genera, and one may legitimately speculate that the evolution of modern bees was intimately related to the evolution of bee-pollinated flowers during the Tertiary period. The archaic lepidopteran family Micropterigidae (to which *Sabatinca* belongs) dates from the Neocomian segment of the Lower Cretaceous, before the earliest known angiosperms, but the presently important lepidopteran pollinators are not ancient types.

With the aid of a little imagination, one can set up a series of morphological types of flowers that represent progressive adaptation to more discriminating pollinators (Leppik, 1957). Starting with relatively amorphous flowers with numerous tepals, as in *Magnolia,* one progresses to flowers with a small and definite number of petals that are all about alike and all more or less in the same plane, as in many polypetalous flowers, to flowers that are regular but markedly three-dimensional, such as daffodils and phloxes, to flowers that are not only three-dimensional but also irregular, such as orchids and snapdragons.

In a very loose way, such a series does actually reflect progressive evolutionary advance, but there are many exceptions and special cases. The flower-heads of many of the Asteraceae compare in form to primitive magnoliid flowers, but the Asteraceae produce abundant nectar, and they are visited by a wide array of pollinators. (I well remember the role of *Chrysothamnus,* in the Asteraceae, in augmenting my collection of insects for high-school biology.) Some of the Asteraceae, such as species of *Bidens* and *Coreopsis,* have five or eight petal-like rays and simulate ordinary polypetalous flowers. Even more than with some other characters, the use of the various groups of pollinators reflects extensive parallelism.

Although we ordinarily think of bees as gatherers of nectar, some of them gather pollen instead. Most members of the large family Melastomataceae are pollinated by pollen-gathering bees. The poricidal anthers in this family open explosively in response to vibration of the wings of the bees. There is good reason to suppose that the usual absence of nectaries in the melastomes is secondary rather than primitive. Other members of the same order (Myrtales) are generally nectariferous. Pollination by pollen-gatherers may set the stage for a change from entomophily to anemophily, as has apparently happened in the subclass Commelinidae of the Liliopsida. The order Commelinales, basal to the subclass, is entomophilous but lacks nectaries and nectar. Anthers of some members of the order are poricidal, as in the Melastomataceae, but others open longitudinally in ordinary fashion. Most of the more advanced orders of the Commelinidae have reduced flowers and are anemophilous. Anemophily in some other groups has no apparent relationship to pollination by pollen-gatherers.

Wind-pollination has evolved from insect-pollination many times, usually associated with reduction of the perianth, as in the Amentiferae. Although a large part of the traditional Amentiferae probably hangs together, the group as a whole comes from at least four different sources, each of which independently adopted wind-pollination in association with floral reduction. Even within the single family Asteraceae, taxonomically far-removed from any of the Amentiferae, wind-pollination has evolved more than once. The most immediately obvious examples are the subtribe Ambrosiinae of the tribe Heliantheae, and the genus *Artemisia,* in the tribe Anthemideae. In these groups also, wind-pollination is associated with floral reduction.

Flowers with the perianth much reduced are not always wind-pollinated. *Populus* and *Salix,* in the same family, both have highly reduced flowers, but *Populus* is wind-pollinated, whereas *Salix* has well developed nectaries and is (at least in part) insect-pollinated. It remains to be seen whether *Salix* has a continuously entomophilous ancestry going back to the Violales and more primitive groups, or whether it has reverted to entomophily after having passed through an anemophilous evolutionary stage. It may be significant that in at least two respects (number of stamens and number of bud-scales) in addition to its usually more reduced growth-form, *Salix* appears to be more advanced than *Populus.* However, the combination of primitive and advanced features in one plant is so common in angiosperms in general that no conclusion can safely be drawn here without further evidence. It may also be noted that although the Fagaceae have reduced flowers and are usually wind-pollinated, insects are attracted to the conspicuous white inflorescences of *Castanea* and some other genera. Presumably *Castanea* is secondarily entomophilous.

Wind-pollination and insect-pollination are not necessarily mutually exclusive. The change from one to the other can take place gradually, without any sudden jumps, especially if adaptation to insect-pollination is generalized and does not involve complex or unusual structure associated with a particular kind of pollinator. The well known genus *Solidago,* like a great many other Asteraceae, is generally insect-pollinated but has no special adaptations for particular pollinators. Some of the species, such as *S. speciosa,* are reported to release a considerable amount of pollen into the air as well. *Solidago speciosa* is not less well adapted to the attraction of insects than other goldenrods; indeed it is one of the most showy species of the genus.

The vast majority of angiosperms are ordinarily cross-pollinated, and there are many mechanisms that restrict or prevent selfing. The most effective of these is dioecism, which we have already discussed. Among species with perfect flowers, common methods of preventing (or minimizing) selfing include self-sterility, heterostyly, exserted styles, exserted stamens, and protandry-protogyny. Each of these devices has evolved repeatedly in different groups, and the term self-sterility masks a variety of different physiological responses. Neither taxonomic nor ecologic affinity unites the diverse species that share any one mechanism for restricting selfing.

It is perfectly obvious that evolutionary progress depends on exchange of genes as well as on mutations per se. On the other hand, selfing is the only certain method of pollination, and any mechanism that inhibits selfing carries the inherent danger of reduced seed-set. Inasmuch as plants cannot seek each other out for pollinating purposes, any restriction of self-pollination puts them in thrall to their pollinators.

Although frequent gene-exchange is clearly an evolutionary desideratum, it is not necessary that selfing be completely eliminated. A mixture of crossing and selfing can keep the evolutionary pot bubbling nearly or quite as well. A single cross-pollination can provide the materials to produce new and different gene-combinations through several generations of selfing. Examples have been adduced in CHAPTER 2.

The diversity of mechanisms favoring outcrossing suggests to me that the angiosperms were originally self-compatible and indiscriminately self- or cross-pollinated. Subsequently, either self- or cross-pollination might be favored, according to the conditions of selection. Self-pollination may provide an immediate advantage for the temporary exploitation of a particular habitat, but it is a blind alley from which escape is possible only by a difficult and unlikely U-turn. Within any particular group, it may reasonably be assumed that self-pollination has been derived from cross-pollination or indiscriminate pollination. Indiscriminate pollination may lead to regular out-crossing by any of several routes, depending on the availability of the necessary mutations and the precise conditions of selection. Outcrossers have the capacity to respond to selective pressures and to speciate, but they are not forever committed. Change of the conditions of selection may lead them back to a more mixed or even an indiscriminate system of pollination, or to obligate selfing.

Carpels and Placentation

The morphological nature of the carpel has been much discussed, and new hypotheses continue to be proposed. The most generally accepted view for many years has been that it is essentially a megasporophyll, and this view continues to command widespread support. The concept of the carpel as a megasporophyll fits very well into the strobilar hypothesis of floral evolution, and indeed any other interpretation would seem to require an extensive reconsideration of the facts and concepts of floral morphology and phylogeny which now seem to be fitting into a harmonious, internally consistent pattern.

For many years it was believed that the primitive, pre-angiospermous open carpel probably had a row of ovules along each margin, and that closure of the carpel brought the two rows of ovules together into a single row along the ventral suture. This view may still prove to be correct, but it seems more likely that the primitive, open carpel had ovules scattered over its upper surface, and that restriction of the ovules to the apposed margins of the carpel represents an early modification from the ancestral condition (Fig. 5.10). The latter view dates from a paper by Bailey and Swamy in 1951 and reflects a reconsideration of the evidence, sparked by the discovery of the archaic genus *Degeneria* in Fiji a few years before.

It seems perfectly clear that one way in which the typical closed angiospermous carpel originated was by conduplicate folding of an open carpel and subsequent closure of the open margin. Among modern members of the Magnoliales, some species of *Tasmannia* (Winteraceae) have thin, unsealed carpels that are merely folded along the midrib, the ovules

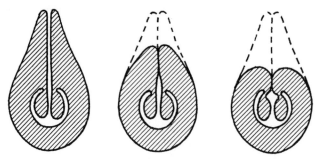

Fig. 5.10. Idealized series of carpellary cross-sections showing derivation of marginal placentation in a closed carpel (RIGHT) from laminar placentation in a conduplicate, unsealed carpel (LEFT). Adapted from Bailey and Swamy, 1951.

being borne on the two inner surfaces of the folded carpel. The carpels of some species of *Bubbia* (Winteraceae) and of *Degeneria* are very much like the *Tasmannia* carpels just mentioned, except for being abaxially somewhat deformed. In these genera a mat of tangled hairs running the length of the unsealed margin of the carpel serves as an elongate stigma on which the pollen germinates. Stages in the development of the typical simple pistil, with closed ovary, style, and terminal (Fig. 5.11) stigma are still preserved among various living members of the Magnoliales.

Whether closure of the carpels may have taken place in any other way is still debatable, if improbable. It was at one time thought that in many angiosperms parietal placentation reflected connation of several open carpels by their lateral margins. Most of the groups to which this concept had been applied now seem better interpreted as derived from forms with axile placentation. After these advanced types have been disposed of, there remain a few taxa in the Magnoliales that have syncarpous, parietal placentation but do not have near relatives with axile placentae. The Canellaceae, for example, do not seem related to any group with axile placentation. Even more strikingly, two genera (*Isolona, Monodora*) of the Annonaceae, an otherwise apocarpous family, have a compound pistil with parietal placentation. Among the archaic monocots, the Hydrocharitaceae, with laminar-parietal placentation in a compound ovary, belong to an otherwise apocarpous complex. In such taxa it seems not unlikely that conduplicate but unsealed carpels have become connate by their margins, after which the initially deeply sulcate ovary-form became more smoothly rounded.

Primitively, the angiosperm gynoecium must have consisted of several or many carpels, spirally arranged on a more or less elongate receptacle. Each of these carpels doubtless had several or many ovules, and it may reasonably be assumed that the carpels spread open at maturity, freeing the seeds. Gynoecia of this type exist in many of the more archaic angiosperms today, both monocots and dicots. Sometimes these spirally arranged carpels became more or less fused into a syncarp, as in species of *Magnolia,* but this line of evolution (as opposed to the union of several

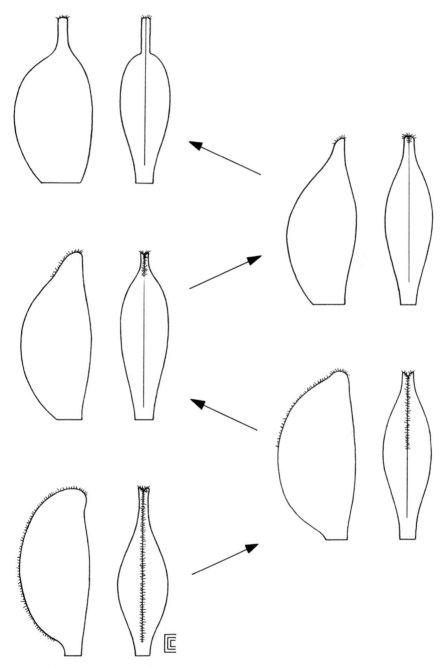

Fig. 5.11. Idealized series from the conduplicate, unsealed carpel of *Degeneria* to a typical simple pistil with ovary, style, and terminal stigma. Transitional forms such as those shown here exist in the Winteraceae and some other families.

carpels to form a compound pistil) did not lead to any further advance. The antiquity of the elongate receptacle with numerous spirally arranged carpels is documented by the Albian-Cenomanian fossil *Archaeanthus* (Dilcher & Crane, 1984), although this fossil does not prove that all early angiosperm flowers were of similar nature.

Reduction of the number of carpels to a single whorl opened new possibilities for further evolution. One theoretical possibility that seems never to have been exploited is the fusion of the carpels into several separate compound pistils within the flower. The carpels in known angiosperms may be separate, or loosely united, or firmly united, or united for only part of their length, but if they are united at all they form a single pistil.

Given insect-pollination and the tendency for several or many grains to be transported collectively in more or less of a lump, a compound pistil is more efficient than several separate pistils. Greater efficiency may not be the whole cause of the evolutionary fusion of carpels, however. This fusion is surely part of a general tendency toward reduction of flowers that permeates the whole angiosperm phylad. Some aspects of this tendency, such as the repeated evolution of wind-pollinated flowers with no perianth, certainly cannot be ascribed to selection for greater efficiency in the entomophilous habit. Nor can entomophily be assigned any clear role in the change from spirally arranged carpels to cyclic carpels, the necessary precursor to the evolution of the compound pistil.

It is interesting that phyletically the ovaries typically fuse before the styles and stigmas, so that it is not at all unusual to find a single ovary with separate styles and stigmas, or a single ovary and style with separate stigmas. Indeed it is unusual to find the stigmas so completely fused as to leave no external trace of the carpellary units. Although the phyletic fusion of the ovaries and possibly the styles might be explained in terms of pollination-efficiency, the subsequent partial or even complete fusion of the stigmas in various groups can hardly be explained in the same way; indeed it would seem instead to be counter-selective. Here, as with some other evolutionary trends in the angiosperms, it would be convenient to invoke the concept of evolutionary momentum, if the concept itself had not fallen into disrepute.

We have noted that although the primitive carpel may have had the ovules scattered over the upper surface, the restriction of the ovules to marginal rows was an early evolutionary step. Thus the presence of several carpels in a whorl, each with a single marginal placenta, is still a fairly primitive condition. Fusion of the members of such a whorl gives a compound pistil with axile placentation. This step has occurred repeatedly in different groups. The partitions in such a compound pistil are, at least phyletically, double membranes, each composed of the connate walls of two adjacent carpels.

Many of the Apocynaceae and Asclepiadaceae have two separate ovaries with a common style or style-head. Here the separation of the bodies of the carpels appears to be secondary rather than primitive. We are not witnessing stages in carpellary fusion from the top down. Whatever may have been the cause of this secondary separation, it apparently could not overcome the selective advantage of having a common set of adjacent pollinating-surfaces for both carpels, and the style-head has remained intact. The deposition of pollen on any of the several stigmatic surfaces of the common style-head may result in fertilization of ovules in either or both of the two separate ovaries.

The most common types of placentation in compound ovaries are axile, parietal, free-central, basal, and apical.[4] The axile type is ancestral to all the others (Fig. 5.12).

As we have noted, in some few groups parietal placentation may also result from marginal fusion of folded carpels, without the phyletic intervention of a truly axile condition.

Parietal placentation typically arises from a failure of the partitions to join in the center of the ovary. These incomplete partitions are often called deeply intruded placentae. The partitions may then be further reduced or even eliminated, so that the placentae are on the wall of the strictly unilocular ovary. On the other hand, the placental edges of the partial partitions may separate and curve away from each other. If these partitions then meet and fuse again in the center of the ovary, axile placentation is restored. This sort of return to axile placentation may actually have occurred in some of the Gentianaceae and Hydrophyllaceae. Another sort of modification of parietal placentation occurs in *Eucrypta,* of the Hydrophyllaceae. In this genus each of the two placentas is attached to the ovary-wall by a median dorsal ridge, but the main body of the placenta is flattened and essentially discoid, with circular margins attached to the ovary-wall. Other variations of parietal placentation also exist.

Free-central placentation arises from axile by abortion of the partitions, usually accompanied by failure of the placental column to reach the top of the ovary. The Caryophyllaceae are usually said to have free-central placentation, but the early ontogenetic stages are typically axile, and vestigial partitions are often visible at the base of the mature capsule. In some other families, such as the Primulaceae, the origin of free-central placentation from axile is not so immediately obvious, but the basic structure is the same.

Basal placentation is easily derived from free-central by reduction of the placental column, usually accompanied by a decrease in the number of ovules to only one or a few. Basal placentation may also arise from axile or parietal or marginal placentation by progressive restriction of the placenta.

Apical placentation arises from axile or parietal (or marginal) by progressive restriction of the placenta from the base upwards. A slight further restriction of the remaining part of the placenta makes it fully apical. Sometimes it is convenient to refer to placentation in a plurilocular ovary as basal-axile, or apical-axile.

---

[4] The term parietal placentation has often been used to apply broadly to both simple and compound pistils. It is here restricted to compound pistils, following much recent and current usage. Simple pistils with the ovules in a line formed by the apposed edges of the carpel, as in the Fabales, are here said to have marginal placentation.

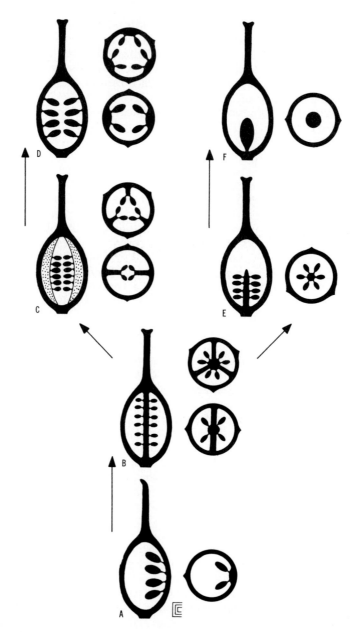

Fig. 5.12. Evolutionary relationships among some types of placentation. **A,** marginal placentation in a simple pistil. **B, C, D, and E** all show compound pistils. **B, C, and D** each show two and three carpels in different cross-sections. **B,** axile placentation. **C,** parietal placentation, with intruded placentas. **D,** parietal placentation. **E,** free-central placentation. **F,** basal placentation. Placentation like that of F can also be derived directly from A.

These several types of placentation do not exhaust the possibilities. The Brassicaceae and some of the Papaveraceae (e.g., *Macleaya*) and Fumariaceae have the ovules attached to the margins of the partition in a bilocular ovary. The evolutionary morphology of such fruits has occasioned much controversy and is still not settled to the satisfaction of all investigators. It may be significant that the placentation in other members of the Papaveraceae ranges from axile through parietal with intruded placentas to ordinary parietal. Many of the Capparaceae, generally regarded as closely allied to but more archaic than the Brassicaceae, have parietal placentation in a unilocular ovary otherwise very much like that of the Brassicaceae.

We must here caution against an uncritical reliance on ontogeny to determine the phylogeny of gynoecial structure. Being the serial homologues of leaves, the carpels in the more archaic angiosperms arise as separate primordia on the floral meristem. Closure of the carpels and union of the carpels result from subsequent ontogenetic changes, which may become phyletically stabilized. Folded but ancestrally unsealed carpels become closed, phyletically, by progressive union of the primordial carpellary margins, from the bottom to the top, as shown by intermediate stages preserved as mature structures in various archaic living angiosperms. Study of such closed carpels in a contextual vacuum has given rise to much nonsense about "ascidiate" carpels, which are in fact not fundamentally different from laminar carpels.

Compound ovaries arise, phyletically, by ontogenetic fusion of folded (and usually closed) carpels. The resulting ovary is plurilocular, with axile placentation. The ontogeny may then be modified so that the carpellary primordia fuse before the formation of the partitions, as in *Pelargonium, Rhamnus,* and *Syringa.* The ontogeny may then be further modified so that the partitions do not meet in the center and are eventually suppressed altogether. Many genera with parietal placentation exemplify this ontogeny. In such ovaries it is ontogenetically simpler to join the carpellary primordia by their lateral margins than to first produce closed carpels, then join the carpels, and then to dissipate the partitions. In some more advanced taxa, such as *Lysimachia,* the gynoecium may arise from a girdling primordium without any initial distinction into carpellary primordia. The plant is under no compulsion to retain a complicated ontogeny in producing a simplified mature morphology. If such complications are in fact preserved (as in some initially plurilocular ovaries that mature to have free-central placentation), they provide strong phylogenetic evidence, but their absence proves nothing.

We have noted on an earlier page that some taxa with numerous stamens have a much smaller number of basic staminal primordia that are supplied by trunk-bundles. Some authors (myself included) consider that such flowers may be in the initial evolutionary stages of reduction in the number of stamens. Comparable condensation from a spiral, multiprimordial ancestry might be postulated for the numerous separate pistils of *Fragaria vesca.* According to Sattler (1973, p. 76), "The gynoecium is initiated by five inconspicuous gynoecial primordia, on which a larger number of pistil primordia (secondary gynoecial primordia) is formed." The series might of course be read the other way, to indicate a secondary increase in the number of pistils of *Fragaria,* but there is no obvious reason to presuppose such a secondary increase. The ontogeny of *Fragaria* is a logically plausible intermediate between an ontogeny such as that of *Ranunculus,* with a separate primordium for each of the numerous pistils, and that of many more advanced taxa with one primordium for each of a limited number of carpels. (No direct phyletic lineage of *Ranunculus* and *Fragaria* is here suggested.) Just as with the androecium, reduction in the number of pistils might well have begun by condensation of the carpellary primordia. There is of course no inherent reason why reduction in the number of pistils of some other groups might not have been accomplished by direct reduction in the number of carpellary primordia, without the intervention of a stage with compound primordia.

The adaptive significance of changes in placentation is obscure. In a few taxa the elastic dehiscence of the fruit requires a particular type of placentation, but in general it makes no obvious difference to the plant whether the placentation is axile, parietal, or free-central. Likewise, in one-seeded, indehiscent fruits, it is hard to see any biological importance in whether the ovule is attached to the top, the bottom, or along the side of the ovary. If these features confer any selective advantage, either in general or in correlation with a particular habitat or way of life, the fact remains to be demonstrated.

Fusion of carpels to form a compound pistil may take place in flowers with two, three, four, five, or more carpels. After the initial fusion has occurred, the number of carpels may be progressively reduced down to two or even one. Decrease in carpel-number may be saltatory, or one or more carpels may be gradually reduced and lost. Several families and individual genera have a pseudomonomerous gynoecium that may or may not show vestiges of lost carpels. *Krameria,* long thought to have a simple (unicarpellate) pistil, is now considered on anatomical evidence to have one well developed fertile carpel and one much reduced sterile one.

Gradual reduction in carpel-number appears to be taking place in *Navarretia,* of the Polemoniaceae. Most species of *Navarretia* have three stigmas and a trilocular, tricarpellate ovary, like other members of the family. In *N. divaricata* two of the three stigmas are often partly connate. The capsule in this species is loculicidally dehiscent by three valves, but it is commonly only two-locular by complete failure of one of the partitions, the odd value also being narrower than the others. *Navarrettia minima* and *N. intertexta* have two stigma-lobes and bilocular, only scarcely or irregularly dehiscent fruits.

Gradual reduction of some of the carpels can also be seen in some of the Caprifoliaceae and the related family Valerianaceae. *Linnaea,* in the Caprifoliaceae, has a trilocular ovary, but two of the locules contain several abortive ovaries each, whereas the third has a single normal ovule. The fruit is one-seeded and unequally three-locular, the two smaller locules being empty. In the Valerianaceae, *Valerianella* has a tricarpellate pistil with a three-lobed stigma; the fruit is trilocular, but two of the locules are sterile and poorly developed. *Valeriana* also has a trilobed stigma and a basically tricarpellate ovary, but two of the carpels are vestigial. In *Plectritis* the stigma is two-lobed or rarely three-lobed, and the ovary is wholly unilocular, with no evident vestige of the two sterile carpels.

Saltatory reduction in carpel-number can also be seen in the Caprifoliaceae, among other families. Some of the American species of *Lonicera,* such as *L. ciliosa* and *L. involucrata,* are tricarpellate, whereas others, such as *L. coerulea* and *L. utahensis,* are bicarpellate. *Triosteum,* in the same family, has three-, four-, and five-carpellate ovaries, sometimes even in the same species, without intermediate stages.

Saltatory changes in the number of carpels are usually downward, but are sometimes upward instead. The plant called *Nicotiana multivalvis,* an Amerindian cultigen of northwestern United States, had six to eight carpels. It is generally believed to have been derived from *N. bigelovii,* a wild species with two carpels, the typical number for the genus and family. Taxonomists now put both of these into the same species with *N. quadrivalvis,* another Amerindian cultigen (of the northern Great Plains) with mostly four carpels. (Because *N. quadrivalvis* is the oldest name in this group, its name must stand for the broadly defined species, in which *N. bigelovii* and *N. multivalvis* are included.) *Leptodactylon pungens* and most other members of the Polemoniaceae have five calyx-lobes, five corolla-lobes, five epipetalous stamens, and a tricarpellate ovary. Most members of the closely related species *L. watsonii* have 6, 6, 6, and 4, although some have 5, 5, 5, and 3. Still another species of the same genus, *L. caespitosum,* characteristically has 4, 4, 4, and 2. One may suspect that the tropical American tree *Chrysophyllum caimito,* with six to eight carpels, has a five-carpellate ancestry.

The adaptive significance of the changes in carpel-number is obscure. The downward changes, which are more frequent than the upward ones, fit into the general pattern of reduction that is expressed in so many different ways in floral evolution. We have seen that some manifestations of this general pattern might well reflect survival-value and selection, but others apparently do not. There is not a close enough correlation between the evidently or probably adaptive and the seemingly nonadaptive manifestations of the pattern to warrant the thought that both types are governed by the identical set of genes. If the explanation is to be found in pleiotropic effect of genes valuable for other functions, the nature of the other functions is yet to be discovered.

Ovules

In all living gymnosperms the ovule typically has the micropyle at the end opposite the stalk. All theories of ovular evolution take this as the primitive orientation. In contrast to these straight, orthotropous ovules of gymnosperms are the ovules of most angiosperms, with the ovule bent back on itself to bring the micropyle alongside the funiculus. It seems perfectly clear that the anatropous condition of angiosperms is derived from the orthotropous condition of gymnosperms. The questions are when and how.

Anatropy must have originated very early in the evolution of angiosperms, because among the living members of the group this appears to be the primitive state, and there is nothing contradictory in the fossil record. Anatropous ovules are standard among the more archaic families of both monocots and dicots, as well as being widely distributed among the more advanced families.

Within the angiosperms, orthotropous, campylotropous, and amphitropous ovules are specialized types derived from an anatropous ancestry. Orthotropous ovules are found chiefly in families in which the ovule is basal and solitary in the ovary—advanced types such as the Juglandaceae, Piperaceae, Polygonaceae, Restionaceae, and Urticaceae, which otherwise have little in common. In at least some groups the orthotropous condition is attained by progressive phyletic migration of the funiculus. The Moraceae have anatropous ovules suspended from the top of the ovary. In the related but more advanced family Urticaceae, *Urtica* and *Boehmeria* have an orthotropous, basal ovule, and other genera show various transitional stages between the two types.

Campylotropous and amphitropous ovules, with the micropyle pointing more or less at right angles to the funiculus, are derived from the anatropous type by differential growth, and an ovule that is campylotropous or amphitropous at the time of fertilization may be anatropous at an earlier ontogenetic stage. Families with these specialized types of ovules are not archaic and not necessarily closely related among themselves. Campylotropous ovules are found, for example, in members of such diverse families as the Capparaceae, Caryophyllaceae, and Geraniaceae.

The most plausible suggestion for the origin of anatropy in angiosperms is that of Gaussen (1946) and Stebbins (1974). As we have noted in CHAPTER 4, these authors see the recurved cupule of *Caytonia* as the forerunner of the angiosperm ovule. This interpretation provides a logical explanation for the origin of the anatropous, bitegmic condition.

An attempt to use the outgroup-comparison method for determination of polarity of anatropy versus orthotropy in angiosperms as a whole would lead to an answer unacceptable to students of morphology and evolution of the group. Inasmuch as angiosperms include both anatropous and orthotropous types, whereas gymnosperms are consistently orthotropous, the orthotropous condition would have to be taken as primitive (plesiomorphic) in angiosperms. By careful selection of taxa for comparison, however, we might be able to support the idea that in particular groups of angiosperms anatropy is primitive and orthotropy derived (apomorphic).

The primitive angiosperm ovule evidently had two integuments. Fusion of the two integuments into one has occurred in many different families, and intermediate stages of fusion can often be seen. The Ranunculaceae, Rosaceae, Salicaceae, Ericaceae, and Arecaceae, among other families, include both unitegmic and bitegmic types. Even when the two integuments are perfectly distinct at the micropylar end of the ovule, the distinction tends to fade out at the chalazal end. In anatropous ovules the outer integument also tends to be adnate to the funiculus, so that in vertical section the ovule appears to have only one integument on the funicular side. Fusion of the two integuments into one may be accompanied by a reduction in the thickness, so that the single integument is no thicker than either of the two ancestral ones, or, as in most of the Asteridae, the single integument may be massive, as thick as or thicker than both of the ancestral integuments together.

The unitegmic condition may also be achieved by abortion of one or the other integument. In *Populus,* for example, the inner integument is sometimes present but poorly developed, and sometimes completely wanting (Mauritzon, 1939, p. 22).

The outgroup-comparison method would give less than satisfactory results in polarizing bitegmic versus unitegmic ovules in angiosperms. The only gymnosperms with clearly bitegmic ovules are the Gneticae, but students of the group maintain that the outer integument here is not homologous (or even homoplasic) with that of angiosperms. Other gymnosperms appear to be unitegmic, although a case can be made that the single integument in cycads actually represents two fused integuments. By outgroup-comparison one would have to take the bitegmic condition in angiosperms as apomorphic, and the unitegmic condition as plesiomorphic.

In the more archaic families of angiosperms the nucellus is usually several or many cells thick and well differentiated from the integuments, recalling the massive nucellus of many gymnosperms. Evolutionary advance leads to tenuinucellate ovules, with a nucellus only one cell thick. In many of the Asteridae the integument appears to abut directly on the embryo-sac, and the nucellus can be distinguished only as a single layer of a few cells forming a cap over the micropylar end of the embryo-sac. Reduction of the nucellus, like many evolutionary advances in the angiosperms, has occurred independently in many different groups.

The specialized cell or group of cells within the young ovule that gives rise to or matures into the spore mother cell is called the archesporium. In gymnosperms and some angiosperms the archesporium is characteristically multicellular, even though typically only one cell actually functions as a megaspore mother cell. In most angiosperms the archesporium is unicellular; there are no wasted potential megaspore mother cells. Clearly this difference is in pattern with the evolutionary loss of other excess baggage in the reproductive apparatus of the angiosperms.

Within the angiosperms, crassinucellate ovules commonly have a multicellular archesporium, and tenuinucellate ovules usually have a unicellular archesporium, but there are many exceptions. The Asteraceae, for example, have tenuinucellate ovules, but a few genera have a multicellular archesporium. The loose correlation between nucellar and archesporial type fits the pattern of a loose correlation among primitive characters in the angiopserms in general. It seems plain enough that within the angiosperms the unicellular archesporium is derived from the multicellular. This is not to deny the possibility of reversion; the multicellular archesporium of some Asteraceae may well be secondary.

Among living angiosperms, the "typical," *Polygonum*-type embryo-sac with 8 nuclei derived from a single megaspore appears to be primitive. It seems perfectly obvious that this type is derived by progressive reduction from a multicellular gametophyte such as is found in gymnosperms. The next step in such a reduction series leads to a four-nucleate embryo-sac such as that of the Onagraceae. In the Onagraceae the two synergic nuclei apparently retain a role in facilitating fertilization of the egg, leaving only one embryo-sac nucleus to fuse with the second sperm nucleus, and the resulting endosperm is diploid. The prospects of any further reduction of the female gametophyte, short of bypassing it altogether, do not seem good. In fact no more reduced type is known.

Other variations in type result from the participation of more than one megaspore in the development of the embryo-sac. We have here an example of the fact that nature is not bound by our ideas of classification of knowledge. In evolutionary theory, the embryo-sac is the female gametophyte of angiosperms. As such, it is a distinct, separate individual that retains its identity even though it is completely enclosed by the sporophyte. It should have n chromosomes and should be derived from a single megaspore. In actual fact, however, the embryo-sac of angiosperms is not a distinct individual; it is merely a stage in the reproduction of the (sporophyte) plant. As such, it is free from some of the restrictions that would be convenient to impose on it from the standpoint of evolutionary theory. The participation of two or four megaspores in the formation of the embryo-sac poses no threat to its reproductive function; neither do variations in the chromosome number of its nuclei, so long as one of these nuclei has n chromosomes and can serve as the egg. Thus, from a functional standpoint, the existence of bisporic and tetrasporic embryo-sacs should not be surprising, and indeed several variations of these two types do exist. One of the tetrasporic types, called the *Peperomia* type, has 16 nuclei. Considered on the basis of the number of nuclei alone, this type should be more primitive than the typical, eight-nucleate, monosporic embryo-sac. However, all tetrasporic embryo-sacs must ultimately be derived from monosporic ones; furthermore, it takes one less set of divisions to produce a 16-nucleate embryo-sac than an 8-nucleate monosporic one.

Most of the evolutionary trends in ovular structure fit into the general pattern of floral reduction that pervades the angiosperms. The resulting economy of structure is on the plus side for general efficiency and survival value, but it is hard to believe that the difference is great enough to provide much driving evolutionary force. Without invoking any discredited mechanisms, it might be possible to think of these reductions as another example of the well known evolutionary tendency for unused structures, or unnecessary complications of structure, to degenerate. Aside from simple economy, this degeneration is believed to result from the accumulation of "loss" mutations that may or may not be useful for any of many other functions, these other functions being generally unspecified and indeed unknown.

Fertilization, Seeds, and Seedlings

Double fertilization and the development of a copious endosperm from a triple fusion nucleus are clearly primitive characters within the angiosperms. The formation of an endosperm nucleus by fusion of a sperm cell with two cells of the embryo-sac is such a standard accompaniment of typical fertilization in angiosperms that the term "double fertilization" has been coined to cover the two processes collectively. Even when the mature seed has no trace of endosperm, an endosperm nucleus is generally formed coincident with fertilization. Aside from apomicts, the most notable exceptions to this rule are provided by some of the orchids, in which the seeds are extremely small, with tiny, undifferentiated embryo and no food storage tissue as such. Orchids are highly advanced in other respects, and the absence of even an endosperm nucleus in some of them is clearly secondary rather than primitive.

In archaic angiosperms the endosperm is a food storage tissue whose nutrients are absorbed by the embryo during germination. In more advanced types the embryo absorbs the food from the endosperm before the seed is ripe, so that in the mature seed the food in the cotyledons or elsewhere in the embryo, and the endosperm is missing. This absorption may take place rather late in ontogeny, as in many of the Sapotaceae, in which the endosperm is obvious in young seeds but wanting or scanty in mature ones. (Some other genera of the Sapotaceae have a copious endosperm at maturity.) In still more advanced types, the endosperm may degenerate early in the ontogeny of the fertilized ovule, and most of the stored food in the mature seed has never been in the endosperm. These changes, like other evolutionary advances in the angiosperms, have occurred repeatedly in different groups.

The nucellus or the integuments may also serve as food storage tissue in the mature seed, forming what is called a perisperm. This is clearly an advanced condition. Many perispermous seeds also have an endosperm, and during germination the food is absorbed from the perisperm by the endosperm and thence is passed on to the embryo.

The evolutionary origin of double fertilization is obscure. It appears to have no forerunner among the gymnosperms, unless the occasional fusion of the second sperm nucleus with a ventral canal nucleus in *Ephedra* be so considered. It may be suggested that inasmuch as two sperm nuclei are regularly delivered to the embryo-sac, it should not be surprising that the one not involved in ordinary fertilization should also find something to fuse with. Why it should fuse with two other nuclei instead of only one, and why this triple fusion nucleus should initiate food storage tissue, are still wholly speculative.

One may speculate that the difference in ploidy-level between the zygote and the endosperm facilitates the physiological distinction between the two in subsequent ontogeny. Against (or perhaps tangential to) this thought is the fact that triple fusion which does not involve a sperm nucleus does not lead to the formation of endosperm. In some tetrasporic embryo-sacs (*Lilium* type) three of the four megaspores fuse soon after being produced. This triple fusion nucleus gives rise eventually to half of the nuclei of the embryo-sac. One of these triploid nuclei and one haploid nucleus of the embryo-sac then fuse with a sperm nucleus to form a pentaploid endosperm nucleus. The origin of the *Lilium* type embryo-sac may itself have been facilitated by evolutionary habituation of the embryo-sac to triple fusion in the formation of the endosperm nucleus.

There is no obvious reason why the precursors of the angiosperms should have continued to deliver two sperms to the female gametophyte before a function had been found for the second one. It may be noted, however, that modern gymnosperms produce two or more sperms per pollen tube, even though only one can function successfully. Reduction of the female gametophyte in protoangiosperms to a size at which it could no longer function effectively as a food storage tissue may have made it possible for the second sperm to find a function instead of being wasted. Why the female gametophyte became so reduced that the origin of a new food storage tissue was necessary remains to be explained. Presumably the explanation would have to invoke either evolutionary momentum (the persistence of a trend beyond the point of usefulness) or some benefit from other effects of the genes governing a decrease in the size of the female gametophyte. The concept of evolutionary momentum is not in favor among most modern students of evolutionary mechanisms, who feel that any evolutionary trend must be related to survival value.

Endosperm is divided into three general types on the basis of its ontogeny. If the formation of cell walls is postponed until after a number of nuclear divisions have occurred, so that there is a free-nuclear stage in early ontogeny, the endosperm is said to be **nuclear**. If cell walls are formed more or less coincident with most or nearly all of the nuclear divisions, the endosperm is said to be **cellular**. A peculiar intermediate type, common in the Alismatidae and some other monocots, is called **helobial**. In this type a cell wall is laid down between the first two nuclei of the developing endosperm, after which development proceeds along the cellular pattern in one-half of the endosperm, and along the nuclear pattern in the other. The distinctions among these three types are not as sharp as the descriptions would suggest; there are many transitional conditions.

There is a continuing difference of opinion about whether nuclear or cellular endosperm is the more primitive. Within the family Gentianaceae, it seems clear enough that nuclear endosperm is primitive and cellular endosperm is advanced. The family as a whole has nuclear endosperm, but two genera, *Voyria* and *Voyriella*, have cellular endosperm. These two genera are mycotrophs without chlorophyll, and they also have highly specialized pollen. It is unlikely that these advanced genera would have retained a primitive character (endosperm ontogeny) that has been lost in the remainder of the family. Investigated members of other families of the Gentianales are almost uniformly nuclear.

What is true for the Gentianaceae may or may not be true for angiosperms in general. It may well be that the ontogeny of the endosperm is subject to reversal, and that in some other family cellular endosperm is primitive and nuclear advanced. There is, however, a loose correlation between nuclear endosperm and other primitive characters, as has been pointed out by Sporne (1954). Furthermore, it may be significant that in the living gymnosperms both the female gametophyte and the embryo have a free-nuclear stage in early ontogeny.

The adaptive significance of the different types of endosperm ontogeny is wholly unknown.

None of the many fossil seeds of pteridosperms has yet been found to contain an embryo. It may therefore be inferred that at the time the seeds were shed the embryo must have been very small or still unformed, as in the modern *Ginkgo*. Fertilization in *Ginkgo* is long delayed after pollination, sometimes until after the ripe seed has fallen to the ground.

Since pteridospermous embryos are unknown, we do not know how many cotyledons they may have had. Modern cycads have two cotyledons, as do the Gneticae and the fossil Bennettitales. Most of the conifers, on the other hand, have several cotyledons. Although most angiosperms have only one or two cotyledons, sporadic tricotyledonous embryos occur in many genera. One genus, *Degeneria,* is typically tricotyledonous; about ⅞ of the embryos have three cotyledons, and nearly all the rest have four, with only rare individuals having only two. Inasmuch as *Degeneria* is also primitive in many other respects, it has been suggested that its embryos are also primitive and that the ancestral stock of the angiosperms had several cotyledons instead of only two. This suggestion may be correct, but at present it is only a speculation. We may note at this point that *Idiospermum* (Laurales) has three or more often four massive cotyledons, whereas other members of the Laurales are uniformly dicotyledonous. The more archaic members of the order have a small embryo and copious endosperm, whereas *Idiospermum* has a large embryo and no endosperm. It seems likely that the polycotyledonous condition in *Idiospermum* is secondary.

Regardless of whether embryos with three or four cotyledons are considered to be primitive or advanced, as compared with dicotyledonous ones, the change from one number to the other apparently takes place at a single jump. It results from a simple change in the symmetry of organization, rather than from a gradual reduction of one or two of the cotyledons.

It is now agreed by all that monocotyledonous embryos are derived from dicotyledonous ones. The change may take place in any of several ways. The following examples are all drawn from the class Magnoliopsida, with the intent of reserving discussion of the origin of monocotyledony in the Liliopsida for a subsequent chapter.

The simplest way for monocotyledony to arise from dicotyledony is by a change in symmetry, comparable to the change in symmetry seen in *Degeneria* and *Idiospermum. Centranthus,* in the advanced family Valerianaceae, has one, two, or three cotyledons in the embryo. No intermediate stages are necessary. Such a change in symmetry may not always be easy to distinguish from abortion of one of the cotyledons. Several genera of the Asteraceae (e.g., *Ambrosia, Calendula, Dimorphotheca*) as well as scattered genera in other families (e.g., *Impatiens, Raphanus*) produce occasional monocotyledonous embryos, with or without a vestige of a second cotyledon. Here the change in number evidently requires only a single step. It should be noted that the presence of a vestige of the second cotyledon proves nothing about the number of steps required to achieve the reduction.

The second cotyledon may also be gradually reduced by a series of short steps. All stages of this reduction can be seen among dicotyledons. In *Trapa, Eranthis*, and *Mamillaria*, representing three different subclasses, one cotyledon is smaller than the other. Such widely differing genera as *Claytonia, Corydalis, Pinguicula*, and *Ranunculus* embrace species with two unequal cotyledons and species that are essentially monocotyledonous.

Two cotyledons may become one by fusion along the lateral margins. This is well illustrated in the Nymphaeales. *Nymphaea* has two separate cotyledons. *Nuphar* has two unequal cotyledons, which are fused by one margin in some species and around the base in others. *Nelumbo* has two similar cotyledons fused by both margins to form a cup-shaped, bilobed unit surrounding the epicotyl.

Finally, monocotyledony can arise by gradual differentiation of two cotyledons for different functions. This sort of change is illustrated by species of *Peperomia*. *Peperomia lucida* has two equal cotyledons, both of which are withdrawn from the seed during germination and become the first functional leaves of the seedling. *Peperomia peruviana* likewise has two initially equal cotyledons, but only one of them is withdrawn from the seed and becomes foliar; the other remains within the seed coat and functions only as an absorbing organ. *Peperomia parvifolia* has two initially unequal cotyledons. The larger one remains within the seed coat and functions as an absorbing organ; the smaller one becomes the first leaf of the seedling. The situation in *P. parvifolia* is hardly to be distinguished from that in many monocots, in which the structure resembling the second cotyledon of *P. parvifolia* is interpreted as the first true leaf.

It is probably significant that newly ripe seeds of most of the more archaic families of angiosperms have a small, poorly differentiated embryo embedded in a copious endosperm. The embryo continues to grow and differentiate during the after-ripening period, but even when the seed is ready to germinate the embryo is small in comparison to the endosperm. Evolutionary progress from the primitive type of seed leads first to endospermous seeds with well differentiated embryo, and then, as we have noted, to nonendospermous seeds with the food stored in the embryo. Perisperm in addition to or in place of endosperm is also advanced rather than primitive. These changes, like other evolutionary advances in the angiosperms, have occurred independently in many different lines.

The primitive cotyledon serves both as a food-absorbing and a food-making organ. It absorbs food from the endosperm during germination, and then it is withdrawn from the seed coat and becomes photosynthetic. Evolutionary specialization of the cotyledons emphasizes food absorption (and sometimes also storage) at the expense of photosynthesis. In the garden bean the cotyledons are chiefly absorbing and storing organs, but they are also brought above the ground during germination and they become weakly photosynthetic for a short time before withering and falling off. In the garden pea the photosynthetic function has been dispensed with and the cotyledons remain below ground within the seed coat. Among the monocotyledons the cotyledon is often complex, with one part remaining in the seed and another part becoming aerial.

Although the seed coat of angiosperms is usually firm and dry, it sometimes has a fleshy covering. This fleshy covering may arise by modification of the integuments (or outer integument), or by elaboration of the funiculus. The first of these types of fleshy covering is called a sarcotesta, the second an aril. The term aril has often been loosely used to include the sarcotesta, and many taxa that are said to be arillate have a sarcotesta instead of a true aril. The same seed may have both a sarcotesta and a true aril, and careful ontogenetic study is often necessary to distinguish the one from the other.

It is uncertain whether the presence of either a sarcotesta or an aril is more primitive than its absence. Corner has maintained, in a series of papers (e.g., 1954), that the truly arillate seed is primitive in the angiosperms, but his view has not been widely adopted. Other botanists have often viewed the aril and sarcotesta, which are obviously adaptations relating to dispersal, as having originated separately in diverse groups. Corner's view is part of a more comprehensive theory (the durian theory), the taxonomic consequences of which have not yet been fully evaluated.

FRUITS AND SEED DISPERSAL

One of the most important functional characters related to fruit structure is whether the fruit opens to release the individually dispersed seeds, or whether the fruit remains closed and is dispersed whole with the included seeds. The former condition is certainly the more primitive. Follicles, legumes, and capsules generally have individually dispersed seeds. Most other fruits, including achenes, grains, samaras, and the various sorts of fleshy fruits, are generally dispersed intact. In a few common families with a compound pistil the carpels (Apiaceae) or half-carpels (Boraginaceae, Lamiaceae, Verbenaceae) separate at maturity and serve as one-seeded disseminules.

It is perfectly clear that the primitive fruit is a follicle, consisting of a single carpel that opens along the ventral suture at maturity, releasing the individually dispersed seeds. The seeds of many follicles have no specialized means of dispersal. Others are plumed (as in *Asclepias*) and are distributed by wind, or have a fleshy outer layer and are eaten by birds or other animals, passing through the digestive tract unharmed. We have noted that it is uncertain whether a fleshy covering on the seed is primitive or advanced. Plumed or winged seeds are clearly secondary as compared to seeds with no specialized means of dispersal.

A simple modification of the follicle is the typical legume, which opens down both the dorsal and the ventral sutures. Many follicles open for a short distance along the distal part of the dorsal suture, as well as along the whole length of the ventral suture. It requires only a progressive elongation of the dorsal opening to convert a follicle into a legume. Many legumes dehisce explosively, throwing the seeds several feet. This explosive dehiscence may well be useful, but its usefulness could hardly take effect before the transition from follicle to legume had been essentially completed. The ancestors of the legumes could not have foreseen that progressive modification of the follicle would eventually produce a fruit that could dehisce explosively. The factors governing the evolution of the follicle into a legume remain obscure.

Unicarpellate dry fruits that dehisce along both sutures (i.e., typical legumes) are very common in the Fabales (Leguminosae). Similar fruits occur in a few other groups, such as the Connaraceae, but are not generally called legumes. As a matter of practical convenience, a legume is defined as the fruit of a member of the Leguminosae. Although these are always monocarpellate, they are not always dehiscent. Indehiscent legumes have the same evolutionary opportunities as other indehiscent dry fruits, and some of these opportunities have been exploited. Some legumes (e.g., *Astragalus crassicarpus*) have even become fleshy. A special type of indehiscent legume is the loment, which breaks transversely into one-seeded segments. Loments are often provided with hooked hairs that adapt them to distribution by animals, or they may be thin and samaroid.

We have noted that there is a general evolutionary tendency for separate carpels to become joined into a compound pistil. This change most commonly occurs in plants with follicular fruits, and the result is to turn the fruit into a capsule. The most primitive type of capsular dehiscence is doubtless septicidal. The carpels merely separate when ripe and open in follicular fashion along the ventral suture. *Veratrum* and scattered other genera have a septicidal capsule, but this is not a common type. From the standpoint of functional engineering, loculicidal dehiscence is much more efficient than septicidal, particularly in pistils with firmly united carpels. Regardless of the cause of the continuing trend toward carpellary fusion, loculicidal dehiscence appears to be the evolutionary answer to the problem it presents in how to liberate the seeds. Some loculicidal capsules are explosively dehiscent, as in *Impatiens*, but others open more gently and merely expose the seeds.

Poricidal dehiscence is obviously derived from loculicidal by restricting the length of the opening. This tends to limit the number of seeds that are liberated at any one time, extending the period of release to several days or even weeks. The survival value of such a change might be debated, but in any case it has occurred independently in a number of families, such as the Papaveraceae and Campanulaceae.

Circumscissile dehiscence is superimposed on other types of dehiscence, rather than resulting from stepwise modification of them. From a morphological standpoint there is no reason why a capsule should not at once be circumscissile and loculicidal, as it can be both septicidal and loculicidal, but in fact such combinations are rare. The advantage, if any, of circumscissile dehiscence over the other types is obscure.

Indehiscent fruits have evolved from dehiscent fruits many times, both in monocarpellate and polycarpellate types. The typical achene, as seen in many members of the Ranunculaceae, is derived from the follicle by failure of dehiscence and reduction of the number of seeds to one. Achenes can also have two or more carpels, as in the Polygonaceae and Asteraceae—the former with superior ovary, the latter with inferior ovary.

Dehiscent fruits with only one seed, and indehiscent fruits with more than one seed are less frequently seen. The infrequency of one-seeded dehiscent fruits is easy enough to explain in teleological terms: It is pointless for the fruit to open and release a single seed; the whole fruit might just as well be the disseminule. Translating this into more acceptably mechanistic terms, one might say that the dehiscence mechanism, having no great usefulness, is easily lost because mutations affecting it are not selected against. The change is in pattern with the general evolutionary principle that useless structures tend to deteriorate through the accumulation of loss mutations. Because genes so commonly have pleiotropic effects, a mutation that is a loss mutation with regard to one character may be useful for some other effect.

The infrequency of several-seeded indehiscent fruits is more directly selective. In most instances it is more efficient for the seeds to be dispersed separately than collectively. Anyone who has ever had to thin sugar-beets will recognize the problems inherent in having several seeds germinate at the same place. Beets produce aggregate fruits, each derived from several flowers, but the dispersal problem is the same as that of indehiscent simple fruits containing several seeds.

The achene is the most generalized type of dry, indehiscent, one-seeded fruit. There are several possibilities for further evolution within this broad category. The achene may develop hooks or barbs that suit it to distribution by animals, e.g., the hooked stylar beak of some species of *Ranunculus,* and the retrorsely barbed pappus-awns of most species of *Bidens.* It may become flattened and winged, forming a samara. It may become enlarged and thick-walled, forming a nut. All of these changes are readily explained in terms of adaptation and survival value, and all have taken place several or many times independently in different lines.

Another type of modified achene is the caryopsis (grain), in which the seed coat is adnate to the pericarp. The vast majority of grasses have this type of fruit. Some grass fruits, such as those of *Sporobolus,* have the seed loose within the pericarp and are by morphological criteria achenes, but purely as a matter of terminology it is customary to define the caryopsis on taxonomic rather than morphologic criteria. A caryopsis is the fruit of a member of the Poaceae. Fruits of a few species or genera in other families have the seed coat adnate to the pericarp but are still called achenes. It is not easy to see survival value in adnation of the seed coat to the pericarp, although the change does no harm; in general it should be selectively neutral. If selection is to be invoked as the explanation, it must be in terms of pleiotropic effect.

It should be noted that the fruit of *Sporobolus* does not appear to be primitive within the grass-family. Instead it is a reversion to an ancestral type, in this one character of loose seed within the fruit. In many other respects *Sporobolus* is advanced within the family, and it is most unlikely that one primitive character persisted while so many others were changed. Many of the evolutionary trends and developments in the angiosperms appear to be selectively neutral, or merely move the plant from one available ecologic niche to another, and the frequency of reversals should not be surprising.

Outgroup comparisons, cladistic style, would give contradictory answers here according to the comprehensiveness of the ingroup. If the grasses as a whole were compared to the Cyperaceae or whatever other family one might choose as the nearest relative, then loose seeds (as in *Sporobolus*) would appear to be primitive among the grasses. If a smaller ingroup, consisting of *Sporobolus* and some immediate relatives, were compared with an outgroup of other grasses, then loose seeds would appear to be advanced. By judicious selection and definition of groups for comparison, one can control the answer.

Fleshy fruits have evolved from dry fruits many times, both in monocarpellate and polycarpellate types. Evolution of fleshiness may proceed concurrently with suppression of dehiscence, or a dry, indehiscent fruit may evolve into a fleshy one. The drupe of *Prunus* and the coherent individual drupelets of *Rubus* are doubtless derived from dry, indehiscent fruits that had only a single seed (i.e., from achenes). On the other hand, the berries of the Solanaceae and many other families appear to be derived from capsules, with the two changes proceeding more or less simultaneously. The berry of *Actaea,* in the Ranunculaceae, is a modified follicle. Neither the dry, indehiscent, many-seeded fruit nor the dehiscent, fleshy fruit has a felicitous combination of characters, and these types are rare.

Fleshiness of fruits is at least ordinarily an adaptation to dissemination by animals (including birds). In most cases the seeds are swallowed along with the pulpy pericarp and pass through the digestive tract unharmed. Obviously this method of seed dispersal entails the development of a protective covering for the seed that is resistant to digestion. This may be the seed coat, or the inner part of the pericarp, or even the whole pericarp. The fleshy covering of the drupe-like fruits of the Elaeagnaceae is formed by the hypanthium, and the true pericarp is wholly stony. Drupes ordinarily have only a single seed, less often two or several. Only one seed can usefully germinate at a given time and place, and natural selection does not favor many-seeded drupes. Seeds with a sarcotesta or aril, mentioned in a previous section, are ecologically comparable to one-seeded fleshy fruits.

SECONDARY METABOLITES

Until a few decades ago, secondary metabolites were generally regarded as being mainly waste products, of no functional importance to the plant.

Physiological and comparative chemical studies during the 1950's cast doubt on this comfortable idea, and in 1959 Fraenkel revived an old but long-neglected view that many secondary metabolites serve to discourage predators or pathogens. Subsequent evidence of rapid intracellular turn-over of the molecules of many secondary metabolites has strengthened Fraenkel's interpretation, which is now widely accepted.

Following up a generalized suggestion by Ehrlich and Raven (1964) I proposed in 1977 that

".... the evolution of chemical repellents plays an important but complex role in the rise and diversification of new families, orders, and subclasses of angiosperms. When one set of repellents loses its effectiveness, the time is ripe for another set. A suitable new set of repellents gives its possessors a competitive advantage and permits their evolutionary expansion. The increased abundance of the new group fosters the evolution of resistance to their repellents by predators. Then another new group of repellents may be exploited, in the continuing struggle between predator and prey. A long period of relative disuse may even permit the revival of an old set of repellents, after the predators have lost their resistance."

Continuing,

"Since every set of repellents gradually loses its effectiveness, opportunities arise for the selective development of new sets. .... the basic pattern in evolution of repellents is one of successive shifts from one major set to another, in response to progressive increase in resistance by the predators. The pattern is blurred by the constant evolutionary experimentation with new repellents and refurbished old ones."

The secondary metabolites of angiosperms are exceedingly diverse chemically. Some, such as hydrocyanic acid, appear to have arisen repeatedly (by diverse chemical routes) in unrelated taxa, without ever fostering the evolution of a major taxonomic group. Others, such as mustard oil, have been vigorously exploited by one major taxon, and less successfully (later?) tried out by additional small taxa.

Two major groups of secondary metabolites show enough taxonomic correlation, enough stepwise chemical progression, and enough interconnection to merit extended consideration here. These are the groups associated with the shikimate pathway and/or with acetic and mevalonic acid.

The shikimate pathway is fundamental to the production of lignin and essential flavonoids, and thus is not restricted to secondary metabolites. Successive steps in the pathway are represented by shikimic acid, chorismic acid, tyrosine and/or phenylalanine, cinnamic acid, and cinnamyl alcohol. At any step in the pathway, some of the product can be diverted to form other substances. Lignin is a set of polymers derived in large part from cinnamyl alcohol. Condensed tannins (proanthocyanins) and flavonoid compounds are derived in large part from cinnamic acid, which is one step short of cinnamyl alcohol on the shikimate pathway. Some of the flavonoids are essential for photosynthesis. Benzyl-isoquinoline alkaloids and betalains come off the shikimate pathway one step earlier, from tyrosine and/or phenylalanine. Another group of alkaloids, called anthranilate-derived alkaloids, relates to chorismic acid. The hydrolyzable tannins (gallo- and ellagi-tannins, which chemically have little to do with condensed tannins) are derived partly from shikimic acid as glucose esters.

Acetate (a 2-carbon acid) and its derivative mevalonate (a 6-carbon acid) are essential for the production of various kinds of terpenoids, including cholesterol. Like the products of the shikimate pathway, these compounds are available, in an evolutionary sense, for diversion to various uses. Secondary metabolites with an acetate or mevalonate foundation include polyacetylenes, sesquiterpene lactones, saponins, steroidal alkaloids, and iridoid compounds. The indole alkaloids combine derivatives of the shikimate pathway with derivatives of mevalonate.

Condensed tannins are widespread in ferns, gymnosperms, and woody members of the Hamamelidae, Rosidae, and Dilleniidae, but are less well represented in the Magnoliidae and only poorly represented in the Asteridae. Hydrolyzable tannins are restricted to the angiosperms, where they are found mainly in the Hamamelidae, Rosidae, and Dilleniidae. Sesquiterpene lactones, polyacetylenes, saponins, steroidal and indole alkaloids, and iridoid compounds are especially well represented in the Asteridae, although not confined to that subclass.

In 1977 I suggested the following general progression among these chemical and taxonomic groups:

"... the isoquinoline alkaloids of the Magnoliidae gave way to the tannins of the Hamamelidae, Rosidae, and Dilleniidae, and these in turn gave way to the iridoid compounds that were most effectively exploited by the Asteridae. Within the Asteridae the rise of the relatively recent family Asteraceae may relate to a shift to polyacetylenes and sesquiterpene lactones in place of the already less effective iridoids."

I would now distinguish between the condensed and hydrolyzable tannins, with the former generally preceding the latter in taxonomic distribution, although both groups may occur together in the same species or higher taxon.

Kubitzki and Gottlieb (1984) are receptive in principle to the concept of evolutionary replacement of one group of secondary metabolites by another, but they raise a problem regarding the position of the isoquinoline alkaloids and related compounds in the evolutionary series. These come off the shikimate pathway one step before the precursors of the condensed tannins. Inasmuch as the angiosperms may have inherited condensed tannins from their gymnospermous ancestors, these authors consider that the Magnoliidae must be an evolutionary side-shoot from a main line that had earlier beginnings.

An inherent weakness in both their scheme and mine is that we do not know what the chemical defenses of the early angiosperms really were. From the fossil record it seems clear that at least some of them had ethereal oil cells like those found in the more archaic members of the modern Magnoliidae, but these oil cells contain a different group of compounds (mainly terpenoids), which do not figure in the present discussion. Modern Magnoliidae with ethereal oil cells commonly also have isoquinoline alkaloids or related compounds. It is the evolutionary status of plants with the isoquinoline alkaloids (and similar compounds) that is in dispute.

From a purely chemical standpoint, it is attractive to join Kubitzki and Gottlieb in visualizing a progressive truncation of the shikimate pathway, with condensed tannins (present also in gymnosperms) being succeeded in evolutionary turn by isoquinoline alkaloids (and related compounds), anthranilate-derived alkaloids, and hydrolyzable tannins. Unfortunately, such a straight-line progression puts the Magnoliidae somewhat above the evolutionary base of the dicotyledons, in contrast to their basal position on morphological grounds. If we assume that the early Cretaceous angiosperms, morphologically suggestive of the modern Magnoliidae, also had similar chemical defenses, then there is indeed a problem in integrating the chemical with the morphological evidence. Not an insoluble problem, perhaps, but one that must be faced.

Kubitzki and Gottlieb do not challenge the morphologically primitive status of the Magnoliidae, but they suppose that there must have been an ancestral group that was chemically as well as morphologically primitive. They put the Magnoliidae on an early sideshoot, and they further associate the Caryophyllidae and the monocotyledons with the magnoliid line. Thus they visualize two major groups of angiosperms, the "magnolialean block" (Magnoliidae, Caryophyllidae, and monocotyledons) and the "rosiflorean block" (Hamamelidae, Rosidae, Dilleniidae, and Asteridae). They consider it "more likely that the magnolialean and rosiflorean blocks, which must have had an old origin, diverged at an early as yet unknown stage in angiosperm evolution." Perhaps one could paraphrase their view by saying that the early angiosperms probably had a magnoliid morphology combined with gymnospermous secondary metabolites (condensed tannins). That would leave open the possibility that condensed tannins were better represented among the early, morphologically magnoliid angiosperms than they are in the modern Magnoliidae. Their presentation might also suggest the possibility that these unknown earliest angiosperms with gymnospermous secondary metabolites were more primitive morphologically than the Magnoliidae in some unspecified way.

I do not believe that such a fundamental dichotomy in early angiosperm evolution is called for by the evidence. The correlation of secondary metabolites with major taxonomic groups is not as good as the authors suggest. Neither is there any chemical necessity to suppose that there was a progressive evolutionary truncation of the shikimate pathway in the formation of secondary metabolites.

The Polygonales are associated with the Caryophyllales in virtually all schemes of classification. Yet the Polygonales are abundantly tanniferous, producing both condensed and hydrolyzable tannins. According to the scheme of Kubitzki and Gottlieb the Polygonales should therefore go with the rosiflorean block, rather than with the nontanniferous magnolialean block to which they assign the Caryophyllales. In counterpoint, isoquinoline alkaloids occur in a few members of the Rutaceae, which otherwise go with their rosiflorean block.

The abundance of the characteristic, otherwise rare isoquinoline alkaloids and chemically related compounds in the Magnoliidae tends to divert attention from the presence of condensed tannins in the group. Some members of the magnoliid families Winteraceae, Magnoliaceae, Annonaceae, Monimiaceae, Lauraceae, Saururaceae, Illiciaceae, and Schisandraceae are reported to produce proanthocyanins (although not always in large amounts) as well as other repellents. Thus the Magnoliidae provide an adequate base for the evolution of other groups containing proanthocyanin (condensed tannins).

There is nothing chemically difficult about the evolutionary re-establishment of proanthocyanins in angiosperms that otherwise lack them. The shikimate pathway must be preserved intact as a major chemical operation in woody plants, in order to sustain the formation of lignin, and it must be maintained as far as cinnamic acid in order to sustain the formation of essential flavonoids. Therefore the proper chemical precursors for condensed tannins must be present in angiosperms in general, and the more so in woody members. The basic machinery continues to be available, capable of being put to work under a proper selective regimen.

Thus the chemistry of shikimate-related secondary metabolites poses no barrier to the thought, based on comparative morphology of both living and fossil angiosperms, that the Magnoliidae stand at the base of the evolutionary scheme and are directly or indirectly ancestral to all other angiosperms. At the present time we must leave open the question of whether the presence of proanthocyanins in many of the Hamamelidae, Rosidae, and Dilleniidae reflects the origin of these subclasses from proanthocyanin-containing members of the Magnoliidae, or a reestablishment of proanthocyanins from the available chemical precursors.

The evolutionary sequence in which the several major groups of secondary metabolites were exploited in a major way by diverse groups of angiosperms appears at the present time to be fortuitous. Granted that the angiosperms inherited proanthocyanins (condensed tannins) from their gymnospermous ancestors, the chemical machinery for exploiting derivatives of any step in the shikimate pathway appears to have been continuously available throughout the history of the group. We must of course add that the indole alkaloids could only arise after both their shikimate-derived and mevalonate-derived precursors were available. A further possible reservation relates to the fact, emphasized by Kubitzki and Gottlieb, that the chemical classes of repellents here discussed are progressively more reduced (and thus harder to detoxify by oxidation) according to their position nearer the beginning of the shikimate pathway. Since the plants must manage to evade the metabolic disturbances caused by their own repellents, it is conceivable that it was easier for the plants, just as for their predators, to learn to live with the more oxidized groups before the more reduced ones. Conceivable, but far from demonstrated.

We should emphasize again at this point that not everything fits the pattern here described for these groups of secondary metabolites. The Myristicaceae and Calycanthaceae produce indole or indole-related alkaloids, which are well advanced in the chemical scheme and are otherwise found mainly in the Asteridae. Steroid alkaloids occur in some monocots (such as the Dioscoreaceae), as well as in dicots that Kubitzki and Gottlieb include in their rosiflorean block. Other such anomalies could be listed. The pattern we perceive (with some difficulty) in the distribution of these secondary metabolites reflects the fact that certain taxonomic groups are more inclined than others to exploit particular opportunities in chemical evolution. The perturbations of the pattern reflect the fact that the chemical machinery for the evolutionary exploitation of particular groups of secondary metabolites is widely available, and under proper conditions can be exploited independently by more than one taxonomic group.

Complex interactions abound in the influence of secondary metabolites on predator-prey relationships. A special group of fungi (the white rusts of crucifers) and a special group of insects (cabbage butterflies) have evolved resistance to mustard oils. Although mustard oils deter most other fungi and insects (not herbarium beetles!), they are not highly effective against herbivorous mammals; many humans like a whiff of mustard oil. The monarch butterfly is famous for its adaptation to the highly poisonous milkweeds (*Asclepias*). The monarch caterpillars sequester the poison in such a way that it does not interfere with their own metabolism but makes them (and the adult butterflies) nauseous to potential predators. Ehrlich and Raven (1964) have explored this sort of plant-insect relationship at some length.

There is an odd sort of competitive exclusion in the use of secondary metabolites for protection. The evolutionary opportunity to exploit a particular set of chemical repellents is initially open to anything that produces the right mutations, and the same set of repellents may sometimes be exploited by more than one taxonomic group at about the same time. The opportunity declines in value, however, as the predators become more resistant. Under special local conditions, or with the aid of happenstance fixation of mutations, individual species or even larger groups may turn to repellents already widely used by other taxa. As Levin (1976) has pointed out, such re-adopted repellents cannot confer any broad-scale advantage on their possessors, and the evolutionary expansion of the taxonomic group that produces them is likely to be blocked by pre-adapted predators. Only a long period of relative disuse of a particular set of repellents might permit their subsequent successful revival by another group of plants.

Here is the nub of the chemical problem about the evolutionary relationship of the Magnoliidae to other angiosperms. Why return to condensed tannins? Had the insect groups that evolved during the Lower Cretaceous as predators of angiosperms lost much of their ancestral resistance to condensed tannins? Or had the initial value of the isoquinoline

alkaloids been so vitiated by evolution among the insects that the proanthocyanins began to seem good by comparison? At the present time these
questions must remain open. We can only say that any barriers there may
have been to a return to heavy exploitation of condensed tannins must
have been more closely related to natural selection than to inherent chemical difficulties in making the change.

The concept of truncation of metabolic pathways and diversion of
materials, suggested by Kubitzki and Gottlieb, does merit some attention.
Thus the absence of anthocyanins from the betalain families of Caryophyllales reflects the suppression of only the last step in the pathway to
anthocyanin—the step from anthoxanthin to anthocyanin. David Giannasi has suggested (unpublished) that the backup of excess phenylalanine
resulting from the blockage of anthocyanin synthesis may have led to a
shunt from phenylalanine to betalain. Likewise, in the Magnoliidae, the
taxa that produce benzyl-isoquinoline alkaloids do not produce myricetin,
a terminal flavonol (comparable in that respect to anthocyanin). The
resulting accumulation of phenylalanine and tyrosine may have set the
stage for a shunt to benzyl-isoquinoline alkaloids. Such truncations of
pathways and diversion of chemical sequences into new side-trails may
turn out to be common.

Secondary metabolites have been discussed here in terms of their protective function. Some of them have other or different functions. In addition to other possible functions, betalains and anthocyanins both serve
to attract pollinators to flowers, as do some anthoxanthins and carotenoids. At the present stage of knowledge, these other functions do not
obviously correlate with broad-scale evolutionary trends in angiosperms.

Macromolecular Data

AMINO ACID SEQUENCES IN VITAL PROTEINS

The sequence of amino acids in vital proteins such as cytochrome c,
plastocyanin, and ferredoxin carries potentially useful taxonomic information, especially at and above the level of family. Unfortunately, the
technique for establishing the sequence is complex, time-consuming, and
subject to error. Enthusiastic efforts a few years ago to acquire and exploit
such sequence data for angiosperms were not well rewarded. Authors such
as Boulter (1973) succumbed to the temptation to extrapolate broadly
from a limited data-base, reaching conclusions unacceptable to the taxonomic community (vide Cronquist, 1976). The subject is now quiescent,
and no revival is in sight. Molecularly minded systematists find a more
exciting prospect in the structure of nucleic acids.

NUCLEIC ACIDS

The presently most promising new approach to the assessment of phylogeny lies in comparison of base-pair sequences in nucleic acids, includ-

ing chloroplast DNA, ribosomal RNA, and even nuclear DNA. The technique, though complex, is less difficult than that for amino acid sequences in proteins. More data can be accumulated with less effort.

One of the great virtues of the nucleic acid sequence method is its relative independence from the more traditional methods and concepts. The only bias carried over from existing ideas lies in the selection of materials to sequence. Subject to the usual problems of computer-manipulation of the data, it is possible to establish a putative cladogram for the tested taxa, based entirely on the nucleic acid sequences.

It must of course be understood that the sequence method will be complementary to other taxonomic methods, rather than replacing them. A parsimony-based cladogram can only roughly approximate unparsimonious evolution. The problem of how far to extrapolate from the dataset will remain. A cladogram, even if guaranteed to be correct, does not specify a precise taxonomy, but merely limits the viable options. Any complex cladogram is compatible with more than one possible taxonomy.

I can foresee two principal uses for the nucleic acid sequence method. One is to help choose between competing taxonomic arrangements. The other is to suggest possibilities that have escaped our attention. If the cladogram seems to call for an arrangement substantially different from what we are accustomed to, then it is time to look again, following the classical Hegelian procedure of thesis, antithesis, and synthesis.

SEROLOGY

Comparative serology provides another useful source of information in plant taxonomy. Extracted proteins of a given species are used to sensitize an experimental animal (typically a rabbit), so that an antiserum is produced in its blood. Reaction of the extracted antiserum to extracted proteins of several other species is then checked by any of several methods. The experimental procedures have been described in numerous publications and need not be discussed here.

Early applications of serology used crude extracts containing a mixture of proteins. Investigators now often separate and isolate the proteins before sensitizing the rabbit. Proteins known to be taxonomically widespread and relatively invariant can then be discarded, and attention focused on the others.

The great virtue of serological data is that they are objectively measurable and absolutely independent of all other characters. One gets results that can be measured in terms of the amount of precipitation or the number of bands on a gel diffusion plate. Furthermore, as the late Marion Johnson was fond of pointing out, the method can be used as either a microscope or a telescope, depending on how strongly you sensitize the rabbit.

Serological methods usually produce results sufficiently harmonious with other kinds of comparisons so that we are encouraged to use them to help resolve some otherwise doubtful questions. Unfortunately, they also sometimes give results so startlingly disharmonious with those from other methods that they cannot be considered definitive. Cristofolini (1980) has discussed the theoretical basis of the method, its uses, and some of its complexities and problems.

A serious problem with serological data is that they exist only as one to one comparisons gathered at the expense of much time and effort. Other kinds of characters, both chemical and morphological, exist independently of comparison. Once the data are gathered for the various taxa or individuals under consideration they can be cross-compared in all sorts of ways by the mind or with the aid of a computer. Each serological comparison, in contrast, requires a separate laboratory test.

It takes only one test to compare two items, but 3 tests for 3 items, 6 tests for 4 items, 10 tests for 5 items, 15 tests for 6 items, and so on at a steeply ascending rate. The formula for the number of tests required to compare each member of a group individually with all other members is $n(n-1)/2$, if n is the number of members of the group. When n is more than about half a dozen, this figure approaches one-half of the square of n. If we consider that there are about 385 families of flowering plants, then it would take nearly 75,000 tests to compare one sample of one species in each family with one sample of one species of each of all the other families. And if we consider that there are about 215,000 species of angiosperms, then it would take more than 2.3×10^{10} tests to check one sample of each species against all other species.

Obviously such large numbers of tests are out of the question. We must content ourselves with a very limited number, and choose our test items carefully. But this choice introduces the very element of subjectivity that the serological method is supposed to avoid.

Serological data are unlike other taxonomic data also in that they are not readily amenable to a phylogenetic approach. One can get a rough check on the degree of similarity (and probable phyletic affinities) among several taxa, but it is hard to proceed from there to establishment of polarity and construction of a cladogram.

Interpretation of Evolutionary Trends

The nature of the forces governing evolutionary trends in the angiosperms is not entirely clear. The orthodox position among students of evolutionary theory per se is that all long-term trends must be explained in terms of survival value. Either the trend is directly useful, or the genes governing it are favored because of other effects. There have been few public challenges to this position since the flowering of the neo-Darwinian school of thought some four decades ago. The neo-Darwinian mechanism (mutation, selection, and fixation in small populations) is now so well worked out, and it so evidently provides the explanation for so much of what is going on, that one can easily believe it provides the full and complete answer.

Easily, that is, until one gets down to cases. Working plant taxonomists during the past several decades have usually paid lip-service to the concept that all evolutionary trends are selective, but their discussions of the trends in the groups they study have commonly lacked any attempt at a selectionist interpretation. Privately, and not for attribution, many of these same people will express doubt as to the universality of survival value as the only guiding force in evolution.

We have noted in our survey of evolutionary trends in the angiosperms that some of them are clearly selective, others more doubtfully so, and others appear to be selectively neutral or even mildly counter-selective. Hidden survival value and pleiotropic effect will have to be worked very hard to provide a neo-Darwinian cover for many of the changes affecting the inflorescence and the structure of the gynoecium, although some few of these changes might well be selective. The difficulty is compounded by the fact that a given trend often operates in a widely differing set of environments, so that it is most difficult to find a common environmental factor which could conceivably be governing. The problem becomes particularly acute when one considers a trend that seems merely to lead 'round and 'round the mulberry bush. For example, all students of the Asteraceae agree that aggregation and reduction are widespread (though not irreversible) trends in the inflorescence of the family. In several different genera, in different tribes, one sees composite composites, with one-flowered, individually involucrate heads aggregated into a secondary head with its own common involucre. The flower head of *Dipsacus* is probably a secondary head, consisting of an aggregation of uniflorous heads.

In order to remember, understand, and interpret what we see, our minds constantly seek patterns, not just in the diversity among angiosperms, but in everything that we consider. In this very paragraph I am trying to elucidate a pattern in human behavior. Sometimes the mind will impose a pattern where none exists, or it will arbitrarily choose one of two or more equally valid possibilities to the exclusion of others. Probably most readers have seen a drawing of a Necker cube (Fig. 5.13), a transparent cube deliberately drawn to be mentally reversible, so that one can at will perceive a view looking into a box, or another view of only the outside of the box, from a different angle. Because of its transparency, the Necker cube is not quite right for either view of the box, but our minds automatically assume that it must be one or the other. There are many tile floors in which one can see different patterns of blocks, according to one's wishes. In these simple cases we recognize the arbitrariness of the choice. In more complex cases the existence of alternative possibilities may escape our attention.

In the section on inflorescences we noted that no existing classification of inflorescences is even approximately satisfactory. We then considered the probable evolutionary history of inflorescences in terms of the traditional classification. If some other classification of inflorescences had been used instead, the analysis of evolutionary trends would necessarily have been quite different. Certainly, then, there is an arbitrary element in our concept of evolutionary patterns in inflorescences.

Should we therefore give up all attempts at logical analysis? Of course not. The mind cannot operate without them. But we should be alert to

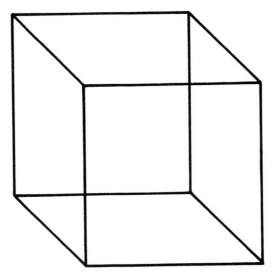

Fig. 5.13. Necker cube, as explained in the text.

the possibility of alternative interpretations, and we should not be disappointed if we can impose only a less than perfect order on the endless diversity of nature. A bit of skepticism about the ultimate correctness of any rational scheme will do no harm.

How do these caveats apply to a consideration of evolutionary trends in angiosperms? We have noted that many of the evolutionary trends bear little apparent relation to survival value, that the same thing often happens in a number of different groups, and that there are some reversals. It might be claimed that among the multitude of evolutionary changes which occur, our minds fasten upon those which can be arranged in stepwise progression, and that the resulting evolutionary trends are mere creations of the mind. This approach implies that each step in such an artificial sequence is useful either for its own sake or through pleiotropic effect, but that the sequential progression of steps, being purely mental and arbitrary, needs no explanation. The occurrence of similar changes in several taxa of a related group would likewise be dismissed as not requiring any explanation. I am not very happy with this outlook, but until a better understanding is reached, it should perhaps not be wholly rejected.

A possibly useful variant of this approach would be to say that there is a limited number of possibilities for morphologic evolution in any one group, that some of the myriad individual selections for obscure physiological characters will pleiotropically affect these morphological characters, and that a stepwise morphological progression, an apparent evolutionary trend of no functional significance, can therefore be produced by a series of scarcely related selections. The viability of this interpretation cannot be fully tested until we know more about the chemical nature of the individual genes that govern the characters affected by evolutionary trends. If the many mutations that are serially fixed to produce a trend are chemically very different from each other, this outlook has possibilities. If, on the other hand, these mutations are chemically related, then their physiological as well as their morphological effects should fall into patterns, and any progressive morphological change caused by pleiotropic effect should be associated with a progressive change of some other sort that has survival value. This brings us back to the fact that efforts to find adaptive trends pleiotropically associated with the seemingly nonadaptive trends in angiosperms have not been well rewarded.

As we have noted in CHAPTER 1, the problem of the causes of evolutionary trends has been eased somewhat by the general recognition among evolutionary theorists that mutation is not mathematically at random. Even on the basis of classic evolutionary theory, mutation provides more material for selection to work on in some directions than in others.

The synthetic theory of evolution, which only a few years ago seemed to be graven in stone, now appears to need substantial revision to provide for new information at the cytological and molecular level. Even the virtually exclusive role of selection is under attack from different positions. The work of Dover and his associates (e.g., 1982) on duplicative transposition and gene conversion (collectively called molecular drive) is of particular interest. It appears that some genes can insert additional copies of themselves at various sites in the genome, without the necessity of external selection. Furthermore, some alleles, when present in heterozygous combination, can in effect replace their allelic mates, again without external selection. One can visualize a sort of molecular peck-order among various alleles at a given locus, and a percentage frequency at which one allele will replace another in the absence of selection.

The importance of molecular drive remains to be determined. If gene conversion were pervasive and efficient, we would not as easily find Mendelian ratios in laboratory experiments. But perhaps a rate of conversion too low to stand out against the statistical noise would still be effective over a period of many generations. The problem of explaining neutral evolutionary changes will certainly be eased if molecular drive turns out to be a significant evolutionary factor. Changes in the sequence of amino acids in vital enzymes might be particularly amenable to such an interpretation. At present the whole matter is speculative.

Studies of isoenzymes and nucleic acid sequences during the past decade or so have overwhelmed the resistance of classical neo-Darwinians to the concept of neutral mutations. Essential neutrality of many of the sequence-changes in nucleic acids is now accepted as a simple fact of life by workers in this field. How such changes become fixed as characteristics of a species is still not entirely clear. Whatever the mechanism, there is no reason to suppose that it is restricted to mutations that do not have a detectable phenetic expression. The way is open to neutralist interpretation of some morphological as well as purely chemical changes. We should immediately add that recognition of some neutral changes must be an addition to the synthetic theory of evolution, rather than a replacement for it.

No one denies that selection is a very important evolutionary force. The question is to what extent selectively neutral or nearly neutral changes might be caused by other forces. The flexible, only loosely integrated morphologic-physiologic system of plants, in contrast to the more rigidly constrained system of animals, might provide the opportunity for internally governed molecular changes to play an important evolutionary role.

The problem of evolutionary trends without a plausible adaptive significance apparently presents itself oftener to botanists than to zoologists. Yet it may be instructive to consider the case of the drongos, a group of tropical birds with weird and wonderful tails. Failing to find any ecologic or other selective significance in the trends they discovered, the impeccably selectionist authors of a careful study (Mayr & Vaurie, 1948) of this group concluded (p. 246) that "throughout the family there is a genetic predisposition toward a lengthening of the tail, toward a modification of the outermost tail feather, and toward the development of a frontal crest, a disposition that is materialized in a certain number of species," and (p. 264) that "evolution within the family has been restricted to the realization of a limited number of trends." Certainly their interpretation of the nature of evolution in the drongos appears to be equally applicable to much of the evolution in angiosperms, both collectively and severally as regards the individual families and orders.

Selected References

Arber, E. A. N. & J. Parkin. 1970. On the origin of angiosperms. J. Linnean Soc., Bot. **38:** 29–80.

Axelrod, D. I. 1959. Poleward migration of early angiosperm flora. Science **130:** 203–207.

Axelrod, D. I. 1966. Origin of deciduous and evergreen habits in temperate forests. Evolution **20:** 1–15.

Baas, P. & M. Gregory. 1985. A survey of oil cells in the dicotyledons with comments on their replacement by and joint occurrence with mucilage cells. Israel J. Bot. **34:** 167–186.

Bailey, I. W. 1944. The development of vessels in angiosperms and its significance in morphological research. Amer. J. Bot. **31:** 421–428.

Bailey, I. W. 1953. Evolution of tracheary tissue in land plants. Amer. J. Bot. **40:** 4–8.

Bailey, I. W. 1956. Nodal anatomy in retrospect. J. Arnold Arbor. **37:** 269–287.

Bailey, I. W. & G. B. L. Swamy. 1951. The conduplicate carpel of dicotyledons and its initial trends of specialization. Amer. J. Bot. **38:** 373–379.

Banks, H. P. 1976. The oldest stomata (paracytic) with paired guard cells. Paleobotanist **25:** 27–31.

Baranova, M. A. 1972. Systematic anatomy of the leaf epidermis in the Magnoliaceae and some related families. Taxon **21:** 447–469.

Baranova, M. A. In press. Printisipy sravnitel'no-stomatograficheskogo izucheniya tsvetkovykh rasteniy. Komarovskie Chteniya 38. Nauka. Leningradskoe otdelenie.

Barghoorn, E. S. 1940–1941. The ontogenetic development and phylogenetic specialization of rays in the xylem of dicotyledons. I, II, III. Amer. J. Bot. **27:** 918–928, 1940; **28:** 273–282, 1941. Bull. Torrey Bot. Club **68:** 317–325, 1941.

Behnke, H.-D. 1975. The bases of angiosperm phylogeny: Ultrastructure. Ann. Missouri Bot. Gard. **62:** 647–663.

Behnke, H.-D. 1981. Sieve-element characters. Nordic J. Bot. **1:** 381–400.

Behnke, H.-D. & W. Barthlott. 1983. New evidence from the ultrastructural and micromorphological fields in angiosperm classification. Nordic J. Bot. **3:** 43–66.

Benzing, D. 1967. Developmental patterns in stem primary xylem of woody Ranales. I. & II. Amer. J. Bot. **54:** 805–813, 813–820.

Bernhardt, P. & L. B. Thien. 1987. Self-isolation and insect pollination in the primitive angiosperms: New evaluations of older hypotheses. Pl. Syst. Evol. **156:** 159–176.

Bessey, C. E. 1915. The phylogenetic taxonomy of flowering plants. Ann. Missouri Bot. Gard. **2:** 109–164.

Boke, N. H. 1964. The cactus gynoecium: A new interpretation. Amer. J. Bot. **51:** 598–610.

Boulter, D. 1973. The use of amino acid sequence data in the classification of higher plants. Pages 211–216 *in* G. Bendz & J. Santesson (eds.), Chemistry in botanical classification. Nobel Symposium 25. Academic Press. New York.

Brewbaker, J. L. 1967. The distribution and phylogenetic significance of binucleate pollen grains in the angiosperms. Amer. J. Bot. **54:** 1069–1083.

Campbell, J. H. 1985. An organizational interpretation of evolution. Pages 133–167 *in* D. J. Depew & B. H. Weber (eds.), Evolution at a crossroads: The new biology and the new philosophy of science. M.I.T. Press. Cambridge, Massachusetts.

Candolle, A. P. de. 1813. Théorie Élémentaire de la Botanique.

Carlquist, S. 1961. Comparative plant anatomy. Holt, Rinehart & Winston. New York.

Carlquist, S. 1969 (1970). Toward acceptable evolutionary interpretations of floral anatomy. Phytomorphology **19:** 332–362.

Carlquist, S. 1975. Ecological strategies of xylem evolution. Univ. Calif. Press. Berkeley.

Carlquist, S. 1980. Further concepts in ecological wood anatomy, with comments on recent work in wood anatomy and evolution. Aliso **9:** 499–553.

Carlquist, S. 1983. Wood anatomy of *Bubbia* (Winteraceae), with comments on the origin of vessels in dicotyledons. Amer. J. Bot. **70:** 578–590.

Carlquist, S. 1987. Presence of vessels in the wood of *Sarcandra* (Chloranthaceae): Comments on vessel origins in angiosperms. Amer. J. Bot. **74:** 1765–1771.

Carr, S. G. M. & D. J. Carr. 1961. The functional significance of syncarpy. Phytomorphology **11:** 249–256.

Corner, E. J. H. 1946. Centrifugal stamens. J. Arnold Arbor. **27:** 423–437.

Corner, E. J. H. 1954. The durian theory extended. II. Phytomorphology **4:** 152–165.

Crepet, W. L. 1984 (1985). Advanced (constant) insect pollination mechanisms: Pattern of evolution and implications vis-à-vis angiosperm diversity. Ann. Missouri Bot. Gard. **71:** 607–630.

Cristofolini, G. 1980. Interpretation and analysis of serological data. Pages 269–288 *in* F. A. Bisby, J. G. Vaughan & C. A. Wright (eds.), Systematics Association Special Volume No. 16. Chemosystematics: Principles and practice. Academic Press. London.

Cronquist, A. 1976. The taxonomic significance of the structure of plant proteins: A classical taxonomist's view. Brittonia **28:** 1–27.

Cronquist, A. 1977. On the taxonomic significance of secondary metabolites in angiosperms. Pl. Syst. Evol. Suppl. **1:** 179–189.

Cutter, E. G. 1965. Recent experimental studies of the shoot apex and shoot morphogenesis. Bot. Rev. **31:** 7–113.

Daniel, E. & R. Sattler. 1978. Development of perianth tubes of *Solanum dulcamara*: Implications for comparative morphology. Phytomorphology **28:** 151–171.

Davis, G. L. 1966. Systematic embryology of the angiosperms. Wiley. New York.

Dickison, W. C. 1975. The bases of angiosperm phylogeny: Vegetative anatomy. Ann. Missouri Bot. Gard. **62:** 590–620.

Dilcher, D. L. & P. R. Crane. 1984. *Archaeanthus*: An early angiosperm from the Cenomanian of the western interior of North America. Ann. Missouri Bot. Gard. **71:** 351–383.

Dobzhansky, Th. 1941. Genetics and the origin of species. 2nd ed. Columbia Univ. Press. New York.

Douglas, G. E. 1957. The inferior ovary. II. Bot. Rev. **23:** 1–46.

Dover, G. 1982. Molecular drive: A cohesive mode of species evolution. Nature **299:** 111–117.

Dover, G., et al. 1982. Dynamics of genome evolution and species differentiation. Pages 343–372 *in* G. Dover & R. B. Flavell (eds.), Genome evolution. Academic Press. London.

Doyle, J. A. 1978. Origin of angiosperms. Ann. Rev. Ecol. Syst. **9:** 365–392.

Doyle, J. A. & L. J. Hickey. 1976. Pollen and leaves from the Mid-Cretaceous Potomac Group and their bearing on early angiosperm evolution. Pages 139–206 *in* C. B. Beck (ed.), Origin and early evolution of angiosperms. Columbia Univ. Press. New York.

Eames, A. J. 1961. Morphology of the angiosperms. McGraw-Hill. New York.

Eckert, G. 1966. Entwicklungsgeschichtliche und blütenanatomische Untersuchungen zum Problem der Obdiplostemonie. Bot. Jahrb. Syst. **85:** 523–604.

Ehrlich, P. R. & P. H. Raven. 1964 (1965). Butterflies and plants: A study in co-evolution. Evolution **18:** 586–608.

Endress, P. K. 1986. Reproductive structures and phylogenetic significance of extant primitive angiosperms. Pl. Syst. Evol. **152:** 1–28.

Endress, P. K. 1987. Floral phyllotaxis and floral evolution. Bot. Jahrb. Syst. **108:** 417–438.

Engler, A. 1926. Die natürlichen Pflanzenfamilien. 2nd ed. 14a.

Esau, K., V. I. Cheadle & E. M. Gifford. 1953. Comparative structure and possible trends of specialization of the phloem. Amer. J. Bot. **40:** 9–19.

Eyde, R. H. 1971. Evolutionary morphology: Distinguishing ancestral structure from derived structure in flowering plants. Taxon **20:** 63–73.

Eyde, R. H. 1975. The bases of angiosperm phylogeny: Floral anatomy. Ann. Missouri Bot. Gard. **62:** 521–537.

Faegri, K. & L. van der Pijl. 1979. Principles of pollination ecology. 3rd ed. Pergamon Press. Oxford, New York.

Fairbrothers, D. E. 1983. Evidence from nucleic acid and protein chemistry, in particular serology, in angiosperm classification. Nordic J. Bot. **3:** 35–41.

Fairbrothers, D. E., et al. 1975. The bases of angiosperm phylogeny: Chemotaxonomy. Ann. Missouri Bot. Gard. **62:** 765–800.

Fraenkel, G. S. 1959. The *raison d'être* of secondary plant substances. Science **129:** 1466–1470.

Friis, E. M., P. R. Crane & K. R. Pedersen. 1986. Floral evidence for Cretaceous chloranthoid angiosperms. Nature **320:** 163–164.

Gaussen, H. 1946. Les Gymnospermes, actuelles et fossiles. Trav. Lab. Forest. Toulouse. Tome II, vol. 1, fasc. 3, chap. 5. Les autres Cycadophytes. L'origine cycadophytique des Angiospermes.

Gershenzon, J. & T. Mabry. 1983. Secondary metabolites and the higher classification of angiosperms. Nordic J. Bot. **3:** 5–34.

Grant, V. 1950. The protection of ovules in flowering plants. Evolution **4:** 179–201.

Heslop-Harrison, J. 1976. The adaptive significance of the exine. Pages 27–37 *in* I. K. Ferguson & J. Muller (eds.), The evolutionary significance of the exine. Linn. Soc. Symp. Ser. 1. Academic Press. London.

Hesse, H. 1981. The fine structure of the exine in relation to the stickiness of angiosperm pollen. Rev. Palaeobot. Palyn. **35:** 81–92.

Hesse, M. 1984. Pollenkitt is lacking in Gnetatae: *Ephedra* and *Welwitschia*; further proof for its restriction to the angiosperms. Pl. Syst. Evol. **144:** 9–16.

Hickey, L. J. 1973. Classification of the architecture of dicotyledonous leaves. Amer. J. Bot. **60:** 17–33.

Hickey, L. J. & J. A. Doyle. 1977. Early Cretaceous fossil evidence for angiosperm evolution. Bot. Rev. **43:** 3–104.

Hickey, L. J. & J. A. Wolfe. 1975. The bases of angiosperm phylogeny: Vegetative morphology. Ann. Missouri Bot. Gard. **62:** 538–589.

Hiepko, P. 1964. Das zentrifugale Androeceum der Paeoniaceae. Ber. Deutsch. Bot. Ges. **77:** 427–435.

Hiepko, P. 1965. Vergleichend-morphologische und entwicklungsgeschichtliche Untersuchungen über das Perianth bei den Polycarpicae. Bot. Jahrb. Syst. **84:** 359–508.

Hilu, K. W. 1983. The role of single-gene mutations in the evolution of flowering plants. Evol. Biol. **16:** 97–128.

Hutchinson, J. 1973. The families of flowering plants. 3rd ed. Oxford Univ. Press. London.

Jeffrey, C. 1983. 'Advances in cladistics.' A review. Kew Bull. **38:** 1–10.

Kasapligil, B. 1951. Morphological and ontogenetic studies of *Umbellularia californica* Nutt. and *Laurus nobilis* L. Univ. Calif. Publ. Bot. **25:** 115–240.

Kaul, R. B. 1967a. Development and vasculature of the flowers of *Lophotocarpus calycinus* and *Sagittaria latifolia* (Alismaceae). Amer. J. Bot. **54:** 914–920.

Kaul, R. B. 1967b. Ontogeny and anatomy of the flower of *Limnorchis flava* (Butomaceae). Amer. J. Bot. **54:** 1223–1230.

Kaul, R. B. 1968. Floral development and vasculature in *Hydrocleis nymphoides* (Butomaceae). Amer. J. Bot. **55:** 236–242.

Krassilov, V., P. V. Shilin & V. A. Vachrameev. 1983. Cretaceous flowers from Kazakhstan. Rev. Palaeobot. Palynol. **40:** 91–113.

Kubitzki, K. 1987. Origin and significance of trimerous flowers. Taxon **36:** 21–28.

Kubitzki, K. & O. R. Gottlieb. 1984. Phytochemical aspects of angiosperm origin and evolution. Acta Bot. Neerl. **33:** 457–468.

Leins, P. & W. Winhard. 1973. Entwicklungsgeschichtliche Studien an Loasaceen-Blüten. Oesterr. Bot. Z. **122:** 145–165.

Leppik, E. E. 1957. Evolutionary relationship between entomophilous plants and anthophilous insects. Evolution **11:** 466–481.

Levin, D. A. 1976. The chemical defenses of plants to pathogens and herbivores. Ann. Rev. Ecol. Syst. **7:** 121–159.

Mauritzon, J. 1939. Die Bedeutung der embryologischen Forschung für das natürliche System der Pflanzen. Lunds Univ. Arrskr. N.F. II. **35(15):** 1–70.

Mayr, B. 1969. Ontogenetische Studien an Myrtales-Blüten. Bot. Jahrb. Syst. **89:** 210–271.

Mayr, E. & C. Vaurie. 1948. Evolution in the family Dicruridae (birds). Evolution **2:** 238–265.

Merxmüller, H. & P. Leins. 1971. Zur Entwicklungsgeschichte männlicher Begonienblüten. Flora **160:** 333–339.

Muller, J. 1981. Fossil pollen records of extant angiosperms. Bot. Rev. **47:** 1–142.

Muller, J. 1984. Significance of fossil pollen for angiosperm history. Ann. Missouri Bot. Gard. **71:** 419–443.

Niklas, K. J. 1985. The aerodynamics of wind pollination. Bot. Rev. **51:** 328–386.

Pacini, E., G. G. Franchi & M. Hesse. 1985. The tapetum: Its form, function, and possible phylogeny in Embryophyta. Pl. Syst. Evol. **149:** 155–185.

Palser, B. F. 1975. The bases of angiosperm phylogeny: Embryology. Ann. Missouri Bot. Gard. **62:** 621–646.

Parkin, J. 1951. The protrusion of the connective beyond the anther and its bearing on the evolution of the stamen. Phytomorphology **1:** 1–18.

Pijl, L. van der. 1960–1961. Ecological aspects of flower evolution. I. Phyletic evolution. Evolution **14:** 403–416, 1960. II. Zoophilous flower classes. Evolution **15:** 44–59, 1961.

Pijl, L. van der. 1966. Ecological aspects of fruit evolution. A functional study of dispersal organs. Proc. Kon. Nederl. Akad. Wetensch. **C69:** 597–640.

Pijl, L. van der & K. Faegri. 1979. The principles of pollination ecology. 3rd ed. Pergamon Press. Oxford, New York.

Puri, V. 1951. The role of floral anatomy in the solution of morphological problems. Bot. Rev. **17:** 471–553.

Puri, V. 1952. Placentation in angiosperms. Bot. Rev. **18:** 603–651.

Raven, P. H. 1975. The bases of angiosperm phylogeny: Cytology. Ann. Missouri Bot. Gard. **62:** 724–764.

Richards, F. 1948. The geometry of phyllotaxis and its origin. Symp. Soc. Exp. Biol. **2:** 217–245.

Rickett, H. W. 1944. The classification of inflorescences. Bot. Rev. **10:** 187–231.

Robbins, C. T., et al. 1987. Role of tannins in defending plants against ruminants: Reduction in protein availability. Ecology **68:** 98–107.

Romero, E. J. & S. Archangelsky. 1986. Early Cretaceous angiosperm leaves from southern South America. Science **234:** 1580–1582.

Sattler, R. 1973. Organogenesis of flowers. A photographic text-atlas. Univ. Toronto Press. Toronto.

Sporne, K. R. 1954. A note on nuclear endosperm as a primitive character among dicotyledons. Phytomorphology **4:** 275–278.

Sporne, K. R. 1956. The phylogenetic classification of the angiosperms. Biol. Rev. Cambridge Phil. Soc. **31:** 1–29.

Stebbins, G. L. 1965. The probable growth habit of the earliest flowering plants. Ann. Misouri Bot. Gard. **52:** 457–468.

Stebbins, G. L. 1967. Adaptive radiation and trends of evolution in higher plants. Evol. Biol. **1:** 101–142.

Stebbins, G. L. 1974. Flowering plants. Evolution above the species level. Belknap Press of Harvard Univ. Press. Cambridge, Massachusetts.

Stebbins, G. L. 1975. Deductions about transspecific evolution from processes at the population and species level. Ann. Missouri Bot. Gard. **62:** 825–834.

Stebbins, G. L. & G. S. Khush. 1961. Variation in the organization of the stomatal complex in the leaf epidermis of monocotyledons and its bearing on their phylogeny. Amer. J. Bot. **48:** 51–59.

Takhtajan, A. 1959. Die Evolution der Angiospermen. Trans. to German by W. Höppner. Gustav Fischer Verlag. Jena.

Thien, L. B. 1980. Patterns of pollination in primitive angiosperms. Biotropica **12:** 1–13.

Thien, L. B., D. A. White & L. Y. Yatsu. 1983. The reproductive biology of a relict—*Illicium floridanum* Ellis. Amer. J. Bot. **70:** 719–727.

Thien, L. B., et al. 1985. The pollination of *Zygogynum* (Winteraceae) by a moth, *Sabatinca* (Micropterigidae): An ancient association? Science **227:** 540–543.

Thompson, D'Arcy W. 1942. On growth and form. 2nd ed. Macmillan. New York.

Thorne, R. F. 1963. Some problems and guiding principles of angiosperm phylogeny. Amer. Naturalist **97:** 287–305.

Upchurch, G. 1984. Cuticle evolution in Early Cretaceous angiosperms from the Potomac group of Virginia and Maryland. Ann. Missouri Bot. Gard. **71:** 522–550.

Walker, J. W. & J. A. Doyle. 1975. The bases of angiosperm phylogeny: Palynology. Ann. Missouri Bot. Gard. **62:** 664–723.

Walker, J. W. & A. G. Walker. 1984. Ultrastructure of Lower Cretaceous angiosperm pollen and the origin and early evolution of flowering plants. Ann. Missouri Bot. Gard. **71:** 464–521.

Wilson, C. L. 1937. The phylogeny of the stamen. Amer. J. Bot. **24:** 686–699.

Wilson, C. L. 1965. The floral anatomy of the Dilleniaceae. I. *Hibbertia* Andr. Phytomorphology **15:** 248–274.

Wilson, T. K. 1964. The comparative morphology of the Canellaceae. III. Pollen. Bot. Gaz. **125:** 192–197.

Winge, Ö. 1917. The chromosomes, their numbers and general importance. Compt.-Rend. Trav. Carlsberg Lab. **13:** 131–275.

Wolfe, J. A., et al. 1975. The bases of angiosperm phylogeny: Paleobotany. Ann. Missouri Bot. Gard. **62:** 801–824.

Young, D. A. 1981. Are the angiosperms primitively vesselless? Syst. Bot. **6:** 313–330.

Zavada, M. S. 1984. Angiosperm origins and evolution based on dispersed fossil pollen ultrastructure. Ann. Missouri Bot. Gard. **71:** 444–463.

Zavada, M. S. & T. N. Taylor. 1986. Pollen morphology of Lactoridaceae. Pl. Syst. Evol. **154:** 31–39.

Zimmermann, W. 1930. Die Phylogenie der Pflanzen. Gustav Fischer Verlag. Jena.

Chapter 6

Drimys winteri, of the family Winteraceae, order Magnoliales. Photo courtesy of Rudolf M. Schuster.

The Subclasses, Orders, and Families of Dicotyledons

Distinction Between Dicots and Monocots

It has been recognized for more than a century that the angiosperms, or flowering plants, form a natural group which consists of two subgroups. These two subgroups have usually been called dicotyledons and monocotyledons (or equivalent names with Latinized endings), from the most nearly constant of the several differences between them. As formal taxa they are here considered to be classes, called Magnoliopsida and Liliopsida. They have also been called Magnoliatae and Liliatae, but the -opsida endings are recommended for classes of higher plants in the *International Code of Botanical Nomenclature.* The terms dicotyledons and monocotyledons, or dicots and monocots, continue to be useful English names. The dicots are much the larger of the two groups. By a rough estimate there are perhaps 165,000 species of dicots, and about 50,000 monocots.

Both groups occur in a wide variety of habitats, but the dicotyledons are the more diverse in habit. About half of all the species of dicots are more or less woody-stemmed, and many of them are definitely trees, usually with a deliquescently branched trunk. The monocots in contrast are predominantly herbaceous. Less than 10% of all monocots are woody, and most of these belong to a single large family, the Arecaceae (Palmae). Woody monocots usually have an unbranched (or sparingly branched) stem with a terminal crown of large leaves, a habit that is rare in dicots. The difference in habit is partly a reflection of the complete absence of typical cambium in monocots, in contrast to its usual presence in dicots.

There are average differences in the underground as well as the aerial parts of dicots and monocots. In monocots the primary root soon aborts, and the mature root system is wholly adventitious. Many dicots likewise have an adventitious root system, but a primary root system, derived from the radicle, is more common.

All of the differences between dicots and monocots are subject to overlap or exception. The most nearly constant difference is the number of cotyledons, but as we have noted there are some dicots with only one cotyledon. The special features of monocots are further discussed in CHAPTER 7. The several differences between dicots and monocots are summarized in the following table.

DICOTS	MONOCOTS
Cotyledons 2 (seldom 1, 3, or 4, or the embryo seldom undifferentiated)	Cotyledon 1 (or the embryo sometimes undifferentiated)
Leaves mostly net-veined	Leaves mostly parallel-veined
Intrafascicular cambium usually present	Intrafascicular cambium lacking; usually no cambium of any sort
Vascular bundles of the stem usually borne in a ring that encloses a pith	Vascular bundles of the stem generally scattered, or in 2 or more rings
Floral parts, when of definite number, typically borne in sets of 5, less often 4, seldom 3 (carpels often fewer)	Floral parts, when of definite number, typically borne in sets of 3, seldom 4, almost never 5 (carpels often fewer)
Pollen typically triaperturate, or of triaperturate-derived type, except in a few of the more archaic families	Pollen uniaperturate or of uniaperturate-derived type
Mature root system either primary or adventitious, or both	Mature root system wholly adventitious

It is widely agreed that the monocots are derived from primitive dicots, and that the monocots must therefore follow rather than precede the dicots in any proper linear sequence. The solitary cotyledon, parallel-veined leaves, absence of a cambium, the dissected stele, and the adventitious root system of monocots are all regarded as apomorphic characters in the angiosperms, and any plant that was plesiomorphic (i.e., more primitive than the monocots) in these several respects would certainly be a dicot. The monocots are more primitive than the bulk of the dicots in having uniaperturate pollen, but several of the more archaic families of dicots also have uniaperturate pollen, so there is no problem here.

The Subclasses of Dicots (Magnoliopsida)

The dicots are here considered to consist of six subclasses, the Magnoliidae, Hamamelidae, Caryophyllidae, Dilleniidae, Rosidae, and Asteridae (Fig. 6.1). These were formally proposed and named by Takhtajan (Fig. 5.1) in 1964, and validated in 1966. His proposal represents a major conceptual advance, which I am happy to adopt. Antecedents to these groupings can of course be seen in earlier publications, tracing back through Takhtajan's and my own earlier work to the work of Bessey, Engler, Bentham and Hooker, A. P. de Candolle, and A. L. de Jussieu. We stand on the shoulders of our predecessors.

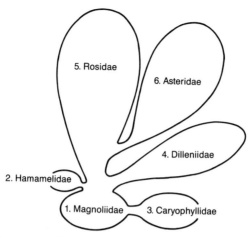

Fig. 6.1. Putative relationships among the subclasses of dicotyledons. The size of the balloons is roughly proportional to the number of species in the subclass.

Some segregate subclasses more recently proposed by Takhtajan and others are in my opinion less useful and are not here accepted. I include the Ranunculidae and Nymphaeidae in the Magnoliidae, and the Lamiidae in the Asteridae.

The several subclasses are groups which hang together on the basis of all of our information, but which cannot be precisely defined phenetically. They can be characterized only in generalities and in terms of critical tendencies. Even more than the families and orders, they are polythetic groups, established by accretion of apparently related members. Our minds demand some sort of organization of the 64 orders of dicots into a smaller number of affinity-groups, even though the resulting groups are poorly characterized.

In general, it may be said that the Magnoliidae are the basal complex, from which all other angiosperms have been derived. The Magnoliidae consist of nearly all of what has been called the Ranalian complex, plus a few other families. In cladistic terms, the subclass is a prime example of a paraphyletic group.

The Hamamelidae are a group of mostly wind-pollinated families with reduced, chiefly apetalous flowers that are often borne in catkins. This subclass consists chiefly of the core of the traditional Amentiferae, after some unrelated families such as the Salicaceae have been excluded. Plants with highly reduced flowers also occur in each of the other subclasses, but the Hamamelidae are an ancient major group with reduced flowers.

The Caryophyllidae are the Caryophyllales and their immediate allies. These families show a strong tendency toward free-central or basal placentation, and many of them have betalains, so far unknown in the other subclasses. Only a few are sympetalous.

The Rosidae and Dilleniidae are parallel groups that are not well distinguished morphologically. Those members of the Rosidae with numer-

ous stamens usually have the stamens developing (or initiated) in centripetal sequence. More advanced members of the group show a strong
tendency toward uniovulate locules and the development of a nectariferous disk that represents a reduced whorl of stamens. The vast majority
of the Rosidae are polypetalous; only a few are sympetalous or apetalous.
Those members of the Dilleniidae with numerous stamens usually have
the stamens developing centrifugally. The Dilleniidae usually have more
than one ovule in each locule, and they seldom have a nectariferous disk
of staminodial origin. Several of the more advanced families of the Dilleniidae are sympetalous, but they are in one way or another less advanced
than the Asteridae.

The Asteridae are the higher sympetalous families, with the stamens
rarely more than as many as the corolla-lobes, and with tenuinucellate
ovules that have a single massive integument. They are the most clearly
characterized of the six subclasses of dicots, but even so they contain a
few apetalous groups.

There are some differences among the subclasses in the most commonly
produced secondary metabolites, but these differences are perhaps even
less stable than the morphological ones. Isoquinoline alkaloids and related
compounds are common in the Magnoliidae but rare elsewhere. Betalains
in the Caryophyllidae have already been mentioned. The Hamamelidae
and the more archaic members of the Rosidae and Dilleniidae (especially
the woody ones) exploit condensed and hydrolyzable tannins as repellents,
but these are found in some members of the other subclasses as well.
Many of the Asteridae (especially the more archaic members of the group)
produce iridoids and related compounds but these also occur in some
members of the Rosidae, Dilleniidae, and Hamamelidae. Various other
groups of secondary metabolites are more or less characteristic of particular orders or families, but the same or similar compounds may occur in
taxa that are otherwise very different.

The subclasses of Magnoliopsida might be treated in any of several
linear sequences, so long as the Magnoliidae come first. It is also well for
the Asteridae to come last, inasmuch as these are the most highly advanced
group. The remaining four subclasses are all derived separately from the
Magnoliidae. I treat the Hamamelidae next after the Magnoliidae because
the Hamamelidae seem to represent the remnants of a very early line of
specialization that waxed and then waned as the other subclasses expanded. This is the only subclass other than the Magnoliidae to have any
primitively vesselless members. The Rosidae are treated just before the
Asteridae, because of the accumulating evidence that the Asteridae are
derived from the Rosidae. That leaves the Caryophyllidae and Dilleniidae
to be inserted between the Hamamelidae and the Rosidae. The Caryophyllidae and Dilleniidae collectively differ from the other subclasses in
having the stamens, when numerous, usually initiated in centrifugal sequence. The Caryophyllidae, being the smaller and less highly evolved
group, are treated before the Dilleniidae. Furthermore, it seems well to
juxtapose the Dilleniidae and Rosidae, because of the poor phenetic distinction between these two groups. Thus we come up with a sequence:

Magnoliidae—Hamamelidae—Caryophyllidae—Dilleniidae—Rosidae—
Asteridae. This sequence is identical to that of Takhtajan (1966).

The fossil record as well as the comparative morphology of modern
angiosperms provides strong support for the concept that the basic radiation of the group began early in the Lower Cretaceous, from plants
roughly comparable to the modern Magnoliidae. I am uneasy about iden-
tifying dispersed Lower Cretaceous pollen with any modern genus or
family, no matter how close the resemblance. Given the relative lack of
morphological integration among angiosperms, we have no assurance that
the plants which produced these early pollen grains were similar in other
respects to modern plants with such pollen. Yet there is no escaping the
fact that the very early fossils of both pollen and leaves of angiosperms
find their closest counterparts in the Magnoliidae.

It appears that by mid-Albian (late Lower Cretaceous) time the Hamamelidae and Rosidae were diverging from the ancestral Magnoliidae. The
Dilleniidae may have begun to diverge at about the same time, although
the evidence here is not so clear. The Caryophyllidae and Asteridae are
evidently more recent. The putative evolutionary history of each of these
several groups is discussed under the appropriate subclass.

The evolutionary origin of the monocots from very early dicots is
discussed in the next chapter.

Synoptical Arrangement of the Subclasses of Magnoliopsida[1]

1 Plants relatively archaic, the flowers typically apocarpous, always polypetalous
   or apetalous (but sometimes synsepalous) and generally with an evident
   perianth, usually with numerous (sometimes laminar or ribbon-shaped) stamens initiated in centripetal sequence, the pollen-grains mostly binucleate
   and often uniaperturate or of uniaperturate-derived type;[2] ovules bitegmic
   and crassinucellar; seeds very often with a tiny embryo and copious endosperm, but sometimes with a larger embryo and reduced or no endosperm;
   cotyledons occasionally more than 2; plants very often accumulating benzyl-
   isoquinoline or aporphine alkaloids, but without betalains, iridoid compounds, or mustard-oils, and only seldom strongly tanniferous . . . .
   . . . . **I. Magnoliidae.**
1 Plants more advanced in one or more respects than the Magnoliidae; pollen-
   grains triaperturate or of a triaperturate-derived type; cotyledons not more
   than 2; stamens not laminar, generally with well defined filament and anther;

---

[1] It should be clearly understood that the keys presented in this book are intended primarily
as conceptual aids rather than as a means of identification. Characters that are difficult to
observe are frequently used, and many of the numerous exceptions are necessarily ignored
or minimized. For a workable but necessarily artificial and repetitive set of keys to the
families of angiosperms on a world-wide basis, the student is referred to the third edition
(1973) of John Hutchinson's *Families of Flowering Plants.*

[2] By established convention, the term uniaperturate-derived is interpreted to exclude
triaperturate pollen, even though the uniaperturate type is phyletically antecedent to the
triaperturate type.

plants only rarely producing benzyl-isoquinoline or aporphine alkaloids, but often with other kinds of alkaloids, or tannins, or betalains, or mustard-oils, or iridoid compounds.

2 Flowers more or less strongly reduced and often unisexual, the perianth poorly developed or wanting, the flowers often borne in catkins, but never forming bisexual pseudanthia, and never with numerous seeds on parietal placentas; pollen-grains often porate and with a granular rather than columellar infratectal structure, but also often of ordinary type .... **II. Hamamelidae.**

2 Flowers usually more or less well developed and with an evident perianth, but if not so, then usually either grouped into bisexual pseudanthia or with numerous seeds on parietal placentas, only rarely with all the characters of the Hamamelidae, as listed above; pollen-grains of various architecture, but rarely if ever both porate and with a granular infrastructure.

3 Flowers polypetalous or less often apetalous or sympetalous, if sympetalous then usually either with more stamens than corolla-lobes, or with bitegmic or crassinucellar ovules; ovules only rather seldom with an integumentary tapetum; carpels 1–many, distinct or more often united to form a compound pistil; plants often tanniferous or with betalains or mustard-oils.

4 Stamens, when numerous, usually initiated in centrifugal (seldom centripetal) sequence; placentation various, often parietal or free-central or basal, but also often axile; species with few stamens and axile placentation usually either bearing several or many ovules per locule, or with a sympetalous corolla, or both.

5 Plants usually either with betalains, or with free-central to basal placentation (in a compound ovary), or both, but lacking both mustard-oils and iridoid compounds, and tanniferous only in the two smaller orders; pollen-grains trinucleate or seldom binucleate; ovules bitegmic, crassinucellar, most often campylotropous or amphitropous; plants most commonly herbaceous or nearly so, the woody species usually with anomalous secondary growth or otherwise anomalous stem-structure; petals distinct or wanting, except in the Plumbaginales; in the largest order (Caryophyllales) the sieve-tubes with a unique sort of P-type plastid, and the seeds usually with perisperm instead of endosperm .... **III. Caryophyllidae.**

5 Plants without betalains, and the placentation only rarely (except in the Primulales) free-central or basal; plants often with mustard-oils or iridoid compounds or tannins; pollen-grains usually binucleate (notable exception: Brassicaceae); ovules various, but seldom campylotropous or amphitropous except in the Capparales; plants variously woody or herbaceous, many species ordinary trees; petals distinct or less often connate to form a sympetalous corolla, seldom wanting; seeds only seldom with perisperm; plastids of the sieve-tubes usually of S-type, but in any case not as in the Caryophyllales .... **IV. Dilleniidae.**

4 Stamens, when numerous, usually initiated in centripetal (seldom centrifugal) sequence; flowers seldom with parietal placentation (notable exception: many Saxifragaceae) and also seldom (except in parasitic species) with free-central or basal placentation in a unilocular, compound ovary, but very often (especially in species with few stamens) with 2–several locules that have only 1 or 2 ovules in each; flowers

polypetalous or less often apetalous, only rarely sympetalous; plants often tanniferous, and sometimes with iridoid compounds, but only rarely with mustard-oils and never with betalains .... **V. Rosidae.**
3 Flowers sympetalous (rarely polypetalous or apetalous); stamens generally isomerous with the corolla-lobes or fewer, never opposite the lobes; ovules unitegmic and tenuinucellar, very often with an integumentary tapetum; carpels most commonly 2, occasionally 3–5 or more; plants only seldom tanniferous, and never with betalains or mustard-oils, but often with iridoid compounds or various other sorts of repellants ...
.... **VI. Asteridae.**

Selected References

Behnke, H.-D. 1977. Transmission electron microscopy and systematics of flowering plants. Pl. Syst. Evol., Suppl. **1:** 155–178.
Bessey, C. E. 1915. The phylogenetic taxonomy of flowering plants. Ann. Missouri Bot. Gard. **2:** 109–164.
Brown, W. H. 1938. The bearing of nectaries on the phylogeny of flowering plants. Proc. Amer. Philos. Soc. **79:** 549–595.
Crane, P. R., E. M. Friis & K. R. Pedersen. 1986. Lower Cretaceous angiosperm flowers: Fossil evidence on early radiation of dicotyledons. Science **232:** 852–854.
Cronquist, A. 1977. On the taxonomic significance of secondary metabolites in angiosperms. Pl. Syst. Evol., Suppl. **1:** 179–189.
Cronquist, A. 1981. An integrated system of classification of flowering plants. Columbia Univ. Press. New York.
Dahlgren, R. M. T. 1980. A revised system of classification of the angiosperms. J. Linn. Soc., Bot. **80:** 91–124.
Dahlgren, R. M. T. 1983. General aspects of angiosperm evolution and macrosystematics. Nordic J. Bot. **3:** 119–149.
Doyle, J. A. & L. J. Hickey. 1976. Pollen and leaves from the Mid-Cretaceous Potomac Group and their bearing on early angiosperm evolution. Pages 139–206 *in* C. B. Beck (ed.), Origin and early evolution of angiosperms. Columbia Univ. Press. New York.
Ferreira, Z. S. & O. R. Gottlieb. 1982. Polyacetylenes as systematic markers in dicotyledons. Biochem. Syst. Ecol. **10:** 155–160.
Gibbs, R. D. 1974. Chemotaxonomy of flowering plants. 4 vols. McGill-Queen's Univ. Press. Montreal & London.
Hallier, H. 1912. L'origine et le système phylétique des angiospermes exposés à l'aide de leur arbre généalogique. Arch. Néerl. Sci. Exact. Nat., Sér. 3, B. **1:** 146–234.
Hartley, R. D. & P. J. Harris. 1981. Phenolic constituents of the cell walls of dicotyledons. Biochem. Syst. Ecol. **9:** 189–203.
Hickey, L. J. & J. A. Doyle. 1977. Early Cretaceous fossil evidence for angiosperm evolution. Bot. Rev. **43:** 3–104.
Hutchinson, J. 1973. The families of flowering plants arranged according to a new system based on their probable phylogeny. 3rd ed. Clarendon Press. Oxford.

Knobloch, E. & D. H. Mai. 1986. Monographie der Früchte und Samen in der Kreide von Mitteleuropa. Rospravy Ústředniho Ústevu Geologického Svazek 47.

Melchior, H. (ed.). 1964. A. Engler's Syllabus der Pflanzenfamilien. Zwölfte Auflage. II Band. Angiospermen. Gebrüder Borntraeger. Berlin.

Muller, J. 1981. Fossil pollen records of extant angiosperms. Bot. Rev. **47:** 1–142.

Pollard, C. J. & K. S. Amuti. 1981. Fructose oligosaccharides: Possible markers of phylogenetic relationships among dicotyledonous plant families. Biochem. Syst. Ecol. **9:** 69–78.

Sattler, R. 1975. Organogenesis of flowers. A photographic text-atlas. Univ. Toronto Press.

Savile, D. B. O. 1979. Fungi as aids in higher plant classification. Bot. Rev. **45:** 377–503.

Smets, E. 1986. Localization and systematic importance of the floral nectaries in the Magnoliatae (Dicotyledons). Bull. Jard. Bot. Natl. Belg. **56:** 51–76.

Stebbins, G. L. 1974. Flowering plants: Evolution above the species level. Belknap Press of Harvard Univ. Press. Cambridge, Massachusetts.

Takhtajan, A. L. 1959. Die Evolution der Angiospermen. Transl. to German by W. Höppner. Gustav Fischer Verlag. Jena.

Takhtajan, A. L. 1966. Systema et phylogenia Magnoliophytorum. Soviet Sciences Press. Moscow, Leningrad. (In Russian)

Takhtajan, A. L. 1980. Outline of the classification of flowering plants (Magnoliophyta). Bot. Rev. **46:** 225–359.

Takhtajan, A. L. 1987. Systema Magnoliophytorum. Soviet Sciences Press. Leningrad Branch. (In Russian.)

Thorne, R. F. 1976. A phylogenetic classification of the Angiospermae. *In* M. K. Hecht, W. C. Steere & B. Wallace (eds.), Evolutionary Biology **9:** 35–106. Plenum Press. New York & London.

Thorne, R. F. 1977. Some realignments in the Angiospermae. Pl. Syst. Evol., Suppl. **1:** 299–319.

Thorne, R. F. 1983. Proposed new realignments in the angiosperms. Nordic J. Bot. **3:** 85–117.

Wunderlich, R. 1959. Zur Frage der Phylogenie des Endospermtypen bei den Angiospermen. Oesterr. Bot. Z. **106:** 203–293.

Subclass I. Magnoliidae

The subclass Magnoliidae as here defined consists of 8 orders (Fig. 6.2), 39 families, and about 12,000 species. Three of the orders (Magnoliales, Laurales, and Ranunculales) make up more than two-thirds of the species. Every order that is here referred to the Magnoliidae now seems securely placed there.

The Magnoliidae consist principally of those dicotyledons that have retained one or more features of a syndrome of primitive morphological characters, and which are not obviously allied to some more advanced group. The most important items of the syndrome are uniaperturate (or

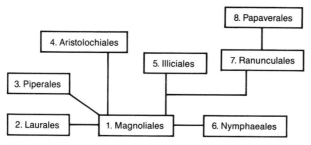

Fig. 6.2.   Putative relationships among the orders of Magnoliidae.

uniaperturate-derived) pollen, an apocarpous (or monocarpous) gynoecium, and numerous stamens that originate in centripetal sequence. All
of the dicotyledons that have uniaperturate or uniaperturate-derived pollen belong to the Magnoliidae, but about one-third of the species of the
subclass have triaperturate or triaperturate-derived pollen. More than
nine-tenths of the species of Magnoliidae have an apocarpous or monocarpous gynoecium, but in some of the less advanced members of the
Hamamelidae, Caryophyllidae, Dilleniidae and Rosidae the gynoecium
is apocarpous as in most of the Magnoliidae. These apocarpous members
of other subclasses are obviously related to syncarpous members of their
respective groups. Something more than half of the Magnoliidae have
numerous stamens that are initiated in centripetal sequence, but in a
considerable number of the Rosidae and a few of the Dilleniidae the
stamens are also numerous and centripetal. With the single debatable
exception of *Barclaya* (Nymphaeales), the Magnoliidae do not have a
sympetalous corolla, but this feature sets them apart only from the Asteridae and more advanced Dilleniidae. The vast majority of the Magnoliidae have bitegmic, crassinucellar ovules, but these features are also
widespread in the other subclasses except the Asteridae. Various other
putatively primitive features, such as vesselless wood, laminar stamens,
laminar placentation, and the presence of more than 2 cotyledons, are
largely or wholly restricted to the Magnoliidae, but are not standard features even within the subclass.

   The Magnoliidae have their own set of chemical defenses. A great many
of them have isoquinoline alkaloids and related compounds, especially
benzyl-isoquinoline and aporphine types. These are rare (though not unknown) in other groups of angiosperms. The various sorts of other alkaloids found in other angiosperms are largely or wholly wanting from
the Magnoliidae. Many of the Magnoliidae have characteristic volatile
oils, often in specialized spherical idioblasts, but some of these same oils
occur in other groups, as for example in the Apiaceae. Cyanogenic members of the Magnoliidae use a tyrosine-based pathway, so far as known.
Most of the cyanogenic monocotyledons resemble the Magnoliidae in this
regard. Other subclasses of dicotyledons have developed other pathways
of cyanogenesis, while retaining the tyrosine-based pathway in some members. Iridoid compounds and mustard-oils are unknown in the Magno-

liidae. As expounded on an earlier page, the chemical arsenal of the Magnoliidae may consist largely of weapons that have been superseded in more advanced groups.

The subclass Magnoliidae conforms in large part to what has often been called the Ranalian complex. Perhaps the most notable exclusion is the family Dilleniaceae, which is often taken as part of the Ranalian complex but which is also well known to be closely allied to the group that has sometimes been called the Guttiferalean complex. On formal morphology they are more at home in the Ranalian complex, but on the basis of transitional forms and close relationships they are better assigned to the advanced instead of the archaic group. The opposite course would require the provision of a new subclass name to replace Takhtajan's name Dillaniidae, but that is a minor nomenclatural matter rather than a factor of critical importance.

The Aristolochiales and Papaverales, which have not generally been included in the Ranalian complex, are here referred to the Magnoliidae, following Takhtajan. These orders are short evolutionary side-branches that have not given rise to other large groups. In a formal classification, they must either be treated as distinct subclasses, or (as here) included in the Magnoliidae. On formal morphology they are admittedly anomalous in the Magnoliidae.

The monotypic families Tetracentraceae and Trochodendraceae are here excluded from the Magnoliidae and assigned to the Hamamelidae, following Takhtajan. Again, they could on natural grounds be assigned to either group. In the Magnoliidae they would be specialized (despite their vesselless wood) and peripheral; in the Hamamelidae they are near-basal. Both families have elongate idioblasts that appear to be homologous with the spherical ethereal oil cells found in many Magnoliidae. In *Tetracentron* these idioblasts are secretory, but in *Trochodendron* they are not.

Within the Magnoliidae, it is clear that the Magnoliales are the most archaic order and should come first in the linear sequence. One can reasonably suppose that if the common ancestor of all the families in any other order of the subclass were alive today, it would be referred to the Magnoliales, or to a group that can be traced back to the Magnoliales. In cladistic terminology, the Magnoliales are a paraphyletic group.

The position and status of the other orders of the Magnoliidae in the system are to a considerable extent measured by how much they have diverged from the Magnoliales. It seems reasonable to put the Laurales next after the Magnoliales in the sequence, since it is the Laurales that are most difficult to distinguish clearly from the Magnoliales. It is equally clear that the Papaverales are derived from the Ranunculales, and that these are the two most advanced orders in the subclass. They therefore terminate the linear sequence.

The Piperales, Aristolochiales, Illiciales, and Nymphaeales appear to be derived directly and individually from the Magnoliales. The sequence among these four is therefore more a matter of convenience than necessity. I have chosen to arrange them in the sequence of my synoptical key. There is some further logic in this in that the Piperales, which are connected to the Magnoliales by the somewhat transitional family Chloranthaceae, come first in the group, and that the Nymphaeales, which are the most divergent from the Magnoliales, come last. Furthermore, it is posible that the closest relationship of the Chloranthacee is with the Laurales, as suggested by Endress (see below). The sequence here presented is compatible with either interpretation. A case might be made for putting the Illiciales immediately before the Ranunculales, inasmuch as the Ranunculales appear to take their origin in or near this group. No complex phylogeny can be accurately reflected in a linear sequence.

Peter Endress (1986) (Fig. 4.1) has selected three groups of families of the Magnoliidae as of particular interest for the study of the possible early evolution of the angiosperms. The first group consists of the Degeneriaceae, Himantandraceae, Eupomatiaceae, and Austrobaileyaceae, all of which are here assigned to the Magnoliales. These have medium-sized to fairly large flowers with numerous floral organs in spiral phyllotaxy. They tend to have laminar stamens, and have well developed inner staminodes with secretory structures that might provide food for insects. The flowers have a strong, often fetid odor and are pollinated by beetles or flies. In all of these respects they conform well to what has in recent decades become the classic concept of the primitive angiosperm flower.

Endress' second group consists of the Trimeniaceae, Amborellaceae, and Chloranthaceae. The Trimeniaceae and Amborellaceae are here considered to be archaic members of the Laurales, and the Chloranthaceae are referred to the Piperales as a distant sister-group to the other two families of that order. These three selected families have small, simple, often unisexual flowers, with an insignificant (or no) perianth and without staminodes. The one to several carpels have each a single ovule. Pollination is variously anemophilous or cantharophilous. Some recent authors have considered that the simple floral structure and often anemophilous pollination of the Chloranthaceae, in particular, might be as primitive and basic to angiosperms as the larger and more complex magnolialean flowers previously discussed. After careful comparison of various members of these several families and their probable relatives in the Laurales, Endress concludes that the floral structure here is reduced, rather than primitively simple. I agree. In any case there does not seem to be any direct connection between the anemophilous Chloranthaceae, with monosulcate pollen, and the anemophilous Hamamelidae, with triaperturate (or triaperturate-derived) pollen.

Endress' third group consists of the family Winteraceae. This family has medium-sized to small flowers of unstable structure. The number of floral organs (tepals, stamens, carpels, ovules) varies considerably within a genus, and sometimes even within a species. The size of the organs, especially the stamens, is likewise variable and unstable. Phyllotaxy is more or less unordered, especially in the androecium, without a fixed, simple geometric pattern. Pollination is variously by Coleoptera, Lepidoptera, Thysanoptera, Diptera, or the wind. Some species are self-pollinated. The family does have a distinctive sort of coarsely reticulate, uniporate pollen, an apparent antecedent of which has recently been discovered in Lower Cretaceous (Albian) deposits (Walker et al., 1983). Pollen comparable to that of some members of the other two groups also dates from the Lower Cretaceous, and indeed the Barremian *Clavatipollenites* appears to be virtually identical with the pollen of the modern genus *Ascarina* in the Chloranthaceae.

Endress considers that it is not possible at the present time to choose any one of these three groups as more archaic than the others. It may well be (my comment, not Endress') that the bulk of the modern angiosperms arose from plants more nearly like Group 1, but even that might be debated.

Synoptical Arrangement of the Orders of Magnoliidae

1 Plants ordinarily with ethereal oil cells in the parenchymatous tissues; pollen (except Illiciales) uniaperturate or derived from a uniaperturate type, not triaperturate; petals, when present, homologous with the sepals and bracts, and very often with 3 or more vascular traces.
   2 Pollen variously uniaperturate, biaperturate, or multiaperturate, or inaperturate, but not triaperturate.
      3 Plants distinctly woody (except *Cassytha,* of the Lauraceae); flowers normally developed, usually with an evident perianth of separate tepals that may or may not be differentiated into sepals and petals (in Eupomatiaceae the tepals all connate to form a deciduous calyptra).
         4 Flowers mostly hypogynous (somewhat perigynous in the Eupomatiaceae, these with numerous ovules); pollen typically uniaperturate or sometimes inaperturate (biaperturate in Eupomatiaceae and some Annonaceae); stamens often laminar, or with a prolonged and enlarged connective, but sometimes of more ordinary type; nodes most commonly trilacunar, sometimes multilacunar or unilacunar; stipules present or absent; flowers mostly solitary or in open, few-flowered inflorescences, in most families rather large; seeds with small embryo and copious endosperm .... **1. Magnoliales.**
         4 Flowers usually perigynous or epigynous (hypogynous in the small families Amborellaceae and Trimeniaceae, and in a few Monimiaceae); pollen mostly inaperturate or biaperturate, less often uniaperturate or multiaperturate; stamens usually of fairly ordinary type, but sometimes more or less laminar and with prolonged connective; ovule solitary (or 2, but only one maturing); nodes unilacunar; stipules wanting; flowers typically smaller and in more numerously flowered inflorescences than in most Magnoliales; seeds as in Magnoliales, or often with a large embryo and little or no endosperm ....2. **Laurales.**
      3 Plants otherwise, most species herbaceous or only secondarily woody.
         5 Flowers with much reduced or no perianth, often crowded into a spadix-like inflorescence; ovules mostly orthotropous; plants without aristolochic acid; seeds often with perisperm .... **3. Piperales.**
         5 Flowers with a well developed perianth, often consisting of a gamosepalous, more or less corolloid calyx, not crowded into a spadix; ovules mostly anatropous; plants commonly accumulating aristolochic acid; seeds with endosperm but not perisperm ....
         .... **4. Aristolochiales.**

2 Pollen triaperturate or sexaperturate; flowers hypogynous; woody plants with unilacunar nodes and without stipules .... **5. Illiciales.**
1 Plants without ethereal oil cells; pollen (except most Nymphaeales) triaperturate or derived from a triaperturate type; petals, when present, mostly apparently staminodial in origin, very often with only a single vascular trace; plants herbaceous, less often woody, and then probably with an herbaceous ancestry.
6 Plants aquatic, lacking vessels (except in the roots of *Nelumbo*); placentation mostly laminar (apical in *Nelumbo*); pollen uniaperturate or inaperturate, or (*Nelumbo*) triaperturate .... **6. Nymphaeales.**
6 Plants terrestrial or occasionally aquatic, with vessels; placentation marginal or parietal to sometimes laminar or axile; pollen triaperturate, or derived from a triaperturate type.
7 Gynoecium mostly apocarpous or seemingly or actually unicarpellate, seldom evidently syncarpous and then with more than 2 carpels; sepals usually more than 2; plants nearly always without protopine ....
.... **7. Ranunculales.**
7 Gynoecium syncarpous, usually of 2 carpels (carpels more numerous in *Papaver* and some other Papaveraceae, numerous and only weakly united in *Platystemon*); sepals mostly 2, occasionally 3, seldom 4; plants commonly producing protopine (an isoquinoline alkaloid) ....
....**8. Papaverales.**

SELECTED REFERENCES

Bailey, I. W. & B. G. L. Swamy. 1951. The conduplicate carpel of dicotyledons and its initial trends of specialization. Amer. J. Bot. **38:** 373–379.

Behnke, H.-D. 1971. Sieve-tube plastids of Magnoliidae and Ranunculidae in relation to systematics. Taxon **20:** 723–730.

Canright, J. E. 1963. Contributions of pollen morphology to the phylogeny of some ranalean families. Grana Palynol. **4:** 64–72.

Endress, P. K. 1973. Arils and aril-like structures in woody Ranales. New Phytol. **72:** 1159–1171.

Endress, P. K. 1983. Dispersal and distribution in some small archaic relic angiosperm families (Austrobaileyaceae, Eupomatiaceae, Himantandraceae, Idiospermoideae-Calycanthaceae). Sonderbd. naturwiss. Ver. Hamburg **7:** 201–271.

Endress, P. K. 1986. Reproductive structures and phylogenetic significance of extant primitive angiosperms. Pl. Syst. Evol. **152:** 1–18.

Erbar, C. 1983. Zum Karpelbau einiger Magnoliiden. Bot. Jahrb. Syst. **104:** 3–31.

Erbar, C. & P. Leins. 1983. Zur Sequenz von Blütenorganen bei einigen Magnoliiden. Bot. Jahrb. Syst. **103:** 433–449.

Hiepko, P. 1965. Vergleichend-morphologische und entwicklungsgeschichtliche Untersuchungen über das Perianth bei den Polycarpicae. Bot. Jahrb. Syst. **84:** 359–508.

Kubitzki, K. & H. Reznik. 1966. Flavonoid-Muster der Polycarpicae als systematisches Merkmal. I. Übersicht über die Familien. Beitr. Biol. Pflanzen **42:** 445–470.

Sastri, R. L. N. 1969. Comparative morphology and phylogeny of the Ranales. Biol. Rev. Cambridge Philos. Soc. **44:** 291–319.

Smith, A. C. 1971 (1972). An appraisal of the orders and families of primitive extant angiosperms. J. Indian Bot. Soc. Golden Jubilee Vol. **50A:** 215–226.

Thien, L. B. 1980. Patterns of pollination in primitive angiosperms. Biotropica **12:** 1–13.

Thorne, R. F. 1974. A phylogenetic classification of the Annoniflorae. Aliso **8:** 147–209.

Walker, J. W. 1974a. Evolution of exine structure in the pollen of primitive angiosperms. Amer. J. Bot. **61:** 891–902.

Walker, J. W. 1974b. Aperture evolution in the pollen of primitive angiosperms. Amer. J. Bot. **61:** 1112–1137.

Walker, J. W. 1976. Comparative pollen morphology and phylogeny of the Ranalean complex. Pages 241–299 *in* C. B. Beck (ed.), Origin and early evolution of angiosperms. Columbia Univ. Press. New York.

Walker, J. W., G. J. Brenner & A. G. Walker. 1983. Winteraceous pollen in the Lower Cretaceous of Israel: Early evidence of a magnolialean angiosperm family. Science **220:** 1273–1275.

West, W. C. 1969. Ontogeny of oil cells in the woody Ranales. Bull. Torrey Bot. Club **96:** 329–344.

Wood, C. E. 1958. The genera of woody Ranales in the southeastern United States. J. Arnold Arbor. **39:** 296–346.

1. Order Magnoliales

The order Magnoliales as here defined consists of 10 families and nearly 3000 species. One family, the Annonaceae, has about 2300 species and makes up about three-fourths of the order. Most of the remaining fraction is made up by only three families, the Myristicaceae (300), Magnoliaceae (220), and Winteraceae (100). The other six families of the order add up to scarcely 30 species in all. Five of the families (Winteraceae, Degeneriaceae, Himantandraceae, Magnoliaceae, and Annonaceae) are generally agreed to be fairly closely related, although sharply distinct. The Canellaceae and Myristicaceae form a pair that may be allied to the Annonaceae. The other three families are more isolated.

The Magnoliales may be briefly characterized as those families of the Magnoliidae that have ethereal oil cells, uniaperturate (or sometimes inaperturate or biaperturate) pollen, and usually hypogynous flowers with a well developed perianth of usually separate tepals. They are all woody plants. All of the putatively primitive features of angiosperms occur in one or another family of Magnoliales, but some of these features occur in other orders as well.

The vast majority of species of Magnoliales occur in tropical and warm-temperate regions, most of them in places with a moist, equable climate. Otherwise they occupy no particular ecological niche in contrast to other angiosperms, at least so far as present knowledge indicates.

Based on the comparative morphology of modern species, and on early Cretaceous fossil pollen and leaves, the Magnoliales must be considered the most archaic existing order of flowering plants. The fossil record clearly shows that the earliest angiosperm pollen-grains were monosulcate, and that simple, entire leaves with relatively unorganized pinnate venation are the ancestral archetype. Among modern angiosperms only the Magnoliales can accommodate this combination of characters.

No one family of Magnoliales can be considered ancestral to the rest of the order. Each family presents its own combination of primitive and advanced characters. It is convenient to begin the sequence of families with the Winteraceae, which are vesselless and have an apparently primitive type of pinnate venation in the leaves, but the sculptured, uniporate (rather than monosulcate) pollen is certainly not primitive in the order. Some other features of the Winteraceae are discussed on page 271.

Synoptical Arrangement of the Families of Magnoliales

1 Stamens distinct (rarely with the filaments connate below into a short tube in some Annonaceae).
  2 Leaves without stipules.
    3 Vessels wanting; pollen-grains uniporate, usually in tetrads; stomates more or less occluded by cutin; flowers seldom trimerous ..... **1. Winteraceae.**
    3 Vessels present in the secondary wood; pollen-grains variously monosulcate or bisulcate or inaperturate, but not uniporate, usually in monads; stomates not occluded; flowers often trimerous, at least as to the perianth.
      4 Carpel solitary, conduplicate, unsealed, the stigma running the length of the apposed margins; cotyledons 3 or 4; stamens laminar; ovules numerous; nodes pentalacunar .... **2. Degeneriaceae.**
      4 Carpels either more than one, or sealed (with a terminal style and stigma), or often both; cotyledons 2.
        5 Stamens more or less laminar or ribbon-shaped, not clearly divided into filament and anther.
          6 Trees or shrubs with alternate leaves; perianth (or apparent perianth) calyptrate in whole or in part.
            7 Each of the two sepals calyptrate (the outer one enclosing the inner), but the petals distinct and not calyptrate; carpels closed, distinct, uniovulate; nodes trilacunar; pollen-grains monosulcate; endosperm not ruminate ....
             .... **3. Himantandraceae.**
            7 Perianth represented or replaced by a single calyptra; carpels individually unsealed, but all closely crowded and more or less connate, thus appearing to be deeply sunken into the broad, flat receptacle; ovules several or many; nodes multilacunar; pollen-grains with 2 (3) parallel equatorial sulci .... **4. Eupomatiaceae.**
          6 Woody vines with opposite or subopposite leaves; perianth not at all calyptrate .... **5. Austrobaileyaceae.**
        5 Stamens usually with a short, thick filament and a well defined anther, the connective surpassing the anther and commonly enlarged above it, or seldom the stamens more or less laminar; perianth not calyptrate; carpels closed, each with 1–many ovules; leaves alternate ....**8. Annonaceae.**

2 Leaves with evident, deciduous stipules.
  8 Stamens numerous, spirally arranged; carpels usually more than 3, spirally arranged; ovules most commonly 2, but sometimes more numerous; nodes multilacunar; pollen-grains in monads . . . . . **6. Magnoliaceae.**
  8 Stamens 6, in 2 whorls of 3; carpels 3, in one whorl; ovules 4–8; nodes unilacunar; pollen-grains in tetrads . . . . **7. Lactoridaceae.**
1 Stamens with the filaments united at the base into a tube or column (connate only at the base in *Brochoneura,* of the Myristicaceae).
  9 Flowers unisexual; carpel solitary; ovule solitary, nearly basal; filaments united into a solid column (except as noted in *Brochoneura*) . . . .
  . . . .**9. Myristicaceae.**
  9 Flowers perfect; carpels 2–6, united into a compound, unilocular pistil with 2–6 parietal placentas; filaments united into a tube around the ovary . .
  . . . .**10. Canellaceae.**

SELECTED REFERENCES

Armstrong, J. E. & S. C. Tucker. 1986. Floral development in *Myristica* (Myristicaceae). Amer. J. Bot. **73**: 1131–1143.

Bailey, I. W. & C. G. Nast. 1943, 1944, 1945. The comparative morphology of the Winteraceae. I–VII. J. Arnold Arbor. **24**: 340–346, 472–481, 1943; **25**: 97–103, 215–221, 342–348, 454–466, 1944; **26**: 37–47, 1945.

Bailey, I. W., C. G. Nast & A. C. Smith. 1943. The family Himantandraceae. J. Arnold Arbor. **24**: 190–206.

Bailey, I. W. & A. C. Smith. 1942. Degeneriaceae, a new family of flowering plants from Fiji. J. Arnold Arbor. **23**: 356–365.

Bailey, I. W. & B. G. L. Swamy. 1949. The morphology and relationships of *Austrobaileya.* J. Arnold Arbor. **30**: 211–226.

Baranova, M. 1972. Systematic anatomy of the leaf epidermis in the Magnoliaceae and some related families. Taxon **21**: 447–469.

Brenner, G. J. & T. Crepet. 1987. Myristicaceous-like pollen in the Lower Cretaceous of Israel. Prepublication ms.

Buchheim, G. 1962. Beobachtungen über den Bau der Frucht der Familie Himantandraceae. Sitzungsber. Ges. Naturf. Freunde Berlin (N.F.) **2**: 78–92.

Canright, J. E. 1952, 1953, 1955, 1960. The comparative morphology and relationships of the Magnoliaceae. I. Trends of specialization in the stamens. Amer. J. Bot. **39**: 484–497, 1952. II. Significance of the pollen. Phytomorphology **3**: 355–365, 1953. III. Carpels. Amer. J. Bot. **47**: 155–165, 1960. IV. Wood and nodal anatomy. J. Arnold Arbor. **36**: 119–140, 1955.

Carlquist, S. 1964. Morphology and relationships of Lactoridaceae. Aliso **5**: 421–435.

Deroin, T. 1985. Contribution à la morphologie comparé du gynécée des Annonaceae-Monodoroideae. Bull. Mus. Hist. Nat. Paris. IV. **7B**(Adansonia): 167–176.

Dickison, W. C. & P. K. Endress. 1983. Ontogeny of the stem—node—leaf vascular continuum of *Austrobaileya.* Amer. J. Bot. **70**: 906–911.

Endress, P. K. 1977. Über Blütenbau und Verwandtschaft der Eupomatiaceae und Himantandraceae (Magnoliales). Ber. Deutsch. Bot. Ges. **90**: 83–103.

Endress, P. K. 1980. The reproductive structures and systematic position of the Austrobaileyaceae. Bot. Jahrb. Syst. **101:** 393–433.

Endress, P. K. 1984. The flowering process in the Eupomatiaceae (Magnoliales). Bot. Jahrb. Syst. **104:** 297–319.

Endress, P. K. 1984. The role of inner staminodes in the floral display of some relic Magnoliales. Pl. Syst. Evol. **146:** 269–282.

Goldblatt, P. A. 1974. A contribution to the knowledge of cytology in Magnoliales. J. Arnold Arbor. **55:** 453–457.

Gottsberger, G. 1970. Beiträge zur Biologie von Annonaceen-Blüten. Oesterr. Bot. Z. **118:** 237–279.

Gottsberger, G., I. Silberbauer-Gottsberger & F. Ehrendorfer. 1980. Reproductive biology in the primitive relic angiosperm *Drimys brasiliensis* (Winteraceae). Pl. Syst. Evol. **135:** 11–39.

Lammers, T. G., T. F. Stuessy & L. M. Silva. 1986. Systematic relationships of the Lactoridaceae, an endemic family of the Juan Fernández Islands, Chile. Pl. Syst. Evol. **152:** 243–266.

Leinfellner, W. 1969. Über die Karpelle verschiedener Magnoliales. VIII. Überblick über alle Familien der Ordnung. Oesterr. Bot. Z. **117:** 107–127.

Le Thomas, A. 1980, 1981. Ultrastructural characters of the pollen grains of African Annonaceae and their significance for the phylogeny of primitive angiosperms. Pollen & Spores **22:** 267–342, 1980; **23:** 5–36, 1981.

Mohana Rao, P. R. 1983. Seed and fruit anatomy in *Eupomatia laurina* with a discussion of the affinities of Eupomatiaceae. Flora **173:** 311–319.

Parameswaran, N. 1962. Floral morphology and embryology in some taxa of the Canellaceae. Proc. Indian Acad. Sci. B, **55:** 167–182.

Swamy, B. G. L. 1949. Further contributions to the morphology of the Degeneriaceae. J. Arnold Arbor. **30:** 10–38.

Tucker, S. C. 1959. Ontogeny of the inflorescence and the flower in *Drimys winteri* var. *chilensis.* Univ. Calif. Publ. Bot. **30:** 257–336.

Vink, W. 1970, 1977, 1978. The Winteraceae of the Old World. I. *Pseudowintera* and *Drimys*—Morphology and taxonomy. II. *Zygogynum*—Morphology and taxonomy. III. Notes on the ovary of *Takhtajania.* Blumea **18:** 225–354, 1970; **23:** 219–250, 1977; **24:** 521–525, 1978.

Walker, J. W. 1971. Pollen morphology, phytogeography, and phylogeny of the Annonaceae. Contr. Gray Herb. **202:** 1–131.

Wilson, T. K. 1960, 1965, 1964, 1966. The comparative morphology of the Canellaceae. I. Synopsis of genera and wood anatomy.Trop. Woods **112:** 1–27, 1960. II. Anatomy of the young stem and node. Amer. J. Bot. **52:** 369–378, 1965. III. Pollen. Bot. Gaz. **125:** 192–197, 1964. IV. Floral morphology and conclusions. Amer. J. Bot. **53:** 336–343, 1966.

Wilson, T. K. & L. M. Maculans. 1967. The morphology of the Myristicaceae. I. Flowers of *Myristica fragrans* and *M. malabarica.* Amer. J. Bot. **54:** 214–220.

Zavada, M. S. 1984. Pollen wall development of *Austrobaileya maculans.* Bot. Gaz. **145:** 11–21.

Zavada, M. S. & T. N. Taylor. 1986. Pollen morphology of Lactoridaceae. Pl. Syst. Evol. **154:** 31–39.

2. Order Laurales

The order Laurales as here defined consists of 8 families and about 2500 species. The Lauraceae, with about 2000 species, are by far the largest family, and the Monimiaceae, with about 450, are next. The remaining families have fewer than a hundred species in all, and three of them (Amborellaceae, Gomortegaceae, and Idiospermaceae) have only a single species each. The Monimiaceae are rather heterogeneous, and some authors see three additional families here (Atherospermataceae, Hortoniaceae, and Siparunaceae).

The Laurales may be briefly characterized as those families of the Magnoliidae that have most or all of the following syndrome of features: ethereal oil cells, perigynous or epigynous flowers with a well developed (though usually not large) perianth of free and distinct tepals, inaperturate or biaperturate pollen, and unilacunar nodes. Except for the anomalous twining parasite *Cassytha,* in the Lauraceae, they are all woody plants.

The vast majority of the species of Laurales occur in tropical or warm-temperate regions, most of them in places with a moist, equable climate. Otherwise they occupy no particular ecological niche in contrast to other woody angiosperms.

The Laurales are obviously allied to the Magnoliales. Several families have been shifted back and forth from one order to the other by various botanists. In trying to formulate a conceptually valid arrangement of the magnoliid families I have found it useful to define the Laurales narrowly, so as to form a fairly well characterized group more advanced than the loosely defined Magnoliales.

Although they are not the largest family of the order, the Monimiaceae are critical to an understanding of the Laurales. Search for relatives of each of the other families leads one into one or another part of the Monimiaceae. Only the Calycanthaceae and Idiospermaceae form a pair collectively somewhat set off from the rest of the order.

The Laurales must be presumed to be nearly as ancient as the Magnoliales, but the early Cretaceous fossil record of the order is scanty and dubious. Fossil leaves do indicate that the order was well diversified in late Maestrichtian time.

SYNOPTICAL ARRANGEMENT OF THE FAMILIES OF LAURALES

1 Seeds with well developed endosperm and small to medium-sized embryo.
  2 Leaves alternate; wood without vessels; flowers unisexual; stamens numerous, opening by longitudinal slits; pollen inaperturate or obscurely uniaperturate; carpels 5–8 .... **1. Amborellaceae.**
  2 Leaves opposite or occasionally subopposite; wood with vessels; flowers various.
    3 Ovary superior; flowers unisexual or less often perfect.
      4 Receptacle hardly differentiated from the pedicel, the 5–25 pairs of opposite, decussate appendages passing without demarcation from

the bracteoles of the pedicel to the tepals of the flower; flowers hypogynous; carpel 1 (2); pollen with 2 or 8–12 poorly marked apertures; anthers opening by longitudinal slits ..... **2. Trimeniaceae.**
4 Receptacle well differentiated from the pedicel, the bracts not passing
  into the tepals; flowers mostly perigynous (varying to essentially
  hypogynous in *Hortonia* and *Xymalos*); pollen inaperturate or rarely
  uniaperturate or biaperturate; anthers opening by slits or valves ..
  .... **3. Monimiaceae.**
3 Ovary inferior; flowers perfect; carpels 2 or 3, united; pollen inaperturate;
  anthers opening by valves .... **4. Gomortegaceae.**
1 Seeds without endosperm and with large embryo.
  5 Leaves opposite; pollen biaperturate; anthers opening by longitudinal slits.
    6 Carpels 5–35; cotyledons 2 .... **5. Calycanthaceae.**
    6 Carpels 1 or 2 (3); cotyledons 3 or 4 .... **6. Idiospermaceae.**
  5 Leaves alternate, very rarely opposite or whorled; pollen inaperturate; an-
    thers nearly always opening by valves; carpel 1; cotyledons 2.
    7 Ovary superior or very rarely inferior; fruit a 1-seeded berry or a drupe,
      only rarely dry and indehiscent .... **7. Lauraceae.**
    7 Ovary inferior; fruit dry, indehiscent .... **8. Hernandiaceae.**

SELECTED REFERENCES

Bailey, I. W. 1957. Additional notes on the vesselless dicotyledon, *Amborella trichopoda* Baill. J. Arnold Arbor. **38**: 374–380.

Blake, S. T. 1972. *Idiospermum* (Idiospermaceae), a new genus and family for *Calycanthus australiensis*. Contr. Queensland Herb. **12**: 1–37.

Endress, P. K. 1972. Zur vergleichenden Entwicklungsmorphologie, Embryo-logie und Systematik bei Laurales. Bot. Jahrb. Syst. **92**: 331–428.

Endress, P. K. 1980a. Floral structure and relationships of *Hortonia* (Monim-iaceae). Pl. Syst. Evol. **133**: 199–221.

Endress, P. K. 1980b. Ontogeny, function and evolution of extreme floral con-struction in Monimiaceae. Pl. Syst. Evol. **134**: 79–120.

Endress, P. K. & D. H. Lorence. 1983. Diversity and evolutionary trends in the floral structure of *Tambourissa* (Monimiaceae). Pl. Syst. Evol. **143**: 53–81.

Endress, P. K. & F. B. Sampson. 1983. Floral structure and relationships of the Trimeniaceae (Laurales). J. Arnold Arbor. **64**: 447–473.

Gottlieb, O. R. 1972. Chemosystematics of the Lauraceae. Phytochemistry **11**: 1537–1570.

Kasapligil, B. 1951. Morphological and ontogenetic studies of *Umbellularia californica* Nutt. and *Laurus nobilis* L. Univ. Calif. Publ. Bot. **25**: 115–239.

Kostermans, A. J. G. H. 1957. Lauraceae. Reinwardtia **4**: 193–256.

Kubitzki, K. 1969. Monographie der Hernandiaceen. Bot. Jahrb. Syst. **89**: 78–209.

Kubitzki, K. & S. Renner. 1982. Lauraceae. Fl. Neotropica Monogr. 31.

Leinfellner, W. 1966, 1968. Über die Karpelle verschiedener Magnoliales. II. *Xymalos, Hedycarya* und *Siparuna* (Monimiaceae). VI. *Gomortega keule* (Gomortegaceae). Oester. Bot. Z. **113**: 448–458, 1966; **115**: 113–119, 1968.

Money, L. L., I. W. Bailey & B. G. L. Swamy. 1950. The morphology and relationships of the Monimiaceae. J. Arnold Arbor. **31**: 372–404.

Nicely, K. A. 1965. A monographic study of the Calycanthaceae. Castanea **30**: 38–81.

Sampson, F. B. 1969. Studies on the Monimiaceae. I. Floral morphology and gametophyte development of *Hedycarya arborea* J. R. et G. Forst. (subfamily Monimioideae). Austral. J. Bot. **17**: 403–424. II. Floral morphology of *Laurelia novae-zelandiae* A. Cunn. (subfamily Atherospermoideae). New Zealand J. Bot. **7**: 214–240. III. Gametophyte development of *Laurelia novae-zelandiae* A. Cunn. (subfamily Atherospermoideae). Austral. J. Bot. **17**: 425–439.

Sampson, F. B. & P. K. Endress. 1984. Pollen morphology in the Trimeniaceae. Grana **23**: 129–137.

Sastri, R. L. N. 1952, 1958, 1962, 1963, 1965. Studies in Lauraceae. I. Floral anatomy of *Cinnamomum iners* Reinw. and *Cassytha filiformis* Linn. II. Embryology of *Cinnamomum* and *Litsea*. J. Indian Bot. Soc. **31**: 240–246, 1952; **37**: 266–278, 1958. III. Embryology of *Cassytha*. Bot. Gaz. **123**: 197–206, 1962. IV. Comparative embryology and phylogeny. Ann. Bot. (London). II. **27**: 425–433, 1963. V. Comparative morphology of the flower. Ann. Bot. (London) II. **29**: 39–44, 1965.

Stern, W. L. 1954. Comparative anatomy of xylem and phylogeny of Lauraceae. Trop. Woods **100**: 1–72.

Stern, W. L. 1955. Xylem anatomy and relationships of Gomortegaceae. Amer. J. Bot. **42**: 874–885.

Weberling, F. 1985. Zur Infloreszenzmorphologie der Lauraceae. Bot. Jahrb. Syst. **107**: 395–414.

Wilson, C. L. 1976. Floral anatomy of *Idiospermum australiense* (Idiospermaceae). Amer. J. Bot. **63**: 987–996.

3. Order Piperales

The order Piperales as here defined consists of 3 families and perhaps as many as 2000 species. The Chloranthaceae and Saururaceae collectively have fewer than a hundred species; the remainder belong to the Piperaceae. The close relationship of the Saururaceae to the Piperaceae is not in dispute.

The Chloranthaceae are a taxonomically isolated group, and their inclusion in the Piperales is debatable. They would be at least equally anomalous in any other order, and the only plausible alternative would be to put them into an order of their own. At the present state of knowledge either choice could be defended.

The Piperales may be briefly characterized as those families of the Magnoliidae that have ethereal oil cells, small flowers with much reduced or no perianth that are often crowded into a spadix-like inflorescence, and mostly orthotropous ovules. More than half of the species are herbs or half-shrubs, in contrast to the mostly woody Laurales and Magnoliales.

The Piperaceae are notable for their strong tendency toward a scattered arrangement of the vascular bundles, as in monocotyledons. The bundles are open, however, rather than closed as in the monocotyledons. The Piperaceae have sometimes figured in speculation about the origin of monocotyledons, but I do not find the outlook promising.

First appearances would suggest that the floral reduction of the Piperales is associated with anemophily, but the situation is complex. *Ascarina* and *Hedyosmum,* in the Chloranthaceae, are anemophilous, but *Chloranthus* and *Sarcandra,* in the same family, are pollinated by beetles or sometimes flies. The flowers of at least some species of Piperaceae are entomophilous, and the pseudanthial inflorescences of *Anemopsis,* in the Saururaceae, also suggest entomophily. Perhaps the order was initially anemophilous, but some members have reverted to entomophily. Aside from the imperfect syndrome of anemophily and floral reduction, there is nothing ecologically distinctive about the order.

The ancestry of the Piperales must be sought in the Magnoliales, or in the ancient transition between the Magnoliales and Laurales. Endress (1986, cited under Magnoliidae) is quite right in noting substantial similarities between the Chloranthaceae and the two most archaic families (Amborellaceae and Trimeniaceae) of the Laurales. These two families, however, have poorly developed (or no) apertures in the pollen, in contrast to the more primitive, monosulcate pollen of many Chloranthaceae. The pluriovulate carpels of *Saururus* suggest an ancestry of at least the Saururaceae and Piperaceae in the pluriovulate Magnoliales rather than in the uniovulate Laurales (including Amborellaceae and Trimeniaceae). If the Chloranthaceae are excluded from the Piperales, then the more narrowly defined order must surely have a magnolialean rather than a Lauralean base. Within the Magnoliales only the family Lactoridaceae shows some tendency toward the special features of the Piperales, having small flowers with 3 sepals, no petals, and 3 + 3 stamens. In counterpoint, the wood of *Lactoris* (the only genus in the family) is already much too advanced for a plausible ancestor of the Piperales, having very short, simply perforate vessel-segments. The wood of *Sarcandra,* in the Chloranthaceae, has been thought to be primitively vesselless, and the vessel-segments of *Saururus* have elongate perforation-plates with many cross-bars. Recently Carlquist (1987) has demonstrated very primitive vessels in the roots of *Sarcandra,* but an ancestry for the family among angiosperms with very primitive wood is still indicated.

Fossil pollen that appears to be securely identified as representing the Chloranthaceae occurs in Maestrichtian and more recent deposits. Other pollen of much greater age, dating back even to the Barremian, is rather closely comparable to that of the modern genus *Ascarina.* This ancient fossil pollen has been called *Clavatipollenites.* If it does in fact represent the Chloranthaceae, then the family antedates all other modern families in the known fossil record. On the other hand, there are several features in which the flowers of the Chloranthaceae must be regarded as reduced rather than primitive, at least under the strobilar hypothesis of floral evolution. Despite their apparently ancient lineage, the Chloranthaceae are not among the most archaic members of the Magnoliidae. It is perfectly possible that some of the now characteristic morphological features of the Chloranthaceae did not evolve until long after the characteristic features of the pollen.

Recently discovered fossil androecia of Albian and Santonian-Campanian age, with pollen in situ, have been plausibly attributed to the Chloranthaceae. These tell us nothing, however, about the structure of the rest of the flower. They do suggest that both anemophily and entomophily have a long history in the family.

Synoptical Arrangement of the Families of Piperales

1 Leaves opposite, with interpetiolar stipules; ovary half to fully inferior (or nude), unicarpellate, with a single pendulous ovule; seed with copious, oily endosperm and no perisperm . . . . **1. Chloranthaceae.**
1 Leaves alternate, or rarely opposite or whorled; stipules adnate to the petiole, or wanting; ovary superior to occasionally inferior (or nude); seed with copious, starchy perisperm and no endosperm.
  2 Ovules (1) 2–10 per carpel; carpels several, distinct above the base or united to form a compound, unilocular ovary with parietal placentation . . . . . .
  . . . . **2. Saururaceae.**
  2 Ovule solitary and basal or nearly so in the single locule of the compound or monomerous ovary . . . . **3. Piperaceae.**

Selected References

Carlquist, S. 1987. Presence of vessels in wood of *Sarcandra* (Chloranthaceae): Comments on vessel origins in angiosperms. Amer. J. Bot. **74**: 1765–1771.

Datta, P. C. & A. Dasgupta. 1977. Comparison of vegetative anatomy of Piperales. I, II. Acta Biol. Acad. Sci. Hung. **28**: 81–96, 97–110.

Endress, P. K. 1971. Bau der weiblichen Blüten von *Hedyosmum mexicanum* Cordemoy (Chloranthaceae). Bot. Jahrb. Syst. **91**: 39–60.

Endress, P. K. 1987. The Chloranthaceae: Reproductive structures and phylogenetic position. Bot. Jahrb. Syst. **109**: 153–226.

Friis, E. M., P. R. Crane & K. R. Pedersen. 1986. Floral evidence for Cretaceous chloranthoid angiosperms. Nature **320**: 163, 164.

Murty, Y. S. 1958, 1959, 1960. Studies in the order Piperales. I. A contribution to the study of vegetative anatomy of some species of *Peperomia*. Phytomorphology **10**: 50–59, 1960. II. A contribution to the study of vascular anatomy of the flower of *Peperomia*. J. Indian Bot. Soc. **37**: 474–491, 1958. III. A contribution to the study of floral morphology of some species of *Peperomia*. J. Indian Bot. Soc. **38**: 120–139, 1959. V. A contribution to the study of floral morphology of some species of *Piper*. VI. A contribution to the study of floral anatomy of *Pothomorphe umbellata* (L.) Miq. Proc. Indian Acad. Sci. B **49**: 52–65, 82–85, 1959. VII. A contribution to the study of morphology of *Saururus cernuus* L. J. Indian Bot. Soc. **38**: 195–203, 1959. VIII. A contribution to the morphology of *Houttuynia cordata* Thunb. Phytomorphology **10**: 329–341, 1960.

Okada, H. 1986. Karyomorphology and relationships in some genera of Saururaceae and Piperaceae. Bot. Mag. Tokyo **99:** 289–299.

Swamy, B. G. L. 1953. The morphology and relationships of the Chloranthaceae. J. Arnold Arbor. **34:** 375–408.

Tucker, S. C. 1976. Floral development in *Saururus cernuus* (Saururaceae). 2. Carpel initiation and floral vasculature. Amer. J. Bot. **63:** 289–301.

Tucker, S. C. 1980. Inflorescence and flower development in the Piperaceae. I. *Peperomia.* Amer. J. Bot. **67:** 686–702.

Tucker, S. C. 1981. Inflorescence and floral development in *Houttuynia cordata* (Saururaceae). Amer. J. Bot. **68:** 1017–1032.

Vijayaraghavan, M. R. 1964. Morphology and embryology of a vesselless dicotyledon—*Sarcandra irvingbaileyi* Swamy, and systematic position of the Chloranthaceae. Phytomorphology **14:** 429–441.

Wood, C. E. 1971. The Saururaceae in the southeastern United States. **52:** 479–485.

4. Order Aristolochiales

The order Aristolochiales consists of the single family Aristolochiaceae, with about 600 species, most of them tropical. Like the previous three orders, the Arisotolochiales have ethereal oil cells. Most of them are woody vines, but some are herbs or shrubs. The structure of the xylem suggests that many or perhaps all of the woody members may have an herbaceous ancestry. The distinctive flowers are epigynous (sometimes only half-epigynous or perigynous), with a well developed, basally tubular, often irregular and corolloid calyx, and usually with strongly reduced or no petals.

Long thought to be taxonomically isolated, the Aristolochiales are now considered to belong to the Magnoliidae. The archaic monotypic genus *Saruma* is particularly instructive in an assessment of affinities of the group. *Saruma* has perigynous flowers with several carpels that are united only at the base. The carpels ripen into follicles. The flowers have well developed petals and monosulcate pollen. These features, together with the ethereal oil cells and numerous ovules of the family as a whole, would seem to exclude all groups but the Magnoliales as possible ancestors. Even the characteristic aristolochic acids of the family are chemically allied to the aporphine alkaloids found in many members of the Magnoliidae.

SELECTED REFERENCES

Gregory, M. P. 1956. A phyletic rearrangement in the Aristolochiaceae. Amer. J. Bot. **43:** 110–122.

Hegnauer, R. 1960. Chemotaxonomische Betrachtung. 11. Phytochemische Hinweise für die Stellung der Aristolochiaceae in System der Dicotyledonen. Die Pharmazie **15:** 634–642.

Johri, B. M. & S. P. Bhatnagar. 1955. A contribution to the morphology and life history of *Aristolochia.* Phytomorphology **5:** 123–137.

Leins, P. & C. Erbar. 1985. Ein Beitrag zur Blütenentwicklung der Aristolochiaceen, einer Vermittlergruppe zu den Monokotylen. Bot. Jahrb. Syst. **107:** 343–368.

5. Order Illiciales

The order Illiciales as here defined consists of two closely related families, the Illiciaceae, with a single genus *Illicium* and about 40 species, and the Schisandraceae, with 2 genera and about 50 species.

The Illiciales may be briefly characterized as those members of the Magnoliidae that have ethereal oil cells and hypogynous flowers with triaperturate or sexaperturate pollen. They are all woody plants with unilacunar nodes. Except for the pollen, the group could readily be accommodated in the Magnoliales.

SYNOPTICAL ARRANGEMENT OF THE FAMILIES OF ILLICIALES

1 Flowers perfect; trees or shrubs, not climbing; carpels in a single whorl; fruits follicular . . . . **1. Illiciaceae.**
1 Flowers unisexual; scrambling or twining woody vines; carpels spirally arranged; fruits fleshy, indehiscent . . . .**2. Schisandraceae.**

SELECTED REFERENCES

Kapil, R. N. & S. Jalan. 1964. *Schisandra* Michaux—its embryology and systematic position. Bot. Not. **117:** 285–306.

Robertson, R. E. & S. C. Tucker. 1979. Floral ontogeny of *Illicium floridanum,* with emphasis on stamen and carpel development. Amer. J. Bot. **66:** 605–617.

Smith, A. C. 1947. The families Illiciaceae and Schisandraceae. Sargentia **7:** 1–224.

White, D. A. & L. B. Thien. 1983. The pollination of *Illicium parviflorum* (Illiciaceae). J. Elisha Mitchell Sci. Soc. **101:** 15–18.

6. Order Nymphaeales

The order Nymphaeales as here defined consists of 5 families and about 65 species. The Nymphaeaceae, with about 50 species, are by far the largest family.

The Nymphaeales may be briefly characterized as those families of the Magnoliidae that are aquatic herbs without ethereal oil cells and without vessels in the shoot. Most of them have uniaperturate or inaperturate pollen, but the distinctive family Nelumbonaceae has triaperturate pollen. Most of the Nymphaeales have long-petiolate leaves with broad, cordate to hastate or peltate, floating blade, but in *Ceratophyllum* the leaves are all slender and submersed, and in *Nelumbo* many of the leaves are emergent.

Unlike most orders of angiosperms, the Nymphaeales have an obvious ecological niche. They inhabit still waters, and many of their characteristics reflect adaptation to this habitat. On the other hand, they do not occupy this habitat to the exclusion of other groups. *Nymphoides,* in the Menyanthaceae, is very nymphaeaceous in aspect and habitat, and *Myriophyllum,* in the Haloragaceae, likewise recalls *Ceratophyllum.*

Based on leaf fossils, it appears that the Nymphaeales have a long history, going back all the way to the Albian stage of the Lower Cretaceous period. The fairly numerous and varied Albian fossils of this sort are coming to be called nymphaeaphylls. The monosulcate pollen of many of the Nymphaeaceae and Cabombaceae bespeaks an ancestry among the more primitive dicotyledons, but does not specify the time of origin. Nymphaealean pollen is in fact not very distinctive, and can be traced with some certainty only to the uppermost Cretaceous. The absence of fossil flowers attributable to the group is not surprising, in view of the scarcity of fossil flowers in general.

The most reasonable interpretation of the evidence, in my opinion, is that the modern Nymphaeales all descend from a group of primitive dicotyledons that took to an aquatic habitat and became herbaceous very early in the history of the angiosperms. There was a subsequent early dichotomy into a line leading to the modern Nelumbonaceae and a line leading eventually to the other 4 families. The modern families of the order thus represent a series of isolated end-lines, comparable on a smaller scale to the series of isolated end-lines that comprise the families of the modern orders Magnoliales and Laurales.

Synoptical Arrangement of the Families of Nymphaeales

1 Plants rooted to the substrate; flowers typically long-pedunculate and reaching or exserted from the surface of the water (seldom wholly submersed), perfect, usually with evident petals; carpels (1) 2–many; ovules bitegmic, anatropous except in Barclayaceae; leaves in most genera alternate (or apparently so), long-petiolate, with floating or emergent, cordate or peltate blade, but some or all of the leaves sometimes submersed, and in *Cabomba* these submersed leaves opposite or whorled, short-petiolate, and strongly dissected.
2 Carpels individually embedded in the enlarged, obconic receptacle; ovule 1 (2); seeds with large embryo, no perisperm, and virtually no endosperm; pollen triaperturate .... **1. Nelumbonaceae.**
2 Carpels not embedded in the receptacle; ovules 2–many; seeds with small embryo, some endosperm, and abundant perisperm; pollen uniaperturate or inaperturate.
3 Plants acaulescent, the leaves all simple and arising directly from the rhizome, usually with floating blade; petals 8–many (rarely none); car-

pels more or less firmly united to form a compound, plurilocular, superior to inferior ovary that ripens into a somewhat spongy, berry-like, irregularly (or scarcely) dehiscent fruit; ovules and seeds numerous.
4 Petals distinct (or none); stamens free from the petals; ovules anatropous; pollen uniaperturate .... **2. Nymphaeaceae.**
4 Petals connate into a lobed tube to which the stamens are attached, the corolla-tube epigynous, arising around the top of the ovary, but the sepals hypogynous; ovules orthotropous; pollen inaperturate ..
.... **3. Barclayaceae.**
3 Plants with long, slender, leafy, distally floating stems in addition to the rhizomes, with or without floating leaf-blades, often some or all of the leaves submersed and dissected; petals (2) 3 (4); carpels distinct, ripening into leathery, indehiscent fruits; ovules and seeds 2 or 3 ......
.... **4. Cabombaceae.**
1 Plants rootless, free-floating, submersed; flowers inconspicuous, sessile, unisexual, apetalous; carpel 1; ovule solitary, unitegmic, orthotropous; pollen inaperturate; leaves all sessile, whorled, dissected ... **5. Ceratophyllaceae.**

SELECTED REFERENCES

Esau, K. & H. Kosakai. 1975. Leaf arrangement in *Nelumbo nucifera*: A reexamination of a unique phyllotaxy. Phytomorphology **25**: 100–112.
Haines, R. W. & K. A. Lye. 1975. Seedlings of Nymphaeaceae. J. Linn. Soc., Bot. **70**: 255–265.
Jones, E. N. 1931. The morphology and biology of *Ceratophyllum demersum*. Stud. Nat. Hist. Iowa Univ. **13(3)**: 11–55.
Kosakai, H., M. F. Moseley & V. I. Cheadle. 1970. Morphological studies of the Nymphaeaceae. VI. Does *Nelumbo* have vessels? Amer. J. Bot. **57**: 487–494.
Li, H.-L. 1955. Classification and phylogeny of the Nymphaeaceae and allied families. Amer. Midl. Naturalist **54**: 33–41.
Melikyan, A. P. 1964. Sravnitel'naya anatomiya spermodermy nekotorykh predstaviteley cemeystva Nymphaeaceae. Bot. Zh. **49**: 432–436.
Moseley, M. F. 1958, 1961, 1971 (1972). Morphological studies of the Nymphaeaceae. I. The nature of the stamens. Phytomorphology **8**: 1–29, 1958. II. The flower of *Nymphaea*. Bot. Gaz. **122**: 233–259, 1961. III. The floral anatomy of *Nuphar*. VI. Development of the flower of *Nuphar*. Phytomorphology **15**: 54–84, 1965; **21**: 253–283, 1971 (1972).
Moseley, M. F. & N. W. Uhl. 1985. Morphological studies of the Nymphaeaceae sensu lato. XV. The anatomy of the flower of *Nelumbo*. Bot. Jahrb. Syst. **106**: 61–98.
Moseley, M. F. et al. 1984. Morphological studies of the Nymphaeaceae (sensu lato). XIII. Contributions to the vegetative and floral structure of *Cabomba*. Amer. J. Bot. **71**: 902–924.
Richardson, F. C. 1969. Morphological studies of the Nymphaeaceae. IV. Structure and development of the flower of *Brasenia schreberi* Gmel. Univ. Calif. Publ. Bot. **47**: 1–101.
Schneider, E. L. 1976. The floral anatomy of *Victoria* Schomb. (Nymphaeaceae). J. Linn. Soc., Bot. **72**: 115–148.

Schneider, E. L. 1978. Morphological studies of the Nymphaeaceae. IX. The seed of *Barclaya longifolia* Wall. Bot. Gaz. **139**: 223–230.

Schneider, E. L. & J. D. Buchanan. 1980. Morphological studies of the Nymphaeaceae. XI. The floral biology of *Nelumbo pentapetala.* Amer. J. Bot. **67**: 182–193.

Schneider, E. L. & E. G. Ford. 1978. Morphological studies of the Nymphaeaceae. X. The seed of *Ondinea purpurea* Den Hartog. Bull. Torrey Bot. Club **105**: 192–200.

Schneider, E. L. & J. M. Jeter. 1982. Morphological studies of the Nymphaeaceae. XII. The floral biology of *Cabomba caroliniana.* Amer. J. Bot. **69**: 1410–1419.

Schneider, E. M. & L. A. Moore. 1977. Morphological studies of the Nymphaeaceae. VII. The floral biology of *Nuphar lutea* subsp. *macrophylla.* Brittonia **29**: 88–99.

Snigirevskaya, N. S. 1964. Materialy k morfologii i sistematike roda *Nelumbo* Adans. Trudy Bot. Inst. AN SSSR, ser. 1, **13**: 104–172.

Wood, C. E. 1959. The genera of the Nymphaeaceae and Ceratophyllaceae in the southeastern United States. J. Arnold Arbor. **40**: 94–112.

7. Order Ranunculales

The order Ranunculales as here defined consists of 8 families and about 3200 species. More than half of the species belong to the single large family Ranunculaceae, and most of the others belong to only two families, the Berberidaceae (650) and Menispermaceae (400). Six of the families (Ranunculaceae, Circaeasteraceae, Berberidaceae, Sargentodoxaceae, Lardizabalaceae, and Menispermaceae), including the three largest ones, clearly belong to the same circle of affinity. The other two families (Coriariaceae and Sabiaceae) are less securely placed.

The Ranunculales may be briefly characterized as those families of the Magnoliidae that have well distributed vessels and triaperturate (or triaperturate-derived) pollen and do not have ethereal oil cells or protopine. The flowers are usually apocarpous and usually have more than 2 sepals. In contrast to the Nymphaeales, most of them are terrestrial, although a few species are aquatic.

With the partial exception of the Sabiaceae (which are only doubtfully included here), woody members of the Ranunculales have broad medullary rays, and the Menispermaceae also have anomalous secondary thickening. The Berberidaceae, which have many woody members, are in most respects more advanced than the more consistently herbaceous Ranunculaceae, and the genera that connect these two families are herbaceous. Thus it seems likely that the order as a whole is primitively herbaceous, and that all of its woody members are only secondarily woody.

It is plain enough that the Ranunculales must be derived from the Magnoliales through some woody group with triaperturate pollen. The Illiciales are the only known candidates to provide such a connection, but their relatively primitive xylem argues against a very close relationship.

The fossils provide no help here. Pollen referred to the Ranunculaceae dates only from the Lower Miocene, and the record is otherwise virtually blank.

Members of the Ranunculales occur in a wide range of habitats, from tropical to arctic, and from strictly terrestrial to aquatic. They also embrace a wide array of growth-forms, from annual or perennial herbs to herbaceous or woody vines or even small trees. Many of the Ranunculales have retained isoquinoline alkaloids from their magnolialean heritage, but other sorts of chemical defenses are also extensively exploited. One cannot even begin to characterize the order ecologically in terms that would not include a great many members of various other orders as well.

SYNOPTICAL ARRANGEMENT OF THE FAMILIES OF RANUNCULALES

1 Gynoecium mostly of separate carpels, or seemingly or actually of a single carpel, rarely (a few Ranunculaceae) of several more or less connate carpels; flowers often with nectariferous petals, but without an intrastaminal nectary-disk; endosperm copious to scanty or none; herbs and herbaceous or woody vines, less often shrubs or small trees.

  2 Leaves mostly alternate (opposite notably in *Clematis,* of the Ranunculaceae); petals not becoming fleshy; flowers never pentamerous throughout; plants without ellagic acid.

    3 Flowers mostly perfect; herbs or less often woody plants; endosperm well developed; plants mostly of temperate or boreal regions, or of tropical mountains.

      4 Leaves with dichotomous, free venation; nodes unilacunar; ovules orthotropous, unitegmic, tenuinucellar; endosperm-development cellular; flowers reduced, without petals or petaloid nectaries . . . . **2. Circaeasteraceae.**

      4 Leaves with net venation, or at least not with dichotomous, free venation; nodes mostly or always trilacunar to multilacunar; ovules anatropous to seldom hemitropous, bitegmic or seldom unitegmic; flowers usually well developed, often with nectariferous petals or with petaloid sepals, but sometimes much reduced and without perianth.

        5 Carpels usually 2 or more and distinct, seldom solitary or weakly united; stamens usually numerous, spirally arranged; anthers opening by longitudinal slits; herbs, rarely woody vines or low shrubs . . . . **1. Ranunculaceae.**

        5 Carpel solitary, or apparently so; stamens 4–18, most often 6, generally of the same number as the nectariferous petals and opposite them (opposite nectarless petals when the flowers do not have nectariferous petals); anthers usually opening by 2 uplifting valves; herbs or more often shrubs or even small trees . . . . **3. Berberidaceae.**

    3 Flowers nearly always unisexual; nearly all woody plants, mostly vines; endosperm present or absent; plants mostly of tropical or warm-temperate regions.

      6 Leaves compound; fruit of berries or fleshy follicles; embryo small,

straight; endosperm copious; flowers racemose; petals, when present, nectariferous.

7 Carpels numerous, spirally arranged; ovule solitary ....
.... **4. Sargentodoxaceae.**

7 Carpels 3 in a single whorl, rarely 6–15 in 2–5 whorls; ovules usually more or less numerous, seldom few .... **5. Lardizabalaceae.**

6 Leaves simple, rarely compound; fruit drupaceous or seldom of nutlets; embryo rather large, very often curved or even coiled; endosperm copious to often scanty or none; flowers cymose or cymose-paniculate, or seldom solitary; petals, when present, not nectariferous; ovules 2, one generally abortive .... **6. Menispermaceae.**

2 Leaves opposite or whorled; petals persistent, enlarging in fruit, becoming fleshy and more or less enveloping the achenes; flowers ordinarily wholly pentamerous; plants with ellagic acid .... **7. Coriariaceae.**

1 Gynoecium evidently of 2 (or 3) carpels united to form a compound ovary; flowers with an intrastaminal nectary-disk surrounding the base of the ovary, but without nectariferous petals; endosperm scanty or none; trees, shrubs, or woody vines .... **8. Sabiaceae.**

Selected References

Ernst, W. R. 1964. The genera of Berberidaceae, Lardizabalaceae, and Menispermaceae in the southeastern United States. J. Arnold Arbor. **45:** 1–35.

Foster, A. S. 1961. The floral morphology and relationships of *Kingdonia uniflora*. J. Arnold Arbor. **42:** 397–415.

Foster, A. S. 1963. The morphology and relationships of *Circaeaster*. J. Arnold Arbor. **44:** 299–327.

Gregory, W. C. 1941. Phylogenetic and cytological studies in the Ranunculaceae. Trans. Amer. Phil. Soc. II. **31:** 443–521.

Janchen, E. 1949. Die systematische Gliederung der Ranunculaceen und Berberidaceen. Österr. Akad. Wiss. Math.-Naturwiss. Kl., Denkschr. **108(4):** 1–82.

Jensen, U. 1968. Serologischer Beiträge zur Systematik der Ranunculaceae. Bot. Jahrb. Syst. **88:** 204–268; 269–310.

Kordyum, E. L. 1961. Sravnitel'no-embriologicheskoe issledovanie cemeystva liutikovykh. V. sb.: Morfogenez rasteniy **2:** 473–477. Moscow Univ. Press. Moscow.

Leinfellner, W. 1956. Zur Morphologie des Gynözeums von *Berberis.* Oesterr. Bot. Z. **103:** 600–612.

Meacham, C. A. 1980. Phylogeny of the Berberidaceae with an evaluation of classifications. Syst. Bot. **5:** 149–172.

Payne, W. W. & J. L. Seago. 1968. The open conduplicate carpel of *Akebia quinata* (Berberidales: Lardizabalaceae). Amer. J. Bot. **55:** 575–581.

Sastri, R. L. N. 1969. Floral morphology, embryology, and relationships of the Berberidaceae. Austral. J. Bot. **17:** 69–79.

Sharma, V. K. 1968. Floral morphology, anatomy and embryology of *Coriaria nepalensis* Wall., with a discussion on the inter-relationships of the family Coriariaceae. Phytomorphology **18:** 143–153.

Tamura, M. 1963–1968. Morphology, ecology and phylogeny of the Ranunculaceae. Parts 1–8. Sci. Rep. S. Coll. N. Coll. Osaka Univ. **11**: 115–126; **12**: 141–156; **13**: 25–35; **14(1)**: 53–71; **14(2)**: 27–48; **15(1)**: 13–35; **16(2)**: 21–43; **17(1)**: 41–56.
Tamura, M. 1972. Morphology and phylogenetic relationship of the Glaucidiaceae. Bot. Mag. (Tokyo) **85**: 29–41.

8. Order Papaverales

The order Papaverales has only two families, the Papaveraceae, with about 200 species, and the Fumariaceae, with about 400. Two small genera, *Hypecoum* and *Pteridophyllum,* tend to connect these otherwise well characterized families. These two genera have variously been referred to the Papaveraceae, or to the Fumariaceae, or have been considered to form one or two additional families.

The Papaverales may be briefly characterized as those families of the Magnoliidae that have well distributed vessels and triaperturate (or triaperturate-derived) pollen and that typically produce the isoquinoline alkaloid protopine. Like the Ranunculales and Nymphaeales, they lack ethereal oil cells. The flowers are syncarpous, most commonly with 2 carpels, and the sepals typically number 2, occasionally 3, seldom 4.

For many years it was customary to include the Papaverales and Capparales as here defined in a single large order, usually under the name Rhoeadales. The frequent presence of a replum in the fruit (an otherwise rare character) was probably an important reason for the association.

Evidence that has accumulated for the past several decades has led most students to separate the Papaverales from the Capparales, and to associate the Papaverales with the Ranunculales. The Papaverales are rich in the benzyl-isoquinoline and aporphine alkaloids that characterize the Ranunculaceae and other Magnoliidae, and diverse species of Papaverales have particular alkaloids, such as berberine, in common with members of the Ranunculales. The Capparales are poor in alkaloids, and they lack isoquinoline alkaloids entirely. The Papaverales have laticifers or elongate secretory cells in which the alkaloids are borne. These are wanting from the Capparales, which instead have scattered cells that produce myrosin, an enzyme involved in the formation of mustard-oil. Serological studies also indicate a relationship of the Papaverales to the Ranunculales, and the isolation of the Capparales from both of these orders. The stamens of the Papaverales originate centripetally, when a sequence can be determined, whereas those of the Capparales originate centrifugally. The pollen of the Papaverales is considered by palynologists to be similar to that of the Ranunculales, and different from that of the Capparales. Significant embryological differences between the Papaverales and Capparales have also been observed. There no longer seems to be any reason to doubt that the Papaverales should be dissociated from the Capparales and associated with the Ranunculales.

A Middle Eocene fossil flower from British Columbia may well represent the Papaveraceae. Otherwise the known fossil record of the order is insignificant.

The Papaverales are ecologically less varied than some of the larger orders, but even so they show no particular ecological unity. Most of them are herbs, but a few are shrubs or even small trees. They occur from subtropical to arctic regions. Some of them grow in moist woods, others in deserts, and others above timberline in the mountains; some of them are ruderal weeds. All of the habitats in which they occur are occupied also by habitally similar species of diverse other orders.

SYNOPTICAL ARRANGEMENT OF THE FAMILIES OF PAPAVERALES

1 Sepals fully enclosing the bud before anthesis; flowers regular; stamens distinct, numerous (only 4–6 in spp. of *Meconella*); nectaries wanting; plants producing milky or colored latex, often in articulated laticifers .... **1. Papaveraceae.**
1 Sepals small, not enclosing the developing bud; flowers strongly irregular, except in *Hypecoum* and *Pteridophyllum*; stamens 6 and diadelphous, or (in *Hypecoum* and *Pteridophyllum*) 4 and distinct; plants without latex or laticifers, but commonly with elongate secretory cells .... **2. Fumariaceae.**

SELECTED REFERENCES

Arber, A. 1931, 1932. Studies in floral morphology. III. On the Fumarioideae, with special reference to the androecium. IV. On the Hypecoideae, with special reference to the androecium. New Phytol. **30:** 317–354, 1931; **31:** 145–173, 1932.

Arber, A. 1938. Studies in flower structure. IV. On the gynaeceum of *Papaver* and related genera. Ann. Bot. (London) II, **2:** 649–663.

Bersillon, G. 1955. Recherches sur les Papavéracées: Contribution à l'étude du développement des dicotylédones herbacées. Ann. Sci. Nat. Bot. sér. 11, **16:** 225–447.

Ernst, W. R. 1962. The genera of Papaveraceae and Fumariaceae in the southeastern United States. J. Arnold Arbor. **43:** 315–343.

Frohne, D. 1962. Das Verhältnis vor vergleichender Serobotanik zu vergleichender Phytochemie, dargestallt an serologischen Untersuchungen im Bereich der "Rhoeadales." Pl. Med. **10:** 283–297.

Günther, K.-F. 1975. Beiträge zur Morphologie und Verbreitung der Papaveraceae. Flora **164:** 185–234; 393–436.

Hegnauer, R. 1961. Die Gliederung der Rhoeadales sensu Wettstein im Lichte der Inhaltstoffe. Pl. Med. **9:** 37–46.

Jensen, U. 1967 (1968). Serologische Beiträge zur Frage der Verwandtschaft zwischen Ranunculaceen und Papaveraceen. Ber. Deutsch. Bot. Ges. **80:** 621–624.

Ryberg, M. 1960. A morphological study of the Fumariaceae and the taxonomic significance of the characters examined. Acta Horti Berg. **19:** 122–248.

Sardulaeva, A. L. 1959. Morfologiya pyl'tsy semeystva makovykh (Papavera-
ceae). Problemy Botaniki **4**: 11–50.
Stockey, R. A. 1987. A permineralized flower from the Middle Eocene of British
Columbia. Amer. J. Bot. **74**: 1878–1887.

Subclass II. Hamamelidae

The subclass Hamamelidae as here defined consists of 11 orders (Fig.
6.3), 26 families, and about 3400 species. Nearly two-thirds of the species
belong to the order Urticales, and another quarter to the Fagales. The
other 9 orders have less than 300 species together. Like the Magnoliidae,
the Hamamelidae have a large proportion of small, taxonomically isolated, presumably relictual families.

The Hamamelidae are a coherent group of dicotyledons with more or
less strongly reduced, often unisexual flowers that are often borne in
catkins and never have numerous seeds on parietal placentas. The pollen
grains are often porate and with a granular rather than columellate infratectal structure, but these are not essential attributes of the group. The
morphological definition is not precise, especially inasmuch as reduced
flowers occur in various other groups of dicotyledons, but even so the
Hamamelidae form a compact, conceptually useful group.

The Hamamelidae can be traced back through the platanoid line to
near the middle of the Albian (final) stage of the Lower Cretaceous period,
more than 100 million years ago. While the platanoids were differentiating
from the ancestral magnoliids (or pre-magnoliids), a sister-group marked
by pinnatifid and eventually compound leaves was differentiating as the
probable ancestors of the modern Rosidae. As here interpreted, the two
emerging subclasses did not become clearly distinct until the appearance
of the *Normapolles* complex near the middle of the Cenomanian (earliest)
stage of the Upper Cretaceous.

The small size, smooth surface, and porate apertures of *Normapolles*
and its allies indicate that the group was adapted to wind-pollination.
Anemophily in this group appears to be an evolutionary reversion to a
pre-angiospermous condition, since early pollen of the triaperturate series
was adapted to transfer by insects rather than by wind. The immediate
ancestry of the *Normapolles* group is not clearly specified. On the still
scanty (or incompletely understood) fossil record it could just as well have
been from pre-rosids as from distinctive pre-hamamelids.

The *Normapolles* group was evidently diversified and successful in the
early part of the Upper Cretaceous. It included a wide array of subtypes,
some of which do and others of which do not appear to have modern
descendants. The ancestry of the modern amentiferous orders of the Hamamelidae appears to be firmly fixed in the *Normapolles* group. By the
Campanian stage of the Upper Cretaceous, some 80 million years ago,
pollen had evolved that appears to be referable to the modern orders
Fagales, Juglandales, and Myricales.

The interpretation here presented is that the Hamamelidae originated

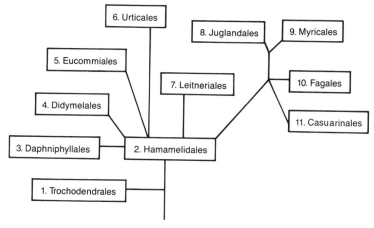

Fig. 6.3.   Putative relationships among the orders of Hamamelidae.

in the Albian stage as a group characterized by floral reduction and incipient wind-pollination, possibly in a climate with alternating wet and dry seasons. The deciduous habit that would be adaptively useful in such a climate would also be compatible with the evolution of anemophily. The combination of deciduous habit and wind-pollination might pre-adapt the early Hamamelidae to invasion of temperate regions, before these had been fully occupied by other groups of angiosperms. With the evolution of pollen more specifically adapted to transfer by wind, the group proliferated and diversified, as shown in the fossil record of the *Normapolles* complex. Later in the Upper Cretaceous the group declined, possibly as a result of increasing adaptation of insect-pollinated Rosidae and Dilleniidae to similar habitats. The continuing co-evolution of insects and entomophilous angiosperms might reasonably be expected to reduce and eventually overcome any initial advantage that the anemophilous Hamamelidae might have acquired in the early part of the Upper Cretaceous. Some of the Hamamelidae have more recently reverted to entomophily, even though the reduced flowers in most of these still suggest anemophily on first inspection. Whatever the balance may be among the controlling factors, the result is that the modern Hamamelidae consist of a few still highly successful groups, plus a series of isolated end-lines.

At some stage in their evolution the Hamamelidae and Rosidae took to exploiting tannins, notably hydrolyzable tannins such as ellagic acid, as an important defense against predators. Only a few of the modern Magnoliidae are significantly tanniferous, and almost none of them produces ellagic acid. In the modern Rosidae tannins are much more important among the archaic families than among the more advanced ones. One may reasonably suppose that the Hamamelidae and Rosidae took up hydrolyzable tannins as a defense when the two groups were still in the nascent stage of differentiation, and that the new weapon had something to do with their rise at the expense of their magnoliid predecessors.

The possible evolutionary history of the Dilleniidae cannot yet be integrated into this speculative account because of our still insufficient understanding of the fossil record.

Physena (2 spp. from Madagascar) fully merits the status of a separate family, as recently proposed by Takhtajan. Its place in the system is more debatable. It is here considered to be most nearly at home in the Hamamelidae, based on its reduced, unisexual flowers, long, latrorse anthers, and other features. The Physenaceae may need to be set apart in their own order within the Hamamelidae, but such action may well await detailed morphological, anatomical, and palynological study. The Physenaceae are here for convenience appended to the Urticales, from which they differ in their exstipulate leaves, axillary racemes, and peculiar ovary, this partitioned only at the base, and with 2 ovules on each of 2 basal-parietal placentas. We may note here for the record that *Physena* has anomocytic stomates (unpublished study by Margarita Baranova), but that scarcely helps to place the genus in the system.

SYNOPTICAL ARRANGEMENT OF THE ORDERS OF HAMAMELIDAE

1 Pistillate (or perfect) flowers either producing more than one fruit, or producing a single dehiscent fruit; ovules 1–many per carpel.
  2 Vessels wanting; leaves with unique, elongate (often branched) idioblasts; flowers (or some of them) perfect; carpels 4 or more, laterally coherent, collectively ripening into a folliceum; ovules several to many in each carpel; stipules wanting or represented only by a pair of flanges on the petiole .... **1. Trochodendrales.**
  2 Vessels present; no conspicuous, elongate idioblasts; flowers perfect to more often unisexual; carpels 2–several, distinct or more or less united to form a compound pistil, ripening into a capsule or into several separate fruits; ovules 1–many; stipules present or less commonly absent ....
.... **2. Hamamelidales.**
1 Pistillate (or perfect) flowers usually producing a single indehiscent fruit; ovules not more than 2 per carpel.
  3 Embryo minute; endosperm copious; ovary bilocular, with 2 ovules in each locule .... **3. Daphniphyllales.**
  3 Embryo well developed, of normal proportions; endosperm fairly abundant to often wanting; ovary various.
    4 Flowers not in aments; ovary unilocular or rarely bilocular; calyx often present; plants woody or herbaceous; endosperm well developed to wanting.
      5 Staminate flowers with 2 stamens and very short, connate filaments; vessel-segments with scalariform perforations; stipules none; ovule solitary .... **4. Didymelales.**
      5 Staminate (or perfect) flowers with distinct stamens, these usually but not always more than 2; vessel-segments with simple perforations.
        6 Ovules in the single locule 2, unitegmic; stipules wanting; flowers naked, racemosely arranged on the proximal, merely bracteate part of a distally leafy shoot .... **5. Eucommiales.**
        6 Ovule solitary (or solitary in each of the 2 locules), bitegmic; stipules

usually present; flowers clustered into inflorescences, usually with a vestigial perianth . . . . **6. Urticales.**

4 Flowers, or at least the staminate flowers, usually in aments (not in Nothofagaceae, of the Fagales); ovary with 1–several locules; calyx mostly wanting or very much reduced; plants woody; endosperm scanty or none.

  7 Pistil apparently of a single carpel, with a single style and locule; ovule solitary, pendulous; plants with well developed secretory canals in the pith, petioles, and leaf-veins . . . . **7. Leitneriales.**

  7 Pistil composed of more than one carpel, as shown by the presence of more than one style and often also more than one locule; plants without secretory canals.

    8 Leaves opposite or alternate, seldom whorled, always more or less well developed; ovules each with a single embryo-sac.

      9 Ovule solitary, orthotropous to less often hemitropous; aromatic plants with resinous-dotted leaves.

        10 Leaves pinnately compound (unique in the subclass); ovary bilocular (seldom trilocular or seemingly quadrilocular) below but unilocular above, the partition not reaching the top of the cavity, the ovule borne at the summit of the partial partition . . . . **8. Juglandales.**

        10 Leaves simple (sometimes pinnately lobed); ovary fully unilocular, with a basal ovule . . . . **9. Myricales.**

      9 Ovules 2 or more, anatropous; plants not aromatic, or not strongly so, the leaves not resinous-dotted; ovary 2- to several-locular at least below, often unilocular above . . . . **10. Fagales.**

    8 Leaves whorled, reduced to scales; ovules with multiple embryo-sacs . . . . **11. Casuarinales.**

Selected References

Abbe, E. C. 1974. Flowers and inflorescences of the "Amentiferae." Bot. Rev. **40:** 159–261.

Axelrod, D. I. 1966. Origin of deciduous and evergreen habits in temperate forests. Evolution **20:** 1–15.

Capuron, R. 1968. Sur le genre *Physena* Noronh. ex Thouars. Adansonia II. **8:** 355–357.

Endress, P. K. 1967. Systematische Studie über die verwandtschaftlichen Beziehungen zwischen den Hamamelidaceen und Betulaceen. Bot. Jahrb. Syst. **87:** 431–525.

Endress, P. K. 1977. Evolutionary trends in the Hamamelidales—Fagales group. Pl. Syst. Evol. Suppl. **1:** 321–347.

Giannasi, D. E. 1986. Phytochemical aspects of phylogeny in Hamamelidae. Ann. Missouri Bot. Gard. **73:** 417–437.

Hjelmqvist, H. 1948. Studies on the floral morphology and phylogeny of the Amentiferae. Bot. Not. Suppl. **2(No. 1):** 1–171.

Janchen, E. 1950. Die Herkunft der Angiospermen-Blüte und die systematische Stellung der Apetalen. Oesterr. Bot. Z. **97:** 129–167.

Kuprianova, L. A. 1965. Palinologiya serezhkotsvetnykh. Soviet Sciences Press. Moscow-Leningrad.

Moseley, M. F. 1973 (1974). Vegetative anatomy and morphology of Amentiferae. Brittonia **25**: 356–370.

Petersen, F. P. & D. E. Fairbrothers. 1985. A serotaxonomic appraisal of the "Amentiferae." Bull. Torrey Bot. Club **112**: 43–52.

Stone, D. E. 1973 (1974). Patterns in the evolution of amentiferous fruits. Brittonia **25**: 371–384.

Tiffney, B. H. 1986. Fruit and seed dispersal and the evolution of the Hamamelidae. Ann. Missouri Bot. Gard. **73**: 394–416.

Wolfe, J. 1973 (1974). Fossil forms of Amentiferae. Brittonia **25**: 334–355.

Zavada, M. S. & D. L. Dilcher. 1986. Comparative pollen morphology and its relationship to phylogeny of pollen in the Hamamelidae. Ann. Missouri Bot. Gard. **73**: 348–381.

1. Order Trochodendrales

The order Trochodendrales as here defined consists of two closely related woody families with a single species each, the Trochodendraceae and Tetracentraceae. Both families differ from all other Hamamelidae in being primitively vesselless, and in the unique, elongate, often branched idioblasts in the leaves. These idioblasts are apparently derived from the ethereal oil cells of the ancestral Magnoliidae. Neither family can be considered ancestral to the other. *Tetracentron* is more primitive in having a perianth, and in that the idioblasts are secretory, but *Trochodendron* is more primitive in having numerous stamens instead of only 4. The pinnate venation of *Trochodendron* may also be more primitive than the palmate venation of *Tetracentron*.

It is now widely agreed that the Trochodendrales form a connecting link between the Magnoliidae and Hamamelidae. The relationship to the Magnoliidae, amply documented by the primitively vesselless wood, was elucidated by Bailey and Nast more than 40 years ago. The connection to *Euptelea* and *Cercidiphyllum* (here referred to the Hamamelidales) has also been evident for many years. Aside from its relatively primitive floral structure, *Cercidiphyllum* also has leaves much like those of *Tetracentron*. Endress (1986) goes so far as to include the Eupteleaceae and Cercidiphyllaceae in the Trochodendrales, along with the family Trochodendraceae (defined to include both *Trochodendron* and *Tetracentron*). He considers that the Trochodendrales as so defined "have common roots with the Hamamelidales and have retained more magnolialean traits than have the Hamamelidales." I find it more useful to include the Eupteleaceae and Cercidiphyllaceae in the Hamamelidales, but either way one must admit a relationship between the two orders.

The fossil record of the Trochodendrales as here defined is scanty and inconclusive. We must suppose that the ancestry of the order lies in the Lower Cretaceous, but there are no Lower Cretaceous fossils to document the idea, and even the Upper Cretaceous fossils referred here are at best debatable. Some Upper Cretaceous (latest Campanian) wood may well represent either *Tetracentron* or *Trochodendron,* but is not firmly identified. Leaves and pollen that appear to belong here go back to the Eocene or Paleocene, and even some mid-Cretaceous fossil leaves have been thought possibly to represent both genera.

SELECTED REFERENCES

Bailey, I. W. & C. G. Nast. 1945. Morphology and relationships of *Trochodendron* and *Tetracentron.* I. Stem, root, and leaf. J. Arnold Arbor. **26:** 143–154.
Endress, P. K. 1986. Floral structure, systematics, and phylogeny in Trochodendrales. Ann. Missouri Bot. Gard. **73:** 297–324.
Nast, C. G. & I. W. Bailey. 1946. Morphology and relationships of *Trochodendron* and *Tetracentron.* II. Inflorescence, flower, and fruit. J. Arnold Arbor. **26:** 267–276.
Smith, A. C. 1945. A taxonomic review of *Trochodendron* and *Tetracentron.* J. Arnold Arbor. **26:** 123–142.

2. Order Hamamelidales

The order Hamamelidales as here defined consists of 5 families. The vast majority of the species belong to the Hamamelidaceae (100+). The Platanaceae have 6 or 7 species, and the Cercidiphyllaceae, Eupteleaceae, and Myrothamnaceae each have two species. The order may be briefly characterized as those members of the Hamamelidae which have vesseliferous wood and flowers that produce several fruits or a single dehiscent fruit. The leaves lack the peculiar idioblasts of the Trochodendrales.

Aside from the fact that they are all woody plants, the members of the Hamamelidales have little in common ecologically. Even the floral reduction that permeates the group has not restricted them to wind-pollination. A number of members of the Hamamelidaceae are pollinated by insects. *Hamamelis* itself appears to be insect-pollinated, although it blooms at a time when few insects are about. I consider the petals in *Hamamelis* and some other genera of the Hamamelidaceae to be of staminodial origin, associated with a reversion from anemophily to entomophily. *Rhodoleia* has pseudanthial inflorescences and is bird-pollinated.

The imperfectly sealed carpels of *Platanus* and especially *Euptelea* must direct our search for the ancestry of the order back toward the Magnoliidae rather than toward anything in the modern Rosidae. On the basis of fossil leaves, inflorescences, unisexual flowers, and pollen, it appears that plants very much like modern *Platanus* have existed since the Albian (Crane et al., 1986). These earliest platanoids had somewhat clumped pollen and a slightly larger perianth than modern *Platanus,* suggesting the possibility of entomophily, but the taxonomic affinity seems clear. Even the incomplete fusion of the adaxial suture of the carpel is evident in the fossils.

Among the other families of the order, the Cercidiphyllaceae date from the Campanian stage of the Upper Cretaceous on the basis of pollen, and from the Paleocene on macrofossils. The Hamamelidaceae date from the Paleocene on both pollen and macrofossils.

SYNOPTICAL ARRANGEMENT OF THE FAMILIES OF HAMAMELIDALES

1 Carpels distinct, or the carpel solitary.
  2 Ovules numerous; fruits follicular; plants dioecious; leaves stipulate, palmately to pinnipalmately veined . . . . **1. Cercidiphyllaceae.**
  2 Ovules 1–4; fruits indehiscent; plants monoecious, or with perfect flowers; leaves various.
    3 Stamens relatively numerous, commonly 7–20; flowers mostly perfect; connective prolonged, but not apically enlarged and peltate; ovules anatropous; leaves exstipulate, pinnately veined, merely toothed; embryo tiny, with poorly differentiated cotyledons . . . . **2. Eupteleaceae.**
    3 Stamens 3–4 (–7); flowers unisexual, the plants monoecious; connective apically enlarged and peltate; ovules orthotropous or nearly so; leaves stipulate, usually palmately lobed and veined; embryo of normal proportions . . . . **3. Platanaceae.**
1 Carpels united (at least below) into a compound pistil.
  4 Carpels 2 (3); leaves alternate (rarely opposite); pollen in monads; flowers perfect or unisexual, often with an evident perianth; ovules 1–many; shrubs or trees . . . . **4. Hamamelidaceae.**
  4 Carpels 3 or 4; leaves opposite; pollen in tetrads; flowers unisexual, the plants dioecious; perianth none; ovules many; low shrubs . . . .
      . . . . **5. Myrothamnaceae.**

SELECTED REFERENCES

Barabe, D. 1984. Application du cladisme à la systématique des Angiospermes: Cas des Hamamelidales. Candollea **39:** 51–70.

Bogle, A. L. 1970, 1986. Floral morphology and vascular anatomy of the Hamamelidaceae: The apetalous genera of Hamamelidoideae. J. Arnold Arbor. **51:** 310–366, 1970. Subfamily Liquidambaroideae. Ann. Missouri Bot. Gard. **73:** 325–347, 1986. (A manuscript on *Rhodoleia* awaits publication.)

Crane, P. R., E. M. Friis & K. R. Pedersen. 1986. Lower Cretaceous angiosperm flowers: Fossil evidence on early radiation of dicotyledons. Science **232:** 852–854.

Crane, P. R. & R. A. Stockey. 1986. Morphology and development of pistillate inflorescences in extant and fossil Cercidiphyllaceae. Ann. Missouri Bot. Gard. **73:** 382–393.

Endress, P. K. 1967. Systematische Studie über die verwandtschaftlichen Beziehungen zwischen Hamamelidaceen und Betulaceen. Bot. Jahrb. Syst. **87:** 431–525.

Endress, P. K. 1969 (1970). Gesichtspunkte zur systematischen Stellung der Eupteliaceen (Magnoliales). Ber. Schweiz. Bot. Ges. **79:** 229–278.

Ernst, W. R. 1963. The genera of Hamamelidaceae and Platanaceae in the southeastern United States. J. Arnold Arbor. **44:** 193–210.

Goldblatt, P. & P. K. Endress. 1977. Cytology and evolution in Hamamelidaceae. J. Arnold Arbor. **58:** 67–71.

Jäger-Zürn, I. 1966. Infloreszenz- und blütenmorphologische, sowie embryologische Untersuchungen an *Myrothamnus* Welw. Beitr. Biol. Pflanzen **42:** 241–271.

Leinfellner, W. 1969. Über die Karpelle verschiedener Magnoliales. VII. *Euptelea* (Eupteleaceae). Oesterr. Bot. Z. **116:** 159–166.

Nast, C. G. & I. W. Bailey. 1946. Morphology of *Euptelea* and comparison with *Trochodendron.* J. Arnold Arbor. **27:** 186–192.

Puff, C. 1978. Zur Biologie von *Myrothamnus flabellifolius* Welw. (Myrothamnaceae). Dinteria **14:** 1–20.

Swamy, B. G. L. & I. W. Bailey. 1949. The morphology and relationships of *Cercidiphyllum.* J. Arnold Arbor. **30:** 187–210.

3. Order Daphniphyllales

The order Daphniphyllales consists of the single family Daphniphyllaceae, with only the genus *Daphniphyllum,* about 9 species native mostly to eastern Asia and the Malay Archipelago. The group may be characterized as Hamamelidae with a drupaceous fruit, abundant endosperm, and a very small embryo. *Daphniphyllum* has no known fossil record.

Daphniphyllum has often been included in the Euphorbiaceae, or in the Euphorbiales as a distinct family. The drupaceous fruit and scalariform vessels, and the absence of an obturator and a caruncle would all be unusual in the Eurphorbiaceae, although these features can be found individually in various members of the family. More importantly, the tiny embryo is wholly out of harmony with the Euphorbiales and suggests a position nearer the base of the evolutionary tree.

The most obvious place for *Daphniphyllum,* once it is dissociated from the Euphorbiaceae, is in the Hamamelidae. Several previous authors, dating back at least to Hallier in 1912, have associated *Daphniphyllum* with the Hamamelidaceae. It may be significant that Zavada and Dilcher (1986, cited under Hamamelidae) found *Daphniphyllum* to group well with other Hamamelidae on the basis of pollen morphology. Although it seems reasonably at home in the Hamamelidae, *Daphniphyllum* does not fit comfortably with anything else in an established order. It appears to be another isolated end-line, comparable in that regard to *Didymeles, Eucommia, Leitneria,* and *Casuarina.*

SELECTED REFERENCES

Bhatnagar, A. K. & M. Gard. 1977. Affinities of *Daphniphyllum*—Palynological approach. Phytomorphology **27:** 92–97.

Carlquist, S. 1982. Wood anatomy of *Daphniphyllum*: Ecological and phylogenetic considerations, a review of Pittosporalean families. Brittonia **34:** 252–266.

Huang, T.-C. 1966. Monograph of *Daphniphyllum.* Taiwania **11:** 57–98; **12:** 137–234.

4. Order Didymelales

The order Didymelales consists of the single family Didymelaceae, with a single genus *Didymeles* and 2 species, confined to Madagascar. The group may be characterized as Hamamelidae with open-paniculate, bistaminate male flowers, very short, connate filaments, and a drupaceous fruit lacking endosperm. Pollen considered to represent *Didymeles* is known from Paleocene and more recent deposits.

Most authors have thought *Didymeles* to be related to the Hamamelidales and/or the Leitneriaceae. Other suggestions have included the Euphorbiaceae and *Aquilaria* (a putatively archaic member of the Thymelaeaceae). Both of these latter suggested ties would seem to require that the gynoecium of *Didymeles* be only pseudomonomerous, rather than simply monomerous as it appears to be. Furthermore, *Didymeles* has relatively primitive wood, with scalariform vessels and other plesiomorphic features that would argue against such affinities. It is simpler and less fraught with difficulty (may I say more parsimonious?) to consider *Didymeles* as related to and probably derived from the Hamamelidales, parallel in some respects to *Leitneria.*

SELECTED REFERENCES

Köhler, E. 1980. Zur Pollenmorphologie und systematische Stellung der Didymelaceae Leandri. Feddes Repert. **91:** 581–591.

Leandri, J. 1937. Sur l'aire et la position systématique du genre malgache *Didymeles* Thouars. Ann. Sci. Nat. Bot. sér. 10, **19:** 309–318.

5. Order Eucommiales

The order Eucommiales consists of the family Eucommiaceae, with a single genus and species *Eucommia ulmoides,* native to montane forests of western China. The order may be characterized as Hamamelidae with naked, unisexual flowers racemosely arranged on the proximal, bracteate part of a distally leafy shoot, with several stamens and a single unilocular ovary containing a pair of unitegmic ovules. *Eucommia,* or something like it, can be traced to the Paleocene on the basis of pollen, and to the Eocene on the basis of leaves and fruits.

The Eucommiaceae have usually been associated with either the Urticales or the Hamamelidales, or sometimes with the Magnoliales. Zavada and Dilcher (1986, cited under Hamamelidae) consider that the pollen links *Eucommia* to the Hamamelidales. On overall morphology, *Eucommia* is perhaps most nearly at home in the Urticales, but Eckardt (1956, 1963) has pointed out a series of features that make it anomalous there also. *Eucommia* is more primitive than the Urticales in having two ovules instead of only one, but more advanced in several other features (unitegmic, not fully crassinucellar ovules, absence of stipules). It seems likely that *Eucommia* originated from the Hamamelidales independently of the Urticales. Because of its combination of advanced and primitive features, *Eucommia* cannot be regarded as directly transitional between the Hamamelidales and Urticales, but it bolsters the idea of an evolutionary link between these two orders.

SELECTED REFERENCES

Eckardt, Th. 1956 (1957). Zur systematischen Stellung von *Eucommia ulmoides*. Ber. Deutsch. Bot. Ges. **69**: 487–498.
Eckardt, Th. 1963. Some observations on the morphology and embryology of *Eucommia ulmoides* Oliv. J. Indian Bot. Soc. **42A**: 27–34.
Tippo, O. 1940. The comparative anatomy of the secondary xylem and the phylogeny of the Eucommiaceae. Amer. J. Bot. **28**: 832–838.

6. Order Urticales

The order Urticales as here defined consists of 6 families and about 2200 species. The Moraceae have about a thousand species, the Urticaceae about 700, and the Cecropiaceae about 300. The Ulmaceae have about 150 species, the Cannabaceae only 3, and the Barbeyaceae only one. The Cecropiaceae have only rather recently (Berg, 1978) been described as a distinct family. Previously they were usually treated as a subfamily (Conocephaloideae) of either the Moraceae or Urticaceae, but they form a discordant element in either group.

The Urticales may be briefly characterized as non-amentiferous Hamamelidae with distinct stamens, one ovule per ovary or locule, 1 (–3) indehiscent fruits per flower, and a well developed embryo of normal proportions.

There is no doubt about the close relationship of the Moraceae, Cannabaceae, Cecropiaceae, and Urticaceae. The Ulmaceae are a little farther removed, but their affinity to the other 4 families is generally admitted. Some authors, such as Grudzinskaya (1967), would segregate a family Celtidaceae from the Ulmaceae, but the two families then stand side by side.

Only the position of the Barbeyaceae is still in dispute, Thorne (1976, cited under Magnoliophyta) considering the family to be incertae sedis. I here follow Dickison and Sweitzer (1970) in considering that the ensemble of characters, including the vascular anatomy, supports inclusion of *Barbeya* in the Urticales. Zavada and Dilcher (1986, cited under Hamamelidae) consider that the pollen also supports placement of *Barbeya* in the Urticales.

The Urticales have usually been associated with some of the other orders here referred to the subclass Hamamelidae, largely on the basis of floral features. Furthermore, Wolfe (1973, cited under Hamamelidae) emphasizes the similarity in leaf-venation between several genera of the Ulmaceae and many other Hamamelidae, notably members of the Fagaceae and Betulaceae. Pollen of the Urticales is said to suggest the fossil *Normapolles* group, as does that of several other orders of Hamamelidae.

There is also a long-standing school of thought, exemplified most recently by Thorne (1973) and Berg (1977), that the Urticales are allied to the Malvales. Such an alliance can be seriously entertained only if *Barbeya* is excluded from the group. The primitive phloem and more or less distinct carpels of *Barbeya* are readily compatible with the Hamamelidae, but would be aberrant in a group to be associated with the Malvales.

The fossil record supports the antiquity of the Urticales. Pollen considered to represent the Ulmaceae can be traced to the Turonian stage of the Upper Cretaceous, some 90 million years BP, within the time-span of the *Normapolles* group. Fruits of the Urticaceae date from the Campanian, and of both subfamilies of the Ulmaceae from the Paleocene.

The Urticales are ecologically diversified. They all have reduced flowers that might be supposed a priori to be wind-pollinated, but many of them are in fact pollinated by insects. There is virtually nothing in the vegetative features to fit the order to any coherent set of habitats or ecological niches.

Synoptical Arrangement of the Families of Urticales

1 Leaves exstipulate, opposite; nodes unilacunar; gynoecium of 1–3 distinct or partly connate pistils, each with a separate style .... **1. Barbeyaceae.**
1 Leaves usually stipulate, variously opposite or alternate; nodes trilacunar or pentalacunar; gynoecium of a single unilocular (rarely bilocular) pistil.
  2 Ovary with 2 styles (but one style sometimes more or less reduced); ovule apical, pendulous, anatropous.
    3 Plants without laticifers, and without milky juice.
      4 Woody plants .... **2. Ulmaceae.**
      4 Herbs (or herbaceous vines) .... **3. Cannabaceae.**
    3 Plants nearly always with laticifers and milky juice ..... **4. Moraceae.**
  2 Ovary with a single style, pseudomonomerous; ovule basal or nearly so, erect, more or less orthotropous.
    5 Stamens more or less erect in bud, not elastically reflexed in dehiscence; woody plants; cystoliths wanting .... **5. Cecropiaceae.**
    5 Stamens inflexed in bud, elastically reflexed in dehiscence; herbs or occasionally half-shrubs, or rarely small, soft-wooded trees; cystoliths generally present .... **6. Urticaceae.**

Selected References

Behnke, H.-D. 1973. Sieve-tube plastids of Hamamelidae—Electron microscopic investigations with special reference to Urticales. Taxon **22:** 205–210.

Berg, C. C. 1977. Urticales, their differentiation and systematic position. Pl. Syst. Evol., Suppl. **1**: 349–374.

Berg, C. C. 1978. Cecropiaceae, a new family of Urticales. Taxon **27**: 39–44.

Corner, E. J. H. 1962. The classification of Moraceae. Gard. Bull. Singapore **19**: 187–252.

Dickison, W. C. & E. M. Sweitzer. 1970. The morphology and relationships of *Barbeya oleoides*. Amer. J. Bot. **57**: 468–476.

Elias, T. S. 1970. The genera of Ulmaceae in the southeastern United States. J. Arnold Arbor. **51**: 18–40.

Giannasi, D. E. 1978. Generic relationships in the Ulmaceae based on flavonoid chemistry. Taxon **27**: 331–344.

Grudzinskaya, I. A. 1967. Ulmaceae i obosnovanie vydeleniya Celtidoideae v samostoyatel'noe semeystvo Celtidaceae Link. Bot. Zh. **52**: 1723–1749.

Kuprianova, L. A. 1962. Palinologicheskie dannye k sistematike poryadkov Fagales & Urticales. V sb.: Dokl. Sov. Palinologov k pervoy Mezhdunarod-noy Palinolog. Konf. 17–25.

Leins, P. & C. Orth. 1979. Zur Entwicklungsgeschichte mañnlicher Blüten von *Humulus lupulus* (Cannabaceae). Bot. Jahrb. Syst. **100**: 372–378.

Miller, N. G. 1970. The genera of Cannabaceae in the southeastern United States. J. Arnold Arbor. **51**: 185–203.

Miller, N. G. 1971. The genera of the Urticaceae in the southeastern United States. J. Arnold Arbor. **52**: 40–68.

Small, E. & A. Cronquist. 1976. A practical and natural taxonomy for *Cannabis*. Taxon **25**: 405–435.

Sweitzer, E. M. 1971. The comparative anatomy of Ulmaceae. J. Arnold Arbor. **52**: 523–585.

Thorne, R. F. 1973 (1974). The "Amentiferae" or Hamamelidae as an artificial group: A summary statement. Brittonia **25**: 395–405.

Tippo, O. 1938. Comparative anatomy of the Moraceae and their presumed allies. Bot. Gaz. **100**: 1–99.

7. Order Leitneriales

The order Leitneriales consists of the single species *Leitneria floridana*, making up the family Leitneriaceae, confined to the coastal plain of the southeastern United States. The order may be briefly characterized as amentiferous Hamamelidae with a single pistil composed of a single carpel with a single style and a solitary ovule. The plants have well developed secretory canals in the pith, petioles, and leaf-veins. The fossil record of *Leitneria* can be traced with some assurance to near the base of the Miocene epoch, and perhaps into the Oligocene.

Leitneria is by all accounts taxonomically isolated, and its relationships are uncertain. The origin of *Leitneria* from a hamamelidalean ancestry has been postulated by several authors, and this possibility seems as likely as any. The multicellular, clavate glands of the leaves might or might not be homologous with the peltate gland-scales of the Juglandales, Myricales, and Fagales. Zavada and Dilcher (1986, cited under Hamamelidae) consider that the pollen fits well into the Hamamelidae and is particularly closely linked to that of *Daphniphyllum*. For a contrary view, linking *Leitneria* to the Sapindales, see Petersen and Fairbrothers (1983).

SELECTED REFERENCES

Abbe, E. C. & T. T. Earle. 1940. Inflorescence, floral anatomy and morphology of *Leitneria floridana*. Bull. Torrey Bot. Club **67**: 173–193.
Channell, R. B. & C. E. Wood. 1962. The Leitneriaceae in the southeastern United States. J. Arnold Arbor. **43**: 435–438.
Petersen, F. P. & D. E. Fairbrothers. 1983. A serotaxonomic appraisal of *Amphipterygium* and *Leitneria*—Two amentiferous taxa of Rutiflorae (Rosidae). Syst. Bot. **8**: 134–148.

8. Order Juglandales

The order Juglandales consists of two families, the Juglandaceae, with about 60 species, and the Rhoipteleaceae, with only one. The order may be briefly characterized as amentiferous Hamamelidae with compound leaves.

In most of the respects in which *Rhoiptelea* differs from the Juglandaceae (stipulate leaves, presence of some perfect flowers, superior ovary, and bitegmic, hemitropous to anatropous ovule) the Rhoipteleaceae are the more archaic group. These features of the Rhoipteleaceae are all compatible with the Urticales, to which the family has sometimes been referred. On the other hand, *Rhoiptelea* has no evident close relatives in the Urticales, whereas its relationship to the Juglandaceae is now obvious to all. Withner (1941) notes that "the flower of *Rhoiptelea* resembles closely the pre-juglandaceous flower hypothesized by Manning."

The Juglandales, Myricales, Fagales, and Casuarinales have a distinctive sort of pollen that appears to take its evolutionary origin in the *Normapolles* complex of middle Cenomanian (early Upper Cretaceous) time. Fruits that appear to represent the Juglandales are almost as ancient, dating from the Santonian stage, some 85 million years BP. Wolfe (1973, cited under Hamamelidae) considers that the Juglandaceae and Rhoipteleaceae had begun to diverge by the Santonian or early Campanian stage, in the middle Upper Cretaceous. Manchester (1987) takes a more cautious view of the fossil record of the Juglandaceae proper. He considers that the first obvious leaves and fruits of the family are mid-Paleocene, but on the basis of fossils of whole flowers as well as pollen he too seats the Juglandaceae in the Upper Cretaceous *Normapolles* complex.

The pinnately compound leaves of the Juglandaceae have led some botanists in the past to seek a relationship to the Anacardiaceae through floral reduction. The wood anatomy, the foliar trichomes, the pollen, and the serological reactions all oppose such a tie, however, and link the Juglandales with the Hamamelidae instead. The long-standing argument about the affinities of the Juglandales may now be laid to rest.

SYNOPTICAL ARRANGEMENT OF THE FAMILIES OF JUGLANDALES

1 Flowers in triplets axillary to the bracts of the catkin, the middle flower of the triplet perfect and fertile, with 4 sepals, 6 stamens, and a superior ovary; lateral flowers pistillate but sterile and more or less reduced; leaves stipulate; ovule bitegmic, hemitropous to anatropous . . . . **1. Rhoipteleaceae.**
1 Flowers unisexual, solitary in the axils of the bracts of the catkin, the staminate ones with (3–) 5–many stamens, the calyx adnate to the bract or wanting; pistillate flowers with an inferior ovary and 1–4 calyx-teeth, or the calyx obsolete; leaves exstipulate; ovule orthotropous, unitegmic . . . .
. . . . **2. Juglandaceae.**

SELECTED REFERENCES

Elias, T. S. 1971. The genera of Juglandaceae in the southeastern United States. J. Arnold Arbor. **53:** 26–51.

Leroy, J.-F. 1955. Étude sur les Juglandaceae. A la recherche d'une conception morphologique de la fleur femelle et du fruit. Mém. Mus. Natl. Hist. Nat., Sér. B, Bot. **6:** 1–246.

Manchester, S. R. 1987. The fossil history of the Juglandaceae. Missouri Bot. Gard. Monogr. Syst. Bot. 21.

Manning, W. E. 1938, 1940, 1948. The morphology of the flowers of the Juglandaceae. I. The inflorescence. II. The pistillate flowers and fruit. III. The staminate flowers. Amer. J. Bot. **25:** 407–419, 1938; **27:** 839–852, 1940; **33:** 606–621, 1948.

Manning, W. E. 1978. The classification within the Juglandaceae. Ann. Missouri Bot. Gard. **65:** 1058–1087.

Petersen, F. P. & D. E. Fairbrothers. 1979 (1980). Serological investigation of selected amentiferous taxa. Syst. Bot. **4:** 230–241.

Polechko, M. A. & R. B. Clarkson. 1986. A serological study of the systematics of the Juglandaceae. Biochem. Syst. Ecol. **14:** 33–39.

Stone, D. E. & C. R. Broome. 1971. Pollen ultrastructure: Evidence for relationship of the Juglandaceae and Rhoipteleaceae. Pollen & Spores **13:** 5–14.

Wing, S. L. & L. J. Hickey. 1984. The *Platycarya* perplex and the evolution of the Juglandaceae. Amer. J. Bot. **71:** 388–411.

Withner, C. L. 1941. Stem anatomy and phylogeny of the Rhoipteleaceae. Amer. J. Bot. **28:** 872–878.

9. Order Myricales

The order Myricales consists of the single family Myricaceae, with three genera and some 50 species. The group may be characterized as amentiferous Hamamelidales with alternate, simple leaves and a compound, unilocular ovary with a solitary basal ovule. The New Caledonian genus *Canacomyrica* is distinctive but clearly belongs to the family.

The Myricaceae are generally considered to be related to the Juglandales, and some authors include them in that order. The pollen, like that of the Juglandales, Fagales, and Casuarinales, is reminiscent of the *Normapolles* complex in the early Upper Cretaceous. Distinctly myricoid pollen dates from the Santonian, and megafossils from the Maestrichtian. The conspicuous, peltate gland-scales of the leaves of Myricales, from which the characteristic odor emanates, are evidently homologous with similar structures in both the Juglandales and the Fagales. For purposes of a conceptual framework it seems more useful to treat the Myricales as a distinct order than to include them in the Juglandales or any other order.

SELECTED REFERENCES

Elias, T. S. 1971. The genera of Myricaceae in the southeastern United States. J. Arnold Arbor. 52: 305–318.
Leroy, J.-F. 1957. Sur deux Amentifères remarquables de la Flore Asiatico-Pacifique et Pacifique. Proc. Eighth Pacific Science Congress 4: 459–464.
Macdonald, A. D. 1977. Myricaceae: Floral hypothesis for *Gale* and *Comptonia*. Canad. J. Bot. 55: 2636–2651.
Macdonald, A. D. & R. Sattler. 1973. Floral development of *Myrica gale* and the controversy over floral concepts. Canad. J. Bot. 51: 1965–1975.

10. Order Fagales

The order Fagales as here defined consists of 4 families and more than 900 species. The Fagaceae have nearly 800 species, the Betulaceae about 120, the Nothofagaceae about 35, and the Balanopaceae only about 9. The order may be briefly characterized as mostly amentiferous Hamamelidae with well developed, simple, usually alternate leaves, and with 2 or more ovules in an ovary with 2 or more locules or semilocules.

The close relationship of the Fagaceae, Nothofagaceae, and Betulaceae is not in dispute. *Nothofagus* has usually been included in the Fagaceae, but as shown in the accompanying synoptical arrangement it stands apart well enough to justify status as a separate family. Pollen attributed to *Nothofagus* is known from the Santonian (or perhaps Coniacian) epoch of the Upper Cretaceous to the present. Recognizable genera of Fagaceae enter the record somewhat later. Early *Nothofagus* pollen also suggests the Betulaceae, further strengthening the linkage among these families that has been based on comparative morphology of modern species.

The position of *Balanops* (the only genus of Balanopaceae) is more debatable. The pollen clearly links it with the Fagales and other amentiferous Hamamelidae. The cupule subtending the drupaceous, somewhat acorn-like fruit resembles the cupule of *Quercus* and other fagaceous genera, but may not be homologous with it. In *Balanops* the cupule evidently consists of a set of well developed bracts in a close spiral, whereas in the Fagaceae it is generally considered to be a modified branch-system with associated bracts. Some authors prefer to put the Balanopaceae in their own order, but the order then stands alongside the Fagales, so that the segregation hardly seems worth while.

Selected References

Abbe, E. C. 1935, 1938. Studies in the phylogeny of the Betulaceae. I. Floral and inflorescence anatomy and morphology. II. Extremes in the range of variation of floral and inflorescence morphology. Bot. Gaz. **97**: 1–67, 1935; **99**: 431–469, 1938.

Brett, D. W. 1964. The inflorescence of *Fagus* and *Castanea* and the evolution of the cupules of the Fagaceae. New Phytol. **63**: 96–118.

Carlquist, S. 1980. Anatomy and systematics of Balanopaceae. Allertonia **2**: 191–246.

Elias, T. S. 1971. The genera of Fagaceae in the southeastern United States. J. Arnold Arbor. **52**: 159–195.

Fey, B. S. & P. K. Endress. 1983. Development and morphological interpretation of the cupule in Fagaceae. Flora **173**: 451–468.

Forman, L. L. 1964. *Trigonobalanus,* a new genus of Fagaceae, with notes on the classification of the family. Kew Bull. **17**: 381–396.

Forman, L. L. 1966. On the evolution of cupules in the Fagaceae. Kew Bull. **18**: 385–419.

Hall, J. W. 1952. The comparative anatomy and phylogeny of the Betulaceae. Bot. Gaz. **113**: 235–270.

Jones, J. H. 1986. Evolution of the Fagaceae: The implications of foliar features. Ann. Missouri Bot. Gard. **73:** 228–275.

Kaul, R. B. 1985. Reproductive morphology of *Quercus* (Fagaceae). Amer. J. Bot. **72:** 1962–1967.

Kaul, R. B. 1986. Evolution and reproductive biology of inflorescences in *Lithocarpus, Castanopsis, Castanea,* and *Quercus* (Fagaceae). Ann. Missouri Bot. Gard. **73:** 284–296.

Langdon, L. M. 1939. Ontogenetic and anatomical studies of the flower and fruit of the Fagaceae and Juglandaceae. Bot. Gaz. **101:** 301–327.

Langdon, L. M. 1947. The comparative morphology of the Fagaceae. I. The genus *Nothofagus.* Bot. Gaz. **108:** 350–371.

Romero, E. J. 1986. Fossil evidence regarding the evolution of *Nothofagus* Blume. Ann. Missouri Bot. Gard. **73:** 276–283.

Tanai, T. 1986. Phytogeographic and phylogenetic history of the genus *Nothofagus* Blume (Fagaceae) in the Southern Hemisphere. J. Fac. Sci., Hokkaido Univ. **21:** 505–582.

11. Order Casuarinales

The order Casuarinales consists of the single family Casuarinaceae, with a single genus *Casuarina,* consisting of about 50 species found mainly in Australia and the Pacific islands. Some recent opinion would divide *Casuarina* into three smaller genera. The order may be briefly characterized as Hamamelidae with whorled leaves that are reduced to mere scales. The group is also notable for having multiple (commonly 20 or more) embryosacs, even though only one is fully developed and fertile. The individual twigs are reminiscent of *Equisetum* in aspect, but very different in anatomical structure.

The Casuarinaceae were considered by Engler to be very primitive dicotyledons, but the consensus among modern workers is that the flowers are reduced rather than primitively simple. The wood is also advanced, by comparison with that of many Magnoliidae. The pollen dates from the Paleocene and is basically similar to that of most other amentiferous Hamamelidae. It is now generally believed that the Casuarinaceae are related to such families as the Betulaceae and Myricaceae, with which they are thought to share a common origin in or near the Hamamelidales.

SELECTED REFERENCES

Flores, E. M. 1960. Shoot vascular system and phyllotaxis of *Casuarina* (Casuarinaceae). Amer. J. Bot. **67:** 131–140.

Moseley, M. F. 1948. Comparative anatomy and phylogeny of the Casuarinaceae. Bot. Gaz. **110:** 231–280.

Swamy, B. G. L. 1948. A contribution to the life history of *Casuarina.* Proc. Amer. Acad. Arts **77:** 1–32.

Ueno, J. 1963. On the fine structure of the pollen walls of Angiospermae. III. *Casuarina.* Grana Palynol. **4:** 189–193.

Subclass III. Caryophyllidae

The subclass Caryophyllidae as here defined consists of 3 orders (Fig. 6.4), 14 families, and about 11,000 species. About nine-tenths of the species belong to the single large order Caryophyllales. Thus in a sense it may be said that the subclass consists of the order Caryophyllales plus two smaller orders (Polygonales and Plumbaginales) that are customarily associated with it.

Each of the three orders is well marked, but no one distinctive feature marks the subclass. The simplest way to characterize the group is to say that it consists of those dicotyledons that have bitegmic, crassinucellar ovules, and either have betalains instead of anthocyanins or have free-central or basal placentation in a compound ovary. It may further be said that most species are herbaceous, and that woody species usually have anomalous secondary growth or otherwise anomalous stem-structure. The stamens, when numerous, originate in centrifugal sequence, and the pollen-grains are usually trinucleate. The food-storage tissue of the seed is typically starchy, and very often has clustered starch-grains.

The families Bataceae, Gyrostemonaceae, and Theligonaceae, sometimes associated with the subclass Caryophyllidae or more directly with the order Caryophyllales, are here excluded from the group. The Bataceae and Gyrostemonaceae together form a small order that is somewhat doubtfully referred to the subclass Dilleniidae. The Theligonaceae are more confidently associated with the Rubiaceae in the order Rubiales (subclass Asteridae). *Rhabdodendron* and *Viviana,* sometimes included in the Caryophyllales, are here referred to the Rosidae. *Rhabdodendron* forms a distinct family in the order Rosales, and *Viviana* is included in the Geraniaceae.

The ancestry of the Caryophyllidae may lie in or near the Ranunculaceae. In the absence of known fossil connections, it may be supposed that the common ancestor of the Caryophyllidae was an herb with hypogynous flowers and separate carpels, and without well developed petals. The number of potentially ancestral groups is thus immediately limited. The possibility that the Ranunculaceae may be at least collateral ancestors is bolstered by the fact that some of them have pollen very much like that of many of the Caryophyllales. The floral trimery of the Polygonaceae also has ample precedent in some of the Ranunculaceae. The evolutionary significance of the centrifugal androecium in the Caryophyllales can scarcely be evaluated until a satisfactory general interpretation of the origin of centrifugality is achieved.

The fossil record as presently interpreted carries the Caryophyllidae back only to the Maestrichtian epoch, some 70 million years ago. This relatively short fossil history, as contrasted to the Magnoliidae, Hamamelidae, and Rosidae, is consonant with the primitively herbaceous habit of the Caryophyllidae. Aside from the Nymphaeales, dicotyledonous herbs apparently played only a negligible role in the vegetation of the Cretaceous.

Further speculation on the ancestry of the Caryophyllidae is hampered by uncertainty about the affinity of the Polygonales and Plumbaginales to the Caryophyllales. It would be easier to see a pattern in the chemical

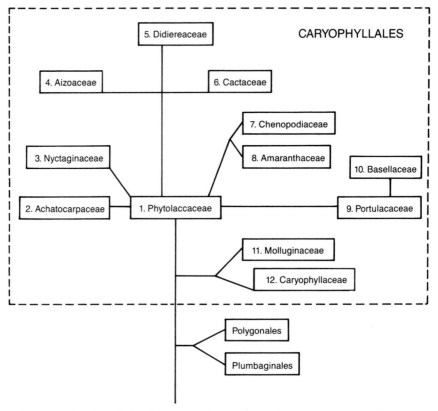

Fig. 6.4. Putative relationships among the families and orders of Caryophyllidae.

evolution if the heavily tanniferous Polygonales and Plumbaginales were divorced from the mostly nontanniferous Caryophyllales. The Plumbaginales could be accommodated in the Dilleniidae, alongside the Primulales, but the Polygonales would be out of place there. The special chemistry of the Caryophyllales may be presumed to have some evolutionary and selective significance and may indicate that the order originated after tannins had passed the peak of their effectiveness as repellents, but then what of the Polygonaceae? I leave the question unresolved.

SYNOPTICAL ARRANGEMENT OF THE ORDERS OF CARYOPHYLLIDAE

1 Ovules 1–many, campylotropous or amphitropous, only rarely anatropous; seeds essentially without true endosperm, the peripheral, straight to much more often curved or annular embryo generally bordering or surrounding a more or less abundant perisperm, or the perisperm sometimes scanty or wanting; sieve-tubes with a characteristic sort of P-type plastid that has a subperipheral ring of proteinaceous filaments; most families producing be-

talains but not anthocyanins; plants without ellagic acid, and only seldom
with proanthocyanin; perianth, ovary and placentation diverse, but the perianth unlike that of typical members of the next two orders . . . .
. . . . **1. Caryophyllales.**

1 Ovule solitary on a basal placenta, anatropous or orthotropous; seeds without
perisperm, the straight or curved, peripheral or embedded embryo commonly
associated with more or less abundant endosperm, or the endosperm sometimes scanty or wanting; sieve-tube plastids of S-type; plants producing anthocyanins, but not betalains, and generally with proanthocyanins or ellagic
acid or both.

2 Perianth not clearly differentiated into calyx and corolla, the 2–6 tepals either
in a single whorl or more often in two more or less similar sets of (2) 3
each; carpels (2) 3 (4); stamens 2–9, rarely more, but only seldom 5,
generally in 2 or 3 whorls; ovule orthotropous, only rarely anatropous;
leaves often with conspicuous, sheathing stipules . . . . . .**2. Polygonales.**

2 Perianth differentiated into a pentamerous, gamosepalous calyx and a pentamerous, generally gamopetalous corolla; carpels 5; stamens 5, opposite
the petals or corolla-lobes; ovule anatropous; leaves exstipulate . . . .
. . . . **3. Plumbaginales.**

SELECTED REFERENCE

Nowicke, J. W. & J. J. Skvarla. 1977. Pollen morphology and the relationship
of the Plumbaginaceae, Polygonaceae, and Primulaceae to the order Centrospermae. Smithsonian Contr. Bot. 37: 1–64.

1. Order Caryophyllales

The order Caryophyllales, as here defined, consists of 12 families and
about 10,000 species. No one family dominates the order, but the three
families Aizoaceae, Cactaceae, and Caryophyllaceae collectively contain
about two-thirds of the species. The Phytolaccaceae, usually considered
to be phyletically basal in the order, have only about 120 species. The
order has often been known by the descriptive name Centrospermae, in
reference to the free-central or basal placentation of many members. The
familiar name Caryophyllales is here retained in preference to the older
names Chenopodiales and Silenales of Lindley (1833).

In addition to the traditional floral characters, the vast majority of
investigated members of the Caryophyllales have a characteristic syndrome of embryological features, which have been listed by Maheshwari
(1950, p. 362, in initial citations) as follows: 1) anther tapetum glandular,
and its cells two- to four-nucleate; periplasmodium absent; 2) divisions
of the microspore mother cells simultaneous; 3) pollen-grains trinucleate;
4) ovules campylotropous with strongly curved and massive nucellus; 5)
micropyle formed by the swollen apex of the inner integument, which
protrudes and approaches the funiculus; 6) a hypodermal archesporial
cell which cuts off a cell wall; 7) formation of a nucellar cap arising from

periclinal divisions of the cells of the nucellar epidermis; 8) functioning of the chalazal megaspore of the tetrad; 9) formation of a monosporic eight-nucleate embryo-sac; 10) functioning of the perisperm as the chief storage region. Each of these features occurs individually in other orders, and sometimes several of them occur together, but the presence of all of them collectively is a good indication that the plant belongs to the Caryophyllales.

All investigated members of the Caryophyllales have a characteristic type of sieve-tube plastid that is unknown in other angiosperms. The plastid contains a set of bundles of proteinaceous filaments that collectively form a subperipheral ring. Often there is also a larger central protein crystalloid, which may be either globular or polyhedral. Sieve-tube plastids with proteinaceous inclusions occur in some other dicotyledons (notably in some members of the Magnoliidae and Fabaceae) and are standard among the monocotyledons, but in these groups the inclusions do not form a ring of filaments. The structure of the sieve-tube plastids has taken on considerable taxonomic importance because of its correlation with taxonomic groups perceived on other grounds. The functional significance of the differences in structure is still wholly obscure.

The Caryophyllales are further noteworthy in that most members of the order produce betalains and lack anthocyanins. Among the angiosperms betalains are known only in the Caryophyllales, although they also occur in some Basidiomycetes. Betalains form two color-groups, betacyanins and betaxanthins, comparable to the anthocyanins and anthoxanthins among the colored flavonoids.

Betalains sometimes coexist with anthoxanthins (flavonoids of yellow to orange-red color), but they have never been demonstrated to coexist with anthocyanins. Betalains and flavonoids are structurally very different (Fig. 6.5), but their seeming antipathy suggests a functional equivalence. They are of course similar in their function as flower-pigments, but it is difficult to see how this function in common should prevent the coexistence of betalains and anthocyanins, while permitting the coexistence of betalains and anthoxanthins. Furthermore, in some other families such as the Asteraceae, flavonoid flower-pigments occur together with the very different carotenoids. Possibly the evolution of betalains was fostered by blockage of the terminal step in the anthocyanin pathway, as suggested on page 246.

Because of the widespread occurrence of betalains in the Caryophyllales and their apparent restriction to this order, their presence has taken on some taxonomic significance. A few years ago some authors proposed to define the order (necessarily under another name) on this feature alone. Under this interpretation the Caryophyllaceae and Molluginaceae, which have anthocyanins but not betalains, would be divorced from the other ten families of the group. This proposal was not well received by students of the Caryophyllales or by students of the general system of classification of flowering plants. Almost immediately it was contradicted by another newly discovered (and even more esoteric) character, the structure of the

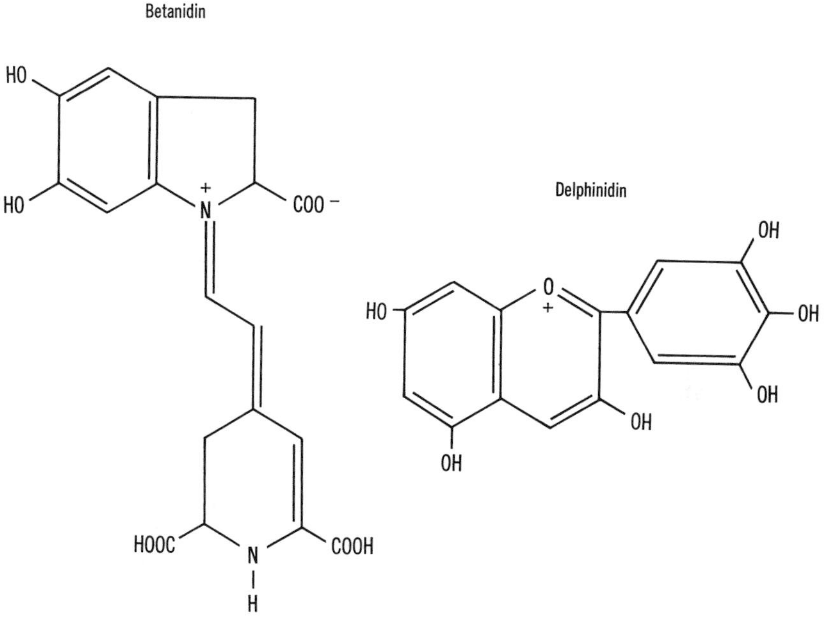

Betanidin

Delphinidin

Fig. 6.5.   Structural formula (LEFT) of betadin, a typical betacyanin, and (RIGHT) of delphinidin, a typical anthocyanin.

sieve-tube plastids. These special plastids (described in an earlier paragraph) occur in the Caryophyllaceae and Molluginaceae as well as in the other families of the order.

The new characters of pigmentation and sieve-tube plastids have helped to clarify the previously uncertain limits of the Caryophyllales. For example, the Cactaceae, in the past often treated as a distinct order, are now regularly included in the Caryophyllales. Both the sieve-tube plastids and the pigments (betalains) give strong support to what was previously a minority opinion—that the Cactaceae belong with the Caryophyllales. The definition of the order here presented is now accepted by virtually all students of the general system of classification of flowering plants. There remain some differences of opinion about the possible division of the Phytolaccaceae into several smaller and more homogeneous families, but the segregate families still remain in the order.

Many of the Caryophyllales, including some (or all) members of eight of the twelve families, have a characteristic spherical, pantoporate type of pollen-grain that has been loosely compared to a golf ball in appearance. This type of pollen is rare among other angiosperms, although not wholly unknown. Except for the Amaranthaceae, which are reported to be uniformly pantoporate, each of these several families has some members with ordinary (mostly triaperturate) pollen as well as some members with the more specialized (apomorphic) pollen. Thus it is clear that pantoporate pollen has arisen independently in each group. We have here a good example of the general principle that characteristics held in common by members of a taxonomic group frequently reflect independent realization of similar evolutionary potentialities, rather than direct inheritance from a common ancestor. If the members of the Caryophyllales with more primitive pollen had all become extinct, it would be easy to suppose that the golf ball type of pollen had originated only once in the order and was a marker of monophylesis.

Some of the evolutionary trends or tendencies in the Caryophyllales are obviously adaptive. C_4 photosynthesis, found in many members, appears to be an adaptation to high temperatures and/or aridity. The succulent habit and associated crassulacean acid metabolism of many other members are clearly adaptations to aridity. Anomalous secondary growth is a means of returning to a woody habit after the cambium has phyletically lost the capacity for prolonged secondary growth. Whether anomalous secondary growth can also be interpreted as a means of protecting the phloem from desiccation, as suggested by Fahn and Shchori (1967), is more debatable. None of these adaptive features is restricted to the Caryophyllales. All can be found in various other groups of angiosperms.

Some of the other characters or evolutionary tendencies of the Caryophyllales, such as those affecting the gynoecium, the pollen, and the sieve-tube plastids, are much more difficult to interpret in Darwinian terms. As we have noted, the functional significance of the substitution of betalains for anthocyanins is still very dubious. Of course the possibility of new insight into the significance of these features cannot be denied.

The Phytolaccaceae are generally (and plausibly) regarded as the most archaic family of the Caryophyllales. Some authors would derive all the other families of the order directly or indirectly from the Phytolaccaceae, but that may be going too far. I am not yet convinced that uniovulate carpels (characteristic of the Phytolaccaceae) are primitive for the Caryophyllales as a whole, or even for the betalain families as a group. The diagram (Fig. 6.4) showing possible relationships should be interpreted with this reservation in mind.

An enigmatic feature of the Caryophyllales is the presence of bound ferulic acid in the cell walls, which is otherwise found only in the Commelinidae, Zingiberidae, the palms, and a few other monocotyledons.

In devising a linear sequence it is convenient to begin with the Phytolaccaceae. The Achatocarpaceae are only marginally distinct from the Phytolaccaceae, and should follow immediately. The Nyctaginaceae, with a monomerous gynoecium, are conveniently placed before the bulk of the families that have a syncarpous gynoecium. The Aizoaceae, Didiereaceae, and Cactaceae are allied inter se and must be linked together, as must also the Portulacaceae and Basellaceae.

Although the Caryophyllaceae and Molluginaceae clearly belong with the other 10 families of the group, the cladistic position of these two families with respect to the others is not clear. They may be an early offshoot from the ancestral stock of the order, as shown in Figure 6.4, or they may be a subsequent branch that has reverted to the production of anthocyanin in association with the loss of betalains. In any case, it is convenient to end the sequence of families with the Caryophyllaceae, so as to juxtapose them to the apparently related Polygonales.

SYNOPTICAL ARRANGEMENT OF THE FAMILIES OF CARYOPHYLLALES

1 Gynoecium either of 1–many distinct carpels, each with a single ovule, or of 2 or more carpels united to form a compound ovary with as many locules and ovules as carpels.
  2 Sepals distinct, or rarely connate below, but not forming a corolloid calyx-tube, generally not at all petaloid; carpels mostly 2–several, less often only one; inflorescence usually racemose or spicate or less commonly paniculate or cymose, not subtended by a conspicuous involucre; leaves alternate
      . . . . **1. Phytolaccaceae.**
  2 Sepals united to form a distally lobed tube that commonly simulates a sympetalous corolla and is sometimes subtended by sepaloid bracts; carpel solitary; inflorescence mostly cymose or head-like, often subtended by a conspicuous involucre; leaves opposite or rarely alternate . . . .
      . . . . **3. Nyctaginaceae.**
1 Gynoecium otherwise, always of 2 or more carpels united to form a compound ovary, the ovary either unilocular or with as many locules as carpels, in the latter case either with more than one ovule per carpel or with some locules empty.
  3 Flowers with 10–20 stamens and a superior, unilocular ovary with 2 styles and a single basal ovule . . . . **2. Achatocarpaceae.**
  3 Flowers either with fewer stamens, or with an inferior or plurilocular ovary, or with more than one ovule, often differing in more than one of these respects.
    4 Ovary with a single fertile locule and 2 (3) empty locules; spiny, cactus-like trees or shrubs with unisexual flowers in a cymose inflorescence; seeds essentially without perisperm . . . . **5. Didiereaceae.**
    4 Ovary without empty locules; other features various, but not combined as in the Didiereaceae.
      5 Flowers epigynous or less often semi-epigynous or distinctly perigynous; tepals (and often also the stamens) usually more or less numerous, but sometimes few and in a single cycle; plants succulent.
        6 Plants leaf-succulents or rarely stem-succulents, in either case nearly always unarmed; ovary superior to inferior, usually plurilocular; mainly Old World . . . . **4. Aizoaceae.**
        6 Plants either stem-succulents or distinctly spiny, usually both; ovary unilocular, nearly always inferior; mainly New World . . . .
         . . . . **6. Cactaceae.**
      5 Flowers hypogynous, or seldom semi-epigynous or weakly perigynous; tepals and stamens mostly few and cyclic, but sometimes more numerous in Portulacaceae; plants succulent or not.
        7 Perianth evidently monochlamydeous, seldom at all petaloid, commonly small and inconspicuous, sometimes even obsolete; ovules mostly solitary (seldom 2–several) on a basal placenta; stem very commonly with anomalous secondary growth; sieve-tube plastids nearly always without a central protein crystalloid.
          8 Perianth mostly green or greenish and more or less herbaceous,

only seldom dry and somewhat scarious or membranous; filaments distinct, or sometimes connate at the base only . . . . .
. . . . **7. Chenopodiaceae.**
8 Perianth generally dry and scarious or membranous; filaments often connate below (the androecial tube sometimes even simulating a small, sympetalous corolla) . . . **8. Amaranthaceae.**
7 Perianth generally dichlamydeous or seemingly so (except notably the Molluginaceae, with axile placentation and usually several or many ovules, otherwise only occasionally monochlamydeous); sieve-tube plastids with a central protein crystalloid.
9 Sepals generally 2, seldom more numerous; stamens most commonly as many as and opposite the petals, seldom more numerous or alternate with the petals; no anomalous secondary thickening; plants producing betalains but not anthocyanins; central protein crystalloid of the sieve-tube plastids globular.
10 Plants not twining or scrambling; ovules (1) 2–many; fruit capsular, or very seldom indehiscent; seldom any of the vascular bundles becoming bicollateral . . . .
. . . . **9. Portulacaceae.**
10 Plants twining or scrambling; ovule solitary; fruit indehiscent; larger vascular bundles becoming bicollateral (with internal phloem) at maturity . . . . **10. Basellaceae.**
9 Sepals 4 or 5; stamens not at once of the same number as and opposite the petals; plants sometimes with anomalous secondary thickening, regularly producing anthocyanins but not betalains; central protein crystalloid of the sieve-tube plastids mostly polyhedral, only seldom globular.
11 Ovary with 2–several locules and axile placentation (but in the upper part of the ovary the partitions sometimes not reaching the placental column); petals small and inconspicuous or more often wanting; leaves opposite, alternate, or whorled . . . . **11. Molluginaceae.**
11 Ovary unilocular (sometimes partitioned at the base), with central or basal placentation; petals usually more or less well developed, but sometimes wanting; leaves nearly always opposite . . . . **12. Caryophyllaceae.**

SELECTED REFERENCES

Bedell, H. G. 1980. A taxonomic and morphological re-evaluation of Stegnospermaceae (Caryophyllales). Syst. Bot. **5:** 419–431.

Behnke, H.-D. 1976. Ultrastructure of sieve-element plastids in Caryophyllales (Centrospermae), evidence for delimitation and classification of the order. Pl. Syst. Evol. **126:** 31–54.

Behnke, H.-D. 1976. A tabulated survey of some characters of systematic importance in centrospermous families. Pl. Syst. Evol. **126:** 95–98.

Bogle, A. L. 1969. The genera of Portulacaceae and Basellaceae in the southeastern United States. J. Arnold Arbor. **50:** 566–598.

Bogle, A. L. 1970. The genera of Molluginaceae and Aizoaceae in the southeastern United States. J. Arnold Arbor. **51:** 431–462.

Bogle, A. L. 1974. The genera of Nyctaginaceae in the southeastern United States. J. Arnold Arbor. **55:** 1–37.

Boke, N. H. 1964. The cactus gynoecium: A new interpretation. Amer. J. Bot. **51:** 598–610.

Bortenschlager, S. 1973. Morphologie pollinique des Phytolaccaceae. Pollen & Spores **15:** 227–253.

Burret, F., Z. Rabesa, P. Zandonella & B. Voirin. 1981. Contribution biochimique à l'ordre des Centrospermales. Biochem. Syst. Evol. **9:** 257–262.

Buxbaum, F. 1961. Vorläufige Untersuchungen über Umfang, systematische Stellung und Gliederung der Caryophyllales (Centrospermae). Beitr. Biol. Pflanzen **36:** 1–56.

Carolin, R. C. 1983. The trichomes of the Chenopodiaceae and Amaranthaceae. Bot. Jahrb. Syst. **103:** 451–466.

Choux, P. 1934. Les Didiéréacées, xerophytes de Madagascar. Mém. Acad. Malgache **XVII:** 1–69.

Cranwell, L. M. 1963. The Hectorellaceae: Pollen type and taxonomic speculation. Grana Palynol. **4:** 195–202.

Eckardt, Th. 1976. Classical morphological features of centrospermous families. Pl. Syst. Evol. **126:** 5–25.

Eggli, U. 1984. Stomatal types of Cactaceae. Pl. Syst. Evol. **146:** 197–214.

Fahn, A. & Y. Shchori. 1967 (1968). The organization of the secondary conducting tissues in some species of Chenopodiaceae. Phytomorphology **17:** 147–154.

Gilbert, M. G. 1987. The taxonomic position of the genera *Telephium* and *Corrigiola.* Taxon **36:** 47–49.

Herre, H. 1971. The genera of the Mesembryanthemaceae. Tafelberg-Uitgewers Beperk. Cape Town.

Hofmann, U. 1973. Centrospermen-Studien 6. Morphologische Untersuchungen zur Umgrenzung und Gliederung der Aizoaceen. Bot. Jahrb. Syst. **93:** 247–324.

Horak, K. E. 1981. Anomalous secondary thickening in *Stegnosperma* (Phytolaccaceae). Bull. Torrey Bot. Club **108:** 189–197.

Ihlenfeldt, H.-D. & H. Straka. 1961 (1962). Über die systematische Stellung und Gliederung der Mesembryanthemen. Ber. Deutsch. Bot. Ges. **74:** 485–492.

Jensen, U. 1965. Serologische Untersuchungen zur Frage der systematischen Einordnung der Didiereaceae. Bot. Jahrb. Syst. **84:** 233–253.

Mabry, T. J., L. Kimler & C. Chang. 1972. The betalains: Structure, function, and biogenesis, and the plant order Centrospermae. *In* V. C. Runeckles & T. C. Tso (eds.), Recent advances in phytochemistry **5:** 105–134. Academic Press. New York.

McNeill, J. 1974. Synopsis of a revised classification of the Portulacaceae. Taxon **23:** 725–728.

Narayana, P. S. & L. L. Narayana. 1986. The embryology of Stegnospermataceae, with a discussion on its status, affinities, and systematic position. Pl. Syst. Evol. **154:** 137–145.

Nowicke, J. W. 1975 (1976). Pollen morphology in the order Centrospermae. Grana **15:** 51–77.

Rodman, J. E., et al. 1984. A taxonomic analysis and revised classification of Centrospermae. Syst. Bot. **9:** 297–323.

Rohweder, O. 1965, 1967, 1970. Centrospermen-Studien. 1. Der Blütenbau bei *Uebelinia kiwuensis* T. C. E. Fries (Caryophyllaceae). 2. Entwicklung und morphologische Deutung des Gynöciums bei *Phytolacca.* 3. Blütenentwicklung und Blütenbau bei Silenoideen (Caryophyllaceae). 4. Morphologie und Anatomie der Blüten, Früchte und Samen bei Alsinoideen und Paronychioideen sens. lat. (Caryophyllaceae). Bot. Jahrb. Syst. **83:** 406–418, 1965; **84:** 509–526, 1965; **86:** 130–185, 1967; **90:** 201–271, 1970.

Rohweder, O. & K. Huber. 1974. Centrospermen-Studien. 7. Beobachtungen und Anmerkung zur Morphologie und Entwicklungsgeschichte einiger Nyctaginaceen. Bot. Jahrb. Syst. **94:** 327–359.

Skvarla, J. J. & J. W. Nowicke. 1976. Ultrastructure of pollen exine in centrospermous families. Pl. Syst. Evol. **126:** 55–78.

Straka, H. 1975. Palynologie et différentiation systématique d'une famille endémique de Madagascar: les Didiéréacées. Boissiera **24:** 245–248.

Thomson, B. F. 1942. The floral morphology of the Caryophyllaceae. Amer. J. Bot. **29:** 333–349.

Wheat, D. 1977. Successive cambia in the stem of *Phytolacca dioica.* Amer. J. Bot. **64:** 1209–1217.

2. Order Polygonales

The order consists of the single family Polygonaceae, with about 30 genera and a thousand species, chiefly of North Temperate regions. *Eriogonum* (250), *Polygonum* (200), *Rumex* (200), and *Coccoloba* (125) are the largest genera. *Polygonum* consists of several well marked sections that are often (and not without reason) treated as distinct genera. *Coccoloba* and some of its allies are unusual in the family in being tropical and woody.

Pollen attributed to the Polygonaceae dates from the Paleocene epoch. The Polygonaceae form a sharply limited and taxonomically rather isolated family. The unilocular ovary with a solitary basal ovule appears to be reduced from a basally partitioned ovary with several ovules on a free-central placenta, quite in agreement with the structure of the Caryophyllaceae and some other families of the Caryophyllales. The usually peripheral embryo which may be curved around the food-storage tissue of the seed is also reminiscent of the Caryophyllales. The pollen shows a morphological series from tricolporate to pantoporate, as in several families of the Caryophyllales. The subfamily Paronychioideae of the Caryophyllaceae is frequently cited as a group pointing toward the Polygonaceae. For these and other reasons most authors are in agreement that the Polygonaceae are allied to the Caryophyllales. Nevertheless, the Polygonaceae differ from the Caryophyllaceae and other Caryophyllales in their mostly orthotropous ovules, in having endosperm instead of perisperm as the principal food-storage tissue in the seed, in having S-type rather than P-type sieve-tube plastids, in having primitively trimerous flowers, in being tanniferous, and in other features. Thus it seems necessary to treat the Polygonaceae as an order by themselves, rather than including them with their only evident allies in the Caryophyllales.

For whatever it may be worth, I should point out that the still very meager data on the structure of cytochrome C_3 suggest a relationship—albeit rather remote—between the Polygonaceae and Caryophyllaceae. We cannot properly place much taxonomic weight on the structure of cytochrome until many more taxa have been studied, but at least in this instance it fits into the picture.

Selected References

Galle, P. 1977. Untersuchungen zur Blütenentwicklung der Polygonaceen. Bot. Jahrb. Syst. **98:** 449–489.
Graham, S. A. & C. E. Wood, Jr. 1965. The genera of Polygonaceae in the southeastern United States. J. Arnold Arbor. **46:** 91–121.
Haraldson, K. 1978. Anatomy and taxonomy in Polygonaceae subfam. Polygonoideae Meisn. emend. Jaretzky. Symb. Bot. Upsal. **22(2):** 1–95.
Roberty, G. & S. Vautier. 1964. Les genres de Polygonacées. Boissiera **10:** 7–128.

3. Order Plumbaginales

The order consists of the single family Plumbaginaceae, with about a dozen genera and perhaps 400 species, depending on one's taxonomic view of some of the larger genera. The family is widely distributed in diverse parts of the world, but best developed from the Mediterranean region to western and central Asia. Many of the species are xerophytic or maritime. There are two well marked subfamilies. The three largest genera, *Limonium* (*Statice*), *Acantholimon,* and *Armeria,* all belong to the Armerioideae. *Plumbago,* with about 20 species, is the largest genus of the Plumbaginoideae.

The Plumbaginaceae enter the fossil record only in the Middle Eocene.

The detailed study of the Plumbaginaceae by Friedrich (1956) appeared at the time to have securely established the relationship of the family to the Caryophyllales. More recently, Corner (1976, in initial citations) also considered that the anatomy of the seed-coat supports an affinity of the Plumbaginaceae with the Caryophyllales.

Some other recent information, however, casts doubt on the relationship. Like the Polygonales, the Plumbaginales have sieve-tubes with S-type rather than P-type plastids, and both of these orders differ from the bulk of the Caryophyllales in having anthocyanins instead of betalains. Nowicke and Skvarla (1977, cited under Caryophyllidae) consider that the pollen of the Plumbaginaceae is distinctive, unlike either the Caryophyllales or the Polygonaceae. The Plumbaginaceae also differ from the Caryophyllales in their sympetalous corolla, and in a series of embryological features (i.e., they do not have the full caryophylloid embryological syndrome). It therefore seems necessary to hold the Plumbaginaceae apart in their own order, rather than to include them in the Caryophyllales as proposed by Friedrich. The possibility even arises that the Plumbaginales should be transferred to the Dilleniidae, where they would have to stand alongside the Primulales, but serological studies by Frohne and John (1978, cited under Primulales) show no affinity between the Plumbaginales and Primulales. Furthermore, the lack of endo-apertures in the pollen of the Plumbaginaceae militates against an assignment of the family to the Dilleniidae but is perfectly compatible with an assignment to the Caryophyllidae.

Data from fungal parasites provide some support for the treatment here presented. According to Savile (1979, in general citations) similar rusts link the Plumbaginaceae, Polygonaceae, and Caryophyllaceae, and similar smuts further link the Polygonaceae, Caryophyllaceae, and Portulacaceae.

SELECTED REFERENCES

Channell, R. B. & C. E. Wood. 1959. The genera of Plumbaginaceae of the southeastern United States. J. Arnold Arbor. 40: 391–397.
Friedrich, H.-C. 1956. Studien über die natürliche Verwandtschaft der Plumbaginales und Centrospermae. Phyton (Horn) 6: 220–263.
Harborne, J. B. 1967. Comparative biochemistry of the flavonoids—IV. Correlations between chemistry, pollen morphology and systematics in the family Plumbaginaceae. Phytochemistry 6: 1415–1428.
Roth, I. 1962. Histogenese und morphologische Deutung der Kronblätter von *Armeria.* Oesterr. Bot. Z. 109: 19–40.

Subclass IV. Dilleniidae

The subclass Dilleniidae as here defined consists of 13 orders (Fig. 6.6), 77 families, and about 25,000 species. More than three-fourths of the species belong to only 5 orders, the Violales (5000), Capparales (4000), Ericales (4000), Theales (3500), and Malvales (3000–3500). The Primulales (1900) and Ebenales (2000) are also fairly large orders, whilst the remaining 6 orders have only about 1300 species collectively.

The orders that make up the Dilleniidae evidently hang together as a natural group, but this group cannot be fully characterized morphologically. Like the Rosidae, the Dilleniidae are more advanced than the Magnoliidae in one or another respect, but less advanced than the Asteridae. Except for the rather small (400 spp.) order Dilleniales, the vast majority of the Dilleniidae are sharply set off from characteristic members of the Magnoliidae by being syncarpous. With a few exceptions, the species of Dilleniidae with numerous stamens have the stamens initiated in centrifugal sequence. In this respect they differ from the Rosidae, in which species with numerous stamens usually have a centripetal sequence of

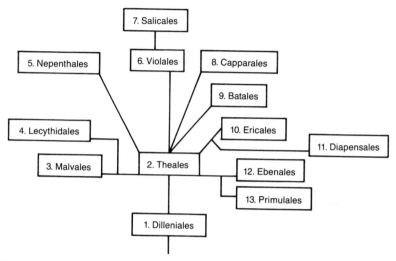

Fig. 6.6. Putative relationships among the orders of Dilleniidae.

development. More than a third of the species of Dilleniidae have parietal placentation, in contrast to the relative rarity of this type in the Rosidae. About a third of the species (not the same third) are sympetalous, but only a very few of these (e.g., *Diapensia*) have isomerous, epipetalous stamens alternate with the corolla lobes and also unitegmic, tenuinucellar ovules as in the Asteridae. The ovules in the Dilleniidae as a whole are bitegmic or less often unitegmic, with various transitional types, and they range from crassinucellar to tenuinucellar. Often they are bitegmic and tenuinucellar, a combination rare outside this group. Aside from the anomalous order Batales, only a single family and order (Salicales) is amentiferous. The Salicales differ from the subclass Hamamelidae in their parietal placentation and more or less numerous seeds.

It is perfectly clear that the Dilleniidae take their origin in the Magnoliidae. The apocarpous order Dilleniales, especially the family Dilleniaceae, forms a connecting link between the two subclasses. If the rest of the subclass Dilleniidae did not exist, the order Dilleniales could easily be accommodated in the Magnoliidae. Within the Magnoliidae, the family Illiciaceae in the order Illiciales may be somewhere near to the ancestry of the Dilleniaceae, but the relationship between the two families is still not particularly close.

The Theales are the central group of Dilleniidae, from which all the other orders except the Dilleniales appear to have evolved. The Malvales, Lecythidales, Violales, Capparales, and Nepenthales all appear to have arisen from a common complex in the Theales. The Salicales are an amentiferous offshoot from the Violales, and the Batales appear to be related to the Capparales. The remaining four orders take their origin in a different part (or parts) of the Theales. The Ericales are evidently allied to the Actinidiaceae (Theales), and the Diapensiales appear to be allied to the Ericales. The Ebenales and Primulales are somewhat more remote, but may be allied to each other and to a lesser extent to the Ericales. Only the Theales provide a reasonably likely origin for these groups. These concepts of relationships may be conveniently expressed in the accompanying phylogenetic tree (Fig. 6.6).

Pollen that appears to represent the Dilleniidae dates from about the beginning of the Upper Cretaceous, but this early pollen is not clearly referable to an order. Otherwise the fossil record as presently understood gives no clear indication of the origin of the group. On grounds of geographical distribution and secondary metabolites, as well as the pollen, I suggest that the Dilleniidae must have diverged from the ancestral Magnoliidae at about the same time as the Hamamelidae and Rosidae, that is, toward the end of the Lower Cretaceous.

The adaptive significance of the characters that mark the Dilleniidae as a group is not immediately obvious. Syncarpy may have some advantage over apocarpy in relation to access of pollen-tubes to the ovules, but it is hard to see how the advantage could be effective in the early stages of the evolution of syncarpy. The biological importance of the sequence of initiation of stamens is obscure, as is also that of the kind of placentation. The number of ovules in a locule would seem a priori to be of some possible significance in relation to seed-dispersal and the choice between quantity and quality of disseminules, but a broad-scale evaluation of that significance remains to be presented.

SYNOPTICAL ARRANGEMENT OF THE ORDERS OF DILLENIIDAE

1 Carpels mostly distinct; stamens mostly numerous; ovules bitegmic, crassinucellar; seeds mostly arillate and with well developed endosperm . . . .
. . . .**1. Dilleniales.**
1 Carpels almost always more or less united (at least at anthesis) to form a compound pistil; other characters various, the stamens numerous to few, the ovules bitegmic or unitegmic, crassinucellar or tenuinucellar, the seeds with or without an aril and with or without endosperm.
   2 Flowers mostly polypetalous or sometimes apetalous, only seldom (mainly the Cucurbitaceae and some other Violales) sympetalous; stamens numerous to few; ovules bitegmic or less often unitegmic, crassinucellar or often tenuinucellar; stipules present or absent.
      3 Plants insectivorous herbs or shrubs, sometimes climbing or epiphytic
      . . . . **5. Nepenthales.**
      3 Plants not obviously insectivorous; habit various.
         4 Placentation mostly axile, seldom parietal.
            5 Flowers normally developed, with an evident perianth, perfect or less often unisexual, not borne in catkins; pollen-grains with more or less distinctly tectate-columellate (or in any case not solid) exine; plants woody or herbaceous, without mustard-oils.
               6 Flowers hypogynous or perigynous, only rarely epigynous.
                  7 Sepals mostly imbricate, only seldom valvate; filaments distinct or connate into groups; plants mostly without stellate or lepidote indument, with or without mucilage, sometimes

with stratified phloem, but only seldom with wedge-shaped rays; seeds not known to contain cyclopropenyl fatty acids
.... **2. Theales.**
7 Sepals valvate, only very seldom imbricate; filaments very often monadelphous, but sometimes distinct or merely connate into groups; young stems usually with stratified phloem and very wide, wedge-shaped phloem-rays; plants usually with mucilage-cells, -sacs, or -cavities; seeds commonly containing cyclopropenyl fatty acids .... **3. Malvales.**
  6 Flowers epigynous or sometimes only semi-epigynous ....
.... **4. Lecythidales.**
  5 Flowers much reduced, unisexual, with tiny or no perianth, borne in catkins; pollen-grains with solid exine; woody plants, producing mustard-oils .... **9. Batales.**
4 Placentation mostly parietal, seldom axile, rarely basal or apical in a unilocular ovary.
  8 Flowers normally developed, with an evident perianth, not borne in catkins; plants woody or herbaceous.
    9 Plants usually without mustard-oil and myrosin-cells; fruits variously dry or fleshy and dehiscent or indehiscent, but without a replum; carpels most often 3; perianth seldom tetramerous; flowers hypogynous to often perigynous or epigynous, sometimes sympetalous .... **6. Violales.**
    9 Plants with mustard-oil and myrosin-cells; fruit most often (but not always) a specialized type of capsule with a distinct replum; carpels most often 2; perianth very often tetramerous; flowers hypogynous to less often perigynous, not sympetalous ......
.... **8. Capparales.**
  8 Flowers much reduced, unisexual, without an evident perianth, borne in catkins; plants woody .... **7. Salicales.**
2 Flowers mostly sympetalous (except mainly some of the Ericales, these with unitegmic ovules and other specialized embryological features); stamens seldom more than 2 or 3 (4) times as many as the corolla-lobes; ovules tenuinucellar; stipules wanting.
  10 Flowers with most or all of the features of the ericoid embryological syndrome (ovules unitegmic, tenuinucellar; endosperm-development cellular; endosperm-haustoria formed at both ends of the embryo-sac; testa a single layer of cells, or even wanting; style hollow, the cavity fluted in alignment with the locules of the ovary; anthers becoming inverted during ontogeny, so that the morphological base appears to be apical, without a fibrous layer in the wall, dehiscing by apparently terminal pores; anther-tapetum of the glandular type, with multinucleate cells; pollen-grains borne in tetrads); filaments very often attached directly to the receptacle; plants strongly mycotrophic and often producing iridoid compounds and other special chemicals of restricted occurrence .... **10. Ericales.**
  10 Flowers with less than half of the features of the ericoid embryological syndrome; filaments nearly always attached to the corolla-tube; plants not strongly mycotrophic, without iridoid compounds and mostly without the special chemicals of the Ericales.
    11 Placentation mostly axile, or less often parietal; functional stamens various, very often more numerous than the corolla-lobes or alternate with them.

12 Perennial herbs or low half-shrubs, accumulating aluminum; functional stamens as many as and alternate with the corolla-lobes; ovules unitegmic; endosperm-development cellular . . . . **11. Diapensiales.**
12 Trees or shrubs, not accumulating aluminum except in the Symplocaceae; functional stamens either more numerous than the corolla-lobes, or as many as the corolla-lobes and then usually opposite them; ovules bitegmic or unitegmic; endosperm-development nuclear or cellular . . . . **12. Ebenales.**
11 Placentation free-central or basal in a unilocular ovary; functional stamens as many as and opposite the corolla-lobes; ovules mostly bitegmic; endosperm-development nuclear . . . . . **13. Primulales.**

1. Order Dilleniales

The order Dilleniales as here defined consists of two families, the Dilleniaceae and Paeoniaceae. The Dilleniaceae have 10 genera and about 350 species, best developed in the Australian region. The Paeoniaceae consist of the single genus *Paeonia,* with about 30 species, best developed in temperate eastern Asia. The small family Crossosomataceae, sometimes included in the Dilleniales, is here referred to the Rosales.

The Dilleniaceae are relatively primitive in many features. They commonly have more or less distinct, conduplicate carpels, and the carpels are sometimes not fully sealed. The ovules are bitegmic and crassinucellar, and they mature into seeds with a tiny embryo and copious endosperm. The stamens are usually more or less numerous, and the connective is sometimes prolonged. The wood has scalariform vessels and a syndrome of other features regarded as primitive. In all of these respects the Dilleniaceae recall the Magnoliidae.

On the other hand, the Dilleniaceae do not closely resemble any one family of the Magnoliidae, and they are sharply set off from the Magnoliidae by a series of chemical features. Unlike the vast majority of the Magnoliidae, the Dilleniaceae have ellagic acid, proanthocyanins, and raphides. The ethereal oil cells so characteristic of the woody Magnoliidae are wanting from the Dilleniaceae. The Dilleniaceae are almost without alkaloids, and the few that have been found in some species have nothing to do with the characteristic benzyl-isoquinoline alkaloids of the Magnoliidae. Furthermore, there is a still unresolved controversy about the ancestry of the multistaminate, centrifugal androecium such as that found in the Dilleniaceae. If, as some authors maintain, this kind of androecium is necessarily derived from an ordinary, cyclic, paucistaminate androecium by secondary increase in the number of stamens, then the gap between the Dilleniaceae and Magnoliidae is further widened.

If the hypothesis of chemical evolution that I presented in 1977 is correct, the Dilleniidae probably originated about the same time as the Hamamelidae and Rosidae. The Hamamelidae and the more archaic members of the Dilleniidae and Rosidae all rely heavily on hydrolyzable tannins as defensive weapons. The more advanced members of these latter two groups have largely discarded tannins in favor of more recently evolved defenses.

The centrifugal androecium and frequently campylotropous or amphitropous ovules of the Dilleniidae recall the Caryophyllidae, but the Caryophyllidae have their own set of specialized features not found in the Dilleniaceae and other Dilleniidae. Any evolutionary relationship between the Dilleniaceae and the Caryophyllidae must be rather remote in time.

In contrast to their evident separation from the Magnoliidae and Caryophyllidae, the Dilleniaceae are obviously allied to such syncarpous families as the Actinidiaceae and Theaceae. For purposes of conceptual organization it is useful, however, to put the largely apocarpous family Dilleniaceae in a separate order from the largely syncarpous Theales. The Dilleniaceae appear to be the modern remnants of the group that gave rise not only to the Theales but also to the rest of the subclass Dilleniidae.

Paeonia has traditionally been referred to the Ranunculaceae, where it is sadly misplaced. The persistent, leathery sepals, sepal-derived rather than staminodial petals, centrifugal stamens, perigynous disk, and arillate seeds are all out of harmony with the Ranunculaceae. The distinction is further reinforced by anatomical, cytological, palynological, and serological features. The idea that *Paeonia* is closely related to the Ranunculaceae can no longer be seriously entertained.

Beginning with Camp (in Gundersen, 1950, cited under dicotyledons), most recent authors have treated *Paeonia* as a separate family to be associated with the Dilleniaceae. This seems reasonable, and no other obvious possibility presents itself. Even so, there are some notable differences between the two families, and it is a matter of opinion whether taxonomic needs are best met by putting them in the same order or by keeping the Paeoniaceae in an order of their own.

Synoptical Arrangement of the Families of Dilleniales

1 Flowers without a nectary-disk; leaves mostly entire, seldom trilobed or pinnatifid; raphides, crystal sand, and proanthocyanin present; embryogeny normal; plants woody (of various form) or rarely herbaceous, occurring in tropical and subtropical regions, especially Australia .... **1. Dilleniaceae.**
1 Flowers with the stamens seated beneath a well developed, perigynous nectary-disk; leaves ternately or ternate-pinnately compound or dissected; raphides, crystal sand, and proanthocyanins wanting; embryo with a free-nuclear stage in early ontogeny (unique among angiosperms); herbs or half-shrubs or soft shrubs, mostly of temperate Eurasia and western North America .... **2. Paeoniaceae.**

Selected References

Carniel, K. 1967. Über die Embryobildung in der Gattung *Paeonia.* Oesterr. Bot. Z. **114:** 4–19.

Dickison, W. C. 1967–1971. Comparative morphological studies in Dilleni-aceae. I. Wood anatomy. II. The pollen. III. The carpels. IV. Anatomy of the node and vascularization of the leaf. V. Leaf anatomy. VI. Stamens and young stem. VII. Additional notes on *Acrotrema*. J. Arnold Arbor. **48:** 1–29, 231–240, 1967; **49:** 317–329, 1968; **50:** 384–400, 1969; **51:** 89–113, 403–418, 1970; **52:** 319–333, 1971.

Dickison, W. C., J. W. Nowicke & J. J. Skvarla. 1982. Pollen morphology of the Dilleniaceae and Actinidiaceae. Amer. J. Bot. **69:** 1055–1073.

Gurni, A. A. & K. Kubitzki. 1981. Flavonoid chemistry and systematics of the Dilleniaceae. Biochem. Syst. Evol. **9:** 109–114.

Hiepko, P. 1964 (1965). Das zentrifugale Androecium der Paeoniaceae. Ber. Deutsch. Bot. Ges. **77:** 427–435.

Hiepko, P. 1966. Zur Morphologie, Anatomie und Funktion des Diskus der Paeoniaceae. Ber. Deutsch. Bot. Ges. **79:** 233–245.

Keefe, J. M. & M. Moseley. 1978. Wood anatomy and phylogeny of *Paeonia* section Moutan. J. Arnold Arbor. **59:** 274–297.

Kubitzki, K. 1968. Flavonoide und Systematik der Dilleniaceen. Ber. Deutsch. Bot. Ges. **81:** 238–251.

Wilson, C. L. 1965, 1973 (1974). The floral anatomy of the Dilleniaceae. I. *Hibbertia* Andr. II. Genera other than *Hibbertia*. Phytomorphology **15:** 248–274, 1965; **23:** 25–42, 1973 (1974).

Yakovlev, M. S. & M. D. Yoffe. 1957. On some peculiar features in the em-bryogeny of *Paeonia* L. Phytomorphology **7:** 74–82.

2. Order Theales

The order Theales as here defined consists of 18 families and nearly 3500 species. Three of the families, the Clusiaceae (1200), Theaceae (600), and Dipterocarpaceae (600), make up fully two-thirds of the order, and most of the remaining species belong to only two additional families, the Ochnaceae (400) and Actinidiaceae (300). The other 13 families contain scarcely 300 species in all, and five of them (Medusagynaceae, Oncotheca-ceae, Paracryphiaceae, Pentaphylacaceae, and Pellicieraceae) have only one or two species each.

The assortment of families amongst the Theales and Violales that is presented here is conditioned partly by obvious affinities between partic-ular pairs of families and sets of families, and partly by the rationale that (with relatively insignificant probable exceptions among the Magnoliidae) parietal placentation always has an axile phyletic antecedent. Phyletic fusion of closed carpels forms a compound, plurilocular ovary with axile placentation. Parietal placentation is derived from axile by failure of the partitions to meet and join in the center. There is no theoretical reason why an ovary with partial partitions might not revert, phyletically, to a plurilocular one, and doubtless this has happened in some groups. The initial working hypothesis, however, must always be to the contrary. A group with parietal placentation should be derived from one with axile placentation, rather than vice versa. In this instance adherence to this rationale gives us an order in which the major families clearly belong together, and the minor ones are at least not obviously misplaced.

The rationale for distinguishing the Malvales from the Theales is discussed under the Malvales.

The characters by which families of Theales differ among themselves are a mixed bag of obviously adaptive, possibly adaptive, and seemingly nonadaptive features. The mangrove habit of the monotypic family Pellicieraceae is obviously adaptive. The accrescent fruiting sepals of the Dipterocarpaceae appear to be associated with wind-dispersal of the fruits, although students of the family say that the mechanism is not very effective. The highly modified floral bracts of the Marcgraviaceae are said to secrete nectar and to attract pollinators such as hummingbirds, but strictly from the standpoint of effective pollination it would seem more advantageous to produce the nectar within the flowers, closer to the anthers and stigmas. The different sorts of fruits in the different families can reasonably be supposed to relate in considerable part to dispersal-mechanisms. The raphides, sclerenchymatous idioblasts, resin or mucilage systems, tannins, and other secondary metabolites of various families are doubtless significant in the continuing evolutionary struggle between plants and their predators. One might argue that the gynobasic style and essentially separate ovary-lobes of many Ochnaceae relate in some way to dispersal mechanisms, but it is more difficult to see interim survival value in the progressive indentation of the ovary that leads to the more specialized, gynobasic structure. Someone with a lively imagination might see some advantage in reducing the number of stamens from numerous to few (or building it up from few to numerous). The prospect for finding survival value in the following features seems to me to be dismal: opposite versus alternate leaves; presence or absence of stipules (absence is advanced!); number of carpels in the gynoecium; bitegmic versus unitegmic ovules; crassinucellar versus tenuinucellar ovules; nuclear versus cellular development of the endosperm; presence of cortical bundles in the young stem.

Pollen considered to represent diverse families of the Theales dates from the Eocene, but the order may well be much more ancient. The existence of 3 well marked subfamilies of the Dipterocarpaceae on 3 separate continents (Dipterocarpoideae in Asia, Monotoideae in Africa, and Pakaraimoideae in South America), together with the evidently relictual nature of the monotypic South American subfamily, calls for an origin of the family before the pieces of Gondwanaland had drifted very far apart. Anything later than the middle of the Upper Cretaceous (or perhaps even earlier) would seem to present problems in dispersal, yet I know of no verified Cretaceous fossils of Dipterocarpaceae. According to Muller (personal communication), the family shows a differentiation of types, both pollen and macrofossil, in the Oligocene. Pollen considered to be dipterocarpaceous suddenly becomes abundant in Miocene deposits in Borneo (on the Laurasian plate). This apparent proliferation in the Miocene may mark the invasion of Laurasia after the Gondwanan plate had drifted within range.

The restricted geographical occurrence of several thealean families in remote parts of the world (including two in Madagascar, two in New Caledonia, one in West Africa, one in the Seychelles Islands, and three in South America) also bespeaks an ancient origin of the order.

SYNOPTICAL ARRANGEMENT OF THE FAMILIES OF THEALES

1 Leaves digitately 3-foliolate; embryo with enlarged, thickened hypocotyl and reduced cotyledons; tropical America .... **5. Caryocaraceae.**
1 Leaves simple, or seldom pinnately compound; embryo usually of more ordinary proportions.
  2 Leaves mostly alternate.
    3 Leaves mostly stipulate.
      4 Connective prominently exserted; sepals, or some of them, very often accrescent and wing-like in fruit; endosperm mostly wanting; interruptedly pantropical .... **4. Dipterocarpaceae.**
      4 Connective not prominently exserted (though sometimes laterally expanded); sepals only seldom accrescent and forming wings about the fruit; endosperm present in most spp.
        5 Flowers with an intrastaminal disk, or without a disk; pollen in monads.
          6 Anthers with normal connective, often opening by terminal pores; stem generally with cortical bundles; mucilage-cells and -channels absent in most genera; staminodes present (internal to the functional stamens) or not, when present either distinct or connate to form a tube or disk around the ovary, but not resembling a gynophore; flowers often with a gynobasic style; pantropical .... **1. Ochnaceae.**
          6 Anthers with broad, glandular connective separating the pollensacs, these dehiscent by longitudinal slits; stem without cortical bundles; mucilage-cells or -channels present; flowers with a prominent, intrastaminal, gynophore-like disk in which the ovary is somewhat embedded; flowers only seldom with a gynobasic style; Madagascar .... **2. Sphaerosepalaceae.**
        5 Flowers generally with an extrastaminal disk; pollen in tetrads; connective normal; anthers dehiscent by longitudinal slits; mucilage-cells and -channels present; cortical bundles absent; style terminal; Madagascar ....**3. Sarcolaenaceae.**
    3 Leaves exstipulate.
      7 Floral bracts not highly modified, though sometimes elongate and petaloid.
        8 Stamens mostly numerous, seldom only 10, very rarely only 5; ovules (1) 2–many in each locule.
          9 Petals imbricate or convolute; styles distinct, or the style solitary and evidently bilobed or cleft, rarely only the stigmas distinct; sepals imbricate, distinct or basally connate; widespread, chiefly in tropical and subtropical regions.
            10 Anthers opening by longitudinal slits, or rarely by short, terminal, pore-like slits, not inverted; ovules bitegmic; plants with sclerenchymatous idioblasts in the parenchymatous

tissues, but not raphides; trees or shrubs, only rarely climbing .... **6. Theaceae.**
10 Anthers inverted, deeply sagittate, opening by seemingly terminal pores (or the pores sometimes eventually elongating
into lateral slits); ovules unitegmic; plants with raphides,
but not sclerenchymatous idioblasts; trees, shrubs, or often
lianas .... **7. Actinidiaceae.**
9 Petals valvate; style solitary, only the stigma shallowly lobed;
calyx-lobes valvate, or the calyx-tube virtually entire; tropical
West Africa .... **8. Scytopetalaceae.**
8 Stamens 4 or 5; ovules 1–4 in each locule, or some locules empty.
11 Corolla of distinct petals; style solitary, only the stigmas sometimes distinct.
12 Pollen-sacs opening by a specialized terminal pore; ovules
2 in each locule; plants with neither raphides nor sclerenchymatous idioblasts; sepals without the specialized
glands of the next group; SE Asia to Sumatra ....
.... **9. Pentaphylacaceae.**
12 Pollen-sacs opening by a longitudinal slit; ovules solitary in
each locule, or some locules empty; plants producing raphides; sepals beset toward the middle of the inner surface
with tiny, embedded, flask-shaped glands.
13 Trees or shrubs, but not mangroves; fruit fleshy, with
one seed in each of the 4 or 5 locules; seeds with
copious endosperm; sepals not petaloid; no sclerenchymatous idioblasts; Malaysian region, and disjunct
in N South America .... **10. Tetrameristaceae.**
13 Mangroves; fruit dry, 1-seeded; seeds without endosperm; sepals petaloid; plants with sclerenchymatous
idioblasts in the cortex and pith; Pacific tropical
America .... **11. Pellicieraceae.**
11 Corolla sympetalous; ovary apically shortly 5-lobed, the lobes
stigmatic ventrally; ovules 2 in each locule; anthers opening
by longitudinal slits; New Caledonia ... **12. Oncothecaceae.**
7 Floral bracts, or some of them, highly modified into pitcher-like, saccate, spurred, or hooded structures; plants mostly lianas and epiphytes, producing raphides and sclerenchymatous idioblasts; tropical
America .... **13. Marcgraviaceae.**
2 Leaves opposite or verticillate (or merely subverticillate in Paracryphiaceae).
14 Leaves stipulate.
15 Trees, shrubs, or lianas; stamens 15–many; ovules 2 in each locule;
fruit fleshy; tropical America .... **14. Quiinaceae.**
15 Herbs or half-shrubs; stamens as many or twice as many as the
petals, fewer than 15; ovules numerous; fruit capsular; cosmopolitan .... **15. Elatinaceae.**
14 Leaves exstipulate (stipulate in *Mahurea,* of the Clusiaceae).
16 Ovary 8–25-locular; no secretory canals or cavities; fruit capsular,
opening septicidally from the base, the carpels united distally and
spreading away from the summit like the ribs of an umbrella.
17 Ovules 4 in each locule; ovary 8–15-locular; stamens mostly 8,
in a single cycle; vessel-segments with scalariform perforations; New Caledonia .... **16. Paracryphiaceae.**

17 Ovules 2 in each locule; ovary 17–25-locular; stamens numerous; vessel-segments with simple perforations; Seychelles Islands . . . . **17. Medusagynaceae.**

16 Ovary (1–) 3–5 (–20+)-locular; well developed secretory canals or cavities present in most or all organs; ovules (1) 2–many in each locule; fruit variously dehiscent or indehiscent, but not as in the previous group; cosmopolitan, mainly tropical and North Temperate . . . . **18. Clusiaceae.**

SELECTED REFERENCES

Agababyan, V. Sh. & E. L. Zavaryan. 1971. K palinosistematike roda *Paracryphia* Bak. f. AN Armyanskoy SSR Biol. Zh. Armenii. **25:** 35–40.

Baretta-Kuipers, T. 1976. Comparative wood anatomy of Bonnetiaceae, Theaceae and Guttiferae. Leiden Bot. Series **3:** 76–101.

Capuron, R. 1962. Révision des Rhopalocarpacées. Adansonia Sér. 2, **2:** 228–267.

Capuron, R. 1970. Observations sur les Sarcolaenacées. Adansonia Sér. 2, **10:** 247–265.

Carlquist, S. 1964. Pollen morphology and evolution of Sarcolaenaceae (Chlaenaceae). Brittonia **16:** 231–254.

Carpenter, C. S. & W. C. Dickison. 1976. The morphology and relationships of *Oncotheca balansae*. Bot. Gaz. **137:** 141–153.

Cavaco, A. 1952. Chlaenacées. *In* H. Humbert (ed.), Flore de Madagascar et des Comores. **126:** 1–37.

Den Outer, R. W. & A. P. Vooren. 1980. Bark anatomy of some Sarcolaenaceae and Rhopalocarpaceae and their systematic position. Meded. Landbouwhogeschool **80(6):** 1–15.

Dickison, W. C. 1972. Observations on the floral morphology of some species of *Saurauia, Actinidia* and *Clematoclethra*. J. Elisha Mitchell Sci. Soc. **88:** 43–54.

Dickison, W. C. 1981. Contributions to the morphology and anatomy of *Strasburgeria* and a discussion of the taxonomic position of the Strasburgeriaceae. Brittonia **33:** 554–580.

Dickison, W. C. 1986. Further observations on the floral anatomy and pollen morphology of *Oncotheca* (Oncothecaceae). Brittonia **38:** 249–259.

Dickison, W. C. & P. Baas. 1977. The morphology and relationships of *Paracryphia* (Paracryphiaceae). Blumea **23:** 417–438.

Erbar, C. 1986. Untersuchungen zur Entwicklung der spiraligen Blüte von *Stewartia pseudocamellia* (Theaceae). Bot. Jahrb. Syst. **106:** 391–407.

Gottwald, H. & N. Parameswaran. 1967. Beiträge zur Anatomie und Systematik der Quiinaceae. Bot. Jahrb. Syst. **87:** 361–381.

Huard, J. 1965. Anatomie des Rhopalocarpacées. Adansonia Sér. 2, **5:** 103–123.

Huard, J. 1965. Remarques sur la position systématique des Rhopalocarpacées d'après leur anatomie et leur morphologie pollinique. Bull. Soc. Bot. France **112:** 252–254.

John, J. & K.-P. Kolbe. 1980. The systematic position of the "Theales" from the viewpoint of serology. Biochem. Syst. Ecol. **8:** 241–248.

Kawano, S. 1965. Anatomical studies on the androecia of some members of the Guttiferae—Moronoboideae. Bot. Mag. (Tokyo) **78:** 97–108.

Keng, H. 1962. Comparative morphological studies in Theaceae. Univ. Calif. Publ. Bot. **33:** 269–384.

Kobuski, C. E. 1951. Studies in the Theaceae. XXIII. The genus *Pelliciera.* J. Arnold Arbor. **32:** 256–262.

Letouzey, R. 1961. Notes sur les Scytopétalacées (Revision des Scytopétalacées de l'herbier de Paris). Adansonia Sér. 2, **1:** 106–142.

Li, H. L. 1952. A taxonomic review of the genus *Actinidia.* J. Arnold Arbor. **33:** 1–61.

Maguire, B., et al. 1972. Botany of the Guayana Highland—Part IX. Tetrameristaceae. Mem. N.Y. Bot. Gard. **23:** 165–192.

Maguire, B. & P. Ashton. 1980. *Pakaraimaea dipterocarpacea* II. Taxon **29:** 225–231.

Maury, G., J. Muller & B. Lugardon. 1975. Notes on the morphology and fine structure of the exine of some pollen types in Dipterocarpaceae. Rev. Palaeobot. Palynol. **19:** 241–289.

Muller, J. 1969. Pollen-morphological notes on Ochnaceae. Rev. Palaeobot. Palynol. **9:** 149–173.

Narayana, L. L. 1975. A contribution to the floral anatomy and embryology of Ochnaceae. J. Jap. Bot. **50:** 329–336.

Pauzé, F. & R. Sattler. 1979. La placentation axillaire chez *Ochna atropurpurea.* Canad. J. Bot. **57:** 100–107.

Prance, G. T. & M. F. da Silva. 1973. A monograph of the Caryocaraceae. Fl. Neotropica Monograph 12.

Schmid, R. 1978a. Reproductive anatomy of *Actinidia chinensis* (Actinidiaceae). Bot. Jahrb. Syst. **100:** 149–195.

Schmid, R. 1978b. Actinidiaceae, Davidiaceae, and Paracryphiaceae: Systematic considerations. Bot. Jahrb. Syst. **100:** 196–204.

Schofield, E. K. 1968. Petiole anatomy of the Guttiferae and related families. Mem. N.Y. Bot. Gard. **18(1):** 1–55.

Shilkina, I. A. 1977. Sravnitel'no-anatomicheskaya kharakteristika drevesiny roda *Oncotheca* Baill. (Por. Theales). Bot. Zh. **62:** 1273–1275.

van Steenis, C. G. G. J. 1956. Pentaphylacaceae. Fl. Males. ser. 1, **5(2):** 121–124.

Straka, H. & F. Albers. 1978. Die Pollenmorphologie von *Diegodendron humbertii* R. Capuron (Diegodendraceae, Ochnales bzw. Theales). Bot. Jahrb. Syst. **99:** 363–369.

Vestal, P. A. 1937. The significance of comparative anatomy in establishing the relationship of the Hypericaceae to the Guttiferae and their allies. Philipp. J. Sci. **64:** 199–256.

Vijayaraghavan, M. R. 1965. Morphology and embryology of *Actinidia polygama,* and systematic position of the family Actinidiaceae. Phytomorphology **15:** 224–235.

Vijayaraghavan, M. R. & U. Dhar. 1976. *Scytopetalum tieghemii*—Embryologically unexplored taxon and affinities of the family Scytopetalaceae. Phytomorphology **26:** 16–22.

3. Order Malvales

The order Malvales as here defined consists of 5 families and about 3000 to 3500 species, cosmopolitan in distribution, but best represented in the tropics. The Malvaceae, with a thousand to 1500 species, and the Sterculiaceae, with about a thousand, are the largest families. The Tiliaceae have about 450 species, the Elaeocarpaceae about 400, and the Bombacaceae about 200.

The Malvales may be briefly characterized as polypetalous dicotyledons with valvate sepals, often monadelphous or polyadelphous filaments, and commonly with cyclopropenyl fatty acids in the seeds. Some vegetative features characteristic of the order are discussed in subsequent paragraph.

Most authors have agreed that all of the families here referred to the Malvales are allied. The Elaeocarpaceae stand somewhat apart from the rest of the order, but even so the relationship is so close that they have often been included in the Tiliaceae. The remaining four families (Tiliaceae, Sterculiaceae, Bombacaceae, and Malvaceae) are even more closely allied, and there has been some controversy about their definition. Individual genera have been shifted from one family to another by various authors. The whole tribe Hibisceae is referable to the Bombacaceae if the structure of the fruit is taken as the critical character, and to the Malvaceae if (as here) the ornamentation of the pollen is stressed instead.

The small families Sarcolaenaceae (Chlaenaceae) and Sphaerosepalaceae (Rhopalocarpaceae) are often also referred to the Malvales. These families have mucilage-cells, as in the Malvales, and the Sarcolaenaceae also have stratified phloem. On the other hand, they have imbricate sepals, and they do not seem closely allied to any family of the Malvales. On balance, I find it more useful to include these two families in the Theales, partly because the Malvales are otherwise relatively homogeneous, whereas the Theales are more heterogeneous. Likewise, I find it more useful to refer the Scytopetalaceae to the Theales than to include them in the Malvales, where they have no obvious relatives.

The nature of the nectaries in the Malvales is evidently correlated with the polypetalous structure of the flowers. According to Brown (1938, in initial citations):

> "In this order, nectary glands are characteristic, multicellular, glandular hairs which are usually packed closely together to form cushion-like growths. In the Tiliaceae, these nectaries are found in various places, including the sepals, petals, and androgynophore. In the Malvaceae, Bombacaceae and Sterculiaceae they have become localized and are found in the sepals. . . . The honey is made available by means of openings between the overlapping bases of the petals. The lack of gam-

opetalous corollas in these families is probably connected with the occurrence of nectaries in the sepals and the necessity for slits between the petals to make the nectar available."

There has been a continuing controversy about whether the large number of stamens and/or carpels found in some or all members of most families of the order reflects a primitive survival or a secondary increase. The monothecal stamens of the Malvaceae and Bombacaceae are widely admitted to represent longitudinal halves of ancestrally dithecal stamens, but there the agreement stops. Polyandrous types commonly have one or more sets of 5 stamen-traces (trunk bundles) with each trace repeatedly forked so that eventually there is one vascular bundle for each stamen. Polycarpellate types sometimes show a similar branching of 5 basic carpel-traces.

Some students of floral anatomy have interpreted this pattern to indicate an increase in the number of stamens and carpels, based on an originally pentamerous flower. I am more attracted to the contrary view that fairly large and indefinite numbers of stamens and carpels in the Malvales are inherited directly from a Thealean ancestry, and that condensation of the vascular supply is merely the first step in a phyletic reduction from numerous stamens and carpels to few. The characteristic compound stamen-trunks that have been interpreted to mean a secondary increase in number are not restricted to the Malvales, but are widespread in the Dilleniidae in general, and they have also been found in the Myrtales, Alismatales, and even the Magnoliales.

At the same time, it must be admitted that when the number of parts of a particular kind is fairly large and indefinite, evolutionary increase as well as decrease may occur. There is no need to suppose that the largest number of dithecal stamens that can be found in any species of Malvales is the minimum ancestral number for the order. Likewise, the arrangement of the numerous carpels of the small tribe Malopeae (Malvaceae) into 5 vertical ranks suggests the likelihood of a secondary increase in the number of carpels in this group.

The Malvales are probably derived from the less modified members of the Theales, from which they differ in the valvate rather than imbricate calyx. The vast majority of the Malvales also share a syndrome of vegetative features that are more sporadic (and less consistently associated) in the Theales. These are the stellate or lepidote indument, the mucilage-cells or -cavities, and the stratified phloem with wedge-shaped rays. Furthermore, the seeds of at least the four core-families of the Malvales have fatty acids containing a cyclopropenyl group. This type of fatty acid now appears to be restricted to the Malvales.

The only other obvious relationship of the Malvales to any large group is with the Violales. These two orders are here regarded as groups that have taken different evolutionary paths from a common ancestry in the Theales. The Elaeocarpaceae are the most archaic family of the Malvales, as judged by the general floral morphology, wood anatomy, absence of stellate hairs, and lack of the specialized type of nectary found in the other families of the order. Some of the Elaeocarpaceae are very similar to some of the Flacourtiaceae, and this similarity extends even to the pollen-morphology. Any common ancestor of the Flacourtiaceae and Elaeocarpaceae would presumably have an imbricate calyx and axile placentation, and thus could appropriately be placed in the Theales.

Aside from the correlation of the type of nectary with the structure of the corolla, the ecological significance of the characters that mark the Malvales is mostly obscure. The mucilage-cells presumably have some function in discouraging predators, but this reasonable speculation is not backed by objective evidence. If the valvate arrangement of the sepals has any importance to the plant, the fact is not obvious. If stellate hairs have any advantage over simple hairs, it has not been demonstrated. The stratified phloem with wedge-shaped rays does not confer any obvious advantage over plants with more conventional phloem. The functional significance of the cyclopropenyl group in some of the fatty acids remains to be elucidated.

The ecological significance of the families that make up the order is scarcely more evident than that of the order as a whole. The Malvaceae are mostly herbaceous or nearly so, whereas the other families are mostly woody, but beyond that the problems are unresolved. The spines on the pollen of most Malvaceae, and the tendency in several families for the filaments to be connate, might relate to the kinds of pollinators, or they might not. It is hard to see how the number of pollen-sacs per anther might affect the competitive ability of the plant, but here as elsewhere the possibility must be entertained that there is a hidden significance which might be discovered by a persistent and perceptive investigator.

The oldest clearly malvalean fossils are Maestrichtian pollen-grains of the Bombacaceae. Since the Bombacaceae are fairly well advanced members of the order, it may reasonably be supposed that the Malvales arose before Maestrichtian time. It may be significant that pollen considered to represent the Malvaceae enters the fossil record only in the late Eocene, distinctly later than the Tiliaceae, Bombacaceae, and Sterculiaceae.

SYNOPTICAL ARRANGEMENT OF THE FAMILIES OF MALVALES

1 Anthers tetrasporangiate and dithecal; epicalyx only seldom present; filaments distinct or connate; mostly trees and shrubs, a few herbs.
  2 Filaments distinct, or only shortly connate at the base into 5 or 10 clusters.
    3 Plants without mucilage-cells, -cavities, and -canals, except that the epidermis of the leaves is often mucilaginous; phloem not stratified, and without wedge-shaped rays; indument not of stellate or peltate hairs; petals valvate or seldom imbricate .... **1. Elaeocarpaceae.**
    3 Plants with well developed mucilage-cells and often also -cavities or -canals; phloem of young stems tangentially stratified into hard and soft layers, and with wedge-shaped rays; indument often of stellate hairs or peltate scales; petals imbricate or convolute or valvate ..... **2. Tiliaceae.**
  2 Filaments all generally connate into a tube around the ovary ....
.... **3. Sterculiaceae.**

1 Anthers bisporangiate and monothecal (but sometimes coalescent in the Bombacaceae); flowers very often with an epicalyx; filaments generally connate into a tube.

4 Pollen-grains generally smooth or merely rugose, only rarely minutely spinulose, of various shapes, triaperturate (colpate, colporate, or porate) to less often pantoporate; trees; fruit a loculicidal capsule, or seldom fleshy and indehiscent .... **4. Bombacaceae.**

4 Pollen-grains generally minutely spiny, only rarely smooth, mostly spherical and pantoporate, but sometimes tricolporate; herbs or soft shrubs, only rarely trees; fruit variously schizocarpic, or septicidally or loculicidally dehiscent, only seldom baccate or samaroid ....**5. Malvaceae.**

SELECTED REFERENCES

Alexandrov, V. G. & A. V. Dobrotvorskaya. 1957. O morfologicheskoi sushchnosti tychinok, lepestkov, i tak nazyvaemoy tychinochnoy trubki v tsvetke mal'vovykh. Trudy Bot. Inst. Komarova AN SSSR, ser. VII, **4**: 83–137.

Bates, D. M. 1968. Generic relationships in the Malvaceae, tribe Malveae. Gentes Herb. **10**: 117–135.

Brizicky, G. K. 1965. The genera of Tiliaceae and Elaeocarpaceae in the southeastern United States. J. Arnold Arbor. **46**: 286–307.

Brizicky, G. K. 1966. The genera of Sterculiaceae in the southeastern United States. J. Arnold Arbor. **47**: 60–74.

Edlin, H. L. 1935. A critical revision of certain taxonomic groups of the Malvales. New Phytol. **34**: 1–20, 122–143.

Fuchs, H. P. 1967. Pollen morphology of the family Bombacaceae. Rev. Palaeobot. Palynol. **3**: 119–132.

Leinfellner, W. 1960. Zur Entwicklungsgeschichte der Kronblätter der Sterculiaceae—Buettnerieae. Oesterr. Bot. Z. **107**: 153–176.

Rohweder, O. 1972. Das Andröcium der Malvales und der "Konservatismus" des Leitgewebes. Bot. Jahrb. Syst. **92**: 155–167.

Sharma, B. D. 1969. Pollen morphology of Tiliaceae in relation to plant taxonomy. J. Palyn. (Lucknow) **5**: 7–29.

Sharma, B. D. 1970. Contribution to the pollen morphology and plant taxonomy of the family Bombacaceae. Proc. Indian Natl. Sci. Acad. **36B**: 175–191.

Shenstone, F. S. & J. R. Vickery. 1961. Occurrence of cyclo-propene acids in some plants of the order Malvales. Nature **190**: 168, 169.

van Heel, W. A. 1966. Morphology of the androecium in Malvales. Blumea **13**: 177–394.

van Heel, W. A. 1978. Morphology of the pistil in Malvaceae—Ureneae. Blumea **24**: 123–127.

Venkata Rao, C. 1949. Floral anatomy of some Sterculiaceae with special reference to the position of the stamens. J. Indian Bot. Soc. **28**: 237–245.

Venkata Rao, C. 1949–1954. Contributions to the embryology of Sterculiaceae. I–V. J. Indian Bot. Soc. **28**: 180–197, 1949; **29**: 163–176, 1950; **30**: 122–131, 1951; **31**: 251–260, 1953; **32**: 208–238, 1953 (1954).

Venkata Rao, C. 1950. Pollen grains of Sterculiaceae. J. Indian Bot. Soc. **29**: 130–137.

Venkata Rao, C. 1952. Floral anatomy of some Malvales and its bearing on the affinities of families included in the order. J. Indian Bot. Soc. **31**: 171–203.

4. Order Lecythidales

The order Lecythidales consists of the single family Lecythidaceae, with about 400 species. Confined to tropical regions, the group is best developed in rain forests, especially in South America. Characteristic members of the order differ from other orders of the Dilleniidae in their combination of polyandrous, epigynous flowers and axile placentation.

The Lecythidaceae have traditionally been referred to the order Myrtales because of their combination of separate petals, numerous stamens, and syncarpous, inferior ovary with axile placentation. They differ from characteristic members of the Myrtales, however, in their alternate leaves, centrifugal stamens, bitegmic, tenuinucellar ovules, lack of internal phloem, lack of vestured pits in the vessels, and in a series of embryological features that have been elucidated by Mauritzon (1939, in bibliography for CHAPTER 5). The differences are too formidable to ignore, and the Lecythidaceae must be removed from the Myrtales. No other order can accommodate the Lecythidaceae without undue strain, and it becomes necessary to recognize an order Lecythidales.

Although no one feature by itself is definitive, the Lecythidales are much more at home in the Dilleniidae than in the Rosidae (the only other subclass in which they might conceivably be placed). The bitegmic, tenuinucellar ovule of the Lecythidales is common in the Theales, Primulales, and Ebenales (all members of the Dilleniidae), but rare and scattered elsewhere. Although centrifugal stamens have been demonstrated in the small family Punicaceae of the Myrtales, this kind of androecium is much more common in the Dilleniidae than in the Rosidae. Stratified phloem, as in the Lecythidales, is common in the Malvales and to some extent in the Theales, much less so in the other subclasses. The complex anatomy of the petiole in Lecythidales is reminiscent of both the Theales and the Malvales. The enlarged hypocotyl of many Lecythidales might be compared with that of the Caryocaraceae and Marcgraviaceae in the Theales. Muller (1972) found that the pollen structure of the Lecythidales is readily compatible with that of the Theales and Malvales (as well as with that of several other orders not under consideration here), but difficult to reconcile with that of the Myrtales. My interpretation of the set of similarities and differences is that the Lecythidales and Malvales have undergone partly parallel and partly divergent specializations from a common ancestry in the Theales.

The striking differences in the androecium of various members of the Lecythidaceae have led some authors to recognize several separate families. This is not really wrong, but the segregates must in any case stand alongside the Lecythidaceae in the system of classification. I see nothing to be gained by elevating the subfamilies to familial rank.

The complex evolutionary series of changes in the androecium of the

Lecythidaceae is considered to reflect progressive restriction of possible pollinators, with emphasis on euglossine bees. The cortical vascular bundles and the bitegmic, tenuinucellar structure of the ovules are more difficult to explain in Darwinian terms. Epigyny among angiosperms in general has been claimed by some authors to help protect the ovules, but I remain skeptical.

Pollen considered to represent the genus *Barringtonia* in the Lecythidaceae is known from Lower Eocene and more recent deposits.

Selected References

Leins, P. 1972. Das zentrifugale Androeceum von *Couroupita guianensis* (Lecythidaceae). Beitr. Biol. Pflanzen. **48:** 313–319.

Mori, S. A., & collaborators. 1987. The Lecythidaceae of a lowland neotropical forest: La Fumée Mountain, French Guiana. Mem. N.Y. Bot. Gard. **44:** 1–190.

Mori, S. A. & G. T. Prance. In press. Lecythidaceae—Part II. The zygomorphic-flowered New World Lecythidaceae. Fl. Neotropica Monogr.

Muller, J. 1972. Pollen morphological evidence for subdivision and affinities of Lecythidaceae. Blumea **20:** 350–355.

Prance, G. T. 1976. The pollination and androphore structure of some Amazonian Lecythidaceae. Biotropica **8:** 235–241.

Prance, G. T. & S. A. Mori. 1979. Lecythidaceae—Part I. The actinomorphic-flowered New World Lecythidaceae. Fl. Neotropical Monogr. 21.

5. Order Nepenthales

The order Nepenthales as here defined consists of 3 well marked small families, scarcely 200 species in all. The Droseraceae have about a hundred species, the Nepenthaceae about 75, and the Sarraceniaceae about 15. None of the three families can be considered ancestral to any of the others. They represent distinct lines that have undergone more or less similar changes from a similar ancestry. A fourth family, the Byblidaceae (including Roridulaceae), has often been referred to the Nepenthales, but is now generally associated with the Pittosporaceae in the Rosales.

The mutual affinity of the three families of Nepenthales has been affirmed and denied by various authors, and competent opinion is still divided. All considered, there is perhaps a little more reason to question the relationship of the Droseraceae to the Sarraceniaceae and Nepenthaceae than the relationship of the latter two families to each other.

Opinion is still divided about the affinities of the Nepenthales. Members of the Theales, Violales, Rosales, and Papaverales have been suggested as allies of one or more of the families. In my opinion the ancestry of the Nepenthales is to be sought in the Theales. Except for their insectivorous habit, the Nepenthales would fit well into the Theales (assuming that the stamens of the Sarraceniaceae turn out to be centrifugal, a point not yet fully established). Inasmuch as two of the families of Nepenthales have axile placentation, the Violales do not seem very likely ancestors. The foliar glands and other vegetative similarities of *Ancistrocladus* and *Dioncophyllum* (Violales) to *Nepenthes* are here regarded as reflecting an eventual common ancestry rather than a more direct relationship.

The insectivorous habit of the Nepenthales may be presumed to be an evolutionary response to their growth in habitats deficient in available nitrogen. The Sarraceniaceae and Droseraceae commonly grow in waterlogged soils containing little or no soluble nitrate. The Nepenthaceae occur in wet, tropical forests, which characteristically have nutrient-poor soils. Many other groups of plants have faced similar problems, but very few have learned to meet them by trapping insects.

Aside from the insect-catching apparatus, the characters that mark the order and the individual families are of doubtful ecological significance.

Synoptical Arrangement of the Families of Nepenthales

1 Leaves, or some of them, modified to form pitchers; ovary plurilocular, with axile placentation; style solitary, or sometimes very short or none.
  2 Flowers perfect; filaments distinct; pollen-grains in monads; ovules tenuinucellar; terrestrial herbs, sometimes scrambling, but otherwise not climbing; New World .... **1. Sarraceniaceae.**
  2 Flowers unisexual; filaments united into a column; pollen-grains in tetrads; ovules crassinucellar; herbs or more often shrubs or half-shrubs, often climbing or epiphytic; Old World .... **2. Nepenthaceae.**
1 Leaves not forming pitchers; ovary unilocular, with parietal or basal placentation; styles usually distinct (and often deeply bifid), only seldom united; cosmopolitan herbs .... **3. Droseraceae.**

Selected References

Arber, A. 1941. On the morphology of the pitcher-leaves in *Heliamphora, Sarracenia, Darlingtonia, Cephalotus,* and *Nepenthes.* Ann. Bot. (London) II, **5:** 563–578.

Bell, C. R. 1949. A cytotaxonomic study of the Sarraceniaceae of North America. J. Elisha Mitchell Sci. Soc. **65:** 137–166.

Carlquist, S. 1981. Wood anatomy of Nepenthaceae. Bull. Torrey Bot. Club **108:** 324–336.

Chanda, S. 1965. The pollen morphology of Droseraceae with special reference to taxonomy. Pollen & Spores 7: 509–528.

DeBuhr, L. E. 1975. Phylogenetic relationships of the Sarraceniaceae. Taxon **24:** 297–306.

DeBuhr, L. E. 1977. Wood anatomy of the Sarraceniaceae; ecological and evolutionary implications. Pl. Syst. Evol. **128:** 159–169.

McDaniel, S. 1971. The genus *Sarracenia* (Sarraceniaceae). Bull. Tall Timbers Res. Sta. **9:** 1–36.

Markgraf, F. 1955. Über Laubblatt-Homologien und verwandtschaftliche Zu-
sammenhänge bei Sarraceniales. Planta **46**: 414–446.
Wood, C. E. 1960. The genera of Sarraceniaceae and Droseraceae in the southeastern United States. J. Arnold Arbor. **41**: 152–163.

6. Order Violales

The order Violales as here defined consists of 24 families and nearly
5000 species. Fully four-fifths of the species belong to only five families:
the Begoniaceae (1000), Flacourtiaceae (800+), Violaceae (800), Cucurbitaceae (700), and Passifloraceae (650). The Loasaceae, Begoniaceae,
Cucurbitaceae, and a few of the smaller families may conceivably prove
to belong somewhere else, but the bulk of the order hangs together as a
natural group with the Flacourtiaceae at its evolutionary base. Among
the larger families, the Passifloraceae and Violaceae are clearly linked to
the Flacourtiaceae, and it appears that the Cucurbitaceae are linked to
the Passifloraceae.

The more archaic members of the Violales are trees with alternate,
stipulate leaves, perfect, hypogynous, polypetalous flowers with numerous
centrifugal stamens, a compound pistil with free styles and parietal placentation, bitegmic, crassinucellar ovules, and seeds with a well developed
endosperm. Such a combination of characters immediately suggests the
Flacourtiaceae, which are usually considered to be the most archaic family
of the order. It may also be interesting to note that a few of the Flacourtiaceae have a plurilocular ovary with axile placentation; on formal morphological characters these would be perfectly at home in the Theales.

Tendencies toward perigyny and epigyny, unisexuality, reduction in the
number of stamens, fusion of filaments into groups, the development of
a corona, reduction in the number of carpels, fusion of styles, and loss of
endosperm can all be seen in the family Flacourtiaceae. These are also
some of the more prominent characters that are used in combination to
define many of the families of the order. Although the more archaic
members of the order have centrifugal stamens (so far as known), the
Begoniaceae and the subfamily Mentzelioideae of the Loasaceae are centripetal. In the Violales and in the Dilleniidae as a whole it appears the
centrifugal stamens are plesiomorphic and centripetal ones apomorphic,
just the reverse of the situation in other polystemonous angiosperms.

The Violales and Capparales may be considered as more or less parallel
offshoots from the Theales, each having mostly parietal instead of axile
placentation. The Violales differ from the Capparales in the absence of a
replum and the usual absence of mustard-oils. Furthermore, the Violales
have a much higher proportion of woody species, they only seldom have
compound leaves, they often have perigynous to epigynous flowers, and
they most commonly have 3 carpels (a rare number in the Capparales),
only seldom 2 (the most common number in the Capparales).

The adaptive significance of most of the characters that distinguish the

Violales as a group is obscure. Placentation, number of carpels, ovular structure, and sequence of initiation of stamens are difficult to relate to survival value. The most important ecological distinction between the Violales and the Capparales is almost surely the nature of their chemical defenses. The Capparales heavily exploit mustard-oils, to the virtual exclusion of most other weapons, whereas the Violales have a wide array of repellents in different families, but only rarely mustard-oils.

Some of the families of Violales do show some ecological correlations. The Fouquieriaceae are spiny xerophytes with small leaves that fall off as the soil dries out. The Tamaricaceae, Frankeniaceae, and many of the Cistaceae meet problems of water-stress by having small, firm, persistent leaves that can survive desiccation, and the Tamaricaceae and Frankeniaceae further have specialized salt-excreting foliar glands. The Passifloraceae and Cucurbitaceae are chiefly tendriliferous vines, and the Dioncophyllaceae and Ancistrocladaceae are woody vines that climb by means of stout hooks from the branch-tips (Ancistrocladaceae) or leaf-tips (Dioncophyllaceae). Some of the families have distinctive chemical defenses. The cucurbitacins appear to be nearly unique to the Cucurbitaceae. The Loasaceae and Fouquieriaceae are unusual in the order in having iridoid compounds, although these are common enough in some other orders (including some in the Dilleniidae). The Flacourtiaceae, Passifloraceae, and probably also the other cyanogenic families produce cyanogens in an unusual way involving special types of fatty acids that have a cyclopentenoid ring. Aside from these features, one sees the familiar pattern of families defined by characters of little or no obvious biological importance, and some of the larger families embrace a wide range of growth-forms that occur in diverse habitats. The Violaceae, in particular, are noteworthy for including one large genus (*Rinorea*) of tropical woody plants found in the understory of rain forests, and another (*Viola*) consisting of herbs that grow mainly in temperate regions and in tropical mountains.

The Flacourtiaceae and the Cistaceae both date from the Miocene, on the basis of fossil pollen. Pollen that might represent the Flacourtiaceae or any of several other dilleniid families extends well back into the Cretaceous.

For those who find it useful to organize the Violales into suborders, I have indicated a scheme in the synoptical arrangement of families.

SYNOPTICAL ARRANGEMENT OF THE FAMILIES OF VIOLALES

1 Ovary usually superior (half-inferior in the Ancistrocladaceae and some Turneraceae, inferior in a very few Flacourtiaceae); plants of various habit.
  2 Flowers mostly polypetalous or apetalous, or the petals seldom shortly connate at the base.
    3 Flowers without a corona, or very rarely (a monotypic genus of Flacourtiaceae) with an intrastaminal corona, mostly hypogynous, seldom evidently perigynous or even epigynous.
      4 Plants mostly not climbing, in any case without hooked or twining leaf-tips or branch-tips.

5 Stamens mostly 10 or more, rarely as few as 5 or even 3 (Violineae, in part).
  6 Styles distinct or united to varying degrees, the stigmas distinct; plants often cyanogenic in association with a cyclopentenoid ring system; endosperm oily, often containing cyclopentenyl (chaulmoogric) fatty acids.
    7 Ovules on parietal (sometimes more or less deeply intruded) or seldom virtually basal or even axile placentas; anthers dithecal; petals variously present or absent; carpels 2–10 .... **1. Flacourtiaceae.**
    7 Ovules pendulous from the top of a unilocular ovary; anthers monothecal; petals wanting; carpels 3–4 .... **2. Peridiscaceae.**
  6 Style solitary, terminated by the simple or lobed stigma, or the stigmas seldom distinct; plants not cyanogenic; endosperm starchy or oily, not known to contain cyclopentenyl fatty acids.
    8 Placentation parietal to more or less distinctly axile; stamens (3–) more or less numerous; petals imbricate or convolute; plants not with the odor of garlic.
      9 Plants with an orange or red latex; anthers opening by pores or short slits; ovules anatropous; leaves alternate, from simple, entire, and palmately veined to palmately lobed or compound .... **3. Bixaceae.**
      9 Plants with colorless juice; anthers opening by longitudinal slits; ovules orthotropous or rarely anatropous; leaves opposite or less often alternate, simple, variously veined, often more or less reduced and ericoid or scale-like ... . **4. Cistaceae.**
    8 Placentation basal; stamens (8) 10; petals induplicate-valvate; plants with a garlic-like odor .... **5. Huaceae.**
5 Stamens 1–8, or sometimes 10 or even more numerous in the Tamaricaceae.
  10 Stamens 1–3; flowers very small, in catkin-like spikes or racemes (Violineae, in part).
    11 Stamen solitary; carpels 2–3; flowers generally perfect .... **6. Lacistemaceae.**
    11 Stamens 3, connate into a column; carpels 8–13; flowers unisexual .... **7. Scyphostegiaceae.**
  10 Stamens 4 or more; flowers variously large or small.
    12 Endosperm oily; leaves of normal proportions, stipulate, without salt-excreting glands; flowers regular or very often irregular (Violineae, in part).
      13 Stamens 8; sepals, petals, and carpels each 4; flowers regular .... **8. Stachyuraceae.**
      13 Stamens (3–) 5; sepals and petals each 5; carpels (2) 3 (–5); flowers regular or very often irregular .... **9. Violaceae.**
    12 Endosperm starchy or none; leaves exstipulate, often much reduced and ericoid or scale-like, commonly with embedded, multicellular, salt-excreting glands; flowers regular (Tamaricineae).
      14 Styles 2–5 (or the stigmas sessile); leaves alternate; sepals

distinct or connate only near the base . . . .
. . . . **10. Tamaricaceae.**
14 Style solitary, slender and elongate; leaves opposite; sepals connate to form a shortly lobed tube . . . .
. . . . **11. Frankeniaceae.**
4 Plants woody climbers with stout, hooked or twining branch-tips or
leaf-tips (Ancistrocladineae).
15 Ovules numerous on the 2–5 parietal placentas, conspicuously
exserted from the developing capsule well before maturity; plants
climbing by hooked or twining leaf-tips; ovary superior . . . . . .
. . . . **12. Dioncophyllaceae.**
15 Ovule solitary, basilateral, included in the mature nut; plants
climbing by hooked or twining branch-tips; ovary half-inferior
. . . . **13. Ancistrocladaceae.**
3 Flowers with an extrastaminal corona (except most Turneraceae), more
or less strongly perigynous; stamens 5 (–numerous) (Passiflorineae, in
part).
16 Corona wanting, or seldom present; flowers without a gynophore or
androgynophore; plants not climbing . . . . **14. Turneraceae.**
16 Corona nearly always present; flowers usually with a gynophore or
androgynophore.
17 Seeds exarillate; undershrubs or herbs, not climbing; sepals and
petals valvate in bud . . . . **15. Malesherbiaceae.**
17 Seeds arillate; herbaceous or woody vines, climbing by tendrils,
or less often erect shrubs or even trees; sepals and petals imbricate in bud, or the petals seldom wanting . . . .
. . . . **16. Passifloraceae.**
2 Flowers evidently sympetalous.
18 Flowers nearly always unisexual; leaves simple (but often lobed) or compound; stamens 10 or fewer (Passiflorineae, in part).
19 Herbs or half-shrubs without a latex-system; fruit capsular; style
solitary, more or less deeply cleft; stamens 3–5 . . . .
. . . . **17. Achariaceae.**
19 Soft-stemmed shrubs or small trees (rarely herbs) with a well developed latex-system; fruit fleshy, melon-like; styles distinct; stamens 10 or seldom only 5 . . . . **18. Caricaceae.**
18 Flowers perfect; leaves simple, entire or nearly so; stamens 10 or more.
20 Spiny, xerophytic shrubs or small, fleshy trees with small, ephemeral
leaves; carpels 3; fruit capsular; stamens 10–18 (–23) (Fouquieri-
ineae) . . . . **19. Fouquieriaceae.**
20 Unarmed trees with large, persistent leaves; carpels 2; fruit drupaceous; stamens about 20–30 (Hoplestigmatineae) . . . .
. . . . **20. Hoplestigmataceae.**
1 Ovary mostly inferior, rarely only half-inferior; plants mostly herbs or herbaceous vines, a few trees and shrubs; endosperm scanty or none except in
Loasaceae.
21 Flowers mostly unisexual (rarely polygamous or perfect); ovules bitegmic,
crassinucellar; plants without iridoid compounds.
22 Stamens apparently 2–5, typically 3 with one monothecal and two
dithecal anthers; mostly tendriliferous vines; corolla mostly sympetalous; styles 1–3; plants producing cucurbitacins; leaves exstipulate (Cucurbitineae) . . . . **21. Cucurbitaceae.**

22 Stamens 4–many, all with dithecal anthers; plants without tendrils; petals distinct or none; styles distinct or merely connate at the base; plants without cucurbitacins (Begoniineae).
  23 Ovary unilocular, with parietal placentas; leaves exstipulate; sepals 4–8 . . . . **22. Datiscaceae.**
  23 Ovary mostly plurilocular, with axile placentas, or seldom unilocular with deeply intruded parietal placentas; leaves stipulate; sepals 2–5 . . . . **23. Begoniaceae.**
21 Flowers perfect; ovules unitegmic, tenuinucellar; leaves exstipulate; style solitary; plants commonly producing iridoid compounds (Loasineae) . . . . **24. Loasaceae.**

SELECTED REFERENCES

Aleshina, L. A. 1971. Palinologicheskie dannye k sistematike i filogenii semeystva Cucurbitaceae Juss. V sb.: Morfologiya pyl'tsy Cucurbitaceae, Thymelaeaceae, Cornaceae. L. A. Kuprianova i M. S. Yakovlev, redaktory: 3–103. Izd. Nauka. Leningradskoe Otdelenie. Leningrad.

Ayensu, E. S. & W. L. Stern. 1964. Systematic anatomy and ontogeny of the stem in Passifloraceae. Contr. U.S. Natl. Herb. **34:** 45–73.

Baas, P. 1972. Anatomical contributions to plant taxonomy. II. The affinities of *Hua* Pierre and *Afrostyrax* Perkins et Gilg. Blumea 20: 161–192.

Badillo, V. M. 1971. Monografía de la familia Caricaceae. Publ. Assoc. Prof. Univ. Central de Venezuela. Maracay.

Behnke, H.-D. 1976. Sieve-element plastids of *Fouquieria, Frankenia* (Tamaricales), and *Rhabdodendron* (Rutaceae), taxa sometimes allied with Centrospermae (Caryophyllales). Taxon **25:** 265–268.

Beijersbergen, A. 1972. Note on the chemotaxonomy of Huaceae. Blumea **20:** 160.

Boesewinkel, F. D. 1984. Ovule and seed structure in Datiscaceae. Acta Bot. Neerl. **33:** 419–429.

Brizicky, G. K. 1961. The genera of Turneraceae and Passifloraceae in the southeastern United States. J. Arnold Arbor. **42:** 204–218.

Brizicky, G. K. 1961. The genera of Violaceae in the southeastern United States. J. Arnold Arbor. **42:** 321–333.

Carlquist, S. 1985. Wood anatomy of Begoniaceae, with comments on raylessness, paedomorphosis, relationships, vessel diameter and ecology. Bull. Torrey Bot. Club **112:** 59–69.

Chevalier, A. 1947. La famille de Huacaceae et ses affinités. Rev. Int. Bot. Appl. Agric. Trop. **27**(No. 291–292): 26–29.

Dahlgren, R., S. R. Jensen & J. B. Nielsen. 1976. Iridoid compounds in Fouquieriaceae and notes on its possible affinities. Bot. Not. **129:** 207–212.

Davidson, C. 1976. Anatomy of xylem and phloem of the Datiscaceae. Los Angeles County Mus. Contr. Sci. **280:** 1–28.

DeWilde, W. J. J. O. 1971. The systematic position of the tribe Paropsieae, in particular the genus *Ancistrothyrsus,* and a key to the genera of Passifloraceae. Blumea **19:** 99–104.

DeWilde, W. J. J. O. 1974 (1975). The genera of tribe Passifloreae (Passifloraceae) with special reference to flower morphology. Blumea **22:** 37–50.

Ernst, W. R. & H. J. Thompson. 1963. The Loasaceae in the southeastern United States. J. Arnold Arbor. **44:** 138–142.

Gmelin, R. & A. Kjaer. 1970. Glucosinolates in the Caricaceae. Phytochemistry **9:** 591–593.

Gottwald, H. & N. Parameswaran. 1968. Das sekundäre Xylem und die systematische Stellung der Ancistrocladaceae und Dioncophyllaceae. Bot. Jahrb. Syst. **88:** 49–69.

Henrickson, J. 1972. A taxonomic revision of the Fouquieriaceae. Aliso **7:** 439–537.

Jeffrey, C. 1962. Notes on Cucurbitaceae, including a proposed new classification of the family. Kew Bull. **15:** 337–371.

Jeffrey, C. 1966. On the classification of the Cucurbitaceae. Kew Bull. **20:** 417–426.

Keating, R. C. 1968, 1970, 1972. Comparative morphology of Cochlospermaceae. I. Synopsis of the family and wood anatomy. Phytomorphology **18:** 379–392, 1968. II. Anatomy of the young vegetative shoot. Amer. J. Bot. **57:** 889–898, 1970. III. The flower and pollen. Ann. Missouri Bot. Gard. **59:** 282–296, 1972.

Keating, R. C. 1973. Pollen morphology and relationships of the Flacourtiaceae. Ann. Missouri Bot. Gard. **60:** 273–305.

Keating, R. C. 1976. Trends in specialization in pollen of Flacourtiaceae with comparative observations of Cochlospermaceae and Bixaceae. Grana **15:** 29–49.

Keng, H. 1967. Observations on *Ancistrocladus.* Gard. Bull. Singapore **22:** 113–121.

Kooiman, P. 1974. Iridoid substances in the Loasaceae and the taxonomic position of the family. Acta Bot. Neerl. **23:** 677–679.

Leins, P. & R. Bonnery-Brachtendorf. 1977. Entwicklungsgeschichtliche Untersuchungen an Blüten von *Datisca cannabina* (Datiscaceae). Beitr. Biol. Pflanzen. **53:** 143–155.

Leins, P. & W. Winhard. 1973. Entwicklungsgeschichtliche Studien an Loasaceen-Blüten. Oesterr. Bot. Z. **122:** 145–165.

Marburger, J. E. 1979. Glandular leaf structure of *Triphyophyllum peltatum* (Dioncophyllaceae): A "fly-paper" insect-trapper. Amer. J. Bot. **66:** 404–411.

Merxmüller, H. & P. Leins. 1971. Zur Entwicklungsgeschichte männlicher Begonien-blüten. Flora **160:** 333–339.

Metcalfe, C. R. 1952. The anatomical structure of the Dioncophyllaceae in relation to the taxonomic affinities of the family. Kew Bull. **1951:** 351–368.

Metcalfe, C. R. 1956. *Scyphostegia borneensis* Stapf. Anatomy of stem and leaf in relation to its taxonomic position. Reinwardtia **4:** 99–104.

Miller, R. B. 1975. Systematic anatomy of the xylem and comments on the relationships of the Flacourtiaceae. J. Arnold Arbor. **56:** 20–102.

Poppendieck, H.-H. 1981. Cochlospermaceae. Fl. Neotropica Monogr. 27.

Prance, G. T. & M. Freitas da Silva. 1973. Caryocaraceae. Fl. Neotropica Monogr. 12.

Presting, D. 1965. Zur Morphologie der Pollenkörner der Passifloraceen. Pollen & Spores **7**: 193–247.

Puri, V. 1947, 1948, 1954. Studies in floral anatomy. IV. Vascular anatomy of the flower of certain species of the Passifloraceae. Amer. J. Bot. **34**: 562–573, 1947. V. On the structure and nature of the corona in certain species of the Passifloraceae. J. Indian Bot. Soc. **27**: 130–149, 1948. VII. On placentation in the Cucurbitaceae. Phytomorphology **4**: 278–299, 1954.

Rao, V. S. 1969. The floral anatomy of *Ancistrocladus*. Proc. Indian Acad. Sci. B **70**: 215–222.

Rehm, S., P. R. Enslin, A. D. J. Meeuse & J. Wessels. 1957. Bitter principles of the Cucurbitaceae. VII. The distribution of bitter principles in this plant family. J. Sci. Food Agric. **12**: 679–686.

Schmid, R. 1964. Die systematische Stellung der Dioncophyllaceen. Bot. Jahrb. Syst. **83**: 1–56.

Sleumer, H. O. 1980. Flacourtiaceae. Fl. Neotropica Monogr. 22.

Spencer, K. C. & D. S. Seigler. 1984. Cyanogenic glycosides of *Carica papaya* and its phylogenetic position with respect to the Violales and Capparales. Amer. J. Bot. **71**: 1444–1447.

Spirlet, M.-L. 1965. Utilisation taxonomique des grains de pollen de Passifloracées. Pollen & Spores **7**: 249–301.

Swamy, B. G. L. 1953. On the floral structure of *Scyphostegia*. Proc. Natl. Inst. Sci. India **19**: 127–142.

van Heel, W. A. 1967. Anatomical and ontogenetic investigations on the morphology of the flowers and fruit of *Scyphostegia borneensis* Stapf (Scyphostegiaceae). Blumea **15**: 107–125.

Vijayaraghavan, M. R. & D. Kaur. 1966. Morphology and embryology of *Turnera ulmifolia* L. and affinities of the family Turneraceae. Phytomorphology **19**: 539–553.

Whalen, M. A. 1987. Wood anatomy of the American frankenias (Frankeniaceae): Systematic and evolutionary implications. Amer. J. Bot. **74**: 1211–1223.

7. Order Salicales

The order consists of the single family Salicaceae, with 2 genera, *Populus* (about 40 species), and *Salix* (perhaps as many as 300 species). The group may be characterized as amentiferous members of the Dilleniidae with parietal placentation and usually more or less numerous ovules and seeds. Other traditional members of the Amentiferae mostly have only one or two ovules per locule; most of these families are here referred to the subclass Hamamelidae.

The wood of Salicaceae is moderately specialized. The vessels have simple perforations, the imperforate tracheary elements have small, mostly simple pits, and the wood-rays are uniseriate.

If one extrapolates backward from the Salicaceae to the hypothetical ancestral type with small but complete flowers, numerous stamens, and a several-carpellate ovary with parietal placentation and separate styles, one arrives at a group that might reasonably be included in the Violales, near the Flacourtiaceae. The Flacourtiaceae have indeed often been cited as possible or probable allies of the Salicaceae, and Takhtajan emphasizes that *Idesia* and related genera of the Flacourtiaceae are particularly suggestive of the Salicaceae. It is interesting and perhaps significant that salicin, which is widespread in the Salicaceae, also occurs in *Idesia* and a few other Flacourtiaceae but is known almost nowhere else. Furthermore, *Idesia* and the Salicaceae play host to similar rust fungi belonging to the genus *Melampsora*. The small family Stachyuraceae may also be mentioned as possibly standing near to the ancestry of the Salicaceae.

Fossil leaves credibly considered to represent the genus *Salix* occur in Eocene deposits in North Dakota, but identifiable salicaceous pollen dates only to the Oligocene.

SELECTED REFERENCES

Fisher, M. J. 1928. The morphology and anatomy of the flowers of the Salicaceae. Amer. J. Bot. **15:** 307–326, 372–394.
Holm, L. 1969. An uredinological approach to some problems in angiosperm taxonomy. Nytt. Mag. Bot. **16:** 147–150.
Maliutina, E. T. 1972. O morfologicheskoy prirode chastey tsvetka nekotorykh vidov roda *Salix* L. i vozmozhnye puti ikh evoliutsii. Bot. Zh. **57:** 524–530.
Meeuse, A. D. J. 1975. Taxonomic relationships of Salicaceae and Flacourtiaceae. Acta Bot. Neerl. **24:** 437–457.
Rowley, J. R. & G. Erdtman. 1967. Sporoderm in *Populus* and *Salix*. Grana Palynol. **7:** 517–567.

8. Order Capparales

The order Capparales as here defined consists of 5 families and nearly 4000 species. By far the largest family is the Brassicaceae, with about 3000 species. Next come the Capparaceae, with about 800. The other three families have fewer than a hundred species in all. The Papaveraceae and Fumariaceae, often in the past associated with the Capparales in a collective order Rhoeadales, are here treated as a distinct order Papaverales in the subclass Magnoliidae. The numerous features that require this separation are discussed under the Papaverales.

The most characteristic feature of the Capparales is the production of one or another sort of mustard-oil. Mustard-oils are isothiocyanates, mostly derived by hydrolysis of glucosinolates through the intervention of the enzyme myrosin. Tyically the myrosin is stored in scattered idioblasts called myrosin-cells. In some taxa only the guard-cells contain myrosin.

In addition to the Capparales, mustard-oils are known in a thin scattering of other groups, a little more than 300 species in all. These are the Bataceae and Gyrostemonaceae (collectively making up the order Batales), Limnanthaceae and Tropaeolaceae (both in the Geraniales), *Bretschnei-*

dera and *Akania* (Sapindales), some Salvadoraceae (Celastrales), *Drypetes* (Euphorbiaceae), and some of the Caricaceae (Violales). Thus 7 orders, in 2 subclasses, contain at least some members that produce mustard-oils. There may be a chemical relationship between the unusual method of cyanogenesis in the Violales and the production of mustard-oils by the Capparales.

One may reasonably speculate that there is a functional correlation between the presence of mustard-oils in the Capparales and the absence or restricted occurrence of other repellents such as tannins, alkaloids, and iridoid compounds. Such specialization in repellents is of course an invitation to the evolution of specialized groups of predators that can tolerate (and may even require) the critical substances. Possibly the cabbage-butterflies represent such a group. The white rusts of crucifers may also be especially adapted to mustard-oil. On the other hand, mustard-oils evidently do not discourage herbarium-beetles, which feed happily on crucifers as well as on a wide range of families in other orders.

Aside from the mustard-oils and some obvious features of habit, most of the characters that mark the families of Capparales and the order as a whole are of doubtful selective significance. Standard evolutionary theory would seem to require that the replum has some adaptive value, and that the difference in the replum between the Capparaceae and Brassicaceae must also be adaptive, but I can not come up with a plausible explanation. What difference does it make to members of the two families whether the replum has a partition or not? How does the gynophore of the Capparaceae confer any advantage or help fit the plants to any particular habitat? What is the value to the Resedaceae in having the ovary open at the top, so that the ovules are exposed? Obviously all these variations in structure function well enough to permit the plants to survive and reproduce and carry on their own kind through long periods of time. But why change? It does not appear that the changes have opened up any new or better way of exploiting the habitat, or enabled the plants to occupy any previously unavailable territory, or given them any advantage in the competition for scarce resources. My imagination is inadequate to the task of providing a Darwinian interpretation.

It is now generally believed that the Capparaceae stand near the base of the order Capparales, and that the Capparales are allied to the Violales and Theales. Some authors, such as Takhtajan, see a close relationship of the Capparaceae to the Flacourtiaceae. This may well be correct, but I believe that the phyletic connection between these two families (and their respective orders) lies in their common origin in the Theales.

As in other groups with centrifugal stamens, it is still an open question whether the fascicled stamens of the Capparaceae represent a stage in androecial reduction or a secondary increase in the number of stamens. I incline toward the former interpretation. It is likewise debatable whether the few Capparaceae with a plurilocular ovary are primitive or secondary in this regard. I incline toward the view that they are primitive. On the other hand, numbers of 6 or more sepals, petals, and carpels may well reflect a secondary increase, as several authors have supposed.

The gynoecium of the Brassicaceae is unique, although species in which the partition fails to develop compare closely with some of the Capparaceae. The morphology of the cruciferous gynoecium has occasioned much controversy and is still not settled to the satisfaction of all concerned. I prefer the 2-carpellary interpretation of Puri (1941). The cruciferous gynoecium is surely homologous with the gynoecium of those Capparaceae that have a replum but lack a partition, and there is no reason to suppose that these latter genera are anything but bicarpellate as they appear to be.

Botanists are agreed that the Brassicaceae are related to the Capparaceae but more advanced in at least some respects. The nature of the connection, however, is debatable. I am not enthusiastic about the possibility of a close relationship between *Stanleya* (Brassicaceae) and *Cleome* (Capparaceae), which has been postulated by some authors.

Fossils thought to represent the Capparaceae date from the Eocene, whereas the more advanced family Brassicaceae dates only from the Oligocene, on present evidence.

SYNOPTICAL ARRANGEMENT OF THE FAMILIES OF CAPPARALES

1 Seeds with fairly well developed endosperm; ovary plurilocular, with typically 6 carpels and proliferating axile placentas; sepals, petals, and stamens mostly 8 each; coarse herbs or soft shrubs with trifoliolate leaves ....
.... **1. Tovariaceae.**
1 Seeds with very scanty or no endosperm; placentas parietal (sometimes intruded), only very rarely axile (or in one small genus of Resedaceae the carpels distinct).
  2 Stigma 1, capitate or slightly lobed, usually elevated above the ovary on a style; ovary closed.
    3 Flowers hypogynous or seldom slightly perigynous, regular or somewhat irregular; sepals (2–) 4 (–6); petals (0–) 4 (–6); carpels 2 (–12); fruit very often with a definite replum.
      4 Ovary and fruit typically unilocular with parietal (sometimes intruded) placentas, or rarely plurilocular with axile placentas, only very rarely cross-partitioned by a septum; stamens 4–many, but never tetradynamous; flowers generally with an evident gynophore or androgynophore; pollen-grains mostly binucleate; leaves simply or trifoliolate or palmately compound, but not much dissected; shrubs, or less often herbs or trees, most species tropical or subtropical .....
.... **2. Capparaceae.**
      4 Ovary and fruit nearly always cross-partitioned by a septum; placentas parietal; stamens 6 and usually tetradynamous (the 2 outer shorter than the 4 inner), seldom fewer or more numerous; flowers only seldom with a gynophore, and never with an androgynophore; pollen-grains mostly trinucleate; leaves simple to often pinnately more or less dissected, only seldom with definite leaflets; herbs, very seldom shrubs, most species of temperate or warm-temperate or boreal regions .... **3. Brassicaceae.**
    3 Flowers perigynous, irregular; sepals, petals, and functional stamens 5

each; carpels (2) 3 (4); no replum; trees with pinnately decompound
leaves and definite leaflets . . . . **4. Moringaceae.**
2 Stigmas as many as the carpels, sessile and well separated; ovary usually
open at the top; flowers irregular; sepals 4–8; carpels (2) 3–6 (7); no replum;
herbs or seldom shrubs, with entire to deeply pinnatifid leaves . . . .
. . . . **5. Resedaceae.**

Selected References

Abdallah, M. S. & H. C. D. de Wit. 1967, 1978. The Resedacae. A taxonomic
revision of the family. Belmontia, New Series, **8(26A & B):** 1–416 + 91 figs.
(Pp. 1–98, figs. 1–17, 1967; pp. 99–416, figs. 18–91, 1978.)

Alexander, I. 1952. Entwicklungsstudien an Blüten von Cruciferen und Papaveraceen. Planta **41:** 125–144.

Behnke, H.-D. 1977. Dilatierte ER-Zisternen, ein micromorphologisches Merkmal der Capparales? Ber. Deutsch. Bot. Ges. **90:** 241–251.

Dvorak, F. 1971. On the evolutionary relationship in the family Brassicaceae.
Feddes Repert. **82:** 357–372.

Dvorak, F. 1973. The importance of the indumentum for the investigation of
evolutional relationships in the family Brassicaceae. Oesterr. Bot. Z. **121:**
155–164.

Ernst, W. R. 1963. The genera of Capparaceae and Moringaceae in the southeastern United States. J. Arnold Arbor. **44:** 81–95.

Feeny, P. 1977. Defensive ecology of the Cruciferae. Ann. Missouri Bot. Gard.
64: 221–234.

Frohne, D. 1962. Das Verhältnis von vergleichender Serobotanik zu vergleichender Phytochemie, dargestellt an serologischen Untersuchungen im Bereich der "Rhoeadales." Pl. Med. **10:** 283–297.

Iltis, H. H. 1957. Studies in the Capparidaceae. III. Evolution and phylogeny
of the western North American Cleomoideae. Ann. Missouri Bot. Gard. **44:**
77–119.

Janchen, E. 1942. Das Systeme der Cruciferen. Oesterr. Bot. Z. **91:** 1–28.

Jørgensen, L. B. 1981. Myrosin cells and dilated cysternae of the endoplasmic
reticulum in the order Capparales. Nordic J. Bot. **1:** 433–445.

Leins, P. & G. Metzenauer. 1979. Entwicklungsgeschichtliche Untersuchungen
an *Capparis*-Blüten. Bot. Jahrb. Syst. **100:** 542–554.

Leins, P. & U. Sobick. 1977. Die Blütenentwicklung von *Reseda lutea.* Bot.
Jahrb. Syst. **98:** 133–149.

Puri, V. 1941. Life-history of *Moringa oleifera* Lamk. J. Indian Bot. Soc. **20:**
263–284.

Puri, V. 1941, 1942, 1950. Studies in floral anatomy. I. Gynaeceum constitution
in the Cruciferae. Proc. Indian Acad. Sci. B **14:** 166–187, 1941. II. Floral
anatomy of the Moringaceae with special reference to gynaeceum constitution. Proc. Natl. Inst. Sci. India **8:** 71–88, 1942. VI. Vascular anatomy of the
flower of *Crataeva religiosa* Forst., with special reference to the nature of the
carpels in the Capparidaceae. Amer. J. Bot. **37:** 363–370, 1950.

Puri, V. 1952. Floral anatomy in relation to taxonomy. Agra. Univ. J. Res., Sci.
1: 15–35.

Sobick, U. 1983. Blütenentwicklungsgeschichtliche Untersuchungen an Resedaceen unter besonderer Berücksichtigung von Androeceum und Gynoeceum. Bot. Jahrb. Syst. **104:** 203–248.

Vaughan, J. G., A. J. McLeod & B. M. G. Jones (eds.). 1976. The biology and chemistry of the Cruciferae. Academic Press. London, New York, San Francisco.

9. Order Batales

The order Batales as here defined consists of 2 small families, the Bataceae and Gyrostemonaceae, only 6 genera and about 19 species in all. They may be simply characterized as dicotyledons with mustard-oils and a solid exine. They are woody plants with small, unisexual flowers that are sometimes borne in catkins.

Both families have often been included in or associated with the Caryophyllales, but they differ from the Caryophyllales in their solid exine, in their very ordinary, S-type sieve-tube plastids, in having mustard-oils, and in lacking both betalains and anthocyanins. As long ago as 1965, before the chemical features and the sieve-tube plastids had been studied, Kuprianova emphasized external pollen-morphology in assigning the Gyrostemonaceae to the Batales along with *Batis.*

The most likely place for the Batales is in the Dilleniidae, alongside the Capparales. Inclusion of the Batales in the Dilleniidae brings no important new character to the subclass, except for the solid exine of the pollen-grains, which would be equally anomalous in all the other subclasses except the Magnoliidae.

Pollen considered to represent *Batis* is known from Maestrichtian deposits in California. Thus the Batales, on the record, appear to be as old as any identifiable order in either the Dilleniidae or the Caryophyllidae.

SYNOPTICAL ARRANGEMENT OF THE FAMILIES OF BATALES

1 Leaves alternate; stamens 6–many; placentation axile; ovary with (1–) usually more or less numerous carpels and as many locules; fruit dry, dehiscent or less often indehiscent; seeds with endosperm . . . . 1. Gyrostemonaceae.
1 Leaves opposite; stamens 4; placentation parietal-basal; ovary with 2 carpels and 4 locules; fruit drupaceous, with 4 pyrenes; seeds without endosperm . . . . 2. Bataceae.

SELECTED REFERENCES

Behnke, H.-D. 1977. Phloem ultrastructure and systematic position of Gyrostemonaceae. Bot. Not. **130:** 255–260.

Behnke, H.-D. 1977. Zur Skulptur der Pollen-Exine bei Centrospermen (*Gisekia, Limeum, Hectorella*), bei Gyrostemonaceen und Rhabdodendraceen. Pl. Syst. Evol. **128:** 227–235.

Behnke, H.-D. & B. L. Turner. 1971. On specific sieve-tube plastids in Caryophyllales. Further investigations with special reference to the Bataceae. Taxon **20:** 731–737.

Carlquist, S. 1978. Wood anatomy and relationships of Bataceae, Gyrostemonaceae, and Stylobasiaceae. Allertonia **1**: 297–330.

Eckardt, Th. 1959 (1960). Das Blütendiagramm von *Batis* P. Br. Ber. Deutsch.
Bot. Ges. **72**: 411–418.

Eckardt, Th. 1971. Anlegung und Entwicklung der Blüten von *Gyrostemon
ramulosus* Desf. Bot. Jahrb. Syst. **90**: 434–446.

Goldblatt, P., J. W. Nowicke, T. J. Mabry & H.-D. Behnke. 1976. Gyrostemonaceae: Status and affinity. Bot. Not. **129**: 201–206.

Kuprianova, L. A. 1965. Palinologiya serezhkotsvetnykh. Izd. Nauka. Moskva-
Leningrad.

Mabry, T. J. & B. L. Turner. 1964. Chemical investigations of the Batidaceae.
Taxon **13**: 197–200.

Prijanto, B. 1970. Gyrostemonaceae. World Pollen Flora **2**: 1–12.

Prijanto, B. 1970. Batidaceae. World Pollen Flora **3**: 1–11.

10. Order Ericales

The order Ericales as here defined consists of 8 families and about 4000
species. About seven-eighths of the species belong to the Ericaceae (3500),
and most of the remainder to the Epacridaceae (400). The other six families have only a little over a hundred species in all.

Most of the members of the Ericales have a long series of embryological
features in common, as enumerated in the synoptical arrangement of
orders of the Dilleniidae. Most of these features are subject to some
exception, and most or all of them occur in certain other orders. It is the
combination of features, rather than any one, that distinguishes the bulk
of the Ericales from other orders. The Ericales are also noteworthy for
progressively more obligate mycotrophy, culminating in the Monotropaceae, which lack chlorophyll and depend on their mycorrhiza for nour-
ishment. Some of the Monotropaceae are in effect parasites once removed,
since their mycorrhizal fungus also penetrates the roots of trees and thus
acts as a bridge for the transfer of nutrients.

The mutual affinity among the Ericaceae, Pyrolaceae, Monotropaceae,
Epacridaceae, and Clethraceae has for many years been evident to all,
and a consensus that the Empetraceae also belong to the group now seems
firmly established. A similar consensus about the Cyrillaceae seems to be
developing, although they are admittedly somewhat removed from the
other families. The position of the Grubbiaceae is more debatable.

In addition to the 8 families here assigned to the Ericales, Takhtajan
refers the Actinidiaceae (together with the segregate family Saurauiaceae)
to the Ericales. This is defensible on grounds of evolutionary relationships,
but it complicates the morphologic definition of the order and is in my
opinion unnecessary. The Actinidiaceae would be aberrant in the Ericales
in their numerous stamens, in their cymose inflorescences, and in having
raphides. All of these features can easily be accommodated in the Theales.
As Takhtajan points out, the Actinidiaceae are closely related to the
Theaceae as well as to the Clethraceae and other Ericales.

Pollen considered to represent the Ericales dates from the Maestrichtian. Some of these early fossil grains are considered to belong to the Cyrillaceae, and others to the Clethraceae–Ericaceae–Epacridaceae complex of families. Fossil seeds attributed to *Rhododendron* and *Vaccinium* have been found in Paleocene deposits in England.

SYNOPTICAL ARRANGEMENT OF THE FAMILIES OF ERICALES

1 Embryo normally developed, with 2 cotyledons; plants more or less woody, always chlorophyllous.
  2 Pollen-grains in monads; petals, when present, distinct or only very shortly connate at the base.
    3 Ovary superior; sepals 5 (–7); petals as many as the sepals; carpels 2–5; leaves alternate.
      4 Ovules 1–3 per locule; intrastaminal nectary-disk present; fruit indehiscent, though often capsule-like in appearance; seed-coat none . . . . **1. Cyrillaceae.**
      4 Ovules numerous; nectary-disk wanting, although the basal part of the ovary is sometimes nectariferous; fruit a loculicidal capsule; seed-coat present, consisting of a single layer of cells . . . **2. Clethraceae.**
    3 Ovary inferior; sepals 4; petals none; carpels 2; leaves opposite . . . . **3. Grubbiaceae.**
  2 Pollen-grains mostly in tetrads, but if in monads or pseudomonads, then the corolla evidently sympetalous; petals, when present, very often united to form a sympetalous corolla.
    5 Perianth weakly or scarcely differentiated into calyx and corolla, consisting of 3–6 separate, distinct members arranged in 1 or 2 cycles; ovules solitary in each locule; many or all of the flowers generally unisexual . . . . **4. Empetraceae.**
    5 Perianth clearly differentiated into calyx and corolla, usually with more than 3 (typically 5) members in each of the 2 cycles, the corolla sympetalous or seldom polypetalous.
      6 Stamens mostly of the same number as the corolla-lobes, often attached to the corolla-tube; anthers mostly bisporangiate, monothecal, and opening by a single longitudinal slit, not appendiculate, or seldom with a single appendage; leaves mostly with palmate or nearly parallel venation . . . . **5. Epacridaceae.**
      6 Stamens mostly twice as many as the corolla-lobes (or petals), seldom of the same number or more than twice as many, usually free from the corolla-tube or attached only at its very base; anthers tetrasporangiate and dithecal, inverted and opening by a pair of pores at the apparent apex, or by more or less elongate slits extending downward from it, only rarely opening longitudinally for their whole length, often provided with 2 (or more) slender appendages; leaves pinnately veined, or seldom pinnipalmately plinerved . . . . **6. Ericaceae.**
1 Embryo very small and undifferentiated, without cotyledons; herbs or (*Chimaphila*, in the Pyrolaceae) half-shrubs, often without chlorophyll.
  7 Plants usually with green leaves; anthers opening by seemingly apical pores; pollen-grains usually in tetrads; petals separate . . . . **7. Pyrolaceae.**
  7 Plants without chlorophyll, the leaves reduced to mere scales; anthers generally opening by elongate, usually longitudinal slits, or rarely by seemingly apical pores; pollen-grains in monads; petals separate or united (or wanting) . . . . **8. Monotropaceae.**

SELECTED REFERENCES

Böcher, T. W. 1981. Evolutionary trends in Ericalean leaf structure. Kongel. Danske Vidensk.-Selsk. Biol. Skr. **23(2):** 1–64.
Carlquist, S. 1977. A revision of Grubbiaceae. J. S. African Bot. **43:** 115–128.
Carlquist, S. 1978. Vegetative anatomy and systematics of Grubbiaceae. Bot. Not. **131:** 117–126.
Copeland, H. F. 1941. Further studies on Monotropoideae. Madroño **6:** 97–119.
Copeland, H. F. 1943. A study, anatomical and taxonomic, of the genera of Rhododendroideae. Amer. Midl. Naturalist **30:** 533–625.
Copeland, H. F. 1947. Observations on the structure and classification of the Pyroleae. Madroño **9:** 65–102.
Copeland, H. F. 1953. Observations on the Cyrillaceae particularly on the reproductive structures of the North American species. Phytomorphology **3:** 405–411.
Copeland, H. F. 1954. Observations on certain Epacridaceae. Amer. J. Bot. **41:** 215–222.
Fagerlind, F. 1947. Die systematische Stellung der Familie Grubbiaceae. Svensk Bot. Tidskr. **41:** 315–320.
Giebel, K. P. & W. C. Dickison. 1976. Wood anatomy of Clethraceae. J. Elisha Mitchell Sci. Soc. **92:** 17–26.
Hagerup, O. 1946. Studies on the Empetraceae. Biol. Meddel. Kongel. Danske Vidensk. Selsk. **20(5):** 1–49.
Hara, N. 1958. Structure of the vegetative shoot apex and development of the leaf in the Ericaceae and their allies. J. Fac. Sci. Univ. Tokyo, Sec. 3, Bot. **7:** 367–450.
Leins, P. 1964. Entwicklungsgeschichtliche Studien an Ericales-Blüten. Bot. Jahrb. Syst. **83:** 57–88.
Luteyn, J. L. 1983. Ericaceae Part I. *Cavendishia.* Fl. Neotropica Monogr. 35.
Nowicke, J. W. 1966. Pollen morphology and classification of the Pyrolaceae and Monotropaceae. Ann. Missouri Bot. Gard. **53:** 213–219.
Palser, B. F. 1951–1967. Studies of floral morphology in the Ericales. I. Bot. Gaz. **112:** 447–485, 1951. II. Bot. Gaz. **114:** 33–52, 1952. III. Phytomorphology **4:** 335–354, 1954. IV. Trans. Illinois Acad. Sci. **51:** 24–34, 1958. V. Bot. Gaz. **123:** 79–111, 1961. VII, with P. S. Ganapathy. Bot. Gaz. **125:** 280–297, 1964. VIII, with Y. S. Murty. Bull. Torrey Bot. Club **94:** 243–320, 1967.
Paterson, B. R. 1961. Studies of floral morphology in the Epacridaceae. Bot. Gaz. **122:** 259–279.
Sleumer, H. 1967. Monographia Clethracearum. Bot. Jahrb. Syst. **87:** 36–175.
Stevens, P. F. 1971. A classification of the Ericaceae: Subfamilies and tribes. J. Linn. Soc., Bot. **64:** 1–53.
Thomas, J. L. 1960. A monographic study of the Cyrillaceae. Contr. Gray Herb. **186:** 1–114.
Thomas, J. L. 1961. The genera of Cyrillaceae and Clethraceae of the southeastern United States. J. Arnold Arbor. **42:** 96–106.
Veillet-Bartoszewska, M. 1963. Recherches embryogéniques sur les Ericales. Comparaison avec les Primulales. Rev. Gén. Bot. **70:** 141–230.

Wallace, G. D. 1975a. Studies of the Monotropoideae (Ericaceae): Taxonomy and distribution. Wasm. J. Biol. **33:** 1–88.

Wallace, G. D. 1975b. Interrelationships of the subfamilies of the Ericaceae and the derivation of the Monotropoideae. Bot. Not. **128:** 286–298.

Watson, L. 1965. The taxonomic significance of certain anatomical variations among Ericaceae. J. Linn. Soc., Bot. **59:** 111–125.

Watson, L. 1967. Taxonomic implications of a comparative anatomical study of Epacridaceae. New Phytol. **66:** 495–504.

Wood, C. E. 1961. The genera of Ericaceae in the southeastern United States. J. Arnold Arbor. **42:** 10–80.

11. Order Diapensiales

The order Diapensiales consists of the single family Diapensiaceae, with only 18 species, found mostly in Arctic and North Temperate regions. The group may be briefly characterized as herbaceous or suffrutescent Dilleniidae with unitegmic, tenuinucellar ovules and with the stamens attached to the corolla-tube alternate with its lobes.

The Diapensiaceae have often been included in the Ericales, but they differ from typical members of that order in a rather long list of embryological and androecial characters. In spite of the differences, however, the two orders may well be related. The unitegmic, tenuinucellar ovules and integumentary tapetum suggest that the Diapensiales belong either with the Asteridae or with the more advanced orders of Dilleniidae. The frequent presence of a set of staminodes in addition to the functional stamens suggests that the group would be more at home among the advanced Dilleniidae than among the Asteridae. That leads us back to the Ericales as the most likely allies, and it may be significant that two genera of the Diapensiales have appendages on the anthers that resemble those of some of the Ericales. It seems probable that the two orders have a common ancestry in the Theales.

The adaptive significance of the characters that mark the Diapensiales is dubious.

SELECTED REFERENCES

Palser, B. F. 1963. Studies of floral morphology in the Ericales. VI. The Diapensiaceae. Bot. Gaz. **124:** 200–219.

Wood, C. E. & R. B. Channell. 1959. The Empetraceae and Diapensiaceae of southeastern United States. J. Arnold Arbor. **40:** 161–171.

12. Order Ebenales

The order Ebenales as here defined consists of 5 families and about 2000 species, chiefly of tropical and subtropical regions. The largest family is the Sapotaceae, with about 1100 species, followed by the Ebenaceae, with about 450. The order may be briefly characterized as woody Dilleniidae with sympetalous flowers that have one or more cycles of stamens, with at least one cycle opposite the corolla-lobes, and in which the ovary is plurilocular with axile placentation and one to few ovules per locule.

Most authors are agreed that the Ebenales as here constituted form a natural group, and there is a developing consensus that the group takes its origin in the Theales. The Ebenales also resemble the Ericales in some respects, but the relationship here is collateral rather than lineal. The Ebenales are more advanced than the bulk of the Ericales in the reduced number of ovules and in having the stamens attached to the corolla-tube, and also in having only a very few polypetalous members, but so far as known they lack the set of specialized embryological features that mark the Ericales. The bitegmic ovules of the Ebenaceae and Styracaceae are not likely to have been derived from the unitegmic ovules of the Ericales. The two orders may be regarded as having undergone certain parallel and other divergent changes from a common ancestry in the Theales.

Aside from the features associated with secondary metabolites, there is nothing ecologically outstanding about the Ebenales or any of the included families. They are all woody and chiefly tropical, but these are typical angiospermous features. The differences in fruit-type that characterize some of the families are obviously related to seed-dispersal, but none of the families has any special adaptation for seed-dispersal that is not well known in other groups as well. The exserted water-cells of the leaves of Symplocaceae are curious, but their functional significance remains to be elucidated. The importance of the differences in pubescence, nodal anatomy, and ovular structure is equally obscure, and if the genes governing these characters are important for other effects, the nature of these other effects is still wholly unknown.

In contrast to the classical morphological characters, the latex of the Sapotaceae and the naphthaquinones of the Ebenaceae are good candidates for interpretation in terms of survival value. Both probably discourage attacks by insects or other predators. The accumulation of aluminum in the Symplocaceae may also have a protective function. The tannins found throughout the order are presumably also protective, but so far as I know there is nothing distinctive about them as compared to the tannins of many other orders.

No one family of the Ebenales is likely to be directly ancestral to any of the others. Each has a combination of relatively primitive and more advanced features that bespeaks collateral relationships with the other families.

Fossil pollen attributed to the Sapotaceae and Symplocaceae dates from the Maestrichtian stage of the Upper Cretaceous, and fruits of Symplocaceae date from the Lower Eocene. Upper Cretaceous leaves attributed to the Ebenaceae need confirmation; leaves, flowers, and pollen clearly referable to this family date from the Eocene.

Synoptical Arrangement of the Families of Ebenales

1 Plants with a well developed latex-system; pubescence of 2-armed (malpighian) hairs (one arm sometimes reduced or obsolete); nodes mostly trilacunar; vessels with simple perforations; ovules unitegmic .... **1. Sapotaceae.**

1 Plants without a latex-system; pubescence not of 2-armed hairs except in some Ebenaceae; nodes unilacunar (nodal anatomy of Lissocarpaceae unknown).
2 Flowers mostly unisexual, rarely perfect; styles more or less deeply cleft, or the styles almost distinct; vessels with simple perforations; ovules bitegmic
   .... **2. Ebenaceae.**
2 Flowers mostly perfect, rarely unisexual; style simple with a capitate or merely lobed stigma; vessels with scalariform perforations, or (Lissocarpaceae) some of the perforations scalariform and others simple.
3 Pubescence characteristically of stellate hairs or peltate scales; fruit mostly dry, seldom fleshy; stamens all in a single series; ovary superior to inferior; anthers more or less linear; ovules bitegmic or unitegmic ..
   .... **3. Styracaceae.**
3 Pubescence neither of stellate hairs nor of peltate scales, sometimes wanting; fruit more or less fleshy; ovary inferior, or seldom only half-inferior.
4 Anthers linear; flowers with a corona; stamens 8, twice as many as the corolla-lobes, all in a single series .... **4. Lissocarpaceae.**
4 Anthers broadly ovate or rotund; flowers without a corona; stamens (4–) 12 to rather numerous, in more than one series, or grouped into fascicles; ovules unitegmic .... **5. Symplocaceae.**

SELECTED REFERENCES

Baehni, C. 1938, 1965. Mémoires sur les Sapotacées. I. Système de classification. Candollea **7**: 394–508, 1938. III. Inventaire des genres. Boissiera **11**: 1–262, 1965.

Basinger, J. F. & D. C. Christophel. 1985. Fossil flowers and leaves of the Ebenaceae from the Eocene of southern Australia. Canad. J. Bot. **63**: 1825–1843.

Copeland, H. F. 1938. The *Styrax* of northern California and the relationships of the Styracaceae. Amer. J. Bot. **25**: 771–780.

Cronquist, A. 1946. Studies in the Sapotaceae. II. Survey of the North American genera. Lloydia **9**: 241–292. VI. Miscellaneous notes. Bull. Torrey Bot. Club **73**: 465–471.

Dickison, W. C. & K. D. Phend. 1985. Wood anatomy of the Styracaceae: Evolutionary and ecological considerations. IAWA Bull. II, **6**: 3–22.

Kolbe, K.-P. & J. John. 1980. Serology and systematics of the Ebenales and the Theales. Biochem. Syst. Ecol. **8**: 249–256.

Lam, H. J. 1939. On the system of the Sapotaceae, with some remarks on taxonomical methods. Recueil Trav. Bot. Néerl. **36**: 509–525.

Nooteboom, H. P. 1975. Revision of the Symplocaceae of the Old World, New Caledonia excepted. Leiden Bot. Ser. 1.

van den Oever, L., P. Baas & M. Zandoe. 1981. Comparative wood anatomy of *Symplocos* and latitude and altitude of provenance. IAWA Bull. II. **2**: 3–24.

Pennington, T. D. In press. Sapotaceae. Fl. Neotropica Monogr.

Schadel, W. E. & W. C. Dickison. 1979. Leaf anatomy and venation patterns of Styracaceae. J. Arnold Arbor. **60**: 8–27.

White, E. B. 1956–1963. Notes on Ebenaceae. I, II. Bull. Jard. Bot. État **26**:

237–246, 277–307, 1956. III. Bull. Jard. Bot. État **27:** 515–531, 1957. IV. Bol. Soc. Brot. II. **36:** 97–100, 1962. V. Bull. Jard. Bot. État **33:** 345–367, 1963.

Wood, C. E. & R. B. Channell. 1960. The genera of the Ebenales in the southeastern United States. J. Arnold Arbor. **41:** 1–35.

Yamazaki, T. 1970–1972. Embryological studies in Ebenales. 1. Styracaceae. 2. Symplocaceae. 3. Sapotaceae. 4. Ebenaceae. J. Jap. Bot. **45:** 267–273, 353–358, 1970; **46:** 161–165, 1971; **47:** 20–28, 1972.

13. Order Primulales

The order Primulales consists of 3 families and about 1900 species. The Myrsinaceae have about 1000 species, the Primulaceae about 800, and the Theophrastaceae about 100. The mangrove genus *Aegiceras* stands somewhat apart from other Myrsinaceae and has sometimes been taken as a separate family, but its relationships are not in dispute.

The Primulales are sympetalous dicotyledons with the functional stamens opposite the corolla-lobes (with or without an alternating set of staminodes), and with a compound ovary that has a single style and several to numerous tenuinucellar, mostly bitegmic ovules on a free-central or basal placenta. No other group has this combination of characters.

No one family of the Primulales is likely to be directly ancestral to either of the others. The Theophrastaceae are more primitive than the other families in consistently having a set of staminodes in addition to the functional stamens, but they stand between the Myrsinaceae and the Primulaceae in the vascular anatomy of the stem, and their leaf-architecture is specialized in a way unlike either of the other two families. It is uncertain whether the characteristic schizogenous secretory system of the Myrsinaceae is a primitive or an advanced feature in the order. Either way, it is difficult to see a straight-line evolutionary series that is harmonious with the distribution of other characters in the order. Either there has been parallel elaboration, or parallel reduction.

Neither the Primulales nor the Ebenales can be considered ancestral to the other, but they might have a common ancestry just short of the Theales. Such an ancestor would be a tropical tree with hypogynous, sympetalous flowers that have two or three sets of epipetalous stamens, a compound ovary, separate styles, and numerous bitegmic, tenuinucellar ovules on axile placentas. Only the sympetalous condition would be at odds with the characters of the Theales. Alternatively, one could suppose that the Ebenales and Primulales achieved the sympetalous condition independently, in which case the nearest common ancestor would be referable to the Theales. The latter assumption would be more nearly in accord with the results of serological studies by Frohne and John (1978), which suggest a mutual affinity among the Primulales, Theales, and Ericales, and a less close affinity of the Ebenales to these three.

The Primulales as a whole do not appear to be adapted to any particular ecological niche, nor are the characters that mark the order of any obvious selective significance. The features of growth-habit and fruit-type that distinguish the Primulaceae from the other two families are evidently adaptive, but there is nothing distinctive about them as compared with other angiosperms. The differences in the fruits are doubtless correlated with different strategies for seed-dispersal, but there is nothing unusual about these strategies as compared with those of other angiosperms. The biological significance of the staminodes of the Theophrastaceae is obscure. The chemical defenses are doubtless adaptive. The special secretory system of the Myrsinaceae may be unlike anything in any other order, but the chemistry of the compounds remains to be elucidated. All 3 families have triterpenoid saponins, but compounds of these groups occur in other orders as well.

SYNOPTICAL ARRANGEMENT OF THE FAMILIES OF PRIMULALES

1   Plants nearly always woody, often arborescent, largely tropical and subtropical; fruits mostly fleshy, often 1-seeded (even though there are several or many ovules in the ovary).
  2   Flowers with staminodes alternate with the corolla-lobes; plants without an evident secretory system in the stems and leaves, the leaves not gland-dotted; leaves commonly with elongate subepidermal fibers and often with a submarginal fibrous strand .... **1. Theophrastaceae.**
  2   Flowers without staminodes; plants with a well developed schizogenous secretory system in the stem and leaves, the leaves gland-dotted; leaves usually without subepidermal fibers and usually without a submarginal fibrous strand .... **2. Myrsinaceae.**
1   Plants herbaceous or rarely half-shrubby, chiefly of temperate or cold regions or altitudes; fruit dry, mostly capsular, with (1–) several or many seeds ...
  .... **3. Primulaceae.**

SELECTED REFERENCES

Channell, R. B. & C. E. Wood. 1959. The genera of the Primulales of the southeastern United States. J. Arnold Arbor. **40:** 268–288.

Dickson, J. 1936. Studies in floral anatomy. III. An interpretation of the gynaecium in the Primulaceae. Amer. J. Bot. **23:** 385–393.

Frohne, D. & J. John. 1978. The Primulales: Serological contributions to the problem of their systematic position. Biochem. Syst. Ecol. **6:** 315–322.

Roth, I. 1959a. Histogenese und morphologische Deutung der Kronblätter von *Primula*. Bot. Jahrb. Syst. **79:** 1–16.

Roth, I. 1959b. Histogenese und morphologische Deutung der Plazenta von *Primula*. Flora **148:** 129–152.

Sattler, R. 1962. Zur frühen Infloreszenz- und Blütenentwicklung der Primulales sensu lato mit besonderer Berücksichtigung der Stamen-Petalum-Entwicklung. Bot. Jahr. Syst. **81:** 358–396.

Spanowsky, W. 1962. Die Bedeutung der Pollenmorphologie für die Taxonomie der Primulaceae—Primuloideae. Feddes Repert. Spec. Nov. Regni Veg. **65:** 149–214.

Subclass V. Rosidae

The subclass Rosidae as here defined consists of 18 orders (Fig. 6.7), 116 families, and more than 60,000 species. It is the largest subclass of angiosperms, in terms of the number of families, but about the same size as the Asteridae in terms of the number of species. About three-fourths of the species in the Rosidae belong to only 5 large orders: Fabales (18,000), Myrtales (9000), Euphorbiales (8000), Rosales (6600), and Sapindales (5400). The remaining orders have a little more than 15,000 species amongst them.

The 18 orders that make up the Rosidae evidently hang together as a natural group. Only the Euphorbiales and Rafflesiales are obviously debatable, the former because of some similarities to the Malvales in the subclass Dilleniidae, the latter because their morphological reduction in association with parasitism makes their affinities hard to establish.

In general, the Rosidae are more advanced than the Magnoliidae in one or another respect, but less advanced than the Asteridae, and they mostly lack the special features that characterize the Hamamelidae and Caryophyllidae. Those Rosidae that are florally similar to the Hamamelidae are clearly linked to more typical members of their subclass. The Julianiaceae, for example, are obviously related to the Anacardiaceae, in spite of their amentiferous floral organization.

The subclass most likely to be confused with the Rosidae is the Dilleniidae. These are likewise more advanced than the Magnoliidae and less advanced than the Asteridae. Compound leaves with distinct, articulated leaflets are much less common in the Dilleniidae than in the Rosidae. Most of the Dilleniidae are polypetalous (as are the vast majority of the Rosidae), but a considerable number are sympetalous, and some are apetalous or even amentiferous. In contrast to the Rosidae, the Dilleniidae usually have centrifugal stamens (when the stamens are numerous), and only a few families of Dilleniidae (notably the Brassicaceae) have trinucleate pollen. Parietal placentation is common in the Dilleniidae (in contrast to its relative rarity in the Rosidae), but other types are also well represented. Uniovulate or biovulate locules are much less common in the Dilleniidae than in the Rosidae, but are well represented in the Malvales, whose position in the Dilleniidae is well established. Not many of the Dilleniidae have a typical nectary-disk of the sort so common in the Rosidae, but other types of nectaries are common.

In the last analysis, the Rosidae and Dilleniidae are kept apart as subclasses because each seems to constitute a natural group separately derived from the ancestral Magnoliidae, rather than because of any definitive distinguishing characters. The same sorts of evolutionary advances have

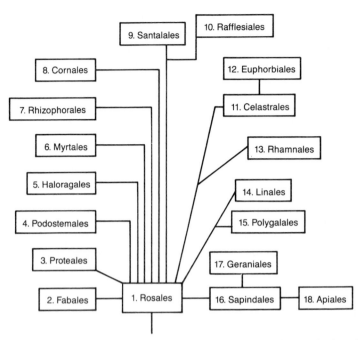

Fig. 6.7. Putative relationships among the orders of Rosidae. Here, as in the other phyletic diagrams, the length of the line between two orders is governed by the requirements of two-dimensional representation and does not indicate closeness of relationship.

occurred in both groups, but with different frequencies. In spite of the lack of solid distinguishing criteria, I believe that it is conceptually more useful to hold the two as separate subclasses than to combine them into one or to abandon any attempt at organization of the Magnoliopsida into subclasses.

The Rosidae are evidently derived from the Magnoliidae, as indicated by the fossil record as well as by comparative morphology. None of the especially primitive characters that we have noted in some of the Magnoliidae is known in the Rosidae. Every significant respect in which any member of the Rosidae differs from the more archaic members of the Magnoliidae appears to be an apomorphy, with the possible exception of the nature of the chemical defenses, on which the phyletic progression among the subclasses is still debatable.

The fossil record suggests that the Rosidae began to diverge from the ancestral Magnoliidae near the middle of the Albian stage of the Lower Cretaceous, as a group with tricolpate pollen and pinnatifid (then compound) leaves. *Sapindopsis* is a good candidate for the earliest recognizable antecedent of the subclass. The implication here is that the pinnate-leaved habit, so common in the Rosidae, is basic to the group, and that modern families of Rosidae with simple leaves have a pinnate ancestry (cf. Hickey & Doyle, 1977, under Magnoliophyta). On the basis of comparative morphology of modern species, there is no doubt that simple leaves have been repeatedly derived from compound leaves in several families of the Rosidae, with unifoliolate compound leaves as an intermediate stage. Extension of this interpretation to all the simple-leaved members of the subclass may seem a bit drastic, but it is entirely compatible with the phyletic arrangement I have proposed for the group. On the other hand, the occurrence of fossil pollen of the Aquifoliaceae in early Upper Cretaceous (Turonian) deposits suggests that simple leaves in the Rosidae have a long evolutionary history.

Two caveats should be entered at this point. One is that in the absence of fossil flowers it is not possible to identify *Sapindopsis* with any modern family or order of Rosidae. Indeed the tricolpate pollen associated with *Sapindopsis* militates against such an identification. In the modern members of the subclass truly tricolpate pollen is relatively rare, and triaperturate types are generally tricolporoidate or tricolporate or triporate. Hickey and Doyle (1977, under Magnoliophyta) consider that the most primitive pollen-type among modern Rosidae is tricolporoidate, and that the few tricolpates in the group are secondary. Tricolporoidate pollen makes its first appearance in the Late Albian, some time after the first appearance of *Sapindopsis* leaves. The second caveat is that these ages are based on fossils of the Potomac Group, which may reflect immigration after a somewhat earlier divergence in Gondwanaland.

The Rosales are the most archaic order of their subclass. All other orders of the Rosidae appear to be derived directly or indirectly from the Rosales, which provide a fine example of a paraphyletic taxon. If the other orders of the subclass were wiped out of existence, the Rosales could be accommodated without great difficulty as a somewhat isolated order of the Magnoliidae. A large proportion of the Rosales are apocarpous, whereas apocarpy is rare in the rest of the group (except for the basically monocarpous orders Fabales and Proteales). On the other hand, the relationship between the Rosales and some of the more advanced orders of the subclass is so obvious, and the difficulty of delimiting these from the Rosales is so great, that it seems necessary to associate the Rosales with their descendants rather than with their collateral ancestors.

Synoptical Arrangement of the Orders of Rosidae

1 Flowers of relatively primitive structure, commonly either apocarpous (with 1–many carpels), or with more or less numerous stamens, often with both of these features; plants never with internal phloem, never parasitic (though sometimes insectivorous) and never highly modified aquatics.
 2 Gynoecium mostly of 2–many carpels, only seldom (but notably in some Connaraceae and in the subfamily Prunoideae of the Rosaceae) of a single carpel, and then the plants not with the special features of the Fabales or Proteales; endosperm variously present or absent . . . . **1. Rosales.**
 2 Gynoecium nearly always of a single carpel; endosperm usually none or scanty, seldom well developed.
  3 Petals usually present; perianth most commonly 5-merous, only seldom

4-merous or of other numbers; stamens most commonly 10, less often 9, seldom fewer or more numerous; leaves mostly compound, seldom simple, mostly stipulate and with a basal pulvinus; fruit of various types, but most commonly dry and dehiscent along both sutures, usually with 2 or more seeds; ovules (1) 2–many .... **2. Fabales.**

3 Petals wanting, or represented only by scales or glands; flowers mostly 4-merous, with not more than 8 stamens; leaves variously simple or compound, but exstipulate and without a pulvinus; fruit of diverse types, very often with only a single seed, dehiscent (if at all) along only one suture; ovules 1–several or seldom many .... **3. Proteales.**

1 Flowers more advanced in one or another respect, mostly syncarpous (seldom pseudomonomerous or with distinct carpels), typically with not more than twice as many stamens as sepals or petals (stamens numerous in some Myrtales—notably the Myrtaceae, which have internal phloem—only rarely numerous in other groups), very often with only 1 or 2 ovules per carpel; plants variously autotrophic or sometimes parasitic, sometimes highly modified aquatics.

4 Stem commonly with internal phloem; flowers usually strongly perigynous or epigynous, often tetramerous, often with numerous stamens and numerous ovules; embryo often of unusual structure, but also often of perfectly ordinary type .... **6. Myrtales.**

4 Stem nearly always without internal phloem; flowers and embryo various.

5 Plants mostly parasitic or hemiparasitic (wholly autotrophic in some Santalales); gynoecium very often unusual in either the number or the arrangement of the ovules, which are often much reduced in structure.

6 Ovules few, commonly 1–8, or up to about 12, often on a free-central or basal placenta, or pendulous from near the summit of a columnar placenta that extends upward beyond the basal partial partitions; seeds solitary, or rarely 2–3; plants with or without chlorophyll .. .. **9. Santalales.**

6 Ovules and seeds very numerous, commonly in the thousands, on parietal, often deeply intruded placentas or in an irregularly plurilocular ovary; plants without chlorophyll ...... **10. Rafflesiales.**

5 Plants (with few exceptions, such as the Krameriaceae) autotrophic.

7 Flowers generally more or less reduced (not very much so in some Euphorbiaceae) and often unisexual, the perianth mostly poorly developed or wanting; styles generally distinct or only basally connate.

8 Endosperm wanting; flowers perfect, hypogynous, generally with numerous ovules; highly modified aquatics .. **4. Podostemales.**

8 Endosperm more or less well developed; flowers with only 1 or 2 ovules per locule, otherwise with very diverse structure; habit various.

9 Flowers epigynous, not grouped into pseudanthia; mostly herbs, often aquatic; no milky juice .... **5. Haloragales.**

9 Flowers hypogynous or naked, often grouped into pseudanthia; herbs, shrubs, or trees, often with milky juice .... **12. Euphorbiales.**

7 Flowers mostly of ordinary type, generally not much reduced except in a few small families such as the Garryaceae and Julianiaceae, very often with a nectary-disk and very often with only one or two ovules per locule; styles distinct, or very often connate for much of their length into a single compound style.

10 Leaves mostly simple and entire or merely toothed, only seldom

pinnatifid (as in *Aralidium,* of the Cornaceae), or compound (as in many of the Vitaceae, order Rhamnales).

11 Flowers epigynous or strongly perigynous, or with such prominently erect-connivent sepals as to appear strongly perigynous.

  12 Ovules bitegmic, 2 (or more) per carpel; leaves stipulate; fruit mostly a berry, seldom a capsule; ovary superior or inferior; plants not known to have iridoid compounds, sometimes of mangrove habit . . . .
. . . .**7. Rhizophorales.**

  12 Ovules unitegmic, one per carpel (2 ovules present in the single locule of the bicarpellate ovary of Garryaceae); leaves nearly always without stipules; fruit usually a drupe, seldom a berry; ovary inferior; plants often producing iridoid compounds, never of mangrove habit .
. . . . **8. Cornales.**

11 Flowers hypogynous, or sometimes half-epigynous or somewhat perigynous.

  13 Flowers regular or nearly so; anthers generally opening by longitudinal slits, only seldom by transverse slits or short distal slits or terminal pores.

    14 Stamens distinct, seldom more than 5; flowers usually with a solitary (sometimes cleft) style, seldom with distinct styles.

      15 Stamens alternate with the petals, or seldom both alternate and opposite the petals . . . .
. . . . **11. Celastrales.**

      15 Stamens opposite the petals . . . **13. Rhamnales.**

    14 Stamens usually connate by their filaments, at least toward the base, often more than 5; styles distinct, or the style sometimes solitary and then variously entire or cleft . . . .**14. Linales.**

  13 Flowers either more or less strongly irregular, or with poricidal anthers, or often both . . . . . **15. Polygalales.**

10 Leaves mostly compound or conspicuously lobed or cleft, only seldom (as in the Balsaminaceae) simple and unlobed.

  16 Ovary superior; pollen-grains binucleate or less often trinucleate.

    17 Plants mostly woody, seldom herbaceous . . . .
. . . . **16. Sapindales.**

    17 Plants mostly herbaceous or nearly so, seldom shrubby or even arborescent . . . .**17. Geraniales.**

  16 Ovary (with the rarest of exceptions) inferior; pollen-grains mostly trinucleate . . . . **18. Apiales.**

Selected References

Heimsch, C. H. 1942. Comparative anatomy of the secondary xylem in the "Gruinales" and "Terebinthales" of Wettstein with reference to taxonomic grouping. Lilloa **8:** 83–198.

Mauritzon, J. 1939. Contributions to the embryology of the orders Rosales and Myrtales. Acta Univ. Lund. N.S. Avd. 2, **35(2):** 1–121.

Rullman, H.-D. 1978. Phytoserologische Untersuchungen zur Gliederung der Geraniales. Dissertation zur Erlangung des Doktorgrades des Fachbereichs Math.-Naturwiss. der Christian-Albrechts-Univ. Kiel.

1. Order Rosales

The order Rosales as here defined consists of 24 families and about 6600 species, widely distributed throughout the world. The Rosaceae, with about 3000 species, are by far the largest family, followed by the Crassulaceae (900) and Saxifragaceae (700). These three well known families together make up about seven-tenths of the order. Another 6 families of moderate size are familiar to botanists generally. These are the Chrysobalanaceae (400), Grossulariaceae (350), Cunoniaceae (350), Connaraceae (350), Pittosporaceae (200), and Hydrangeaceae (170). The remaining small, much less familar families have only about 225 species in all and collectively constitute less than 4% of the order. These are the Bruniaceae (75), Brunelliaceae (50), Anisophylleaceae (40), Neuradaceae (10), Crossosomataceae (8 or 9), Surianaceae (6), Alseuosmiaceae (5), Eucryphiaceae (5), Byblidaceae (4), Columelliaceae (4), Rhabdodendraceae (3), Greyiaceae (3), Cephalotaceae (1), Davidsoniaceae (1), and Dialypetalanthaceae (1).

The Rosales form an exceedingly diverse order, standing at the evolutionary base of their subclass. In effect, they are what is left over after all the more advanced, specialized orders have been delimited. Aside from internal phloem and a parasitic or highly modified aquatic habit, most of the features that mark the more advanced orders of the subclass Rosidae (and indeed even some of the features of the Asteridae) can be found individually within the order Rosales, but in the Rosales these features do not occur in the combinations that mark the more advanced groups. Two characters that are very common in the Rosales are much less common among the other orders of the subclass. These are a polymerous androecium and an apocarpous gynoecium (although the gynoecium is monocarpous in the large order Fabales). Furthermore, a great many of the Rosales have more or less numerous ovules per carpel, and relatively few have only one or two. In contrast, many of the other orders of Rosidae have only one or two ovules per carpel, and most of those that have numerous ovules are well differentiated from the Rosales in other respects.

Despite the diversity of the order, and despite the lability of the critical characters even within some of the larger families, the 24 families all appear to be interrelated. None of the families is notably archaic within the order. Each family has its own combination of relatively primitive and relatively advanced features. The subordinal groupings are, I think, for the most part useful and reasonably in accord with probable phylogenetic relationships, but the Connaraceae may be as closely allied to the Rosineae and even to the Fabales as they are to the Cunoniineae. It would be possible to elevate the 5 suborders here recognized to full ordinal status, but I would be reluctant to see the Rosaceae and Saxifragaceae referred to different orders, and if these two are kept together it is difficult to extricate any of the other suborders. Conceptually I find it more useful to delimit the order broadly and to recognize suborders within it, than to fragment the order and lose sight of the interrelationships among its parts.

The Saxifragaceae have been variously defined in different systems of classification. Engler and his followers took a very broad view, and included not only herbaceous genera but also the woody genera here segregated into the familes Grossulariaceae and Hydrangeaceae. Many recent authors have found the Englerian concept too broad to be useful, and have therefore defined the family more narrowly. As many as 20 different families have been recognized by some authors. The three families here recognized (Saxifragaceae, Grossulariaceae, and Hydrangeaceae) are the smallest number consistent with a logical scheme for the order as a whole.

The herbaceous family Saxifragaceae as here defined may be a relatively recent (Eocene or Oligocene) derivative of the Rosaceae, rather than being closely allied to the Grossulariaceae or Hydrangeaceae. Largely on the basis of presumed evolutionary progression in heteroecious rusts, Savile (1975) thinks that *Astilbe* may be the most archaic member of the Saxifragaceae. *Astilbe* is remarkably similar in aspect and some technical features to the clearly rosaceous genus *Aruncus*.

The relationship of the Crassulaceae to the Saxifragaceae has long been plain for all to see. There is even a transitional genus, *Penthorum* (1–3 spp.) that has variously been included in one or the other family or treated as a separate family Penthoraceae.

It is possible that the Chrysobalanaceae would be more at home in the Theales, as suggested by Tobe and Raven (1984). The bitegmic, tenuinucellar ovules found in the family by these authors support the proposed transfer.

Despite their relatively primitive morphology, the Rosales are not clearly represented in the pre-Tertiary fossil record. Recognizably rosalean pollen dates only from the Eocene. Megafossils of the fairly advanced genus *Rosa* appear in the Paleocene or Eocene of North America, and are widespread by the Oligocene.

Synoptical Arrangement of the Families of Rosales

1 Seeds mostly with more or less well developed (seldom rather scanty) endosperm, or the endosperm wanting in a few Connaraceae and a few Saxifragaceae.
  2 Plants more or less strongly woody, and not succulent (herbaceous only in some Byblidaceae and some Hydrangeaceae).
    3 Leaves mostly pinnately compound or trifoliolate, seldom unifoliolate or simple, mostly stipulate except in Connaraceae (simple but with prominent stipules in Dialypetalanthaceae); flowers mostly hypogynous or only slightly perigynous (epigynous in Dialypetalanthaceae, half-epigynous in a few Cunoniaceae) (Cunoniineae).
      4 Carpels distinct, or united only at the very base, or the carpel solitary; ovules 2 in each carpel, collateral.

5 Leaves opposite or sometimes ternate, with stipules and stipellules; stigma elongate, decurrent on the style ...... **1. Brunelliaceae.**
5 Leaves alternate, without stipules or stipellules; stigma terminal, capitate .... **2. Connaraceae.**
4 Carpels with few exceptions united into a compound ovary with axile placentas; ovules (1) 2–many in each carpel.
   6 Flowers hypogynous or rarely (some Cunoniaceae) half-epigynous; styles as many as the carpels, mostly distinct.
      7 Carpels 4–14 (–18), pluriovulate; stamens numerous; ovules epitropous; flowers solitary, axillary, large, with showy petals ..
         .... **3. Eucryphiaceae.**
      7 Carpels 2 (3–5), (1) 2- to several-ovulate; stamens 8–10, or seldom numerous; ovules mostly apotropous; flowers in various sorts of inflorescences (only seldom solitary and axillary), mostly small, the petals mostly shorter than the sepals, or the petals sometimes wanting .... **4. Cunoniaceae.**
   6 Flowers epigynous, bicarpellate, with a single style and numerous ovules; stamens 16–25 .... **6. Dialypetalanthaceae.**
3 Leaves simple, entire to deeply cleft, exstipulate or nearly so; flowers variously hypogynous to strongly perigynous or epigynous, with united carpels and axile to parietal placentas.
   8 Flowers hypogynous; plants (at least the Pittosporaceae) with well developed schizogenous secretory canals; ovules tenuinucellar, unitegmic at least in Pittosporaceae; leaves alternate, but sometimes closely clustered at the tips of the branches (Pittosporineae).
      9 Leaves without insect-catching hairs; mostly shrubs or trees or woody vines, seldom half-shrubs; endosperm-development nuclear; flowers often with a more or less definite corolla-tube ....
         .... **7. Pittosporaceae.**
      9 Leaves with insect-catching hairs; herbs or half-shrubs; endosperm-development cellular; petals very nearly distinct ....
         ....**8. Byblidaceae.**
   8 Flowers usually half to fully epigynous, or seldom merely perigynous or (Greyiaceae, some Hydrangeaceae) virtually hypogynous; plants without secretory canals (Grossulariineae).
      10 Leaves opposite or seldom whorled, only rarely alternate; ovules unitegmic, tenuinucellar.
         11 Petals distinct; stamens (4–) 8–many; styles various, sometimes as in the next group, but more often as many as the carpels and distinct, or connate below into a common style with distinct stigmatic branches ....**9. Hydrangeaceae.**
         11 Petals shortly connate below; stamens 2; stylé solitary, short and thick, with a merely lobed stigma ....
            .... **10. Columelliaceae.**
      10 Leaves mostly alternate, only seldom opposite; ovules various.
         12 Petals distinct (rarely shortly connate at the base), or sometimes wanting.
            13 Ovules mostly numerous; leaves normally developed, the plants not ericoid in aspect.
               14 Flowers perigynous to more often epigynous; gynoecium of 2–3 (–7) carpels; usually some or all of the vessel-segments with scalariform perforations; imperforate tracheary elements with bordered pits, often septate .... **11. Grossulariaceae.**

      14 Flowers hypogynous; gynoecium of 5 (6) carpels; vessel-segments with simple perforations; imperforate tracheary elements with simple pits, not septate . .
.... **12. Greyiaceae.**
    13 Ovules 1–2 (–8) in each locule of the 2–3-locular (seldom pseudomonomerous) ovary; leaves small, closely set, commonly imbricate, the plants typically of ericoid aspect .... **13. Bruniaceae.**
   12 Petals united below to form a corolla-tube ....
.... **15. Alseuosmiaceae.**
2 Plants either herbaceous, or succulent or both (Saxifragineae).
  15 Plants distinctly succulent; carpels as many as the petals, distinct or united only at the base; flowers hypogynous or seldom slightly perigynous ....**16. Crassulaceae.**
  15 Plants only slightly or not at all succulent; carpels seldom of the same number as the petals, variously distinct or united; flowers almost hypogynous in *Parnassia* (Saxifragaceae), otherwise perigynous to often partly or wholly epigynous.
    16 Carpels 6, distinct, mostly with a single basal ovule; sepals 6; petals none; stamens 12; some of the leaves modified into small pitchers
.... **17. Cephalotaceae.**
    16 Carpels 2–4 (–7), usually more or less united at least below (seldom wholly distinct), and usually with numerous ovules on parietal or axile placentas; flowers mostly 4–5-merous, with 1 or 2 cycles of stamens and usually (not always) with petals; leaves not modified into pitchers .... **18. Saxifragaceae.**
1 Seeds mostly with very scanty or no endosperm (endosperm copious in Crossosomataceae and a few Rosaceae). (Rosineae, except that the Davidsoniaceae belong with the Cunoniineae, and the Anisophylleaceae belong with the Grossulariineae.)
  17 Style or styles not gynobasic, sometimes (some Rosaceae) basiventral, but then the separate carpels usually more than 5.
    18 Flowers hypogynous; gynoecium of 2 carpels united to form a compound, bilocular ovary with distinct styles; leaves very large, pinnately compound; trees .... **5. Davidsoniaceae.**
    18 Flowers perigynous to epigynous; other characters various, but not combined as above.
      19 Stamens mostly 8; ovary inferior, with mostly 4 carpels; woody plants with simple leaves ....**14. Anisophylleaceae.**
      19 Stamens mostly 10 or more, but if less than 10 then the other features not as in the foregoing group.
        20 Seeds arillate, with well developed endosperm; desert shrubs with small leaves .... **21. Crossosomataceae.**
        20 Seeds not arillate, usually with little or no endosperm; plants of various habit and habitat.
          21 Gynoecium apocarpous, or syncarpous with 2–5 styles; stamens usually more than 10, but sometimes as few as 5 or even only 1; flowers perigynous or less often epigynous
.... **19. Rosaceae.**
          21 Gynoecium syncarpous, with 10 styles; stamens 10; flowers epigynous .... **20. Neuradaceae.**
  17 Style or styles gynobasic or basiventral; carpels 1–5, distinct or united only by a common style.
    22 Leaves not punctate; ovules 2 (–5); stigmas short.

23 Flowers with a nectary-disk lining the hypanthium below the stamens; gynoecium ancestrally (and in a few modern species) tricarpellate, with the carpels united only by their common gynobasic style, but 2 of the carpels generally more or less reduced, so that the ovary may appear to be monomerous with a basal style; plants commonly with silica-bodies in some of the cells of the parenchyma and epidermis, and often with some of the cell-walls silicified .... **22. Chrysobalanaceae.**

23 Flowers without a nectary-disk; gynoecium of 1–5 distinct carpels, each with a basiventral style; plants without silica bodies, and the cell walls not silicified .... **23. Surianaceae.**

22 Leaves pellucid-punctate; ovule solitary; stigma long-decurrent on the style; nectary-disk wanting .... **24. Rhabdodendraceae.**

SELECTED REFERENCES

Agababyan, V. Sh. 1964. Evoliutsiya pyl'tsy v poryadkakh Cunoniales i Saxifragales v svyazi c nekotorymi voprosami ikh sistematiki i filogenii. Izv. AN Armyanskoy SSR, Biol. Nauki 17: 59–72.

Bange, G. G. J. 1952. A new family of dicotyledons: Davidsoniaceae. Blumea 7: 293–296.

Bate-Smith, E. C. 1977. Chemistry and taxonomy of the Cunoniaceae. Biochem. Syst. Ecol. 5: 95–105.

Bausch, J. 1938. A revision of the Eucryphiaceae. Kew Bull. Misc. Inform. 1938: 317–349.

Bensel, C. R. & B. F. Palser. 1975. Floral anatomy in the Saxifragaceae sensu lato. I. Introduction, Parnassioideae and Brexioideae. II. Saxifragoideae and Iteoideae. III. Kirengeshomoideae, Hydrangeoideae and Escallonioideae. IV. Baueroideae and conclusions. Amer. J. Bot. 62: 176–185, 661–675, 676–687, 688–694.

Brizicky, G. K. 1961. A synopsis of the genus *Columellia* (Columelliaceae). J. Arnold Arbor. 42: 363–372.

Carlquist, S. 1976. Wood anatomy of Byblidaceae. Bot. Gaz. 137: 35–38.

Carlquist, S. 1976. Wood anatomy of Roridulaceae: Ecological and phylogenetic implications. Amer. J. Bot. 63: 1003–1008.

Carlquist, S. 1978. Wood anatomy of Bruniaceae: Correlations with ecology, phylogeny, and organoography. Aliso 9: 323–364.

Carlquist, S. 1981. Wood anatomy of Pittosporaceae. Allertonia 2: 355–392.

Cuatrecasas, J. 1970. Brunelliaceae. Fl. Neotropica Monogr. 2.

DeBuhr. L. E. 1978. Wood anatomy of *Forsellesia* (*Glossopetalon*) and *Crossosoma* (Crossosomataceae, Rosales). Aliso 9: 179–184.

Dickison, W. C. 1971–1974. Anatomical studies in the Connaraceae. I. Carpels. II. Wood anatomy. III. Leaf anatomy. IV. The bark and young stem. J. Elisha Mitchell Sci. Soc. 87: 77–86, 1971; 88: 120–136, 1972; 89: 121–138, 1973; 166–171, 1973 [1974].

Dickison, W. C. 1975. Floral morphology and anatomy of *Bauera*. Phytomorphology 25: 69–76.

Dickison, W. C. 1975. Leaf anatomy of Cunoniaceae. J. Linn. Soc., Bot. **71:** 275–294.

Dickison, W. C. 1978. Comparative anatomy of Eucryphiaceae. Amer. J. Bot. **65:** 722–735.

Dickison, W. C. 1979. A survey of pollen morphology of the Connaraceae. Pollen & Spores **21:** 31–79.

Dickison, W. C. 1986. Wood anatomy and affinities of the Alseuosmiaceae. Syst. Bot. **11:** 214–221.

Ferguson, I. K. & D. A. Webb. 1970. Pollen morphology in the genus *Saxifraga* and its taxonomic significance. J. Linn. Soc., Bot. **63:** 295–311.

Forero, E. 1983. Connaraceae. Fl. Neotropica Monogr. 36.

Gardner, R. O. 1978. Systematic notes on the Alseuosmiaceae. Blumea **24:** 138–142.

Gelius, L. 1967. Studien zur Entwicklungsgeschichte an Blüten der Saxifragales sensu lato mit besonderer Berücksichtigung des Androeceums. Bot. Jahrb. Syst. **87:** 253–303.

Grund, C. & U. Jensen. 1981. Systematic relationships of the Saxifragales revealed by serological characteristics of seed proteins. Pl. Syst. Evol. **137:** 1–22.

Gutzwiller, M.-A. 1961. Die phylogenetische Stellung von *Suriana maritima* L. Bot. Jahrb. Syst. **81:** 1–49.

Haskins, M. L. & W. J. Hayden. 1987. Anatomy and affinities of *Penthorum.* Amer. J. Bot. **74:** 164–177.

Hideux, M. J. & I. K. Ferguson. 1976. The stereostructure of the exine and its evolutionary significance in Saxifragaceae sensu lato. Pages 327–377 *in* I. K. Ferguson & J. Muller (eds.), The evolutionary significance of the exine. Linn. Soc. Symp. Ser. No. 1. Academic Press. London & New York.

Huber, H. 1963. Die Verwandtschaftsverhältnisse der Rosifloren. Mitt. Bot. Staatssamml. München **5:** 1–48.

Kania, W. 1973. Entwicklungsgeschichtliche Untersuchungen an Rosaceenblüten. Bot. Jahrb. Syst. **93:** 175–246.

Klopfer, K. 1968–1972. Beiträge zur floralen Morphogenese und Histogenese der Saxifragaceae. 1. Die Infloreszens-Entwicklung von *Tellima grandiflora.* 2. Die Blütenentwicklung von *Tellima grandiflora.* 4. Die Blütenentwicklung einiger *Saxifragen*-Arten. 7. *Parnassia palustris* und *Francoa sonchifolia.* Florea B **157:** 461–476, 1968; **158:** 1–21, 1969; **159:** 347–365, 1970; **161:** 320–332, 1972.

Klopfer, K. 1973. Florale Morphogenese und Taxonomie der Saxifragaceae sensu lato. Feddes Repert. **84:** 475–516.

Komar, G. A. 1967. O prirode nizhney zavyazi kryzhovnikovykh (Grossulariaceae). Bot. Zh. **52:** 1611–1629.

Krach, J. E. 1977. Seed characters in and affinities among Saxifragineae. Pl. Syst. Evol. Suppl. **1:** 141–153.

Morf, E. 1950. Vergleichend-morphologische Untersuchungen am Gynoeceum der Saxifragaceen. Ber. Schweiz. Bot. Ges. **60:** 516–590.

Narayana, L. L. & M. Radhakrishnaiah. 1976. Floral anatomy of Pittosporaceae. 1. J. Jap. Bot. **51:** 278–282.

Pillans, N. S. 1947. Revision of Bruniaceae. J. S. African Bot. **13**: 121–206.

Pires, J. M. & W. A. Rodriguez. 1971. Notas sôbre os gêneros *Polygonanthus* e *Anisophyllea.* Acta Amazonica **1(2):** 7–15.

Prance, G. T. 1965. The systematic position of *Stylobasium* Desf. Bull. Jard. Bot. État **35:** 435–448.

Prance, G. T. 1968. The systematic position of *Rhabdodendron* Gilg & Pilg. Bull. Jard. Bot. Natl. Belg. **38(2):** 127–146.

Prance, G. T. 1970. The genera of Chrysobalanaceae in the southeastern United States. J. Arnold Arbor. **51:** 521–528.

Prance, G. T. 1972. Chrysobalanaceae. Fl. Neotropica Monogr. 9.

Prance, G. T. 1972. Rhabdodendraceae. Fl. Neotropica Monogr. 11.

Puff, C. & A. Weber. 1976. Contributions to the morphology, anatomy, and karyology of *Rhabdodendron,* and a reconsideration of the systematic position of the Rhabdodendraceae. Pl. Syst. Evol. **125:** 195–222.

Richardson, P. E. 1970. The morphology of the Crossosomataceae. 1. Leaf, stem, and node. Bull. Torrey Bot. Club **97:** 34–39.

Rizzini, C. T. & P. Occhioni. 1949. Dialypetalanthaceae. Lilloa **17:** 243–286.

Robertson, K. R. 1974. The genera of Rosaceae in the southeastern United States. J. Arnold Arbor. **55:** 303–332, 344–401, 611–662.

Savile, D. B. O. 1975. Evolution and biogeography of Saxifragaceae with guidance from their rust parasites. Ann. Missouri Bot. Gard. **62:** 354–361.

Schaeppi, H. 1970. Untersuchungen über den Habitus von *Aruncus, Astilbe,* und einiger ähnlicher Pflanzen. Beitr. Biol. Pflanzen **46:** 371–387.

Schaeppi, H. 1971. Zur Gestaltung des Gynoeceums von *Pittospora tobira.* Ber. Schweiz. Bot. Ges. **81:** 40–51.

Schaeppi, H. & F. Steindl. 1950. Vergleichend-morphologische Untersuchungen am Gynoecium der Rosoideen. Ber. Schweiz. Bot. Ges. **60:** 15–50.

Sleumer, H. 1968. Die Gattung *Escallonia* (Saxifragaceae). Verh. Kon. Ned. Akad. Wetensch. Afd. Natuurk., Tweede Sect. **59(2):** 1–146.

Spongberg, S. A. 1972. The genera of Saxifragaceae in the southeastern United States. J. Arnold Arbor. **53:** 409–498.

Spongberg, S. A. 1978. The genera of Crassulaceae in the southeastern United States. J. Arnold Arbor. **59:** 197–248.

Steenis, C. G. G. J. van. 1984. A synopsis of Alseuosmiaceae in New Zealand, New Caledonia, Australia, and New Guinea. Blumea **29:** 387–394.

Sterling, C. 1969. Comparative morphology of the carpel in the Rosaceae. X. Oesterr. Bot. Z. **116:** 46–54.

Stern, W. L. 1974, 1978. Comparative anatomy and systematics of woody Saxifragaceae. *Escallonia.* J. Linn. Soc., Bot. **68:** 1–20, 1974. *Hydrangea.* J. Linn. Soc., Bot. **76:** 83–113, 1978.

Stern, W. L., G. K. Brizicky & R. H. Eyde. 1969. Comparative anatomy and relationships of Columelliaceae. J. Arnold Arbor. **50:** 36–75.

Stern, W. L., E. M. Sweitzer & R. E. Phipps. 1970. Comparative anatomy and systematics of woody Saxifragaceae. *Ribes.* Pages 215–237 *in* N. K. B. Robson, D. F. Cutler & M. Gregory (eds.), New research in plant anatomy. J. Linn. Soc., Bot. 63. Suppl. 1. Academic Press. London & New York.

Thorne, R. F. & R. Scogin. 1978. *Forsellesia* Greene (*Glossopetalon* Gray), a third genus in the Crossosomataceae, Rosineae, Rosales. Aliso **9:** 171–178.

Tobe, H. & P. H. Raven. 1984. An embryological contribution to systematics of the Chrysobalanaceae. I. Tribe Chrysobalaneae. Bot. Mag. (Tokyo) **97**: 397–411.

Tobe, H. & P. H. Raven. 1987. Systematic embryology of the Anisophylleaceae. Ann. Missouri Bot. Gard. **74**: 1–26.

Vani-Hardev (no initial). 1972. Systematic embryology of *Roridula gorgonias* Planch. Beitr. Biol. Pflanzen **48**: 339–351.

2. Order Fabales

The order Fabales consists of 3 families and about 18,000 species, widely distributed throughout the world. The Fabaceae comprise more than 12,000 species, the Mimosaceae about 3000, and the Caesalpiniaceae more than 2000. The three families have often been considered to be subfamilies of a single large family Leguminosae. Under such a definition the name Fabaceae is conserved over the older names Caesalpiniaceae and Mimosaceae, for use by those who prefer to base all names of families on genera.

The existence of the three major groups (here called families), which collectively constitute a larger group (here called an order), is widely admitted. It is only the taxonomic rank of the groups on which opinion remains sharply divided. I prefer the treatment here presented as being more in harmony with the customary definitions of families in angiosperms.

The Fabales may be briefly characterized as dicotyledons with a single carpel and compound, stipulate leaves. The fruit is most commonly dry and dehiscent along both sutures, forming what is called a typical legume. Many members of the order bear root-nodules that harbor nitrogen-fixing bacteria, a feature otherwise restricted to a few small families.

Many authors have treated the Leguminosae as a family of a broadly defined order Rosales. This is not really wrong, but I believe the organization here presented is conceptually more useful. The legumes, whether treated as one family or three, form such a coherent group with such an abundance of genera and species that the assignment of the group to any other order raises questions of what is tail and what is dog.

The Fabales are by all accounts closely related to the Rosales as here defined. The Connaraceae, here referred to the Rosales, are often cited as a family having much in common with the Fabales. The rusts and smuts of the Fabales emphasize their distinction from the Rosaceae, with which they have often been associated (Savile, 1979, cited under Magnoliopsida).

The Fabaceae (sensu stricto) are obviously the most advanced family of the Fabales. The Mimosaceae and Caesalpiniaceae apparently diverge from a common base, with neither family being ancestral to the other. In a linear sequence it is customary to start with the Mimosaceae and finish with the Fabaceae. The Caesalpiniaceae are connected to both of the other families, and the Fabaceae may reasonably be regarded as derived from the Caesalpiniaceae.

Pollen considered to represent the Caesalpiniaceae enters the fossil record at widely separated localities in the Maestrichtian stage of the

Upper Cretaceous. Fossil inflorescences and tetradinous pollen considered to represent fairly well advanced members of the Mimosaceae are known from Middle Eocene and more recent deposits in North America, and several kinds of mimosaceous pollen occur in Upper Eocene and more recent deposits in Africa. Flowers and inflorescences apparently representing both the Mimosaceae and the Fabaceae (sensu stricto) have recently been discovered in deposits of marginal Paleocene–Eocene age in Tennessee.

SYNOPTICAL ARRANGEMENT OF THE FAMILIES OF FABALES

1 Flowers hypogynous or slightly perigynous, regular (at least as to the corolla); petals mostly valvate, often connate below to form a tube; stamens often more than 10, the filaments often colored and long-exserted and forming the conspicuous part of the inflorescence; ovules anatropous or sometimes hemitropous; leaves mostly bipinnately compound (sometimes reduced to phyllodes); plants mainly tropical and woody .... **1. Mimosaceae.**
1 Flowers slightly to evidently perigynous, only rarely essentially hypogynous, the corolla usually more or less strongly irregular; petals imbricate, distinct or only the 2 lower ones connate; stamens most commonly 10, less often 9, or sometimes fewer, but only seldom more numerous, not forming the most conspicuous part of the inflorescence; ovules anatropous or hemitropous to often amphitropous or campylotropous; leaves and habit various.
    2 Corolla not papilionaceous; adaxial (upper) petal usually borne internally to the lateral petals and smaller than them; sepals mostly distinct; filaments distinct or variously connate, but not usually forming a definite sheath around the pistil; plants mainly tropical and woody, with pinnately or bipinnately compound (seldom unifoliolate or simple) leaves .... **2. Caesalpiniaceae.**
    2 Corolla mostly papilionaceous, the adaxial petal (called the banner or standard) borne externally to the others and generally the largest, folded along the midline so as to embrace the other petals in bud; 2 lateral petals (called wings) similar inter se and mostly distinct; 2 lower petals innermost, similar inter se, mostly connate distally to form a keel enfolding the androecium and gynoecium; sepals mostly connate below to form a tube (beyond the hypanthial base); stamens mostly 10 (seldom fewer, but not more), usually connate by their filaments to form an open or closed sheath around the pistil, the uppermost one often more or less separate from the others so that the androecium is diadelphous (9 + 1), or the uppermost stamen sometimes obsolete, or sometimes the filaments all distinct; plants of varying habit and habitat, often herbaceous and extratropical, the leaves pinnately or less often palmately compound or trifoliolate, seldom unifoliolate or simple .... **3. Fabaceae.**

SELECTED REFERENCES

Bell, E. A., J. A. Lackey & R. M. Polhill. 1978. Systematic significance of canavanine in the Papilionoideae (Fabaceae). Biochem. Syst. Ecol. **6:** 201–212.

Buss, P. A. & N. R. Lersten. 1975. Survey of tapetal nuclear number as a taxonomic character in Leguminosae. Bot. Gaz. **136**: 388–395.
Crepet, W. L. & D. L. Dilcher. 1977. Investigations of angiosperms from the Eocene of North America. A mimosoid inflorescence. Amer. J. Bot. **64**: 714–725.
Crepet, W. L. & D. W. Taylor. 1985. The diversification of the Leguminosae: First fossil evidence of the Mimosoideae and Papilionoideae. Science **228**: 1087–1089.
Elias, T. S. 1974. The genera of Mimosoideae (Leguminosae) in the southeastern United States. J. Arnold Arbor. **55**: 67–118.
Guinet, P. 1969. Les mimosacées. Étude de palynologie fondamentale, corrélations, évolution. Trav. Sect. Sci. Techn. Inst. Franç. Pondichery (India) **9**: 1–293.
Harborne, J. B., D. Boulter & B. L. Turner (eds.). 1971. Chemotaxonomy of the Leguminosae. Academic Press. London, New York.
Lackey, J. A. 1977. A revised classification of the tribe Phaseoleae (Leguminosae: Papilionoideae), and its relation to canavanine distribution. J. Linn. Soc., Bot. **74**: 163–178.
Leinfellner, W. 1970. Zur Kenntnis der Karpelle der Leguminosen. 2. Caesalpiniaceae und Mimosaceae. Oesterr. Bot. Z. **118**: 108–120.
Pettigrew, C. J. & L. Watson. 1977. On the classification of Caesalpinioideae. Taxon **26**: 57–64.
Polhill, R. M. & P. H. Raven (eds.). 1981. Advances in legume systematics. 2 vols. Royal Botanic Gardens. Kew.
Robertson, K. R. & Y.-T. Lee. 1976. The genera of Caesalpinioideae (Leguminosae) in the southeastern United States. J. Arnold Arbor. **57**: 1–53.
Yakovlev, G. P. 1972. Dopolneniya k sisteme poryadka Fabales Nakai (Leguminales Jones). Bot. Zh. **57**: 585–595.

3. Order Proteales

The order Proteales as here defined consists of two families, the Proteaceae, with more than a thousand species, and the Elaeagnaceae, with about fifty. The order may be briefly characterized as dicotyledons with a single carpel, mostly 4-merous flowers with not more than 8 stamens, no petals (or reduced and modified petals), and exstipulate leaves.

It is not certain that the two families belong together. Despite an impressive number of technical features in common, they do not look much alike. Instead the Elaeagnaceae look remarkably like some of the Thymelaeaceae. Any relationship between these latter two families would imply that the pistil in the Elaeagnaceae is only pseudomonomerous, whereas the pistil in Proteaceae clearly consists of a single carpel, which is often not fully sealed. The alternative to including the Elaeagnaceae in the Proteales would be to recognize a unifamilial order Elaeagnales. The Elaeagnaceae would be a clearly discordant element in the Myrtales, to which the Thymelaeaceae are assigned.

Fossil pollen regarded as proteaceous dates from the Maestrichtian or possibly the Santonian stage of the Upper Cretaceous. The Elaeagnaceae enter the record distinctly later, in the Oligocene.

SYNOPTICAL ARRANGEMENT OF THE FAMILIES OF PROTEALES

1 Plants provided with a vesture of peltate scales or stellate hairs; fruit typically a pseudodrupe, the dry achene surrounded by the persistent, thickened, externally fleshy or mealy base of the hypanthium; stamens as many as an alternate with the sepals, or twice as many as the sepals; nodes unilacunar . . . . **1. Elaeagnaceae.**
1 Plants without peltate scales or stellate hairs; fruits diverse, but not as in the Elaeagnaceae; stamens as many as and opposite the sepals; nodes trilacunar . . . . **2. Proteaceae.**

SELECTED REFERENCES

Graham, S. A. 1964. The Elaeagnaceae in the southeastern United States. J. Arnold Arbor. **45:** 274–278.

Haber, J. M. 1959–1966. The comparative anatomy and morphology of the flowers and inflorescences of the Proteaceae. I. Some Australian taxa. II. Some American taxa. III. Some African taxa. Phytomorphology **9:** 325–358, 1959 (1960); **11:** 1–16, 1961; **16:** 49–527, 1966.

Hawker, L. E. & J. Fraymouth. 1951. A re-investigation of the root-nodules of species of *Elaeagnus, Hippophae, Alnus,* and *Myrica,* with special reference to morphology and life histories of causative organisms. J. Gen. Microbiol. **5:** 369–386.

Johnson, L. A. S. & B. G. Briggs. 1975. On the Proteaceae—the evolution and classification of a southern family. J. Linn. Soc., Bot. **70:** 83–182.

Rao, V. S. 1974. The nature of the perianth in *Elaeagnus* on the basis of floral anatomy, with some comments on the systematic position of the Elaeagnaceae. J. Indian Bot. Soc. **53:** 156–161.

Venkata Rao, C. 1960–1971. Studies in the Proteaceae. I–IV, XIII. Proc. Natl. Inst. Sci. India **26B:** 300–337, 1960; **27B:** 126–151, 1961; **29B:** 489–510, 1963; **30B:** 197–244, 1964; **35B:** 471–486, 1969. V, VI. J. Indian Bot. Soc. **44:** 244–270, 479–494, 1965. XIV. Proc. Indian Natl. Sci. Acad. **36B:** 345–363, 1971.

Venkata Rao, C. 1967. Origin and spread of the Proteaceae. Proc. Natl. Inst. Sci. India **33B:** 219–351.

4. Order Podostemales

The order Podostemales consists of the single family Podostemaceae, with 200+ species, mainly of tropical regions. The group may be briefly characterized as highly modified (often thalloid) aquatic herbs with very small, perfect, hypogynous, apetalous flowers that usually have numerous, bitegmic ovules on axile placentas.

The Podostemales are taxonomically isolated, but most authors agree that they are related to the Saxifragaceae and Crassulaceae. The family Hydrostachyaceae, which has in the past often been associated with the Podostemaceae, is now generally considered to belong to the subclass Asteridae. It is here referred to the order Callitrichales.

Selected References

Graham, S. A. & C. E. Wood. 1975. The Podostemaceae in the southeastern United States. J. Arnold Arbor. **56**: 456–465.
Jäger-Zürn, I. 1967. Embryologische Untersuchungen an vier Podostemaceen. Oesterr. Bot. Z. **114**: 20–45.
Jäger-Zürn, I. 1970. Morphologie der Podostemaceae I. *Tristicha trifaria* (Bory ex Willd.) Spreng. Beitr. Biol. Pflanzen **47**: 11–52.
Royen, P. van. 1951–1955. The Podostemaceae of the New World. Meded. Bot. Mus. Herb. Rijks Univ. Utrecht **107**: 1–151, 1951; **115**: 1–21, 1953; **119**: 215–263, 1955.
Schnell, R. 1967. Études sur l'anatomie et la morphologie des Podostémacées. Candollea **22**: 157–225.

5. Order Haloragales

The order Haloragales as here defined consists of 2 families, the Haloragaceae and Gunneraceae, probably fewer than 200 species in all. Two other families that have often been associated with these two are now considered to belong elsewhere. The Theligonaceae are allied to the Rubiaceae, and the Hippuridaceae are associated with the Callitrichaceae and Hydrostachyaceae to form an order (Callitrichales) of the Asteridae. The Haloragales may be briefly characterized as dicotyledons with minute flowers and an inferior ovary with 1–4 locules and 2–4 distinct styles, each locule with a single pendulous ovule. Most of them are herbs, many are aquatic, and none of them has milky juice. The fruits separate into 1-seeded mericarps.

The Haloragales have often been considered to be allied to the Myrtales, or even included in that order. In addition to their reduced flowers, however, the Haloragales differ from the Myrtales in having distinct styles (a primitive feature) rather than a common style, and they further differ from characteristic members of the Myrtales in having a well developed endosperm and in lacking internal phloem and vestured pits. The embryo of the Gunneraceae is very small in relation to the endosperm, as in archaic angiosperms in general. Thus it does not seem likely that the Haloragales are florally reduced, aquatic derivatives of the Myrtales. Both orders must instead be derived from a generalized Rosalean ancestry.

Based on the fossil pollen alone, the Haloragales appear to be one of the older orders of the Rosidae. Pollen considered to represent *Gunnera* dates from the Turonian stage, well below the middle of the Upper Cretaceous. Pollen clearly referable to the Haloragaceae dates only from the Paleocene, but some Upper Cretaceous pollen may also belong here.

1 Ovary 2- to 4-locular, with as many styles as locules; stamens (3) 4 or 8; embryo-sac monosporic, 8-nucleate; embryo straight, cylindric; flowers individually subtended by a pair of bracteoles; stem monostelic; plants commonly cyanogenic and producing proanthocyanins, often aquatic or amphibious or of marshes, with small to medium-sized, alternate or often opposite or whorled leaves lacking stipules and axillary scales; leaf-venation tending to be pinnate . . . . **1. Haloragaceae.**
1 Ovary unilocular, with 2 styles; stamens 1–2; embryo-sac tetrasporic, 16-nucleate; embryo tiny, obcordate; flowers not bracteolate; stem polystelic; plants neither cyanogenic nor with proanthocyanins, terrestrial, with alternate, palmately veined, often very large leaves which have an axillary scale that is sometimes considered to be stipular . . . . **2. Gunneraceae.**

SELECTED REFERENCES

Bawa, S. B. 1969. Embryological studies on the Haloragidaceae. II. *Laurembergia brevipes* Schindl. and a discussion of systematic considerations. Proc. Natl. Inst. Sci. India **35B:** 273–290.
Behnke, H.-D. 1986. Contributions to the knowledge of sieve-element plastids in Gunneraceae and allied families. Pl. Syst. Evol. **151:** 215–222.
Jarzen, D. M. 1980. The occurrence of *Gunnera* pollen in the fossil record. Biotropica **12:** 117–123.
Orchard, A. E. 1975. Taxonomic revisions in the family Haloragaceae. I. The genera *Haloragis, Haloragodendron, Glischrocaryon, Meziella* and *Gonocarpus.* Bull. Auckland Inst. Mus. 10.
Praglowski, J. 1970. The pollen morphology of the Haloragaceae with special reference to taxonomy. Grana **10:** 159–239.

6. Order Myrtales

The order Myrtales as here defined consists of 14 families and more than 9000 species. About three-fourths of the species belong to only 2 large families, the Melastomataceae (4000) and Myrtaceae (3000). Another 4 families, the Onagraceae, Combretaceae, Lythraceae, and Thymelaeaceae, have 400 to 600 species each. The remaining 8 families have only about 60 species in all, and 6 of them have only a single genus each. The Sonneratiaceae, with 2 genera and 10 species, notable for being adapted to pollination by bats, are sometimes included in the Lythraceae. In addition to the mostly strongly perigynous to epigynous flowers and the overlapping similarities among the constituent families, the order is marked by two otherwise uncommon anatomical features: internal phloem and vestured pits in the vessel-segments.

The most discordant family, and the only one that still provokes controversy about its possible inclusion in the order, is the Thymelaeaceae. The Thymelaeaceae are marked by their usually pseudomonomerous ovary, often unusual pollen, and a distinctive set of secondary metabolites, commonly including the simple coumarin daphnin (or allied compounds). Furthermore, some few members of the family are unusual in the Myrtales in having essentially hypogynous flowers. More ordinary kinds of pollen and gynoecium, with transitional types, also occur in the family, however. Thus it is unnecessary to seek the placement of the Thymelaeaceae in another order. Indeed the internal phloem, vestured pits, and strongly perigynous, polypetalous to apetalous flowers of characteristic members of the family would be out of harmony with any other order that might be suggested as a haven for it. Furthermore, the characteristic obturator of the Thymelaeaceae, though not identical in detail, might be compared with the obturator of the Combretaceae; and the glandular-punctate leaves of some Thymelaeaceae recall those of the Myrtaceae. It would of course be possible to recognize an order Thymelaeales to provide for this one family, as some authors have done, but the segregate order would still stand alongside the Myrtales.

Martin and Dowd (1986) link the Thymelaeaceae to the other families of the Myrtales on the basis of the sequence of amino-acids in the terminal 40 residues of the smaller subunit of ribulose biphosphate carboxylase. We must be wary of taking these results, or any other single sort of evidence, as definitive, but they do weight the scales toward a myrtalean position for the family.

An ecological interpretation of the Myrtales is difficult and unsatisfying. Tannins, including ellagic acid and often proanthocyanins, play a major role, for most species, in discouraging predators. A number of other orders rely on these same substances. The habitat and growth-habit of the Myrtales embrace most of the possibilities available to angiosperms. Only some of the smaller, highly specialized families, such as the Trapaceae, are ecologically distinctive. Members of the Myrtales seem to be peculiarly susceptible to fixation of disturbances in the development of the embryo-sac, embryo, and endosperm, but the adaptive significance of these unusual types of ontogeny remains to be elucidated. The adaptive significance of perigyny and epigyny in protecting the ovules has been inconclusively debated. The functional importance of internal phloem is wholly obscure, especially inasmuch as it occurs in plants of diverse habit in diverse habitats, which grow intermingled with plants of similar aspect belonging to orders that do not have internal phloem.

Pollen attributed to the Myrtaceae dates from the Santonian stage of the Upper Cretaceous, some 85 million years BP, and a generalized type of onagraceous pollen makes its appearance in the Maestrichtian. Pollen referred to other families of Myrtales does not antedate the Tertiary. The only Cretaceous macrofossils referred to the order are the distinctive fruits of *Trapa,* which extend some distance back into the Upper Cretaceous.

SYNOPTICAL ARRANGEMENT OF THE FAMILIES OF MYRTALES

1 Ovary generally superior both at anthesis and in fruit, only the very base
  sometimes adnate to the hypanthium.
  2 Ovules 2–many per carpel; ovary generally 2–several-locular; fruit com-
    monly capsular, seldom indehiscent.
    3 Stamens numerous, in more than 2 cycles, seldom only 12; carpels 4–20;
      trees, often of mangrove habit . . . . **1. Sonneratiaceae.**
    3 Stamens mostly bicyclic or unicyclic, rarely more than 12, seldom reduced
      to 1; carpels 2–4 (–6); not mangroves.
      4 Stamens either more numerous than the sepals (commonly twice as
        many), or as many as and opposite the sepals, seldom reduced to 1
        . . . . **2. Lythraceae.**
      4 Stamens as many as and alternate with the sepals.
        5 Flowers perfect.
          6 Petals present; flowers 6-merous, bicarpellate, multiovulate . . .
          . . . . **3. Rhynchocalycaceae.**
          6 Petals absent; flowers 4–5-merous.
            7 Carpels 2, each with numerous ovules; embryo-sac bisporic,
              8-nucleate (unique in the order, except for *Heteropyxis,* in
              the Myrtaceae); nodes trilacunar (unique in the order) . . . .
              . . . . **4. Alzateaceae.**
           7 Carpels 4, each with 2–4 ovules; embryo-sac tetrasporic, 16-
              nucleate (unique in the order); nodes unilacunar . . . .
              . . . . **5. Penaeaceae.**
        5 Flowers largely unisexual, the plants polygamo-dioecious; carpels 2,
          each with numerous ovules . . . . **6. Crypteroniaceae.**
  2 Ovule solitary in the pseudomonomerous ovary, or the ovules solitary in
    each of 2 or more locules; fruit commonly indehiscent, less often capsular
    . . . . **7. Thymelaeaceae.**
1 Ovary half to more often fully inferior, or in a relatively few genera and species
  of some families superior.
  8 Plants annual aquatics; ovary bilocular, with a single pendulous apical-axile
    ovule in each locule, half-inferior at anthesis, becoming almost wholly
    inferior in fruit; fruits horned; cotyledons very unequal; haplostemonous
    . . . . **8. Trapaceae.**
  8 Plants woody or herbaceous, terrestrial, or less often aquatic; other features
    not combined as above.
    9 Stamens mostly numerous, seldom only as many or twice as many as the
      sepals or petals.
      10 Leaves glandular-punctate; carpels mostly 2–5 (–16); fruit various,
        but only rarely many-seeded and indehiscent, in any case the seeds
        without a proliferating sarcotesta . . . . **9. Myrtaceae.**
      10 Leaves not glandular-punctate; carpels rather numerous, commonly
        7–9 (–15); fruit indehiscent, with a firm rind and many seeds embed-
        ded in a pulpy mass representing the proliferating sarcotestas . . .
        . . . . **10. Punicaceae.**
    9 Stamens usually not more than twice as many as the sepals or petals.
      11 Placentation axile to less often basal or parietal; fruit only seldom
        1-seeded and indehiscent; plants woody or herbaceous.
        12 Anthers opening by longitudinal slits; connective without ap-
          pendages; leaves pinnately veined.
          13 Embryo-sac 4-nucleate, the endosperm diploid (unique in the

order); ovules usually numerous, seldom only 1 or 2 per carpel; fruit usually capsular, less often indehiscent, but not drupaceous; plants with raphides; most species herbaceous
....**11. Onagraceae.**
13 Embryo-sac 8-nucleate, the endosperm triploid; ovules 2 (3) per carpel; fruit drupaceous; plants without raphides; shrubs or trees ....**12. Oliniaceae.**
12 Anthers mostly opening by a terminal pore or pores, only seldom by longitudinal slits; connective commonly provided with conspicuous appendages; leaves mostly with 3–9 prominent longitudinal veins, only seldom pinnately veined ....
....**13. Melastomataceae.**
11 Placentation apical in a unilocular ovary; ovules 2 (–6); fruit indehiscent, 1-seeded; trees, shrubs, or woody vines ....
....**14. Combretaceae.**

SELECTED REFERENCES

Behnke, H.-D. 1984. Ultrastructure of sieve-element plastids of Myrtales and allied groups. Ann. Missouri Bot. Gard. **71:** 824–831.
Brown, C. A. 1967. Pollen morphology of the Onagraceae. Rev. Palaeobot. Palynol. **3:** 163–180.
Bunniger, L. 1972. Untersuchungen über die morphologische Natur des Hypanthiums bei Myrtales- und Thymelaeales-Familien. II. Myrtaceae. III. Vergleich mit den Thymelaeaceae. Beitr. Biol. Pflanzen **48:** 79–156.
Bunniger, L. & F. Weberling. 1968. Untersuchungen über die morphologische Natur des Hypanthiums bei Myrtales-Familien. I. Onagraceae. Beitr. Biol. Pflanzen **44:** 447–477.
Carlquist, S. 1975. Wood anatomy of Onagraceae, with notes on alternative modes of photosynthate movement in dicotyledon woods. Ann. Missouri Bot. Gard. **62:** 386–424.
Carlquist, S. & L. DeBuhr. 1977. Wood anatomy of Penaeaceae (Myrtales): Comparative, phylogenetic, and ecological implications. J. Linn. Soc., Bot. **75:** 211–227.
Cronquist, A. 1984. A commentary on the definition of the order Myrtales. Ann. Missouri Bot. Gard. **71:** 780–782.
Dahlgren, R. & R. F. Thorne. 1984. The order Myrtales: Circumscription, variation, and relationships. Ann. Missouri Bot. Gard. **71:** 633–699.
Exell, A. W. & C. A. Stace. 1966. Revision of the Combretaceae. Bol. Soc. Brot. Ser. 2, **40:** 5–26.
Eyde, R. H. 1977, 1978. Reproductive structures and evolution in *Ludwigia* (Onagraceae). I. Androecium, placentation, merism. II. Fruit and seed. Ann. Missouri Bot. Gard. **64:** 644–655, 1977; **65:** 656–675, 1978.
Eyde, R. H. & J. T. Morgan. 1973. Floral structure and evolution in Lopezieae (Onagraceae). Amer. J. Bot. **60:** 771–787.
Eyde, R. H. & J. A. Teeri. 1967. Floral anatomy of *Rhexia virginica* (Melastomataceae). Rhodora **69:** 163–178.
Graham, A. & S. A. Graham. 1971. The geologic history of the Lythraceae. Brittonia **23:** 335-346.

Graham, A., et al. 1985, 1987. Palynology and systematics of the Lythraceae. I, II. Amer. J. Bot. **72:** 1012–1031, 1985; **74:** 829–850, 1987.

Graham, S. A. 1984. Alzateaceae, a new family of Myrtales in the American tropics. Ann. Missouri Bot. Gard. **71:** 757–779.

Heinig, K. H. 1951. Studies in the floral morphology of the Thymelaeaceae. Amer. J. Bot. **38:** 113–132.

Johnson, L. A. S. & B. G. Briggs. 1984. Myrtales and Myrtaceae—A phylogenetic analysis. Ann. Missouri Bot. Gard. **71:** 700–756.

Keating, R. C. 1984. Leaf histology and its contribution to relationships in the Myrtales. Ann. Missouri Bot. Gard. **71:** 801–823.

Martin, P. G. & J. M. Dowd. 1986. Phylogenetic studies using protein sequences within the order Myrtales. Ann. Missouri Bot. Gard. **73:** 442–448.

Mayr, B. 1969. Ontogenetische Studien an Myrtales-Blüten. Bot. Jahrb. Syst. **89:** 210–271.

Miki, S. 1959. Evolution of *Trapa* from ancestral *Lythrum* through *Hemitrapa*. Proc. Imp. Acad. Japan **35(6):** 289–294.

Mújica, M. B. & D. F. Cutler. 1974. Taxonomic implications of anatomical studies on the Oliniaceae. Kew Bull. **29:** 93–123.

Muller, J. 1978. New observations on pollen morphology and fossil distribution of the genus *Sonneratia* (Sonneratiaceae). Rev. Palaeobot. Palyn. **26:** 277–300.

Nevling, L. I. 1962. The Thymelaeaceae in the southeastern United States. J. Arnold Arbor. **43:** 428–434.

Patel, V. C., J. J. Skvarla & P. H. Raven. 1984. Pollen characters in relation to the delimitation of Myrtales. Ann. Missouri Bot. Gard. **71:** 858–969.

Rao, V. S. & R. Dahlgren. 1969. The floral anatomy and relationships of Oliniaceae. Bot. Not. **122:** 160–171.

Raven, P. H. 1964. The generic subdivision of Onagraceae, tribe Onagreae. Brittonia **16:** 276–288.

Raven, P. H. 1976. Generic and sectional delimitation in Onagraceae, tribe Epilobieae. Ann. Missouri Bot. Gard. **63:** 326–340.

Schmid, R. 1984. Reproductive anatomy and morphology of Myrtales in relation to systematics. Ann. Missouri Bot. Gard. **71:** 832–835.

Stern, W. L. & G. K. Brizicky. 1958. The comparative anatomy and taxonomy of *Heteropyxis*. Bull. Torrey Bot. Club **85:** 111–123.

Ting, W. S. 1966. Pollen morphology of Onagraceae. Pollen & Spores **8:** 9–36.

Tobe, H. & P. H. Raven. 1983. An embryological analysis of Myrtales; its definition and characteristics. Ann. Missouri Bot. Gard. **70:** 71–94.

Tobe, H. & P. H. Raven. 1984a. The embryology and relationships of *Rhynchocalyx* Oliv. (Rhynchocalycaceae). Ann. Missouri Bot. Gard. **71:** 836–843.

Tobe, H. & P. H. Raven. 1984b. The embryology and relationships of *Alzatea* Ruiz & Pav. (Alzateaceae, Myrtales). Ann. Missouri Bot. Gard. **71:** 844–852.

Tobe, H. & P. H. Raven. 1984c. The embryology and relationships of Oliniaceae. Pl. Syst. Evol. **146:** 105–116.

Tobe, H. & P. H. Raven. 1984d. The embryology and relationships of Penaeaceae (Myrtales). Pl. Syst. Evol. **146:** 181–195.

Tobe, H. & P. H. Raven. 1985. The histogenesis and evolution of integuments in Onagraceae. Ann. Missouri Bot. Gard. **72:** 451–458.

Tobe, H. & P. H. Raven. 1987a. Embryology and systematic position of *Heteropyxis* (Myrtales). Amer. J. Bot. **74:** 197–208.

Tobe, H. & P. H. Raven. 1987b. The embryology and relationships of *Dactylocladus* (Crypteroniaceae) and a discussion of the family. Bot. Gaz. **148:** 103–111.

van Vliet, G. J. C. M. & P. Baas. 1984. Wood anatomy and classification of the Myrtales. Ann. Missouri Bot. Gard. **71:** 783–800.

de Vos, O. C. 1981. Ontogeny and vascularization of the flower of *Oenothera* (Onagraceae). Acta Bot. Neerl. **30:** 219–229.

Weberling, F. 1963. Ein Beitrag zur systematischen Stellung der Geissolomataceae, Penaeaceae und Oliniaceae sowie der Gattung *Heteropyxis* (Myrtaceae). Bot. Jahrb. Syst. **82:** 119–128.

Wilson, K. A. 1960. The genera of Myrtaceae in the southeastern United States. J. Arnold Arbor. **41:** 270–278.

7. Order Rhizophorales

The order Rhizophorales consists of the single family Rhizophoraceae, with about a hundred species, widely distributed in tropical regions. The mangrove genera (tribe Rhizophoreae, 4 genera, ca. 17 spp.) are the most familiar members of the family, but the majority of the genera and species are inland plants that are not mangroves. The group may be briefly characterized as dicotyledonous woody plants with simple, entire, opposite leaves, interpetiolar stipules, separate petals, at least twice as many stamens as petals, and a plurilocular ovary with mostly 2 apical-axile, bitegmic ovules in each locule.

The proper taxonomic disposition of the Rhizophoraceae presents a difficult problem. Traditionally they have been referred to a broadly defined and poorly characterized order Myrtales. In the present system the Myrtales are a more homogeneous group, and the Rhizophoraceae would be as out of place as a giraffe in a herd of bison. The Rhizophoraceae have neither the internal phloem nor the vestured pits of the Myrtales, and the Myrtales mostly lack the stipulate leaves, frequently scalariform vessels, diversified alkaloids, and well developed endosperm of the Rhizophoraceae. The Cornales and Rosales are equally inhospitable to the Rhizophoraceae, although both the Rhizophoraceae and the Cornales probably take their origin in the Rosales near the Grossulariaceae and Hydrangeaceae. The only reasonable alternative is to treat the Rhizophorales as a distinct order.

Pollen considered to represent the Rhizophoraceae dates from the Upper Eocene.

SELECTED REFERENCES

Graham, S. A. 1964. The genera of Rhizophoraceae and Combretaceae in the southeastern United States. J. Arnold Arbor. **45:** 285–301.

Juncosa, A. M. & P. B. Tomlinson. 1987. Floral development in mangrove Rhizophoraceae. Amer. J. Bot. **74**: 1263–1279.

Muller, J. & C. Caratini. 1977. Pollen of *Rhizophora* (Rhizophoraceae) as a guide fossil. Pollen & Spores **19**: 361–389.

Prance, G. T., et al. 1975. Revisao taxonômica des espécies amazonicas de Rhizophoraceae. Acta Amazonica **5**: 5–22.

van Vliet, G. J. C. M. 1976. Wood anatomy of the Rhizophoraceae. Leiden Bot. Ser. **3**: 20–75.

8. Order Cornales

The order Cornales as here defined consists of 3 families and scarcely 150 species. The Cornaceae, with about 100 species, are the largest family, with which the other families are to be associated individually. The family Cornaceae is only loosely knit, and 11 of the 14 genera have been treated by one or another author as monotypic families.

The Cornales may be briefly characterized as woody (rarely herbaceous) dicotyledons with simple, mostly exstipulate leaves, epigynous, often 4-merous flowers, distinct (or no) petals, and a pluricarpellate, usually plurilocular ovary with as many ovules as carpels, the ovules unitegmic and usually crassinucellar.

The families of the Cornales have often been included in a broadly defined order Apiales or Umbellales. The merits of that treatment, as opposed to the one presented here, have been extensively discussed in the taxonomic literature. In my opinion the Apiales are derived from the Rosales via the Sapindales, whereas the Cornales are derived directly from the Rosales, in the vicinity of the Hydrangeaceae and Grossulariaceae. Features of the gross morphology, wood-anatomy, palynology, and chemistry combine to support this view of the relationship of the Cornales, as does the existence of the non-missing link *Corokia* (Cornaceae, as here defined), which has with good reason been compared to *Argophyllum* in the Grossulariaceae (Escalloniaceae).

Eyde (1988) redefines the Cornaceae to include only *Cornus* (sensu lato), *Mastixia, Nyssa, Camptotheca,* and *Davidia.* He allows *Alangium* to stand uncomfortably in the vicinity of the Cornaceae (as a family Alangiaceae), and appears to be ambivalent about the relationship of *Garrya* (Garryaceae) to the Cornaceae. All of the other genera here included in the Cornaceae are excluded, some with posited allies in the Rosales (as here defined), others left twisting in the wind.

It is easy enough to follow Eyde in including the Nyssaceae in the Cornaceae, but the exclusion of other genera is more difficult when one is trying to produce a general system. I do not think it is helpful to have a passel of minuscule families or even orders, as some other authors have proposed. These must in any case stand near to the Cornaceae as fellow derivatives from the Rosales.

It appears that diversification of the Cornales into families and genera was underway in the late Upper Cretaceous. Stones of Campanian age from the fruits of *Cornus* have recently been found in Sweden. Stones of

Mastixia (or something allied to it) date back at least to the Maestrichtian of Europe. Pollen very much like that of *Cornus* (but also resembling that of some Grossulariaceae) has been found in Paleocene deposits in South Africa. The Garryaceae, with the most reduced flowers in the order, enter the fossil record only in the Miocene.

SYNOPTICAL ARRANGEMENT OF THE FAMILIES OF CORNALES

1 Ovules solitary in each of the 1–several locules, or some locules empty; flowers not in aments.
   2 Plants with articulated laticifers, and producing emetine alkaloids but not iridoid compounds; vessel-segments usually with simple perforations; fruit drupaceous, but the stone not opening by valves; leaves alternate . . . . . .
   . . . . **1. Alangiaceae.**
   2 Plants without laticifers (except *Mastixia*) and without alkaloids, but often with iridoid compounds; vessel-segments usually with scalariform perforations; fruit a drupe or less often a berry, the stone in drupaceous fruits often opening by subapical valves; leaves alternate or more often opposite
   . . . . **2.   Cornaceae.**
1 Ovules two in the single locule of the ovary; flowers in unisexual aments; leaves opposite; plants producing iridoid compounds . . . . **3.   Garryaceae.**

SELECTED REFERENCES

Brunner, F. & D. E. Fairbrothers. 1978. A comparative serological investigation within the Cornales. Serol. Mus. Bull. **53:** 2–5.

Chao, C.-Y. 1954. Comparative pollen morphology of the Cornaceae and allies. Taiwania **5:** 93–106.

Dahling, G. V. 1978. Systematics and evolution of *Garrya.* Contr. Gray Herb. **209:** 1–104.

Eyde, R. H. 1963. Morphological and paleobotanical studies of the Nyssaceae. I. A survey of the modern species and their fruits. J. Arnold Arbor. **44:** 1–59.

Eyde, R. H. 1964. Inferior ovary and generic affinities of *Garrya.* Amer. J. Bot. **51:** 1083–1092.

Eyde, R. H. 1966. The Nyssaceae in the southeastern United States. J. Arnold Arbor. **47:** 117–125.

Eyde, R. H. 1966. Systematic anatomy of the flower and fruit of *Corokia.* Amer. J. Bot. **53:** 833–847.

Eyde, R. H. 1967 (1968). The peculiar gynoecial vasculature of Cornaceae and its systematic significance. Phytomorphology **17:** 172–182.

Eyde, R. H. 1968. Flowers, fruits, and phylogeny of Alangiaceae. J. Arnold Arbor. **49:** 167–192.

Eyde, R. H. 1972. Pollen of *Alangium:* Toward a more satisfactory synthesis. Taxon **21:** 471–477.

Eyde, R. H. 1988. Comprehending *Cornus:* Puzzles and progress in the systematics of the dogwoods. Bot. Rev. **54(3):** 233–351.

Eyde, R. H. & E. S. Barghoorn. 1963. Morphological and paleobotanical studies of the Nyssaceae. II. The fossil record. J. Arnold Arbor. **44:** 328–376.

Eyde, R. H., A. Bartlett & E. S. Barghoorn. 1969. Fossil record of *Alangium.* Bull. Torrey Bot. Club **96:** 288–314.

Ferguson, I. K. 1966. The Cornaceae in the southeastern United States. J. Arnold Arbor. **47:** 106–116.

Kapil, R. N. & P. R. Mohana Rao. 1966. Studies of the Garryaceae. II. Embryology and systematic position of *Garrya* Douglas ex Lindley. Phytomorphology **16:** 564–578.

Maekawa, F. 1965. *Aucuba* and its allies—The phylogenetic consideration on the Cornaceae. J. Jap. Bot. **40:** 41–47.

Markgraf, F. 1963. Die phylogenetische Stellung der Gattung *Davidia.* Ber. Deutsch. Bot. Ges. **76:** (63)–(69).

Mohana Rao, P. R. 1972 (1973). Embryology of *Nyssa sylvatica* and systematic consideration of the family Nyssaceae. Phytomorphology **22:** 8–21.

Moseley, M. F. & R. M. Beeks. 1955. Studies of the Garryaceae. I. The comparative morphology and phylogeny. Phytomorphology **5:** 314–346.

9. Order Santalales

The order Santalales as here defined consists of 10 families and about 2000 species. The Medusandraceae and Dipentodontaceae, with a single species each, are somewhat doubtfully included in the order, and the position of the small family Balanophoraceae has been debated. The remaining 7 families, making up the great bulk of the order, are generally considered to form a highly natural group showing progressive adaptation to parasitism. The largest family is the Loranthaceae (900), followed by the Santalaceae (400), Viscaceae (300), and Olacaceae (250). None of the other families has as many as a hundred species.

The ovary of members of the Santalales contains only a few ovules. These are often borne on (or in) a free-central or basal placenta, or are pendulous from near the summit of a columnar placenta that extends upward beyond the basal partial partitions. The embryology is often complex and unusual.

Ontogenetic and anatomical studies suggest that the inferior ovary in members of the Santalales is at least partly receptacular rather than appendicular; i.e., the ovary is sunken into the receptacle.

Fossil pollen of the Olacaceae dates from the Maestrichtian, and macrofossils from the Eocene. The Santalaceae follow, with pollen in the late Paleocene and macrofossils in the Oligocene. Pollen of the Loranthaceae and/or Viscaceae dates from the early Eocene, and of the Balanophoraceae from the early Miocene. Thus the fossil record gives some support to the thought that the Olacaceae are basal to most of the other families of the order, and that the Balanophoraceae are relatively late comers to the scene.

SYNOPTICAL ARRANGEMENT OF THE FAMILIES OF SANTALALES

1 Fruit capsular; leaves with small stipules; plants autotrophic; ovules 6–8.
2 Fertile stamens opposite the petals, alternating with well developed stami-

nodes; petals and sepals well differentiated; flowers in slender, catkin-like
racemes .... **1. Medusandraceae.**
2 Fertile stamens alternate with the petals, and alternate with a set of nectary-
glands; petals and sepals very much alike; flowers in globose umbels ...
.... **2. Dipentodontaceae.**
1 Fruit indehiscent, often fleshy; leaves without stipules; plants partly or wholly
parasitic, except some Olacaceae; ovules 1–5 in most families, up to 12 in
Loranthaceae.
3 Plants chlorophyllous and photosynthetic; shoot of fairly ordinary construction, with obvious nodes and internodes, the leaves well developed or
reduced to small scales; inflorescence with an ordinary (not an extremely
large) number of flowers.
4 Plants terrestrial, (autotrophic or) attached to the roots of their host, except
in a few Santalaceae; ovules well differentiated from the placenta (except
in *Exocarpos,* of the Santalaceae), variously bitegmic or unitegmic, or
not differentiated into nucellus and integument.
5 Perianth mostly dichlamydeous; leaves alternate; ovary superior or less
often inferior.
6 Ovary with partitions at the base (rarely throughout), thus partly
(rarely wholly) 2–5-locular, with one ovule per locule or semiloc-
ule; leaves often with silicified cells borne singly or in groups in
the mesophyll, and also often with spicular sclereids, but without
a branching system of lignified cells connecting the veins ......
.... **3. Olacaceae.**
6 Ovary strictly unilocular, with one ovule; leaves with a branching
system of lignified cells connecting the veins, but without silicified
cells or spicular sclereids .... **4. Opiliaceae.**
5 Perianth strictly monochlamydeous; leaves opposite or less commonly
alternate; ovary inferior or less often superior .... **5. Santalaceae.**
4 Plants aerial, attached to the branches of their host (terrestrial in a few
Loranthaceae); fruit various; ovules not differentiated into nucellus and
integument.
7 Ovules well differentiated from the placental column; fruit dry, without
viscid tissue, airborne by 3 strongly accrescent, feathery staminodes;
leaves alternate; inflorescence catkin-like ..... **6. Misodendraceae.**
7 Ovules embedded in and scarcely differentiated from the large, free-
central or basal placenta; fruit fleshy, the seed or stone usually surrounded or capped at one end by viscid tissue; leaves and inflorescence various.
8 Flowers perfect, only rarely unisexual, generally dichlamydeous, often
large and showy; endosperm compound, usually lacking chlorophyll; ovules several, commonly 4–12; embryo-sac monosporic;
leaves opposite or sometimes alternate ...... **7. Loranthaceae.**
8 Flowers strictly unisexual, generally small and inconspicuous; perianth monochlamydeous; endosperm simple, chlorophyllous; ovules
2; embryo-sac bisporic.
9 Leaves opposite; inflorescence not catkin-like; placental column
present ....**8. Viscaceae.**
9 Leaves mostly alternate; inflorescence catkin-like; placental column absent, the ovules embedded in the base of the ovary ..
.... **9. Eremolepidaceae.**
3 Plants wholly without chlorophyll; shoot often fungoid in aspect; inflorescence massive, with numerous or very numerous, often minute flowers;
plants terrestrial .... **10. Balanophoraceae.**

SELECTED REFERENCES

Agarwal, S. 1963. Morphological and embryological studies in the family Olacaceae. I. *Olax* L. II. *Strombosia* Blume. Phytomorphology **13**: 185–196, 348–356.

Baas, P., E. van Oosterhoud & C. J. L. Scholtes. 1982. Leaf anatomy and classification of the Olacaceae, *Octoknema,* and *Erythropalum.* Allertonia **3**: 155–210.

Barlow, B. A. 1964. Classification of the Loranthaceae and Viscaceae. Proc. Linn. Soc. New South Wales II, **89**: 268–272.

Barlow, B. A. & D. Wiens. 1971. The cytogeography of the loranthaceous mistletoes. Taxon **20**: 291–312.

Bhatnagar, S. P. & P. C. Joshi. 1965. Morphological and embryological studies in the family Santalaceae. VII. *Exocarpus bidwellii* Hook. f. Proc. Natl. Inst. Sci. India **31B**: 34–44.

Brenan, J. P. M. 1952. Plants of the Cambridge Expedition 1947–1948. II. A new order of flowering plants from the British Cameroons. Kew Bull. **1952**: 227–236.

Carlquist, S. 1985. Wood and stem anatomy of Misodendraceae: Systematic and ecological conclusions. Brittonia **37**: 58–75.

Cocucci, A. E. 1983. New evidence from embryology in angiosperm classification. Nordic J. Bot. **3**: 67–73.

Dixit, S. N. 1958, 1961. Morphological and embryological studies in the family Loranthaceae. IV. *Amyema* Van-Tiegh. V. *Lepeostegeres gemmiflorus* (Bl.) Bl. VIII. *Tolypanthus* Bl. Phytomorphology **8**: 346–364, 365–376, 1958; **11**: 335–345, 1961.

Fagerlind, F. 1945. Blüte und Blütenstand der Gattung *Balanophora.* Bot. Not. **1945**: 330–350.

Fagerlind, F. 1947. Gynöceummorphologische und embryologische Studien in der Familie Olacaceae. Bot. Not. **1947**: 207–230.

Fagerlind, F. 1948. Beiträge zur Kenntnis der Gynäceummorphologie und Phylogenie der Santalales-Familien. Svensk Bot. Tidskr. **42**: 195–229.

Fener, S. 1981. Pollen morphology and relationships of Misodendraceae (Santalales). Nordic J. Bot. **1**: 731–734.

Hansen, B. 1972. The genus *Balanophora* J. R. & G. Forster. A taxonomic monograph. Dansk Bot. Ark. **28(1)**: 1–188.

Hansen, B. 1980. Balanophoraceae. Fl. Neotropica Monogr. 23.

Hansen, B. & K. Engell. 1978. Inflorescences in Balanophoroideae, Lophophytoideae and Scybalioideae (Balanophoraceae). Svensk Bot. Tidskr. **72**: 177–187.

Hiepko, P. 1971. Die Gattungsabgrenzung bei den Opiliaceae. Ber. Deutsch. Bot. Ges. **84**: 661–663.

Hiepko, P. 1985. A revision of Opiliaceae. III. Bot. Jahrb. Syst. **107**: 137–152.

Johri, B. M. & S. Agarwal. 1965. Morphological and embryological studies in the family Santalaceae. VIII. *Quinchamalium chilense* Lam. Phytomorphology **15**: 360–372.

Johri, B. M. & S. P. Bhatnagar. 1960. Embryology and taxonomy of the Santalales. Proc. Natl. Inst. Sci. India **26B**, Suppl.: 199–220.

Kuijt, J. 1968. Mutual affinities of Santalalean families. Brittonia 20: 136–147.
Kuijt, J. 1969. The biology of parasitic flowering plants. Univ. Calif. Press. Berkeley.
Kuijt, J. 1988. Monograph of the Eremolepidaceae. Syst. Bot. Monogr. 18.
Lobreau-Callen, D. 1982. Structures et affinités polliniques des Cardiopterygaceae, Dipentodontaceae, Erythropalaceae et Octoknemataceae. Bot. Jahrb. Syst. 103: 371–412.
Maheshwari, P., B. M. Johri & S. N. Dixit. 1957. The floral morphology and embryology of the Loranthoideae (Loranthaceae). J. Madras Univ. 27B: 121–136.
Merrill, E. D. 1941. Dipentodontaceae. Pages 69–73 *in* Plants collected by Captain F. Kingdon Ward on the Vernay-Cutting Expedition, 1938–39. Brittonia 4: 20–188.
Ram, M. 1957, 1959. Morphological and embryological studies in the family Santalaceae. I. *Comandra umbellata* (L.) Nutt. II. *Exocarpus*, with a discussion on its systematic position. III. *Leptomeria* R. Br. Phytomorphology 7: 24–35, 1957; 9: 4–19, 20–33, 1959.
Reed, C. 1955. The comparative morphology of the Olacaceae, Opiliaceae and Octoknemataceae. Mem. Soc. Brot. 10: 29–79.
Sleumer, H. O. 1984. Olacaceae. Fl. Neotropica Monogr. 38.
Smith, F. H. & E. C. Smith. 1943. Floral anatomy of the Santalaceae and some related forms. Oregon State Monogr. Stud. Bot. 5.
Wiens, D. & B. A. Barlow. 1971. The cytogeography and relationships of the viscaceous and eremolepidaceous mistletoes. Taxon 20: 313–332.

10. Order Rafflesiales

The order Rafflesiales as here defined consists of 3 families and perhaps 60 species. The Mitrastemonaceae are obviously allied to the Rafflesiaceae and have often been included in that family. The Hydnoraceae are clearly distinctive, but their relationship to the other families is generally admitted. Aside from the features common to the order, *Prosopanche* (Hydnoraceae) resembles *Mitrastemon* in its dome-like synandrium covering the gynoecium, although the details of the structure are different.

The Rafflesiales may be briefly characterized as nongreen parasites with very numerous ovules on parietal, often deeply intruded placentas or in an irregularly plurilocular ovary. The plants are vegetatively much reduced and modified, often with only the flowers or the inflorescence emergent from the host. The pollen is extraordinarily diverse, ranging from monosulcate or uniporate to bisulcate, 2-, 3-, or 4-porate, irregularly multiaperturate, or inaperturate, with equally varied structure and ornamentation of the exine. On the basis of the pollen Takhtajan et al. (1985) propose to revive the families Apodanthaceae and Cytinaceae, which have usually been included in the Rafflesiaceae.

The relationships of the Rafflesiales are disputed and doubtful. If we take the pollen at face value, then the ancestry of the group must be sought directly in the monosulcate segment of the Magnoliidae, where they have no obvious allies. On the other hand, the diversity and instability of the pollen structure here suggest that not too much weight should be put upon it. Perhaps the pervasive simplification in the group, associated with the parasitic habit, has led to the reappearance of seemingly primitive pollen.

If one can bypass the problem of monsulcate pollen in *Hydnora,* then in my opinion the most likely relatives of the Rafflesiales are the Santalales. If one mentally extrapolates backward from existing Rafflesiales to suppose what their less specialized ancestors might have been like, one visualizes green, tanniferous root-parasites with perfect, hypogynous, regular, monochlamydeous flowers that have more or less numerous bitegmic, tenuinucellar ovules in a compound ovary on deeply intruded parietal placentas (or possibly axile placentas), and with fleshy fruits that have more or less numerous seeds with a well developed endosperm. The only features on the list that are out of harmony with the Santalales are the nature of the placentas and the number of ovules and seeds. The very large number of ovules and seeds in the Rafflesiales is clearly an apomorphy derived from some smaller number, and the complex placental organization of the group is obviously associated with the increase in number of ovules. Thus these features by themselves do not seem to present an insuperable barrier to a relationship with the Santalales. The tendency toward simplification of the ovules and the embryo in both orders may simply reflect parallel adaptations to a parasitic habit, but not all groups of parasites show these changes. The endotropic, mycelium-like haustorial body of the Rafflesiaceae and Mitrastemonaceae is very reminiscent of that in many of the Viscaceae. Here we are clearly dealing with parallel adaptations to parasitism, but no other parasitic group has developed a similar structure. As pointed out in an earlier chapter, parallelism is in itself some indication of relationship, to be considered along with other evidence.

At the same time, it is clear that the Rafflesiales cannot be derived from any of the more advanced members of the Santalales. Some of the Rafflesiales have bitegmic ovules, and nothing in the Santalales more advanced than the Olacaceae has more than one integument—indeed most of them have none at all. Furthermore, all of the branch-parasites in the Santalales are immediately excluded as likely ancestors; only root-parasites will do.

SYNOPTICAL ARRANGEMENT OF THE FAMILIES OF RAFFLESIALES

1 Plants essentially ectoparasitic, the vegetative body consisting of a coarse, rhizome-like pilot-root from which the numerous slender, unbranched haustorial roots emerge; leaves strictly wanting; style none; flowers perfect; ovary inferior . . . . **1. Hydnoraceae.**
1 Plants essentially endoparasitic, the vegetative body much branched and mycelium-like, permeating the tissues of the host; no external roots or rhizome-like structures; scale-leaves present on the emergent flowering shoot; stylar column more or less well developed, often large and conspicuous.
   2 Ovary superior; flowers perfect; stamen-tube free from the pistil and en-

closing it, except for a small apical opening, but deciduous after the pollen has been shed .... **2. Mitrastemonaceae.**
2 Ovary inferior or half-inferior; flowers mostly unisexual; stamens adnate to the stylar column, or sometimes forming a sheath around it, the androecium not deciduous as a unit .... **3. Rafflesiaceae.**

SELECTED REFERENCES

Cocucci, A. E. 1965–1976. Estudios en el género *Prosopanche* (Hydnoraceae). I, II, III. Kurtziana **2:** 53–74, 1965; **8:** 7–15, 1975; **9:** 19–39, 1976.
Cocucci, A. E. 1983. New evidence from embryology in angiosperm classification. Nordic J. Bot. **3:** 67–73.
Matuda, E. 1947. On the genus *Mitrastemon.* Bull. Torrey Bot. Club **74:** 133–141.
Meijer, W. 1958. A contribution to the taxonomy and biology of *Rafflesia arnoldi* in west Sumatra. Ann. Bogor. **3:** 33–44.
Olah, L. von. 1960. Cytological and morphological investigations in *Rafflesia arnoldi* R. Br. Bull. Torrey Bot. Club **87:** 406–416.
Takhtajan, A. L., N. R. Meyer & V. N. Kosenko. 1985. Morfologiya pyl'tsy i klassifikatsiya semeystva Rafflesiaceae s. l. Bot. Zhurn. **70:** 153–162.

11. Order Celastrales

The order Celastrales as here defined consists of 12 families and a little more than 2000 species. The Celastraceae (800), Hippocrateaceae (300), Aquifoliaceae (300+), and Icacinaceae (400) are fairly closely related and make up the bulk of the order. The Hippocrateaceae might with some reason be submerged in the Celastraceae. The Dichapetalaceae (200) stand somewhat apart from the other families and are by some authors excluded from the Celastrales. The remaining 7 families have fewer than 50 species altogether. The position of the Salvadoraceae (12) and Stackhousiaceae (20–25) as members of the Celastrales is generally accepted, but the affinities of the Corynocarpaceae (5), Tepuianthaceae (5), Cardiopteridaceae (3), Aextoxicaceae (1) and Geissolomataceae (1) are more debatable. The Cardiopteridaceae may well be better placed in the Solanales, as suggested by Lobreau-Callen (1982).

The Celastrales may be briefly characterized as mostly woody dicotyledons with simple leaves, mostly hypogynous or somewhat perigynous, regular flowers, a single set of distinct stamens mostly alternate with the distinct or shortly connate petals (less often 2 or even 3 sets of stamens), and a mostly plurilocular ovary with 1 or 2 (seldom several) axile (or axile-apical or axile-basal) ovules in each locule. There is nothing ecologically distinctive about the order nor (aside from the ensemble of secondary metabolites) any of its major families.

Fossil pollen attributed to the genus *Ilex* (Aquifoliaceae) first appears in Turonian (early Upper Cretaceous) deposits in Australia. By Coniacian time it is also in Africa, and by the beginning of the Tertiary the type is cosmopolitan. Hu (1967) considers that "The evolutionary lines that involve the widespread groups of the family were well established in the Oligocene." Pollen of the other families does not antedate the Tertiary. The Icacinaceae (Paleocene) come in somewhat before the Celastraceae and Hippocrateaceae (Oligocene). Cretaceous macrofossils attributed to the Celastraceae need to be re-examined. *Sphenostemon* (Aquifoliaceae), with more or less laminar stamens and embedded microsporangia, seems particularly archaic, but neither this genus nor any other in the order displays all the putatively primitive characters of the group.

SYNOPTICAL ARRANGEMENT OF THE FAMILIES OF CELASTRALES

1 Flowers diplostemonous, with 4 + 4 functional stamens; petals none; disk none; habit ericoid . . . . **1. Geissolomataceae.**
1 Flowers mostly haplostemonous (except for the Tepuianthaceae and a few Celastraceae, these differing from Geissolomataceae in other respects), sometimes (Corynocarpaceae) with a set of staminodes in addition to the functional stamens; petals present or rarely absent; disk often present; habit not ericoid.
  2 Ovules mostly erect and basal-axile, or several and superposed in 2 rows on the axile placenta in each locule (seldom apical-axile in Celastraceae), bitegmic; disk well developed except in Salvadoraceae; leaves opposite or less often alternate.
    3 Flowers with a well developed nectary-disk, pentamerous or less often tetramerous; carpels mostly 3–5, seldom only 2.
      4 Woody plants; flowers hypogynous or only slightly perigynous (but the disk sometimes enveloping the ovary); leaves opposite or alternate.
        5 Disk intrastaminal, or the stamens seated on the disk, only rarely the disk extrastaminal; stamens 4–5 (–10); seeds mostly with endosperm; plants with or often without a latex-system; seeds mostly arillate . . . . **2. Celastraceae.**
        5 Disk extrastaminal; stamens (2) 3 (–5); seeds without endosperm; plants generally with a well developed latex-system . . . . **3. Hippocrateaceae.**
      4 Herbs; flowers distinctly perigynous, the disk lining the hypanthium; leaves alternate; seeds with endosperm . . . . . . **4. Stackhousiaceae.**
    3 Flowers without a fully developed nectary-disk (but the stamens sometimes alternating with nectariferous glands), mostly tetramerous; carpels 2; seeds without endosperm . . . . **5. Salvadoraceae.**
  2 Ovules pendulous, apical or apical-axile, 1–2 per locule, bitegmic or more often unitegmic; disk mostly wanting, or represented only by nectary-glands alternating with the stamens, fully developed only in Tepuianthaceae and some Dichapetalaceae; leaves alternate or rarely opposite.
    6 Stipules wanting or vestigial; seeds with endosperm except in some Icacinaceae.
      7 Woody plants, without milky juice; corolla polypetalous or sometimes more or less sympetalous.
        8 Fruit capsular; nectary disk well developed, of 5–10 discrete but contiguous fleshy glands . . . . **6. Tepuianthaceae.**
        8 Fruit drupaceous or samaroid.
          9 Flowers not enclosed by a calyptrate bracteole; ovules unitegmic;

no disk or nectary-glands except in some Icacinaceae; endosperm not ruminate.
10 Locules (2–) 4–6 or more, each with a solitary (rarely 2) ovule;
pedicel not articulated at the summit . **7. Aquifoliaceae.**
10 Fertile locule solitary (rarely 3), with (1) 2 ovules; pedicel
articulated at the summit .... **8. Icacinaceae.**
9 Flowers enclosed in bud by a calyptrate bracteole; ovules bitegmic; nectary-glands well developed, alternating with the stamens; endosperm ruminate; ovary bilocular, one locule with 2
ovules, the other empty .... **9. Aextoxicaceae.**
7 Climbing herbs with milky juice; fruit samaroid; corolla distinctly sympetalous .... **10. Cardiopteridaceae.**
6 Stipules present; endosperm wanting; disk present and intrastaminal, or
more often represented by nectary-glands alternating with the stamens.
11 Flowers with petaloid staminodes alternating with the functional stamens, which are opposite the petals; ovary bicarpellate, but one
carpel usually more or less reduced; ovule solitary, or solitary in
each of the two locules; ovules crassinucellar; pollen grains dicol-
porate .... **11. Corynocarpaceae.**
11 Flowers without staminodes; stamens alternate with the petals; ovary
with 2–3 (4) equal carpels and locules, each locule with 2 tenuinucellar ovules; pollen grains tricolporate ....**12. Dichapetalaceae.**

Selected References

Baas, P. 1973. The wood anatomical range in *Ilex* (Aquifoliaceae) and its ecological and phylogenetic significance. Blumea **21**: 193–258.

Baas, P. 1975. Vegetative anatomy and the affinities of Aquifoliaceae, *Sphenostemon, Phelline,* and *Oncotheca.* Blumea **22**: 311–407.

Bailey, I. W. & R. A. Howard. 1941. The comparative morphology of the
Icacinaceae. I–IV. J. Arnold Arbor. **22**: 125–132, 171–187, 432–442, 556–
568.

Barker, W. R. 1977. Taxonomic studies in *Stackhousia* Sm. (Stackhousiaceae)
in South Australia. J. Adelaide Bot. Gard. **1**: 69–82.

Berkeley, E. 1953. Morphological studies in the Celastraceae. J. Elisha Mitchell
Sci. Soc. **69**: 185–206.

Bernardi, L. 1964. La position systématique du genre *Sphenostemon* Baillon
sensu van Steenis. Candollea **19**: 199–205.

Boesewinkel, F. D. & F. Bouman. 1980. Development of ovule and seed-coat
of *Dichapetalum mombuttense* Engl. with notes on other species. Acta Bot.
Neerl. **29**: 103–115.

Brizicky, G. K. 1964. The genera of Celastrales in the southeastern United States.
J. Arnold Arbor. **45**: 206–234.

Carlquist, S. 1975. Wood anatomy and relationships of Geissolomataceae. Bull.
Torrey Bot. Club **102**: 128–134.

Dahl, A. O. 1952. The comparative morphology of the Icacinaceae. VI. The
pollen. J. Arnold Arbor. **33**: 252–295.

Dahlgren, R. & V. S. Rao. 1969. A study of the family Geissolomataceae. Bot.
Not. **122**: 207–227.

Fagerlind, F. 1945. Bau des Gynöceums, den Samenanlage und des Embryo-sackes bei einigen Repräsentanten der Familie Icacinaceae. Svensk Bot. Tidskr. **39:** 346–364.

Goldblatt, P., H. Tobe, S. Carlquist & V. C. Patel. 1985. Familial position of the Cape genus *Empleuridium*. Ann. Missouri Bot. Gard. **72:** 167–183.

Hartog, R. M. den & P. Baas. 1978. Epidermal characters of the Celastraceae sensu lato. Acta Bot. Neerl. **27(5/6):** 355–388.

Hu, S.-y. 1967. The evolution and distribution of the species of Aquifoliaceae in the Pacific area. J. Jap. Bot. **42:** 13–32, 49–59.

Lobreau, D. 1969. Les limites de l'"ordre" des Célastrales d'après le pollen. Pollen & Spores **11:** 499–555.

Lobreau-Callen, D. 1977. Nouvelle interpretation de l'"ordre" des Célastrales à l'aide de la palynologie. Compt. Rend. Hebd. Séances Acad. Sci. **284D:** 915–918.

Lobreau-Callen, D. 1982. Structures et affinités polliniques des Cardiopteryga-ceae, Dipentodontaceae, Erythropalaceae et Octoknemataceae. Bot. Jahrb. Syst. **103:** 371–412.

Mauritzon, J. 1936. Embryologische Angaben über Stackhousiaceae, Hippocrat-eaceae und Icacinaceae. Svensk Bot. Tidskr. **30:** 541–550.

Metcalfe, C. R. 1956. The taxonomic affinities of *Sphenostemon* in the light of the anatomy of its stem and leaf. Kew Bull. **1956:** 249–253.

Narang, N. 1953. The life-history of *Stackhousia linariaefolia* A. Cunn. with a discussion on its systematic position. Phytomorphology **3:** 485–493.

Prance, G. T. 1972. Dichapetalaceae. Fl. Neotropica Monogr. 10.

Robson, N. 1965. Taxonomic and nomenclatural notes on Celastraceae. Bol. Soc. Brot., ser. 2, **39:** 5–55.

Stant, M. Y. 1952. Notes on the systematic anatomy of *Stackhousia*. Kew Bull. **1951:** 309–318.

12. Order Euphorbiales

The order Euphorbiales as here defined consists of 4 families, domi-nated by the very large family Euphorbiaceae (8000 spp.), to which the other families are attached as small satellites. Of these satellite families, only the Pandaceae are without question allied to the Euphorbiaceae. The Buxaceae have usually been associated with the Euphorbiaceae, and both the pollen-morphology and the floral anatomy have been interpreted to favor such an affinity, but an alternative position in the Hamamelidae can also be defended. Behnke (1982) considers that the Buxaceae are well isolated from the other families here referred to the Euphorbiales, and Carlquist (1982) considers that on anatomical grounds the Buxaceae would fit more comfortably in the Hamamelidae. The affinities of *Simmondsia* are uncertain, but its inclusion in the Euphorbiales brings no significant new characters to the order. Serological studies (Scogin, 1980) support a relationship to the Euphorbiaceae. *Daphniphyllum,* often included in the Euphorbiales or even in the family Euphorbiaceae, is here considered to form a distinct family and order in the Hamamelidae.

Leaving aside the satellite families, the position of the Euphorbiaceae in the general scheme of classification is also debatable. In the twelfth edition of the Engler Syllabus they are included in a broadly defined order Geraniales. Takhtajan allies them with the Malvales, in the subclass Dilleniidae. Each of these assignments has a substantial body of tradition and respectable opinion behind it. In 1967 Webster cautiously favored a rosid rather than a dilleniid affinity for the family. Twenty years later (1987) he proposed to resolve the problem by associating "the Euphorbiales with the Malvales and Geraniales [sensu Engler], and possibly with the Celastrales, in a superorder that straddles the arbitrary boundary between the Dilleniidae and Rosidae." Vogel (1986) also uses the apparently diverse affinities of the Euphorbiaceae to promote a proposed abandonment of the Rosidae-Dilleniidae organization. I cannot agree. The phenetic distinction between the two subclasses is weak, but the existence of two affinity-groups here seems clear enough, despite the doubtful position of a few taxa.

The Euphorbiaceae are so diverse in vegetative and chemical features and in pollen-morphology that one could compare some member of the group to any of a wide range of families and orders of dicotyledons. The euphorbiad gynoecium, in contrast, is much more stable, as is also the nectary-disk in flowers that are not highly reduced and aggregated into pseudanthia. These features should therefore provide a better guide to the affinities of the group, and in these respects the Euphorbiaceae compare well with the Celastrales and Sapindales. Similar gynoecia are much less common in the Dilleniidae, and occur mainly in groups which have other specialized features that militate against a close relationship with the Euphorbiaceae. The malvalean gynoecium is more or less comparable to that of the Euphorbiaceae, but the nectaries in the two groups are wholly different. Therefore I prefer to assign the Euphorbiaceae to the Rosidae rather than to the Dilleniidae. Although some euphorbiads have compound leaves, simple leaves appear to be basic for the group. Thus it seems better to associate the Euphorbiales more closely with the Celastrales than with the Sapindales or Geraniales. It may also be noted that some tendency toward dioecism is well established in the Celastrales, and that two celastralean families, the Aextoxicaceae and Dichapetalaceae, have often been thought to be related to the Euphorbiaceae.

The huge genus *Euphorbia* (perhaps 1500 species) has very strongly reduced flowers that are aggregated into bisexual pseudanthia commonly called cyathia. The cyathium has a solitary, terminal pistillate flower composed essentially of a naked pistil, surrounded by (4) 5 staminate cymes. The bracts subtending these staminate cymes are connate into a campanulate or hemispheric involucre (simulating a hypanthium), and the tips of the bracts alternate with nectary-glands that may each have a small petaloid appendage. Each male cyme produces 1–10+ closely aggregated flowers; each such flower consists of a single stamen that may or may not be seated in its own small cup (vestigial perianth). The pistillate flower at the center of the cyathium may at first appear to be sessile or nearly so, but its pedicel commonly elongates with increasing maturity, so that the trilocular ovary hangs out of the cyathium on a stalk.

The Euphorbiaceae are highly diversified ecologically as well as morphologically and chemically. Some of the African species of *Euphorbia* are spiny, essentially leafless, arborescent succulents that are ecologically comparable to some of the cacti. Some genera are tropical forest trees. Some species are extreme xerophytes. Many are ordinary herbaceous mesophytes. Various members of the family contain diverse sorts of secondary metabolites, including various kinds of alkaloids (benzyl-isoquinoline alkaloids in *Croton*), tannins, and even (*Drypetes*) mustard-oils. More often they contain laticifers, with different contents in different genera or sections. The milky juice and the alkaloids found in so many members of the family can readily be believed to help protect the plants from predators. Otherwise it is difficult or impossible to find any unifying ecological features in the group. We still await a convincing Darwinian explanation of the progressive reduction of the euphorbiaceous flower, culminating unexpectedly and very successfully in pseudanthia that are functionally comparable to ordinary flowers in other families.

Pollen considered to represent the Buxaceae dates from the Campanian stage of the Upper Cretaceous. Pollen of two subfamilies of Euphorbiaceae (Crotonoideae and Phyllanthoideae) comes in somewhat later, in the Paleocene. Macrofossils considered to represent the Euphorbiaceae are known only from Eocene and more recent deposits.

SYNOPTICAL ARRANGEMENT OF THE FAMILIES OF EUPHORBIALES

1 Ovules apotropous, the raphe dorsal.
  2 Ovules 2 per carpel; endosperm copious; vessels with scalariform perforations; styles borne on or forming continuations of the apical margin of the ovary (in this respect resembling *Daphniphyllum*); secondary growth of normal type; sieve-tubes with P-type plastids .... **1. Buxaceae.**
  2 Ovules one per carpel; endosperm very scanty or none; vessels with simple perforations; stigmas sessile, deciduous, clustered at the top of the ovary; secondary growth anomalous, concentric; sieve-tubes with S-type plastids .... **2. Simmondsiaceae.**
1 Ovules epitropous, the raphe ventral, or rarely (*Panda*) the ovule orthotropous; ovary with a single common style, or with the styles or stigmas clustered at the top of the ovary.
  3 Obturator wanting; fruit drupaceous; flowers without a disk; seeds without a caruncle; plants without milky juice; leaves arranged in flat sprays that simulate pinnately compound leaves .... **3. Pandaceae.**
  3 Obturator well developed; fruit usually a capsular schizocarp, only seldom drupaceous; flowers usually with a disk, or naked and aggregated into cyathia; seeds often with a caruncle; plants often with milky juice; leaves simple or less often compound, or much reduced, only seldom arranged in flat sprays that simulate pinnately compound leaves .... **4. Euphorbiaceae.**

SELECTED REFERENCES

Bailey, D. C. 1980. Anomalous growth and vegetative anatomy of *Simmondsia chinensis*. Amer. J. Bot. **67**: 147–161.

Baranova, M. A. 1980. Sravnitel'no-stomatograficheskoe issledovanie semeystv Buxaceae i Simmondsiaceae. Pages 68–75 *in* Sistematika i evoliutsiya vysshikh rasteniy. Nauka. Leningrad.

Behnke, H. -D. 1982. Sieve-element plastids, exine sculpturing, and the systematic affinities of the Buxaceae. Pl. Syst. Evol. **139:** 257–266.

Buchmann, S. L. 1987. Floral biology of jojoba (*Simmondsia chinensis,*) an anemophilous plant. Desert Plants **8:** 111–124.

Carlquist, S. 1982. Wood anatomy of Buxaceae: Correlations with ecology and phylogeny. Flora **172:** 463–491.

Forman, L. L. 1966. The reinstatement of *Galearia* Zoll. & Mor. and *Microdesmis* Hook. f. in the Pandaceae. With appendices by C. R. Metcalfe and N. Parameswaran. Kew Bull. **20:** 309–321.

Forman, L. L. 1968. The systematic position of *Panda* Pierre. Proc. Linn. Soc. London **179:** 269–270.

Hayden, W. J., et al. 1984. Systematics and palynology of *Picrodendron*: Further evidence of relationship with the Oldfieldioideae (Euphorbiaceae). J. Arnold Arbor. **65:** 105–127.

Köhler, E. 1965. Die Pollenmorphologie der biovulaten Euphorbiaceae und ihre Bedeutung für die Taxonomie. Grana Palynol. **6:** 26–120.

Köhler, E. & P. Brückner. 1983. Zur Pollenmorphologie und systematischen Stellung der Gattung *Simmondsia* Nutt. Wiss. Z. Friedrich-Schiller-Univ. Jena, Math.-Naturwiss. Reihe **32:** 945–955.

Mathou, T. 1939. Recherches sur la famille des Buxacées: Étude anatomique, microchimique et systématique. Thése Fac. Sci. Toulouse.

Melikyan, A. P. 1968. Polozhenie semeystv Buxaceae i Simmondsiaceae v sisteme. Bot. Zhurn. **53:** 1043–1047.

Nowicke, J. W. 1984. A palynological study of the Pandaceae. Pollen & Spores **26:** 31–42.

Nowicke, J. W. & J. J. Skvarla. 1984. Pollen morphology and the relationships of *Simmondsia chinensis* to the order Euphorbiales. Amer. J. Bot. **71:** 210–215.

Punt, W. 1962. Pollen morphology of the Euphorbiaceae with special reference to taxonomy. Wentia **7:** 1–116.

Radcliffe-Smith, A. 1987. Segregate families from the Euphorbiaceae. Bot. J. Linn. Soc. **94:** 47–66.

Scogin, R. 1980. Serotaxonomy of *Simmondsia chinensis* (Simmondsiaceae). Aliso **9:** 555–559.

Vaughan, J. G. & J. A. Rest. 1969. Note on the testa structure of *Panda* Pierre, *Galearia* Zoll. & Mor. and *Microdesmis* Hook. f. (Pandaceae). Kew Bull. **23:** 215–218.

Vogel, C. 1986. Phytoserologische Untersuchungen zur Systematik der Euphorbiaceae; Beiträge zur infrafamiliären Gliederung und zu Beziehungen im extrafamiliären Bereich. Dissert. Bot. 98.

Webster, G. L. 1967. The genera of Euphorbiaceae in the southeastern United States. J. Arnold Arbor. **48:** 303–430.

Webster, G. L. 1987. The saga of the spurges: A review of classification and relationships in the Euphorbiales. Bot. J. Linn. Soc. **94:** 3–46.

13. Order Rhamnales

The order Rhamnales as here defined consists of 3 families and about 1700 species. There are about 900 species of Rhamnaceae, 700 of Vitaceae, and 70 of Leeaceae. Most members of the order are readily recognizable by the combination of dichlamydeous, polypetalous, haplostemonous flowers with the stamens opposite the petals, and with 1 or 2 ovules in each locule of a compound ovary. There is nothing ecologically distinctive about the group, and there is a considerable ecological diversity among its members, most of which are woody.

The close relationship of the Leeaceae to the Vitaceae is not in dispute. The Rhamnaceae are generally thought to be a little more distantly related, and some modern students would remove them from any association with the other two families.

Fossil pollen of the Rhamnales (both Rhamnaceae and Vitaceae) dates only from the Oligocene. Macrofossils of both of these families date from the Eocene, and Jones and Dilcher (1980) maintain that the fossil leaves "support the hypothesis that modern tribes and possibly genera of Rhamnaceae had evolved by the Middle Eoncene."

The origin of the Rhamnales is to be sought in the Rosales, in a common complex with the ancestors of the Celastrales and Sapindales. There may well have been a diplostemonous common ancestor of the Rhamnales and Celastrales (a very few of the Celastrales are in fact diplostemonous). Differentiation of the two orders from this common ancestor would involve loss of the antesepalous stamens by the Rhamnales, and loss of the antepetalous stamens by the Celastrales.

SYNOPTICAL ARRANGEMENT OF THE FAMILIES OF RHAMNALES

1 Flowers perigynous to sometimes essentially epigynous; fruits mostly drupaceous or separating into mericarps, not baccate; plants without raphides; embryo rather large; sieve-tubes with S-type plastids; ovules mostly solitary in each chamber of the ovary; mostly shrubs or trees, often thorny, but sometimes scrambling or tendriliferous vines . . . . **1. Rhamnaceae.**
1 Flowers hypogynous; fruits baccate (though sometimes rather dry); plants with raphide-sacs in the parenchymatous tissues; embryo small; sieve-tubes with P-type plastids.
  2 Ovules solitary in each chamber of the ovary; filaments connate into a tube; plants erect, without tendrils . . . . **2. Leeaceae.**
  2 Ovules paired in each chamber of the ovary; filaments distinct; plants mostly (not always) tendriliferous vines . . . .**3. Vitaceae.**

SELECTED REFERENCES

Behnke, H.-D. 1974. P- und S-Typ Siebelement-plastiden bei Rhamnales. Beitr. Biol. Pflanzen **50:** 457–464.

Bennek, C. 1958. Die morphologische Beurteilung der Staub- und Blumenblätter der Rhamnaceen. Bot. Jahrb. Syst. **77:** 423–457.

Brizicky, G. K. 1964. The genera of Rhamnaceae in the southeastern United States. J. Arnold Arbor. **45:** 439–463.

Brizicky, G. K. 1965. The genera of Vitaceae in the southeastern United States. J. Arnold Arbor. **46:** 48–67.

Jones, J. H. & D. L. Dilcher. 1980. Investigations of angiosperms from the Eocene of North America: *Rhamnus marginatus* (Rhamnaceae) reexamined. Amer. J. Bot. **67:** 959–967.

Kashyap, G. 1955–1958. Studies in the family Vitaceae. I. Floral morphology of *Vitis trifolia* L. Agra Univ. J. Res., Sci. **4**(Suppl.): 777–783, 1955. II. Floral anatomy of *Vitis trifolia* Linn., *Vitis latifolia* Roxb., and *Vitis himalayana* Brandis. III. Floral morphology of *Vitis latifolia* Roxb., *Vitis himalayana* Brandis and *Vitis trifolia* Linn. J. Indian Bot. Soc. **36:** 317–323, 1957; **37:** 240–248, 1958.

Moore, M. O. & D. E. Giannasi. 1987. Foliar flavonoids of selected *Vitis* taxa in the southeastern United States. Biochem. Syst. Ecol. **15:** 79–83.

Nair, N. C. 1968. Contribution to the floral morphology and embryology of two species of *Leea* with a discussion on the taxonomic position of the genus. J. Indian Bot. Soc. **47:** 193–205.

Nair, N. C. & P. N. N. Nambisan. 1957. Contribution to the floral morphology and embryology of *Leea sambucina* Wild. Bot. Not. **110:** 160–172.

Nair, N. C. & V. S. Sarma. 1961. Organography and floral anatomy of some members of the Rhamnaceae. J. Indian Bot. Soc. **40:** 47–55.

Prichard, E. C. 1955. Morphological studies in Rhamnaceae. J. Elisha Mitchell Sci. Soc. **71:** 82–106.

Tiffney, B. H. & E. S. Barghoorn. 1976. Fruits and seeds of the Brandon Lignite. I. Vitaceae. Rev. Paleobot. Palynol. **22:** 169–191.

14. Order Linales

The order Linales as here defined consists of 5 families and about 550 species. The two largest families are the Linaceae (220) and Erythroxylaceae (200). The other 3 families are distinctive small groups that have often been included in the Linaceae. Of the 3, the Humiriaceae in particular form a well marked, coherent group that seems to be most appropriately treated as a distinct family. Once the Humiriaceae are removed from the Linaceae, then the Ixonanthaceae and Hugoniaceae also appear as aberrant groups that might more reasonably be treated as separate families. Each of the 5 families of the order then appears as a well defined group. The mutual interrelationships among the 5 families are not in serious dispute.

The families of Linales have often been included in a broadly defined order Geraniales, distinguished from the Sapindales by the epitropous rather than apotropous ovules. Under the concepts that I have developed and presented earlier, the orientation of the ovules is considered to be a feature of less than ordinal significance, and the more narrowly defined order Geraniales is considered to be a largely herbaceous offshoot from the mostly woody order Sapindales. Both the Sapindales and the Geraniales characteristically have compound or evidently lobed leaves, and the forms with simple, entire or merely toothed leaves are considered to be apomorphic within the order. The Linales, on the other hand, all have simple, entire or merely toothed leaves, and the habit ranges from distinctly woody (and sometimes with scalariform vessels) in the more archaic members to herbaceous in the more advanced ones. Thus the Linales cannot be included in or derived from the Geraniales as here conceived, but they might possibly be a simple-leaved offshoot from archaic, extinct members of the Sapindales with scalariform vessels, well developed stipules, and distinct styles. A perhaps more likely alternative is that the Linales are derived directly from simple-leaved members of the Rosales, parallel to the compound-leaved Sapindales. In any case it seems clear enough that the Sapindales, Geraniales, and Linales are all derived eventually from the Rosales.

SYNOPTICAL ARRANGEMENT OF THE FAMILIES OF LINALES

1 Petals usually with a ligular appendage toward the base on the inner side; usually only one locule of the ovary ovuliferous; disk and nectary-glands wanting; trees or shrubs; stamens 10; fruit a drupe; vessel-segments with simple perforations . . . . .1. **Erythroxylaceae.**
1 Petals not appendaged; all locules ovuliferous; disk or nectary-glands present.
  2 Style solitary, simple, only the stigmas sometimes separate; disk intrastaminal, well developed, or sometimes represented only by 2–5 glands; trees or shrubs.
    3 Fruit a drupe; seeds neither arillate nor winged; filaments connate for much of their length into a tube; anthers often of unusual structure; sepals connate into a lobed or toothed cup or tube; vessel-segments with scalariform perforations; stamens 10–many . . . **2. Humiriaceae.**
    3 Fruit a capsule with arillate or winged seeds; filaments distinct; anthers of normal structure; sepals distinct or only basally connate; vessel-segments with simple perforations; stamens 5–20 . . . . . **3. Ixonanthaceae.**
  2 Style more or less deeply cleft, or often the styles distinct; disk extrastaminal, often represented only by 2–5 glands; sepals distinct or only basally connate.
    4 Trees, shrubs, or often woody vines; fruit a drupe or a nut; vessel-segments with simple or scalariform perforations; stamens (5–) 10 (–15) . . . . . .
      . . . . .4. **Hugoniaceae.**
    4 Herbs, or seldom shrubs; fruit usually a capsule (of indehiscent mericarps in *Anisadenia*); vessel-segments with simple perforations; functional stamens (4) 5 . . . . 5. **Linaceae.**

SELECTED REFERENCES

Boesewinkel, F. D. 1980. Development of ovule and testa of *Linum usitatissimum* L. Acta Bot. Neerl. 29: 17–32.

Boesewinkel, F. D. 1985. The ovule and seed of *Humiria balsamifera* (Aubl.) St. Hil. Acta Bot. Neerl. **34**: 183–191.

Boesewinkel, F. D. & J. Geenen. 1980. Development of ovule and seed-coat of *Erythroxylum coca* Lamk. Acta Bot. Neerl. **29**: 231–241.

Cuatrecasas, J. 1961. A taxonomic revision of the Humiriaceae. Contr. U.S. Natl. Herb. **35**: 25–214.

Forman, L. L. 1965. A new genus of Ixonanthaceae with notes on the family. Kew Bull. **19**: 517–526.

Narayana, L. L. & D. Rao. 1969–1977. Contributions to the floral anatomy of Humiriaceae 1–6. J. Jap. Bot. **44**: 328–335, 1969; **48**: 143–146, 242–276, 1973; **51**: 12–15, 42–44, 1976; **52**: 145–153, 1977.

Narayana, L. L. & D. Rao. 1969–1978. Contributions to the floral anatomy of the Linaceae. [13 parts.] J. Jap. Bot. **44**: 289–294, 1969; **48**: 205–208, 1973; **51**: 92–96, 349–352, 1976; **52**: 56–59, 231–234, 315–317, 1977; **53**: 12–14, 161–163, 213–218, 1978. Phytomorphology **21**: 64–67, 1971 (1972). Curr. Sci. **43**: 226–227, 391–393, 1974.

Nooteboom, H. P. 1967. The taxonomic position of Irvingioideae, *Allantospermum* Forman and *Cyrillopsis* Kuhlm. Adansonia sér. 2, **7**: 161–168.

Oltmann, O. 1968 (1969). Die Pollenmorphologie der Erythroxylaceae und ihre systematische Bedeutung. Ber. Deutsch. Bot. Ges. **81**: 505–511.

Robertson, K. R. 1971. The Linaceae in the southeastern United States. J. Arnold Arbor. **52**: 649–665.

Rogers, C. M. & K. S. Xavier. 1972. Parallel evolution in pollen structure in *Linum*. Grana **12**: 41–46.

Saad, S. I. 1962. Pollen morphology of *Ctenolophon*. Bot. Not. **115**: 49–57.

Suryakanta (no initial). 1974. Pollen morphological studies in the Humiriaceae. J. Jap. Bot. **49**: 112–122.

Van Welzen, P. C. & P. Baas. 1984. A leaf-anatomical contribution to the classification of the Linaceae complex. Blumea **29**: 453–479.

15. Order Polygalales

The order Polygalales as here defined consists of 7 families and about 2300 species. Most of the species belong to only 3 families, the Malpighiaceae (1200+), Polygalaceae (750), and Vochysiaceae (200). The other 4 families have only a little more than a hundred species in all.

The order may be briefly characterized as dicotyledons with simple leaves, hypogynous or merely perigynous, often strongly irregular flowers, distinct (or only basally connate), often clawed petals, often poricidal anthers, and a compound, usually plurilocular ovary with mostly only 1 or 2 ovules per locule. The filaments are often connate into a cleft tube or into 2 groups.

The mutual affinity of 5 of the families of Polygalales has been widely accepted. These are the Polygalaceae, Xanthophyllaceae, Vochysiaceae, Trigoniaceae, and Tremandraceae. The Tremandraceae are unusual in the order in having regular flowers. In other respects, however, including the wood-anatomy and the poricidal anthers, they fit well into the Polygalales, and they do not appear to be closely allied to any other order.

The other two families, the Malpighiaceae and Krameriaceae, are more controversial. There has been a long-standing difference of opinion as to whether the Krameriaceae are more closely allied to the Polygalaceae or Caesalpiniaceae. The issue now appears to be resolved in favor of the polygalaceous relationship. Heimsch (1942, cited under Rosidae) considered that the wood-anatomy of *Krameria* is similar to that of the Polygalaceae, but very different from that of legumes. The general floral structure, although it superficially suggests that of legumes, is actually more compatible with that of the Polygalaceae. More importantly, Leinfellner (1971) and Milby (1971) have shown that the pistil is basically bicarpellate, with one fertile and one sterile carpel. Milby also notes that the general floral anatomy of *Krameria* (the only genus of its family) is very different from that of legumes, but he does not make any comparison with the Polygalaceae. Recent serological studies also support a relationship of *Krameria* to the Polygalaceae.

It is interesting and perhaps significant that *Krameria* is pollinated primarily by bees of the genus *Centris,* which collect oil from the flowers. The same species of *Centris* also collects oil from species of Malpighiaceae. Simpson and Neff (1978) consider that the association of *Centris* with Malpighiaceae is phyletically ancestral, and that with *Krameria* derived.

The Malpighiaceae are morphologically transitional between the Linales and Polygalales, and they might with some justification be included in either order. In the Linales they would be advanced, in the Polygalales more archaic. They cannot be considered as directly ancestral to the rest of the Polygalales, however, because their seeds lack endosperm, whereas the Polygalaceae and some of the other families have endospermous seeds. I opt for including the Malpighiaceae in the Polygalales, because they (the Malpighiaceae) are apparently allied to the Vochysiaceae and Trigoniaceae, and because their inclusion to the Polygalales is less disturbing to the homogeneity of the order than their inclusion in the Linales would be to that group.

The Polygalales and Linales are here regarded as a pair of closely related, basically simple-leaved offshoots from the Rosales, parallel in some respects to the compound-leaved Sapindales on the one hand, and to the simple-leaved Celastrales and Rhamnales on the other. The Polygalales differ from the other simple-leaved orders in having irregular flowers, or poricidal anthers, or both. These are of course advanced features. Primitively woody, the order has given rise to herbaceous forms in the Polygalaceae, Vochysiaceae, and Krameriaceae. These three families include both woody and herbaceous species, but only the Polygalaceae have a large proportion of herbs.

Ecologically the Polygalales have little in common beyond the possible similarities in pollinating mechanisms as suggested by the structure of the flowers. The family Polygalaceae is indeed highly diverse ecologically, as it includes small trees, shrubs, ordinary herbs, climbers, and even a few nongreen mycoparasites. The several families (and sometimes genera within the families) differ in the number of carpels, number of ovules per locule, and presence or absence of stipules and endosperm, but these characters are difficult to assess in terms of ecological adaptation or survival value.

The differences in habit and type of fruit that mark some of the genera are apparently adaptive but are duplicated in many other groups of dicotyledons.

The Polygalaceae can be traced to the Paleocene on the basis of pollen, and to the Eocene on the basis of fruits thought to belong to the modern genus *Securidaca*. Fossil flowers of Malpighiaceae occur in Middle Eocene deposits in Tennessee. Since this family is regarded as originally South American, its ancestry presumably antedates the Tennessee fossils.

SYNOPTICAL ARRANGEMENT OF THE FAMILIES OF POLYGALALES

1 Anthers mostly opening by longitudinal slits, seldom by terminal pores; gynoecium of (2) 3 (–5) carpels, rarely pseudomonomerous; stipules usually present and more or less well developed, but small or wanting in some Vochysiaceae and Malpighiaceae.
  2 Styles generally distinct or connate only at the base, only rarely (as in spp. of *Bunchosia*) fully connate; plants generally with malpighian hairs; sepals usually with a pair of prominent abaxial glands near the base; embryo-sac often tetrasporic and 16-nucleate; flowers mostly irregular, the 5 petals commonly clawed, usually with ciliate, toothed, or fringed margins; ovules solitary in each locule . . . . **1. Malpighiaceae.**
  2 Style solitary, with a capitate or lateral stigma; plants seldom with malpighian hairs; sepals without abaxial glands; embryo-sac not known to be tetrasporic or 16-nucleate; ovules often more than 1 per locule.
    3 Flowers obliquely irregular, but not papilionaceous; stamens distinct or connate into 2 groups, very often only one stamen antheriferous; plants commonly accumulating aluminum . . . . **2. Vochysiaceae.**
    3 Flowers papilionaceous, with a 2-petaled keel, 2 wings, and a basally saccate or spurred standard; stamens collectively unilateral on the anterior side of the flower, monadelphous by their filaments, 5–8 of them with anthers; plants not accumulating aluminum . . . **3. Trigoniaceae.**
1 Anthers mostly opening by terminal or subterminal pores or short slits, less frequently (Xanthophyllaceae, some Polygalaceae) by longitudinal slits; gynoecium of 2 (less often 3–5 or even 8) carpels, or sometimes pseudomonomerous; stipules mostly wanting or poorly developed.
  4 Flowers regular, with distinct, induplicate-valvate petals; pollen-grains tricolporate; plants mostly of ericoid aspect . . . . **4. Tremandraceae.**
  4 Flowers usually evidently irregular, commonly papilionaceous in aspect; plants not ericoid.
    5 Ovules solitary in each of the (1) 2–5 (–8) locules of the ovary; filaments generally forming a cleft tube; seeds with or less often without endosperm; pollen-grains polycolporate . . . .**5. Polygalaceae.**
    5 Ovules 2 or more in the single locule of the ovary; filaments not forming a tube; seeds without endosperm.
      6 Ovary with 2 parietal placentas and 2–16 ovules in all; anthers opening by elongate longitudinal slits; pollen-grains polycolporate; fruit unarmed; small trees, commonly accumulating aluminum . . . .
. . . . **6. Xanthophyllaceae.**
      6 Ovary with a pair of pendulous subapical ovules; anthers opening by terminal pores or short slits; pollen-grains with 3 (4) apertures; fruit generally covered with bristles or spines that are often retrorsely barbed; hemiparasitic shrubs and perennial herbs . . . .
. . . . **7. Krameriaceae.**

SELECTED REFERENCES

Anderson, W. R. 1979. Floral conservatism in neotropical Malpighiaceae. Biotropica **11:** 219–223.
Boesewinkel, F. D. 1987. Ovules and seeds of Trigoniaceae. Acta Bot. Neerl. **36:** 81–91.
Carlquist, S. 1977. Wood anatomy of the Tremandraceae: Phylogenetic and ecological implications. Amer. J. Bot. **64:** 704–713.
Dickison, W. C. 1973. Nodal and leaf anatomy of *Xanthophyllum* (Polygalaceae). J. Linn. Soc., Bot. **67:** 103–115.
Erdtman, G., P. Leins, R. Melville & C. R. Metcalfe. 1969. On the relationships of *Emblingia.* J. Linn. Soc., Bot. **62:** 169–186.
Leinfellner, W. 1971. Das Gynözeum von *Krameria* und sein Vergleich mit jenem der Leguminosae und der Polygalaceae. Oesterr. Bot. Z. **119:** 102–117.
Leinfellner, W. 1972. Zur Morphologie des Gynözeums der Polygalaceen. Oesterr. Bot. Z **120:** 51–76.
Lleras, E. 1978. Trigoniaceae. Fl. Neotropica Monogr. 19.
Lobreau-Callen, D. 1984. Pollen et paléobotanique des Malpighiaceae. Rev. Paleobiol. Vol. Spécial: 131–138.
Milby, T. H. 1971. Floral anatomy of *Krameria lanceolata.* Amer. J. Bot. **58:** 569–576.
Miller, N. G. 1971. The Polygalaceae in the southeastern United States. J. Arnold Arbor. **52:** 267–284.
Robertson, K. R. 1972. The Malpighiaceae in the southeastern United States. J. Arnold Arbor. **53:** 101–112.
Robertson, K. R. 1973. The Krameriaceae in the southeastern United States. J. Arnold Arbor. **54:** 322–327.
Simpson, B. B. & J. L. Neff. 1978. Dynamics and derivation of the pollination syndrome of *Krameria* (Krameriaceae). Bot. Soc. Amer. Misc. Ser. Publ. **156:** 14.
Singh, B. 1959, 1961. Studies in the family Malpighiaceae. I. Morphology of *Thryallis glauca* Kuntze. II. Morphology of *Malpighia glabra* Linn. III. Development and structure of seed and fruit of *Malpighia glabra* Linn. Hort. Advance **3:** 1–19, 1959; **5:** 83–96, 145–155, 1951.
Stafleu, F. A. 1948–1954. A monograph of the Vochysiaceae. 1–4. Recueil Trav. Bot. Néerl. **41:** 397–540, 1948. Acta Bot. Neerl. **1:** 222–242, 1952; **2:** 144–217, 1953; **3:** 459–480, 1954.
Subra Rao, A. M. 1940, 1941. Studies in the Malpighiaceae. I. Embryo-sac development and embryogeny in the genera *Hiptage, Banistera* and *Stigmatophyllum.* J. Indian Bot. Soc. **18:** 145–156. 2. Structure and development of the ovules and embryo-sacs of *Malpighia coccifera* Linn. and *Tristellateia australis* Linn. Proc. Natl. Inst. Sci. India, Pt. B, Biol. Sci. **7:** 393–404.
Taylor, D. W. & W. L. Crepet. 1987. Fossil floral evidence of Malpighiaceae and an early plant-pollinator relationship. Amer. J. Bot. **74:** 274–286.
Verkerke, W. 1984. Ovule and seed of *Xanthophyllum* (Polygalaceae). Blumea **29:** 409–421.
Verkerke, W. 1985. Ovules and seeds of the Polygalaceae. J. Arnold Arbor. **66:** 353–394.

16. Order Sapindales

The order Sapindales as here defined consists of 15 families and about 5400 species. More than half of these belong to only two families, the Sapindaceae and Rutaceae, each with about 1500 species. Another 2300 species belong to 6 well known but not large families, the Anacardiaceae (600), Burseraceae (600), Meliaceae (550), Zygophyllaceae (250), Simaroubaceae (150), and Aceraceae (110). The remaining 7 families have less than a hundred species in all, and most of these belong to the Staphyleaceae (60) or Hippocastanaceae (16).

The features common to most members of the Sapindales, which make it useful to distinguish them as a group from the Rosales, are the compound or cleft leaves, haplostemonous or diplostemonous androecium, well developed nectary-disk, and syncarpous ovary with a limited number of ovules (usually only 1 or 2) in each locule. All of these features can be found individually in the Rosales, but not in combination (except some members of the Cunoniaceae). Many of the Sapindales produce characteristic triterpenoid bitter substances, and the Rutaceae are notable for their wide variety of alkaloids in addition to the triterpenoids.

Although a number of the now included families have in the past been referred to other orders, the Sapindales are in my opinion a well characterized natural group. Only two families are really peripheral. The Staphyleaceae connect the Sapindales to the ancestral Rosales, in the vicinity of the Cunoniaceae, and the Zygophyllaceae are suggestive of the Geraniales. These two families also differ from the bulk of the order in often having more than 2 ovules per locule. Collectively they constitute less than 6% of the order.

Ecologically the members of the Sapindales have little in common beyond their usually woody habit and the limited number of seeds in each fruit. The nectary-disk is of course an adaptation to insect-pollination, but several related orders have a similar disk, and there is no reason to suppose that the pollinators of the Sapindales are in any way distinctive.

Pollen regarded as sapindaceous dates from the Coniacian stage, below the middle of the Upper Cretaceous. Otherwise nothing in the order is known to antedate the Tertiary. Pollen and wood considered to represent the Anacardiaceae enter the record in the Paleocene, and macrofossils of several families in the Eocene. A leaf referred to the modern genus *Akania* (Akaniaceae) comes from uppermost Paleocene deposits in Argentina.

SYNOPTICAL ARRANGEMENT OF THE FAMILIES OF SAPINDALES

1 Leaves usually stipulate, often conspicuously so; ovules often more than 2 per carpel; seeds with endosperm, except some Zygophyllaceae.
  2 Stamens mostly bicyclic or tricyclic, seldom unicyclic; ovules mostly epitropous, seldom apotropous; compound leaves usually without a terminal leaflet; plants generally not tanniferous .... **15. Zygophyllaceae.**
  2 Stamens unicyclic; ovules apotropous; compound leaves with a terminal leaflet; plants usually tanniferous.

    3 Leaves opposite, seldom alternate; disk annular, mostly intrastaminal (rarely poorly developed or wanting); flowers regular; carpels 2–3 (4); pollen-grains binucleate; vessel-segments with scalariform perforations; plants not producing ellagic acid . . . . **1. Staphyleaceae.**

    3 Leaves alternate; disk unilateral, extrastaminal; flowers irregular; carpels 4 (5); pollen-grains trinucleate; vessel-segments with simple perforations; plants producing ellagic acid . . . . **2. Melianthaceae.**

1 Leaves mostly exstipulate, the stipules when present small and caducous; ovules seldom more that 2 per carpel; seeds with or often without endosperm.

    4 Disk mostly extrastaminal (and often unilateral) or wanting; ovules apotropous except in Akaniaceae; flowers regular or very often somewhat irregular; stamens very often 8; plants very often accumulating quebrachitol.

        5 Leaves alternate (opposite in a few Sapindaceae).

            6 Flowers perigynous; plants producing myrosin-cells and mustard-oils; most of the wood-rays multiseriate, 4–6 (–10) cells wide . . . . **3. Bretschneideraceae.**

            6 Flowers hypogynous.

                7 Seeds with endosperm and without an aril or sarcotesta; plants producing myrosin-cells and mustard-oils; wood-rays mainly multiseriate; nectary-disk wanting; ovules epitropous, 2 in each locule . . . . **4. Akaniaceae.**

                7 Seeds without endosperm, often with an aril or sarcotesta; myrosin-cells and mustard-oils wanting; wood-rays mostly uniseriate, seldom 2–3 (–6)-seriate; nectary-disk generally present; ovules apotropous, 1 or seldom 2 (rarely several) in each locule . . . . **5. Sapindaceae.**

        5 Leaves opposite.

            8 Flowers evidently irregular; fruit a (2) 3 (4)-carpellate, usually 1-seeded capsule; leaves palmately compound . . . . . . **6. Hippocastanaceae.**

            8 Flowers regular; fruit a winged schizocarp, mostly of 2 carpels, typically a double samara; leaves simple and usually palmately lobed or veined, in a few species either pinnately or palmately 3–5 foliolate . . . . **7. Aceraceae.**

    4 Disk mostly intrastaminal, annular or sometimes modified into a gynophore, rarely extrastaminal or (Julianiaceae) wanting; ovules mostly epitropous except in Anacardiaceae and Julianiaceae; plants not known to accumulate quebrachitol, except some Anacardiaceae.

        9 Plants strongly resinous, with vertical intercellular resin-canals in the bark and often also horizontal ones in the wood-rays, usually also with similar resin-ducts in the phloem of the larger veins of the leaves; ovules often attached to a short, broad placental obturator; plants only seldom producing alkaloids and only seldom with triterpenoid compounds.

           10 Flowers of ordinary structure, perfect or unisexual, always with a perianth and usually or always with a nectary-disk or gynophore; plants only seldom saponiferous.

                11 Ovary with 2 (rarely only one) epitropous ovules in each of the (2) 3–5 locules; resin not notably allergenic or poisonous . . . . **8. Burseraceae.**

                11 Ovary with a single apotropous ovule in each of the (2) 3 locules, or more often only one locule ovuliferous, or the carpels rarely distinct or solitary and each (or one of them) with a single ovule; resin often allergenic or poisonous to the touch . . . . **9. Anacardiaceae.**

10 Flowers much reduced, unisexual, the pistillate ones without perianth; disk and gynophore wanting; ovary tricarpellate, unilocular, with a single ovule; plants saponiferous .... **10. Julianiaceae.**
9 Plants resinous or not, but without resin-ducts in the bark, wood-rays, and veins of the leaves; ovules with or more often without an obturator; plants very often producing triterpenoid substances and/or alkaloids, but only seldom saponiferous.
12 Leaves not glandular-punctate; plants often with scattered secretory cells, but generally without secretory cavities.
13 Stamens distinct; other features various, but not combined as in the Meliaceae.
14 Seeds without endosperm; leaves mostly compound, seldom simple; bark generally bitter; plants mostly producing characteristic triterpenoid lactones called quassinoids; flowers 3–8-merous, most commonly 5-merous; style solitary or often the styles several and distinct; pollen-grains binucleate .... **11. Simaroubaceae.**
14 Seeds with copious endosperm; leaves simple; bark not bitter; plants not producing quassinoids; flowers trimerous or sometimes tetramerous; style solitary; pollen-grains trinucleate .... **12. Cneoraceae.**
13 Stamens mostly connate by their filaments, seldom distinct; leaves usually compound; bark bitter; seeds usually with well developed endosperm; ovary with a single style; leaves commonly with resinous secretory cells at the boundary of the palisade and spongy mesophyll .... **13. Meliaceae.**
12 Leaves glandular-punctate, the plants commonly with secretory cavities containing aromatic ethereal oils, these cavities scattered throughout the parenchymatous tissues and in the pericarp .....
.... **14. Rutaceae.**

SELECTED REFERENCES

Boesewinkel, F. D. 1984. Development of ovule and seed-coat in *Cneorum tricoccon* L. (Cneoraceae). Acta Bot. Neerl. **33**: 61–70.
Brizicky, G. K. 1962. The genera of Rutaceae in the southeastern United States. J. Arnold Arbor. **43**: 1–22.
Brizicky, G. K. 1962. The genera of Simaroubaceae and Burseraceae in the southeastern United States. J. Arnold Arbor. **43**: 173–186.
Brizicky, G. K. 1962. The genera of Anacardiaceae in the southeastern United States. J. Arnold Arbor. **43**: 359–375.
Brizicky, G. K. 1963. The genera of Sapindales in the southeastern United States. J. Arnold Arbor. **44**: 462–501.
Copeland, H. F. 1961. Observations on the reproductive structures of *Anacardium occidentale*. Phytomorphology **11**: 315–325.
Cronquist, A. 1944. Studies in Simaroubaceae. IV. Resume of the American genera. Brittonia **5**: 128–147.
Cronquist, A. 1945. Additional notes on the Simaroubaceae. Brittonia **5**: 469–470.
Dickison, W. C. 1986. Floral morphology and anatomy of Staphyleaceae. Bot. Gaz. **147**: 312–326.

Dickison, W. C. 1987. A palynological study of the Staphyleaceae. Grana **26:** 11–24.

Fish, F. & P. G. Waterman. 1973. Chemosystematics in the Rutaceae. II. The chemosystematics of the *Zanthoxylum/Fagara* complex. Taxon **22:** 177–203.

Guédès, M. 1973. Carpel morphology and axis-sharing in syncarpy in some Rutaceae, with further comments on "New Morphology." J. Linn. Soc., Bot. **66:** 55–74.

Gut, B. J. 1966. Beiträge zur Morphologie des Gynoeceums und der Blütenachse einiger Rutaceen. Bot. Jahrb. Syst. **85:** 151–247.

Hardin, J. W. 1957. A revision of the American Hippocastanaceae. Brittonia **9:** 145–195.

Heimsch, C. 1940. Wood anatomy and pollen morphology of *Rhus* and allied genera. J. Arnold Arbor. **21:** 279–291.

Jensen, U. 1974. Close relationships between Ranunculales and Rutales? Systematic considerations in the light of new results of comparative serological research. Serol. Mus. Bull. **50:** 4–7.

Lobreau-Callen, D., S. Nilsson, F. Albers & H. Straka. 1978. Les Cneoraceae (Rutales): Étude taxonomique, palynologique et systématique. Grana **17:** 125–139.

Mauritzon, J. 1936. Zur Embryologie und systematischen Abgrenzung der Reihen Terebinthales und Celastrales. Bot. Not. **1936:** 161–212.

Muller, J. & P. W. Leenhouts. 1976. A general survey of pollen types in Sapindaceae in relation to taxonomy. Pages 407–445 *in* I. K. Ferguson & J. Muller (eds.), The evolutionary significance of the exine. Linn. Soc. Symp. Ser. No. 1. Academic Press. London & New York.

Nair, N. C. 1959–1963. Studies on Meliaceae. I. Floral morphology and embryology of *Naregamia alata* W. & A. II. Floral morphology and embryology of *Melia azedarach* Linn.—A reinvestigation. V. Morphology and anatomy of the flower of the tribes Melieae, Trichileae and Swietenieae. VI. Morphology and anatomy of the flower of the tribe Cedrelieae and discussion of the floral anatomy of the family. J. Indian Bot. Soc. **38:** 353–366, 367–378, 1959; **41:** 226–242, 1962; **42:** 177–189, 1963.

Pennington, T. D. 1981. Meliaceae. Fl. Neotropica Monogr. 28.

Pennington, T. D. & B. T. Styles. 1975. A generic monograph of the Meliaceae. Blumea **22:** 419–540.

Polonsky, J. 1966. Les principes amers des Simarubacées. Pl. Med. **14:** 107–116.

Porter, D. M. 1972. The genera of Zygophyllaceae in the southeastern United States. J. Arnold Arbor. **53:** 531–552.

Ramp, E. 1987. Functionelle anatomie des Gynoeciums bei *Staphylea.* Bot. Helvet. **97:** 89–98.

Romero, E. J. & L. J. Hickey. 1976. A fossil leaf of Akaniaceae from Paleocene beds in Argentina. Bull. Torrey Bot. Club **103:** 126–131.

Saleh, N. A. M. & M. N. El-Hadidi. 1977. An approach to the chemosystematics of the Zygophyllaceae. Biochem. Syst. Ecol. **5:** 121–128.

Spongberg, S. 1971. The Staphyleaceae in the southeastern United States. J. Arnold Arbor. **52:** 196–203.

Stern, W. L. 1952. The comparative anatomy of the xylem and the phylogeny of the Julianiaceae. Amer. J. Bot. **39:** 220–229.

Straka, H., F. Albers & A. Mondon. 1976. Die Stellung und Gliederung der Familie Cneoraceae (Rutales). Beitr. Biol. Pflanzen **52:** 267–310.

Waterman, P. G. 1975. Alkaloids of the Rutaceae: Their distribution and systematic significance. Biochem. Syst. Ecol. **3:** 149–180.

Waterman, P. G. & M. F. Grundon (eds.). 1983. Chemistry and chemical taxonomy of the Rutales. Academic Press. London & New York.

Weberling, F. & P. W. Leenhouts. 1965. Systematisch-morphologische Studien an Terebinthales-Familien (Burseraceae, Simaroubaceae, Meliaceae, Anacardiaceae, Sapindaceae). Akad. Wiss. Abh. Math.-Naturwiss. Kl. 1965. Nr. 10: 495–584.

Wolfe, J. A. & T. Tanai. 1987. Systematics, phylogeny, and distribution of *Acer* (maples) in the Cenozoic of western North America. J. Fac. Sci., Hokkaido Univ. **22:** 1–246.

Young, D. A. 1976. Flavonoid chemistry and the phylogenetic relationships of the Julianiaceae. Syst. Bot. **1:** 149–162.

17. Order Geraniales

The order Geraniales as here defined consists of 5 families and about 2600 species. The 3 largest families are the Oxalidaceae (900), Balsaminaceae (900), and Geraniaceae (700). The definition here adopted is identical to that of Hutchinson. In this instance I believe his emphasis on growth habit provides a better distinction between the Geraniales (mainly herbaceous) and Sapindales (mainly woody) than does the emphasis on the orientation of the ovules in the traditional Englerian system. It may also be noted that none of the Geraniales as here defined has the annular or unilateral nectary-disk found in so many of the Sapindales.

The close relationship of the Geraniaceae and Oxalidaceae has been evident to all. The tribe Geranieae and the large genus *Oxalis* are distinctive enough, but these two groups are connected by a series of smaller genera that are variously apportioned between the two families by different authors. I do not think it improves our understanding of relationships to recognize some of these small connecting groups as distinct families, as some authors have proposed. What we gain in sharpening the definition of the major groups we lose by increasing the number of families to be remembered.

Although the Tropaeolaceae are obviously distinctive, their relationship to the Geraniaceae is generally admitted. The characteristic spur on one of the sepals in the Tropaeolaceae is apparently homologous with a similar spur found in the large genus *Pelargonium* of the Geraniaceae, the chief difference being that the spur of *Pelargonium* is adnate to the petiole and is therefore easily overlooked. Cytological evidence also supports the concept that the Oxalidaceae, Geraniaceae, and Tropaeolaceae are closely related.

The Limnanthaceae and Balsaminaceae are more controversial. Both are morphologically and cytologically somewhat removed from the core families of the order and from each other, without having any obvious affinities elsewhere. It may be significant that the Limnanthaceae and

Tropaeolaceae are alike in producing mustard-oil and erucic acid, which are otherwise mainly confined to the Capparales. A direct connection of these families to the Capparales is strongly contra-indicated by the 9 differences in amino-acid sequence of the cytochrome *c* of *Tropaeolum* and *Brassica*. On a purely morphological basis the Balsaminaceae might be accommodated in either the Geraniales or the Polygalales as here conceived. They would be wholly isolated in the Polygalales, however, whereas they do have some similarity to the Tropaeolaceae in the Geraniales.

There is nothing ecologically distinctive about the Geraniales. Nearly all of the species are herbs or soft shrubs, but this growth-form is well known in diverse other orders. Many of the Geraniales prefer moist or shady places, but *Erodium,* in the Geraniaceae, is a familiar vernal weed of dry regions. The curious, elastically dehiscent fruits of *Impatiens* (Balsaminaceae) are reminiscent of the technically very different but also elastically dehiscent fruits of *Geranium.* The Oxalidaceae have still another way of expelling the seeds mechanically, by means of a basil aril, but none of these methods of dispersal is highly effective. The long-awned, spirally twisting mericarps of *Erodium* are evidently well adapted to animal-transport and self-planting, but they also help to illustrate the diversity rather than any unity of seed-dispersal mechanisms within the order.

Pollen of the Geraniaceae makes a late entry into the fossil record, in the Upper Miocene. Otherwise the fossil record of the order is insignificant.

Synoptical Arrangement of the Families of Geraniales

1 Flowers regular and not spurred, or in *Pelargonium* (Geraniaceae) somewhat irregular and with an inconspicuous spur adnate to the pedicel; stamens mostly 2 or 3 times as many as the sepals or petals, sometimes some of them staminodial; leaves mostly compound or deeply cleft, seldom simple and entire or merely toothed.
2 Annual or more often perennial herbs, generally with a sclerenchymatous sheath in the pericycle and sometimes with a functional cambium, or seldom woody plants, in any case not producing mustard-oil; ovules bitegmic, epitropous, usually pendulous when solitary or few; filaments connate at the base; style or styles terminal on the ovary, or (many Geraniaceae) the style gynobasic but strongly thickened to form a column.
3 Ovary generally with distinct, terminal styles, rarely (*Hypseocharis*) with a single terminal style; fruit a loculicidal capsule, or rarely a berry; endosperm usually copious; ovules tenuinucellar ... **1. Oxalidaceae.**
3 Ovary with a single (often thickened, columnar, and gynobasic) style, or rarely (*Biebersteinia*) with distinct styles; fruit typically of 5 1-seeded mericarps that separate elastically from the persistent central column (the mericarps often opening ventrally to release the seed), or in some of the smaller genera separating into mericarps but without a persistent column, or in some other small genera a loculicidal capsule; endosperm scanty or none, except in *Viviana*; ovules crassinucellar ....
.... **2. Geraniaceae.**

2 Small annual herbs with a parenchymatous pericycle and without cambium, characteristically producing mustard-oil; ovules unitegmic, apotropous, solitary in each locule and erect or ascending; filaments distinct; style gynobasic, uniting the otherwise essentially distinct carpels . . . .
. . . . **3. Limnanthaceae.**
1 Flowers more or less strongly irregular, one of the sepals with a conspicuous free spur; stamens 5 or 8, less than twice as many as the basic (unmodified) number of sepals or petals; leaves simple, not deeply lobed except in some Tropaeolaceae.
  4 Leaves palmately veined, peltate or sometimes palmately lobed or cleft; stamens 8, with distinct filaments; carpels 3, each with a single epitropous ovule, the fruit schizocarpic; plants producing mustard-oil, but without raphides; endosperm-development nuclear; seeds with erucic acid, but without parinaric or acetic acid . . . . **4. Tropaeolaceae.**
  4 Leaves pinnately veined, not peltate; stamens 5, with more or less connate filaments; carpels (4) 5, each with 3–many apotropous ovules; fruit an elastically dehiscent capsule, or seldom a berrylike septicidal capsule; plants with raphides, but without mustard-oil; endosperm-development cellular; seeds with parinaric and acetic acid, but without erucic acid . . . .
. . . . **5. Balsaminaceae.**

SELECTED REFERENCES

Behnke, H. -D. & T. J. Mabry. 1977. S-Type sieve-element plastids and anthocyanins in Vivianiaceae: Evidence against its inclusion in the Centrospermae. Pl. Syst. Evol. **126:** 371–375.

Boesewinkel, F. D. 1985. Development of ovule and seed-coat in *Averrhoa* (Oxalidaceae) with notes on some related genera. Acta Bot. Neerl. **34:** 413–424.

Grey-Wilson, C. 1980. Studies in Balsaminaceae. V. *Hydrocera triflora,* its floral morphology and relationships with *Impatiens.* VI. Some observations on the floral vascular anatomy of *Impatiens.* Kew Bull. **35:** 213–219, 221–227.

Herr, J. M. 1972. An extended investigation of the megagametophyte in *Oxalis corniculata* L. Adv. Pl. Morph. **1972:** 92–101.

Hoffman, U. & J. Ludewig. 1985. Morphologie und systematische Stellung von *Limnanthes douglasii* R. Brown, einem repräsentativen Vertreter der Limnanthaceae. Bot. Jahrb. Syst. **105:** 401–431.

Huynh, K.-L. 1968, 1969. Morphologie du pollen des Tropaeolacées et des Balsaminacées. I, II, III. Grana Palyn. **8:** 88–184, 277–516, 1968; **9:** 34–49, 1969.

Huynh, K.-L. 1969. Étude du pollen des Oxalidaceae. Bot. Jahrb. Syst. **89:** 272–303, 304–334.

Kjaer, A., J. O. Madsen & Y. Maeda. 1978. Seed volatiles within the family Tropaeolaceae. Phytochemistry **17:** 1285–1287.

Lefor, M. W. 1975. A taxonomic revision of the Vivianiaceae. Univ. Connecticut Occas. Papers **2:** 225–255.

Léonard, J. 1950. *Lepidobotrys* Engl., type d'une famille nouvelle de spermatophytes: Les Lepidobotryaceae. Bull. Jard. Bot. État **20:** 31–40.

Maheshwari, P. & B. M. Johri. 1956. The morphology and embryology of

Floerkea proserpinacoides Willd. with a discussion on the systematic position of the family Limnanthaceae. Bot. Mag. (Tokyo) **69**: 410–423.

Mason, C. T. 1952. A systematic study of the genus *Limnanthes* R. Br. Univ. Calif. Publ. Bot. **25**: 455–512.

Narayana, L. L. 1963, 1965. Contributions to the embryology of Balsaminaceae. I. J. Indian Bot. Soc. **42**: 102–109, 1963. 2. J. Jap. Bot. **40**: 104–116, 1965.

Narayana, L. L. 1966. A contribution to the floral anatomy of Oxalidaceae. J. Jap. Bot. **41**: 321–328.

Narayana, L. L. 1974. A contribution to the floral anatomy of Balsaminaceae. J. Jap. Bot. **49**: 315–320.

Ornduff, R. 1971. Systematic studies of Limnanthaceae. Madroño **21**: 103–111.

Robertson, K. R. 1972. The genera of Geraniaceae in the southeastern United States. J. Arnold Arbor. **53**: 182–201.

Robertson, K. R. 1975. The Oxalidaceae in the southeastern United States. J. Arnold Arbor. **56**: 223–239.

Warburg, E. F. 1938. Taxonomy and relationship in the Geraniales in the light of their cytology. New Phytol. **37**: 130–159, 189–210.

Wood, C. E. 1975. The Balsaminaceae in the southeastern United States. J. Arnold Arbor. **56**: 413–426.

18. Order Apiales

The order Apiales (often known under the irregular name Umbellales) consists of 2 families and about 3700 species. The Araliaceae have about 700 species, and the Apiaceae about 3000. The order may be briefly characterized as dicotyledons with mostly compound or cleft leaves, separate petals, and an inferior, plurilocular ovary with a single ovule in each locule. The flowers are commonly borne in umbels that are very often arranged into secondary umbels, but other types of inflorescences also occur in the order. The seeds contain considerable amounts of petroselinic acid, a compound otherwise apparently limited to a few members of the Sapindales and Cornales.

The families of Apiales have in the past often been submerged in the order Cornales. In my opinion this assignment reflects an overemphasis on the epigynous floral structure, a condition that has been independently attained in many different groups of angiosperms. In other respects the Apiales are much more like the Sapindales than like the Cornales. The Araliaceae would in fact fit comfortably into the Sapindales, near the Burseraceae, if the flowers were hypogynous instead of epigynous. On chemical grounds the Apiales stand apart from the Cornales and might well be derived from the Sapindales.

It is widely agreed that the Apiaceae take their origin directly from the Araliaceae, although probably not from any modern genus. All the features that have been used to distinguish the Apiaceae as a family can be found individually in the Araliaceae. In particular, the small genus *Myodocarpus*, of New Caledonia, has bicarpellate, schizocarpic fruits with a central carpophore as in the Apiaceae, but has the inflorescence and vegetative structure of the Araliaceae. Indeed the wood of *Myodocarpus* is relatively primitive, with scalariform vessels. Eyde and Tseng (1971) speculate that *Myodocarpus* and its immediate allies belong to an evolutionary line that "diverged from the other Araliaceae perhaps as long ago as the Cretaceous Period."

The Apiaceae consist of one large subfamily, the Apioideae (250 genera), and two much smaller ones, the Saniculoideae (9 genera) and Hydrocotyloideae (34 genera). The latter two subfamilies mostly do not have the characteristic compound umbel that makes the Apioideae so obviously distinctive. The Hydrocotyloideae, in particular, stand apart because of their chiefly Southern Hemisphere distribution and because of their fruit, which has a woody endocarp and lacks a free carpophore. The fruit is thus somewhat intermediate between that of typical Apiaceae and that of the Araliaceae. It has been argued that the Hydrocotyloideae originated from the Araliaceae independently of the other Apiaceae, and that therefore one should either recognize an additional family Hydrocotylaceae or submerge the Apiaceae in the Araliaceae. The great majority of the Apiaceae form such an obvious group that I would not find it useful to put them into the same family with the Araliaceae, but the possibility that the Hydrocotyloideae should be recognized as a distinct family merits careful consideration by those with special knowledge of the order.

The most nearly distinctive ecological feature of the Apiales is their means of chemical warfare. They forego such common weapons as tannins, HCN, iridoid compounds, and (in most genera) alkaloids, depending instead on monoterpenes, sesquiterpenes, triterpenoid saponins, polyacetylenes, coumarins, and phenyl-propanoid compounds. Their schizogenous secretory canals provide transport and delivery of at least some of these substances. These chemicals and canals are by no means unique to the Apiales, being shared in part with some members of the Sapindales as well as other orders (including notably the otherwise very dissimilar Asterales), but neither is the package common and widespread among angiosperms in general. Like other chemical defenses, those of the Apiales are only partly effective. Many species of Apiaceae are palatable to livestock and to herbarium-beetles.

In other respects the Apiales are not outstanding ecologically. The adaptive significance of epigyny is dubious at best, and there are of course many other epigynous groups of angiosperms. The fruit of the Apiaceae is morphologically unique, but ecologically undistinguished. In a few genera it is beset with hooks or barbs that adapt it to distribution by animals; in other genera it is dispersed by wind, and in others it has no very obvious means of dispersal.

The Araliaceae have an extensive fossil record. Megafossils considered to represent various genera of the family occur throughout the Tertiary and even into the Upper Cretaceous. Pollen referred to the Araliaceae dates from the Paleocene. Pollen of the Apiaceae comes in one epoch later, in the Lower Eocene. Appropriately, the Sapindales somewhat antedate the Apiales in the record.

1 Carpels 1–many, most often 5; fruit usually a drupe or berry, only rarely a schizocarp with a more or less well developed carpophore; flowers commonly in umbels or heads that are often grouped into various sorts of compound inflorescences, but only seldom forming regular compound umbels; trees, shrubs, or woody vines, only seldom perennial herbs ...... **1. Araliaceae.**
1 Carpels consistently 2; fruit a dry schizocarp, the mericarps usually attached apically to a persistent carpophore; flowers in the larger subfamily generally arranged into compound umbels, but in the 2 smaller subfamilies in heads or simple umbels or other sorts of inflorescences; herbs, rarely shrubs or trees .... **2. Apiaceae.**

SELECTED REFERENCES

Baumann, M. G. 1946. *Myodocarpus* und die Phylogenie der Umbelliferen-Frucht. Ber. Schweiz. Bot. Ges. **56**: 13–112.
Cerceau-Larrival, M. T. 1962. Plantules et pollens d'Ombellifères. Leur intérêt systématique et phylogénique. Mém. Mus. Natl. Hist. Nat., Ser. B, Bot. **14**: 1–166.
Crowden, R. K., J. B. Harborne & V. H. Heywood. 1969. Chemosytematics of the Umbelliferae—A general survey. Phytochemistry **8**: 1963–1984.
Dilcher, D. L. & G. E. Dolph. 1970. Fossil leaves of *Dendropanax* from Eocene sediments of southeastern North America. Amer. J. Bot. **57**: 153–160.
Erbar, C. & P. Leins. 1985. Studien zur Organsequenz in Apiaceen-Blüten. Bot. Jahrb. Syst. **105**: 379–400.
Eyde, R. H. & C. C. Tseng. 1969. Flower of *Tetraplasandra gymnocarpa*: Hypogyny with epigynous ancestry. Science **166**: 506–508.
Eyde, R. H. & C. C. Tseng. 1971. What is the primitive floral structure of Araliaceae? J. Arnold Arbor. **52**: 205–239.
Graham, S. A. 1966. The genera of Araliaceae in the southeastern United States. J. Arnold Arbor. **47**: 126–136.
Heywood, V. H. (ed.). 1971. The biology and chemistry of the Umbelliferae. J. Linn. Soc., Bot. 64 (Suppl. 1). Academic Press. London.
Jackson, G. 1933. A study of the carpophore of the Umbelliferae. Amer. J. Bot. **20**: 121–144.
Leins, P. & C. Erbar. 1985. Zur frühen Entwicklungsgeschichte des Apiaceen-Gynoeceums. Bot. Jahrb. Syst. **106**: 53–60.
Lindsey, A. H. 1984. Reproductive biology of the Apiaceae. I. Floral visitors to *Thaspium* and *Zizia* and their importance in pollination. Amer. J. Bot. **71**: 375–387.
Magin, N. 1977. Das Gynoecium der Apiaceae—Modell und Ontogenie. Ber. Deutsch. Bot. Ges. **90**: 53–66.
Mohana Rao, P. R. 1972 (1973). Morphology and embryology of *Tieghemopanax sambucifolius* with comments on the affinities of the family Araliaceae. Phytomorphology **22**: 75–87.
Philipson, W. R. 1970. Constant and variable features of the Araliaceae. Pages

87–100 *in* N. K. B. Robson, D. F. Cutler & M. Gregory (eds.), New research in plant anatomy. J. Linn. Soc., Bot. 63 (Suppl. 1). Academic Press. London.

Pickering, J. L. & D. E. Fairbrothers. 1970. A serological comparison of Umbelliferae subfamilies. Amer. J. Bot. **57:** 988–992.

Rodriguez, R. L. 1957. Systematic anatomical studies on *Myrrhidendron* and other woody Umbellales. Univ. Calif. Publ. Bot. **29:** 145–318.

Thorne, R. F. 1973. Inclusion of the Apiaceae (Umbelliferae) in the Araliaceae. Notes Roy. Bot. Gard. Edinburgh **32:** 161–165.

Tseng, C. C. 1967. Anatomical studies of flower and fruit in the Hydrocotyloideae (Umbelliferae). Univ. Calif. Publ. Bot. **42:** 1–79.

Subclass VI. Asteridae

The subclass Asteridae as here delimited consists of 11 orders (Fig. 6.8), 49 families, and nearly 60,000 species. In terms of number of species it is about the same size as the Rosidae, but in terms of number of families it is surpassed by both the Rosidae and the Dilleniidae. About a third of the species of Asteridae belong to the family Asteraceae, which is the largest family of dicotyledons and one of the two largest families of plants.

The bulk of the Sympetalae of the traditional Englerian system belongs to the Asteridae, but the Diapensiales, Ericales, Ebenales, Primulales, Plumbaginales, and Cucurbitales are removed to other subclasses. Orders 6 to 11 of the Sympetalae in the current (1964) edition of the Engler Syllabus are collectively almost coextensive with the Asteridae as here defined.

From the standpoint of practical recognition, the vast majority of the Asteridae can be distinguished from the vast majority of other dicotyledons by their sympetalous flowers, in which the stamens are isomerous and alternate with the corolla-lobes, or fewer than the corolla-lobes. Much less than 1% of the species of Asteridae fail this test, and probably no more than 1% of the species that meet this test do not belong to the Asteridae. The tenuinucellar ovule with a massive single integument is a further marker of the group, but there are more exceptions to this feature, both within and without the Asteridae.

The Asteridae are the most advanced subclass of dicotyledons, and possibly the most recently evolved (only the Caryophyllidae may be more recent). More than any other subclass, they exploit specialized pollinators and specialized means of presenting the pollen. It seems likely that the rise of the Asteridae is closely correlated with the evolution of insects capable of recognizing complex floral patterns.

Chemically, the Asteridae are noteworthy for the frequent occurrence of iridoid compounds, the usual absence of ellagic acid and proanthocyanins, and the apparently complete absence of betalains, mustard-oils, and benzyl-isoquinoline alkaloids. The absence of betalains and benzyl-isoquinoline alkaloids tends to set the Asteridae off from most of the Caryophyllidae and Magnoliidae, respectively, and the usual absence of

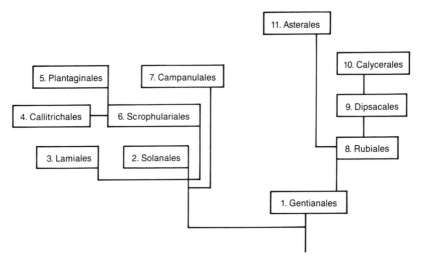

Fig. 6.8.   Putative relationships among the orders of Asteridae.

ellagic acid and proanthocyanins tends to set them off from the Rosidae, Dilleniidae, and Hamamelidae. The distinction is far from absolute, however because these substances are missing from many members of the subclasses they are supposed to characterize. Iridoid compounds are certainly better represented in the Asteridae than in any other subclass, but they are lacking from the very large family Asteraceae, and will probably prove to occur in not more than about half the species of the subclass. Iridoids also occur in some members of the Rosidae and Dilleniidae, and even a few of the Hamamelidae.

It may be reasonable to surmise that in the continuing struggle between plants and their predators, the Asteridae abandoned the familiar weapons of tannins, saponins, and cyanide, in favor of the previously not much-exploited iridoid compounds and the alkaloids related to them. Continuing the speculation, one may suppose that, by the time the Asteraceae originated (toward the end of the Oligocene), predators had already become adapted to tolerate iridoids and their allied alkaloids, so that the stage was set for another massive shift in defensive weapons. The tremendous success of the Asteraceae might well depend more on their chemical arsenal than on their specialized floral structure.

The ancestry of the Asteridae very probably lies in the order Rosales, sensu latissimo. Iridoid compounds, a sympetalous corolla, stamens isomerous and alternate with the petals, a compound pistil with numerous ovules on axile placentas, unitegmic ovules, and tenuinucellar ovules all occur in this order, but not in combination. The nectary-disk of many Asteridae also finds a ready precedent in the Rosales, as do the simple, stipulate, opposite leaves of the more archaic members of the group. The combination of these features into a functional whole marks the transition from the ancestral Rosales to the first members of the Asteridae. All the other orders of Rosidae are already too advanced to serve as possible ancestors of the Asteridae.

The Asteridae make a relatively late entrance into the fossil record. There is no reason to suppose that the group originated before the beginning of the Tertiary period. Fossil pollen referred to the Apocynaceae dates from the Paleocene, and pollen or macrofossils of families in several other orders turn up in the Eocene. The Asteridae began to play a prominent role in the flora of the world only during the Oligocene epoch.

Synoptical Arrangement of the Orders of Asteridae

1 Flowers much reduced, nearly or quite without a perianth, either unisexual, or perfect and epigynous; stamen solitary; or seldom stamens 2–3; plants mostly aquatic . . . .**4. Callitrichales.**
1 Flowers generally with a more or less well developed perianth (typically a sympetalous corolla and a calyx or a pappus) but if essentially without perianth, then the stamens more than 3; plants terrestrial or seldom aquatic.
  2 Ovary with some exceptions (mainly some Gesneriaceae) superior.
    3 Plants nearly always with opposite or whorled leaves, and nearly always with internal phloem; flowers mostly regular or nearly so and with as many stamens as corolla-lobes; endosperm-development nuclear, rarely cellular; ovules usually without an integumentary tapetum, except in Apocynaceae; plants commonly producing alkaloids or iridoid compounds or both . . . .**1. Gentianales.**
    3 Plants only rarely at once with opposite (or whorled) leaves and internal phloem, and then with irregular flowers that have fewer stamens than corolla-lobes; endosperm-development cellular or much less often nuclear; ovules often with an integumentary tapetum; plants with or without alkaloids and iridoid compounds.
      4 Ovary generally consisting of 2 (–14) biovulate carpels with twice as many uniovulate lobes or locelli as carpels (a few exceptions among the Verbenaceae, but the carpels in any case with not more than 2 ovules each), very often (most Boraginaceae and Lamiaceae) the ovary consisting of 4 essentially distinct, half-carpellary lobes united mainly by their gynobasic style; fruit typically consisting of separate, closed half-carpels (nutlets) or of a drupe in which each seed has its own stone or its own locule of a compound stone; plants nearly always without internal phloem . . . . **3. Lamiales.**
      4 Ovary consisting of 2–4 (–8) carpels with (1) 2–many ovules each (rarely the ovary pseudomonomerous), but the carpels only rarely divided into uniovulate segments; fruits diverse, most commonly capsular or baccate, not consisting of half-carpellary nutlets except in a few Convolvulaceae and Myoporaceae; plants sometimes (the Convolvulaceae consistently) with internal phloem.
        5 Corolla scarious, persistent, generally regular; flowers mostly anemophilous, generally tetramerous as to the calyx, corolla, and androecium; leaves phyllodial, more or less parallel-veined, or sometimes much-reduced, very often all basal . . . .
. . . . **5. Plantaginales.**
        5 Corolla otherwise; flowers mostly entomophilous or ornithophilous,

variously pentamerous or tetramerous or otherwise, with isomerous or anisomerous stamens; leaves various in form and structure,
sometimes much reduced, but not phyllodial and parallel-veined,
and only seldom all basal.

6 Flowers mostly regular or nearly so and with as many functional
stamens as corolla-lobes, typically pentamerous; the principal
exceptions are some Solanaceae with an irregular, 5-lobed corolla, but the Solanaceae have internal phloem, and the carpels,
when (as usually) 2, are oblique to the median axis of the flower;
plants often producing alkaloids, but only seldom iridoid compounds, and without orobanchin .... **2. Solanales.**

6 Flowers mostly irregular and with fewer functional stamens than
corolla-lobes, or sometimes with a regular, tetramerous corolla
and 2 or 4 stamens, or the corolla rarely wanting; carpels, when
(as usually) 2, median, not oblique; plants commonly producing
orobanchin and iridoid compounds, but only seldom alkaloids
.... **6. Scrophulariales.**

2 Ovary mostly inferior, seldom only half-inferior, superior only in a few
Campanulales and Rubiales.

7 Flowers borne in various sorts of inflorescences, but if in involucrate
heads then the heads generally basically cymose in structure; flowers
with or without a specialized pollen-presentation mechanism similar
to that of the next group; ovary with 1–several locules and 1–many
ovules in each locule (or some locules empty).

8 Leaves, with few exceptions, alternate; stamens free from the corolla,
or attached at the base of the tube (higher in the Pentaphragmataceae); flowers very often with a specialized pollen-presentation mechanism, the anthers connivent into a tube around the style, which
pushes out the pollen; plants usually herbaceous, sometimes secondarily woody, characteristically storing carbohydrates as inulin
.... **7. Campanulales.**

8 Leaves, with few exceptions, opposite or whorled; stamens attached to
the corolla-tube, usually well above the base; flowers without the
sort of pollen-presentation mechanism described above, except in
the subfamily Ixoroideae of the Rubiaceae; plants variously woody
or herbaceous, without inulin.

9 Stipules usually present and interpetiolar, bearing colleters on the
inner surface (sometimes intrapetiolar, or reduced to mere interpetiolar lines, or enlarged into leaves); corolla typically regular
and with isomerous stamens (much-reduced or wanting in Theligonaceae); endosperm-development nearly always nuclear; plants
chiefly tropical and woody, but some members herbaceous, or of
temperate regions, or both .... **8. Rubiales.**

9 Stipules typically none, when present usually small and adnate (at
least basally) to the petiole, in any case without colleters; corolla
regular or more often irregular, the stamens as many as or often
fewer or more numerous than the corolla-lobes; endosperm-development cellular; plants woody or often herbaceous, of temperate or less often tropical regions .... **9. Dipsacales.**

7 Flowers borne in involucrate, centripetally flowering (rarely uniflorous)
heads; anthers connate (or connivent) into a tube around the style, which
pushes out the pollen; ovary unilocular, with a solitary ovule; plants
characteristically storing carbohydrate as inulin.

10 Ovule apical and pendulous; pollen-grains binucleate; plants without a well developed secretory system, producing iridoid compounds but not polyacetylenes or sesquiterpene lactones; herbs with alternate leaves .... **10. Calycerales.**

10 Ovule basal and erect; pollen-grains trinucleate; plants with a well developed secretory (either resiniferous or laticiferous) system, characteristically producing sesquiterpene lactones, usually also polyacetylenes, and often other chemical repellents, but without iridoid compounds; woody or herbaceous, with alternate, opposite, or whorled leaves .... **11. Asterales.**

SELECTED REFERENCES

Dahlgren, R. 1977. A note on the taxonomy of the "Sympetalae" and related groups. Cairo Univ. Herb. **7 & 8:** 83–102.

Wagenitz, G. 1977. New aspects of the systematics of Asteridae. Pl. Syst. Evol. Suppl. **1:** 375–395.

1. Order Gentianales

The order Gentianales as here defined consists of 5 families and about 5500 species. The Apocynaceae and Asclepiadaceae have about 2000 species each, the Gentianaceae about 1000, the Loganiaceae about 500, and the Saccifoliaceae only one. The four larger families form a distinctive group whose members are obviously allied inter se. The Saccifoliaceae are discussed in a subsequent paragraph.

The Gentianales may be briefly characterized as Asteridae with opposite or whorled leaves, internal phloem, a superior ovary, and a regular corolla with isomerous stamens. They usually have nuclear endosperm, and except for the Apocynaceae they generally lack an integumentary tapetum. They commonly produce alkaloids or iridoid compounds, or both.

The Buddlejaceae, Menyanthaceae, and Oleaceae, which have often been included in the Gentianales, are here excluded. They lack internal phloem, and they have an integumentary tapetum and cellular endosperm. The Menyanthaceae further differ in having alternate leaves, and the Oleaceae usually have only 2 stamens. Furthermore, there is good reason to believe that the tetramerous, regular flower of most Buddlejaceae reflects reduction from a flower with pentamerous, irregular corolla and 4 stamens. The Menyanthaceae are here referred to the Solanales, and the Buddlejaceae and Oleaceae to the Scrophulariales.

Reasons for excluding the Rubiaceae from the Gentianales are discussed under the Rubiales.

The biological significance of the morphological and anatomical characters that distinguish the Gentianales as a group is doubtful. Diverse species of the order occur in a wide range of habitats that are also occupied by species of various other orders, and there is no obvious difference in the way that the Gentianales use these habitats, in contrast to the other orders. The Gentianales heavily exploit iridoid compounds, cardiotonic glycosides, and certain groups of alkaloids as repellents of would-be predators, but repellents of these groups also occur in various other orders that are not closely allied to the Gentianales.

The principal characters marking the family Asclepiadaceae are clearly related to pollination, ensuring that many pollen-grains are transported in a group. The usually large number of ovules in an ovary is an obvious corollary of the method of pollination, but there is no evident advantage in having the carpels virtually distinct. The mechanism of pollination is so complex and subject to interruption that it frequently fails to function (as in the orchids), and many flowers do not bear fruit. The large number of species of Asclepiadaceae bears witness to the viability of the mechanism of pollination, yet the Asclepiadaceae are no more successful than the equally large, closely related family Apocynaceae, in which pollination occurs in a more ordinary way. It seems reasonable to surmise that once the method of mass-pollination has been adopted there is a selective pressure toward perfecting the mechanism. Thus it should not be surprising that within the Asclepiadaceae the subfamily Periplocoideae, with imperfectly developed pollinia, is a much smaller group than the Asclepiadoideae.

There is a fairly straight-line evolutionary series in floral morphology within the Apocynaceae and Asclepiadaceae collectively, from the Plumerioideae to the Apocynoideae to the Periplocoideae to the Secamoneae and thence to the other tribes of the Asclepiadoideae. A determined splitter could recognize 5 families here, and an equally determined lumper might see only one. It has long been customary, and I believe it is conceptually useful, to recognize just two families in this group. The distinction is drawn on the method of pollination, specifically on the presence of a translator in the Asclepiadaceae and its absence from the Apocynaceae. The several other differences between characteristic members of the two families present finely graded series or are subject to exception. The selective value of the progressive evolutionary separation of the carpels is obscure. The evolutionary sequence of the separation, from the bottom of the gynoecium toward the top, is unique.

The affinities of *Saccifolium* are debatable. The sympetalous corolla, isomerous stamens alternate with the corolla-lobes, and tenuinucellar ovules with a single massive integument clearly mark it as a member of the Asteridae. The pentamerous, regular flowers and superior, bilocular ovary with a terminal style and numerous ovules restrict the choice of orders to the Gentianales and Solanales. These are also the only orders of Asteridae with internal phloem in a stem of otherwise normal anatomy (as in *Saccifolium*). The Solanaceae are rich in alkaloids, but like most other members of the Solanales they lack iridoid compounds. Preliminary chemical investigations suggest the presence of an iridoid compound in *Saccifolium*, whereas they do not disclose the presence of an alkaloid. Furthermore, the wood-structure of *Saccifolium*, without apparent medullary rays, resembles that of woody Gentianaceae but is unlike that of Solanaceae. Although there are only a few woody genera of Gentianaceae, these are well represented in the Guayana Highlands. Thus it seems advisable to consider a possible relationship of *Saccifolium* to the Gentianales, and particularly to the Gentianaceae.

Aside from the alternate leaves (which do occur in a few species of *Swertia,* in the Gentianaceae), *Saccifolium* appears to be perfectly at home in the Gentianales, on chemical as well as morphological grounds. No established family of the order can easily accommodate it, however. Perhaps the best comparison is with the Gentianaceae, from which it differs inter alia in its imbricate corolla-lobes and bilocular ovary with axile placentas. The unique leaves of course bespeak the isolated taxonomic position of *Saccifolium.*

The fossil record as presently known and interpreted casts a modest amount of light on the evolutionary history of the Gentianales. The Apocynaceae can be traced back to the Paleocene on the basis of pollen, and to the Eocene on the basis of macrofossils. Pollen referred to the Asclepiadaceae dates from the Oligocene. Macrofossils of the Loganiaceae are recognized in the Eocene, of the Asclepiadaceae in the Oligocene, and of the Gentianaceae in the Miocene. Thus it appears that the group as a whole does not antedate the Tertiary, that the Apocynaceae and Loganiaceae may be of roughly comparable age, and that the Asclepiadaceae and Gentianaceae are more recently evolved. Such a pattern is, at least, compatible with the present day morphology and chemistry of the order. The Gentianales are the only order of Asteridae that can be traced back beyond the Eocene on the basis of pollen.

Synoptical Arrangement of the Families of Gentianales

1 Plants without a latex-system, and without cardiotonic glycosides; style not especially thickened and modified distally; carpels fully united except for the often distinct or lobed stigmas, or seldom the style more deeply cleft.
  2 Leaves not saccate-vaginate, nearly always opposite or whorled.
    3 Leaves mostly with interpetiolar stipules, these sometimes reduced to mere connecting lines; ovary 2–3 (–5)-locular, with axile placentas (the partition sometimes imperfect in the upper part of the ovary); plants of diverse habit, often woody, often producing alkaloids as well as iridoid compounds .... **1. Loganiaceae.**
    3 Leaves exstipulate; ovary generally unilocular, with parietal (often deeply intruded) or rarely free-central placentas, only seldom bilocular and with axile placentas; plants usually herbaceous, seldom woody ......
.... **2. Gentianaceae.**
  2 Leaves saccate-vaginate, alternate, exstipulate; pulvinate subshrub; ovary bilocular, with axile placentas ....**3. Saccifoliaceae.**
1 Plants with a well developed latex-system, and commonly producing cardiotonic glycosides as well as alkaloids; style, except in some Apocynaceae, thickened and modified at the tip; carpels often distinct toward the base and united only distally.
  4 Androecium without translators, the pollen not forming pollinia; androecial corona wanting; carpels often united by part or all of the style below the thickened style-head, or even wholly united; plants commonly producing iridoid compounds .... **4. Apocynaceae.**

4 Androecium provided with translators, the pollen coherent to form pollinia; androecial corona usually well developed, seldom wanting; carpels united only by the thickened style-head; plants without iridoid compounds ... .5. Asclepiadaceae.

SELECTED REFERENCES

Bissett, N. G. 1958, 1961. The occurrence of alkaloids in the Apocynaceae. Ann. Bogor. **3:** 105–236, 1958; **4:** 65–144, 1961.

Chang, F. & D. Frame. 1987. The identity of *Lithophytum* (Loganiaceae, Plocospermeae). Brittonia **39:** 260–262.

Fallen, M. E. 1986. Floral structure in the Apocynaceae: Morphological, functional, and evolutionary aspects. Bot. Jahrb. Syst. **106:** 245–286.

Gopal Krishna, G. & V. Puri. 1962. Morphology of the flower of some Gentianaceae with special reference to placentation. Bot. Gaz. **124:** 42–57.

Maguire, B. & J. M. Pires. 1978. Saccifoliaceae. *In* The botany of the Guayana Highland—Part X. Mem. New York Bot. Gard. **29:** 230–245.

Nilsson, S. 1967. Pollen morphological studies in the Gentianaceae—Gentianinae. Grana Palynol. **7:** 46–143.

Pichon, M. 1948–1950. Classification des Apocynacées. I. Carissées et Ambélaniées. IX. Rauvolfiées, Alstoniées, Allemandées et Tabernémontanoidées. XXV. Échitoidées. Mém. Mus. Natl. Hist. Nat. N. Sér. **24:** 111–181, 1948; **27:** 153–251, 1948; Sér. B. **1:** 1–174, 1950.

Punt, W. & P. Leenhouts. 1967. Pollen morphology and taxonomy in the Loganiaceae. Grana Palynol. **7:** 469–516.

Safwat, F. M. 1962. The floral morphology of *Secamone* and the evolution of the pollinating apparatus in Asclepiadaceae. Ann. Missouri Bot. Gard. **49:** 95–129.

Tournay, R. & A. Lawalrée. 1952. Une classification nouvelle des familles appartenant aux ordres des Ligustrales et des Contortées. Bull. Soc. Bot. France **99:** 262–263.

Vijayaraghavan, M. R. & U. Padmanaban. 1969. Morphology and embryology of *Centaurium ramosissimum* Druce and affinities of the family Gentianaceae. Beitr. Biol. Pflanzen **46:** 15–37.

Woodson, R. E. 1930. Studies in the Apocynaceae. I. A critical study of the Apocynoideae (with special reference to the genus *Apocynum*). Ann. Missouri Bot. Gard. **17:** 1–212.

Woodson, R. E. 1941. The North American Asclepiadaceae. I. Perspective of the genera. Ann. Missouri Bot. Gard. **28:** 193–244.

Woodson, R. E. & J. A. Moore. 1938. The vascular anatomy and comparative morphology of apocynaceous flowers. Bull. Torrey Bot. Club **65:** 135–166.

2. Order Solanales

The order Solanales as here defined consists of 9 families and about 5000 species. More than four-fifths of the species belong to only 2 large families, the Solanaceae (2800) and Convolvulaceae (1500). The order may be briefly characterized as Asteridae with mostly alternate leaves, mostly regular, typically pentamerous flowers with as many stamens as corolla-lobes, and a superior ovary that does not have the special features of the Lamiales. As with other orders, all the characters are subject to exception.

It has been widely agreed in the past that the Nolanaceae, Solanaceae, and Convolvulaceae are closely related inter se, that the Polemoniaceae and Hydrophyllaceae form a pair, and that these two groups are related to each other. The relationship of the Cuscutaceae to the Convolvulaceae is also generally accepted; indeed the Cuscutaceae have often been submerged in the Convolvulaceae. Not all of these families remain associated in some of the newer systems of classification, but here I think the old ways are best. A relationship between the Hydrophyllaceae and Boraginaceae has also been generally perceived. Without denying the relationship, I find it conceptually more useful to put the Boraginaceae in an allied order.

The affinities of the small families Menyanthaceae, Duckeodendraceae, and Retziaceae (the latter two with only a single species each) are more debatable. The Menyanthaceae have often been associated with or included in the Gentianaceae, but they differ from characteristic members of that family (and from most other members of the order Gentianales as well) in their alternate leaves, integumentary tapetum, cellular endosperm, more dissected stele without internal phloem, and absence of gentiopicriside. Only the presence of an iridoid compound in the Menyanthaceae is out of harmony with the Solanales and suggests a position in the Gentianales. Other orders can be excluded on other grounds. I believe the weight of the evidence favors a position in the Solanales.

Duckeodendron is taxonomically isolated and insufficiently studied. Its embryology and chemistry are yet unknown. At the present state of knowledge *Duckeodendron* fits better into the Solanales than into any other order.

Retzia is also taxonomically isolated. Its affinities have been inconclusively debated. Association with or inclusion in the Loganiaceae, Solanaceae, and Stilbaceae (a segregate from the Verbenaceae) has been proposed. The organization of the gynoecium in *Retzia* is distinctive, and unlike all the groups with which the genus might be compared. The placement of *Retzia* in the Solanales in this treatment is influenced by studies in progress by Dennis Stevenson, which show that it has the peculiar oblique orientation of the carpels that characterizes the Solanaceae. The whorled leaves of *Retzia* and its production of iridoid compounds are admittedly anomalous in the Solanales. Further study is in order.

The Solanales are evidently related to the Gentianales. Aside from the general similarities of floral structure, the two orders are linked by the common possession of internal phloem in most species of Solanales and nearly all of the Gentianales. Except for these two orders and the taxonomically remote order Myrtales, only a few widely scattered groups of dicots have internal phloem. Embryologically the Gentianales are more primitive than the Solanales; so far as these characters are concerned, the one order might well be directly ancestral to the other. Although in the angiosperms as a whole alternate leaves are more primitive than opposite leaves, I will hazard the guess that in this pair of orders, as in the Asterales, opposite leaves are primitive and alternate leaves derived. However, any common ancestor of the families of Solanales would probably be more primitive than the vast majority of both groups in having 5 carpels. The few 5-carpellate members of these orders do not appear to be especially primitive in other respects. The two orders should therefore be considered to have diverged from a common ancestor that combined the more primitive features of both.

The Solanales differ from the Gentianales in their mostly alternate leaves, in their often cellular (rather than nuclear) endosperm, in often having an integumentary tapetum, and in the less consistent presence of internal phloem. Furthermore, the Gentianales generally produce iridoid compounds or cardiotonic glycosides or both, whereas the Solanales do not have cardiotonic glycosides, and only the small families Menyanthaceae and Retziaceae have iridoids.

The Lamiales differ from the Solanales in their characteristic gynoecium and fruit, and the Scrophulariales differ in usually having an irregular corolla with fewer stamens than corolla-lobes. These two orders represent the realization of morphological tendencies that are evident but less fully developed in some of the Solanales. The Scrophulariales further differ from the Solanales in commonly having iridoid compounds and sometimes cardiotonic glycosides, but not alkaloids. These chemical features tend to link the Scrophulariales more directly to the Gentianales than to the Solanales.

The order Solanales as a whole is ecologically varied, and the adaptive significance of the characters that mark the group is at best debatable. Only a few members of the order are trees, but otherwise the group embraces a wide range of ecological types that also occur in other orders. In comparison with other Asteridae there is nothing unusual in the arrangement and structure of the leaves, the anatomy of the ovules, or the ontogeny of the endosperm of most members of the Solanales. They lack the specialized features of corolla, androecium, and gynoecium found in various combinations in more advanced orders of the Asteridae, but so do many of the Gentianales. Among the features that distinguish the Solanales from the Gentianales, only the nature of the secondary metabolites is obviously important to the plants, but there is some overlap in the classes of alkaloids present in the Solanaceae and Loganiaceae.

Several of the individual families of Solanales do have some ecological significance. The Menyanthaceae are adapted to aquatic life, but most of the formal characters that mark the family are not obviously related to the habitat. The Convolvulaceae have exploited the twining vine habit more consistently and more successfully than most large families of plants, although they also show a wide range of other growth-forms. The Cuscutaceae have gone on from the twining vine habit of the Convolvulaceae to become parasitic. Both the Polemoniaceae and the Hydrophyllaceae have produced many annuals adapted to deserts and semideserts, but the members of these families also occur in many other habitats, and the biological significance of the characters that distinguish the two families from each other is still unknown. The pollen of the Polemoniaceae is diverse in structure and surface-ornamentation, but Taylor and Levin (1975) could find no correlation with the equally diverse means of pollination.

The fossil record of the Solanales is still scanty. Macrofossils attributed to the Solanaceae occur in Eocene and more recent deposits, but there is no significant record of fossil pollen for the family. D'Arcy (in Hawkes et al., 1979) doubts the identification of all purportedly solanaceous fossils. Pollen attributed to the Convolvulaceae goes back to the Lower Eocene, but without accompanying macrofossils. Pollen attributed to the Polemoniaceae, likewise without accompanying macrofossils, dates only from the Upper Miocene. Other members of the order appear only in post-Miocene deposits, if at all. Thus it appears that the order does not antedate the Tertiary period, and that most of its evolutionary diversification into families is post-Eocene.

Synoptical Arrangement of the Families of Solanales

1 Tall tree; fruit drupaceous, only one of the two locules fertile; Amazonian South America . . . . **1. Duckeodendraceae.**
1 Herbs, shrubs, vines, or seldom small trees, only rarely (1 sp. of Convolvulaceae) tall trees; fruit of various types, most commonly capsular or baccate, only rarely drupaceous.
   2 Stem with internal phloem; plants often producing alkaloids, but not iridoid compounds; always autotrophic.
      3 Carpels (3–) 5 (or in sets of 5); ovary with a terminal style and ripening into a schizocarp, or more often the gynoecium with a gynobasic style and ripening into 5 (or more) nutlets, each with 1–several locelli and seeds; endosperm-development cellular; Pacific slope of South America . . . . **2. Nolanaceae.**
      3 Carpels 2 (rarely 3–5 or casually more); fruits diverse, but not schizocarpic; style not gynobasic except in a few bicarpellate Convolvulaceae; widely distributed.
         4 Ovules and seeds (1–) more or less numerous; carpels, when 2, obliquely oriented, neither median nor collateral; plants without latex; cotyledons not plicate; style simple, the stigma only shortly or scarcely lobed; endosperm-development most commonly cellular, but sometimes nuclear or helobial; herbs, shrubs, vines, or small trees . . . . **3. Solanaceae.**
         4 Ovules mostly 2 per carpel, basal and erect, only rarely more numerous; carpels, when 2, median (one anterior, the other posterior); plants generally with latex-canals or latex-cells; cotyledons plicate; style simple or often more or less deeply cleft, or the styles distinct; endosperm-development nuclear; plants most commonly twining herbaceous vines, but sometimes erect herbs or shrubs or even trees . . . . **4. Convolvulaceae.**

2 Stem without internal phloem; plants sometimes producing iridoid compounds, but without alkaloids; autotrophic or (Cuscutaceae) parasitic.
  5 Twining stem-parasites, not rooted in the ground at maturity, nearly or
  quite without chlorophyll; embryo without well differentiated cotyledons .... **5. Cuscutaceae.**
  5 Autotrophic plants, rooted in the ground; embryo with evident cotyledons.
    6 Ovary bilocular in the lower third or half, unilocular above, with 4
    (–6) ovules attached in 2 pairs (or trios) at the slightly expanded
    summit of the partial partition, one ovule of each pair ascending into
    the unilocular part of the ovary, the other one (or 2) descending into
    one of the semilocules; low shrubs with whorled leaves, producing
    iridoid compounds; South Africa .... **6. Retziaceae.**
    6 Ovary of more ordinary structure; more widespread.
      7 Aquatic or semi-aquatic herbs, often with scattered vascular bundles
      in the stem; plants producing iridoid compounds; corolla-lobes
      valvate or induplicate-valvate or sometimes imbricate; carpels 2;
      ovules numerous on parietal placentas .... **7. Menyanthaceae.**
      7 Terrestrial to semi-aquatic herbs or subshrubs; vascular bundles of
      the stem in a ring, or the xylem forming a continuous ring; plants
      without iridoid compounds; corolla-lobes imbricate or convolute.
        8 Carpels (2) 3 (4); placentation axile; flowers generally with a nec-
        tary-disk around the ovary; corolla-lobes convolute; endo-
        sperm-development nuclear .... **8. Polemoniaceae.**
        8 Carpels 2; placentation parietal or rarely axile; flowers without a
        nectary-disk; corolla-lobes imbricate or less often convolute;
        endosperm-development cellular or less often nuclear ......
        .... **9. Hydrophyllaceae.**

SELECTED REFERENCES

Alfaro, M. E. & A. Mesa. 1979. El origen morfológico del floema intraxilar en
Nolanaceae y la posición sistemática de esta familia. Bol. Soc. Argent. Bot.
18: 123–126.

Bondeson, W. E. 1986. Gynoecial morphology and funicular germination plugs
in the Nolanaceae. Nordic J. Bot. **6:** 183–198.

Carlquist, S., V. M. Eckhart & D. C. Michener. 1983. Wood anatomy of Hydrophyllaceae. I. *Eriodictyon.* Aliso **10:** 397–412.

Constance, L. 1939. The genera of the tribe Hydrophylleae of the Hydrophyllaceae. Madroño **5:** 28–33.

Constance, L. & T. I. Chuang. 1982. SEM survey of pollen morphology and
classification in Hydrophyllaceae (Waterleaf family). Amer. J. Bot **69:**
40–53.

Crété, P. 1946, 1947. Embryogénie des Hydrophyllacées. Développement de
l'embryon chez le *Phacelia tanacetifolia* Benth. Développement de l'embryon
chez le *Nemophila insignis* Benth. Compt. Rend. Hebd. Séances Acad. Sci.
223: 459–460, 1946; **224:** 749–751, 1947.

Dahlgren, R., B. J. Nielsen, P. Goldblatt & J. P. Rourke. 1979. Further notes
on Retziaceae: Its chemical contents and affinities. Ann. Missouri Bot. Gard.
66: 545–556.

D'Arcy, W. G. (ed.). 1986. Solanaceae. Biology and systematics. Columbia Univ.
Press. New York.

Goldblatt, P. & R. C. Keating. 1976. Chromosome cytology, pollen structure, and relationships of *Retzia capensis*. Ann. Missouri Bot. Gard. **63**: 321–325.

Govil, C. M. 1972. Morphological studies in the family Convolvulaceae. IV. Vascular anatomy of the flower. Proc. Indian Acad. Sci. B, **75**: 271–282.

Grant, V. 1959. Natural history of the Phlox family. Systematic Botany. Martinus Nijhoff. The Hague.

Grant, V. & K. A. Grant. 1965. Flower pollination in the Phlox family. Columbia Univ. Press. New York & London.

Hawkes, J. G., R. N. Lester & A. D. Skelding (eds.). 1979. The biology and taxonomy of the Solanaceae. Linn. Soc. Symposium 7. Academic Press. London, New York, San Francisco.

Johnston, I. M. 1936. A study of the Nolanaceae. Proc. Amer. Acad. Arts **71**: 1–87.

Kuhlmann, J. G. 1947. Duckeodendraceae Kuhlmann (nova familia). Arq. Serv. Florest. **3**: 7–8.

Lindsey, A. A. 1938. Anatomical evidence for the Menyanthaceae. Amer. J. Bot. **25**: 480–485.

Mason, H. L. 1945. The genus *Eriastrum* and the influence of Bentham and Gray upon the problem of generic confusion in Polemoniaceae. Madroño **8**: 65–91.

Mesa, A. 1981. Nolanaceae. Fl. Neotropica Monogr. 26.

Nilsson, S. & R. Ornduff. 1973. Menyanthaceae Dum. World Pollen and Spore Flora **2**: 1–20.

Sengupta, S. 1972. On the pollen morphology of Convolvulceae, with special reference to taxonomy. Rev. Palaeobot. Palynol. **13**: 157–212.

Taylor, T. N. & D. A. Levin. 1975 (1976). Pollen morphology of Polemoniaceae in relation to systematics and pollination systems: Scanning electron microscopy. Grana **15**: 91–112.

Tiagi, B. 1966. Floral morphology of *Cuscuta reflexa* Roxb. and *C. lupuliformis* Krocker with a brief review of the literature on the genus *Cuscuta*. Bot. Mag. (Tokyo) **79**: 89–97.

Tucker, W. G. 1969. Serotaxonomy of the Solanaceae: A preliminary survey. Ann. Bot. (London) II, **33**: 1–23.

van der Velde, G. & L. A. van der Heijden. 1981. The floral biology and seed production of *Nymphoides peltata* (Gmel.) O. Kuntze (Menyanthaceae). Aquatic Bot. **10**: 261–293.

Wilson, K. A. 1960a. The genera of Hydrophyllaceae and Polemoniaceae in the southeastern United States. J. Arnold Arbor. **41**: 197–212.

Wilson, K. A. 1960b. The genera of Convolvulaceae in the southeastern United States. J. Arnold Arbor. **41**: 298–317.

Yuncker, T. G. 1932. The genus *Cuscuta*. Mem. Torrey Bot. Club **18**: 113–331.

3. Order Lamiales

The order Lamiales as here defined consists of 4 families and about 7800 species. The Lamiaceae (3200), Verbenaceae (2600) and Boraginaceae (2000) are all large families. The Lennoaceae (4) are a much smaller group. The order may be briefly characterized as Asteridae with a superior ovary consisting of 2 (–4) biovulate carpels with twice as many uniovulate locelli as carpels. The fruit very often consists of 1-seeded, half-carpellary nutlets.

The Verbenaceae and Lamiaceae are a closely related pair of families, which together include about three-fourths of the species in their order. Most authors agree that the Lamiaceae represent the realization and culmination of trends that begin in the Verbenaceae. The boundary between the two families is arbitrary and in part merely conventional, and it seems impossible to draw a sharp line, but the conceptual utility of recognizing two groups rather than only one has seldom been challenged.

Three small tribes that are customarily referred to the Lamiaceae are transitional between the Lamiaceae and Verbenaceae in gynoecial structure. These are the Prostanthereae, Ajugeae, and Rosmarineae, collectively embracing less than 10% of the species of Lamiaceae. In these tribes the ovary is more or less strongly lobed, but the carpels are united below, so that the style is terminal and impressed rather than truly gynobasic. These tribes resemble the Lamiaceae rather than the Verbenaceae in odor and in the aspect of the flowers, although these features do not reliably separate the two families, even among genera whose position is clear on the basis of the gynoecium.

The Verbenaceae are diverse in habit and gynoecial structure, and several peripheral groups have often been extracted as distinct families. Notable among the segregates are the Avicenniaceae (*Avicennia*, ca. 12 spp.), Dicrastylidiaceae or Chloanthaceae (14 genera, ca. 90 spp.), Phrymaceae (1 or 2 spp.), Stilbaceae (5 genera, 12 spp.), and Symphoremataceae (3 genera, 35 spp.). These segregate families collectively include less than 6% of the species of the more broadly defined family Verbenaceae. Their relationships are not in dispute, and the taxonomic rank at which they should be recognized is purely a matter of taste. My taste is to reduce them to less than familial rank.

The Boraginaceae stand somewhat apart from the Verbenaceae-Lamiaceae in their alternate leaves and in some chemical features. The Boraginaceae produce alkannin and pyrrolizidine alkaloids, and are not known to produce iridoid compounds, whereas the other two families frequently produce iridoid compounds, but not alkannin and only seldom alkaloids (these not of the same group as those of the Boraginaceae). Even so, some of the tropical, woody Boraginaceae with a terminal style are remarkably similar to some of the tropical, woody Verbenaceae. The gynoecium of the Boraginaceae covers the complete range from like that of typical Verbenaceae to like that of typical Lamiaceae, with the majority of species having a gynobasic style as in the Lamiaceae.

The gynoecium of the Lamiales provides another example of the evolutionary parallelism that permeates the angiosperms. If the more archaic members of the order were to die out, then the gynobasic style and half-carpellary nutlets of the bulk of the Boraginaceae and Lamiaceae would appear to be a unique synapomorphy.

The Lamiales are related to the Solanales and Gentianales. As noted in the discussion of the Solanales, the Lamiales reflect the realization of some morphological trends that are nascent in the former order. Many authors have noted a probable relationship between the Hydrophyllaceae (Solanales) and Boraginaceae. On purely morphological grounds, there is no obvious reason why the Lamiales might not be derived directly from the Solanales. The chemical picture is more complex. In the light of the distribution of alkaloids and iridoid compounds in the Gentianales, Solanales, and Lamiales, it might be safer to consider the relationship of the Lamiales to the Solanales to be more nearly fraternal than filial, with both orders coming from an ancestry near or in the Gentianales. If opposite leaves are primitive in this group of orders, as I have speculated, then it would be logical to suppose that the Verbenaceae and Lamiaceae have retained the ancestral decussate phyllotaxy, whereas the Boraginaceae and the bulk of the Solanales have reverted to the spiral phyllotaxy that is primitive for the angiosperms as a whole.

On the basis of the fossil pollen, it appears that the Boraginaceae can be traced back to the Oligocene, the Verbenaceae to the Lower Miocene, and the Lamiaceae to the Upper Miocene. The appearance of the Verbenaceae before the Lamiaceae is of course in harmony with what might be expected on the basis of present-day morphology.

The biological importance of the characters that mark the Lamiales is doubtful. The structure of the mature gynoecium obviously influences the means of seed-dispersal, but we have yet to see a comprehensive explanation of the progressive competitive advantage to be obtained by the intrusion of false partitions in the ovary and the subsequent stepwise change from a drupaceous, unlobed fruit to separating, half-carpellary nutlets. The three major families of the order differ to some degree in the nature of their chemical repellents, but the functional significance of these differences remains to be elucidated. Judging by their abundance, diversity, and geographic and ecologic distribution, it does not appear that any one of the three major families has any obvious advantage over the others, although the Verbenaceae are more predominantly tropical than the other two.

The parasitic habit of the Lennoaceae is obviously a specialization. The possible advantage to the Lennoaceae in the increased number of carpels is wholly obscure. It is true enough that the increase in number of carpels increases the potential number of seeds, but this is a most unusual way to produce such an increase, if that is what is being selected for. The order is locked into a close relationship between the number of carpels and the number of ovules, but the three large families have obviously found it possible to govern the number of seeds by the number of flowers.

Synoptical Arrangement of the Families of Lamiales

1 Leaves mostly alternate, usually entire; flowers mostly regular or nearly so and with as many stamens as corolla-lobes; stems not square; plants neither aromatic nor with iridoid compounds.

2 Plants parasitic, without chlorophyll and with reduced, scale-like leaves;

carpels 6–16; fruit a fleshy, eventually irregularly circumscissile capsule; seeds with well developed endosperm and globose, undifferentiated embryo . . . . **1. Lennoaceae.**
2   Plants autotrophic, with chlorophyll and normal leaves; carpels 2 (–5); fruit usually drupaceous or of separating, half-carpellary nutlets, rarely capsular; seeds with a dicotyledonous embryo and well developed to much more often scanty or no endosperm . . . . **2. Boraginaceae.**
1   Leaves mostly opposite (or whorled), entire or often toothed or cleft, or sometimes compound; flowers mostly more or less irregular and with 2–4 stamens, the exceptions (regular corolla and/or 5 stamens) being found chiefly among the Verbenaceae; young stems commonly square; iridoid and aromatic compounds common, though not universal.
3   Style terminal or nearly so, the ovary only shortly or not at all lobed at the top; plants seldom aromatic; fruit variously drupaceous, or capsular, or achenial, or often of half-carpellary nutlets as in the next family . . . .
. . . . **3. Verbenaceae.**
3   Style commonly gynobasic, uniting the otherwise essentially distinct lobes of the ovary, or less commonly the ovary lobed only part way (one-third or more) to the base; plants commonly aromatic; fruit of (1–) 4 half-carpellary nutlets or (rarely) drupelets . . . . **4. Lamiaceae.**

SELECTED REFERENCES

Cantino, P. D.   1982.   Affinities of the Lamiales: A cladistic analysis. Syst. Bot. 7: 237–248.
Cantino, P. D. & D. Sanders.   1986.   Subfamilial classification of Labiatae. Syst. Bot. 11: 155–162.
Carlquist, S.   1970.   Wood anatomy of *Echium* (Boraginaceae). Aliso 7: 183–199.
Copeland, H. F.   1935.   The structure of the flower of *Pholisma arenarium*. Amer. J. Bot. 22: 366–383.
Drugg, W. S.   1962.   Pollen morphology of the Lennoaceae. Amer. J. Bot. 49: 1027–1032.
El-Gazzar, A. & L. Watson.   1970.   A taxonomic study of Labiatae and related genera. New Phytol. 69: 451–486.
Hillson, C. J.   1959.   Comparative studies of floral morphology of the Labiatae. Amer. J. Bot. 46: 451–459.
Johri, B. M. & I. K. Vasil.   1956.   The embryology of *Ehretia laevis* Roxb. Phytomorphology 6: 134–143.
Kapil, R. N. & R. S. Vani.   1966.   *Nyctanthes arbor-tristis* Linn.: Embryology and relationships. Phytomorphology 16: 553–563.
Kooiman, P.   1975.   The occurrence of iridoid glycosides in the Verbenaceae. Acta Bot. Neerl. 24: 459–468.
Rao, V. S.   1952.   The floral anatomy of some Verbenaceae with special reference to the gynoecium. J. Indian Bot. Soc. 31: 297–315.
Stant, M. Y.   1952.   Anatomical evidence for including *Nyctanthes* and *Dimetra* in the Verbenaceae. Kew Bull. 1952: 273–276.
Thieret, J. W.   1972.   The Phrymaceae in the southeastern United States. J. Arnold Arbor. 53: 226–233.

Whipple, H. L. 1972. Structure and systematics of *Phryma leptostachya* L. J. Elisha Mitchell Sci. Soc. **88**: 1–17.

Yatskievych, G. & C. T. Mason, Jr. 1986. A revision of the Lennoaceae. Syst. Bot. **11**: 531–548.

4. Order Callitrichales

The order Callitrichales as here defined consists of 3 families and a little more than 50 species. Each family consists of only a single genus. The affinities of all three families have been debated in the past, and it has not been customary to associate them in a single order. Embryological data for all three, and chemical data for the Callitrichaceae and Hippuridaceae, strongly suggest that each of the three groups belongs to the Asteridae, rather than with the rosidan families to which they had been thought to be allied.

Once the three families have been transferred to the Asteridae, it becomes useful to think of them collectively as forming a group that has undergone vegetative and floral reduction in association with an aquatic habitat. The differences among them, although substantial, are not so great as to preclude such a classification. *Callitriche* resembles the Lamiales in the basic structure of its gynoecium, aside from the fact that the carpels are collateral rather than median, but it does not seem closely allied to any family of that order. Tendencies toward the lamialean gynoecium can be seen in some other orders of the Asteridae, including the Solanales (Nolanaceae and a few Convolvulaceae), Scrophulariales (some Globulariaceae), and Plantaginales (spp. of *Plantago*). Therefore the structure of the gynoecium does not require the inclusion of *Callitriche* in the Lamiales. The gynoecium of *Hydrostachys* is perfectly compatible with that of the Scrophulariales, and a number of recent authors have included the Hydrostachyaceae in that order. Aside from its aquatic habitat, *Hydrostachys* is habitally suggestive of *Plantago,* which is now generally conceded to be related to the Scrophulariaceae. The pseudomonomerous, inferior ovary of *Hippuris* is hard to reconcile with any petaliferous order of the Asteridae, but on chemical grounds Hegnauer (1969) concludes that "Like *Callitriche, Hippuris* is most probably a wholly aquatic offshoot of the Tubiflorae which might have its nearest relatives in the Plantaginaceae (compare *Littorella*)." Thus all three genera can be associated in some way with the Plantaginaceae. The Plantaginaceae, in comparison with the more or less directly ancestral Scrophulariaceae, have taken the road of floral reduction, and *Littorella* has even become aquatic. The Callitrichales may be considered to have exploited more fully the tendencies toward floral reduction and aquatic habitat that are already evident in the Plantaginaceae. It is not required that the Plantaginaceae as we now know them be directly ancestral to the Callitrichales, but at least a collateral relationship seems to be indicated.

For purposes of a linear sequence of orders, it is convenient to put the

Callitrichales and Plantaginales before the Scrophulariales, although from a strictly phylogenetic standpoint the Scrophulariales ought to come before the other two.

1 Gynoecium seemingly of a single carpel, the ovary unilocular, with a single terminal ovule and a single style; flowers perfect and epigynous, or some or all of them unisexual; fruit an achene or drupelet ..... **1. Hippuridaceae.**
1 Gynoecium bicarpellate, the ovary with 4 or more ovules and 2 styles; flowers all unisexual.
  2 Ovary compartmented into 4 locelli, each locellus with a single pendulous, axile ovule; carpels collateral; fruit of 4 separating nutlets; pollen monadinous .... **2. Callitrichaceae.**
  2 Ovary unilocular, with 2 parietal placentas and numerous ovules; carpels median; fruit capsular; pollen tetradinous .... **3. Hydrostachyaceae.**

SELECTED REFERENCES

Cusset, C. 1973. Révision des Hydrostachyaceae. Adansonia II, **13**: 75–119.
Hegnauer, R. 1969. Chemical evidence for the classification of some plant taxa. Pages 121–138 *in* J. B. Harborne & T. Swain (eds.), Perspectives in phytochemistry. Academic Press. London & New York.
Jørgensen, C. A. 1923. Studies on Callitrichaceae. Bot. Tidsskr. **38**: 81–122.
Rauh, W. & I. Jäger-Zürn. 1967. Le problème de la position systématique des Hydrostachyacées. Adansonia II, **6**: 515–523.
Tron, E. Zh. 1967. Anatomicheskoe stroenie steblya *Hippuris vulgaris.* Bot. Zhurn. **52**: 811–819.

5. Order Plantaginales

The order Plantaginales consists of the single family Plantaginaceae, with 3 genera of very unequal size. The familiar cosmopolitan genus *Plantago* has about 250 species. *Littorella,* which is more or less aquatic, has only 3 species, and *Bougeria* only one. The order may be briefly characterized as Asteridae with a superior ovary, mostly anemophilous flowers with a scarious, persistent, generally regular, mostly tetramerous corolla, and phyllodial, more or less parallel-veined (or much reduced), very often all basal leaves.

The affinities of the Plantaginaceae have been disputed in the past. Most present-day authors agree that they are related to the Scrophulariaceae, and Takhtajan includes them in the order Scrophulariales. Although I agree as to the relationships, I find it conceptually more useful to maintain the Plantaginales as a distinct order.

Derivation of the Plantaginaceae from the Scrophulariaceae or some similar ancestral group would imply the same sort of reduction from an irregular, 5-lobed corolla with 4 stamens to a regular corolla with 4 stamens that appears to have taken place in the Buddlejaceae. The floral anatomy of some species suggests a pentamerous ancestry.

The anemophilous habit of the Plantaginaceae must be of considerable importance to the plants, but the reasons for a change from entomophily to anemophily are obscure. The Plantaginaceae grow in the same sorts of places as entomophilous plants, and there is nothing in their general structure, aside from the reduced corolla, that does not appear to be equally compatible with entomophily. The functional significance of the phyllodial leaves (the apparent blade representing a flattened petiole) is wholly obscure.

Pollen attributed to *Plantago* occurs in middle or late Miocene and more recent deposits.

SELECTED REFERENCES

Carlquist, S. 1970. Wood anatomy of insular species of *Plantago* and the problem of raylessness. Bull. Torrey Bot. Club **97**: 353–361.
Cooper, G. O. 1942. Development of the ovule and formation of the seed in *Plantago lanceolata*. Amer. J. Bot. **29**: 577–581.
Misra, R. C. 1966. Morphological studies in *Plantago*. III. Nodal anatomy. Proc. Indian Acad. Sci. **63B**: 271–274.

6. Order Scrophulariales

The order Scrophulariales as here defined consists of 12 families and more than 11,000 species. About three-fourths of the species belong to only 3 large families, the Scrophulariaceae (4000), Acanthaceae (2500), and Gesneriaceae (2500). The Columelliaceae, often associated with the families of the Scrophulariales, are here referred to the Rosales.

The Scrophulariales differ from the closely related order Solanales in usually having an irregular (often bilabiate) corolla with fewer stamens than corolla-lobes, in the much less frequent presence of internal phloem, and in commonly producing iridoid compounds and orobanchin, but only seldom alkaloids. Exceptions can be found to all of these characters, but the clustering of families is clear. It may reasonably be supposed that the floral differences between the two orders reflect increasing specialization by the Scrophulariales for pollination by specific insects or birds. The chemical differences presumably indicate a different choice of weapons in the necessary defense against predators. It may be noted that the Gentianales, which are more primitive in some respects than either the Scrophulariales or the Solanales, produce alkaloids as well as iridoid compounds, but are not known to have orobanchin. The ecological significance of internal phloem is obscure.

The Scrophulariaceae are not only the largest family in the order, but are also central to it. Four of the other families (Acanthaceae, Bignoniaceae, Globulariaceae, and Orobanchaceae) are connected to the Scrophulariaceae by transitional genera or groups of genera that have by different authors been referred to the central or the peripheral family. Although the remaining families of the order are more sharply limited, most of them may logically be considered to be specialized derivatives of the Scrophulariaceae. The Bignoniaceae may be more primitive than the Scrophulariaceae in being mainly woody, but in other respects such as the lack of endosperm, the often climbing habit, the often compound leaves, and the commonly winged seeds, the Bignoniaceae appear to be more advanced.

The Acanthaceae diverge from the Scrophulariaceae primarily in their specialized funiculus and explosively dehiscent fruit. The small subfamilies Nelsonioideae and Thunbergioideae (here referred to the Acanthaceae) represent way-stations along the route to typical Acanthaceae. The ecological significance of the loss of endosperm and development of cystoliths in the Acanthaceae is obscure. Perhaps the cystoliths serve a defensive function.

The Orobanchaceae diverge from the Scrophulariaceae in their parasitic habit and parietal placentation. The evolutionary journey toward parasitism obviously begins with chlorophyllous root-parasites in the Scrophulariaceae; the Orobanchaceae merely occupy the house at the end of the road. The ecological significance of the concurrent change to parietal placentation is obscure.

The Globulariaceae and Myoporaceae have taken the route of reduction in the number of ovules and formation of indehiscent, 1-seeded fruits or mericarps. The change obviously has ecological overtones, but it is not unusual in terms of the Asteridae as a whole, and it does not fit these families to any particular way of life not shared with other groups. These two families also share a special type of glandular hair, the ecological significance of which is unknown. The connection of the Globulariaceae (here defined to include the Selaginoideae) to the Scrophulariaceae is through the tribe Manuleae of the latter family.

The Lentibulariaceae have become insectivorous and mostly aquatic. The ecologic significance of the concurrent change to free-central placentation is unknown.

The Gesneriaceae diverge from the Scrophulariaceae in their basically parietal placentation and frequently more or less inferior ovary. The selective significance of these changes is obscure. We have no idea of what drives the change in the subfamily Cyrtandroideae (Gesneriaceae) to unequal cotyledons, culminating in the large, foliar cotyledon of otherwise leafless species of *Streptocarpus*.

The specialized, mucilaginous trichomes of the Pedaliaceae, which make the herbage somewhat slimy, may well serve a protective function. The ornamentation of the fruits in many Pedaliaceae is obviously an adaptation for zoochorous distribution of the seeds.

The Buddlejaceae and Oleaceae may have restored the ancestral regular corolla by supressing one of the 5 lobes of an irregular corolla and becoming tetramerous. *Sanango*, in the Buddlejaceae, provides a possibly intermediate stage, with a slightly irregular, 5-lobed corolla and only 4 functional stamens, the 5th stamen being small and staminodial or vestigial. The selective forces that could drive such a change in floral structure are obscure.

The Scrophulariales are poorly represented in the fossil record. As befits a fairly advanced group in the Asteridae, nothing in the order antedates the Eocene. Flowers, fruits, and pollen of putative Bignoniaceae date from the Eocene. Pollen of the Acanthaceae comes in during the Lower Miocene, and of the Oleaceae during the Upper Miocene. The appearance of pollen of the Bignoniaceae and Acanthaceae before the other families may simply reflect the distinctiveness of the pollen of many genera of these two groups.

Synoptical Arrangement of the Families of Scrophulariales

1 Plants not insectivorous, and only occasionally aquatic; placentation various, but not free-central.
  2 Corolla mostly 4-lobed and regular or nearly so, wanting in some Oleaceae; mostly woody plants with opposite or whorled leaves, rarely herbs.
    3 Stamens 4; ovules more or less numerous in each locule .... **1. Buddlejaceae.**
    3 Stamens 2, rarely 4; ovules most commonly 2 in each locule, sometimes 1–4, seldom numerous .... **2. Oleaceae.**
  2 Corolla mostly 5-lobed and/or more or less strongly irregular, rarely wanting; habit and leaves various.
    4 Seeds mostly with well developed endosperm (except many Gesneriaceae, these without the special features of any of the families of the next group).
      5 Placentation basically axile, the ovary typically bilocular, sometimes with one locule more or less reduced, or even supressed so that the ovary is pseudomonomerous.
        6 Fruit usually a capsule, rarely a berry or a schizocarp; ovules (2–) more or less numerous in each locule .... **3. Scrophulariaceae.**
        6 Fruit of 2 separating, often unequal nutlets or drupelets, or of a small nut or achene; ovules solitary (2) in each locule, or one locule empty or suppressed .... **4. Globulariaceae.**
      5 Placentation basically parietal, seldom secondarily axile.
        7 Plants parasitic, without chlorophyll; embryo minute, undifferentiated, leaves reduced and alternate; ovary superior ....**6. Orobanchaceae.**
        7 Plants autotrophic; embryo well developed, with 2 cotyledons; leaves opposite, or rarely whorled or alternate, or the plants of anomalous vegetative structure; ovary superior to inferior .... **7. Gesneriaceae.**
    4 Seeds with scanty or no endosperm.
      8 Fruit explosively dehiscent, the seeds with an enlarged and specialized funiculus that is typically developed into a jaculator; characteristic cystoliths usually present in some epidermal and parenchymatous cells .... **8. Acanthaceae.**
      8 Fruit indehiscent or dehiscent, but not explosively so, the funiculus of ordinary type; cystoliths wanting.

9 Herbs (rarely shrubs) with specialized mucilaginous hairs, the herbage commonly slimy; fruits very often with hooks or horns or prickles, or sometimes winged .... **9. Pedaliaceae.**
9 Trees, shrubs, or woody vines, only rarely herbs, without specialized mucilaginous hairs; fruit otherwise.
   10 Ovules more or less numerous in each locule; fruit usually a capsule, or seldom fleshy and indehiscent but not a drupe, plants erect or often climbing, with simple or more often compound, opposite or whorled or rarely alternate leaves .. .. **10. Bignoniaceae.**
   10 Ovules (1) 2–8 in each locule, or one locule empty; fruit a drupe, or sometimes separating into 1-seeded, drupe-like segments; leaves simple.
      11 Twiners, without specialized secretory cavities; leaves opposite .... **11. Mendonciaceae.**
      11 Erect shrubs or small trees, most genera with scattered secretory cavities; leaves alternate, seldom opposite .... **5. Myoporaceae.**
1 Insectivorous herbs, aquatic or of wet places; placentation free-central .... **12. Lentibulariaceae.**

SELECTED REFERENCES

Attawi, F. 1977. Morphologisch-anatomische Untersuchungen an den Haustorien einiger *Orobanche*-Arten. Ber. Deutsch. Bot. Ges. **90:** 173–182.

Baas, P. & Zhang Xinying. 1986. Wood anatomy of trees and shrubs from China. I. Oleaceae. IAWA Bull. II, **7:** 195–220.

Behnke, H.-D. 1986. Contributions to the knowledge of P-type sieve-element plastids in dicotyledons. IV. Acanthaceae. Bot. Jahrb. Syst. **106:** 499–510.

Bremekamp, C. E. B. 1953. The delimitation of the Acanthaceae. Proc. Kon. Nederl. Akad. Wet. **C56:** 533–546.

Bunting, G. S. & J. A. Duke. 1961. *Sanango*: New Amazonian genus of the Loganiaceae. Ann. Missouri Bot. Gard. **48:** 269–274.

Burtt, B. L. 1963, 1970. Studies on the Gesneriaceae of the Old World. XXIV. Tentative keys to the tribes and genera. XXXI. Some aspects of functional evolution. Notes Roy. Bot. Gard. Edinburgh **24:** 205–220, 1963; **30:** 1–9, 1970.

Burtt, B. L. 1977. Classification above the genus, as exemplified by Gesneriaceae, with parallels from other groups. Pl. Syst. Evol., Suppl. **1:** 97–109.

Buurman, J. 1977. Contribution to the pollenmorphology of the Bignoniaceae, with special reference to the tricolpate type. Pollen & Spores **19:** 447–519.

Casper, S. J. 1963. "Systematisch massgebende" Merkmale für die Einordnung der Lentibulariaceen in das System. Oesterr. Bot. Z. **110:** 108–131.

Crété, P. 1955. L'application de certaines données embryologiques à la systématique des Orobanchacées et de quelques familles voisins. Phytomorphology **5:** 422–435.

De, A. 1966–1968. Cytological, anatomical and palynological studies as an aid in tracing affinity and phylogeny in the family Acanthaceae. I. Cytological studies. II. Floral anatomy. III. General anatomy. IV. Palynology and final conclusion. Trans. Bose Research Inst. **29:** 139–175, 1966; **30:** 27–43, 51–65, 1967; **31:** 17–29, 1968.

Farooq, M. 1964. Studies in the Lentibulariaceae. I. The embryology of *Utricularia stellaris* Linn. f. var. *inflexa* Clarke. Proc. Natl. Inst. Sci. India **30B:** 263–299. III. The embryology of *Utricularia uliginosa* Vahl. Phytomorphology **15:** 123–131.

Gentry, A. H. 1974. Coevolutionary patterns in Central America Bignoniaceae. Ann. Missouri Bot. Gard. **61:** 728–759.

Gentry, A. H. & A. S. Tomb. 1979 (1980). Taxonomic implications of Bignoniaceae palynology. Ann. Missouri Bot. Gard. **66:** 756–777.

Goldblatt, P. & A. H. Gentry. 1979. Cytology of Bignoniaceae. Bot. Not. **132:** 475–482.

Guédès, M. 1965. Remarques sur la placentation des Orobanchacées. Bull. Soc. Bot. France **111:** 257–261.

Hartl, D. 1956. Die Beziehungen zwischen den Plazenten der Lentibulariaceen und Scrophulariaceen nebst einem Exkurz über die Spezialisationsrichtungen der Plazentation. Beitr. Biol. Pflanzen **32:** 471–490.

Heckard, L. R. 1962. Root parasitism in *Castilleja*. Bot. Gaz. **124:** 21–29.

Huynh, K.-L. 1968. Étude de la morphologie du pollen du genre *Utricularia* L. Pollen & Spores **10:** 11–55.

Ivanina, L. I. 1965 (1966). Application of the carpological method to the taxonomy of Gesneriaceae. Notes Roy. Bot. Gard. Edinburgh **26:** 383–403.

Johnson, L. A. S. 1957. A review of the family Oleaceae. Contr. New South Wales Natl. Herb. **2:** 395–418.

Junell, S. 1961. Ovarian morphology and taxonomical position of Selagineae. Svensk Bot. Tidskr. **55:** 168–192.

Karrfaldt, E. E. & A. S. Tomb. 1983. Air spaces, secretory cavities, and the relationship between Leucophylleae (Scrophulariaceae) and Myoporaceae. Syst. Bot. **8:** 29–32.

Kshetrapal, S. & Y. G. Tiagi. 1970. Structure, vascular anatomy and evolution of the gynoecium in the family Oleaceae and their bearing on the systematic position of the genus *Nyctanthes* L. Acta Bot. Acad. Sci. Hung. **16:** 143–151.

Li, H.-L. 1954. Trapellaceae, a familial segregate from the Asiatic flora. J. Wash. Acad. Sci. **44:** 11–13.

Long, R. W. 1970. The genera of Acanthaceae in the southeastern United States. J. Arnold Arbor. **51:** 257–309.

Moore, R. J. 1948. Cytotaxonomic studies in the Loganiaceae. II. Embryology of *Polypremum procumbens* L. Amer. J. Bot. **35:** 404–410.

Musselman, L. J. & W. C. Dickison. 1975. The structure and development of the haustorium in parasitic Scrophulariaceae. J. Linn. Soc., Bot. **70:** 183–212.

Rao, V. S. 1953, 1954. The floral anatomy of some Bicarpellatae. I. Acanthaceae. II. Bignoniaceae. J. Univ. Bombay **21**(N.S.)**, part 5B:** 1–34, 1953; **22**(N.S.)**, part 5B:** 55–70, 1954.

Ratter, J. A. 1975. A survey of chromosome numbers in the Gesneriaceae of the Old World. Notes Roy. Bot. Gard. Edinburgh **33:** 527–543.

Sax, K. & E. C. Abbe. 1932. Chromosome numbers and the anatomy of the secondary xylem in the Oleaceae. J. Arnold Arbor. **13:** 37–48.

Singh, S. P. 1960. Morphological studies in some members of the family Pedaliaceae. I. *Sesamum indicum* DC. Phytomorphology **10**: 65–81.

Skog, L. E. 1976. A study of the tribe Gesnerieae, with a revision of *Gesneria* (Gesneriaceae: Gesnerioideae). Smithsonian Contr. Bot. **29**: 1–182.

Straka, H. & H.-D. Ihlenfeldt. 1965. Pollenmorphologie und Systematik der Pedaliaceae R. Br. Beitr. Biol. Pflanzen **41**: 175–207.

Taylor, H. 1945. Cyto-taxonomy and phylogeny of the Oleaceae. Brittonia **5**: 337–367.

Thieret, J. W. 1967. Supraspecific classification in the Scrophulariaceae: A review. Sida **3**: 87–106.

Thieret, J. W. 1971. The genera of Orobanchaceae in the southeastern United States. J. Arnold Arbor. **52**: 404–434.

Thieret, J. W. 1977. The Martyniaceae in the southeastern United States. J. Arnold Arbor. **58**: 25–39.

Tiagi, B. 1963. Studies in the family Orobanchaceae. IV. Embryology of *Boschniackia himalaica* Hook. and *B. tuberosa* (Hook.) Jepson, with remarks on the evolution of the family. Bot. Not. **116**: 81–93.

Weber, H. C. 1980. Zur Evolution des Parasitismus bei den Scrophulariaceae und Orobanchaceae. Pl. Syst. Evol. **136**: 217–232.

Wilson, C. L. 1974. Floral anatomy in Gesneriaceae. I. Cyrtandroideae. II. Gesnerioideae. Bot. Gaz. **135**: 247–256; 256–268.

Wilson, K. A. & C. E. Wood. 1959. The genera of Oleaceae in the southeastern United States. J. Arnold Arbor. **40**: 369–384.

7. Order Campanulales

The order Campanulales as here defined consists of 7 families and about 2500 species. About four-fifths of the species belong to the single family Campanulaceae, and most of the remainder belong to the Goodeniaceae (300). The Stylidiaceae have about 150 species, the Pentaphragmataceae about 30, the Sphenocleaceae and Donatiaceae only 2 each, and the Brunoniaceae only one. The last four families have only a single genus each.

There are two well marked subfamilies of Campanulaceae, the Campanuloideae and Lobelioideae, connected by a small group of transitional genera that are sometimes treated as a third subfamily Cyphioideae. The existence of the two major groups, and the close relationship between them, are not in dispute. The Lobelioideae are the more advanced group, marked by their highly irregular, resupinate flowers and connate anthers. Whether to treat the lobeliads as a family or a subfamily is purely a matter of taste.

The Campanulales are Asteridae with a typically inferior ovary, mostly alternate leaves, and stamens mostly either free from the corolla or attached at the base of the corolla-tube. They characteristically store carbohydrate as inulin. They do not heavily exploit iridoids or tannins as repellents, and except for the pyridine alkaloids of some Lobelioideae, alkaloids are not important constituents. The vast majority of the species are herbaceous, and the woody species appear to have an herbaceous ancestry.

Three of the families and more than nine-tenths of the species of Campanulales have a specialized pollen-presentation mechanism of a type that appears to have been independently evolved also in the Asteraceae, Calyceraceae, and the subfamily Ixoroideae of the Rubiaceae. Even within the Campanulales, the mechanism may well have arisen separately in the Campanulaceae and Goodeniaceae, inasmuch as it is claimed that the collecting hairs of the style of the first family are not homologous with the stylar indusium of the second. The same evolutionary possibility has evidently been exploited several times within the Asteridae.

The pollen-presentation mechanism of the Campanulales would seem a priori to be of great importance to the plant. Certainly differences in its nature furnish important taxonomic characters in the delimitation of families within the order. On the other hand, it is not easy to see how this complex mechanism is a real improvement over more ordinary arrangements. A study of the kinds of pollinators in the order as a whole might be instructive. The basically herbaceous habit of the order is of course significant ecologically, but it is also far from unique. The other characters that collectively distinguish the Campanulales from the other orders of Asteridae are also difficult to interpret in terms of survival-value.

The ancestry of the Campanulales is to be sought in or near the Solanales. Members of the Campanulales that have regular flowers would fit fairly comfortably into the Solanales if they were deprived of the advanced features of epigyny and specialized pollen-presentation.

Pollen referred to the Goodeniaceae occurs in late Oligocene and subsequent deposits. Otherwise the order is scarcely represented in the fossil record.

SYNOPTICAL ARRANGEMENT OF THE FAMILIES OF CAMPANULALES

1 Style without an indusium, but often with collecting hairs.
    2 Stamens as many as the corolla-lobes, typically 5, free from the style; anthers introrse.
        3 Style glabrous, and with a single stigma (or the stigma sessile); plants without a latex system.
            4 Corolla-lobes valvate; fruit a berry; flowers borne in dense, sympodial, helicoid cymes that have conspicuous bracts ....**1. Pentaphragmataceae.**
            4 Corolla-lobes imbricate; fruit a circumscissile capsule; flowers borne in dense, terminal, inconspicuously bracteate spikes .... **2. Sphenocleaceae.**
        3 Style with well developed collecting hairs just below the 2–3 (–5) stigmas; plants with a well developed latex-system ...... **3. Campanulaceae.**
    2 Stamens 2 or 3, fewer than the corolla-lobes or petals; anthers extrorse; plants without a latex-system.
        5 Petals united to form a 5-lobed corolla; stamens wholly adnate to the style, together with which they form a column ..... **4. Stylidiaceae.**
        5 Petals 5–10, distinct; stamens free from the style; filaments distinct ... . **5. Donatiaceae.**

1 Style with a more or less cupulate indusium just beneath the stigmas, but without collecting hairs.
  6 Flowers regular, borne in involucrate, cymose heads; endosperm wanting; ovary superior, unilocular, with a single basal ovule ...... **6. Brunoniaceae.**
  6 Flowers irregular, borne in various sorts of inflorescences, but not in involucrate heads; endosperm well developed; ovary mostly inferior, seldom only half-inferior, rarely essentially superior, (1) 2 (–4)-locular, with 2 or more ovules .... **7. Goodeniaceae.**

SELECTED REFERENCES

Brizicky, G. K. 1966. The Goodeniaceae in the southeastern United States. J. Arnold Arbor. **47**: 293–300.
Carlquist, S. 1969a. Studies in Stylidiaceae: New taxa, field observations, evolutionary tendencies. Aliso **7**: 13–64.
Carlquist, S. 1969b. Wood anatomy in Goodeniaceae and the problem of insular woodiness. Ann. Missouri Bot. Gard. **56**: 358–390.
Carlquist, S. 1969c. Wood anatomy of Lobelioideae (Campanulaceae). Biotropica **1**: 47–72.
Carlquist, S. 1976. New species of *Stylidium,* and notes on Stylidiaceae from southwestern Australia. Aliso **8**: 447–463.
Carlquist, S. 1979. *Stylidium* in Arnhem Land: New species, modes of speciation on the sandstone plateau, and comments on floral mimicry. Aliso **9**: 411–461.
Carolin, R. C. 1959. Floral structure and anatomy in the family Goodeniaceae Dumort. Proc. Linn. Soc. New South Wales **84**: 242–255.
Carolin, R. C. 1960a. Floral structure and anatomy in the family Stylidiaceae Swartz. Proc. Linn. Soc. New South Wales **85**: 189–196.
Carolin, R. C. 1960b. The structures involved in the presentation of pollen to visiting insects in the order Campanulales. Proc. Linn. Soc. New South Wales **85**: 197–207.
Carolin, R. C. 1967. The concept of the inflorescence in the order Campanulales. Proc. Linn. Soc. New South Wales **92**: 7–26.
Carolin, R. C. 1978. The systematic relationships of *Brunonia.* Brunonia **1**: 9–29.
Dunbar, A. 1975. On pollen of Campanulaceae and related families with special reference to the surface ultrastructure. I. Campanulaceae subfam. Campanuloideae. II. Campanulaceae subfam. Cyphioideae and subfam. Lobelioideae; Goodeniaceae; Sphenocleaceae. Bot. Not. **128**: 73–101, 102–118.
Dunbar, A. 1978. Pollen morphology and taxonomic position of the genus *Pentaphragma* Wall. (Pentaphragmataceae). Grana **17**: 141–147.
Gupta, D. P. 1959. Vascular anatomy of the flower of *Sphenoclea zeylanica* Gaertn. and some other related species. Proc. Natl. Inst. Sci. India **25B**: 55–64.
Kapil, R. N. & M. R. Vijayaraghavan. 1965. Embryology of *Pentaphragma horsfieldii* (Miq.) Airy Shaw with a discussion on the systematic position. Phytomorphology **15**: 93–102.

Kaplan, D. R. 1967. Floral morphology, organogenesis and interpretation of the inferior ovary in *Downingia bacigalupii*. Amer. J. Bot. **54:** 1274–1290.

Rapson, L. J. 1953. Vegetative anatomy in *Donatia, Phyllacne, Forstera* and *Oreostylidium* and its taxonomic significance. Trans. & Proc. Roy. Soc. New Zealand **80:** 399–402.

Rosén, W. 1949. Endosperm development in Campanulaceae and closely related families. Bot. Not. **1949:** 137–147.

Shetler, S. G. 1979. Pollen-collecting hairs of *Campanula* (Campanulaceae). Taxon **28:** 205–215.

Shulkina, T. V. 1980. The significance of life-form characters for systematics, with special reference to the family Campanulaceae. Pl. Syst. Evol. **136:** 233–246.

Vijayaraghavan, M. R. & U. Malik. 1972. Morphology and embryology of *Scaevola frutescens* K. and affinities of the family Goodeniaceae. Bot. Not. **125:** 241–254.

8. Order Rubiales

The order Rubiales consists of the very large family Rubiaceae (6500 species) and the very small satellite family Theligonaceae (a single genus with 3 species).

The Rubiaceae are Asteridae with opposite leaves and interpetiolar stipules, or with whorled leaves and no stipules. The flowers have an inferior ovary and a regular corolla with isomerous stamens attached to the tube. These features distinguish the bulk of the Rubiaceae from all other families. As additional characters it may be noted that the stipules commonly bear colleters, that the majority of the species have well developed endosperm, and that the endosperm nearly always follows the nuclear pattern of development.

The Rubiaceae form a connecting link between the Gentianales and the Dipsacales, and would be an aberrant element in either order. Each of these orders is relatively homogeneous and well defined without the Rubiaceae. In my opinion the Loganiaceae (Gentianales) stand near to the ancestry of the Rubiaceae, which in turn stand near to the ancestry of the Caprifoliaceae. The other families of the Dipsacales appear to be derived from the Caprifoliaceae. Further explication of this concept is given in *Integrated System* (Cronquist, 1981).

Pollen considered to represent the Rubiaceae is known from Eocene and more recent deposits. Stipulate leaves that have been referred to the Rubiaceae are also known from Middle Eocene strata in southeastern United States. Even if these identifications are correct, however, the evolutionary radiation of the group appears to be largely post-Eocene.

The taxonomic affinity of *Theligonum,* long uncertain and controversial, was clarified by Wunderlich (1971). Accepting her view of the relationships, I still find it useful to treat the Theligonaceae as a distinct family. The status of *Theligonum* as a florally much reduced derivative of the Rubiaceae is now widely accepted.

SYNOPTICAL ARRANGEMENT OF THE FAMILIES OF RUBIALES

1   Flowers perfect or rarely unisexual, zoophilous (mainly entomophilous) or rarely anemophilous, usually with both a calyx and a sympetalous corolla, or the calyx sometimes obsolete; stamens as many as and alternate with the corolla-lobes, attached to the corolla-tube; ovary composed of 2 (or more) carpels, with a terminal style, and with 1–many anatropous to hemitropous ovules in each locule; embryo straight, or seldom curved .... **1. Rubiaceae.**
1   Flowers unisexual, anemophilous, the staminate ones (perhaps pseudanthia) with 6–30 stamens free from the small, inconspicuous perianth (or involucre) of 2–5 segments, the pistillate ones pseudomonomerous, with a basilateral style surrounded by a tubular, 2–4-toothed perianth; ovule solitary, basal, campylotropous; embryo strongly curved .... **2. Theligonaceae.**

SELECTED REFERENCES

Behnke, H.-D. 1975. Elektronenmikroskopische Untersuchungen zur Frage der verwandtschaftlichen Beziehungen zwischen *Theligonum* und Rubiaceae: Feinbau der Siebelement-Plastiden und Anmerkungen zur Struktur der Pollenexine. Pl. Syst. Evol. **123:** 317–326.

Bremekamp, C. E. B. 1966. Remarks on the position, delimitation, and subdivision of the Rubiaceae. Acta Bot. Neerl. **15:** 1–33.

Darwin, S. P. 1976. The subfamilial, tribal, and subtribal nomenclature of the Rubiaceae. Taxon **25:** 595–610.

Koek-Noorman, J. 1972. The wood anatomy of Gardenieae, Ixorieae and Mussaendeae (Rubiaceae). Acta Bot. Neerl. **21:** 301–320.

Koek-Noorman, J. & P. Hogeweg. 1974. Wood anatomy of Vanguerieae, Cinchoneae, Condamineae, and Rondeletieae (Rubiaceae). Acta Bot. Neerl. **23:** 627–653.

Koek-Noorman, J. & C. Puff. 1983. The wood anatomy of Rubiaceae tribes Anthospermeae and Paederieae. Pl. Syst. Evol. **143:** 17–45.

Lee, Y. S. & D. E. Fairbrothers. 1978. Serological approaches to the systematics of the Rubiaceae and related families. Taxon **27:** 159–185.

Mabry, T. J., I. J. Eifert, C. Chang, H. Mabry & C. Kidd. 1975. Theligonaceae: Pigment and ultrastructural evidence which excludes it from the order Centrospermae. Biochem. Syst. Ecol. **3:** 53–55.

Neubauer, H. F. 1981. Der Knotenbauer einiger Rubiaceae. Pl. Syst. Evol. **139:** 103–111.

Praglowski, J. 1973. The pollen morphology of the Theligonaceae with reference to taxonomy. Pollen & Spores **15:** 385–396.

Robbrecht, E. & C. Puff. 1986. A survey of the Gardenieae and related tribes (Rubiaceae). Bot. Jahrb. Syst. **108:** 63–137.

Roth, J. L. & D. L. Dilcher. 1979. Investigations of angiosperms from the Eocene of North America: Stipulate leaves of the Rubiaceae including a probable polyploid population. Amer. J. Bot. **66:** 1194–1207.

Verdcourt, B. 1958. Remarks on the classification of the Rubiaceae. Bull. Jard. Bot. État **28:** 209–290.

Wagenitz, G. 1959. Die systematische Stellung der Rubiaceae. Ein Beitrag zum System der Sympetalen. Bot. Jahrb. Syst. **79**: 17–35.

Wunderlich, R. 1971. Die systematische Stellung von *Theligonum*. Oesterr. Bot. Z. **119**: 329–394.

9. Order Dipsacales

The order Dipsacales as here defined consists of 4 families and nearly a thousand species. The Caprifoliaceae (400), Valerianaceae (300), and Dipsacaceae (270) are all in the same size-range. The small family Adoxaceae consists of 3 monotypic genera, two of them (*Sinadoxa* and *Tetradoxa*) only recently discovered and named. Some authors extract the genus *Morina* sensu lato (13 spp., including the segregate genera *Acanthocalyx* and *Cryptothladia*) from the Dipsacaceae as a family Morinaceae. This is defensible, but not necessary. The Morinaceae would necessarily stand alongside the more narrowly defined Dipsacaceae in the order Dipsacales.

The Dipsacales are Asteridae with an inferior (or half-inferior) ovary, opposite or whorled, mostly exstipulate leaves, and without the specialized pollen-presentation mechanism of the Asterales and Calycerales. They commonly produce iridoid compounds, and sometimes various sorts of alkaloids, as do the Rubiales.

The Dipsacales are usually considered to be allied to the Rubiales, from which they differ in their more often herbaceous habit, usually anomocytic stomates, usual absence of stipules and complete absence of colleters, often irregular corolla and often anisomerous stamens, and cellular endosperm-development. All of these features are apomorphic as compared to the condition in the Rubiaceae.

The affinities of *Adoxa* have been debated, some authors favoring an alliance with the Saxifragaceae, others an alliance with the Caprifoliaceae through *Sambucus*. Features of classical morphology might permit either interpretation, with the distinct styles favoring the Saxifragaceae, and the sympetalous corolla favoring the Caprifoliaceae. *Adoxa* and *Sambucus* also have similar pollen, and they share the rare *Adoxa*-type tetrasporic embryo-sac. The secondary metabolites of *Adoxa*, which include iridoid compounds but not ellagic acid, also favor an alliance with the Caprifoliaceae rather than the Saxifragaceae. The gynoecium of the newly discovered genus *Sinadoxa* is very suggestive of the Valerianaceae.

Association of *Adoxa* with *Sambucus* does not guarantee the inclusion of the Adoxaceae in the Dipsacales, however. Although *Sambucus* and *Viburnum* have traditionally been included in the Caprifoliaceae, their relationship to the rest of the family has repeatedly been questioned. *Viburnum* is remarkably like some species of *Cornus* and *Hydrangea* in aspect, but there are numerous critical technical differences, listed on page 1008 of *Integrated System*. If *Sambucus* and *Viburnum* are excluded, there seems little doubt that the remainder of the Caprifoliaceae should be associated with the Valerianaceae and Dipsacaceae sensu lato. The structure of the nectaries, in particular, has been adduced (Wagenitz & Laing, 1984) to support this association.

Thorne (1983, cited in the bibliography for Magnoliopsida) has recently proposed to include both *Sambucus* and *Viburnum* in the Adoxaceae, along with *Adoxa, Sinadoxa,* and *Tetradoxa.* The resulting family is poorly characterized, however. Among other features, the nectaries, which unite the remainder of the Dipsacales, separate *Viburnum* from *Sambucus,* and both of these genera from *Adoxa, Sinadoxa,* and *Tetradoxa* collectively. *Viburnum* has an ordinary nectary-disk like that found in many of the Asteridae and Rosidae. *Sambucus* has no nectaries, or only a suggestion of a nectary around the top of the ovary. *Adoxa, Sinadoxa,* and *Tetradoxa* have distinctive nectaries, consisting of a cushion-like group of multicellular, sessile or short-stalked, clavate glands at the inner base of each corolla-lobe. Although the traditional inclusion of *Sambucus* and *Viburnum* in the Caprifoliaceae is debatable, their transfer to the Adoxaceae is even more dubious at the present state of knowledge.

Donoghue (1983) has recently explored in some detail the possible relationship of *Adoxa, Sambucus,* and *Viburnum* to each other and to the core group of Caprifoliaceae. Although he apparently favors some sort of association of these several groups, his rigorous application of cladistic methodology led him to no firm taxonomic conclusion.

The adaptive significance of most of the characters that distinguish the Dipsacales from the other orders of Asteridae is doubtful. If the Dipsacales are derived from the Rubiales, then they (the Dipsacales) have given up the stipular colleters that may reasonably be supposed to help protect the terminal bud in the Rubiales. Within the Dipsacales there is a progression from woody to herbaceous habit, from regular to irregular corolla, from isomerous to anisomerous stamens, from several fertile locules to only one, and from endospermous to nonendospermous seeds. Each of these changes has also taken place in other orders of angiosperms, and there is nothing ecologically distinctive about the order or any of its families. The involucel or epicalyx of the Dipsacaceae is morphologically distinctive, but its functional significance, especially in the dense heads of most genera of the family, is obscure.

On the basis of both pollen and seeds, it appears that the Caprifoliaceae can be traced back to the Middle Eocene. Dipsacaceous pollen dates from the Middle Miocene.

SYNOPTICAL ARRANGEMENT OF THE FAMILIES OF DIPSACALES

1 Plants mostly woody, seldom herbaceous; stamens mostly as many as the
  corolla-lobes, seldom fewer; ovules often more than 1 per locule . . . .
  . . . . **1. Caprifoliaceae.**
1 Plants herbaceous, or rarely shrubby; stamens seldom (except some Dipsacaceae) of the same number as the corolla-lobes; ovules not more than 1 per
  locule.
  2 Stamens twice as many as the corolla-lobes and paired at the sinuses of the

corolla, each with only a single pollen sac, or the stamens as many as the corolla-lobes but each filament divided nearly half way to the base, so that the 2 pollen-sacs are well separated; nectaries consisting of a cushion-like group of multicellular, sessile or short-stalked, clavate glands at the inner base of each corolla-lobe . . . . **2. Adoxaceae.**

2 Stamens as many as or usually fewer than the corolla-lobes, of normal struc-ture, each with 2 pollen-sacs; nectary or nectaries of one or more secretory areas toward the base of the corolla tube, covered with unicellular hairs.

3 Flowers without an epicalyx or involucel (except in *Triplostegia*), borne in various sorts of inflorescences, but not in involucrate heads; ovary basically tricarpellate, often more or less evidently trilocular, with 1 fertile and 2 sterile locules, or pseudomonomerous, with a single locule . . . . **3. Valerianaceae.**

3 Flowers nearly always individually enclosed or subtended by a more or less cupulate epicalyx or involucel, mostly borne in compact, involu-crate, basically cymose heads (in axillary verticillasters in *Morina*); ovary basically bicarpellate, but pseudomonomerous and strictly uni-locular . . . . **4. Dipsacaceae.**

Selected References

Böhne-Gütlein, E. & F. Weberling. 1981. Palynologische Untersuchungen an Caprifoliaceae. I. Sambuceae, Viburneae und Diervilleae. Trop. & Subtrop. Pflanzenwelt **34:** 133–189.

Cannon, M. J. & J. F. Cannon. 1984. A revision of the Morinaceae (Magno-liophyta—Dipsacales). Bull. Brit. Mus. (Nat. Hist.) Bot. Ser. **12:** 1–35.

Carlquist, S. 1982. Wood anatomy of Dipsacaceae. Taxon **31:** 443–450.

Clarke, G. 1978. Pollen morphology and generic relationships in the Valerian-aceae. Grana **17:** 61–75.

Donoghue, M. J. 1983. The phylogenetic relationships of *Viburnum.* Adv. Cla-distics **2:** 143–166.

Ferguson, I. K. 1965. The genera of Valerianaceae and Dipsacaceae in the southeastern United States. J. Arnold Arbor. **46:** 218–231.

Ferguson, I. K. 1966. The genera of Caprifoliaceae in the southeastern United States. J. Arnold Arbor. **47:** 33–59.

Gütlein, R. & F. Weberling. 1982. Fruchtanatomische Untersuchungen an Va-lerianaceae. Ber. Deutsch. Bot. Ges. **95:** 35–43.

Hillebrand, G. R. & D. E. Fairbrothers. 1970. Serological investigation of the systematic position of the Caprifoliaceae. I. Correspondence with selected Rubiaceae and Cornaceae. Amer. J. Bot. **57:** 810–815.

Hillebrand, G. R. & D. E. Fairbrothers. 1970. Phytoserological systematic survey of the Caprifoliaceae. Brittonia **22:** 125–133.

Jensen, S. R. & B. J. Nielsen. 1979. Iridoid glucosides in *Adoxa moschatellina.* Biochem. Syst. Ecol. **7:** 103–104.

Kamelina, O. P. 1980. Sravnitel'naya embriologiya semeystv Dipsacaceae i Morinaceae. Nauka. Leningrad.

Patel, V. C. & J. J. Skvarla. 1979. Valerianaceae pollen morphology. Pollen & Spores **21:** 81–103.

Troll, W. & F. Weberling. 1966. Die Infloreszenzen der Caprifoliaceen und ihre systematische Bedeutung. Akad. Wiss. Abh. Math.-Naturwiss. Kl. 1966. Nr. 4: 459–605.

Wagenitz, G. & B. Laing. 1984. Die Nektarien der Dipsacales und ihre systematische Bedeutung. Bot. Jahrb. Syst. **104:** 483–507.

Weberling, F. 1961. Die Infloreszenzen der Valerianaceen und ihre systematische Bedeutung. Akad. Wiss. Abh. Math.-Naturwiss. Kl. 1961. Nr. **5:** 151–281.

Wilkinson, A. M. 1948. Floral anatomy and morphology of the genus *Viburnum* of the Caprifoliaceae. Amer. J. Bot. **35:** 455–465.

Wilkinson, A. M. 1949. Floral anatomy and morphology of *Triosteum* and of the Caprifoliaceae in general. Amer. J. Bot. **36:** 481–489.

Wu, C.-Y. 1981. Another new genus of Adoxaceae, with special references on the infrafamiliar evolution and systematic position of the family. Acta Bot. Yunnanica **3:** 383–388. (In Chinese; English summary.)

Wu, C.-Y., Z. L. Wu & R. F. Huang. 1981. *Sinadoxa* C.-Y. Wu, Z. L. Wu et R. F. Huang, genus novum familiae Adoxacearum. Acta Phytotax. Sinica **19:** 203–210. (In Chinese.)

10. Order Calycerales

The order Calycerales consists of the single family Calyceraceae, with about 60 species native to Central and South America. The family has attracted botanical attention mainly because of its role in speculation about the ancestry and relationships of the Asteraceae.

The Calyceraceae have variously been included in the Campanulales, the Dipsacales, or a separate order Calycerales. They resemble the Campanulales, and differ from the Dipsacales, in their alternate leaves, in producing inulin, and in their specialized pollen-presentation mechanism. (A somewhat similar pollen-presentation mechanism also exists in the subfamily Ixoroideae of the Rubiaceae, and a very similar one in the Asteraceae.) They resemble the Dipsacales, and differ from characteristic members of the Campanulales, in having the filaments attached near the summit of the corolla-tube, and in a series of embryological features that have been commented on by Poddubnaya-Arnol'di (1964, p. 376). The unilocular ovary with a single apical, pendulous ovule is fully in harmony with the Dipsacales, but would be unique in the Campanulales.

The involucrate, centripetally flowering heads and the pollen-presentation mechanism of the Calyceraceae strongly suggest the Asteraceae, and the pollen is also very much like that of many Asteraceae in the structure and ornamentation of the wall (Skvarla et al., 1977). On the other hand, the two families differ in ways which suggest that the relationship between them is only collateral. The solitary ovule is apical in the Calyceraceae, and basal in the Asteraceae. Conceivably the ovule might have moved (phyletically) from the apex to the base of the ovary, or vice versa, after the uniovulate condition had been achieved, but parallel reductions from an ancestor with a bilocular, pluriovulate ovary seem more likely. The Asteraceae appear to be primitively woody and opposite-leaved. Herbaceous Asteraceae with alternate leaves, comparable in habit to the Calyceraceae, are advanced within their family in these respects. In counterpoint, however, the Calyceraceae are more primitive than the Asteraceae in their binucleate pollen and fairly well developed endosperm. The two families have very different chemical defenses. The Calyceraceae produce iridoid compounds but do not have an evident secretory system, and they apparently lack the polyacetylenes and sesquiterpene lactones that are so common in the Asteraceae. The Asteraceae, in contrast, do not produce iridoid compounds, and they have a well developed secretory system (either resiniferous or laticiferous). Thus it seems likely that the admitted similarities between the two families reflect parallelism from a fairly remote common ancestry.

The difficulties in placing the Calyceraceae properly in the system provide another example of the pervasive parallelism that besets our efforts to decipher relationships among the angiosperms. The whole subclass Asteridae forms a closely knit group, which resists ill-conceived efforts to dismember it on the basis of a limited set of data.

In my view, the Calyceraceae are related to and probably derived from the Dipsacales. Their nearest common ancestry with the Asteraceae probably lies in or near the Rubiales. In this connection we should note that Poddubnaya-Arnol'di (1964) considers that the inclusion of the Dipsacaceae and Calyceraceae in the Rubiales would be in accord with the embryological data, and that from an embryological point of view the Calyceraceae, Dipsacaceae, and Asteraceae are closely related.

The very modest evolutionary success of the Calyceraceae, as contrasted to the tremendous success of the Asteraceae, is a legitimate subject for inquiry and speculation. I suggest that the explanation lies not in the morphology but in the chemistry. According to the principles of chemical evolution expounded in an earlier chapter, the chemical defenses of the Asteraceae probably evolved after the iridoids found in many other members of the subclass had begun to lose their effectiveness. The Calyceraceae are presumably latecomers to the evolutionary scene. At least they probably do not antedate the Asteraceae. Their floral and vegetative morphology should be just as effective as that of herbaceous Asteraceae, but with a limited and outmoded chemical arsenal they do not have a strong competitive position.

SELECTED REFERENCES

Avetisyan, E. M. 1980. Palinomorfologiya cemeystva Calyceraceae. *V kn.*: Sistematika i evoliutsiya vysshykh rasteniy: 57–64. Nauka. Leningrad.
Poddubnaya-Arnol'di, V. A. 1964. Obshchaya embriologiya pokrytosemennykh rasteniy. Nauka. Moskva.
Skvarla, J. J., B. L. Turner, V. C. Patel & A. S. Tomb. 1977 (1978). Pollen morphology in the Compositae and in morphologically related families. Pages 141–248 *in* V. H. Heywood, J. B. Harborne & B. L. Turner (eds.), The biology

and chemistry of the Compositae. Academic Press. London, New York & San Francisco.

11. Order Asterales

The order Asterales consists of the single cosmopolitan family Asteraceae (Compositae), with perhaps as many as 20,000 species, best represented in temperate or subtropical regions that are not densely forested. The family is characterized by its pseudanthial flower-heads with a specialized pollen-presentation mechanism. The anthers are connate (or connivent) into a tube; the pollen is released into the interior of the tube and is pushed out by growth of the style. The solitary ovule is basal, and the dry fruit has only a very thin and inconspicuous layer of endosperm. The family is otherwise so highly diversified that neophytes often think it must be an unnatural group. Synantherologists, in contrast, uniformly consider the family to be highly natural, and resistant to efforts at dismemberment. Only the tribe Lactuceae stands somewhat apart from the others, on the basis of its ligulate (rather than merely radiate) heads in which all five corolla-lobes are represented in the ligule. The Lactuceae are also marked by their well developed latex (instead of resin) system, and by the ornamentation of the pollen, but the Mutisieae form a bridge to the rest of the family.

The Asteraceae are one of the most successful families of flowering plants, represented by numerous genera, species, and individuals. Not many of them are forest trees, and only a few are aquatic, but otherwise they exploit most of the obvious kinds of ecological opportunities available to angiosperms.

I believe that the chemistry is more important than the morphology in fostering the evolutionary success of the Asteraceae. Their initial success may have grown out of their discovery of the effective defensive combination of polyacetylenes and sesquiterpene lactones, before these had been exploited by any other group. The continued expansion of the family has been fostered by its chemical evolutionary lability, which has permitted it to develop and exploit new repellents. It is probably no accident that the largest and most diversified genus in the family is *Senecio*. *Senecio* and its immediate allies have a special set of alkaloids, shared with only a few other families (most notably the Boraginaceae, in which they probably also play a major role in the success of the group). The Lactuceae have retained the sesquiterpene lactones, but introduced a latex-system in place of the polyacetylene-bearing resin-system of the other tribes. The Anthemideae have their own characteristic odor (properly a set of similar odors), as does the subtribe Tagetinae of the Heliantheae, indicating an intensive exploitation of various possibilities among volatile monoterpenes and terpenoids. The future role of the Asteraceae in the vegetation of the world will probably depend more on their continuing chemical evolution than on morphological changes in the group.

The affinities of the Asteraceae have been vigorously but inconclusively debated. Traditionally they have been thought to be allied to the Campanulaceae, and often even included in the same order. The specialized pollen-presentation mechanism in the two families has often been used to bolster such an association. Unfortunately for this argument, a similar mechanism also exists in the Calyceraceae and in the subfamily Ixoroideae of the Rubiaceae. This mechanism is not so well developed in the Ixoroideae as it is in the Asteraceae, Calyceraceae, and the subfamily Lobelioideae of the Campanulaceae, being more nearly comparable to that in the Campanuloideae, but it indicates the evolutionary possibilities within the Rubiaceae.

Patterns of relationship within the Asteraceae strongly suggest that their immediate ancestors must have been shrubs or small trees with opposite leaves and a cymose inflorescence. The basically herbaceous, alternate-leaved Campanulaceae and their immediate allies therefore do not provide a suitable starting point. Furthermore the two families differ in a set of embryological details, which tend to associate the Asteraceae with the Calyceraceae, Dipsacales, and Rubiales (Crété, 1956; Poddubnaya-Arnol'di, 1964, cited under Calycerales). Both the Calyceraceae and the Dipsacaceae are removed from serious consideration as possible ancestors of the Asteraceae because of their herbaceous habit and apical (rather than basal) ovule. Nothing in the Dipsacales more advanced than the Caprifoliaceae is morphologically suitable to be ancestral to the Asteraceae. The frequently nuclear endosperm of the Asteraceae suggests that even the Caprifoliaceae may be too advanced, and that we must look farther back, to the vicinity of the Rubiaceae, for the origin of the Asteraceae.

Before complacently accepting a rubialean affinity for the Asteraceae, we should emphasize again that the Asteraceae are chemically as well as morphologically distinctive. On chemical grounds nothing in the Asteridae seems a very likely ancestor for them, although some similarities can be pointed out to the Campanulales (inulin, polyacetylenes) and Boraginaceae (*Senecio* alkaloids). The family that may be chemically most like the Asteraceae is the Apiaceae, in the subclass Rosidae, but the morphological differences make any effort to link these two families patently absurd.

Studies of chloroplast DNA in the Asteraceae and some other taxa, recently initiated by Robert Jansen and Jeffrey Palmer, have begun to cast some light on the affinities of the family. The data (1988, and previously in public meetings) are still too scanty to carry much weight, but so far as they go they tend to favor a relationship with the Rubiaceae, and strongly oppose a relationship with the Apiaceae. They do not yet bear significantly on the possibility of a relationship with the Campanulaceae, because a complex set of sequence apomorphies in the latter family has until now frustrated efforts at comparison. The position of *Barnadesia* and some allied small genera (subtribe Barnadesiinae of the tribe Mutisieae) as the sister-group of all other Asteraceae, postulated by these same authors, is more difficult to integrate with other information and will require careful consideration in the future.

All considered, I am convinced that the Asteraceae properly belong to the large subclass to which they give their name. Their distinctive chemical features can easily be interpreted as a new and successful set of weapons, developed at a time when predators were becoming resistant to the iridoid compounds of more ancient members of the subclass. I believe that the ancestry of the Asteraceae probably lies in or near the Rubiaceae, along a line parallel in some respects to the line leading to the Dipsacales and Calycerales.

The fossils tell us nothing about the ancestry of the Asteraceae except that their origin is probably relatively recent. Pollen representing the group enters the fossil record at many places in the world at about the end of the Oligocene epoch. A macrofossil of about this same age from Montana appears to be a composite head, and has been described as *Viguiera cronquistii* H. Becker, but its identity as a composite has been challenged. Older fossils ascribed to the Asteraceae are probably incorrectly identified. The Lactuceae may be the most recently evolved tribe in the family. Their distinctive pollen does not enter the fossil record until about the middle of the Miocene epoch, some 18 million years ago.

SELECTED REFERENCES

Bremer, K. 1987. Tribal relationships of the Asteraceae. Cladistics **3:** 210–253.

Carlquist, S. 1966. Wood anatomy of Compositae: A summary, with comments on factors controlling wood evolution. Aliso **6:** 25–44.

Carlquist, S. 1976. Tribal interrelationships and phylogeny of the Asteraceae. Aliso **8:** 465–492.

Crepet, W. L. & T. F. Stuessy. A reinvestigation of the fossil *Viguiera cronquistii* (Compositae). Brittonia **30:** 483–491.

Crété, R. 1956. Contribution à l'étude de l'albumen et de l'embryon chez les Campanulacées et les Lobéliacées. Bull. Soc. Bot. France **103:** 446–454.

Cronquist, A. 1955. Phylogeny and taxonomy of the Compositae. Amer. Midl. Naturalist **53:** 478–511.

Cronquist, A. 1977. The Compositae revisited. Brittonia **29:** 137–153.

Grau, J. & H. Hopf. 1985. Das Endosperm der Compositae. Bot. Jahrb. Syst. **107:** 251–268.

Heywood, V. H., J. B. Harborne & B. L. Turner (eds.). 1977 (1978). The biology and chemistry of the Compositae. Two volumes. Academic Press. London, New York, & San Francisco.

Jansen, R. K. & J. D. Palmer. 1988. Phylogenetic implications of chloroplast DNA restriction site variation in the Mutisieae (Asteraceae). Amer. J. Bot. **75:** 753–766.

Wagenitz, G. 1975 (1976). Systematics and phylogeny of the Compositae (Asteraceae). Pl. Syst. Evol. **125:** 29–46.

Chapter 7

Cypripedium acaule, an orchid. The Orchidaceae are one of the largest families of flowering plants, notable for diverse and even bizarre adaptations to specific pollinators, but they are not among the most successful families in terms of biomass or number of individuals.

The Subclasses, Orders, and Families of Monocotyledons

Origin of the Group and Diversification into Subclasses

The Liliopsida (monocots) are here considered to consist of five sub-classes, the Alismatidae, Arecidae, Commelinidae, Zingiberidae, and Liliidae. The characteristics of the monocots as a group are discussed along with those of dicots at the beginning of CHAPTER VI.

It is now widely agreed that the monocots were derived from primitive dicots, and that the monocots must therefore follow rather than precede the dicots in any proper linear sequence. The single cotyledon, parallel-veined leaves, absence of a cambium, the dissected stele, and the adventitious root system of monocots are all regarded as apomorphies within the angiosperms, and any plant more primitive (plesiomorphic) than the monocots in these several respects would certainly be a dicot.

The fossil pollen record suggests that the origin of monocots from primitive dicots in Aptian-Albian time was the first significant dichotomy in the evolutionary diversification of the angiosperms. The wide variety of monocotyledonous leaves found in late Lower Cretaceous and throughout the Upper Cretaceous attests to the continuing diversification of the group during this time, but most of these leaves cannot be referred with any certainty to modern groups. The first modern family of monocots to be clearly represented in the fossil record is the Arecaceae (subclass Arecidae), near the base of the Santonian (or perhaps in the Coniacian) epoch, but palms are surely not primitive monocots. Their large, distinctive, readily fossilized leaves merely make the group easy to recognize from its inception. Pollen that probably represents the Cyperales or Restionales

451

Fig. 7.1.   Rolf M. T. Dahlgren (1932–1986), senior author of a major work on the general system of classification of monocotyledons. Photo courtesy of Gertrud Dahlgren.

(subclass Commelinidae) appears in the late Upper Cretaceous, probably before the Maestrichtian, and the distinctive leaves of the Zingiberales show up in the Maestrichtian. Pollen thought to represent *Pandanus* occurs in Maestrichtian deposits in North America. The Alismatidae and Liliidae are not certainly recognizable before the Tertiary, but some of the miscellaneous Upper Cretaceous fossil monocot leaves might well belong to one or the other of these groups. We can be reasonably sure that the palms and the Zingiberales did not arise long before the first appearance of their characteristic leaves in the fossil record, but we cannot be so confident that other large groups did not long antedate their first identifiable fossils. Thus the fossil record as presently understood is compatible with any of several different views about the Cretaceous diversification of the monocots. The principal constraint is the recognition of a very early dichotomy between monocots and dicots.

The dicots that gave rise to the monocots may have had apocarpous flowers with a fairly ordinary (not highly specialized) perianth, and with uniaperturate pollen. They must have been herbs without a very active cambium, and they presumably had laminar placentation. The only modern order of dicots that meets these specifications is the Nymphaeales.

It is not here suggested that the Nymphaeales are directly ancestral to the monocots as a whole, but rather that the premonocotyledonous dicots were probably something like the modern Nymphaeales. It is noteworthy that an aquatic group of angiosperms with leaves much like those of the modern Nymphaeales was already proliferating in the Albian epoch of the Lower Cretaceous. The modern Nymphaeales are aquatic, they mostly lack vessels, and they show tendencies toward the fusion of two cotyledons into one. Although the idea has never gained wide acceptance, some botanists still insist that the Nymphaeales are better grouped with the monocotyledons than with the dicotyledons.

The monocots are here considered to be of aquatic ancestry, and the typical parallel-veined leaf is considered to be a modified, bladeless petiole. This morphological interpretation for the leaves of *Sagittaria* was proposed a century and a half ago by de Candolle (1827, vol. 1, p. 286). It was further elaborated in evolutionary terms and applied to the monocots as a whole by Arber in 1925. It is the only hypothesis known to me that permits all the information about monocots to fall into place and make sense. Even the ontogeny of the typical monocot leaf is highly compatible with the petiolar hypothesis, although this fact seems to have escaped those who have elucidated the ontogeny. The blade typically develops from a portion of the leaf-primordium somewhat behind the tip and matures basipetally; the primordial tip is inactive or produces only a terminal point or small appendage (Vorläuferspitze) on the blade.

Several species of *Sagittaria* show all transitions, within a single local population, between a normal leaf with blade and petiole, and a typical monocotyledonous leaf with parallel veins. The transitional series, which was reported by de Candolle and which I have observed in other species in the United States, is conspicuous and impressive. Depending mainly on the depth of the water, the blade is well developed or progressively reduced and lost, with a concomitant change in the structure of the petiole. Here the parallel-veined, submerged leaf is clearly nothing but a modified, bladeless petiole. The blade of *Sagittaria* itself is probably only a secondarily expanded petiole-tip, not strictly homologous with the blade of dicots, but the present structure is nonetheless that of a petiolate leaf with a well defined, palmately veined blade. It is perfectly clear that in *Sagittaria*, plants with the genetic potentiality to produce normal leaves with blade and petiole can be induced to produce instead typical monocotyledonous leaves that are merely flattened petioles. Genetic (and eventually evolutionary) fixation of a character that first appeared as a direct response to the environment is amply provided for in modern evolutionary theory.

Whether the interpretation that fits *Sagittaria* can be extended to the whole class Liliopsida is of course another question. I believe that it can and should be so extended. Under this concept terrestrial monocots with a well defined, net-veined blade are considered to be derived from ancestors with narrow, parallel-veined leaves lacking a well defined blade, and indeed all transitional stages can be seen in several families. An attempt to read the system the other way means that we must start with broad, more or less net-veined leaves in diverse groups of monocots having little to do with each other, and have these all converge in both floral and vegetative characters into a hopelessly polyphyletic core of typical monocots. The resulting system, if it could be called that, would be shot full of internal contradictions.

There are three principal ways by which the typical monocot leaf can become broad and more or less net-veined. One way is to spread the main veins farther apart near the middle of the blade and amplify the cross-connections among them. Subsequently the main veins can fade out before reaching the leaf-tip, so that a more or less palmate venation is established. *Alisma, Sagittaria, Dioscorea, Smilax, Trillium,* and many aroids exemplify this type of change. A second way is for each of the many closely set parallel veins to diverge in turn toward the margin, the outermost ones first, those nearest the midrib last. The result is a pinnately veined leaf with numerous closely parallel primary lateral veins. The Zingiberales reflect this sort of change. The third way, known only in the palms and Cyclanthales, differs from the second way in the intercalation of new tissue between the lateral veins during the early growth of the leaf. The plicate structure of palm and cyclanth leaves reflects this ontogeny.

An interesting difference between monocots and dicots is that whereas in dicots the vessels appear first (phyletically) in the secondary wood of the stem and spread thence to other tissues and organs, in monocots they appear first in the roots. This fact has lead Cheadle (1953) and others to suppose that vessels originated independently in the two classes. They therefore consider that the evolutionary divergence of the two classes preceded the origin of vessels.

On the same facts, plus some others, I come to a different conclusion. I suggest that in the ancestral premonocots, as in their probable relatives the Nymphaeales, vessels were phyletically lost in association with the aquatic habitat. Loss of the cambium eliminated at one stroke all vessels that had not worked their way (phyletically) into the primary tissues. The same factors that operated to produce a primitive, vesselless xylem structure in the Nymphaeales (q.v.) operated in the monocots to leave vestigial, seemingly primitive vessels in the roots. (Indeed *Nelumbo,* alone among the Nymphaeales, has elongate, scalariform vessel elements in the roots, just as in many monocots.) It was only after returning to a land habitat that some of the monocots developed an effective vessel-system in the shoot. In this as in other features, the aquatic ancestry is the key to understanding the monocotyledons.

If the interpretation here presented is correct, the aquatic ancestry of the monocots has had a profound effect on the subsequent evolutionary history of the group. As aquatic herbs, the early monocots were preadapted to evolve terrestrial herbaceous forms, filling a niche (or set of niches) not then effectively occupied by dicots. Nevertheless, the evolution of an efficient water-conducting system, of expanded, net-veined leaves, a branching, arborescent habit, and a means of secondary thickening have not been easy for them. No monocot has evolved a coherent syndrome of these features that would permit a broad-scale competitive challenge to woody dicotyledons. Even among those monocots that have evolved a broad, more or less net-veined leaf-blade, traces of the ancestral parallel-veined pattern usually persist. We have noted that aroids, palms, and the Zingiberales have taken three essentially different routes in the evolutionary expansion of leaves, and the difference is reflected in the mature morphology.

Although the monocots are here considered to have an aquatic ancestry, the situation is not simple. It appears that terrestrial monocots, derived from aquatic early monocots, have themselves repeatedly given rise to groups which have returned to the water. Among the modern Alismatidae there appears to be a progressive adaptation to an aquatic and eventually marine habitat. In the subclass Arecidae, the mainly terrestrial family Araceae has some secondarily aquatic forms that point toward the thalloid, aquatic family Lemnaceae. In a third subclass, the Commelinidae, such aquatic families as the Mayacaceae, Sparganiaceae, and Typhaceae appear to be derived from terrestrial ancestors within the group. The aquatic habit of the Pontederiaceae, in the subclass Liliidae, may likewise prove to be secondary.

The adventitious, fibrous root-system of monocots is a consequence of the absence of cambium. Having no adequate means of secondary thickening, the individual roots cannot persist, enlarge, and ramify. The roots of some monocots do manage to penetrate deeply into the soil, but the largest single family, the Orchidaceae, is shallow-rooted and mycorrhizal, and the next largest family, the Poaceae, tends to exploit mainly the upper part of the soil, forming a dense turf. Another large family, the Liliaceae, often has contractile roots that pull the bulb progressively deeper into the soil as the years go by. Creeping rhizomes, which may penetrate to any depth, serve as rootstocks for many of the Poaceae, Cyperaceae, Liliaceae, and other monocots.

The nature of the single cotyledon in the monocots has occasioned much study and controversy, and is not yet fully resolved. Like the foliage leaves, the cotyledon often has a basal sheath surmounted on one side by a limb that may or may not be divided into blade and petiole. Typically the sheath is closed and tubular, at least near the base. The vascular supply typically consists of two near-median bundles, as in the individual cotyledons of dicots. This implies that the monocot cotyledon is equivalent to a single leaf, and is not a double structure as has sometimes been supposed. The sheathing base of the cotyledon is thus left unexplained, except that it is comparable to the sheathing base of a foliage leaf.

Drawing on evidence from the living members of the Nymphaeales (dicots) I suggest another alternative: Two ancestral cotyledons have become connate by their margins toward the base, forming a bilobed, basally tubular, compound cotyledon. One of the lobes has subsequently been reduced and lost, and its vascular supply suppressed, so that the embryo has in effect a single cotyledon with a sheathing, tubular base. I further suggest that this modified cotyledonary structure has so firmly impressed itself on the growth pattern of the embryo that subsequent leaves are also built on the same plan. The sheathing base of monocot leaves is therefore a reflection of cotyledonary structure, rather than the reverse. I have no idea of the causes or survival value of these evolutionary changes.

Regardless of the morphological nature of the single cotyledon, it appears that throughout the Liliopsida it is basically the same organ. Highly modified though the cotyledon may be in such plants as grasses, there is no need to assume that the monocotyledonous condition of the Liliopsida is of more than one origin. A more ample discussion of the nature and possible evolutionary history of the cotyledon in the Liliopsida may be found in the books by Arber (1925) and Eames (1961) that have previously been cited.

The unique septal nectary of many Liliopsida is an interesting and neglected feature that helps not only to unify the class but also to strengthen the concept that the Alismatidae are near-basal. The structure is apparently unknown in the Magnoliopsida.

According to Brown (1938), septal nectaries

"occur in the septa between two carpels and represent places where the adjacent walls of the carpels have not fused. They discharge nectar to the outside by means of small openings. They are such complicated structures that they would seem to indicate a relationship between all plants having them. . . . The openings of the septal glands may be near the base of the ovary, but often they are at the top of the ovary or even in the style. Where the glands are at the top of the ovary, it would seem that they would not interfere with the fusion of the ovary and torus. This may be connected with the fact that the higher monocotyledons frequently have inferior ovaries."

Septal nectaries are characteristic of those Arecaceae which are nectariferous, and of the Liliales, Bromeliales, and Zingiberales. Not every genus in every family of these orders has septal nectaries, but they are common enough so that their absence is exceptional rather than typical. (The Smilacaceae and the tribe Tulipeae of the Liliaceae may be mentioned among the more notable exceptions.) The complex, external nectaries of some of the Zingiberales are evidently derived from septal nectaries (Rao, 1970). Some of the Orchidales also have modified septal nectaries. It will be noted that septal nectaries occur in three of the four subclasses of Liliopsida that are typically syncarpous. (Most of the Commelinidae lack nectaries entirely.)

Septal nectaries probably take their origin in the mostly apocarpous subclass Alismatidae. As Brown has pointed out, *Sagittaria* and other Alismatidae have nectaries between the petals and staminodes and between and around the staminodes and lower carpels. *Alisma* itself, with a single whorl of separate carpels, has a nectary at the base of the slit between any two adjacent carpels. The palms, which range from apocarpous to syncarpous, have correspondingly alismatoid to septal nectaries. Presumably a similar change occurred in the line(s) leading to the Zingiberidae and Liliidae.

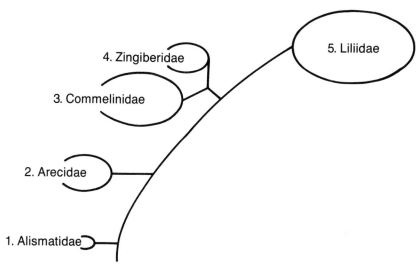

Fig. 7.2. Putative relationships among the subclasses of monocotyledons. The size of the balloons is roughly proportional to the number of species in the subclass.

Because of the evolutionary pattern discussed in the foregoing pages, recognition of major groups of monocots by their aspect is not so consistently difficult and frustrating as a comparable effort among the dicots. Such recognition therefore becomes a feasible addition to the other objectives of the system of monocots. A taxonomic system should always be as simple and easy to use as is consistent with naturalness. The scheme here presented reflects my attention to these matters.

None of the subclasses of monocots can be considered ancestral to any of the others (Fig. 7.2). The Alismatidae, Commelinidae, Zingiberidae, and Liliidae are fairly well characterized, but the Arecidae are a more loosely knit affinity-group.

Synoptical Arrangement of the Subclasses of Liliopsida

1 Plants either with apocarpous (sometimes monocarpous) flowers, or more or less aquatic, or very often both, always herbaceous, but never thalloid; vascular system generally not strongly lignified, often much reduced, the vessels confined to the roots, or wanting; endosperm mostly wanting, not starchy when present; subsidiary cells mostly 2; pollen trinucleate . . **I. Alismatidae.**
1 Plants with syncarpous (or seldom pseudomonomerous) flowers except in some arborescent taxa, usually terrestrial (or epiphytic), much less often more or less aquatic, although sometimes not only aquatic but also thalloid and free-

floating; vessels, endosperm, stomates, and pollen various, but not combined as in the Alismatidae.

2 Flowers mostly numerous, usually small, and subtended by a prominent spathe (or several spathes), often aggregated into a spadix (but the inflorescence much reduced in the Lemnaceae); plants very often either arborescent, or with relatively broad leaves that do not have typical parallel venation, or both (but sometimes lacking both of these features, and in the Lemnaceae even thalloid and free-floating); septal nectaries wanting except in many Arecaceae; subsidiary cells typically 4, less often 2 or more than 4; vessels generally present in all vegetative organs, except among the Arales; endosperm not starchy except in some Arales . . . . **II. Arecidae.**

2 Flowers few to numerous and small to large, but never aggregated into a spadix, and usually without a distinct spathe (inflorescence with 1 or more spathe-like bracts in many Zingiberidae, but the flowers then larger and showy); plants herbaceous or much less often arborescent; leaves narrow and parallel-veined, or less often broader and more or less net-veined, or with a special type of pinnate-parallel venation; nectaries, stomates, vessels, and endosperm various, but not combined as in typical Arecidae.

3 Nectar and nectaries mostly wanting; perianth in the more archaic families trimerous and with well differentiated sepals and petals, in the more advanced families reduced and chaffy and often not obviously trimerous, or wanting, the families with reduced perianth typically adapted to wind-pollination; ovary always superior (or nude); vessels generally present in all vegetative organs; endosperm wholly or in large part starchy, commonly mealy and with compound starch grains, without significant reserves of hemicellulose and usually also without significant reserves of oil, or rarely the endosperm wanting; stomates mostly with 2 subsidiary cells, seldom without subsidiary cells or with more than 2 . . . . **III. Commelinidae.**

3 Nectar and nectaries of one or another sort (often septal nectaries) generally present; perianth generally well developed, not reduced and chaffy, the flowers typically adapted to pollination by insects or other kinds of animals; ovary superior or very often inferior; vessels most often confined to the roots, but sometimes occurring also in the stem or in all vegetative organs; endosperm and stomates various.

4 Sepals usually well differentiated from the petals, often green and herbaceous, sometimes petaloid in texture but still unlike the petals; endosperm typically starchy and mealy, with compound starch grains, only seldom hard and presumably with reserves of hemicellulose; subsidiary cells (2–) 4 or more; plants not obviously mycotrophic; leaves narrow and parallel-veined, or equally often with a broad, expanded, petiolate blade and a characteristic pinnate-parallel venation . . . . **IV. Zingiberidae.**

4 Sepals usually petaloid in form and texture, sometimes differentiated from the petals but still petaloid in appearance, only rarely green and herbaceous; endosperm when present typically very hard, with reserves of hemicellulose, protein and oil, less commonly starchy, but not mealy in texture, the starch grains typically simple rather than compound, or very often the endosperm wanting; subsidiary cells 2 or often none, only seldom 4; plants often strongly mycotrophic; leaves typically narrow and parallel-veined, seldom broader and even more or less net-veined, but without the characteristic pinnate-parallel venation of many Zingiberidae . . . . . . **V. Liliidae.**

Selected References

Arber, A. 1925. Monocotyledons. A morphological study. Cambridge Univ. Press. Cambridge.

Brown, W. H. 1938. The bearing of nectaries on the phylogeny of flowering plants. Proc. Amer. Philos. Soc. **79:** 549–595.

Burger, W. C. 1977. The Piperales and the monocots—Alternate hypotheses for the origin of monocotyledonous flowers. Bot. Rev. **43:** 345–393.

Candolle, A. P. de. 1827. Organographie végétale. 2 vols.

Cheadle, V. I. 1942. The occurrence and types of vessels in the various organs of the plant in the Monocotyledoneae. Amer. J. Bot. **29:** 441–450.

Cheadle, V. I. 1953. Independent origin of vessels in the monocotyledons and dicotyledons. Phytomorphology **3:** 23–44.

Clifford, H. T. 1977. Quantitative studies of inter-relationships amongst the Liliatae. Pl. Syst. Evol. Suppl. **1:** 77–95.

Dahlgren, R. M. T., H. T. Clifford & P. F. Yeo. 1985. The families of monocotyledons. Springer-Verlag. Berlin, New York.

Daghlian, C. P. 1981. A review of the fossil record of monocotyledons. Bot. Rev. **47:** 517–555.

Daumann, E. 1970. Das Blütennektarium der Monocotyledonen unter besonderer Berücksichtigung seiner systematischen und phylogenetischen Bedeutung. Feddes Repert. **80:** 463–590.

Deyl, M. 1955. The evolution of the plants and the taxonomy of the monocotyledons. Acta Mus. Natl. Prag. 11B(6), Botanica **3:** 1–143.

Doyle, J. A. 1973. Fossil evidence on early evolution of the monocotyledons. Quart. Rev. Biol. **48:** 399–413.

Haines, R. W. & K. A. Lye. 1979. Monocotylar seedlings: A review of evidence supporting origin by fusion. J. Linn. Soc., Bot. **78:** 123–140.

Harris, P. J. & R. D. Hartley. 1980. Phenolic constituents of the cell walls of monocotyledons. Biochem. Syst. Ecol. **8:** 153–160.

Hegnauer, R. 1963. Chemotaxonomie der Pflanzen. Band 2. Monocotyledoneae. Birkhauser Verlag. Basel.

Huber, H. 1977. The treatment of the monocotyledons in an evolutionary system of classification. Pl. Syst. Evol. Suppl. **1:** 285–298.

Kaplan, D. R. 1973. The problem of leaf morphology and evolution in the monocotyledons. Quart. Rev. Biol. **48:** 437–457.

Rao, V. S. 1970. Floral anatomy in some monocotyledonous taxa. Proc. Autumn School in Bot., Mahabaleshwar. **1966:** 295–302.

Slater, J. A. 1976. Monocots and chinch bugs: A study of host plant relationships in the Lygaeid subfamily Blissinae (Hemiptera: Lygaeidae). Biotropica **8:** 143–165.

Tomlinson, P. B. 1974. Development of the stomatal complex as a taxonomic character in the monocotyledons. Taxon **23:** 109–128.

Tomlinson, P. B. & M. H. Zimmermann. 1969. Vascular anatomy of monocotyledons with secondary growth—An introduction. J. Arnold Arbor. **50:** 159–179.

Wagner, P. 1977. Vessel types of the monocotyledons: A survey. Bot. Not. **130:** 383–402.

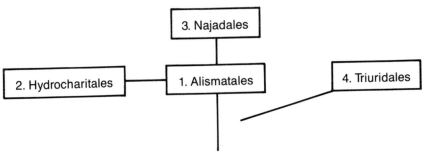

Fig. 7.3.   Putative relationships among the orders of Alismatidae.

Zavada, M. S.   1983. Comparative morphology of monocot pollen and evolutionary trends of apertures and wall structures. Bot. Rev. **49**: 331–371.
Zimmermann, M. H. & P. B. Tomlinson. 1972. The vascular system of monocotyledonous stems. Bot. Gaz. **133**: 141–155.

Subclass I. Alismatidae

The subclass Alismatidae as here defined consists of 4 orders (Fig. 7.3), 16 families, and scarcely 500 species. The Alismatales, Hydrocharitales, and Najadales are closely related; these have often been treated as parts of a single order, usually under the name Helobiae. The Triuridales are a more isolated group. The characters of the subclass have been summarized in the synoptical arrangement.

The Alismatidae have often been considered to be the most archaic group of Liliopsida. They can scarcely be on the main line of evolution of the class, however, because a primitive monocot should have binucleate pollen and endospermous seeds. They are here considered to be a nearbasal side-branch, a relictual group that has retained a number of primitive characters. The apocarpous gynoecium of most members of the Alismatidae combined with the uniaperturate pollen of the Liliopsida as a whole, indicates that any connection of the Liliopsida to the Magnoliopsida must be to the archaic subclass Magnoliidae. It should be noted, however, that the ontogeny of the pleiomerous androecium in the Alismatidae is quite different from that in the Magnoliidae, so that the evolutionary homology can be questioned.

Within the Magnoliidae the aquatic order Nymphaeales presents the closest approach to the Alismatidae. The concept that the Liliopsida as a whole are of aquatic origin has already been discussed.

The trinucleate pollen of the Alismatidae may well relate to their aquatic habitat. Trinucleate pollen typically requires specialized conditions for germination, and a disproportionately high number of aquatic angiosperms have trinucleate pollen. However, judged by the presently extant members of the subclass, it appears that trinucleate pollen in the group may have antedated subsurface pollination. The trinucleate condition should probably therefore be regarded as preadapted to subsurface pollination, rather than as evolved in response to it.

The biological significance of the helobial pattern of endosperm-development in many members of the Alismatidae is wholly obscure, as is also the usual disappearance of the endosperm before maturity of the seed.

Synoptical Arrangement of the Orders of Alismatidae

1 Seeds without endosperm; plants aquatic or semi-aquatic, green, not myco-trophic.
  2 Perianth generally differentiated into evident sepals and petals; flowers often bracteate.
    3 Flowers hypogynous; carpels distinct or only basally connate ....
    ....**1. Alismatales.**
    3 Flowers epigynous, with a compound ovary and parietal or often a modified sort of laminar placentation ....**2. Hydrocharitales.**
  2 Perianth, when present, not differentiated into sepals and petals; bracts wanting or small and inconspicuous, except in Scheuchzeriaceae, but the perianth sometimes consisting of only a single, bract-like tepal ....
  ....**3. Najadales.**
1 Seeds with well developed endosperm; plants terrestrial, mycotrophic, without chlorophyll ....**4. Triuridales.**

Selected References

Kaul, R. B. 1978. Morphology of germination and establishment of aquatic seedlings in Alismataceae and Hydrocharitaceae. Aquatic Bot. **5:** 139–147.
Tomlinson, P. B. 1982. *In* C. R. Metcalfe (ed.), Anatomy of the monocotyledons. VII. Helobiae (Alismatidae). Clarendon Press. Oxford.
Wilder, G. J. 1975. Phylogenetic trends in the Alismatidae (Monocotyledoneae). Bot. Gaz. **136:** 159–170.

1. Order Alismatales

The order Alismatales as here defined consists of 3 families and fewer than a hundred species, of cosmopolitan distribution. The Alismataceae are by far the largest family. The order may be briefly characterized as chlorophyllous Alismatidae with hypogynous flowers, a perianth that is differentiated into 3 sepals and 3 petals, and 3–many distinct or only basally connate carpels. They are all aquatic or semi-aquatic.

The 3 families of Alismatales exploit essentially similar habitats in essentially similar ways. It is reasonable to suppose that the laticifers of the Limnocharitaceae and Alismataceae serve some sort of protective function, and one could further speculate that they may be an important factor in the greater success of these two families, as compared to the monotypic family Butomaceae. It is also possible to surmise that there is some survival-value in having pollen-grains with several apertures instead of only one, although the survival-value may well be only for the individual pollen grain rather than for the species (like the red throats of nestling birds). It might also be possible to see a difference in adaptive strategies between follicular and achenial fruits, although in this instance there is no obvious difference in the results. A more determined imagination is required to see survival-value or ecologic differentiation in the disposition of the ovules, the shape of the embryo, and the number of megaspores involved in the development of the embryo-sac.

The fossil record takes the Alismatales back to the Oligocene and probably the Paleocene. A single leaf that looks very much like *Sagittaria* comes from much older (Cenomanian) deposits in Kansas (personal communication from David Dilcher), but in the absence of other material it would be premature to make a positive identification.

Synoptical Arrangement of the Families of Alismatales

1 Pollen-grains monosulcate; embryo-sac monosporic; embryo straight; plants without secretory canals; leaves linear, not differentiated into blade and petiole; placentation laminar .... **1. Butomaceae.**
1 Pollen-grains (2–) 4–many-porate, or sometimes inaperturate; embryo-sac bisporic; embryo horseshoe shaped; plants usually with schizogenous secretory canals that are lined with an epithelium; leaves typically but not always with a petiole and an expanded blade; placentation various.
  2 Ovules several or many, scattered over the inner surface of the carpel; fruits dehiscent .... **2. Limnocharitaceae.**
  2 Ovules solitary, seldom 2–several, generally ventral-basal; fruits indehiscent, or seldom dehiscent at the base .... **3. Alismataceae.**

Selected References

Argue, C. L. 1976. Pollen studies in the Alismataceae with special reference to taxonomy. Pollen & Spores **18**: 161–201.

Charlton, W. A. 1968, 1973. Studies in the Alismataceae. I. Developmental morphology of *Echinodorus tenellus*. II. Inflorescences of Alismataceae. Canad. J. Bot. **46**: 1345–1360, 1968; **51**: 775–789, 1973.

Charlton, W. A. & A. Ahmed. 1973. Studies in the Alismataceae. III. Floral anatomy of *Ranalisma humile*. IV. Developmental morphology of *Ranalisma humile* and comparisons with two members of the Butomaceae, *Hydrocleis nymphoides* and *Butomus umbellatus*. Canad. J. Bot. **51**: 891–897, 899–910.

Kaul, R. B. 1976. Conduplicate and specialized carpels in the Alismatales. Amer. J. Bot. **63**: 175–182.

Leins, P. & P. Stadler. 1973. Entwicklungsgeschichtliche Untersuchungen am Androeceum der Alismatales. Oesterr. Bot. Z. **121**: 51–63.

Sattler, R. & V. Singh. 1978. Floral organogenesis of *Echinodorus amazonicus*

Rataj and floral construction of the Alismatales. J. Linn. Soc., Bot. **77**: 141–156.

Singh, V. & R. Sattler. 1973. Nonspiral androecium and gynoecium of *Sagittaria latifolia.* Canad. J. Bot. **51**: 1093–1095.

Stant, M. Y. 1964. Anatomy of the Alismataceae. J. Linn. Soc., Bot. **59**: 1–42.

Stant, M. Y. 1967. Anatomy of the Butomaceae. J. Linn. Soc., Bot. **60**: 31–60.

2. Order Hydrocharitales

The order consists of the single family Hydrocharitaceae, with nearly a hundred species, which grow submerged or partly emergent in fresh water and coastal marine water. It is the only group of Alismatales with epigynous flowers, and is further marked by its compound ovary with parietal placentation. Often the placentas are intruded to form partial or nearly complete partitions with the ovules scattered over the surface.

The three marine genera (*Enhalus, Halophila,* and *Thalassia*) are of particular interest, since there are so few marine angiosperms. *Thalassia testudinum,* the Caribbean turtle-grass, grows at depths of as much as 30 m. The chains of pollen-grains of *Thalassia* and *Halophila* appear to be functionally comparable to the filamentous grains of the marine family Zosteraceae.

Seeds confidently assigned by paleobotanists to the modern genus *Stratiotes* occur in deposits of Eocene and more recent age. Pollen assigned to *Stratiotes* dates from the Oligocene. Remains of *Ottelia* have also been recorded from the Eocene.

SELECTED REFERENCES

Ancibor, E. 1979. Systematic anatomy of vegetative organs of the Hydrocharitaceae. J. Linn. Soc., Bot. **78**: 237–266.

Cook, C. D. K. & K. Urmi-König. 1983. A revision of the genus *Stratiotes* (Hydrocharitaceae). Aquatic Bot. **16**: 213–249.

Kaul, R. B. 1968. Floral morphology and phylogeny in the Hydrocharitaceae. Phytomorphology **18**: 13–35.

Kaul, R. B. 1970. Evolution and adaptation of inflorescences in the Hydrocharitaceae. Amer. J. Bot. **57**: 708–715.

3. Order Najadales

The order Najadales as here defined consists of 10 families and a little more than 200 species. The largest family is the Potamogetonaceae, with perhaps as many as a hundred species in the single genus *Potamogeton.*

The Najadales are Alismatidae in which the perianth, when present, is not differentiated into evident sepals and petals. Except in *Scheuchzeria* the flowers are not individually subtended by bracts, but the perianth sometimes consists of a single bract-like tepal.

Scheuchzeria forms a sort of connecting link between the Alismatales and Najadales. It resembles the Alismatales in its biseriate perianth and in having each flower subtended by a bract, but otherwise it appears to be a relatively archaic member of the Najadales. The Aponogetonaceae stand somewhat apart from the rest of the order and may perhaps represent a separate reduction from the Alismatales. The remaining families of the Najadales all evidently hang together, although the differences among them are sharp enough.

The tepals of *Potamogeton* have sometimes been interpreted as appendages of the stamens. I see no need for such a complicated interpretation, and the separate ontogenetic origin of tepals and stamens argues against it. The interpretation of the flower as pseudanthial is equally unnecessary.

The evolutionary history of the Najadales is in large part a story of floral reduction associated with progressive adaptation to aquatic and eventually marine habitats. The Scheuchzeriaceae and Juncaginaceae are typically emergent plants of marshy places. The Aponogetonaceae and Potamogetonaceae are fresh-water aquatics with submerged or floating leaves, but often with emergent inflorescences. The Najadaceae, Ruppiaceae, and Zannichelliaceae are submerged aquatics of fresh or brackish water, and the Posidoniaceae, Zosteraceae and Cymodoceaceae are submerged marine plants.

The reduction of the perianth in the Najadales is associated with the abandonment of insect-pollination, but the concomitant reduction in number of stamens, carpels, and ovules is more difficult to interpret in ecologicial terms. The thread-like pollen-grains of the Posidoniaceae, Zosteraceae and Cymodoceaceae may well be related to the submersed, marine habitat of these three families. It is not hard to believe that in moving water a long thread has more chance of brushing against a stigma than does a little ball.

Fruits attributed to the Potamogetonaceae occur in Paleocene and more recent deposits, and *Potamogeton* is represented by leaves, fruits, seeds and pollen of Oligocene age in both England and the USSR. Seeds thought to represent *Najas* occur sparsely in Oligocene and more recent deposits in England and the USSR.

SYNOPTICAL ARRANGEMENT OF THE FAMILIES OF NAJADALES

1 Ovules (1) 2–several in each of the (2) 3–several distinct or proximally connate carpels; fruits follicular; stamens 6 or more.
  2 Aquatic plants with floating leaf-blades or with wholly submersed leaves; tepals 1–3 (–6), sometimes petaloid; inflorescence typically a simple or basally forking spike, bractless, although the perianth sometimes consists of a single bract-like tepal; pollen-grains monosulcate, borne in monads
    . . . . **1. Aponogetonaceae.**
  2 Emergent marsh-plants; tepals 6, never petaloid; inflorescence a raceme, each pedicel subtended by a bract (unique in the order); pollen-grains inaperturate (holoaperturate) borne in dyads . . . . . **2. Scheuchzeriaceae.**

1 Ovules solitary in each distinct carpel or in each locule of a compound ovary; fruits mostly indehiscent or only tardily and irregularly dehiscent, except in the Juncaginaceae; stamens fewer than 6, except commonly in the Juncaginaceae.

  3 Leaves all basal, the plants scapose and with a terminal spike or raceme, commonly largely emergent . . . . **3. Juncaginaceae.**

  3 Leaves, or many of them, cauline, sometimes with a floating blade, but not emergent (sometimes exposed at low tide); inflorescence various.

    4 Pollen-grains globose or isobilateral, not thread-like; plants of fresh or alkaline or brackish water (*Ruppia* seldom marine).

      5 Flowers perfect.

        6 Tepals 4; stamens 4; pollen-grains globose; fruiting carpels sessile; ovule ventromarginal, generally near the base; plants of fresh water . . . . **4. Potamogetonaceae.**

        6 Tepals 0; stamens 2; pollen-grains of a unique, isobilateral type; fruiting carpels long-stipitate; ovule pendulous from the apex; plants chiefly of brackish or alkaline water . . . . . **5. Ruppiaceae.**

      5 Flowers unisexual.

        7 Pistil solitary, forming a unilocular ovary surmounted by 2–4 elongate stigmas; ovule basal, erect . . . . **6. Najadaceae.**

        7 Pistils (1) 3–4 (–9), each with a short or elongate style and stigma; ovule ventral-apical, pendulous . . . . **7. Zannichelliaceae.**

    4 Pollen-grains thread-like; plants marine.

      8 Flowers perfect; stamens 3, distinct; gynoecium of a single unicarpellate pistil . . . . **8. Posidoniaceae.**

      8 Flowers unisexual; stamen solitary or stamens 2 and connate; carpels 2.

        9 Gynoecium of 2 separate pistils; stamens 2, united back to back; tanniferous cells present . . . . **9. Cymodoceaceae.**

        9 Gynoecium of a single unilocular, bicarpellate pistil; stamen solitary; tanniferous cells wanting . . . . **10. Zosteraceae.**

SELECTED REFERENCES

Agrawal, J. S. 1952. The embryology of *Lilaea subulata* H.B.K. with a discussion on its systematic position. Phytomorphology 2: 15–29.

Bruggen, H. W. E. van. 1985. Monograph of the genus *Aponogeton* (Aponogetonaceae). Bibl. Bot. 137.

Daumann, E. 1963. Zur Frage nach dem Ursprung der Hydrogamie. Zugleich ein Beitrag zur Blütenökologie von *Potamogeton*. Preslia 35: 23–30.

DeCock, A. W. A. M. 1980. Flowering, pollination and fruiting in *Zostera marina* L. Aquatic Botany 9: 201–220.

Hartog, C. den. 1970. Sea-grasses of the world. Verh. Kon. Ned. Akad. Wetensch. Aft. Natuurk. Tweede Sect. 59(1): 1–275.

Haynes, R. R. 1977. The Najadaceae in the southeastern United States. J. Arnold Arbor. 58: 161–170.

Haynes, R. R. 1978. The Potamogetonaceae in the southeastern United States. J. Arnold Arbor. 59: 170–191.

Kay, Q. O. N. 1971. Floral structure in the marine angiosperms *Cymodocea serrulata* and *Thalassodendron ciliatum* (*Cymodocea ciliata*). J. Linn. Soc., Bot. 64: 423–429.

Kuo, J. 1978. Morphology, anatomy and histochemistry of the Australian seagrasses of the genus *Posidonia* König (Posidoniaceae). I. Leaf blade and leaf sheath of *Posidonia australis* Hook. f. Aquatic Bot. **5**: 163–170.

Posluzny, U. & R. Sattler. 1974. Floral development of *Potamogeton richardsonii*. Amer. J. Bot. **61**: 209–216.

Posluzny, U. & R. Sattler. 1974. Floral development of *Ruppia maritima* var. *maritima*. Canad. J. Bot. **52**: 1607–1612.

Posluzny, U. & R. Sattler. 1976. Floral development of *Zannichellia palustris*. Canad. J. Bot. **54**: 651–662.

Posluzny, U. & R. Sattler. 1976. Floral development of *Najas flexilis*. Canad. J. Bot. **54**: 1140–1151.

Posluzny, U. & P. B. Tomlinson. 1977. Morphology and development of floral shoots and organs in certain Zannichelliaceae. J. Linn. Soc., Bot. **75**: 21–46.

Singh, V. 1964–1966. Morphological and anatomical studies in Helobiae. I. Vegetative anatomy of some members of Potamogetonaceae. III. Vascular anatomy of the node and flower of Najadaceae. IV. Vegetative and floral anatomy of Aponogetonaceae. V. Vascular anatomy of the flower of *Lilaea scilloides* (Poir.) Hamm. VII. Vascular anatomy of the flower of *Butomus umbellatus* Linn. Proc. Indian Acad. Sci. B, **60**: 214–231, 1964; **61**: 98–108, 147–159, 316–325, 1965; **63**: 313–320, 1966. II. Vascular anatomy of the flower of Potamogetonaceae. Bot. Gaz. **126**: 137–144, 1965.

Takaso, T. & F. Bouman. 1984. Ovule ontogeny and seed development in *Potamogeton natans* L. (Potamogetonaceae), with a note on the campylotropous ovule. Acta Bot. Neerl. **33**: 519–533.

Tomlinson, P. B. & U. Posluzny. 1976. Generic limits in the Zannichelliaceae (sensu Dumortier). Taxon **25**: 273–279.

Tomlinson, P. B. & U. Posluzny. 1978. Aspects of floral morphology and development in the seagrass *Syringodium filiforme* (Cymodoceaceae). Bot. Gaz. **139**: 333–345.

Vijayaraghavan, M. R. & T. Kapoor. 1985. Embryogenesis in *Najas marina* L.: Structural and histochemical approach. Aquatic Bot. **22**: 45–60.

4. Order Triuridales

The order Triuridales as here defined consists of only the Triuridaceae (7 genera, ca. 70 species) and Petrosaviaceae (1 genus, 3 or 4 species). Members of the Triuridales are terrestrial, mycotrophic Alismatidae, without chlorophyll, and with well developed endosperm. The two families have not always been associated in taxonomic schemes, and their relationships are discussed separately.

Aside from their probable relationship with the Petrosaviaceae, the Triuridaceae stand off sharply from all other groups. The more or less numerous, separate carpels suggest that the family should be associated with the Alismatidae, and the trinucleate pollen is quite compatible with such an association. On the other hand, the terrestrial, mycotrophic habit and the well developed endosperm of the seeds are out of harmony with the other orders of the subclass. The nature of the nectaries is not reported.

It may well eventually become necessary to establish the Triuridales as a distinct subclass, but at the present state of knowledge I do not think it is useful.

Petrosavia has often been included in the Liliaceae, subfamily Melanthoideae. Even such a devotee of narrowly limited families of monocots as Dahlgren (in Dahlgren et al., 1985, cited under Liliopsida) makes it only a subtribe of Melanthiaceae, albeit with 2 genera instead of only one. *Petrosavia* is anomalous in the Liliaceae sensu lato not only in its mycotrophic, achlorophyllous habit, but also in its nearly distinct carpels, which are united only at the very base. It does have septal nectaries, which would be perfectly compatible with the Liliales. *Petrosavia* is anatomically very similar to the Triuridaceae. Stant (1970) comments that "My recent investigations ... have revealed a striking identity between the anatomical structure of the stem, root and leaf of the Triuridaceae and Petrosaviaceae. The resemblance is so complete that I would have no hesitation in placing *Petrosavia* in the family Triuridaceae on the basis of anatomical evidence." Perhaps a study of the sequence of amino acids in cytochrome *c* might help resolve the disagreement about the affinities of *Petrosavia*. Plastocyanin and chloroplast DNA are obviously not available for consideration here.

One of the problems of multiple authorship is exemplified by the fact that Dahlgren, Clifford and Yeo (1985, cited under Liliopsida) treat *Sciaphila* as a member of the Triuridaceae (where it is fully illustrated on p. 291) and also (p. 215) as a member of the Thismiaceae, in a quite different order.

An extraordinary new genus of (or allied to) the Triuridaceae, with central stamens and peripheral carpels, has recently been discovered in Mexico. It is in train to publication by Esteban Martínez, Clara Hilda Ramos, and Gerrit Davidse.

Synoptical Arrangement of the Families of the Triuridales

1 Carpels 3, each with numerous marginal ovules, united only at the very base; seeds numerous; flowers perfect; tepals 6, in 2 sets of 3 . . . .
. . . . **1. Petrosaviaceae.**
1 Carpels 6–50, distinct, each with a single basal ovule; seed solitary; flowers unisexual or seldom perfect; tepals 3–10, in a single cycle . . . .
. . . . **2. Triuridaceae.**

Selected References

Greene, P. S. & O. Solbrig. 1966. *Sciaphila dolichostyla* (Triuridaceae). J. Arnold Arbor. **47:** 266–269.

Stant, M. Y. 1970. Anatomy of *Petrosavia stellaris* Becc., a saprophytic monocotyledon. Pages 147–161 *in* N. K. B. Robson, D. F. Cutler & M. Gregory

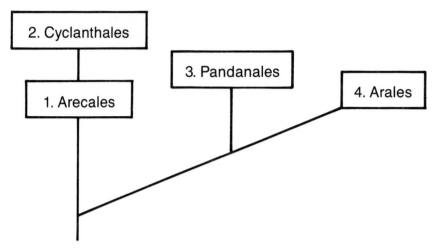

Fig. 7.4.   Putative relationships among the orders of Arecidae.

(eds.), New research in plant anatomy. J. Linn. Soc., Bot. 63, Suppl. 1.
Academic Press. London & New York.

Sterling, C. 1978. Comparative morphology of the carpel in the Liliaceae: He-
wardieae, Petrosavieae, and Tricyrteae. J. Linn. Soc., Bot. **77**: 95–106.

Subclass II. Arecidae

The subclass Arecidae as here defined consists of 4 orders (Fig. 7.4)
and only 6 families, about 5600 species in all. More than half of the
species belong to the single order Arecales, which includes only the family
Arecaceae (palms). A loose affinity among the 4 orders is widely recognized, but the group is morphologically and ecologically diverse. The
palms have the longest fossil record in the subclass, but it is difficult to
visualize them as being ancestral to any group other than possibly the
Cyclanthales.

Synoptical Arrangement of the Orders of Arecidae

1 Leaves characteristically with an expanded, plicate blade that has a unique
    ontogeny.
    2 Inflorescence usually large and branched, although the branches are some-
        times somewhat spadix-like; perianth usually well developed (though typ-
        ically rather small), only seldom vestigial or wanting; ovules solitary in
        each of the (1–) 3 (–10) locules; endosperm-development nuclear; plants
        very often arborescent and with a terminal crown of large leaves, less often
        climbing or acaulescent; leaves seldom merely bifid, except in the seedling
        stage; vessels typically present in all vegetative organs . . . . . **1. Arecales.**

2 Inflorescence a spadix; perianth minute or none; ovules more or less numerous in the single locule; endosperm-development helobial; plants typically herbaceous and acaulescent or with a short, erect stem, less often
erect half-shrubs or lianas; leaves often bifid, but sometimes flabellately
lobed or entire; vessels wanting from the leaves and usually also from the
stems .... **2. Cyclanthales.**
1 Leaves with or without an expanded blade, but in any case not plicate; inflorescence a spadix, except in some Pandanales; vessels mostly confined to the
roots, sometimes also in the stems, or sometimes wanting.
3 Leaves appearing to be in 3 or 4 spirals because of the unique, spiral growth
of the stem, parallel-veined, narrow and usually elongate, very often firm
and xeromorphic, often spiny margined; endosperm-development nuclear;
woody, very often arborescent or coarsely shrubby plants, or sometimes
woody climbers .... **3. Pandanales.**
3 Leaves not appearing to be spiralled, unarmed, sometimes narrow and parallel-veined, but very often with an expanded and more or less distinctly
net-veined blade, or the plant thalloid and without leaves; endosperm-
development cellular or sometimes helobial; herbs or scrambling slender
shrubs or climbing vines, never arborescent .... **4. Arales.**

1. Order Arecales

The order consists of a single family Arecaceae (Palmae), with nearly
3000 species, largely restricted to tropical or warm-temperate regions.
The organization of the genera of palms into tribes and subfamilies is still
fluid. Moore (1973) considers that there are 15 major groups.

Palms are the only monocotyledons to combine an arborescent habit,
a broad leaf-blade, and a well developed vascular system that has vessels
in all vegetative organs. This obviously functional syndrome approaches
that of woody dicotyledons, but palms lack an adequate means of secondary growth and a means of expanding the coverage of the crown.
Furthermore, palms have never developed the deciduous habit, and with
minor exceptions they have not adapted to temperate or cold climates.
Thus their ecological amplitude is limited, as compared with that of woody
dicots. They do well in tropical regions that are moist enough to support
evergreen tree-growth, but not moist enough to support a dense forest,
and they are also common components of the understory in tropical rain-
forests. It is not difficult to suppose that the Cyclanthaceae have a common
ancestry with some of these smaller palms of the forests.

The palms have a continuous fossil record extending well back into the
Upper Cretaceous period, near the base of the Santonian (or perhaps the
Coniacian) stage. The distinctive pollen of the modern genus *Nypa* is
found in rocks of Maestrichtian and younger age. As noted at the beginning
of this chapter, however, palms are not primitive monocots. The leaves
fossilize easily and are readily identifiable to family, but they are long
antedated in the record by other monocot fossils not so easily placed in
a family.

SELECTED REFERENCES

Corner, E. J. H. 1966. The natural history of palms. Univ. Calif. Press. Berkeley.
Ferguson, I. K. 1986. Observations on the variation in pollen morphology of Palmae and its significance. Canad. J. Bot. **64**: 3079–3090.
Henderson, A. 1986. A review of pollination studies in the palms. Bot. Rev. **52**: 221–259.
Moore, H. E. 1973. The major groups of palms and their distribution. Gentes Herb. **11**: 27–141.
Moore, H. E. & N. W. Uhl. 1982. Major trends of evolution in palms. Bot. Rev. **48**: 1–69.
Periasamy, K. 1962. Morphological and ontogenetic studies in palms. I. Development of the plicate condition in the palm leaf. Phytomorphology **12**: 54–64.
Read, R. W. & L. J. Hickey. 1972. A revised classification of fossil palm and palm-like leaves. Taxon **21**: 129–137.
Thanikomai, G. 1970. Pollen morphology, classification and phylogeny of Palmae. Adansonia sér. 2, **10**: 347–365.
Tomlinson, P. B. 1960–1962. Essays on the morphology of palms. Principes **4**: 55–61, 140–143, 1960; **5**: 8–12, 46–53, 83–89, 117–124, 1961; **6**: 44–52, 122–124, 1962.
Tomlinson, P. B. 1961. Vol. 2. Palmae. *In* C. R. Metcalfe (ed.), Anatomy of the monocotyledons. Clarendon Press. Oxford.
Uhl, N. W. & J. Dransfield. 1987. Genera palmarum. Bailey Hortorium. Ithaca, New York.

2. Order Cyclanthales

The order consists of the single family Cyclanthaceae, with some 11 genera and about 180 species, confined to tropical America. Most of the species occur in wet forests or along streams.

Authors are agreed that the Cyclanthaceae are allied to the palms, but sufficiently distinct to warrant being placed in a separate, unifamilial order. A less close relationship to the Pandanales and Arales has also been suggested.

Macrofossils referred to the Cyclanthaceae date from the Eocene epoch, but fossil pollen of the family has yet to be recognized.

SELECTED REFERENCES

Harling, G. 1958. Monograph of the Cyclanthaceae. Acta Horti Berg. **18**: 1–428.
Schremmer, F. 1982. Blühverhalten und Bestäubungsbiologie von *Carludovica palmata* (Cyclanthaceae)—Ein ökologisches Paradoxon. Pl. Syst. Evol. **140**: 95–107.
Tomlinson, P. B. & G. J. Wilder. 1984. Systematic anatomy of Cyclanthaceae (Monocotyledoneae). Bot. Gaz. **145**: 535–549.

Wilder, G. J. 1981. Morphology of adult leaves in the Cyclanthaceae (Mono-cotyledoneae). Bot. Gaz. **142:** 564–588.

Wilder, G. J. 1984. Anatomy of noncostal portions of lamina in the Cyclan-thaceae (Monocotyledoneae). V. Bot. Mus. Leafl. **30:** 103–133.

Wilder, G. J. 1985. Anatomy of noncostal portions of lamina in the Cyclan-thaceae (Monocotyledoneae). I–IV. Bot. Gaz. **146:** 82–105, 213–231, 375–394, 545–563.

Wilder, G. J. 1986. Anatomy of first-order roots in the Cyclanthaceae (Mono-cotyledoneae). I and II. Canad. J. Bot. **64:** 2622–2644, 2848–2864.

3. Order Pandanales

The order consists of the single family Pandanaceae, with about 700 species, entirely confined to the Old World, best developed in tropical regions. The group can be traced back to the Maestrichtian on the basis of fossil pollen, and judging by the pollen it had a much wider distribution in the past than it does now.

Some Eocene fruits from India may represent the Pandanaceae, although they are similar in some respects to the Araceae as well. Nambudiri and Tidwell (1978) suggest that these fruits might indeed be an evolutionary link between the two families. Daghlian (1981, cited under Liliopsida) is skeptical about the identification.

SELECTED REFERENCES

Jarzen, D. M. 1983. The fossil pollen record of the Pandanaceae. Gard. Bull. **36:** 163–175.

Nambudiri, E. M. & W. D. Tidwell. 1978. On probable affinities of *Viracarpon* Sahni from the Deccan Intertrappean flora of India. Paleontographica **166:** 30–43.

Pijl, L. van der. 1956. Remarks on pollination by bats in *Freycinetia, Duabanga* and *Haplophragma,* and on chiropterophily in general. Acta Bot. Neerl. **5:** 135–144.

Stone, B. C. 1972. A reconsideration of the evolutionary status of the family Pandanaceae and its significance in monocotyledon phylogeny. Quart. Rev. Biol. **47:** 34–45.

Zimmermann, M. H., P. B. Tomlinson & J. LeClaire. 1974. Vascular construc-tion and development in the stems of certain Pandanaceae. J. Linn. Soc., Bot. **68:** 21–41.

4. Order Arales

The order Arales consists of 3 well defined families of very unequal size. The Araceae are generally considered to have about 1800 species, but the probable error of the estimate is greater than the total number of species in the Lemnaceae (ca. 9) and Acoraceae (2).

The Araceae form a well characterized family marked by their inflorescence (a spadix) and their more or less expanded leaf-blades that lack the special peculiarities of the Arecaceae and Cyclanthaceae. Most aroids are herbs of the forest floor, or vines climbing on forest trees. Their relatively broad and veiny leaves (for a monocot) are consonant with the habitat.

Acorus has usually been included in the Araceae as an aberrant genus, but it differs in so many ways that I must follow Grayum (1984) in treating it as a separate family. Even its relationship to the Araceae has been questioned. Some botanists have thought it might be related to the Typhales, but serological studies by Lee and Fairbrothers (1972, cited under Typhales) disclose no such affinity.

The Lemnaceae occupy a distinctive ecological niche that has scarcely been entered by other angiosperms. Their structure and reproduction reflect the habitat. It has been widely agreed that the Lemnaceae are related to and derived from the Araceae. *Pistia,* a free-floating aquatic aroid with a relatively small and few-flowered spadix, is seen as pointing the way toward *Spirodela,* the least reduced genus of Lemnaceae. More recently, Grayum (1984) has rejected a direct link between *Pistia* and *Spirodela,* and sees the Lemnaceae as no more than a sister-group of the Araceae. Although a reasonably close relationship of some sort between the two families seems evident, the Lemnaceae are so highly reduced in both vegetative and floral features that their customary inclusion in the Arales makes the order morphologically indefinable.

The known fossil record of the Arales does not antedate the Tertiary. Leaves plausibly referred to *Philodendron* and *Peltandra* have been found in Eocene deposits in the United States, and some fragments of leaves from the Paleocene of Kazakhstan are considered to be araceous. Some small spadices from the Middle Eocene of Tennessee are thought to represent the Acoraceae. Verified araceous pollen dates only from the Miocene, although some Paleocene pollen may also belong here.

SYNOPTICAL ARRANGEMENT OF THE FAMILIES OF ARALES

1 Plants with roots, stems, and leaves, terrestrial (or epiphytic) or sometimes more or less aquatic, but only rarely free-floating; flowers very numerous in a spadix; vascular system well developed, the plants commonly with vessels in the roots and tracheids in all vegetative organs; ovary usually with more than one carpel, only rarely apparently monomerous.
    2 Leaves ensiform, unifacial; plants with ethereal oil cells but not raphides; anthers introrse; placentation apical-axile; fruit dry . . . . . **1. Acoraceae.**
    2 Leaves with a more or less expanded, bifacial blade; plants with raphides but not ethereal oil cells; anthers extrorse; placentation in plurilocular ovaries axile or basal-axile; fruit usually fleshy . . . . **2. Araceae.**
1 Plant thalloid, free-floating, with or without 1–several short, slender roots; flowers (rarely produced) only 2–3 (4) in an inflorescence; vascular system

much reduced, the plants lacking both vessels and tracheids, or sometimes with tracheids in the roots; ovary pseudomonomerous .... **3. Lemnaceae.**

SELECTED REFERENCES

Bogner, J. 1987. Morphological variation in aroids. Aroideana **10(2):** 4–16.
Crepet, W. L. 1978. Investigations of angiosperms from the Eocene of North America: An aroid inflorescence. Rev. Palaeobot. Palynol. **25:** 241–252.
Dilcher, D. L. & C. P. Daghlian. 1977. Investigations of angiosperms from the Eocene of southeastern North America: *Philodendron* leaf remains. Amer. J. Bot. **64:** 526–534.
Eyde, R. H., D. H. Nicolson & P. Sherwin. 1967. A survey of floral anatomy in Araceae. Amer. J. Bot. **54:** 478–497.
French, J. C. 1987. Systematic occurrence of a sclerotic hypodermis in roots of Araceae. Amer. J. Bot. **74:** 891–903.
Grayum, M. H. 1984. Palynology and phylogeny of the Araceae. Ph.D. Thesis. Univ. Massachusetts. Amherst, Massachusetts.
Hartog, C. den & F. von der Plas. 1970. A synopsis of the Lemnaceae. Blumea **18:** 355–368.
Ivanova, I. E. 1973. K sistematike semeystva Lemnaceae S. F. Gray. Bot. Zh. **58:** 1413–1423.
Kaplan, D. R. 1970. Comparative foliar histogenesis in *Acorus calamus* and its bearing on the phyllode theory of monocotyledonous leaves. Amer. J. Bot. **57:** 331–361.
Maheshwari, S. C. 1956. The endosperm and embryo of *Lemna* and systematic position of Lemnaceae. Phytomorphology **6:** 51–55.
Maheshwari, S C. 1958. *Spirodela polyrhiza*: The link between the aroids and the duckweeds. Nature **181:** 1745–1746.
Maheshwari, S. C. & P. P. Khanna. 1956. The embryology of *Arisaema wallichianum* Hook. f. and the systematic position of the Araceae. Phytomorphology **6:** 379–388.
Ray, T. S. 1987. Leaf types in the Araceae. Amer. J. Bot. **74:** 1359–1372.
Savchenko, M. I. & E. N. Manya. 1970. Sravintel'no-anatomicheskie issledovaniya i osi sotsvetiya nekotorykh aroidykh (Araceae). Bot. Zh. **55:** 406–521.
Wilson, K. A. 1960. The genera of the Arales in the southeastern United States. J. Arnold Arbor. **41:** 47–72.

Subclass III. Commelinidae

The subclass Commelinidae as here defined consists of 7 orders (Fig. 7.5), 16 families, and about 15,000 species. More than half of the species belong to the single family Poaceae (grasses), and the Poaceae and the Cyperaceae (sedges) together account for about four-fifths of the species. The most archaic order of the group, the Commelinales, has flowers pollinated by pollen-gathering insects. The other orders show varying degrees of floral reduction associated with adaptation to wind-pollination.

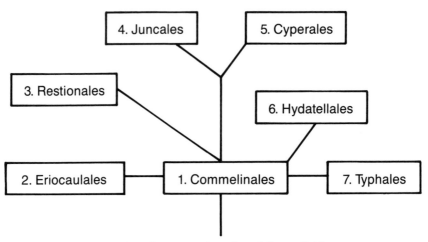

Fig. 7.5.   Putative relationships among the orders of Commelinidae.

Some of the Eriocaulales have reverted to insect-pollination and have developed nectaries just within the tip of the tiny petals, quite unlike the septal nectaries that are common in other groups of monocotyledons.

Among the outstanding features of the Commelinidae are the usual presence of vessels in all vegetative organs, and the starchy endosperm, which often has compound starch-grains and is then mealy in texture. Most of the Zingiberidae have a similar endosperm, but the Arecidae and Liliidae depend more on hemicellulose, protein, and oil.

Smooth, monoporate pollen thought to represent anemophilous Commelinidae first appears in the fossil record in the Campanian, above the middle of the Upper Cretaceous. Pollen more clearly assignable to modern families does not appear until the Maestrichtian and early Tertiary. It is possible that some Cretaceous macrofossils also belong to the Commelinidae, but macrofossils more certainly identifiable with the group do not antedate the Tertiary.

Synoptical Arrangement of the Orders of Commelinidae

1 Flowers commonly perfect, and with more or less showy petals that are well
   differentiated from the sepals, adapted to pollination by insects . . . .
   . . . . **1. Commelinales.**
1 Flowers perfect or unisexual, without showy petals, the perianth (when present)
   sometimes in 2 series, but dry and chaffy, the flowers (except some Eriocaulaceae) adapted to wind-pollination or self-pollination or pollination by water.
   2 Ovules various, but never at once solitary, pendulous from near the summit
      of the ovary, and anatropous; plants terrestrial or less often aquatic.
      3 Ovary with 1–3 fertile locules and as many stigmas, each fertile locule
         with a single pendulous, orthotropous ovule; embryo peripheral to the
         endosperm.

4 Flowers aggregated into dense, pseudanthial, involucrate heads (usually both sexes in the same head), pollinated by wind or often by insects; ovules tenuinucellar; anthers usually tetrasporangiate and dithecal; leaves all basal, without a well differentiated sheath . . . .
. . . . **2. Eriocaulales.**
4 Flowers seldom aggregated into dense heads, usually or always wind-pollinated or self-pollinated; ovules crassinucellar to sometimes tenuinucellar; anthers bisporangiate and monothecal, or less often tetrasporangiate and dithecal; leaves cauline or basal, and with a more or less well differentiated basal sheath . . . . **3. Restionales.**
3 Ovary otherwise, either with more stigmas than locules, or with more than one ovule per locule, or with ascending, anatropous ovules; embryo peripheral (Poaceae) or embedded (Cyperaceae, Juncales) in the endosperm; flowers perfect or unisexual.
5 Ovary with 1–3 locules and 3–many ovules; fruit capsular; pollen-grains in tetrads; flowers with an evident (though small) biseriate, chaffy perianth, borne in open or compact inflorescences unlike those of the Cyperales . . . . **4. Juncales.**
5 Ovary with a single locule and ovule; fruit indehiscent; pollen-grains in monads or pseudomonads; flowers borne in characteristic spikes or spikelets, without a clearly biseriate, chaffy perianth . . . .
. . . . **5. Cyperales.**
2 Ovules solitary (or solitary in each locule), pendulous from near the summit of the ovary, anatropous; plants aquatic or semiaquatic.
6 Seeds with well developed perisperm and virtually no endosperm (unique in the subclass); flowers hydrophilous (unique in the subclass) or autogamous . . . . **6. Hydatellales.**
6 Seeds with well developed endosperm and no perisperm; vascular system well developed, with vessels in all vegetative organs, and with numerous vascular bundles in the stem; flowers anemophilous (or autogamous)
. . . . **7. Typhales.**

1. Order Commelinales

The order Commelinales as here defined consists of 4 families and about 1000 species. The Commelinaceae, with about 700 species, are by far the largest family, followed by the Xyridaceae (200+), Rapateaceae (100), and Mayacaceae (4). Within the order, the Rapateaceae and Xyridaceae are a closely related pair, the Xyridaceae perhaps derived from the Rapateaceae. It should be noted, however, that Tiemann (1985) sees the Xyridaceae as being more nearly allied to the Eriocaulaceae (Eriocaulales).

Ecologically, the Commelinales are characterized by having relatively simple adaptations favoring pollination by pollen-gathering insects. The other orders of the subclass have more or less reduced flowers that in most families are wind-pollinated or self-pollinated. Members of the Zingiberidae and Liliidae, in contrast, commonly have nectariferous flowers, often with more complex adaptations for pollination.

Aside from pollination, the Commelinales are ecologically diverse. They are all essentially herbaceous, but they occur in a wide range of habitats.

The Mayacaceae are basically aquatic. The Xyridaceae mostly occur in wet or marshy places but are rarely truly aquatic. The Rapateaceae and Commelinaceae range from ordinary mesophytes to marsh-plants or occasional xerophytes.

The status of *Cartonema,* sometimes taken as a separate family, has been adequately dealt with by Brenan (1966), Rohweder (1969), and Grootjen (1983). *Cartonema* and *Triceratella* individually stand somewhat apart from the bulk of the Commelinaceae, but their affinity is clear, and there is no need to fragment the family.

It is possible that some of the generalized monocotyledonous fossils from the Tertiary and Upper Cretaceous represent members of the Commelinales, but equally possible that they do not. Otherwise the fossil record of the order is virtually blank.

Synoptical Arrangement of the Families of Commelinales

1 Leaf-sheath open, often not well differentiated from the blade, or (Mayacaceae) the leaf without a sheath.
  2 Leaves mostly or all clustered at the base, with a basal, open sheath and narrow blade; flowers usually in a compact inflorescence terminating a long scape or peduncle.
    3 Stamens 6, opening by apical pores or short, pore-like slits; inflorescence generally a compact cluster (often a head) of spikelets, each spikelet with several bracts subtending the single flower .... **1. Rapateaceae.**
    3 Stamens generally 3, often accompanied by 3 staminodes, rarely 6 and all polliniferous; anthers opening by longitudinal slits; inflorescence usually a simple, racemose head or short, stout spike, rarely open ...
    .... **2. Xyridaceae.**
  2 Leaves well distributed along the stem, numerous and often linear or filiform, without a sheath; flowers pedicellate in the axils of crowded, bract-like leaves at the stem-tips; stamens 3; anthers opening by apical pores or short, pore-like slits .... **3. Mayacaceae.**
1 Leaf with a closed sheath and a well defined (narrow or broad), commonly somewhat succulent blade .... **4. Commelinaceae.**

Selected References

Brenan, J. P. M. 1966. The classification of Commelinaceae. J. Linn. Soc., Bot. **59**: 340–370.

Carlquist, S. 1961. Pollen morphology of Rapateaceae. Aliso **5**: 39–66.

Carlquist, S. 1966. Anatomy of Rapateaceae—Roots and stems. Phytomorphology **16**: 17–38.

Cheadle, V. I. & H. Kosakai. 1982. Occurrence and specialization of vessels in Xyridales. Nordic J. Bot. **2**: 97–109.

Grootjen, C. J. 1983. Development of ovule and seed in *Cartonema spicatum* R. Br. (Cartonemataceae). Austral. J. Bot. **31**: 297–305.

Hamann, U. 1961. Merkmalbestand und Verwandtschaftbeziehungen der Farinosae. Willdenowia **2**: 639–768.

Hamann, U. 1962. Weiteres über Merkmalsbestand und Verwandtschaftsbeziehungen der "Farinosae." Willdenowia **3**: 169–207.

Jones, K. & C. Jopling. 1972. Chromosomes and the classification of the Commelinaceae. J. Linn. Soc., Bot. **65**: 129–162.

Lourteig, A. 1952. Mayacaceae. Notul. Syst. (Paris) **14**: 234–248.

Murty, Y. S., N. P. Saxena & V. Singh. 1974. Floral morphology of the Commelinaceae. J. Indian Bot. Soc. **53**: 127–136.

Rohweder, O. 1969. Beiträge zur Blütenmorphologie und -anatomie der Commelinaceen mit Anmerkungen zur Begrenzung und Gliederung der Familie. Ber. Schweiz. Bot. Ges. **79**: 199–220.

Thieret, J. W. 1975. The Mayacaceae in the southeastern United States. J. Arnold Arbor. **56**: 248–255.

Tiemann, A. 1985. Untersuchungen zur Embryologie, Blütenmorphologie und Systematik der Rapataceen und der Xyridaceen-Gattung *Abolboda* (Monocotyledoneae). Dissert. Bot. **82**: 1–201.

Tomlinson, P. B. 1969. Vol. 3. Commelinales-Zingiberales. In C. R. Metcalfe (ed.), Anatomy of the monocotyledons. Clarendon Press. Oxford.

2. Order Eriocaulales

The order Eriocaulales consists of the single family Eriocaulaceae, with about 1200 species mostly of tropical and subtropical regions. The Eriocaulaceae are much like the Xyridaceae in habit, with clustered basal leaves and a terminal, racemose head on a long peduncle or scape. There is no obvious reason why the Eriocaulaceae might not have been derived directly from the Xyridaceae or from some similar common ancestor with 6 functional stamens. The relationship between the two families is generally admitted, and some authors, such as Dahlgren et al. (1985, cited under Liliopsida), include the Eriocaulaceae in the Commelinales along with the Xyridaceae. I find it conceptually more useful in the context of the Commelinidae to emphasize the apomorphies of the Eriocaulaceae (pseudanthial heads, unisexual flowers, reduced perianth, anemophily, or entomophily in association with petalar nectaries) and keep the family in an order by itself. The nectaries of *Eriocaulon,* borne just within the petal-tips, are distinctive and quite unlike the septal nectaries found in other syncarpous subclasses of monocots.

The Eriocaulales apparently do not have a significant fossil record.

SELECTED REFERENCES

Hare, C. L. 1950. The structure and development of *Eriocaulon septangulare* With. J. Linn. Soc., Bot. **53**: 422–448.

Kral, R. 1966. Eriocaulaceae of continental North America north of Mexico. Sida **2**: 285–332.

Ramaswamy, S. N. & G. D. Arekal. 1982. Embryology of *Eriocaulon xeranthemum* Mart. (Eriocaulaceae). Acta Bot. Neerl. **31**: 41–54.

Stützel, T. & F. Weberling. 1982. Untersuchungen über Verzweigung und Infloreszenzaufbau von Eriocaulaceen. Flora **172:** 105–112.

Thanikomonai, G. 1965. Contribution to the pollen morphology of Eriocaulaceae. Pollen & Spores **7:** 181–191.

3. Order Restionales

The order Restionales as here defined consists of 4 families and about 450 species, best developed in tropical and south-temperate parts of the Old World. About nine-tenths of the species belong to the single family Restionaceae.

The Restionaceae are somewhat grass-like in aspect and are often rather loosely called Southern Hemisphere grasses. Although some sort of relationship between the Restionaceae and Poaceae is widely conceded, they have different sets of apomorphies. The Restionaceae are more primitive (plesiomorphic) than the grasses in typically having a perianth of 2 sets of small, scale-like tepals, whereas the perianth of Poaceae is reduced to 2 or 3 tiny lodicules. The restionaceous gynoecium is also more primitive than that of grasses, having 1–3 carpels and locules, with as many ovules and (usually) styles (or style branches) as locules. The small, lenticular embryo of Restionaceae, capping the endosperm, resembles that of the Commelinales, Eriocaulales, and the other families of Restionales, and is quite unlike the unique, enigmatic embryo of grasses. Most of the Restionaceae are more advanced than the grasses, however, in their unisexual flowers, in that the leaf-blade is much reduced or vestigial, and in that the anthers are bisporangiate and monothecal. The characteristic sclerenchymatous sheath in the stem of Restionaceae also appears to be an apomorphy. Other differences between the two families could also be listed.

Pollen of modern Restionales is round, smooth, and uniporate. Efforts to distinguish among these several families and the grasses on the basis of pollen are still progressing (see Linder & Ferguson, 1985), and all but the most recent identifications to family in this group need to be reconsidered. Pollen that may represent the Restionaceae appears in the Maestrichtian, whereas pollen that may represent the Centrolepidaceae dates from the Paleocene. Pollen of *Flagellaria* (and possibly *Joinvillea*) is more recent, dating from the Miocene.

SYNOPTICAL ARRANGEMENT OF THE FAMILIES OF RESTIONALES

1 Stamens 6; anthers tetrasporangiate and dithecal; flowers perfect; perianth present; leaves chiefly or wholly cauline, with a well developed blade.
  2 Perianth somewhat petaloid; solid-stemmed lianas; leaf-blade circinately inrolled in bud, cirrhose at the tip; sheath closed   . . . **1. Flagellariaceae.**
  2 Perianth chaffy; hollow-stemmed, erect, coarse herbs; leaves plicate in bud, not cirrhose; sheath open . . . .**2. Joinvilleaceae.**

1 Stamens 1–3 (4); anthers, except in a few Restionaceae, bisporangiate and monothecal; flowers unisexual or rarely perfect.
3 Perianth usually present; stamens (1–) 3 (4); leaves in most genera largely cauline, with an open sheath and much reduced or no blade . . . .
. . . .**3. Restionaceae.**
3 Perianth wanting; stamens 1 (2); leaves clustered at the base, with a more or less well defined open sheath and an elongate, slender blade . . . .
. . . . **4. Centrolepidaceae.**

Selected References

Chanda, S. 1966. On the pollen morphology of the Centrolepidaceae, Restionaceae and Flagellariaceae, with special reference to taxonomy. Grana Palynol. **6**: 355–415.

Cutler, D. F. 1966. Anatomy and taxonomy of the Restionaceae. Jodrell Lab. Notes **4**: 1–25.

Hamann, U. 1975. Neue Untersuchungenen zur Embryologie und Systematik der Centrolepidaceae. Bot. Jahrb. Syst. **96**: 154–191.

Kircher, P. 1986. Untersuchungen zur Blüten- und Infloreszenzmorphologie, Embryologie und Systematik der Restionaceen im Vergleich mit Gramineen und Verwandten Familien. Dissert. Bot. **94**: 1–219.

Lee, D. W., Yap Kim Pin & Liew Foo Yew. 1975. Serological evidence on the distinctness of the monocotyledonous families Flagellariaceae, Hanguanaceae and Joinvilleaceae. J. Linn. Soc., Bot. **70**: 77–81.

Linder, H. P. & I. K. Ferguson. 1985. On the pollen morphology and phylogeny of the Restionales and Poales. Grana **24**: 65–76.

Newell, T. K. 1969. A study of the genus *Joinvillea* (Flagellariaceae). J. Arnold Arbor. **50**: 527–555.

Smithson, E. 1957. The comparative anatomy of the Flagellariaceae. Kew Bull. **1956**: 491–501.

Tomlinson, P. B. & A. C. Smith. 1970. Joinvilleaceae, a new family of monocotyledons. Taxon **19**: 887–889.

4. Order Juncales

The order Juncales as here defined consists of 2 families, the Juncaceae, with about 300 species, and the Thurniaceae, with only 3. The probable error in estimating the number of species of Juncaceae is greater than the number of species of Thurniaceae, and the order Juncales may therefore be said to have about 300 (rather than 303) species.

The Juncales may be characterized as Commelinidae with small, chaffy, usually trimerous and biseriate perianth, tetradinous pollen, and capsular fruits with 3 or more seeds. *Thurnia,* although anatomically distinctive, is thought to form a sort of connecting link between the Juncaceae and Rapateaceae.

The Juncaceae have played a key role in phylogenetic speculation about the families of monocotyledons. Subsequent to (and consequent upon) the general recognition of the importance of floral reduction in the evolution of angiosperms, it became customary to consider the Juncaceae as florally reduced derivatives of the Liliaceae or some lily-like ancestor. There is indeed a superficial resemblance between these two groups, but they characteristically differ in their vascular architecture (vessels in all vegetative organs in Juncaceae, confined to the roots in Liliaceae), stomatal structure (paracytic in Juncaceae, usually anomocytic in Liliaceae), and food-reserves of the seed (starch in the Juncaceae, protein or oil or hemicellulose in Liliaceae). In all of these respects the Juncaceae resemble typical Commelinidae rather than typical Liliaceae. Furthermore, if the Thurniaceae are related to the Juncaceae, as is now generally believed, we must take note of the fact that the silica-bodies of *Thurnia* are similar to those of the Rapateaceae, Restionaceae, and some Cyperaceae. Somewhat different silica-bodies occur in the Poaceae. Silica-bodies are virtually unknown in the Liliidae. The Juncales are fully at home in the Commelinidae, where they are here placed, but would be highly aberrant in the Liliidae. The relationship of the Juncales to the Cyperales is discussed under the latter order.

If there is anything ecologically distinctive about the Juncales, as contrasted to the other orders of Commelinidae with reduced, wind-pollinated flowers, the fact has escaped detection. The adaptive significance of the known differences between the Juncaceae and Cyperaceae, for example, is obscure. The reasons why the Juncaceae are less successful than the more abundant and varied Cyperaceae remain to be discovered.

The fossil record of the Juncaceae is scanty and does not certainly carry the family back beyond the Miocene.

SYNOPTICAL ARRANGEMENT OF THE FAMILIES OF JUNCALES

1 Inflorescence of one or more dense heads subtended by spreading, leafy bracts; vascular bundles of the leaf in vertical pairs, the lower (and smaller) bundle of a pair with the phloem on top (adaxial), facing the phloem of the upper bundle; silica-bodies present in some of the cells of the parenchyma and epidermis .... **2. Thurniaceae.**
1 Inflorescence of diverse sorts, but not as in the Thurniaceae; vascular bundles of the leaf of ordinary structure, with abaxial phloem, not as in the Thurniaceae; cells without silica-bodies .... **1. Juncaceae.**

SELECTED REFERENCES

Barnard, C. 1958. Floral histogenesis in monocotyledons. III. The Juncaceae. Austral. J. Bot. **6:** 285–298.

Cutler, D. F. 1965. Vegetative anatomy of Thurniaceae. Kew Bull. **19:** 431–441.

Cutler, D. F. 1969. Vol. 4. Juncales. *In* C. R. Metcalfe (ed.), Anatomy of the monocotyledons. Clarendon Press. Oxford.

Wulff, H. D. 1939. Die Pollenentwicklung der Juncaceen nebst einer Auswertung der embryologischen Befunde hinsichtlich einer Verwandtschaft zwischen den Juncaceen und Cyperaceen. Jahrb. Wiss. Bot. **87:** 533–556.

5. Order Cyperales

The order Cyperales as here defined consists of 2 large and widely distributed families, the Cyperaceae (nearly 4000 species) and Poaceae (8000). The Poaceae are even more successful, as compared to the Cyperaceae, than the number of species would suggest. Grasses (Poaceae) form the dominant vegetation over considerable portions of the earth. The Cyperales may be characterized as Commelinidae with a pluricarpellate but unilocular ovary containing a single ovule, ripening into an indehiscent fruit. They ordinarily have a well developed, partly or wholly starchy endosperm.

If the formal morphological characters usually cited as distinguishing the Poaceae from the Cyperaceae have any great adaptive significance, the fact remains to be established. One may reasonably speculate that it is the intercalary meristem of the leaf that plays a major role in the greater success of the grasses. The leaves of monocots in general mature from the tip downwards; in grasses the base of the leaf-blade remains more or less permanently immature and meristematic. Some of the Cyperaceae, notably species of *Carex,* share this feature to some extent, but in general it is much less developed in the Cyperaceae than in the Poaceae. Anyone who has pushed a lawn-mower should recognize the significance of the intercalary meristem in permitting a plant to withstand grazing.

Although the Cyperaceae and Poaceae have traditionally been associated in older systems of classification, in recent years several authors have taken each family to represent a separate, unifamilial order, or have associated the Cyperaceae with the Juncales and the Poaceae with the Restionales. Neither of these alternatives is really wrong, but I am not convinced that the change is necessary.

Perhaps the most important features linking the Cyperaceae to the Juncales are the tetradinous pollen and diffuse centromere. The pollen of Cyperaceae superficially appears to be monadinous as in the Poaceae, but it is ontogenetically tetradinous; three of the four microspores of the tetrad degenerate and are retained within the common wall. Tetradinous pollen is not inherently of great phylogenetic moment, however. No one seems unduly concerned about the presence of tetradinous and monadinous species in the well characterized and very natural genus *Typha.* Like other characters, this one must be evaluated in the context of other similarities and differences.

The diffuse centromere may prove to be more significant, since this is a rare feature indeed in embryophytes. It is not certain, however, that either the Cyperaceae or the Juncaceae consistently have diffuse centromeres. *Luzula* (Juncaceae) is diffuse, but the behavior of *Juncus* is not yet clarified. Some genera of the Cyperaceae (including *Carex*) are diffuse, but perhaps not all. Instead of a true synapomorphy, we may have here another example of the familiar pattern of parallelism in allied groups. If the diffuse centromere does prove to be consistent in both families, and is also found in the Thurniaceae but not in any of the Poaceae or Restionales, then it may become proper to use the diffuse centromere and the ontogenetically tetradinous pollen to characterize an expanded order Juncales, including the Cyperaceae. The Poaceae could then appropriately be included in the Restionales. This is the option recently taken by Dahlgren et al. (1985, cited under Liliopsida).

I am not enthusiastic about taking the Cyperales and Poales as unifamilial orders. The several families in the Commelinales-Juncales-Restionales group are so clearly allied to each other and to both the grasses and sedges that it seems pointless to recognize a series of orders with a single family each.

At the present state of knowledge, I think it prudent to retain the traditional association of the grasses and sedges in an order apart from other Commelinidae. If further information eventually supports a recasting of the orders along the lines suggested above, so be it.

Some authors maintain that the apparently perfect flowers of *Scirpus* and some other genera of the Cyperaceae are actually pseudanthia, partial inflorescences in which the apparent perianth represents ancestral bracts, each stamen represents a separate flower, and the pistil represents still another flower. Under this interpretation, the true flowers of all Cyperaceae are unisexual and without perianth. Even if the pseudanthial interpretation were correct (which Occam's Razor makes me doubt), it would be more useful from a purely descriptive standpoint to follow the classical interpretation that the flowers and flower-parts are just what they seem. Descriptive morphology loses its function if it is intelligible only to a limited coterie of specialists.

The pistillate spikes of *Carex* (Cyperaceae) do clearly represent compound inflorescences. Each pistillate flower is subtended by a bract, and enclosed by another bract, open at the top, which has its back toward the axis of the spike and often shows an evident suture (the connate margins) toward the summit on the abaxial side. The style protrudes through the apical orifice of the enclosing bract, which is called the perigynium. In a few species of *Carex,* the solitary pistillate flower within the perigynium is evidently lateral on a small rachilla that is prolonged beyond the ovary. The rachilla is considered to represent a vestigial ultimate branch of a compound inflorescence.

The morphology of the grass spikelet has been variously interpreted, partly because of differing views on the general course of evolution in flowering plants. The interpretation here adopted reflects the view that grasses are derived from ancestors with trimerous flowers and two cycles of tepals, and draws on the work of a series of botanists from Celakovsky (1889) onwards.

The taxonomic organization of the grasses into subfamilies and tribes is in a state of flux. The classic work of Avdulov (1931) and Prat (1936) forms a turning point in grass taxonomy. Many microscopic anatomical characters, as well as chromosome-number, have proved to be of critical importance in assessing relationships, and some of the traditional tribes now appear to be heterogeneous and unnatural. A minimum of 3 subfamilies must be recognized. These are the Bambuseae, Pooideae, and Panicoideae. Further study will doubtless lead to a narrower definition of the Pooideae and the recognition of some additional subfamilies, but at present there is no agreement as to the number and definition of these other groups.

Dating the grasses and sedges in the fossil record is complicated by the difficulty of distinguishing fossil pollen of these two groups from that of the Restionaceae. Pollen that appears to represent the Poaceae enters the record in the Paleocene. Pollen and megafossils of both the Cyperaceae and Poaceae are clearly recognizable in the Eocene. Major diversification of the grasses may be more recent, but was evidently well under way in the Miocene.

SYNOPTICAL ARRANGEMENT OF THE FAMILIES OF CYPERALES

1 Flowers spirally or less often distichously arranged on the axis of the spike or spikelet, usually each flower seemingly or actually subtended by only a single scale, without an evident scale between the flower and the axis; seed-coat generally free from the pericarp; leaf-sheath usually closed; stem usually solid, very often triangular; carpels 3 or less often 2; embryo embedded in the endosperm; pollen-grains borne in pseudomonads; chromosomes often with a diffuse centromere .... **1. Cyperaceae.**
1 Flowers distichously arranged on the axis of the spikelet (or only one per spikelet), each flower ordinarily subtended by a pair of scales (lemma and palea), the palea inserted between the flower and the axis; seed-coat usually adnate to the pericarp; leaf-sheath usually open; stem usually hollow, never triangular; carpels 2, seldom 3, embryo peripheral to the endosperm; pollen-grains borne in true monads; chromosomes monocentric ..... **2. Poaceae.**

SELECTED REFERENCES

Avdulov, N. P. 1931. Kario-sistematicheskoe issledovanie cemeystva zlakov. Prilozhenie 44 k Trudam po prikladnoy botanike, genetike i selektsii.
Blaser, H. W. 1941, 1944. Studies in the morphology of the Cyperaceae. I. Morphology of flowers. A. Scirpoid genera. B. Rynchosporoid genera. II. The prophyll. Amer. J. Bot. **28:** 542–551, 832–838, 1941; **31:** 53–64, 1944.
Brown, W. V. 1965. The grass embryo—A rebuttal. Phytomorphology **15:** 274–284.
Butzin, F. 1965. Neue Untersuchungen über die Blüte der Gramineae. Inaugural-Dissertation. Berlin.
Calderón, C. E. & T. R. Soderstrom. 1980. The genera of Bambusoideae (Poaceae) of the American continent: Keys and comments. Smithsonian Contr. Bot. **44:** 1–27.

Celakovsky, L. 1889. Über den Ahrchenbau der brasilianische Grasgattung *Streptochaeta* Schrad. Sitzungsber. Konigl. Böhm. Ges. Wiss. Prag. Math.-Naturwiss. Cl. **1:** 14–42.

Cheadle, V. I. & H. Kosakai. 1972. Vessels in the Cyperaceae. Bot. Gaz. **133:** 214–223.

Clifford, H. T. 1961. Floral evolution in the family Gramineae. Evolution **15:** 455–460.

Dunbar, A. 1973. Pollen development in the *Eleocharis palustris* group (Cyperaceae). I. Ultrastructure and ontogeny. Bot. Not. **126:** 197–254.

Eiten, L. T. 1976. Inflorescence units in the Cyperaceae. Ann. Missouri Bot. Gard. **63:** 81–112.

Goetghebeur, P. 1986. Genera Cyperacearum: Ein bijdrage tot de kennis van de morfologie, systematiek en fylogenese van de Cyperaceae-genera. Rijksuniversiteit van Gent, Proefschrift, Gent.

Hartley, W. 1958, 1973. Studies on the origin, evolution, and distribution of the Gramineae. II. The tribe Paniceae. V. The subfamily Festucoideae. Austral. J. Bot. **6:** 343–357, 1958; **21:** 201–234, 1973.

Koyama, T. 1961. Classification of the family Cyperaceae (1). J. Fac. Sci. Univ. Tokyo, Sect. 3, Bot. **8:** 37–148.

Metcalfe, C. R. 1960. Vol. 1. Gramineae. *In* C. R. Metcalfe (ed.), Anatomy of the monocotyledons. Clarendon Press. Oxford.

Metcalfe, C. R. 1971. Vol. 5. Cyperaceae. *In* C. R. Metcalfe, ed. Anatomy of the monocotyledons. Clarendon Press. Oxford.

Page, V. M. 1951. Morphology of the spikelet of *Streptochaeta*. Bull. Torrey Bot. Club **78:** 22–37.

Philipson, W. R. 1985. Is the grass gynoecium monocarpellary? Amer. J. Bot. **72:** 1954–1961.

Prat, H. 1936. La systematique des Graminées. Ann. Sci. Nat. Bot. Sér. 10. **18:** 165–258.

Prat, H. 1960. Vers une classification naturelle des Graminées. Bull. Soc. Bot. France **107:** 32–79.

Schultze-Motel, W. 1959. Entwicklungsgeschichtliche und vergleichend-morphologische Untersuchungen im Blütenbereich der Cyperaceae. Bot. Jahrb. Syst. **78:** 129–170.

6. Order Hydatellales

The order Hydatellales consists of the single family Hydatellaceae, with 7 species native to Australia, New Zealand, and Tasmania. The two genera (*Hydatella* and *Trithuria*) have customarily been assigned to the Centrolepidaceae, which they resemble in habit, but from which they differ in numerous other ways. The affinities of the Hydatellaceae are uncertain, but they seem to be best accommodated in the Commelinidae. The opercular swelling of the seed-coat suggests a possible eventual relationship with the Commelinales, in which the families Commelinaceae and Mayacaceae have a similar swelling.

SELECTED REFERENCES

Hamann, U. 1976. Hydatellaceae—A new family of Monocotyledoneae. New Zealand J. Bot. **14**: 193–196.

Hamann, U., K. Kaplan & T. Rübsamen. 1979. Über die Samenschalenstruktur der Hydatellaceae (Monocotyledoneae) und die systematische Stellung von *Hydatella filamentosa*. Bot. Jahrb. Syst. **100**: 555–563.

7. Order Typhales

The order Typhales consists of 2 closely related small families of emergent aquatics, the Sparganiaceae and Typhaceae, each with but a single genus. There are only about 2 dozen species in all. A good case can be made for including *Sparganium* in the Typhaceae, but it is sufficiently different from *Typha* so that there is no serious harm in continuing the customary practice of putting each of the two genera into its own family.

The Typhales are taxonomically isolated. Serological tests emphasize the remoteness of the order from others, without providing a clear guide to its affinities. It may be significant that the cell walls contain bound ferulic acid. Among the monocotyledons bound ferulic acid is consistently present in the Commelinidae, the Zingiberidae, and the families Arecaceae, Haemodoraceae, Philydraceae, and Pontederiaceae, but is lacking in other tested groups. Its potential importance as a unique synapomorphy is compromised by its occurrence also in the Caryophyllales, alone among the dicots.

The Pandanales, in which the Typhales have often been included, differ in their arborescent habit, spiral growth-pattern, mostly tetracytic stomates, and nonstarchy endosperm, as well as in the absence of bound ferulic acid in the cell walls. There is some similarity in the inflorescence of the two groups, but the evolutionary development of the spadix of the Pandanaceae can be traced within the family itself. Therefore any similarity that may exist in this regard reflects parallelism or convergence, rather than inheritance from a common ancestry. On the basis of embryological features, Asplund (1972) considers the Typhales well removed from the Pandanales. The cytological similarities between the two orders (both have small chromosomes with a probable base-number of 15) can not outweigh the differences in other respects.

The Typhales are here included in the Commelinidae because of their floral reduction associated with wind-pollination, their paracytic stomates, the presence of vessels in all vegetative organs, their mealy, starch-bearing endosperm, and the bound ferulic acid in their cell walls. All of these features are perfectly fine for the Commelinidae, but collectively they are difficult to reconcile with any other subclass of monocotyledons.

Interpretation of the fossil record of the Typhales is beset by differences of opinion. Some Paleocene pollen is generally considered to represent the order, but its identity as to family is more debatable. Some late

Paleocene fruits are confidently referred to the Sparganiaceae, and both families are represented by pollen and megafossils from the Eocene onwards. Some authors optimistically refer some late Upper Cretaceous fruits to the Typhaceae, and other fruits of similar age to the Sparganiaceae. Other authors doubt the accuracy of the identifications.

SYNOPTICAL ARRANGEMENT OF THE FAMILIES OF TYPHALES

1 Inflorescence of dense, globose heads; perianth of the pistillate flowers of 2–6 small tepals; fruits sessile or nearly so, hydrochorous or endozoochorous ...
....**1. Sparganiaceae.**
1 Inflorescence a dense, elongate, cylindric spike; perianth of the pistillate flowers mostly of numerous capillary bristles; fruits long stipitate, anemochorous ..
....**2. Typhaceae.**

SELECTED REFERENCES

Asplund, I. 1972. Embryological studies in the genus *Typha*. Svensk. Bot. Tidskr. **66:** 1–17.
Lee, D. W. & D. E. Fairbrothers. 1972. Taxonomic placement of the Typhales within the monocotyledons: Preliminary serological investigation. Taxon **21:** 39–44.
Müller-Doblies, D. 1970. Über die Verwandtschaft von *Typha* und *Sparganium* im Infloreszens- und Blütenbau. Bot. Jahrb. Syst. **89:** 451–562.

Subclass IV. Zingiberidae

The subclass Zingiberidae as here defined consists of 2 orders, 9 families, and about 3800 species. The two orders, Bromeliales and Zingiberales, are of nearly equal size in terms of number of species, but the Bromeliales all belong to the single family Bromeliaceae, whereas the Zingiberales are organized into 8 families.

The two orders of Zingiberidae have in the past usually been associated with the orders of the Commelinidae or Liliidae, sometimes the Bromeliales with one group (Commelinidae) and the Zingiberales with the other (Liliidae). They are discordant elements in either group. They resemble the Liliidae (and differ from the Commelinidae) in commonly having septal nectaries and in usually having the vessels confined to the roots. They resemble the Commelinidae (and differ from most Liliidae) in their starchy endosperm with compound starch-grains, and they further differ from typical Liliidae (and resemble the Commelinales) in having the sepals well differentiated from the petals, often green and herbaceous in texture. They differ from both the Liliidae and the Commelinidae in that the number of subsidiary cells around the stomates is usually 4 or more.

The definition of both the Commelinidae and the Liliidae can be considerably sharpened by excluding the Bromeliales and Zingiberales. Although these two orders differ in general appearance and ecological adaptation, they agree in the several features that separate them collectively from the Liliidae and Commelinidae. The inflorescence in characteristic members of the Bromeliales and Zingiberales also has a certain similarity of aspect (relating to the large, showy bracts), and differs from that of most other monocotyledons. Williams and Harborne (1977, under Zingiberales) see a possible association of the Zingiberales and Bromeliales on the basis of the flavonoids. Thus it appears that the purposes of taxonomy are best served by grouping the two orders into a separate subclass.

A putative common ancestor of the Bromeliales and Zingiberales might have been much like some of the more archaic, terrestrial Bromeliaceae, but less xerophytic.

Synoptical Arrangement of the Orders of Zingiberidae

1 Functional stamens 6; flowers regular or sometimes somewhat irregular; xerophytes and epiphytes with narrow, parallel-veined, often firm and spiny-margined leaves, the blade continuous with the sheath, not petiolate; subsidiary cells most commonly 4 .... **1. Bromeliales.**
1 Functional stamens 1 or 5, very rarely 6; flowers more or less strongly irregular; mesophytes (or emergent aquatics), very often growing on the forest floor; leaves with a sheath, petiole, and expanded, entire blade that has a prominent midrib and numerous primary lateral veins in a characteristic pinnate-parallel arrangement; subsidiary cells most commonly more than 4 ....
.... **2. Zingiberales.**

Selected Reference

Cronquist, A. 1978. The Zingiberidae, a new subclass of Liliopsida (Monocotyledons). Brittonia **30:** 505.

1. Order Bromeliales

The order Bromeliales consists of the single family Bromeliaceae, with about 2000 species. The group is wholly American (mainly tropical and subtropical) except for a single species of West Tropical Africa (*Pitcairnia feliciana*).

Terrestrial xerophytic bromeliads such as *Puya* are regarded as the most archaic members of the family. The xerophytic habit may be regarded as a pre-adaptation to the epiphytic habit of most of the species. Smith sees an eventual connection of the Bromeliaceae to the Rapateaceae, with *Navia* (Pitcairnioideae) as the most nearly connecting genus.

It is customary to recognize 3 subfamilies, but some authors recognize

Navia as an additional subfamily. The Bromelioideae have about as many species as the other subfamilies collectively.

1 Ovary superior or seldom half-inferior; fruit a capsule.
  2 Plants mostly terrestrial; seeds mostly winged or with other sorts of ap-
    pendages, but not with a plumose crown (unappendaged in *Navia*); leaves
    entire or often spiny-toothed .... **Pitcairnioideae.**
  2 Plants mostly epiphytic; seeds with a plumose crown of hairs; leaves entire
    .... **Tillandsioideae.**
1 Ovary inferior, or rarely only half-inferior; fruit a berry, or seldom multiple
  and fleshy; seeds without wings or other appendages; leaves mostly spiny-
  toothed; epiphytes or less often terrestrial plants .... **Bromelioideae.**

SELECTED REFERENCES

Benzing, D. H., J. Seemann & A. Renfrow. 1978. The foliar epidermis in Til-
landsioideae (Bromeliaceae) and its role in habitat selection. Amer. J. Bot.
65: 359–365.
Ehler, N. & R. Schill. 1973. Die Pollenmorphologie der Bromeliaceae. Pollen
& Spores **15:** 13–49.
Smith, L. B. & R. J. Downs. 1974, 1977, 1979. Bromeliaceae. Part I. Pitcair-
nioideae. Part 2. Tillandsioideae. Part 3. Bromelioideae. Fl. Neotropica
Monogr. 14, 1974. Monogr. 14, Part 2, 1977. Monogr. 14, Part 3, 1979.
Smith, L. B. & C. E. Wood. 1975. The genera of Bromeliaceae in the southeastern
United States. J. Arnold Arbor. **56:** 375–397.

2. Order Zingiberales

The order Zingiberales is well characterized and sharply defined; its limits have occasioned no controversy. The order is here considered (following Tomlinson, 1962) to consist of 8 families, with a total of about 1800 species. The largest family is the Zingiberaceae, with about 1000 species, followed by the Marantaceae, with about 400. The Strelitziaceae and Heliconiaceae have often been included in the Musaceae, and the Costaceae in the Zingiberaceae, but these segregate families are as distinctive as the families that have traditionally been recognized. One could wish that the families in all orders were as well marked and sharply defined as those in the Zingiberales.

In the Zingiberales the septal nectaries characteristic of so many monocots have been modified to open at the top of the inferior ovary. In the Zingiberaceae the nectaries are further modified to form projections atop the ovary, and their septal evolutionary origin is not immediately evident.

The Zingiberales are almost exclusively tropical. Most members of the order occur in moist forests or in wet open places, but some are adapted to seasonally dry habitats. The broad but fragile leaf-blade of the group may reflect adaptation to a forest habitat, with low light-intensity and little wind.

Leaves that represent the Zingiberales date from the Maestrichtian; some of these Maestrichtian leaves have characters of the Zingiberaceae. Fruits considered to be clearly of the Zingiberaceae date from the Eocene, and fruits believed to represent the Musaceae also date from the Eocene. Here as elsewhere we should keep in mind the possibility of error in assigning fossil organs to modern families. Because of the relatively low level of morphological integration in angiosperms in general, the characters that in combination mark modern families may not always have been associated in the past.

SYNOPTICAL ARRANGEMENT OF THE FAMILIES OF ZINGIBERALES

1 Functional stamens 5 or seldom 6, each with 2 pollen-sacs; plants with raphide-sacs; guard cells symmetrical except in Lowiaceae.
  2 Ovary not prolonged into a hypanthium-like neck; inflorescence with 1–many folded or boat-shaped or spathe-like main bracts, each subtending or enfolding a compact, few-flowered, monochasial cyme; flowers nectariferous, sweet-smelling, adapted to pollination by birds, bats, or insects; some of the tepals often more or less connate.
    3 Flowers perfect; leaves distichous; plants without laticifers, fruit capsular or schizocarpic.
      4 Ovules numerous in each locule; fruit capsular; seeds arillate; median sepal anterior (abaxial) .... **1. Strelitziaceae.**
      4 Ovules solitary in each locule; fruit schizocarpic; seeds not arillate; median sepal posterior (adaxial) .... **2. Heliconiaceae.**
    3 Flowers functionally unisexual; leaves spirally arranged; plants with laticifers; fruit fleshy, indehiscent; seeds not arillate .... **3. Musaceae.**
  2 Ovary conspicuously prolonged into a slender, hypanthium-like neck; inflorescence of irregularly branched axillary cymes, these without specialized subtending bracts; flowers malodorous, presumably adapted to pollination by flies; tepals all distinct .... **4. Lowiaceae.**
1 Functional stamen 1, with 1 or 2 pollen-sacs; plants without raphide-sacs; guard-cells asymmetrical except in most Cannaceae.
  5 Stamen with 2 pollen-sacs, often not strongly petaloid; flowers bilaterally symmetrical; endosperm-development helobial; sepals connate below.
    6 Leaves distichous; sheaths mostly open; plants aromatic, with abundant ethereal oil cells; labellum formed from 2 connate staminodes of the inner staminal cycle; two stamens of the outer cycle often developed as small or petaloid staminodes flanking the fertile stamen or adnate to the labellum; exine much reduced, vestigial ....**5. Zingiberaceae.**
    6 Leaves spirally arranged; sheaths initially closed; plants not aromatic, without ethereal oil cells; labellum formed from 5 connate staminodes (2 from the inner cycle, all 3 of the outer cycle); exine thickened, stratified (unique in the order) .... **6. Costaceae.**
  5 Stamen with a single pollen-sac, the blade strongly petaloid; flowers asymmetrical, endosperm-development nuclear; sepals distinct.
    7 Ovules more or less numerous in each of the 3 locules of the ovary; stem

with mucilage-canals; leaves spirally arranged; embryo straight; seeds
not arillate; flowers not paired . . . .**7. Cannaceae.**
7 Ovule solitary in the single locule or in each of the 3 locules of the ovary;
stem without mucilage-canals; leaves more or less distichous; embryo
usually strongly curved or plicate; seeds mostly arillate; flowers borne
in mirror-image pairs . . . .**8. Marantaceae.**

SELECTED REFERENCES

Andersson, L. 1981. The neotropical genera of Marantaceae. Circumscription
and relationships. Nordic J. Bot. **1:** 218–245.
Grootjen, C. J. 1983. Development of ovule and seed in Marantaceae. Acta Bot.
Neerl. **32:** 69–86.
Hickey, L. J. & R. K. Peterson. 1978. *Zingiberopsis,* a fossil genus of the ginger
family from Late Cretaceous to Early Eocene sediments of western interior
North America. Canad. J. Bot. **56:** 1136–1152.
Kirchoff, B. K. 1983. Floral organogenesis in five genera of the Marantaceae
and in *Canna* (Cannaceae). Amer. J. Bot. **74:** 508–523.
Lane, I. E. 1955. Genera and generic relationships in Musaceae. Mitt. Bot.
Staatssamml. München **2(Heft 13):** 114–131.
Maas, P. J. M. 1972. Costoideae (Zingiberaceae). Fl. Neotropica Monogr. 8.
Mahanty, H. K. 1970. A cytological study of the Zingiberales with special ref-
erence to their taxonomy. Cytologia **35:** 13–49.
Rao, V. S. 1963. The epigynous glands of Zingiberaceae. New Phytologist **62:**
342–349.
Rao, V. S., et al. 1954–1961. The floral anatomy of some Scitamineae. Part I.
J. Indian Bot. Soc. **33:** 118–147, 1954. II, III, IV. J. Univ. Bombay **28**(New
Series): 82–114, 1959; 1–19, 1960. **29**(New Series): 134–150, 1961.
Skvarla, J. J. & J. R. Rowley. 1970. The pollen wall of *Canna* and its similarity
to the germinal apertures of other pollen. Amer. J. Bot. **57:** 519–529.
Stone, D. E., S. C. Sellers & W. J. Kress. 1979 (1980). Ontogeny of exineless
pollen in *Heliconia,* a banana relative. Ann. Missouri Bot. Gard. **66:** 731–
755.
Tomlinson, P. B. 1962. Phylogeny of the Scitamineae—Morphological and an-
atomical considerations. Evolution **16:** 192–213.
Weber, A. 1980. Die Homologie des Perigons der Zingiberaceen. Ein Beitrag
zur Morphologie und Phylogenie des Monokotylen-Perigons. Pl. Syst. Evol.
133: 149–179.
Williams, C. A. & J. B. Harborne. 1977. The leaf flavonoids of the Zingiberales.
Biochem. Syst. Ecol. **5:** 221–229.

Subclass V. Liliidae

The subclass Liliidae as here defined consists of 2 orders, 19 families,
and about 25,000 species. More than four-fifths of the species belong to
only two families, the Orchidaceae and Liliaceae.

The Liliidae characteristically (though not always) have showy flowers, with the tepals all petaloid, and they have intensively exploited insect-pollination. With few exceptions, they have not taken the path of floral reduction, and none of them has a spadix. Although some few Liliidae are arborescent, some have broad, net-veined leaves, and some have vessels throughout the shoot as well as in the root, none of them has coordinated these features into a working system that could present a competitive challenge to woody dicotyledons.

SYNOPTICAL ARRANGEMENT OF THE ORDERS OF LILIIDAE

1 Plants not obviously mycotrophic; seeds of ordinary number and structure, usually with well developed embryo and endosperm; most families and genera with septal nectaries, sometimes with other kinds of nectaries in addition or instead; ovary superior or inferior . . . .**1. Liliales.**
1 Plants strongly mycotrophic, sometimes without chlorophyll; seeds very numerous and tiny, with minute, usually undifferentiated embryo and very little or no endosperm; nectaries diverse, but only seldom septal; ovary inferior . . . . **2. Orchidales.**

1. Order Liliales

The order Liliales as here defined consists of 15 families and nearly 8000 species, of cosmopolitan distribution. About half of the species belong to the single broadly defined family Liliaceae, which is often considered to be the most "typical" family of monocotyledons. The next largest family is the Iridaceae, with about 1500 species. The Agavaceae, Aloaceae, Dioscoreaceae, Smilacaceae, and Velloziaceae are middle-sized families, with 250 to 600 species each. The small families Cyanastraceae, Haemodoraceae, Hanguanaceae, Philydraceae, Pontederiaceae, Stemonaceae, Taccaceae, and Xanthorrhoeaceae have fewer than 250 species collectively.

I take the narrow, parallel-veined leaf to be primitive within the Liliales. Broader, more or less net-veined types have evolved repeatedly, but still show traces of the ancestral condition. Often they have several main veins that arch out from the base and converge toward the tip. It is not difficult to envisage the evolution of this type of venation by increase in the width of the blade, without any increase in the number of main veins. Concomitantly, the connecting cross-veins are elaborated to vasculate the expanded space between the main veins.

I take the primitive type of endosperm in the Liliales to be fleshy or cartilaginous, with food-reserves of protein, oil, and possibly some starch, but not hemicellulose. This type is readily compatible with the endosperm of archaic dicotyledons. Both strongly starchy endosperm and very hard endosperm with reserves of hemicellulose in the thickened cell-walls appear to be advanced features.

Although the Dioscoreaceae and Taccaceae do not appear to be primitive in other respects, they have a more primitive embryo than the other families of the order. The embryo is slipper-shaped or obliquely ovate, the cotyledon is evidently lateral, and the plumule is more or less distinctly terminal. In the other families the embryo is mostly barrel-shaped or ellipsoid to ovoid or cylindric, with a terminal cotyledon and a tiny, lateral, often scarcely distinguishable plumule that may be sunken into a small pocket.

Except possibly for the Hanguanaceae, all the families here referred to the Liliales evidently belong together, but I have not been able to resolve the evidence on their relationships into a coherent phylogenetic scheme. The Haemodoraceae, Pontederiaceae, and Philydraceae have relatively primitive endosperm, but each of these three families is specialized in its own way and cannot be regarded as basal to the order. The Liliaceae are central to most or all of the rest of the group. The Iridaceae, Aloaceae, Agavaceae, and Velloziaceae appear to be derived directly from the Liliaceae. Although the last three of these families are habitally somewhat similar, each probably originated independently of the others. The Xanthorrhoeaceae may have originated from the Agavaceae, or perhaps more directly from the Liliaceae. The Cyanastraceae are linked to the Liliaceae through such genera as *Tecophilaea* and *Cyanella,* which have poricidal anthers resembling those of the Cyanastraceae. The Smilacaceae seem to originate directly from the Liliaceae, but they also resemble the Stemonaceae and Dioscoreaceae. The embryo, the broad, net-veined leaves, and the inferior ovary link the Taccaceae to the Dioscoreaceae, but the endosperm of the Taccaceae lacks the specialized hemicellulose reserves that characterize the Dioscoreaceae and most other families of Liliales. The Hanguanaceae may be related to the Xanthorrhoeaceae, or they may be misplaced in the Liliales.

The delimitation of the family Liliaceae is much disputed. In the traditional Englerian system most of the lilioid monocots with a superior ovary were put into the Liliaceae, and those with an inferior ovary into the Amaryllidaceae. All hands now agree, however, that a cleavage on this basis is unnatural, since the genera with an inferior ovary properly belong in several groups that relate separately to the ancestral group with a superior ovary.

There is enough diversity within the traditional Liliaceae + Amaryllidaceae to provide for several families, but the problem is how to go about the dismemberment. The separation of *Smilax* and its allies as a distinct family (or cluster of smaller families) now seems to be generally accepted. Most authors now also accept the Agavaceae, but they are not agreed as to its delimitation. If the Agavaceae are defined cytologically ($x = 5$ large and 25 small chromosomes), then they include about 8 genera of coarse plants with firm, perennial leaves, plus the habitally very different genus *Hosta.* If, on the other hand, the Agavaceae are defined largely on the basis of habit and chemistry, then the number of genera goes up to about 18, and the chromosome number is more variable but still comprises a few large chromosomes and many small ones. A consistent treatment then requires the recognition of the Aloaceae as another line that has independently undergone the same sort of habital changes as the Agavaceae.

I have chosen to recognize the Agavaceae, Aloaceae, and Smilacaceae as distinct families, and to relegate the remainder of the traditional Liliaceae + Amaryllidaceae to a single rather inchoate family Liliaceae. I would be happy enough to divide this group into several families, if I could find a reasonable way to do it, but I have not found the way. Dahlgren et al. (1985) distribute the Liliaceae sensu meo into 27 families in 4 orders (Melianthales, part of the Liliales, part of the Dioscoreales, and part of the Asparagales) with such minimal differences that I have not been able to comprehend the essential nature of the groups. The 16 differences that they list between the Liliales and Asparagales are so vague and indefinite (e.g., Liliales occasionally with a sarcotesta, Asparagales never with a sarcotesta) that I get no feeling as to which order should receive a particular family. We still await a comprehensive reorganization of the lilies into several families comparable to other recognized families of angiosperms.

Among the most distinctive possible segregates from the Liliaceae as here defined are the Asparagaceae (with much reduced leaves and evident phylloclades), Trilliaceae (with whorled, more or less net-veined leaves and green, herbaceous sepals), Amaryllidaceae and Alstroemeriaceae (both with inferior ovary, said to have been achieved by different routes, and the former group with a distinctive set of alkaloids), and Alliaceae (with superior ovary, amaryllis-like, umbelloid, involucrate inflorescence, *Allium* also with articulated laticifers). Even these groups are not easily definable, however. The small genus *Scoliopus* (2 spp.) is included in the Trilliaceae (order Dioscoreales) by Dahlgren et al. (1985), but said by them to have "obvious affinities to *Medeola* and other Liliaceae s. str. in the order Liliales." Takhtajan (1986), in contrast, includes *Scoliopus* in another lilioid family, the Uvulariaceae. Similar problems beset the definition of the other segregate families.

The fossil record as presently interpreted does not clearly establish either the time of origin of the Liliales or the nature of the connection to other monocots. Muller (1981) considers that fossil pollen of the Liliales makes its first certain appearance in the Eocene, but concedes that some Maestrichtian pollen may also belong here. Some Upper Cretaceous leaves are thought to represent either the Smilacaceae or the Dioscoreaceae.

SYNOPTICAL ARRANGEMENT OF THE FAMILIES OF LILIALES

1 Food reserves of the seed consisting mainly or wholly of starch, sometimes with lesser amounts of protein, oil, and hemicellulose; endosperm never very hard; stomates most commonly paracytic, sometimes tetracytic or anomocytic; herbs.
  2 Stamen solitary; staminodes none; tepals apparently 4 and distinct; flowers without septal nectaries; principal leaves with an ensiform or subulate, unifacial blade . . . . **1. Philydraceae.**

2 Stamens (including staminodes) at least 3, more often 6; tepals usually 6 (very rarely 4), distinct or often connate below to form a perianth-tube; flowers mostly with septal nectaries.

   3 Seeds with endosperm, not chalazosperm; plants usually with raphides; anthers usually opening by longitudinal slits, seldom by terminal pores; fruit with (1–) several or many seeds.

      4 Aquatic or semi-aquatic plants; leaves mostly with a distinct (sometimes inflated) petiole and an expanded, bifacial blade with curved-convergent main veins and evident cross-veins; inflorescence glabrous, or at least not conspicuously long-hairy; vessels confined to the roots .... **2. Pontederiaceae.**

      4 Terrestrial geophytes; leaves mostly linear and parallel-veined, with an equitant, unifacial blade; inflorescence usually conspicuously long-hairy, seldom glabrous; vessels present in all vegetative organs ... . **3. Haemodoraceae.**

   3 Seeds with chalazosperm, not endosperm; plant without raphides; anthers opening by terminal pores or short slits; fruit mostly 1-seeded; leaves with an expanded, bifacial blade, curved-convergent main veins, and evident cross-veins .... **4. Cyanastraceae.**

1 Food reserves of the seed consisting mainly or wholly of protein, oil, and usually also hemicellulose (the latter in the thickened cell-walls), only occasionally with a significant amount of starch; endosperm typically very hard; stomates most commonly anomocytic, but sometimes paracytic or tetracytic; herbs, woody or herbaceous vines, shrubs, or even trees.

   5 Leaves mostly narrow, parallel-veined, and without a distinct petiole, the blade sessile or with a basal sheath, sometimes broader and even net-veined (as in *Trillium*), but only seldom (as in *Hosta*) with a broad, net-veined blade on a distinct petiole.

      6 Habit mostly lilioid, i.e., the plants geophytes with soft, annual (rarely perennial) leaves, the stem herbaceous or nearly so and usually without secondary growth; only seldom approaching the next group in habit.

         7 Stamens mostly as many as the tepals (typically 6), seldom more numerous or only 3; ovary superior or less often inferior; plants very often with raphides in some of the cells .... **5. Liliaceae.**

         7 Stamens 3, opposite the outer tepals; ovary inferior except in the monotypic Tasmanian genus *Isophysis*; plants commonly with prismatic crystals of calcium oxalate in some of the cells, but without raphides .... **6. Iridaceae.**

      6 Habit agavoid or yuccoid, i.e., the plants coarse, often shrubby or arborescent xerophytes, with firm or succulent, mostly perennial leaves, the stem very often with secondary growth.

         8 Plants without secondary growth, and without raphides; lower part of the stem covered by persistent adventitious roots; ovary inferior ... . **7. Velloziaceae.**

         8 Plants generally with secondary growth (not in *Kniphofia,* of the Aloaceae) and with raphides; aerial stem without persistent adventitious roots; ovary superior except in many Agavaceae.

            9 Perianth evidently corolloid, often showy.

               10 Ovules orthotropous to sometimes hemitropous; plants commonly producing anthraquinones but not steroid saponins; vascular bundles of the leaves at least typically with a large cap of wide, thin-walled cells at the phloem pole (the colored

sap, when present, borne in these cells); plants mostly of Africa, Madagascar, and nearby places .... **8. Aloaceae.**

  10 Ovules anatropous to sometimes campylotropous; plants commonly producing steroid saponins but not anthraquinones; vascular bundles of the leaves with a well developed fibrous cap at the phloem pole; plants widespread in warm, dry regions .... **9. Agavaceae.**

  9 Perianth dry and chaffy, usually small, only the inner tepals seldom somewhat petaloid; plants of Australia and some of the islands of the southwestern Pacific .... **10. Xanthorrhoeaceae.**

5 Leaves mostly with a well defined petiole and a broad, more or less netveined blade.

  11 Leaves chiefly or all basal; stem or scape terminating in an inflorescence; flowers without nectar.

    12 Ovary superior; flowers small, unisexual, borne in a large, terminal panicle; perianth more or less chaffy, scarcely corolloid; ovules orthotropous, solitary in each locule; fruit drupaceous; stomates tetracytic .... **11. Hanguanaceae.**

    12 Ovary inferior; flowers larger, perfect, borne in an involucrate cymose umbel; perianth more or less distinctly corolloid; ovules anatropous to campylotropous, more or less numerous; fruit a berry to seldom a capsule; stomates anomocytic .... **12. Taccaceae.**

  11 Leaves chiefly or all cauline; flowers in various sorts of inflorescences, often producing nectar; plants very often climbing.

    13 Flowers dimerous, with 4 tepals, 4 stamens, and 2 carpels united to form a unilocular ovary with basal or apical placentation; vessels mostly confined to the roots .... **13. Stemonaceae.**

    13 Flowers trimerous, with 6 tepals, 6 stamens, and 3 carpels united to form a trilocular (seldom unilocular) ovary with axile (parietal) placentation; vessels usually present in all vegetative organs.

      14 Ovary superior (inferior in the monotypic Australian genus *Petermannia*); plants climbing, herbaceous or slenderly woody vines, or less often erect herbs or branching shrubs, usually with petiolar tendrils (tendrils leaf-opposed in *Petermannia,* wanting in some other genera); rhizome often tuberous, but plants without the characteristic basal "tuber" of the next family; plants without alkaloids; septal nectaries wanting .. .. **14. Smilacaceae.**

      14 Ovary inferior; plants twining-climbing herbaceous vines without tendrils, or sometimes erect herbs; plants commonly with a large basal "tuber" derived from the lowest internodes and/or the hypocotyl; plants often producing alkaloids; both septal and tepalar nectaries commonly present ..... **15. Dioscoreaceae.**

SELECTED REFERENCES

Ayensu, E. S. 1968. Comparative vegetative anatomy of the Stemonaceae (Roxburghiaceae). Bot. Gaz. **129:** 160–165.

Ayensu, E. S. 1972. Vol. 6. Dioscoreales. *In* C. R. Metcalfe (ed.), Anatomy of the monocotyledons. Clarendon Press. Oxford.

Ayensu, E. S. 1974. Leaf anatomy and systematics of New World Velloziaceae. Smithsonian Contr. Bot. **15:** 1–125.

Berg, R. Y. 1962. Contribution to the comparative embryology of the Liliaceae: *Scoliopus, Trillium, Paris,* and *Medeola.* Skr. Norske Vidensk.-Akad. Oslo, Mat.-Naturvidensk. Kl. Ny. Ser. **4:** 1–64.

Blunden, G. & K. Jewers. 1973. The comparative leaf anatomy of *Agave, Beschorneria, Doryanthes* and *Furcraea* species (Agavaceae: Agaveae). J. Linn. Soc., Bot. **66:** 157–179.

Burkill, I. L. 1960. The organography and evolution of Dioscoreaceae, the family of the yams. J. Linn. Soc., Bot. **56:** 319–412.

Buxbaum, F. 1954. Morphologie der Blüte und Frucht von *Alstroemeria* und Anschluss der Alstroemerioideae bei dene echten Liliaceae. Oesterr. Bot. Z. **101:** 337–352.

Cave, M. S. 1964. Cytological observations on some genera of the Agavaceae. Madroño **17:** 163–170.

Chanda, S. & K. Ghash. 1976. Pollen morphology and its evolutionary significance in Xanthorrhoeaceae. Pages 527–559 *in* I. K. Ferguson & J. Muller (eds.), The evolutionary significance of the exine. Linn. Soc. Symp. Ser. No. 1. Academic Press. London & New York.

Cheadle, V. I. 1937. Secondary growth by means of a thickening ring in certain monocotyledons. Bot. Gaz. **98:** 535–555.

Cheadle, V. I. 1968 (1969). Vessels in Haemodorales. Phytomorphology **18:** 412–420.

Cheadle, V. I. 1970. Vessels in Pontederiaceae, Ruscaceae, Smilacaceae and Trilliaceae. Pages 45–50 *in* N. K. B. Robson, D. F. Cutler & M. Gregory (eds.), New research in plant anatomy. J. Linn. Soc., Bot. **63,** Suppl. 1. Academic Press. London & New York.

Cheadle, V. I. & H. Kosakai. 1971 (1972). Vessels in Liliaceae. Phytomorphology **21:** 320–333.

Clausen, R. T. 1940. A review of the Cyanastraceae. Gentes Herb. **4:** 293–304.

Conran, J. G. & H. T. Clifford. 1985. The taxonomic affinities of the genus *Ripogonum.* Nordic J. Bot. **5:** 215–219.

Dahlgren, R. & A. Lu. 1985. *Campynemanthe* (Campynemaceae): Morphology, microsporogenesis, early ovule ontogeny and relationships. Nordic J. Bot. **5:** 321–330.

Daumann, E. 1965. Das Blütennektarium bei den Pontederiaceen und die systematische Stellung dieser Familie. Preslia **37:** 407–412.

Drenth, E. 1972. A revision of the family Taccaceae. Blumea **20:** 367–406.

Eckenwalder, J. E. & S. C. H. Barrett. 1986. Phylogenetic systematics of Pontederiaceae. Syst. Bot. **11:** 373–391.

Fahn, A. 1954. The anatomical structure of the Xanthorrhoaceae Dumort. J. Linn. Soc., Bot. **55:** 158–184.

Goldblatt, P. 1971. Cytological and morphological studies in the southern African Iridaceae. J. S. African Bot. **37:** 317–460.

Goldblatt, P., J. E. Henrich & P. Rudall. 1984. Occurrence of crystals in Iridaceae and allied families and their phylogenetic significance. Ann. Missouri Bot. Gard. **71:** 1013–1020.

Hamann, U. 1966. Embryologische, morphologisch-anatomische und systematische Untersuchungen an Philydraceen. Willdenowia Beih. **4:** 1–178.

Huber, H. 1969. Die Samenmerkmale und Verwandtschaftsverhältnisse der Liliifloren. Mitt. Bot. Staatssamml. München **8:** 219–538.

Kapil, R. N. & K. Walia. 1965. The embryology of *Philydrum lanuginosum* Banks, ex Gaertn. and the systematic position of the Philydraceae. Beitr. Biol. Pflanzen **41:** 381–404.

McKelvey, S. D. & K. Sax. 1933. Taxonomic and cytological relationships of *Yucca* and *Agave*. J. Arnold Arbor. **14:** 76–81.

Menezes, N. L. de. 1980. Evolution in Velloziaceae, with special reference to androecial characters. Linn. Soc. Symp. Ser. **8:** 117–138.

Nietsch, H. 1941. Zur systematische Stellung von *Cyanastrum*. Oesterr. Bot. Z. **90:** 31–52.

Pollard, C. J. 1982. Fructose oligosaccharides in monocotyledons: A possible delimitation of the order Liliales. Biochem. Syst. Ecol. **10:** 245–249.

Rao, V. S. 1969 The vascular anatomy of the flowers of *Tacca pinnatifida*. J. Univ. Bombay **38**(New Series), Part 5B: 18–24.

Rasmussen, H. 1983. Stomatal development in families of Liliales. Bot. Jahrb. Syst. **104:** 261–287.

Rutishauser, R. 1983. *Hydrothrix gardneri*: Bau und Entwicklung einer eigenartigen Pontederiacee. Bot. Jahrb. Syst. **104:** 115–141.

Schlittler, J. 1949. Die systematische Stellung der *Petermannia* F. v. Muell. und ihrer phylogenetische Beziehungen zu den Luzuriagoideae Engl. und den Dioscoreaceae Lindl. Vierteljahrsschr. Naturf. Ges. Zurich 94, Beih. **1:** 1–28.

Schnarf, K. 1948. Der Umfang der Lilioideae in natürlichen System. Oesterr. Bot. Z. **95:** 257–269.

Schulze, W. 1971. Beiträge zur Pollenmorphologie der Iridaceae und ihre Bedeutung für die Taxonomie. Feddes Repert. **82:** 101–124.

Sen, S. 1975. Cytotaxonomy of Liliales. Feddes Repert. **86:** 255–305.

Simpson, M. G. 1983. Pollen ultrastructure of the Haemodoraceae and its taxonomic significance. Grana **22:** 79–103.

Smith, L. B. & E. S. Ayensu. 1974. Classification of Old World Velloziaceae. Kew Bull. **29:** 181–205.

Smith, L. B. & E. S. Ayensu. 1976. A revision of American Velloziaceae. Smithsonian Contr. Bot. **30:** 1–172.

Sterling, C. 1972–1977. Comparative morphology of the carpel in Liliaceae. J. Linn. Soc., Bot. **65:** 163–171, 1972. **66:** 75–82; 213–221, 1972, 1973. **67:** 149–156, 1973. **68:** 115–125, 1974. **70:** 341–349, 1975. **74:** 345–354, 1977.

Stevens, P. F. 1978. Generic limits in the Xeroteae (Liliaceae sensu lato). J. Arnold Arbor. **59:** 129–155.

Swamy, B. G. L. 1964. Observations on the floral morphology and embryology of *Stemona tuberosa* Lour. Phytomorphology **14:** 458–468.

Tomlinson, P. B. & E. S. Ayensu. 1968. Morphology and anatomy of *Croomia pauciflora* (Stemonaceae). J. Arnold Arbor. **49:** 260–275.

Tomlinson, P. B. & E. S. Ayensu. 1969. Notes on the vegetative morphology and anatomy of Petermanniaceae (Monocotyledones). J. Linn. Soc., Bot. **62:** 17–26.

2. Order Orchidales

The order Orchidales as here defined consists of 4 families of very unequal size. The total number of species in the 3 smaller families (less than 150) is much less than the probable error in estimating the number of species of Orchidaceae (15,000 or more).

The Orchidales differ from the Liliales essentially in their strongly mycotrophic habit, and in their very numerous, tiny seeds with a minute, mostly undifferentiated embryo and no endosperm. The reduction of the embryo is at least in part a consequence of mycotrophy; these two features are also associated in other groups of angiosperms. The large number of seeds, their small size, and the lack of endosperm are presumably due to other factors. At least there are many other mycotrophic angiosperms with seeds of ordinary size and a well developed endosperm. The ovary in the Orchidales is always inferior, and only seldom has typical septal nectaries, although the ovarian nectaries of some Burmanniaceae and Orchidaceae may well be derived from septal nectaries.

The combination of mycotrophy and numerous, tiny seeds offers certain evolutionary opportunities as well as imposing some limitations. The plants are physiologically dependent on their fungal symbionts, sometimes even for food, sometimes only for other factors as yet not fully understood, but in any case they can grow only where their fungal symbiont finds suitable conditions. The dust-like seeds of the Orchidaceae are admirably adapted to being carried by the wind and lodging in the bark of trees, and many orchids are epiphytes. The production of many ovules is of course of no value if the ovules do not get fertilized. One way to increase the likelihood of fertilization is to offer special attractants to a limited set of pollinators, and to have the pollen-grains stick together in masses so that many are transported at once. This strategy puts the plants in thrall to their pollinators, but it opens the door to explosive speciation.

Only the Orchidaceae have efficiently exploited the evolutionary opportunities of the order. The floral characters that distinguish the Orchidaceae from their immediate allies clearly reflect progressive specialization for the massive transfer of pollen by specific pollinators.

The Orchidales are evidently derived from the Liliales as here defined. All the characters in which the Orchidales differ from the Liliales represent evolutionary advances, i.e., they are apomorphies. Within the Liliales, only the epigynous segment of the Liliaceae has the characters from which the Orchidaceae, Burmanniaceae, and Corsiaceae might well have arisen. Although the Orchidaceae never have more than 3 stamens, 2 of these are considered to come from the ancestral inner cycle, and one from the outer. Thus a hexandrous ancestry seems likely. The Geosiridaceae (a single achlorophyllous species from Madagascar), with 3 antesepalous stamens, might have arisen through the Iridaceae rather than directly from the Liliaceae (Goldblatt et al., 1987). I have expounded elsewhere the concept that absolute monophylesis is unattainable in a reasonable taxonomic system.

The Orchidales have no significant fossil record. Neither the pollen (with thin or no exine) nor the flowers are well adapted to fossilization, and fossil leaves and stems of orchids might be hard to distinguish from those of various other monocots.

The Orchidaceae consist of 3 well marked subfamilies of very unequal size, sometimes taken as 3 closely related families. The Apostasioideae have only 2 genera and about 20 species. The Cypripedioideae have 4 genera and a little more than a hundred species. All of the remaining genera belong to the Orchidoideae as here defined, but some authors divide the Orchidoideae into several smaller and less well characterized subfamilies such as the Neottioideae, Epidendroideae, and Vandoideae.

SYNOPTICAL ARRANGEMENT OF THE SUBFAMILIES OF THE ORCHIDACEAE

1 Stamens 2 or 3; all 3 stigma-lobes equally developed; no rostellum; pollen-grains in monads, and not aggregated into pollinia.
  2 Perianth only slightly or scarcely irregular, without a saccate lip; placentation axile; style-column short, the free part of the style more elongate; pollen-grains not cohering . . . . **Apostasioideae.**
  2 Perianth strongly irregular, with a deeply saccate lip; placentation parietal; style column more elongate, the free part of the style short; pollen-grains sticky, tending to cohere irregularly . . . . **Cypripedioideae.**
1 Stamen 1; one of the stigma-lobes, or part of it, modified into a rostellum; pollen-grains in tetrads, and aggregated into pollinia; perianth usually strongly irregular; placentation parietal . . . . **Orchidoideae.**

SYNOPTICAL ARRANGEMENT OF THE FAMILIES OF ORCHIDALES

1 Stamens 3 or 6, symmetrically arranged and free from the style; pollen-grains not cohering in pollinia; terrestrial plants, most species with reduced leaves and without chlorophyll.
  2 Flowers regular or only moderately irregular; stamens 3 or 6.
    3 Stamens 3, opposite the sepals . . . . **1. Geosiridaceae.**
    3 Stamens 6, or more often 3 and opposite the petals . . . .
     . . . . **2. Burmanniaceae.**
  2 Flowers highly irregular, the upper sepal large, cordate-ovate, and enclosing the other 5 tepals in bud; stamens 6 . . . . **3. Corsiaceae.**
1 Stamen usually solitary, seldom the stamens 2, or rarely 3, in any case all on the same side of the flower; pollen-grains usually but not always cohering in pollinia; terrestrial or very often epiphytic plants, with or less often without chlorophyll; flowers with few exceptions strongly irregular . . . .
 . . . . **4. Orchidaceae.**

SELECTED REFERENCES

Benzing, D. H. & J. T. Atwood, Jr. 1984. Orchidaceae: Ancestral habitats and current status in forest canopies. Syst. Bot. **9:** 155–165.

Burns-Balogh, P. & P. Bernhardt. 1985. Evolutionary trends in the androecium of the Orchidaceae. Pl. Syst. Evol. **149:** 119–134.

Dodson, C. H. 1962. The importance of pollination in the evolution of the orchids of tropical America. Amer. Orchid Soc. Bull. **31:** 525–534, 641–649, 731–735.

Dressler, R. L. 1961. The structure of the orchid flower. Missouri Bot. Gard. Bull. **49:** 60–69.

Dressler, R. L. & C. H. Dodson. 1960. Classification and phylogeny in the Orchidaceae. Ann. Missouri Bot. Gard. **47:** 25–68.

Garay, L. A. 1960, 1972. On the origin of the Orchidaceae. Bot. Mus. Leafl. **19:** 57–96, 1960. II. J. Arnold Arbor. **53:** 202–215, 1972.

Goldblatt, P., P. Rudall, V. I. Cheadle, L. A. Dorr & C. A. Williams. 1987. Affinities of the Madagascan endemic *Geosiris.* Iridaceae or Geosiridaceae. Bull. Mus. Nat. Hist. Naturelle, sér. 4, section B, Adansonia **9:** 239–248.

Jonker, F. P. 1938. A monograph of the Burmanniaceae. Meded. Bot. Mus. Herb. Rijks Univ. Utrecht **51:** 1–279.

Jonker, F. P. 1939. Les Géosiridacées, une nouvelle famille de Madagascar. Recueil Trav. Bot. Néerl. **36:** 473–479.

Poddubnaya-Arnol'di, V. A. 1967 (1968). Comparative embryology of the Orchidaceae. Phytomorphology **17:** 312–320.

Rao, V. S. 1969. Certain salient features in the floral anatomy of *Burmannia, Gymnosiphon,* and *Thismia.* J. Indian Bot. Soc. **48(1–2):** 22–29.

Rübsamen, T. 1983. Nectaries of the Burmanniaceae (Burmannieae). Acta Bot. Neerl. **32:** 351.

Schmid, R. & M. J. Schmid. 1973. Fossils attributed to the Orchidaceae. Amer. Orchid Soc. Bull. **42:** 17–27.

Vermeulen, P. 1966. The system of the Orchidales. Acta Bot. Neerl. **15:** 224–253.

Williams, N. H. 1979. Subsidiary cells in the Orchidaceae: Their general distribution with special reference to development in the Oncidieae. J. Linn. Soc., Bot. **78:** 41–66.

Withner, C. L. (ed.). 1959. The orchids: A scientific survey. The Ronald Press. New York. (Vol. 32 of Chronica Botanica.)

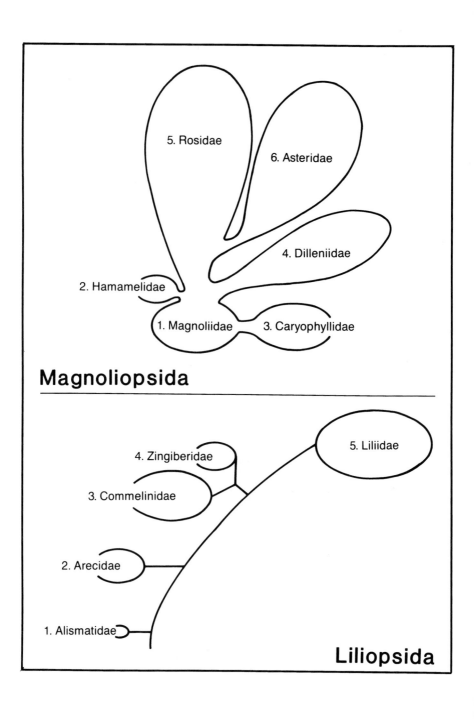

5. Rosidae

6. Asteridae

4. Dilleniidae

2. Hamamelidae

1. Magnoliidae   3. Caryophyllidae

Magnoliopsida

5. Liliidae

4. Zingiberidae

3. Commelinidae

2. Arecidae

1. Alismatidae

Liliopsida

Outline of Classification of *Magnoliophyta*

Class MAGNOLIOPSIDA

Subclass I. Magnoliidae

Order 1. Magnoliales
Family 1. Winteraceae
      2. Degeneriaceae
      3. Himantandraceae
      4. Eupomatiaceae
      5. Austrobaileyaceae
      6. Magnoliaceae
      7. Lactoridaceae
      8. Annonaceae
      9. Myristicaceae
    10. Canellaceae

Order 2. Laurales
Family 1. Amborellaceae
      2. Trimeniaceae
      3. Monimiaceae (Atherospermataceae, Hortoniaceae, Siparunaceae)
      4. Gomortegaceae
      5. Calycanthaceae
      6. Idiospermaceae
      7. Lauraceae (Cassythaceae)
      8. Hernandiaceae (Gyrocarpaceae)

Order 3. Piperales
Family 1. Chloranthaceae
      2. Saururaceae
      3. Piperaceae (Peperomiaceae)

Order 4. Aristolochiales
Family   1. Aristolochiaceae

Order 5. Illiciales
Family   1. Illiciaceae
            2. Schisandraceae

Order 6. Nymphaeales
Family   1. Nelumbonaceae
            2. Nymphaeaceae (Euryalaceae)
            3. Barclayaceae
            4. Cabombaceae
            5. Ceratophyllaceae

Order 7. Ranunculales
Family   1. Ranunculaceae (Glaucidiaceae, Helleboraceae, Hydras-
                tidaceae)
            2. Circaeasteraceae (Kingdoniaceae)
            3. Berberidaceae (Leonticaceae, Nandinaceae, Podophyl-
                laceae)
            4. Sargentodoxaceae
            5. Lardizabalaceae
            6. Menispermaceae
            7. Coriariaceae
            8. Sabiaceae (Meliosmaceae)

Order 8. Papaverales
Family   1. Papaveraceae (Chelidoniaceae, Eschscholziaceae, Platy-
                stemonaceae)
            2. Fumariaceae (Hypecoaceae, Pteridophyllaceae)

Subclass II. Hamamelidae

Order 1. Trochodendrales
Family   1. Tetracentraceae
            2. Trochodendraceae

Order 2. Hamamelidales
Family   1. Cercidiphyllaceae
            2. Eupteleaceae
            3. Platanaceae
            4. Hamamelidaceae (Altingiaceae, Rhodoleiaceae)
            5. Myrothamnaceae

Order 3. Daphniphyllales
Family   1. Daphniphyllaceae

Order 4. Didymelales
Family 1. Didymelaceae

Order 5. Eucommiales
Family 1. Eucommiaceae

Order 6. Urticales
Family 1. Barbeyaceae
      2. Ulmaceae (Celtidaceae)
      3. Cannabaceae
      4. Moraceae
      5. Cecropiaceae
      6. Urticaceae
      * Physenaceae, appended here pro tempore

Order 7. Leitneriales
Family 1. Leitneriaceae

Order 8. Juglandales
Family 1. Rhoipteleaceae
      2. Juglandaceae

Order 9. Myricales
Family 1. Myricaceae

Order 10. Fagales
Family 1. Balanopaceae
      2. Fagaceae
      3. Nothofagaceae
      4. Betulaceae (Carpinaceae, Corylaceae)

Order 11. Casuarinales
Family 1. Casuarinaceae

Subclass III. Caryophyllidae

Order 1. Caryophyllales (Centrospermae)
Family 1. Phytolaccaceae (Agdestidaceae, Barbeuiaceae, Gisekiaceae, Petiveriaceae, Stegnospermaceae)
      2. Achatocarpaceae
      3. Nyctaginaceae
      4. Aizoaceae (Ficoidaceae, Mesembryanthemaceae, Sesuviaceae, Tetragoniaceae)
      5. Didiereaceae
      6. Cactaceae
      7. Chenopodiaceae (Dysphaniaceae, Halophytaceae, Salicorniaceae)

     8. Amaranthaceae
     9. Portulacaceae (Hectorellaceae)
  10. Basellaceae
  11. Molluginaceae
  12. Caryophyllaceae (Alsinaceae, Illecebraceae, Silenaceae)

Order 2. Polygonales
Family 1. Polygonaceae

Order 3. Plumbaginales
Family 1. Plumbaginaceae (Limoniaceae)

Subclass IV. Dilleniidae

Order 1. Dilleniales
Family 1. Dilleniaceae
         2. Paeoniaceae

Order 2. Theales
Family 1. Ochnaceae (Diegodendraceae, Lophiraceae, Luxem-
           burgiaceae, Strasburgeriaceae, Sauvagesiaceae, Wal-
           laceaceae)
         2. Sphaerosepalaceae (Rhopalocarpaceae)
         3. Sarcolaenaceae
         4. Dipterocarpaceae
         5. Caryocaraceae
         6. Theaceae (Asteropeiaceae, Bonnetiaceae, Camelliaceae,
           Sladeniaceae, Ternstroemiaceae)
         7. Actinidiaceae (Saurauiaceae)
         8. Scytopetalaceae (Rhaptopetalaceae)
         9. Pentaphylacaceae
       10. Tetrameristaceae
       11. Pellicieraceae
       12. Oncothecaceae
       13. Marcgraviaceae
       14. Quiinaceae
       15. Elatinaceae
       16. Paracryphiaceae
       17. Medusagynaceae
       18. Clusiaceae (Guttiferae, a permitted alternative name;
           Garciniaceae, Hypericaceae)

Order 3. Malvales
Family 1. Elaeocarpaceae (Aristoteliaceae)
         2. Tiliaceae
         3. Sterculiaceae (Byttneriaceae)

      4. Bombacaceae
      5. Malvaceae

Order 4. Lecythidales
  Family 1. Lecythidaceae (Asteranthaceae, Barringtoniaceae, Foe-tidiaceae, Napoleonaeaceae)

Order 5. Nepenthales
  Family 1. Sarraceniaceae
      2. Nepenthaceae
      3. Droseraceae (Dionaeaceae)

Order 6. Violales
  Family 1. Flacourtiaceae (Berberidopsidaceae, Neumanniaceae, Plagiopteridaceae, Soyauxiaceae)
      2. Peridiscaceae
      3. Bixaceae (Cochlospermaceae)
      4. Cistaceae
      5. Huaceae
      6. Lacistemaceae
      7. Scyphostegiaceae
      8. Stachyuraceae
      9. Violaceae (Leoniaceae)
    10. Tamaricaceae
    11. Frankeniaceae
    12. Dioncophyllaceae
    13. Ancistrocladaceae
    14. Turneraceae
    15. Malesherbiaceae
    16. Passifloraceae
    17. Achariaceae
    18. Caricaceae
    19. Fouquieriaceae
    20. Hoplestigmataceae
    21. Cucurbitaceae
    22. Datiscaceae (Tetramelaceae)
    23. Begoniaceae
    24. Loasaceae (Gronoviaceae)

Order 7. Salicales
  Family 1. Salicaceae

Order 8. Capparales
  Family 1. Tovariaceae
      2. Capparaceae (Cleomaceae, Koeberliniaceae, Pentadi-plandraceae)

        3. Brassicaceae (Cruciferae, a permitted alternative name)
        4. Moringaceae
        5. Resedaceae

Order 9. Batales
Family 1. Gyrostemonaceae
        2. Bataceae

Order 10. Ericales
Family 1. Cyrillaceae
        2. Clethraceae
        3. Grubbiaceae
        4. Empetraceae
        5. Epacridaceae (Prionotaceae, Stypheliaceae)
        6. Ericaceae (Vacciniaceae)
        7. Pyrolaceae
        8. Monotropaceae

Order 11. Diapensiales
Family 1. Diapensiaceae

Order 12. Ebenales
Family 1. Sapotaceae (Achraceae, Boerlagellaceae, Bumeliaceae, Sarcospermataceae)
        2. Ebenaceae
        3. Styracaceae
        4. Lissocarpaceae
        5. Symplocaceae

Order 13. Primulales
Family 1. Theophrastaceae
        2. Myrsinaceae (Aegicerataceae)
        3. Primulaceae (Coridaceae)

Subclass V. Rosidae

Order 1. Rosales
Family 1. Brunelliaceae
        2. Connaraceae
        3. Eucryphiaceae
        4. Cunoniaceae (Baueraceae)
        5. Davidsoniaceae
        6. Dialypetalanthaceae
        7. Pittosporaceae
        8. Byblidaceae (Roridulaceae)
        9. Hydrangeaceae (Kirengeshomaceae, Philadelphaceae, Pottingeriaceae)

10. Columelliaceae
11. Grossulariaceae (Argophyllaceae, Brexiaceae, Carpodetaceae, Dulongiaceae, Escalloniaceae, Iteaceae, Montiniaceae, Phyllonomaceae, Polyosmataceae, Pterostemonaceae, Rousseaceae, Tetracarpaeaceae, Tribelaceae)
12. Greyiaceae
13. Bruniaceae (Berzeliaceae)
14. Anisophylleaceae (Polygonanthaceae)
15. Alseuosmiaceae
16. Crassulaceae
17. Cephalotaceae
18. Saxifragaceae (Eremosynaceae, Francoaceae, Lepuropetalaceae, Parnassiaceae, Penthoraceae, Vahliaceae)
19. Rosaceae (Amygdalaceae, Drupaceae, Malaceae, Pomaceae)
20. Neuradaceae
21. Crossosomataceae
22. Chrysobalanaceae
23. Surianaceae (Stylobasiaceae)
24. Rhabdodendraceae

Order 2. Fabales (Leguminosae, a permitted alternative name at the rank of family)
Family 1. Mimosaceae
        2. Caesalpiniaceae
        3. Fabaceae (Papilionaceae, a permitted alternative name)

Order 3. Proteales
Family 1. Elaeagnaceae
        2. Proteaceae

Order 4. Podostemales
Family 1. Podostemaceae (Tristichaceae)

Order 5. Haloragales
Family 1. Haloragaceae (Myriophyllaceae)
        2. Gunneraceae

Order 6. Myrtales
Family 1. Sonneratiaceae (Duabangaceae)
        2. Lythraceae
        3. Rhynchocalycaceae
        4. Alzateaceae
        5. Penaeaceae
        6. Crypteroniaceae

     7. Thymelaeaceae
     8. Trapaceae
     9. Myrtaceae (Heteropyxidaceae, Kaniaceae, Psiloxylaceae)
   10. Punicaceae
   11. Onagraceae
   12. Oliniaceae
   13. Melastomataceae (Memecylaceae, Mouririaceae)
   14. Combretaceae (Strephonemataceae)

Order 7. Rhizophorales
Family 1. Rhizophoraceae

Order 8. Cornales
Family 1. Alangiaceae
     2. Cornaceae (Aralidiaceae, Aucubaceae, Curtisiaceae, Davidiaceae, Griseliniaceae, Helwingiaceae, Mastixiaceae, Melanophyllaceae, Nyssaceae, Toricelliaceae)
     3. Garryaceae

Order 9. Santalales
Family 1. Medusandraceae
     2. Dipentodontaceae
     3. Olacaceae (Aptandraceae, Cathedraceae, Chaunochitonaceae, Coulaceae, Erythropalaceae, Heisteriaceae, Octoknemaceae, Schoepfiaceae, Scorodocarpaceae, Strombosiaceae, Tetrastylidaceae)
     4. Opiliaceae (Cansjeraceae)
     5. Santalaceae (Anthobolaceae, Canopodaceae, Exocarpaceae, Osyridaceae, Podospermaceae)
     6. Misodendraceae
     7. Loranthaceae
     8. Viscaceae
     9. Eremolepidaceae
   10. Balanophoraceae (Cynomoriaceae, Dactylanthaceae, Sarcophytaceae)

Order 10. Rafflesiales
Family 1. Hydnoraceae
     2. Mitrastemonaceae
     3. Rafflesiaceae (Apodanthaceae, Cytinaceae)

Order 11. Celastrales
Family 1. Geissolomataceae
     2. Celastraceae (Canotiaceae, Chingithamnaceae, Goupiaceae, Lophopyxidaceae, Siphonodontaceae)

   3. Hippocrateaceae
   4. Stackhousiaceae
   5. Salvadoraceae
   6. Tepuianthaceae
   7. Aquifoliaceae (Phellinaceae, Sphenostemonaceae)
   8. Icacinaceae (Phytocrenaceae)
   9. Aextoxicaceae
  10. Cardiopteridaceae
  11. Corynocarpaceae
  12. Dichapetalaceae

Order 12. Euphorbiales
Family 1. Buxaceae (Pachysandraceae, Stylocerataceae)
   2. Simmondsiaceae
   3. Pandaceae
   4. Euphorbiaceae (Androstachydaceae, Hymenocardi-
      aceae, Picrodendraceae, Putranjivaceae, Scepaceae,
      Stilaginaceae, Uapacaceae)

Order 13. Rhamnales
Family 1. Rhamnaceae (Camarandraceae, Frangulaceae, Phylica-
      ceae)
   2. Leeaceae
   3. Vitaceae

Order 14. Linales
Family 1. Erythroxylaceae (Nectaropetalaceae)
   2. Humiriaceae
   3. Ixonanthaceae
   4. Hugoniaceae (Ctenolophonaceae)
   5. Linaceae

Order 15. Polygalales
Family 1. Malpighiaceae
   2. Vochysiaceae
   3. Trigoniaceae
   4. Tremandraceae
   5. Polygalaceae (Diclidantheraceae, Disantheraceae, Em-
      blingiaceae, Moutabeaceae)
   6. Xanthophyllaceae
   7. Krameriaceae

Order 16. Sapindales
Family 1. Staphyleaceae (Tapisciaceae)
   2. Melianthaceae
   3. Bretschneideraceae

 4. Akaniaceae
 5. Sapindaceae (Ptaeroxylaceae)
 6. Hippocastanaceae
 7. Aceraceae
 8. Burseraceae
 9. Anacardiaceae (Blepharocaryaceae, Pistiaceae, Podoaceae)
10. Julianiaceae
11. Simaroubaceae (Irvingiaceae, Kirkiaceae)
12. Cneoraceae
13. Meliaceae (Aitoniaceae)
14. Rutaceae (Flindersiaceae)
15. Zygophyllaceae (Balanitaceae, Nitrariaceae, Peganaceae, Tetradiclidaceae, Tribulaceae)

Order 17. Geraniales
Family 1. Oxalidaceae (Averrhoaceae, Hypseocharitaceae, Lepidobotryaceae)
2. Geraniaceae (Biebersteiniaceae, Dirachmaceae, Ledocarpaceae, Rhynchothecaceae, Vivianiaceae)
3. Limnanthaceae
4. Tropaeolaceae
5. Balsaminaceae

Order 18. Apiales
Family 1. Araliaceae
2. Apiaceae (Umbelliferae, a permitted alternative name; Hydrocotylaceae, Saniculaceae)

Subclass VI. Asteridae

Order 1. Gentianales
Family 1. Loganiaceae (Antoniaceae, Desfontainiaceae, Potaliaceae, Spigeliaceae, Strychnaceae)
2. Gentianaceae
3. Saccifoliaceae
4. Apocynaceae (Plocospermataceae, Plumeriaceae)
5. Asclepiadaceae (Periplocaceae)

Order 2. Solanales
Family 1. Duckeodendraceae
2. Nolanaceae
3. Solanaceae (Goetziaceae, Salpiglossidaceae, Sclerophylacaceae)
4. Convolvulaceae (Dichondraceae, Humbertiaceae)

       5. Cuscutaceae
       6. Retziaceae
       7. Menyanthaceae
       8. Polemoniaceae (Cobaeaceae)
       9. Hydrophyllaceae

Order 3. Lamiales
Family 1. Lennoaceae
       2. Boraginaceae
       3. Verbenaceae (Avicenniaceae, Chloanthaceae, Dicrastylidiaceae, Nyctanthaceae, Phrymaceae, Stilbaceae, Symphoremataceae)
       4. Lamiaceae (Labiatae, a permitted alternative name; Menthaceae, Tetrachondraceae)

Order 4. Callitrichales
Family 1. Hippuridaceae
       2. Callitrichaceae
       3. Hydrostachyaceae

Order 5. Plantaginales
Family 1. Plantaginaceae

Order 6. Scrophulariales
Family 1. Buddlejaceae
       2. Oleaceae (Fraxinaceae, Syringaceae)
       3. Scrophulariaceae (Ellisiophyllaceae, Rhinanthaceae)
       4. Globulariaceae (Selaginaceae)
       5. Myoporaceae (Spielmanniaceae)
       6. Orobanchaceae
       7. Gesneriaceae (Cyrtandraceae)
       8. Acanthaceae (Thunbergiaceae)
       9. Pedaliaceae (Martyniaceae, Trapellaceae)
     10. Bignoniaceae
     11. Mendonciaceae
     12. Lentibulariaceae (Pinguiculaceae, Utriculariaceae)

Order Campanulales
Family 1. Pentaphragmataceae
       2. Sphenocleaceae
       3. Campanulaceae (Cyphiaceae, Cyphocarpaceae, Lobeliaceae, Nemacladaceae)
       4. Stylidiaceae
       5. Donatiaceae
       6. Brunoniaceae
       7. Goodeniaceae

Order 8. Rubiales
Family 1. Rubiaceae (Henriqueziaceae, Naucleaceae)
2. Theligonaceae (Cynocrambaceae)

Order 9. Dipsacales
Family 1. Caprifoliaceae (Carlemanniaceae, Sambucaceae, Vibur-
naceae)
2. Adoxaceae
3. Valerianaceae (Triplostegiaceae)
4. Dipsacaceae (Morinaceae)

Order 10. Calycerales
Family 1. Calyceraceae

Order 11. Asterales
Family 1. Asteraceae (Compositae, a permitted alternative name;
Ambrosiaceae, Carduaceae, Cichoriaceae)

Class LILIOPSIDA

Subclass I. Alismatidae

Order 1. Alismatales
Family 1. Butomaceae
2. Limnocharitaceae
3. Alismataceae

Order 2. Hydrocharitales
Family 1. Hydrocharitaceae (Haplophilaceae, Thalassiaceae)

Order 3. Najadales
Family 1. Aponogetonaceae
2. Scheuchzeriaceae
3. Juncaginaceae (Lilaeaceae, Maundiaceae, Triglochina-
ceae)
4. Potamogetonaceae
5. Ruppiaceae
6. Najadaceae
7. Zannichelliaceae
8. Posidoniaceae
9. Cymodoceaceae
10. Zosteraceae

Order 4. Triuridales
Family 1. Petrosaviaceae
2. Triuridaceae

Subclass II. Arecidae

Order 1. Arecales
Family 1. Arecaceae (Palmae, a permitted alternative name; Ny-
paceae, Phytelephasiaceae)

Order 2. Cyclanthales
Family 1. Cyclanthaceae

Order 3. Pandanales
Family 1. Pandanaceae

Order 4. Arales
Family 1. Acoraceae
2. Araceae
3. Lemnaceae

Subclass III. Commelinidae

Order 1. Commelinales
Family 1. Rapateaceae
2. Xyridaceae (Abolbodaceae)
3. Mayacaceae
4. Commelinaceae (Cartonemataceae)

Order 2. Eriocaulales
Family 1. Eriocaulaceae

Order 3. Restionales
Family 1. Flagellariaceae
2. Joinvilleaceae
3. Restionaceae (Anarthriaceae, Ecdeiocoleaceae)
4. Centrolepidaceae

Order 4. Juncales
Family 1. Juncaceae
2. Thurniaceae

Order 5. Cyperales
Family 1. Cyperaceae (Kobresiaceae)
2. Poaceae (Gramineae, a permitted alternative name; An-
omochloaceae, Bambusaceae, Streptochaetaceae)

Order 6. Hydatellales
Family 1. Hydatellaceae

Order 7. Typhales
Family 1. Sparganiaceae
2. Typhaceae

Subclass IV. Zingiberidae

Order 1. Bromeliales
Family   1. Bromeliaceae (Tillandsiaceae)

Order 2. Zingiberales (Scitamineae)
Family   1. Strelitziaceae
       2. Heliconiaceae
       3. Musaceae
       4. Lowiaceae (Orchidanthaceae)
       5. Zingiberaceae
       6. Costaceae
       7. Cannaceae
       8. Marantaceae

Subclass V. Liliidae

Order 1. Liliales
Family   1. Philydraceae
       2. Pontederiaceae
       3. Haemodoraceae (Conostylidaceae)
       4. Cyanastraceae
       5. Liliaceae (Agapanthaceae, Alliaceae, Alstroemeriaceae, Amaryllidaceae, Aphyllanthaceae, Anthericaceae, Asparagaceae, Asphodelaceae, Aspidistraceae, Asteliaceae, Blandfordiaceae, Calochortaceae, Campynemaceae, Colchicaceae, Convallariaceae, Dianellaceae, Eriospermaceae, Funkiaceae, Hemerocallidaceae, Herreriaceae, Hesperocallidaceae, Hyacinthaceae, Hypoxidaceae, Ixoliriaceae, Medeolaceae, Melanthiaceae, Nartheciaceae, Ruscaceae, Tecophilaeaceae, Uvulariaceae)
       6. Iridaceae (Gladiolaceae, Hewardiaceae, Isophysidaceae, Ixiaceae)
       7. Velloziaceae
       8. Aloaceae
       9. Agavaceae (Doryanthaceae, Dracaenaceae, Nolinaceae, Phormiaceae, Sansevieriaceae)
     10. Xanthorrhoeaceae (Calectasiaceae, Dasypogonaceae)
     11. Hanguanaceae
     12. Taccaceae
     13. Stemonaceae (Croomiaceae, Roxburghiaceae)
     14. Smilacaceae (Lapageriaceae, Luzuriagaceae, Petermanniaceae, Philesiaceae, Rhipogonaceae)

15. Dioscoreaceae (Cladophyllaceae, Stenomeridaceae, Tamaceae, Trichopodaceae)

Order 2. Orchidales

Family 1. Geosiridaceae
2. Burmanniaceae (Tripterellaceae, Thismiaceae)
3. Corsiaceae
4. Orchidaceae (Apostasiaceae, Cypripediaceae, Limodoraceae, Neottiaceae, Thyridiaceae, Vanillaceae)

Glossary

The definitions in the glossary are principally for usage within the angiosperms. Many of the terms also have a broader meaning, or a different meaning in some other group.

a-, ab-   Latin prefix, meaning not, or different from, or away from, or without.

abaxial   On the side away from the axis, or turned away from the axis. (Compare *adaxial.*)

abortive   Hardly or imperfectly developed, usually implying that development begins normally but stops short of normal maturity.

accrescent   Increasing in size with age, as for example a calyx that continues to enlarge after anthesis.

achene   The most generalized type of dry, indehiscent fruit, lacking the specialized features that mark a caryopsis, nut, samara, or utricle.

acotyledonous   Without cotyledons.

acropetal   Near the tip or distal end, as opposed to near the base or proximal end; proceeding from the proximal toward the distal end.

ad-   Latin prefix, meaning to or toward.

adaxial   On the side toward the axis, or turned toward the axis. (Compare *abaxial.*)

adnate   Grown together, or attached; applied only to unlike organs, as stipules adnate to the petiole, or stamens adnate to the corolla. (Compare *connate.*)

adventitious   Originating from mature nonmeristematic tissues, especially if such a development would not ordinarily be expected.

aestivation   The arrangement of flower parts in the bud, especially the position of the petals (or sepals) with respect to each other.

alkaloid   Any of a large, chemically diverse group of nitrogenous, pharmacologically active ring-compounds produced by plants.

alloploid, allopolyploid   A polyploid containing genomes derived from two or more species (Compare *autoploid.*)

ament   A dense, bracteate spike or raceme with a nonfleshy axis bearing many small, naked or apetalous flowers; a catkin.

Amentiferae A group (now considered to be artificial) of dicotyledons characterized by the production of flowers in aments.

amphitropous ovule An ovule with the body half-inverted, so that the funiculus is attached near the middle, and the micropyle points at right angles to the funiculus; hemianatropous.

anatropous ovule An ovule with the body fully inverted, so that the micropyle is basal, adjoining the funiculus.

androecium All of the stamens of a flower, considered collectively.

androgynophore A common stalk, arising from the receptacle, on which both the androecium and the gynoecium are borne.

anemophilous Pollinated by wind.

aneuploid Having a number of chromosomes that is not an exact multiple of a basic haploid number within the group.

angiosperm A member of a group of plants (Magnoliophyta) characterized by having the ovules enclosed in an ovary.

anisomerous With a different number of parts; usually applied to parts of a small and definite number that is less than the number of some other kind of part. E.g., if there are five sepals and five petals, but fewer than five stamens, the stamens are anisomerous.

anomocytic stomate A stomate without differentiated subsidiary cells.

antepetalous In front of (on the same radius as) the petal(s).

antesepalous In front of (on the same radius as) the sepal(s).

anther The part of a stamen that bears the pollen, consisting of one or usually two pollen sacs and a connecting layer between them.

anthesis The period during which a flower is fully expanded and functional, ready to shed or receive pollen.

anthocyanin A chemical class of flavonoid pigments, ranging in color from blue or violet to purple or red, often found in the central vacuole of a cell, especially in petals.

anthoxanthin A group of flavonoid pigments closely allied to anthocyanin, but ranging in color from yellow to orange or orange-red, differing chemically from the anthocyanins primarily in that the heterocyclic ring is more oxidized.

aperturate Having one or more apertures or openings; as applied to pollen-grains, having one or more thin spots in the wall or gaps in the exine.

apetalous Without petals.

apocarpous With the carpels separate from each other (or with only one carpel).

apomixis The setting of seed without fertilization.

apomorphy An advanced character or state, as contrasted to the ancestral plesiomorphy (more primitive character or state). (Compare *plesiomorphy*.)

apotropous ovule An ovule which (if erect) has the raphe ventral (between the partition and the body of the ovule, or which (if pendulous) has the raphe dorsal. (Compare *epitropous*).

appendiculate Having one or more appendages.

archaic Having a relatively large proportion of primitive characters.

archegonium A specialized structure, composed of more than one cell, within which an egg is produced.

aril A specialized, usually fleshy outgrowth from the funiculus that covers or is attached to the mature seed; more loosely, any appendage or fleshy thickening of the seed-coat.

autoploid, autopolyploid   A polyploid in which all the chromosomes are derived from a single species, typically by simple duplication of entire genomes. (Compare *alloploid*.)

autotrophic   Nutritionally independent, making its own food from raw materials obtained more or less directly from the substrate; usually interpreted to include mycorhizal as well as nonmycorhizal plants, so long as they are photosynthetic.

axile placenta   A placenta along the central axis (or along the vertical midline of the septum) of an ovary with two or more locules.

Bauplan (a word borrowed from German)   Ground-plan, or fundamental structural organization.

berry   The most generalized type of fleshy fruit, derived from a single ovary, and with the pericarp wholly fleshy.

betacyanin   A chemical class of nitrogenous, water-soluble pigments, ranging in color from blue or violet to purple or red, found in the central vacuole of a cell, especially in petals, in some kinds of plants.

betalain   A chemical class of nitrogenous, water-soluble pigments, consisting of betacyanins and betaxanthins.

betaxanthin   A chemical class of pigments closely allied to betacyanins, but ranging in color from yellow or orange to orange-red.

bisporangiate strobilus   A strobilus with both micro- and megasporangia.

bisporic embryo-sac   An embryo-sac derived from two megaspores.

bitegmic ovule   An ovule with two integuments.

bract   Any more or less reduced or modified leaf associated with a flower or an inflorescence, but not part of the flower itself.

calyptra   A cap with a closed top, usually deciduous as a unit from the circumscissile base.

calyx   All of the sepals of a flower collectively.

campylotropous ovule   An ovule with the body distorted by unequal growth, so that the micropyle and the adjacent funiculus appear to lie along one side of the ovule instead of at the base.

capsule   A dry, dehiscent fruit composed of more than one carpel.

carpel   The fertile leaf (megasporophyll) of an angiosperm, which bears the ovules.

carpophore   The part of the receptacle that in some kinds of flowers is prolonged between the carpels as a central axis.

caruncle   An excrescence near the hilum of some seeds; a sort of aril.

caryopsis   The fruit of a member of the grass family, typically dry, indehiscent, and with the seed-coat of the single seed adnate to the pericarp.

catkin   An ament.

cellular endosperm   Endosperm in which the formation of partitions (cell walls) follows immediately after mitosis, even in the earliest ontogeny, so that there is no initial free-nuclear endosperm. (Compare *nuclear endosperm*.)

chalaza   The part of the ovule or seed that lies at the opposite end from the micropyle, in line with the antipodal end of the embryo-sac.

clade Any individual evolutionary lineage, from beginning to end.

cladism A taxonomic approach that emphasizes clade at the expense of grade.

cladogram An evolutionary diagram showing sequential branch-points in the putative history of a group; a sort of phylogenetic tree. (See *dendrogram, phenogram.*)

cleistogamous flower A self-pollinating flower that remains closed, never opening.

colleter A mucilage-secreting stout trichome found on stipules or bud-leaves of some angiosperms.

colpate pollen-grain A pollen-grain with one or more furrows in the exine, through which germination can take place.

colporate pollen-grain A colpate pollen-grain that also has a pore or thinner spot in the colpus, associated with germination.

compound ovary or pistil An ovary or pistil composed of more than one carpel.

condensed tannins Tannins that are not hydrolyzable with acid.

connate Grown together or attached; applied only to like organs, as filaments connate into a tube, or leaves connate around the stem. (Compare *adnate.*)

connective The tissue that connects the pollen-sacs of an anther.

contorted (aestivation) Same as convolute.

convolute (aestivation) Arranged so that one edge of each petal (or sepal) is covered, and the other exposed.

corolla All of the petals of a flower collectively.

corona A set of petal-like structures or appendages between the corolla and the androecium, derived by modification of the corolla or of the androecium.

cotyledon A leaf of the embryo of a seed.

crassinucellar, crassinucellate With the nucellus several cells thick, at least at the micropylar end.

cultivar A horticultural variant, either selected from the wild, or produced in cultivation.

cyanogenic Producing cyanide, or capable of doing so under proper conditions.

cyme A broad class of inflorescences characterized by having the terminal flower bloom first, commonly also with the terminal flower of each branch blooming before the others on that branch.

decussate Arranged oppositely, with each pair set at right angles to the pair above and the pair below.

dehiscent Opening at maturity, releasing or exposing the contents.

deliquescent With the central axis melting away irregularly into a series of smaller branches.

dendrogram A phyletic or phenetic representation, typically showing successive dichotomies, of the putative evolutionary history or degrees of similarity and difference within a group. (See *cladogram, phenogram.*)

determinate inflorescence An inflorescence in which the terminal flower blooms first; a cyme. (Compare *indeterminate inflorescence.*)

dichasium A triad of flowers, the central one blooming before the opposite or subopposite lateral ones.

dichotomous Forking more or less regularly into two branches of about equal size.

dioecious   Producing male and female flowers on separate individuals.

diplostemonous   With two cycles of stamens.

disk (of a flower)   An outgrowth from the receptacle, surrounding the base of the ovary; often derived by reduction and modification of the innermost set of stamens.

distichous   Arranged in two opposite, vertical or longitudinal rows, as the leaves of an iris.

distinct (as applied to plant organs)   Not connate with similar organs. (Compare *free.*)

dithecal   Having or composed of two thecae.

division (in taxonomy)   The highest compulsory rank in the taxonomic hierarchy for plants.

drupaceous   Of the nature of a drupe.

drupe   A fleshy fruit with a firm endocarp that permanently encloses the usually solitary seed, or with separate portions of the endocarp enclosing each of two or more seeds.

dyad   A set or group of two.

ecotype   An infraspecific population genetically adapted to a particular habitat or set of similar habitats.

embryo-sac   The female gametophyte of an angiosperm, within which the embryo begins to develop.

encyclocytic stomate   A stomate surrounded by a narrow ring of 4 or more subsidiary cells.

endosperm   The food storage tissue of a seed that is derived from the triple fusion nucleus of the embryo-sac.

entomophagus   Insect-eating; insectivorous.

entomophilous   Pollinated by insects.

epigynous   With the perianth and stamens attached at the top of the ovary, rather than beneath it, i.e., with the ovary inferior.

epipetalous   Attached to the petals or corolla.

epiphyte   A plant without connection to the soil, growing attached to another plant but not deriving its food or water from it.

epitropous ovule   An ovule which (if erect) has the raphe dorsal, or which (if pendulous) has the raphe ventral (between the partition or axis and the body of the ovule). (Compare *apotropous ovule.*)

eukaryotic   With a vesicular nucleus and a set of differentiated cytoplasmic organelles. (Compare *prokaryotic.*)

exarillate   Without an aril.

exine   The outer wall of a pollen-grain, composed of carotenoid polymers called sporopollenin.

exomorphic   Pertaining to external form.

exstipulate   Without stipules.

extrastaminal   Outside of (as opposed to within) the androecium.

extrorse   Turned outward.

family   One of the necessary ranks (above the genus and below the order) in the taxonomic hierarchy for plants.

flavonoid   A class of chemical compounds consisting essentially of two simple or modified benzene rings that share one side in common.

follicetum   A group of lightly cohering follicles, or a whorl of follicles.

follicle   A fruit, derived from a single carpel, which dehisces along the seed-bearing suture at maturity.

free (as applied to plant organs)   Not attached to another kind of organ, as stamens free from the corolla. (See *distinct*.)

free-central placenta   A placenta consisting of a free-standing column or projection from the base of a compound, unilocular ovary.

free-nuclear   With scattered nuclei that are not separated by partitions or cell walls.

funiculus   The stalk of an ovule.

gametophyte   The generation that has *n* chromosomes and produces gametes as reproductive bodies. In angiosperms the female gametophyte is the embryo-sac and the male gametophyte is the pollen-grain.

gamophyllous   With the leaves (or segments) connate.

gamopetalous   With the petals connate, at least toward the base; sympetalous.

gamosepalous   With the sepals connate, at least toward the base; synsepalous.

genus   The next compulsory rank above the species in the taxonomic hierarchy.

gymnosperm   A member of a group of plants characterized by having ovules that are not enclosed in an ovary.

gynobasic style   A style that is attached directly to the receptacle as well as to the base of the carpel(s).

gynoecium   All of the carpels of a flower, collectively.

gynophore   A central stalk in some flowers, bearing the gynoecium.

halophyte   A plant adapted to growth in salty soil.

haplostemonous   With a single cycle of stamens.

helobial endosperm   Endosperm in which the first division of the triple fusion nucleus is followed by the formation of a partition, after which one chamber develops along the nuclear pattern, and the other along the cellular pattern.

heterochrony   A change in the timing or sequence of certain ontogenetic processes as compared to others.

heterostyly   A condition in which some individuals of a population have a relatively long style and short stamens, and others have a relatively short style and long stamens.

heterotrophic   Parasitic or saprobic, as opposed to autotrophic.

hydrolyzable tannins   Tannins that are hydrolyzable with acid.

hydrophyte   A plant adapted to life in the water.

hypanthium   A ring or cup around the ovary, formed either by marginal expansion of the receptacle or by the union of the lower parts of the calyx, corolla, and androecium; when the petals and stamens appear to arise from the calyx-tube, that part of the apparent calyx-tube which is below the attachment of the petals is the hypanthium.

hypogynous   With the perianth and stamens attached directly to the receptacle; more generally, beneath the gynoecium.

idioblast   An individual cell that is markedly different from those surrounding it, without being an essential part of an obviously integrated, functioning system.

imbricate   Arranged in a tight spiral, so that the outermost member has both edges exposed, and at least the innermost member has both edges covered; more loosely, a shingled arrangement.

inaperturate   Without apertures.

indeterminate inflorescence   An inflorescence that blooms from the base upwards, so that theoretically it could continue to elongate indefinitely. (Compare *determinate inflorescence.*)

indusium   A more or less cupulate outgrowth from the style, below the stigmas.

inferior ovary   An ovary with the other floral parts (calyx, corolla, and androecium) attached to its summit; an epigynous flower has an inferior ovary.

integument   One of the one or two layers that partly enclose the nucellus of the ovule; the forerunner of the seed coat.

intercalary meristem   A meristem, separated from the apical meristem, that produces primary tissues; e.g., the meristem at the base of the leaf-blade in grasses.

internal phloem   Primary phloem that lies between the primary xylem and the pith; intraxylary phloem.

intrastaminal   Within (as opposed to outside of) the androecium.

introgression   The leakage or flow of genes from one species to another through hybridization and back-crossing.

introrse   Directed or turned inward.

involucel   Diminutive of involucre; an involucre of the second order.

involucre   Any structure that surrounds the base of another structure; in angiosperms usually applied to a set of bracts beneath an inflorescence.

irregular flower   A flower in which the petals (or less often the sepals) are dissimilar in form or orientation.

isomerous   With the same number of parts as something else; a flower that has isomerous stamens has the same number of stamens as sepals or petals.

jaculator   A modified funiculus that expels the seeds in the Acanthaceae.

karyotype   All of the chromosomes of a nucleus, with reference to relative size and shape as well as number.

laminar   Thin and flat, as in a leaf-blade.

laminar placentation   An arrangement of the ovules on the ventral surface (rather than the margins) of the carpel.

laterocytic stomate   A stomate flanked by three or more subsidiary cells all bordering on the lateral sides of the guard-cell pair; the anticlinal walls separating adjacent subsidiary cells radiate from the guard-cell pair.

latex   A colorless to more often white, yellow, or reddish liquid, produced by some plants, characterized by the presence of colloidal particles of terpenes dispersed in water.

laticifer   A tube containing latex.

legume   The fruit of a member of the Fabales, composed of a single carpel, typically dry, several-seeded, and dehiscing down both sutures.

liana A climbing, woody vine.

lignin A high polymer of several compounds derived from phenyl propane; an essential strengthening component of the walls of many cells, especially xylem.

locule A seed-cavity (chamber) in an ovary or fruit; a compartment in any container.

loculicidal Dehiscing along the midrib or outer median line of each locule, i.e., "through" the locules.

lycopsid A member of a group of plants characterized by alternate or opposite microphylls and axillary sporangia.

lysigenous Originating by dissolution or degeneration of cells or tissue.

manoxylic wood Wood with multiseriate, very high rays, a relatively high proportion of parenchyma, and relatively large tracheids with either circular-bordered or more often scalariform-bordered pits.

marginal placenta A placenta along the suture of the ovary of a simple pistil. (Compare *parietal placenta.*)

megaphyll A leaf of the type associated with leaf gaps in the stele, typically with a branching vein system; opposite of microphyll.

megaphyte A thick-stemmed, simple or sparingly branched, soft shrub that is anatomically much like an herb.

megasporangium A sporangium that produces megaspores.

megaspore A spore that may develop into a female gametophyte.

megasporophyll A sporophyll that bears one or more megasporangia.

mericarp An individual carpel of a schizocarp.

mesophyte A plant adapted to an ordinary amount of water stress; intermediate between hydrophyte and xerophyte.

microphyll A leaf, usually small, with an unbranched midvein whose departure from the stele does not leave a gap; opposite of megaphyll.

micropyle The opening through the integument(s) of an ovule to the nucellus.

microsporangium A sporangium that produces microspores.

microspore A spore that develops into a male gametophyte.

microsporophyll A sporophyll that bears one or more microsporangia.

mixed panicle A branching inflorescence, panicle-like in form, but with a mixed determinate and indeterminate sequence of flowering.

monad One of many individuals that are free from each other rather than attached in groups.

monadelphous stamens Stamens with the filaments connate.

monadinous Borne in monads. (Compare *tetradinous.*)

monocarpic Blooming only once and then dying; usually applied to certain perennials, such as the century plant, but technically applicable to annuals and biennials as well.

monochasium A pair of flowers, one terminal and one lateral, the terminal one blooming first; like a dichasium but lacking one of the lateral flowers.

monochlamydeous With a single series of tepals.

monoecious With unisexual flowers, both types borne on the same individual.

monophyletic With a unified evolutionary ancestry.

monopodial With the branches or appendages arising from a simple axis. (Compare *sympodial.*)

monosporic   Derived from a single spore.

monosulcate pollen-grain   A pollen grain with a single sulcus (furrow) through which germination can occur.

monothecal   Having or composed of a single theca.

multilacunar node   A node with more than three gaps.

mycorhiza   A symbiotic association of a fungus and the root of a vascular plant; by extension, other symbiotic associations of fungi with higher plants.

mycotrophic   Evidently modified as a result of mycorhizal association; dependent on mycorhizal association.

myrosin   An enzyme involved in the formation of mustard oil.

nectary   A structure that produces nectar, usually but not always in association with a flower.

neoteny   A type of heterochrony in which a plant attains sexual maturity while remaining permanently juvenile in some vegetative features; more loosely, any sort of heterochrony.

node   A place on a stem where a leaf is (or has been) attached.

nucellus   The megasporangial wall of a seed plant, which typically encloses the female gametophyte.

nuclear endosperm   Endosperm that has a free-nuclear stage in early ontogeny, the formation of partitions being delayed until several or many mitotic divisions have occurred. (Compare *cellular endosperm*.)

nut   A relatively large, dry, indehiscent fruit with a hard wall, usually containing only one seed.

obturator   A swelling of the ovary wall or placenta which grows towards the micropyle of an ovule, often fitting like a hood over the nucellus, facilitating growth of the pollen tube into the ovule.

oligomerous   With few parts of a kind.

ontogeny   The developmental history of an individual.

order   One of the required ranks in the taxonomic hierarchy, next above family and below class.

ornithophilous   Pollinated by birds.

orthotropous ovule   A straight (unbent) ovule with the funiculus at one end and the micropyle at the other.

outgroup   In cladistic procedure, a group used for comparison with the group under study, in an effort to establish polarity of characters; an outgroup should be the sister group or a close ally of the group under study.

paedomorphosis   A type of heterochrony in which certain structures remain permanently juvenile (or display ancestral characteristics).

panicle   A branching indeterminate inflorescence, usually broadest near the base and tapering upwards. The term is often loosely applied also to mixed panicles, q.v.

paracytic stomate   A stomate accompanied on each side by one (or more) subsidiary cells parallel to the long axis of the guard cells.

paraphyletic   A subset of monophyletic, in which a group is defined so as to exclude some of its descendants.

parietal placenta A placenta along the walls or on the intruded partial partitions of a compound, unilocular ovary. (See *marginal placenta.*)

parsimony Minimal complexity in proividing an explanation or interpretation of a set of data.

peltate Attached by a portion of the surface (typically the center) instead of by the margin.

pentalacunar node A node with five gaps.

pentamerous With five parts of a kind.

perfect flower A flower with both an androecium and a gynoecium.

perianth All of the sepals and petals (or tepals) of a flower, collectively.

pericarp The matured ovary wall of a fruit.

perigynous Having the perianth and stamens united into or borne on a basal saucer or cup (the hypanthium) distinct from the ovary; more generally, around the base of the gynoecium, as a perigynous disk.

perisperm Food storage tissue in the seed, derived from the nucellus.

petal A member of the second set of floral leaves (i.e., the set just internal to the sepals), usually colored or white and serving to attract pollinators.

phenetic Pertaining to the expressed characteristics of an individual, without regard to its genetic nature.

phenogram A dendrogram designed to show phenetic clustering, without regard to possible phylogeny. (See *cladogram, dendrogram.*)

phylad A natural group, of whatever rank, considered from the standpoint of its evolutionary history or prospects; a clade or evolutionary line.

phyllosporous With the ovules borne on specialized or modified leaves, rather than on the ends of telomes.

phylogeny The evolutionary history of a group.

pillar complex A group of related populations or taxa in which the morphologic differences among the diploids are obscured by continuity among the derived polyploids. The metaphorical reference is to diploid pillars supporting a polyploid roof.

pistil The female organ of a flower, composed of one or more carpels, and ordinarily differentiated into ovary, style, and stigma.

placenta The tissue of the ovary to which the ovules are attached.

pleiomerous With several or many parts of a kind.

plesiomorphy A primitive character or state, as compared to the derived apomorphy.

plurilocular Having more than one locule.

polarity The direction of evolutionary change in a particular feature.

pollen The mass of young male gametophytes (pollen-grains) of a seed plant, at the stage when they are released from the anther or microsporangium.

pollinium A coherent cluster of many pollen-grains, transported as a unit during pollination.

polyandrous Having many stamens.

polycarpellate Having many carpels.

polypetalous With the petals separate from each other.

polyphyletic Of more than one evolutionary origin.

polyploid Having three or more sets of chromosomes.

polystemonous With many stamens.

poricidal   Opening by pores.

prokaryotic   Without a vesicular nucleus and without the cytoplasmic organelles that characterize the eukaryotes. (See *eukaryotic*.)

proterandrous (or protandrous) flower   A flower in which the pollen is shed before the stigma is receptive.

proterogynous (or protogynous) flower   A flower in which the stigma is receptive only before the pollen is shed.

pseudanthium   A cluster of small or reduced flowers, collectively simulating a single flower.

pseudomonomerous ovary   An ovary seemingly composed of a single carpel, but phyletically derived from a compound ovary.

pteridosperm   A seed fern; a member of the class Lyginopteridopsida.

pteropsid   A member of a group of vascular plants characterized by having megaphylls and leaf gaps.

pycnoxylic wood   Wood with narrow rays and small tracheids with circular bordered pits.

quincuncial   Consisting of five members in a 2/5 phyllotaxy, so that two members have both margins exposed, two have both margins covered, and one has one margin exposed and the other covered.

raceme   An inflorescence with pedicellate flowers arising in acropetal sequence from an unbranched central axis.

racemose   Pertaining to a broad class of inflorescences characterized by flowering in acropetal sequence.

rachis   A main axis, such as that of a compound leaf.

raphe   The part of the funiculus that is permanently adnate to the integument of the ovule, commonly visible as a line or ridge on the mature seed coat.

raphide   A needle-shaped crystal; raphides occur in certain cells of some kinds of plants.

receptacle   The end of the stem, to which the other flower parts are attached.

replum   A frame-like placenta that persists after the sides (valves) of the fruit have fallen, as in the Brassicaceae and Capparaceae.

rudimentary   Poorly developed, in a phyletically nascent state, without any history of better development. (Compare *vestigial*.)

ruminate   Irregularly ridged and sulcate, looking as though chewed.

samara   An indehiscent, winged fruit.

sarcotesta   A thickened, fleshy seed-coat.

scalariform   Ladderlike, with cross-bars connecting vertical members; a scalariform vessel has the secondary wall in a ladderlike pattern.

schizocarp   A fruit that splits into separate carpels at maturity.

schizogenous   Originating by splitting or separation of tissue.

sclerophyll   A firm leaf, with a relatively large amount of strengthening tissue, which retains its firmness (and often also its shape) even when physiologically wilted.

secondary metabolite   A metabolically produced substance that has no essential metabolic function.

sepal   A member of the outermost set of floral leaves, typically green or greenish and more or less leafy in texture.

septicidal   Splitting through the septa, so that the carpels are separated.

septum   A partition; in an ovary, a partition formed by the connate walls of adjacent carpels.

sieve-tube   A phloem-tube formed from several sieve-elements set end to end.

sister groups   Taxa or clades that share an extinct common ancestor not shared by any other taxon or clade.

spadix   A spike with small, crowded flowers on a thickened, fleshy axis.

spathe   A large, usually solitary bract subtending and often enclosing an inflorescence; the term is used only in the monocotyledons.

species   The smallest groups that are consistently and persistently distinct, and distinguishable by ordinary means.

sphenopsid   A member of a group of vascular plants characterized by whorled leaves and terminal strobili.

sporophyll   A leaf (often more or less modified) that bears one or more sporangia.

stachyosporous   With the ovules borne terminally on telomes, rather than on specialized or modified leaves.

stamen   The microsporophyll of an angiosperm.

staminode   A modified, infertile stamen.

stele   The primary vascular structure of a stem or root, together with any other tissues (such as the pith) that may be enclosed.

stigma   The part of the pistil that is receptive to pollen.

stipule   One of a pair of basal appendages found on or in association with many leaves.

strobilus   A cluster of sporophylls arranged along an axis; a cone.

subsidiary cells (of the stomatal apparatus)   The modified epidermal cells immediately adjoining the guard cells.

subspecies   A major infraspecific taxon; often a group of varieties.

succulent   A plant that accumulates reserves of water in the fleshy stems or leaves, due largely to the high proportion of hydrophilic colloids in the cell sap.

superior ovary   An ovary that is attached to the receptacle above the level of attachment of the other flower parts.

Sympetalae   A group (now considered to be artificial) of dicotyledons characterized by having the petals connate at least toward the base.

sympetalous   With the petals connate, at least toward the base.

sympodial   With the apparent main axis consisting of a series of usually short axillary branches. (See *monopodial*.)

synapomorphy   An apomorphy shared by two or more species through a common inheritance.

syncarpous   With the carpels united to form a compound pistil.

synsepalous   With the sepals connate, at least toward the base; gamosepalous.

tannins   A chemically diverse group of secondary metabolites characterized by their ability to combine with proteins and deactivate them.

tapetum   A nutritive tissue of the anther or ovule which degenerates during the development of the pollen or the post-fertilization embryo-sac.

taxon (pl. taxa)   Any taxonomic entity, of whatever rank.

taxonomy   A study aimed at producing a system of classification of organisms that best reflects the totality of their similarities and differences; a classification produced by such a study.

tectate   Provided with a roof or elevated covering.

tectate-columellate   Provided with a roof or covering supported by columns or pillars.

telome   An ultimate branch of a dichotomously branching stem.

tenuinucellar, tenuinucellate   With the nucellus consisting of a single layer of cells.

tepal   A sepal or petal, or a member of an undifferentiated perianth.

tetrad   A group of four; especially a group of four spores or pollen-grains.

tetradinous   Coherent in tetrads. (See *monadinous*.)

tetrasporic embryo-sac   An embryo-sac derived from four megaspores.

thalloid   Resembling or consisting of a thallus.

thallus   A plant body that is not clearly differentiated into roots, stems, and leaves.

theca   A compartment or locule, as in an anther.

tracheid   The most characteristic cell type in xylem, being long, slender, and tapered at the ends, with a lignified secondary wall and a definite lumen, but without living contents at maturity.

translator   A structure connecting the pollinia of adjacent anthers in the Asclepiadaceae.

triaperturate   With three apertures.

trilacunar node   A node with three gaps.

trilocular   With three locules.

trimerous   With parts in sets of three.

umbel   A racemose inflorescence with greatly abbreviated axis and elongate pedicels; in a compound umbel the primary branches are again umbellately branched at the tip.

uniaperturate   With a single aperture.

unilacunar node   A node associated with a single gap.

unilocular   With a single locule.

unisexual   With androecium but not gynoecium, or with gynoecium but not androecium.

unitegmic ovule   An ovule with a single integument.

utricle   A small, bladderlike, dry, indehiscent fruit with a single seed.

valvate (aestivation)   Arranged with the margins of the petals (or sepals) adjacent throughout their lengths, without overlapping.

variety   An infraspecific taxon with persistent populational significance.

vasicentric   Concentrated around the vessels.

vessel   A xylem-tube formed from several vessel-segments (modified tracheids with imperfect or no end-walls) set end to end.

vestigial   Poorly developed, as a result of evolutionary reduction from a better developed state. (Compare *rudimentary*.)

xeromorphic   With a form suggesting adaptation to dry conditions.

xerophyte   A plant adapted to life in dry places.

Appendix

Two photographs that I wished to use in CHAPTER 2 became available too late to incorporate into the regular text. These are shown below, both courtesy of the HUNT Institute for Botanical Documentation.

Fig. App. 1. LEFT, Göte Turesson (1892–1970), who developed the concept and proposed the term ecotype. RIGHT, Øjvind Winge (1866–1964), who first recognized polyploidy.

A remarkable new genus of Hamamelidae from Costa Rica is in train to publication by Jorge Gómez-Laurito and Luis D. Gómez P. It is an amentiferous tree with simple leaves, a well developed resinous secretory system in the bark, and plum-sized, drupaceous fruits. It lacks the specialized, basally embedded gland-scales of the Juglandales, Myricales, and some Fagales. In SEM view the pollen is compatible with that of the *Normapolles*-related families of the Hamamelidae. It is possible that after further study the new genus will be considered to form a monotypic family and order. Its name is compounded from tico (a colloquial term for a Costa Rican) and the Greek word for tree.

We must begin to give more serious attention to the neglected hypothesis of Friedrich Ehrendorfer (Pl. Syst. Evol. Suppl. 1: 227–234. 1977) that the Rosidae and Dilleniidae take their origin not directly from the Magnoliidae, but instead from the Hamamelidae. Under this hypothesis the floral reduction in the Hamamelidae preceded a secondary elaboration of floral structure in the Rosidae and Dilleniidae on a hamamelid base. The problems inherent in such a concept have not been fully resolved, but they may prove capable of resolution. No change in the formal organization of the subclasses of dicotyledons would be required, but the phylogenetic scheme would have to be revised to intercalate the Hamamelidae between the Magnoliidae and these other two groups. The Caryophyllidae would remain as a direct offshoot from the Magnoliidae.

Index

For each taxon of family rank or higher, an attempt has been made to have the first (**bold face**) index entry (as well as the last one) lead to its place in the system. An *italic* number indicates an illustration.

535